W9-BCP-882

# WEBSTER'S RED SEAL CROSSWORD DICTIONARY

Compiled and Edited by Norman Hill

WARNER BOOKS

A Time Warner Company

## EDITORIAL STAFF

Norman Hill, Editor
Laura M. Engle, Associate Editor
Lili Fenyves Hill, Consulting Editor
Naomi Bloom, Assistant Editor

WARNER BOOKS EDITION

**Copyright © 1971 by Webster's Red Seal Publications, Inc.**
All rights reserved.

Published by arrangement with Webster's Red Seal Publications, Inc.

Warner Books, Inc.
1271 Avenue of the Americas
New York, N.Y. 10020

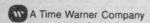 A Time Warner Company

Printed in the United States of America

**First Warner Books Printing:** December, 1982

Reissued: July, 1983

15  14  13  12

### ATTENTION: SCHOOLS AND CORPORATIONS

WARNER books are available at quantity discounts with bulk purchase for educational, business, or sales promotional use. For information, please write to: SPECIAL SALES DEPARTMENT, WARNER BOOKS, 1271 AVENUE OF THE AMERICAS, NEW YORK, N.Y. 10020.

### ARE THERE WARNER BOOKS
### YOU WANT BUT CANNOT FIND IN YOUR LOCAL STORES?

You can get any WARNER BOOKS title in print. Simply send title and retail price, plus 95¢ per order and 95¢ per copy to cover mailing and handling costs for each book desired. New York State and California residents add applicable sales tax. Enclose check or money order only, no cash please, to: WARNER BOOKS, P.O. BOX 690, NEW YORK, N.Y. 10019.

# FOREWORD

During the past decade the editors of this publication have done extensive research in lexicography, have edited tens of thousands of crossword puzzles, checked and evaluated hundreds of thousands of definitions and words. Now it is with great pride and pleasure that we present this new and unique reference book—a crossword puzzle dictionary conceived, designed and painstakingly compiled to best accomplish the single purpose for which a crossword puzzle dictionary is intended: to provide efficient, simplified help for the puzzle solver.

*Webster's Red Seal Crossword Dictionary* contains thousands of entries which are used by leading professional crossword constructors, and which appear most frequently in crossword puzzles published in magazines, books and newspapers. The definitions have been carefully edited by a staff of some of America's most experienced, most expert editors.

We have included those definitions which will be of maximum usefulness to the puzzle solver. As a result we believe you will find *Webster's Red Seal Crossword Dictionary* to be a complete, handy, reliable guide and solving aid.

Definitions are listed alphabetically, and worded just as they appear in puzzles. Where more than one answer word might fit the definition, additional possibilities are offered.

There is no confusing clutter of so-called "special categories" —no detours and confusing road signs; no meandering listings of Indian tribes, mythological beings or foreign weights and measures. What you hold in your hand is the easiest-to-use, most efficient alphabetical dictionary of crossword puzzle definitions available anywhere. We commend it to you with our best wishes for many hours of pleasurable puzzle solving.

Norman Hill
Editor

# A

aardvark ANTEATER
aardvark's diet ANTS
aardwolf HYENA
Aare SWISS RIVER
Aaron BIBLICAL PRIEST
Ab HEBREW MONTH
abaca MANILA HEMP
abalone MOLLUSK, ORMER
abandon DESERT, STRAND, MAROON
abandoned (law) DERELICT
abase DEGRADE, DEMEAN, LOWER, HUMBLE
abasement SHAME, DISHONOR
abash DISCONCERT
abate DIMINISH, EBB, SLACKEN, LET UP, DEDUCT, SUBSIDE
abatement REDUCTION, DECREASE
abbey head ABBOT, ABBESS
abbreviate SHORTEN, ABRIDGE, REDUCE
abdicate RESIGN, RENOUNCE
abdomen BELLY, STOMACH PAUNCH
Abe Lincoln symbol (2 wds.) STOVEPIPE HAT
Abel's brother CAIN, SETH
abet ENCOURAGE, HELP, INCITE, SANCTION
abhor HATE, LOATHE, DETEST, DESPISE
abject BASE, WRETCHED
able CAPABLE, COMPETENT, QUALIFIED, SKILLED
able to be examined TESTABLE
able to fly VOLANT
abluent CLEANER, CLEANSER
ablution BATH, WASHING, CLEANSING
ably EFFICIENTLY, CAPABLY COMPETENTLY
Abner's friend LUM
abode DWELLING, RESIDENCE, HOME, HEARTH
abolish ANNUL
abomasum RUMINANT
abominable ODIOUS, HORRIBLE

abominable snowman YETI
abomination DETESTATION, ABHORRENCE
aborigine PRIMITIVE, NATIVE
about ANENT
above ATOP, ON, UPON, OVER, OVERHEAD, SUPERIOR
aboveboard OPEN, FRANK, CANDID
abrade SAND, SCRAPE, RUB OFF
Abraham's father TERAH
abrasion EROSION
abroad OVERSEAS
abrogate ANNUL, CANCEL
abrupt SUDDEN, BRUSQUE
abscond RUN OFF, DECAMP
absconding soldier DESERTER
absence LACK
absence of sound SILENCE
absent AWAY, LACKING
absolute ENTIRE, COMPLETE
absolutely PURELY, WHOLLY, REALLY
absolute ruler DESPOT, DICTATOR, TYRANT
absolve PARDON, FORGIVE
absorb CONSUME, SWALLOW
absorb information DIGEST, LEARN
absorb moisture IMBIBE
abstain from ESCHEW
abstain from food FAST
abstain from meat (those who) VEGETARIAN
abstract STEAL, DIVERT
abstract being ESSE
abstruse PROFOUND, SUBTLE, RECONDITE
abundantly supplied REPLETE
abuse DAMAGE, INJURE
abusive speech TIRADE
abyss CHASM, PIT, GULF
Abyssinian ruler AMEER, AMIR, EMIR
accelerate SPEED
accelerate a motor REV
accent STRESS
accented part of a verse ARSIS
accept as true BELIEVE
accepted rule CANON
access DOOR
access to a mine ADIT
acclaim ECLAT, APPLAUD, HAIL, WELCOME

| | | | |
|---|---|---|---|
| accredited | APPROVED | across (prefix) | TRANS |
| accrue | INCREASE | acrostic | PUZZLE |
| accumulate | AMASS, STORE | act | FEAT, DEED, |
| accumulated matter | HEAP | PERFORMANCE, BEHAVIOR, | |
| | ACCRETION | DO, PERFORM, BEHAVE, | |
| accurate | EXACT | EMOTE, PRETEND, PRETENSE | |
| accuse | BLAME | Actaeon | HUNTER, STAG |
| accustom | INURE, ENURE | act against | OPPOSE |
| accustomed | WONT | act as a bearer | CARRY |
| ace | CARD | act as a butler | BUTTLE |
| acerbity | RANCOR | act as a model | POSE |
| ache | PAIN, HURT, | act as chairman | PRESIDE |
| | YEARN, LONGING | act as mediator | INTERCEDE |
| accommodate | SERVE, OBLIGE | actin | PROTEIN |
| accompany | ESCORT, ATTEND | acting a role (2 wds.) | ON STAGE |
| accomplice | ALLY | actinia | RAY, SEA ANEMONE |
| accomplish | DO, COMPLETE, | actinolite | ASBESTOS, |
| | PERFECT | | AMPHIBOLE |
| accomplishment | DEED, FEAT | action | DEED |
| accord | UNISON, HARMONIZE, | active | VIGOROUS, AGILE, |
| AGREE, GRANT, BESTOW | | LIVELY, BUSY, SPRY | |
| according to fact | TRUE | active person | DOER |
| according to law | LEGAL | activity | MOTION |
| accost | GREET | act of daring | FEAT |
| account | TAB | act of learning | LOAN |
| accountable | LIABLE | act of stealing | THEFT |
| account book | LEDGER | act of taking for | |
| accounting | BILL | one's own | ADOPTION |
| accounting term | DEBIT, CREDIT, | actor | THESPIAN |
| | NET, PROFIT, | actor Ameche | DON |
| | LOSS, ASSET | actor Andrews | DANA |
| account juggler | EMBEZZLER | actor Arness | JAMES |
| achieve | DO, PERFORM | actor Astaire | FRED |
| achievement | DEED, FEAT | actor Autry | GENE |
| achromatic | COLORLESS | actor Backus | JIM |
| acid | SOUR, TART | actor Barry | GENE |
| aciform | SHARP | actor Blore | ERIC |
| acknowledge | AVOW, OWN | actor Brand | NEVIL |
| acknowledge a greeting | NOD | actor Brynner | YUL |
| acorn | NUT | actor Burr | RAYMOND |
| acorn tree | OAK | actor Cameron | ROD |
| acquaint | INFORM, TELL | actor Carney | ART |
| acquiesce | COMPLY, AGREE, | actor Crabbe | BUSTER |
| | GAIN, GET | actor Dailey | DAN |
| acquire by labor | EARN | actor Drury | JAMES |
| acquired skill | ART | actor Duryea | DAN |
| acquire knowledge | LEARN | actor Ferrer | JOSE, MEL |
| acquisitive | GREEDY | actor Flynn | ERROLL |
| acquit | PARDON, ABSOLVE | actor Fonda | HENRY, PETER |
| acrid | BITTER, TART | actor Ford | GLENN |
| acrimony | BITTERNESS | actor Grant | CARY |
| acrobatic performer | TUMBLER | actor Graves | PETER |
| | ROPEDANCER | actor Guinness | ALEC |
| acrobat's bar | TRAPEZE | actor Heflin | VAN |
| acrobat's feat | STUNT, SPLIT | actor Holbrook | HAL |
| acrobat's garment | LEOTARD | actor Hudson | ROCK |
| acrogen | FERN, MOSS, PLANT | actor Hunter | TAB |
| acrolith | STATUE | actor Jannings | EMIL |
| acromion | SHOULDER, SCAPULA | actor Janssen | DAVID |

| | | | |
|---|---|---|---|
| actor Jourdan | LOUIS | actress Chase | ILKA |
| actor Keith | BRIAN | actress Christian | LINDA |
| actor Karloff | BORIS | actress Claire | INA |
| actor Knotts | DON | actress Collins | JOAN |
| actor Kruger | OTTO, HARDY | actress Dahl | ARLENE |
| actor Ladd | ALAN | actress Davis | BETTE |
| actor Lancaster | BURT | actress Day | DORIS |
| actor Lugosi | BELA | actress Dee | SANDRA |
| actor MacAuthur | JAMES | actress Dennis | SANDY |
| actor MacDowell | RODDY | actress Dickinson | ANGIE |
| actor MacMurray | FRED | actress Drew | ELLEN |
| actor March | HAL, FREDRIC | actress Duke | PATTY |
| actor Massey | RAYMOND | actress Dunne | IRENE |
| actor McQueen | STEVE | actress Farrow | MIA |
| actor Milland | RAY | actress Feldon | BARBARA |
| actor Mineo | SAL | actress Fisher | GAIL |
| actor Mitchum | ROBERT | actress Fleming | RHONDA |
| actor Montand | YVES | actress Foch | NINA |
| actor Murray | DON, JAN, KEN | actress Fontaine | JOAN |
| actor Newman | PAUL | actress Gabor | EVA, ZSA ZSA |
| actor Nielsen | LESLIE | actress Gam | RITA |
| actor Nimoy | LEONARD | actress Gardner | AVA |
| actor O'Brien | PAT | actress Hagen | UTA |
| actor O'Toole | PETER | actress Harding | ANNE |
| actor Parker | FESS | actress Haver | JUNE |
| actor Perkins | TONY | actress Havoc | JUNE |
| actor Powell | WILLIAM | actress Hayworth | RITA |
| actor Price | VINCENT | actress Hepburn | AUDREY, |
| actor Randall | TONY | | KATHARINE |
| actor Sharif | OMAR | actress Hopkins | MIRIAM |
| actor Shatner | WILLIAM | actress Jeanmaire | RENEE |
| actor Sinatra | FRANK | actress Jones | JENNIFER, |
| actor Sparks | NED | | SHIRLEY |
| actor Steiger | ROD | actress Lanchester | ELSA |
| actor Stewart | JAMES | actress Lange | HOPE |
| actor Taylor | ROD, ROBERT | actress Leigh | JANET, VIVIEN |
| actor Torn | RIP | actress Louise | TINA, ANITA |
| actor Van Dyke | DICK | actress Lupino | IDA |
| actor Wallach | ELI | actress Magnani | ANNA |
| actor Wayne | JOHN | actress Mayo | VIRGINIA |
| actor Weaver | DENNIS | actress Medford | KAY |
| actor West | ADAM | actress Merkel | UNA |
| actor's audition | TRYOUT | actress Merrill | DINA |
| actor's hint | CUE | actress Mills | JULIET, HAYLEY |
| actor's part | ROLE | actress Moore | TERRY, MELBA |
| actors in a play | CAST | actress Moorehead | AGNES |
| act pretentiously | | actress Neal | PATRICIA |
| (2 wds.) | SHOW OFF | actress Novak | KIM |
| actress Albright | LOLA | actress Oberon | MERLE |
| actress Angeli | PIER | actress O'Hara | MAUREEN |
| actress Arden | EVE | actress Parker | ELEANOR |
| actress Balin | INA | actress Pitts | ZASU |
| actress Bancroft | ANNE | actress-playwright | |
| actress Baxter | ANNE | Gordon | RUTH |
| actress Benaderet | BEA | actress Rainer | LUISE |
| actress Bernhardt | SARAH | actress Raines | ELLA |
| actress Blake | AMANDA | actress Redgrave | VANESSA, |
| actress Cannon | DYAN | | LYNN |
| actress Charisse | CYD | actress Ritter | THELMA |

| | |
|---|---|
| actress Rush | **BARBARA** |
| actress Shearer | **NORMA** |
| actress Sheridan | **ANNE** |
| actress Sommars | **JULIE** |
| actress Southern | **ANN** |
| actress Stanwyck | **BARBARA** |
| actress Storm | **GALE** |
| actress Taylor | **LIZ, ELIZABETH** |
| actress Thomas | **MARLO** |
| actress Tierney | **GENE** |
| actress Toren | **MARTA** |
| actress Turner | **LANA** |
| actress Welch | **RAQUEL** |
| actress Weld | **TUESDAY** |
| actress West | **MAE** |
| actual | **REAL** |
| actuality | **FACT** |
| aculeus | **STING, PRICKLE** |
| acumen | **INSIGHT** |
| acuminate | **SHARPEN, TAPER** |
| acute | **SHARP** |
| adage | **PROVERB, SAYING** |
| Adam and Eve's home | **EDEN** |
| Adam's ale | **WATER** |
| Adam's grandson | **ENOS** |
| Adam's mate | **EVE** |
| adapt | **ADJUST** |
| add | **TOTAL, SUM UP** |
| addax | **ANTELOPE** |
| adder | **VIPER, SNAKE, ASP** |
| addict | **USER** |
| addicted | **DEVOTED,** |
| **ATTACHED, HABITUATED** | |
| addition | **INCREASE** |
| additional | **EXTRA, MORE,** |
| **SUPPLEMENTARY** | |
| addition to a house | **ELL** |
| addle | **MUDDLE, CONFUSE,** |
| **SPOIL** | |
| add on | **ANNEX, APPEND** |
| address | **SPEAK, SPEECH** |
| address with friendliness | **GREET** |
| add salt | **SEASON** |
| add sugar | **SWEETEN** |
| ade | **FRUIT DRINK** |
| adduce | **CITE** |
| adequate | **SUITABLE** |
| adhere | **STICK, CLEAVE** |
| adherent of a king | **ROYALIST,** |
| **TORY** | |
| adhesive | **STICKY** |
| adhesive strip | **TAPE** |
| adhesive substance | **PASTE,** |
| **GLUE** | |
| adieu | **FAREWELL** |
| adjacent | **NEAR, NEXT** |
| adjoin | **ABUT, CONTIGUOUS** |
| adjuration | **APPEAL, COMMAND** |

| | |
|---|---|
| adjust | **ALINE, ALIGN, ADAPT** |
| adjutant bird | **ARGALA,** |
| **MARABOU, STORK** | |
| administer | **MANAGE** |
| administer corporal | |
| punishment | **SPANK, LASH** |
| **WHIP, PADDLE** | |
| admirer | **BEAU, SWAIN** |
| admiring group | |
| (2 wds.) | **FAN CLUB** |
| admissible | **WORTHY, PROPER,** |
| **ACCEPTABLE** | |
| admission | **ENTRY** |
| admit | **ALLOW, OWN** |
| admit being | |
| true | **ACKNOWLEDGE** |
| admonish | **WARN** |
| admonition | **REBUKE** |
| adnate | **JOINED** |
| ado | **FUSS, HUBBUB, TO-DO** |
| adobe | **BRICK, MUD** |
| adolescent | **TEEN** |
| adopt | **ASSUME, ACCEPT** |
| adorable | **CUTE** |
| adorably pretty (5 wds.) | **AS** |
| **CUTE AS A BUTTON** | |
| adore | **IDOLIZE, LOVE,** |
| **WORSHIP, DOTE** | |
| adorn | **DECORATE, TRIM,** |
| **EMBELLISH** | |
| Adriatic port of Italy | **BARI** |
| adroit | **DEXTEROUS** |
| adulterate | **MIX, DEBASE** |
| adult female | **WOMAN** |
| adult insect | **IMAGO** |
| adult male | **MAN** |
| advance | **GAIN, PROCEED, GO** |
| advanced in years | **AGED, OLD** |
| advancement | **PROGRESS** |
| advantage | **EDGE, HEAD START** |
| advantageous | **USEFUL** |
| advantageous | |
| purchase | **BARGAIN** |
| adventure | **INCIDENT, EVENT,** |
| **EXPERIENCE** | |
| adventurous deed | **GEST, GESTE** |
| adversary | **FOE, ENEMY** |
| adverse | **HOSTILE,** |
| **UNFAVORABLE** | |
| adversity | **DISASTER,** |
| **CALAMITY** | |
| advertisement | **NOTICE** |
| advertising sign | **POSTER,** |
| **BILLBOARD, BILL** | |
| advice | **COUNSEL** |
| advise | **COUNSEL, SUGGEST** |
| advise (arch.) | **REDE** |
| advise of danger | **WARN, ALERT** |
| advocate | **SUPPORT** |

| | |
|---|---|
| Aegean Island, former name | NIOS |
| aerial toy | KITE |
| aerie | NEST |
| aery | ETHEREAL |
| Aesop's island home | SAMOS |
| affable | EASY, POLITE |
| affair | INCIDENT |
| affectation | POSE |
| affected manner | AIRS |
| affection | LOVE, FONDNESS |
| affectionate | LOVING, DEMONSTRATIVE |
| affirm | ASSERT, ATTEST, AVOW, ACKNOWLEDGE, AVER |
| affirmative reply | YES, YEA, AY, AYE |
| affix a signature | SIGN, ENDORSE |
| afflatus | IMPULSE |
| affliction | TROUBLE, SORROW |
| affluent | WEALTHY |
| afford | SPARE |
| affray | MELEE, BRAWL |
| affright | TERROR |
| affront | INSULT |
| Afghan prince | AMIR, AMEER, EMIR |
| aflame | BURNING |
| afoot | BREWING |
| afoul | TANGLED |
| afraid | SCARED |
| African antelope | ELAND, GNU |
| African-Arabian waters (2 wds.) | RED SEA |
| African dialect | BANTU, SWAHILI, BEMBA, LINGALA, CONGO, HAUSA, MANDINGO |
| African hemp | IFE |
| African hunting expedition | SAFARI |
| African land | ALGERIA, BOTSWANA, BURUNDI, CAMEROON, CHAD, CONGO, DAHOMEY, EGYPT, ETHIOPIA, GABON, GAMBIA, GHANA, GUINEA, KENYA, LESOTHO, LIBERIA, LIBYA, MALAWI, MALI, MAURITANIA, MOROCCO, NIGER, NIGERIA, RHODESIA, RWANDA, SENEGAL, SOMALIA, SUDAN, TANZANIA, TOGO, TUNISIA, UGANDA, ZAMBIA |
| African land (2 wds.) | IVORY COAST, SOUTH AFRICA, UPPER VOLTA |
| African lily | ALOE |

| | |
|---|---|
| African nut tree | KOLA, COLA |
| African river | CONGO, JUBA, NIGER, NILE, SHIRE, VAAL, VOLTA, VELE |
| African tree | SHEA |
| Afrikaans | LANGUAGE |
| Afrikander | BOER |
| aft | ASTERN |
| after | FOLLOWING, BEHIND, LATER |
| after-dinner candy | MINT |
| aftermath | RESULT |
| aftermost | LAST |
| afternoon beverage | TEA |
| afternoon party | TEA |
| afternoon performance | MATINEE |
| afternoon show | MATINEE |
| afternoon sleep | SIESTA, NAP |
| afternoon snack | TEA |
| aftersong | EPODE |
| afterthought (abbr.) | PS |
| aftertime | FUTURE |
| afterward | LATER |
| again | ANEW, OVER, ENCORE |
| against | ANTI, CON |
| agama | LIZARD |
| agapanthus | LILY |
| agape | LOVE |
| agar | GEL, MEDIUM |
| age | ERA, EPOCH, LIFETIME, EON |
| aged | OLD, ANCIENT, RIPENED, MATURED |
| aged, as meat | CURED |
| aged beer | LAGER |
| ageless | ETERNAL |
| agenda | PROGRAM |
| agenesis | ABSENCE |
| agent | DEPUTY, REPRESENTATIVE |
| age-old | ANCIENT |
| age on the vine | RIPEN |
| agglomeration | HEAP, MASS |
| agglutinant | GLUE |
| aggrandize | EXALT |
| aggregate | SUM, TOTAL |
| aggressive | PUSHY |
| agile | NIMBLE, LIVELY, SPRY, ACTIVE |
| agitate | STIR |
| Agnes Moorehead role | ENDORA |
| ago | PAST |
| agony | TORTURE |
| agree | ACCORD, ASSENT, CONCUR, CONSENT |
| agreeable | PLEASANT |
| agreement | PACT |

| | |
|---|---|
| agreement between nations | TREATY |
| agrestic | RURAL, RUSTIC |
| agricultural home | FARM |
| agricultural implement | HOE, HARROW, PLOW, REAPER, SICKLE |
| agriculture | FARMING, HUSBANDRY |
| agrimony | FLOWER |
| aguardiente | BRANDY |
| ague | FEVER |
| ahead | FORWARD |
| ah me! | ALAS |
| aid | ABET, ASSIST, HELP |
| Aida role | RADAMES, AMNERIS, AMONASRO |
| aide | ASSISTANT |
| aid in diagnosing | X-RAY |
| aiguille | DRILL |
| ail | SICKEN, TROUBLE |
| ailanthus | TREE |
| ailment | DISEASE |
| aim | OBJECTIVE, DIRECT, GOAL, POINT, END |
| air | AURA, ATMOSPHERE, VENTILATE, TUNE, MELODY |
| airborne | ALOFT, FLYING |
| air circulator | FAN |
| aircraft | AIRPLANE, GLIDER, HELICOPTER, JET |
| airedale | DOG, BREED |
| air hero | ACE |
| airman | AVIATOR, FLIER, PILOT |
| airplane (Fr.) | AVION |
| airplane enclosure | COCKPIT |
| airplane space | SEAT |
| airplane varnish | DOPE |
| air pollution | SMOG |
| airport, for short | DROME |
| air rifle | BB |
| airscrew | PROPELLER |
| airstrip | RUNWAY |
| Air Traffic Control (abbr.) | ATC |
| air travel term | NONSTOP |
| airy | LIGHT, LOFTY |
| airy farewell | TATA |
| ait | ISLET, EYOT |
| aitch | "H" |
| ajar | OPEN |
| akin | RELATED |
| Akkadian sun god | SHAMASH |
| alacrity | SPEED |
| alae | WINGS |
| alar | WINGED, WINGLIKE |
| alarm | FEAR, WARN, ALERT |
| Alaskan native | ALEUT, ESKIMO |
| Alaskan transportation | SLED, SKIDOO |
| alate | WINGED |
| alb | ROBE, CLOAK |
| albacore | TUNA |
| Albanian currency | LEK |
| albeit | ALTHOUGH |
| albite | FELDSPAR |
| alcoholic beverage | GIN, SCOTCH, BOURBON, VODKA, RUM, MEAD, SPIRITS, WHISKEY |
| alcohol lamp | ETNA |
| alcove | NICHE, NOOK |
| alder (var.) | OWLER |
| alegar | VINEGAR |
| alehouse | PUB, TAVERN, INN, BAR |
| ale mug | TOBY |
| alert | ATTENTIVE, WATCHFUL, WARN, ALARM |
| Aleutian island | ATTU |
| Aleut's home | IGLOO |
| alewife | HERRING |
| alexipharmic | ANTIDOTAL |
| alfalfa | GRASS, FODDER |
| alga | SEAWEED |
| Algerian governor | DEY |
| Algerian port | ORAN |
| alien | FOREIGN, STRANGE, FOREIGNER |
| alienate | ESTRANGE |
| alight | DISMOUNT |
| alike | SIMILAR, SAME |
| aline | STRAIGHTEN |
| alive | VITAL |
| all | EVERYBODY, EVERYTHING |
| allargando | SLOWER |
| allay | SLAKE |
| allege | AVER, STATE |
| allegiance | LOYALTY |
| allegorical work | FABLE |
| allegro | FASTER |
| alleviate | EASE, RELIEVE |
| all excited | AGOG |
| alley | LANE |
| alliance | UNION |
| allied | UNITED |
| alligator | CROCODILE |
| alligator pear | AVOCADO |
| all male party | STAG |
| allot | APPORTION, ASSIGN, DISTRIBUTE. METE, DOLE |
| allow | LET, PERMIT, OWN, ADMIT |
| allowable | PERMISSIBLE |
| allowable under law | LEGAL, LICIT |
| allowance | SHARE, RATION |

allowance for cash payment **DISCOUNT**
allowance for waste **TRET**
allow as a discount **REBATE**
allow liquid to fall **SPILL**
allow to fall **DROP**
allow to go free **RELEASE**
alloy **COMBINE, MIX, DEBASE**
all right **OK, OKAY, ROGER**
allspice **MYRTLE, PIMIENTO**
all the time (3 wds.) **DAY AND NIGHT**
all tied up (2 wds.) **EVEN STEVEN**
allude **REFER**
allure **ATTRACT, ENTICE, VAMP**
allurement **FASCINATION**
alluring sea creature **MERMAID, SIREN**
alluring woman **SIREN**
alluvion **FLOOD**
ally **CONFEDERATE**
almandine **GARNET**
almond **NUT**
almost **NEARLY, NIGH**
almost alike **SIMILAR**
alms box **ARCA**
almshouse **POORHOUSE**
aloe **LILY**
aloft **ABOVE, UP**
aloha state **HAWAII**
aloha symbol **LEI**
alone **SOLITARY, SOLO, UNACCOMPANIED**
along in years **AGED, OLD**
aloof **REMOVED**
alphabet **LETTERS**
alphabetic character **LETTER**
Alpine cottage **CHALET**
Alpine country **FRANCE, SWITZERLAND, AUSTRIA, ITALY**
Alpine peak **MATTERHORN, JUNGFRAU**
Alpine primrose **AURICULA**
Alpine region **TIROL, TYROL**
alsike **CLOVER**
also **AND, TOO, PLUS**
also-ran **LOSER**
alter **ADAPT, CHANGE, VARY, AMEND**
alterant **DYE**
alter, as a dress (2 wds.) **MAKE OVER**
altercation **QUARREL, SCRAP**
alternate **STANDBY**
alternately (2 wds.) **BY TURNS**
alternating current (abbr.) **AC**

alternative **OPTION, CHOICE**
alternative word **OR**
althea **FLOWER, HOLLYHOCK**
alto **VIOLA**
alum **ASTRINGENT, STYPTIC**
always **EVER, FOREVER**
always (poet.) **EER**
alyssum **MUSTARD**
amadavat **SONGBIRD**
amadou **PUNK, TINDER**
amalgam **ALLOY, MIXTURE, BLEND**
amalgamation **UNION, BLEND**
amass **ACCUMULATE, GATHER**
amass and conceal **HOARD**
amateur **DILETTANTE**
amateur radio operator **HAM**
amaze **ASTONISH, STUN, AWE**
amazement **SURPRISE**
Amazon tributary **APA, ICA**
ambassador **ENVOY**
ambiguous **UNCLEAR, VAGUE**
ambition **DESIRE**
amble **STROLL, MEANDER**
ambo **PULPIT**
ambush **TRAP**
amend **CORRECT, REVISE, ALTER, CHANGE**
American Beauty **ROSE**
American bird **EAGLE**
American black snake **RACER**
American blackbird **GRACKLE**
American buffalo **BISON**
American cheese **CHEDDAR**
American dish **HOTDOG, HAMBURGER**
American eagle **BALD**
American folk singer **IVES, SEEGER, GUTHRIE**
American humorist **ADE, TWAIN**
American in Britain **YANK**
American Indian **CREE, HOPI, UTE, ERIE, NAVAJO, OTO, APACHE, POHO, SIOUX, OMAHA, CROW**
American Indian tent **TEPEE, TIPI, TIPEE**
American ivy **CREEPER**
American patriot **OTIS, HALE, HENRY**
American soldiers **GI'S**
American spotted cat **MARGAY**
American symbol **EAGLE**
American vegetable **CORN, MAIZE, SQUASH**
America's uncle **SAM**
amiable **CORDIAL, AGREEABLE**
amianthus **ASBESTOS**

| | | | |
|---|---|---|---|
| amicable | FRIENDLY | ancient Mexican | MAYA, AZTEC, |
| amid | AMONG | | TOLTEC |
| amidone | METHADONE | ancient musical | |
| amiss | ASTRAY, WRONG | instrument | LYRA, LYRE, |
| amity | PEACE, FRIENDSHIP | | LUTE |
| ammonia compounds | AMINES | ancient name of Vich | AUSA |
| ammonite | FOSSIL | Ancient of Days | GOD |
| ammunition | SHOT, SHELLS | ancient Peruvian | INCA |
| among | AMID, MID | ancient Phoenician port | SIDON, |
| amoretto | CUPID | | TYRE |
| amorous look | OGLE | ancient poet | BARD, PSALMIST |
| amorphous | SHAPELESS | ancient port of Rome | OSTIA |
| amort | SPIRITLESS | ancient psalmist | DAVID |
| amortize | PRORATE | ancient Roman garments | TOGAS |
| amount | SUM, TOTAL | ancient Roman | |
| amount carried | LOAD | magistrate | AEDILE, EDILE |
| ampere (abbr.) | AMP | ancient sacred writings | |
| ampersand | AND | of Persia | AVESTA |
| amphibian | TOAD, FROG, | ancient serf | HELOT, ESNE |
| | SALAMANDER | ancient stringed | |
| amphitheater | ARENA | instrument | LUTE, LYRA, |
| ample | PLENTIFUL, ENOUGH | | LYRE, KITHARA |
| amplify | ENLARGE, MAGNIFY | ancient Sudanese | NUBIANS, |
| amplitude | BREADTH, SCOPE | | NUBA |
| amulet | CHARM | ancient Syria | ARAM |
| amuse | DIVERT, ENTERTAIN | ancient theatres | ODEON, |
| amusement | GAME | | ODEUM |
| amusement | | ancient two-wheeled | |
| enterprise | CARNIVAL | chariot | ESSED, ESSEDA |
| amusing | COMICAL, FUNNY | ancient writing | RUNE |
| amusing play | COMEDY | ancon | CONSOLE |
| amylaceous | STARCHY | and | ALSO, NEXT, PLUS |
| amylum | STARCH | and (Fr.) | ET |
| analyze grammatically | PARSE | Andaman Islands' | |
| analyze ore | ASSAY | neighbor | NICOBAR |
| Ananias | LIAR | andante | MODERATE |
| anaphora | REPETITION | Andes animal | LLAMA |
| anarchy | DISORDER | Andes country | PERU, BOLIVIA, |
| anasarca | DROPSY | | CHILE, VENEZUELA, |
| anatomical networks | RETIA | | ECUADOR, ARGENTINA |
| anatomical pouch | SAC | andesite | FELDSPAR, GRANITE |
| ancestor of the pharaohs | RA, RE | Andes mountain | SORATA |
| ancestry | FAMILY, LINEAGE | Andes vulture | CONDOR |
| anchor | MOOR, FIX, TIE | and not | NOR |
| anchor chain | CABLE | and others (2 wds., | |
| ancient | OLD, OLDEN, AGED | Lat. abbr.) | ET AL |
| ancient British chariot | ESSED, | Andrew Jackson's nickname | |
| | ESSEDA | (2 wds.) | OLD HICKORY |
| ancient Chinese capital | SIAN | android | ROBOT |
| ancient Greek coin | OBOL | andromeda | STAR |
| ancient Hebrew ascetic | ESSENE | and sign | AMPERSAND |
| ancient Irish capital | TARA | and so on (2 wds., | |
| ancient Italian | LATIN, ROMAN | Lat. abbr.) | ETC. |
| | OSCAN, ETRUSCAN | Andy's partner | AMOS |
| ancient Italian family | ESTE | anecdote | TALE, YARN |
| ancient king | ARTHUR, | anechoic | SOUNDPROOF |
| | DAVID, SAUL | anele | ANOINT |
| ancient kingdom on | | anemone | BUTTERCUP |
| Persian Gulf | ELAM | anent | CONCERNING, ABOUT |

anesthetic **ETHER, CHLOROFORM, GAS**
anew **AFRESH, OVER**
angel **CHERUB, SPIRIT**
angelic **HEAVENLY, GOOD**
angelic child **CHERUB**
angelica **PARSLEY**
angel's headdress **HALO**
angel's instrument **HARP**
anger **ENRAGE, IRE, WRATH, RAGE, MADDEN**
angina **SPASM**
angioma **TUMOR**
angle **BEVEL, FISH, CORNER**
angle of a leaf **AXIL**
anglepod **MILKWEED**
angler's bait **LURE**
angleworm **BAIT**
Anglo-Saxon Letter **EDH**
Anglo-Saxon slave **ESNE**
angry **CROSS, IRATE, MAD, ENRAGED, WRATHFUL**
anguish **DISTRESS, PAIN**
angular **GAUNT**
angwantibo **LEMUR**
anhydrous **WATERLESS**
ani **CUCKOO, BLACKBIRD**
anil **INDIGO**
anile **INFIRM, WEAK**
aniline product **DYE**
animal **BRUTE, BEAST, BIPED**
animal claw **TALON**
animal doctor **VET**
animal enclosure **CAGE, PEN**
animal fat **TALLOW**
animal flesh **MEAT, BEEF, PORK, HAM, VEAL, BACON, LAMB**
animal food **FODDER**
animal foot **PAW, PAD, HOOF**
animal garden **ZOO**
animal hair **FUR, MANE**
animal hide **PELT**
animal home **LAIR, DEN, BURROW, NEST**
animal nail **CLAW**
animal of South America **TAPIR, LLAMA, APARA, COATI, PACO, ALPACA**
animal of the cat family **LION, CHEETAH, TIGER, PANTHER, COUGAR, JAGUAR, OCELOT, CARACAL, LEOPARD**
animal park **ZOO**
animal's coat **FUR, PELT, HIDE, PELAGE**
animal's den **LAIR**

animal skin **PELT, FUR**
animal's limb **LEG**
animal trainer **TAMER**
animate **INSPIRE, CHEER, PROMPT**
animated **ALIVE, LIVELY**
animato (mus.) **ANIMATED**
anime **RESIN**
animosities **ENMITIES**
animus **SOUL**
anisette **LIQUEUR**
anjou **PEAR**
anklebone **TALUS**
ankle coverings **SPATS**
ankle mishap **SPRAIN**
anklet **SOCK**
annals **ARCHIVES**
Anne Bancroft role (2 wds.) **MIRACLE WORKER**
annex **ADD**
annihilate **ANNUL, EXTINGUISH, DESTROY**
announce **REVEAL, REPORT, TELL**
annoy **IRK, PESTER, TEASE, RILE**
annoying **TIRESOME**
annoying bird **PIGEON**
annoying child **BRAT**
annoying feeling **ITCH**
annoying insect **GNAT, MITE**
annoying one **PEST, NUISANCE**
annual **YEARLY**
annual contest (2 wds.) **MISS AMERICA**
annually **YEARLY**
annuity **PAYMENT**
annul **ABOLISH**
annulus **CIRCLE**
anomalous **ABNORMAL, DEVIANT**
anon **PRESENTLY, SOON, SUBSEQUENTLY**
anonymous **NAMELESS, ANON**
anopheles **MOSQUITO**
another name **ALIAS**
another name for Candia **HERAKLION**
another way around **DETOUR**
answer **RESPOND, REPLY**
answer the purpose **SERVE**
ant **EMMET, PISMIRE, TERMITE**
antagonism **ENMITY**
antagonist **RIVAL**
antarctic bird **PENGUIN**
Antarctic explorer **BYRD**
Antarctic sea **ROSS**

| | | | |
|---|---|---|---|
| ant cow | APHID | apology | PLEA |
| antecedent | ANCESTOR | apoplexy | PARALYSIS, STROKE |
| Anthony's nickname | TONY | Apostle Paul | SAUL |
| anthracite | COAL | apothecary's weight | DRAM |
| antiaircraft fire | FLAK | appall | DISMAY |
| antiar | UPAS, POISON | apalling | TERRIBLE |
| antibiotic | SULFA | apparel | DRESS, RAIMENT, |
| antic | CAPER, DIDO, PRANK | | GARB, SUIT, COAT |
| anticipate | AWAIT, WAIT | apparel of skins | PELT |
| anticipation | HOPE | apparent | SEEMING |
| antidote | REMEDY | apparition | GHOST, SHADE, |
| antimacassar | DOILY | | SPECTRE |
| antipasto | APPETIZER, SALAD | appeal | PLEAD |
| antipathy | HATE, HATRED | appear | SEEM, SPRING UP, |
| antiprohibitionists | WETS | | TURN UP |
| antiquated | OLD, PASSE, | appear again | RECUR |
| | AGED, ANCIENT | appearance | ASPECT, FACET, |
| antique | ANCIENT, QUAINT, OLD | | LOOK |
| antiquity | YORE | appease | PACIFY |
| antiseptic liquid | IODINE | appel | DARE, CHALLENGE |
| antithesis | CONTRAST, | appellation | TITLE, NAME |
| | OPPOSITE | append | ADD, ATTACH, ANNEX |
| antler | HORN | appendage | TAIL, LIMB |
| antlered animal | DEER, ELK, | appetite | DESIRE, RELISH |
| | MOOSE | applaud | CLAP, CHEER |
| antre | CAVE, CAVERN | apple (Fr.) | POMME |
| antrum | CAVITY | apple center | CORE |
| anvil (ant.) | INCUS | apple drink | CIDER |
| anxiety | CARE, WORRY, FEAR | applejack | CIDER, BRANDY |
| anxious | EAGER | apple of one's eye | PET, |
| any | SOME | | FAVORITE |
| apace | SWIFTLY, QUICKLY | apple-pie order | NEAT |
| apart from | ASIDE, SEPARATE | apple seed | PIP |
| apartment | FLAT | Appleseed | JOHNNY |
| apartment (abbr.) | APT | appliance | DEVICE, MACHINE, |
| apartment building | TENEMENT | | TOOL |
| apartment occupant | TENANT | applique | DECORATE |
| apart (prefix) | DIS | apply | SPREAD, PLACE, |
| apathy | INDIFFERENCE, | | REQUEST |
| | PASSIVITY | apply lightly | DAB |
| ape | GORILLA, CHIMPANZEE, | apply powder | DUST |
| SIMIAN, ORANGUTAN, MIMIC, | | appoint | NAME, FURNISH |
| IMITATE, MONKEY, MOCK, | | appointment | DATE, TRYST |
| | COPY | apportion | DOLE, ALLOT, METE |
| apeak | VERTICAL | apposite | APT |
| aper | COPYCAT, MIMIC | appraise | RATE |
| apercu | INSIGHT | appreciate | ESTEEM, |
| aperitif | LIQUEUR, WINE | | ESTIMATE, NOTICE |
| aperture | GAP, OPENING, | appreciative | GRATEFUL |
| | ORIFICE | apprehend | DISCERN |
| apex | SUMMIT, TOP, ACME | apprehension | FEAR, |
| aphid | INSECT, LOUSE | | TREPIDATION |
| aphorism | MAXIM, ADAGE | apprentice | TRAINEE, NOVICE |
| apiary dweller | BEE | apprise | TEACH, INFORM |
| apiece | EACH | approach | NEAR, COME |
| apish | SILLY | approachable | RECEPTIVE |
| aplomb | POISE | approbate | APPROVE |
| apocryphal | SPURIOUS | | |

| | |
|---|---|
| appropriate | **ADOPT, SEEMLY, FIT, FITTING** |
| approve | **OK, OKAY** |
| approved model | **STANDARD** |
| approximal | **ADJOINING** |
| approximately | **ABOUT, AROUND** |
| approximation | **LIKENESS, NEARNESS** |
| April shower | **RAIN** |
| apron-like garment | **SMOCK** |
| apropos | **TIMELY, APT** |
| apt | **LIKELY, APROPOS** |
| apteryx | **KIWI** |
| aquarium | **TANK** |
| aquarium fish | **MOLLY, GUPPY, GOURAMI, PLATY** |
| aquatic animal | **OTTER, SEAL, WHALE, SEACOW, SEALION, SEA ELEPHANT, WALRUS, HIPPOPOTAMUS** |
| aquatic bird | **SWAN, TERN, DUCK, TEAL, DRAKE, GULL, PENGUIN, FALK** |
| aquatic rodent | **MUSKRAT, BEAVER** |
| aquatic sport | **SWIM, DIVE, BOAT, SAIL, FISH, SURF, WATER SKI** |
| aquatint | **ETCHING** |
| aquavit | **LIQUOR, APERITIF** |
| aqua vitae | **LIQUOR, ALCOHOL** |
| aqueous | **WATERY** |
| Ara | **CONSTELLATION, MACAW** |
| Arab | **BEDOUIN, SEMITE, YEMENITE** |
| Arab chieftain | **EMIR, AMIR, AMEER** |
| Arab chieftain's domain | **EMIRATE** |
| Arab country | **YEMEN, OMAN, ADEN, SYRIA, LEBANON, EGYPT, JORDAN, MOROCCO, ALGERIA, TUNISIA, LIBYA, SUDAN, IRAQ, KUWAIT, MUSCAT** |
| Arab garment | **ABA, BURNOOSE** |
| Arabian coffee | **MOCHA** |
| Arabian coin | **DINAR** |
| Arabian gazelle | **ARIEL** |
| Arabian gulf | **ADEN, AQABA** |
| Arabian name | **SAUD** |
| Arabian port | **ADEN** |
| Arabian prince | **EMIR, AMIR, AMEER, EMEER** |
| Arabian ship | **DHOW** |
| Arabian territory | **OMAN** |
| arable grassland | **LEA, LEY** |
| arachnid | **SPIDER, MITE, TICK, SCORPION** |
| araneid | **SPIDER** |
| arbalest | **CROSSBOW** |
| arbiter | **UMPIRE** |
| arbitrary | **ABSOLUTE, DESPOTIC** |
| arbitrary assertion (colloq.) | **SAY-SO** |
| arbor | **BOWER** |
| arcane | **HIDDEN, SECRET** |
| arch (Scot.) | **PEND** |
| Archbishop of Canterbury | **ANSELM, BECKET** |
| arched way | **ARCADE, LOGGIA, PORTICO** |
| archer | **BOWMAN** |
| archer's missile | **ARROW** |
| archimage | **MAGICIAN, WIZARD** |
| archives | **ANNALS** |
| arch of a circle | **SECTOR** |
| Arctic abode | **IGLOO, IGLU** |
| Arctic bird | **SKUA** |
| Arctic charr | **TROUT** |
| Arctic expanse | **ICE** |
| Arctic inhabitant | **ESKIMO, ALEUT** |
| arctics | **BOOTS, OVERSHOES** |
| Arctic vehicle | **SLED, SLEIGH, DOGSLED** |
| ardent affection | **LOVE** |
| ardor | **ELAN, ZEAL** |
| arduous journey | **TREK** |
| are | **EXIST** |
| area | **REGION, SURFACE** |
| area in a house | **ROOM** |
| areca | **PALM** |
| arena | **AMPHITHEATER** |
| arenaceous | **SANDY** |
| argala | **STORK, MARIBOU** |
| Argentine dance | **TANGO** |
| Argentine plains | **PAMPAS** |
| argol | **TARTAR** |
| argot | **CANT, SLANG** |
| argue | **DEBATE, REBUT, FIGHT, QUARREL** |
| argument | **SPAT, QUARREL, DEBATE, FIGHT** |
| arid | **DRY, SERE** |
| arid expanse | **DESERT** |
| Aries | **RAM** |
| Arikara | **REE** |
| ariose | **MELODIC** |
| arise | **GET UP, COME UP, ASCEND** |
| arithmetic, for short | **MATH** |
| arithmetic sign | **PLUS, MINUS, EQUAL** |
| Arizona college town | **TEMPE** |

Arizona Indian **APACHE, PIMA, PAPAGO, HOPI, NAVAJO**
Arizona lizard (2 wds.) **GILA MONSTER**
Arizona river **GILA, SALT, COLORADO**
ark **BOAT**
ark builder **NOAH**
arkose **SANDSTONE**
ark's landing place **ARARAT**
arm **LIMB, BRANCH, TENTACLE**
armada **FLEET**
arm and hand joint **WRIST**
armature **DEFENSE, COVERING**
arm bone **ULNA**
arm covering **SLEEVE**
armed band **POSSE**
armed conflict **WAR, BATTLE**
Armenian cap **CALPAC, CALPACK, KALPAK**
Armenian mountain **ARARAT, ARA, ARAGATIS, TAURUS**
Armenian people **GOMER**
arm extremity **HAND**
armistice **TRUCE**
armorbearer **SQUIRE, ARMIGER**
armored mammal **ARMADILLO**
arms **WEAPONS**
arms and legs **LIMBS**
army **FORCES, TROOPS**
army acronym **AWOL**
army base **CAMP**
army bed **COT**
army chaplain **PADRE**
army group **UNIT, CADRE**
army meal **MESS**
army officer **CAPTAIN, COLONEL, MAJOR, GENERAL, LIEUTENANT**
army shoe **BOOT**
army trader **SUTLER**
Army Transport Service (abbr.) **A.T.S.**
army unit **CORPS, REGIMENT**
aroid **TARO**
aroma **BOUQUET, ODOR, FRAGRANCE, SCENT, SMELL**
aromatic **REDOLENT, FRAGRANT**
aromatic beverage **TEA**
aromatic gum resin **MYRRH**
aromatic herb **MINT, DILL, SPEARMINT, SAGE, CARUM**
aromatic medicinal ingredient (2 wds.) **BAY RUM**
aromatic ointment **NARD**
aromatic product **SPICE**

aromatic seed **ANISE, CUMIN**
around **ABOUT**
around (prefix) **PERI**
arouse a response (3 wds.) **RING A BELL**
arraign **CHARGE, ACCUSE**
arrange **ASSORT**
arrange and edit **COMPILE**
arrange in folds **DRAPE**
arrange in layers **TIER, LAMINATE**
arrange in order **SORT**
arrange in rows **ALINE, ALIGN**
arrangement **SETUP, DISPOSITION**
Arras **TAPESTRY**
array **DRESS, DECK, ADORN**
arrears **BEHIND**
arrest **NAB, STOP, CHECK**
arrive **COME**
arrive at **REACH**
arrive by plane **LAND**
arrogance **PRIDE**
arrogant **PROUD, HAUGHTY**
arrogant manner **HAUTEUR**
arrogate **USURP, TAKE**
arrow **DART, SPEAR, SHAFT**
arrow case **QUIVER**
arrow point **BARB**
arrow poison **CURARE, INEE, URARI, UPAS, ANTIAR**
arrow-shaped **HASTATE**
arroyo **BROOK, CREEK, GULCH**
art **CUNNING, KNACK**
art (Lat.) **ARS**
artery **AORTA**
art gallery **SALON, MUSEUM**
article **AN, THE, ITEM**
article of apparel **SHIRT, BLOUSE, DRESS, ROBE, JACKET, VEST, SKIRT, WAIST**
article of bedding **SHEET, SPREAD, BLANKET, PILLOWCASE**
article of cosmetics **ROUGE, LIPSTICK, MASCARA, LINER, POWDER**
article of faith **TENET, DOCTRINE, DOGMA**
article of food **CORN, RICE, BREAD, STEAK, CHOP, VEGETABLE, FRUIT**
article of furniture **TABLE, CHAIR, SOFA, SETTEE, DAVENPORT, BOOKCASE, BED, DRESSER**

article of jewelry **RING, NECKLACE, BRACELET, EARRING**
articles of merchandise **WARES**
artifice **RUSE, SUBTERFUGE**
artificer **ARTISAN, SMITH**
artificial **FALSE**
artificial butter **OLEO**
artificial coloring **DYE**
artificial front **FACADE**
artificial hairpiece **WIG, TOUPEE, FALL**
artificial ice floor **RINK**
artificial language **IDO, ESPERANTO**
artificially high voice **FALSETTO**
artificially sprouted grain **MALT**
artificial silk **RAYON**
artificial water channel **FLUME**
artificial waterway **CANAL**
artillery **CANNON**
artillery emplacement **BATTERY**
artillery fire **SALVO**
artisan **CRAFTSMAN**
artist **PAINTER, SCULPTOR**
artiste **ACTOR, PERFORMER**
artistic person **AESTHETE**
artist's cap **BERET**
artist's equipment **EASEL, PALETTE**
artist's medium **INK, OIL, TEMPERA**
artist's paint holder **PALETTE**
artist's specialty **PAINTING, LANDSCAPE, PORTRAIT, STILL LIFE, SCULPTURE, ETCHING**
artist's stand **EASEL**
artist's work **COLLAGE, PAINTING, MASTERPIECE, PORTRAIT, MINIATURE**
artist's workshop **ATELIER, STUDIO**
artless **OPEN, CANDID**
artlessness **NAIVETE**
art of discourse **RHETORIC**
art of government **POLITICS**
art of self-protection **DEFENSE**
arui **AOUDAD**
arum **CUCKOOPINT, CALLAS**
as **WHILE**
asa **PHYSICIAN, HEALER**
as a certainty **FOR SURE, SURELY**

as a close race (3 wds.) **NIP AND TUCK**
as a rule **NORMALLY**
ascend **ARISE, CLIMB, RISE**
ascenseur **ELEVATOR, LIFT**
ascertain **LEARN, PROVE**
ascertain bearing **ORIENT**
ascertain the dimensions **MEASURE**
ascertain the number **COUNT**
ascetic **HERMIT, AUSTERE**
ascot **TIE, CRAVAT, SCARF**
ascribable **DUE, ATTRIBUTABLE**
ascribe **ASSIGN**
asea **BEFUDDLED, BEWILDERED**
as far as **TO**
ash **TREE**
ash can (Brit.) **DUSTBIN**
ash-colored **GRAY**
ashen **PALE, LIVID**
Asia Minor mountain **IDA**
Asia Minor sea **AEGEAN, BLACK**
Asian country **IRAN, LAOS, VIETNAM, CHINA, THAILAND, INDIA, PAKISTAN, IRAQ, ADEN, AFGHANISTAN, CAMBODIA, JAPAN, QATAR, NEPAL, CEYLON, KOREA, KUWAIT, MACAO, MALAYSIA, PHILIPPINES**
Asian sea **ARAL, CASPIAN, DEAD**
Asian treeless tract **STEPPE**
Asian Turk **TATAR**
Asiatic fiber plant **HEMP**
Asiatic mountains **PAMIRS, ALTAI, ELBURZ, HIMALAYA, KARAKORUM, KUNLUN, TAURUS, URALS**
ask **INQUIRE, INVITE, REQUEST**
ask alms **BEG**
askew **ALOP, AWRY, OBLIQUE**
ask for **SOLICIT**
ask for a job **APPLY**
ask for charity **BEG**
ask forcibly **DEMAND**
ask for payment **DUN**
as of now (2 wds.) **TO-DATE**
aspect **APPEARANCE, PHASE, FACET, SIDE**
aspen **POPLAR**
asperity **ACRIMONY, ROUGHNESS**

asperse **DEFAME, SLANDER**
aspersion **CALUMNY**
asphalt **BITUMEN**
aspiration **HOPE**
aspiring actress **STARLET**
asp **SNAKE, ADDER, VIPER**
ass **DOLT, FOOL**
assail **BESET**
Assam worm **ERIA**
assault **ATTACK**
assemblage **CREW**
assemble **COLLECT, GATHER, MEET, MUSTER**
assembly **COMPANY, MEETING**
assent **CONSENT, AGREEMENT, COMPLY**
assert **AFFIRM, AVER, AVOW, ALLEGE, CLAIM**
assert as fact **POSIT**
assertion **DECLARATION, STATEMENT**
assertion of right **CLAIM**
assess **CHARGE, LEVY, ESTIMATE**
assess taxes **LEVY**
asset **PROPERTY, RESOURCE**
assign **ASCRIBE, DELEGATE**
assign a portion **ALLOT**
assignation **TRYST**
assigned chore **TASK, STINT, JOB**
assignment **TASK**
assimilate **ABSORB**
assist **AID, HELP, ABET**
assistance **AID, HELP, WELFARE**
assistant **AIDE, HELPER**
associate **COMRADE, COMPANION, PARTNER, COLLEAGUE**
Associated Press (abbr.) **AP**
associates **KITH**
association **CLUB, LEAGUE, ORGANIZATION**
assort **CLASSIFY**
assortment **VARIETY**
assuage **ALLAY**
assume an attitude **POSE**
assume an upright position **STAND**
assume control (2 wds.) **TAKE OVER**
assumed manner **AIRS**
assumed name **ALIAS**
assurance **APLOMB, TRUST**
asterisk **STAR**
astern **AFT**

asthmatic **WHEEZY**
astir **ACTIVE, UP**
astonish **AMAZE, ASTOUND, STUN**
astound **AMAZE**
astral **STARRY, STELLAR**
astride **ASTRADDLE**
astringent **ALUM, STYPTIC**
astronaut Cooper **LEROY**
astronaut's "all right" **AOK**
astronaut's feat (2 wds.) **SPACE WALK**
astronaut's ferry **LEM**
astronaut's garment (2 wds.) **SPACE SUIT**
astronaut's report (2 wds.) **NO GO**
astronomer's tool **TELESCOPE**
astute **SHREWD**
asunder **APART**
Aswan sight **DAM**
Aswan's river **NILE**
as well **ALSO, TOO, AND**
asylum **HAVEN**
at **NEARBY**
at a disadvantage (4 wds.) **OUT ON A LIMB**
at a distance **AFAR, OFF**
at all **EVER**
at all events (3 wds.) **IN ANY CASE**
at all times **EVER**
at bat **UP**
ate **DINED, CONSUMED, GOBBLED**
at ease **POISED, RELAXED, COMFORTABLE**
atelier **STUDIO**
ates **SWEETSOP**
at flood level **AWASH**
at full speed **ALL-OUT**
at hand **NEAR**
Athena **PALLAS**
Athenian historian **XENOPHON**
Athenian lawgiver **SOLON**
Athenian statesman **PERICLES**
Athens' rival **SPARTA**
at highest point **ZENITH, APEX, APOGEE**
athletic center **GYMNASIUM, GYM**
athletic contest **TOURNAMENT, GAME, BOUT, MATCH, MEET**
athletic star **ACE, PRO**
at home **IN**
atimon **MUSKMELON**
Atlantic fish **SALEMA**

| | | | |
|---|---|---|---|
| Atlantic island | CANARY | at that place | THERE |
| atlas chart | MAP | at that time | THEN |
| at last | FINALLY | at the back | AFT, ASTERN |
| at liberty | FREE | at the front | |
| at long last | FINALLY | (3 wds.) | TO THE FORE |
| atmosphere | AIR, AURA, | at the middle | CENTRAL |
| | AMBIANCE | at the middle point | MID |
| atmospheric disturbance | | at the peak | ATOP |
| | STATIC, STORM | at the same time | TOGETHER |
| atmospheric weight | | at the summit | ATOP |
| (2 wds.) | AIR PRESSURE | at the tip | APICAL |
| at no cost | FREE, GRATIS | at this place | HERE |
| at no time | NEVER | at this time | NOW |
| at odds | OUT | attic | GARRET |
| atoll | ISLET, REEF | Attila's followers | HUNS |
| atom | WHIT, PARTICLE | attire | DRESS, GARB, |
| atomic | MINUTE, SMALL | | CLOTHING, ARRAY |
| atomic device | REACTOR, BOMB | attired | |
| atomic number (abbr.) | AT. NO. | | CLAD, DRESSED, |
| atomic particle | PROTON, | | GARBED, BEDECKED |
| | NEUTRON, ELECTRON, | attitude | AIR, SLANT |
| | ION | attorney | LAWYER, COUNSELOR |
| atomize | SPRAY | attorney's charge | FEE |
| atone | EXPIATE | attract | ALLURE, LURE, |
| atonement | AMENDS | | ENTICE, INVITE |
| atop | ON. UPON. OVER, | attraction | CHARM, LURE |
| | SURMOUNTING | attractive | CUTE, MAGNETIC, |
| at present | NOW | | INVITING |
| at rest | EASE | attrap | ADORN, ARRAY |
| atrocious | CRUEL, WICKED | attribute | PROPERTY, REFER, |
| attach | APPEND, ANNEX | | ASSIGN, CREDIT |
| attachment | AFFINITY | attrition | FRICTION |
| attach to | ANNEX | at what place | WHERE |
| attack | SET ON, BESET, | at what time | WHEN |
| | ASSAULT, ASSAIL | auberge | INN |
| attack by waiting | SIEGE | auction | SALE |
| attacker | ASSAILANT | auctioneer | SELLER |
| attack on all sides | BESET | auctioneer's word | SOLD, |
| attack repeatedly | PELT, | | GOING, GONE |
| | ASSAIL | auction participant | BIDDER |
| attain | REACH | audacious | BOLD, INSOLENT |
| attainment | ARRIVAL | audacity | GALL, NERVE, |
| attain recognition | ARRIVE | | CHEEK |
| attain success | WIN | audible respiration | SIGH |
| attempt | TRY, ESSAY | audibility | ALOUD |
| attend | ESCORT, LISTEN | audience | EAR, ATTENTION |
| attendance | PRESENCE | auditorium | HALL |
| attendant | ESCORT, SERVANT | auditory | OTIC, AURAL |
| attendant on board | | auger | TOOL, BORE |
| ship | STEWARD | augment | EKE, ADD, SWELL |
| attending | AT, WITH | augury | OMEN, FORETOKEN, |
| attend to | SEE | | PORTENT, SIGN |
| attention | EAR, AUDIENCE | aura | ATMOSPHERE, AIR, |
| attention-getting sound | AHEM, | | EMANATION |
| | PST | auricle | EAR, PINNA |
| attentive | ALERT | auricular | OTIC |
| attestation | TESTIMONY | Aurora | EOS |
| atter | POISON. VENOM. STING | auspices | EGIS, AEGIS |

| | | | |
|---|---|---|---|
| austere | **SEVERE, HARSH** | auto power source | **BATTERY** |
| Australian animal | **KOALA,** | autumn | **FALL** |
| **KANGAROO, PLATYPUS,** | | autumn pear | **BOSC** |
| | **ECHIDNA** | autumnal beverage | **CIDER** |
| Australian badger | **WOMBAT** | auxiliary | **HELPER, AID, ALLY** |
| Australian beverage | **KAVA** | auxiliary verb | **HAD, WAS,** |
| Australian bird | **EMU** | | **ARE, MAY, CAN, WILL,** |
| Australian capital | **CANBERRA,** | | **HAS, MUST, IS, SHALL,** |
| | **PERTH** | | **SHOULD, COULD** |
| Australian cedar | **TOON** | available | **READY, HANDY** |
| Australian city | **ADELAIDE,** | available, as fresh | |
| **SYDNEY, GEELONG,** | | fruit | **IN SEASON** |
| | **BRISBANE** | available money | **CAPITAL** |
| Australian dog | **DINGO** | available space | **ROOM** |
| Austrian capital | **VIENNA** | avalanche | **SLIDE, FALL** |
| authentic | **REAL** | avarice | **GREED** |
| author Bellow | **SAUL** | avaricious | **MISERLY, STINGY** |
| authoress Ferber | **EDNA** | avatar | **ARCHETYPE** |
| author Fleming | **IAN** | avaunt | **ADVANCE** |
| author Gardner | **ERLE** | ave | **HAIL!** |
| author Harte | **BRET** | avenge | **VINDICATE** |
| author Hunter | **EVAN** | avenge a wrong (3 wds.) | |
| authoritative | | | **SETTLE A SCORE** |
| example | **PRECEDENT** | avenue | **STREET, BOULEVARD,** |
| authoritative rule | **LAW** | | **ROADWAY** |
| authoritative standard | **NORM** | aver | **AFFIRM, ASSERT,** |
| authority | **POWER, SAY** | | **DECLARE** |
| authority on governmental | | average | **MEAN, NORM,** |
| law | **PARLIAMENTARIAN** | | **MEDIAN, SO-SO,** |
| authorize | **LICENSE** | | **PAR, ORDINARY** |
| author Levin | **IRA** | averse | **RELUCTANT** |
| author of "The Inferno" | **DANTE** | aversion | **DISLIKE** |
| author of "Picnic" | **INGE** | avert (2 wds.) | **WARD OFF** |
| author of "Pygmalion" | **SHAW** | aviary | **BIRDHOUSE,** |
| author of "Robinson | | | **SANCTUARY** |
| Crusoe" | **DEFOE** | aviation | **FLYING** |
| author of "The Raven" | **POE** | aviator | **AIRMAN, PILOT** |
| author of "The Song of | | avid | **EAGER, ENTHUSIASTIC,** |
| Hiawatha" | **LONGFELLOW** | | **GREEDY** |
| author Tolstoy | **LEO** | avoid | **AVERT, EVADE, SHUN,** |
| author Turgenev | **IVAN** | | **STEER CLEAR OF** |
| author unknown (abbr.) | **ANON** | avoid as hurtful | **ESCHEW** |
| author's alias | | avoirdupois weight | **TON** |
| (2 wds.) | **PEN NAME** | avow | **DECLARE, AVER,** |
| authoritative command | **FIAT,** | | **CONFESS** |
| | **DECREE** | awabi | **ABALONE** |
| auto | **CAR** | awaft | **AFLOAT, ADRIFT** |
| autocracy | **MONARCHY** | awaiting | **PENDING** |
| autocrat | **DESPOT** | awaken | **ROUSE, STIR** |
| auto frame | **CHASSIS** | award | **GRANT, PRIZE,** |
| auto fuel | **GAS, PETROL,** | | **MEDAL, RECOGNIZE** |
| | **GASOLINE** | aware of | **ONTO, COGNIZANT,** |
| autograph | **SIGNATURE** | | **CONSCIOUS** |
| automation | **ROBOT** | away | **ABSENT, OUT** |
| auto part | **STARTER, CHOKE,** | away (prefix) | **APO, AP, DE** |
| **TRANSMISSION, SPARK** | | away from | **ABSENT, OUT** |
| **PLUG, CARBURETOR,** | | away from the coast | **INLAND** |
| **RADIATOR, HORN** | | away from the wind | **ALEE** |

| | |
|---|---|
| awe | DREAD, FEAR |
| awful | TERRIBLE, HORRIBLE, BAD, GRISLY |
| awkward | MALADROIT, CLUMSY, UNGAINLY, INEPT, GAUCHE |
| awkward person | LOUT, CLOD |
| awning | TILT, SHELTER |
| awry | AGEE, AMISS, WRONG |
| ax | ADZ(E), HATCHET |
| axiom | MAXIM, SAW, LAW |
| axis | LINE |
| axle | PIN, SPINDLE |
| aye | YES, YEA |
| azure | BLUE |

## B

| | |
|---|---|
| baa | BLEAT |
| ba-ba | CAKE |
| babacoote | LEMUR |
| babble | PRATE, PRATTLE |
| baboon | APE |
| baby bear | CUB |
| baby carriage | PRAM, BUGGY |
| baby frog | TADPOLE |
| babyish | CHILDISH, PUERILE |
| Babylonian deity | ANU, ISHTAR, BEL, NEBO, MAROUK, BAAL |
| Babylonian people | ELAMITE |
| baby powder | TALC, TALCUM |
| baby rabbit | BUNNY |
| baby's apron | BIB |
| baby's bed | CRADLE, CRIB, BASSINET |
| baby's game | PEEKABOO |
| baby's good-bye | TATA |
| baby's hat | BONNET |
| baby sheep | LAMB |
| baby shoe | BOOTEE, BOOTIE |
| baby's napkin | BIB |
| baby's plaything | RATTLE, TOY |
| baby's supervisor | NURSEMAID, NANNY |
| baby's toy | RATTLE |
| baby's underclothing | DIAPER |
| Bacchanals' cry | EVOE |
| bachelor | CELIBATE |
| bachelor's last words (2 wds.) | I DO |
| bacillus | GERM, MICROBE, BACTERIA |
| back | SUPPORT, UPHOLD, AFT, AID, ENDORSE |
| backbone | SPINE |

| | |
|---|---|
| back country | HINTERLAND, STICKS, BUSH |
| back end | REAR |
| background | REAR, EXPERIENCE |
| background of a play | SETTING |
| backless chair | STOOL |
| backless top | HALTER |
| back of the foot | HEEL |
| back of the neck | NAPE |
| back out | WITHDRAW |
| back pain | NOTALGIA |
| back street | ALLEY |
| back talk | SASS |
| back up | ACCUMULATE, REVERSE |
| backward | REVERSE, SHY |
| backwater | BAYOU |
| backyard barrier | FENCE |
| bacon portion | RASHER |
| bacteria | GERMS |
| bacterial culture | AGAR |
| bad | EVIL, NAUGHTY |
| bad dream | NIGHTMARE |
| bade | ORDERED, COMMANDED, SUMMONED |
| badge | EMBLEM, TOKEN, INSIGNIA |
| badger | TEASE |
| badgerlike animal | RATEL |
| Badger State | WISCONSIN |
| badinage | BANTER, REPARTEE |
| badly | ILL |
| badness | EVIL |
| baffle | OUTWIT |
| baffling question | POSER |
| bag | POKE, SAC(K), POUCH, PURSE |
| bagatelle | TRIFLE |
| bag closure | DRAWSTRING |
| baggage | LUGGAGE, SUITCASES, CASES, GRIPS, TRUNKS, VALISES |
| baggage handler | PORTER, BELL HOP |
| baggy | LOOSE |
| baggy knickers (2 wds.) | PLUS FOURS |
| bagpipe horn | DRONE |
| bail | SCOOP |
| bait | LURE |
| bake | COOK, ROAST |
| bake eggs | SHIRR |
| baker's dozen | THIRTEEN |
| baker's shovel | PEEL |
| bakery item | PIE, CAKE, CREAM PUFF, BREAD, ROLL, BUN, TART, DANISH, PASTRY, COOKIE |

baking dish **RAMEKIN, SHEET, CASSEROLE**
baking ingredient **SODA, YEAST, FLOUR, SALT**
baking chamber **OVEN, OAST, KILN**
baking item **PIN, ROLLER,**
baking pit **IMU, UMU**
baking soda **SALERATUS**
baking tin (2 wds.) **PIE PAN, CAKE PAN, COOKIE SHEET**
baksheesh **TIP, ALMS**
Balaam's mount **ASS**
balance **POISE**
balance-sheet loss **DEFICIT**
balance unsteadily **TEETER**
bald **HAIRLESS**
balderdash **NONSENSE**
bald head **PATE**
bale **BUNDLE**
Balearic island **MAJORCA**
baleful **EVIL, SINISTER, DIRE, HARMFUL, MALIGNANT**
balk **FOIL**
ball **DANCE**
ballad **SONG**
ballast **WEIGHT**
ballerina **DANCER**
ballerina's strong points **TOES**
ballet **DANCE**
ball of medicine **PILL**
ball of paper **WAD**
ball of yarn **CLEW**
ballot **VOTE, TICKET**
ballot caster **VOTER**
ball park events (2 wds.) **HOME RUN, DOUBLE PLAY, TRIPLE PLAY, BASE HIT, DOUBLE HEADER, LADY'S DAY, SHUTOUT**
ballroom dance **FOX TROT, RUMBA, SAMBA, WALTZ, TANGO, TWO STEP, CARIOCA, POLKA**
balls of fringe **TASSELS**
ball team **NINE**
ballyhoo **PUBLICITY**
balmy **MILD, INSANE**
balsam tree **FIR**
Baltic city **DANZIG**
Baltic port **RIGA**
Baltic river **ODER, NEVA, NARVA, NEMAN, DAL, VISTULA, UME, TORNE**
Baltimore **PORT**
Baltimore bird **ORIOLE**
balustrade **RAILING**
Bambi **DEER**

bambino **BABY**
Bambi's mother **DOE**
bamboolike grass **REEDS**
bamboo medicine **TABASHEER, TABASHIR**
bamboo stem **CANE**
bamboozle **HOAX**
ban **INTERDICTION, INTERDICT, PROHIBIT, PROHIBITION, FORBID, EXCOMMUNICATE**
banal **HACKNEYED, TRITE**
banana **PLANTAIN**
banana republic **HONDURAS**
band **ORCHESTRA, GROUP**
bandage **BIND, TOURNIQUET**
bandicott **RAT**
band instrument **DRUM, SNARE, DRUM, SAX, TUBA, FIFE, BUGLE, FLUTE, HORN**
bandit **OUTLAW, ROBBER**
bandleader **CONDUCTOR**
bandleader Arnaz **DESI**
bandleader Weems **TED**
bandleader's stick **BATON**
bandleader's wand **BATON**
bandy **CART**
bane **RUIN, HARM, WOE**
baneful **HARMFUL**
bang **BEAT, SLAM**
bang a door **SLAM**
banishment **EXILE**
banister **RAIL, RAILING**
bank **RIVERSIDE, MOUNT, RIDGE**
bank employee **TELLER, GUARD**
bank payment (abbr.) **INT**
bankrupt **RUIN**
bank safe **VAULT**
bank transaction **LOAN**
banner **FLAG**
banquet **FEAST, REPAST**
bantam car **JEEP**
banter **BADINAGE**
Bantu language **ILA**
baptismal vessel **FONT**
baptismal water **LAVER**
bar **COUNTER, STRIPE, TAVERN, INN**
barb **THORN**
barbarian **GOTH**
barbarous **CRUEL**
barbecue **COOKOUT**
barber's concern **HAIR, BEARD**
barber's tool **RAZOR, CLIPPER**
barb of feather **PINNULA, PINNULE**

| | | | |
|---|---|---|---|
| bard | MINSTREL, POET | baseballer Hodges | GIL |
| Bard's river | AVON | baseballer Kaline | AL |
| bare | EMPTY, NUDE, | baseballer Koufax | SANDY |
| | UNDECORATED, UNVEIL | baseballer Mantle | MICKEY |
| barefaced | IMPUDENT, | baseballer Maris | ROGER |
| | SHAMELESS | baseballer Musial | STAN |
| barely | HARDLY | baseballer Ott | MEL |
| barely audible | FAINT | baseballer Robinson | JACK, |
| bargain | DICKER | | FRANK, BROOKS |
| bargain basement event | SALE | baseballer Ruth | BABE |
| barge | SCOW, BOAT | baseballer Seaver | TOM |
| barge-load of coal | KEEL | baseballer Slaughter | ENOS |
| bar item | ALE, BEER | baseballer Williams | TED |
| bark | SKIN, YELP | baseball fan | ROOTER |
| bark at | BAY | baseball field | DIAMOND |
| bark-like | CORTEX | baseball game | |
| barnyard bird | ROOSTER, | divisions | INNINGS |
| | GOOSE, HEN, DUCK, | baseball glove | MITT |
| | GANDER, CHICKEN | baseball goal | HOME |
| barnyard sound | MOO, OINK, | baseball hit | HOMER, DOUBLE, |
| | CLUCK, BAA, MAA, | | TRIPLE, SINGLE |
| | QUACK, WHINNY, CROW | baseball nickname | BABE, |
| bar of metal | INGOT | | LEFTY |
| bar of soap | CAKE | baseball nine | TEAM |
| barometer line | ISOBAR | baseball official | UMPIRE, UMP |
| baronet's title | SIR | baseball player | FIELDER, |
| barracks | CASERN | | PITCHER, SHORTSTOP, |
| barrage | CANNONADE | | INFIELDER, OUTFIELDER, |
| barranca | RAVINE | | CATCHER, BATTER, |
| barrel | KEG, CASK | | CENTER FIELDER, RIGHT |
| barrel band | HOOP | | FIELDER |
| barrel organ | HURDY-GURDY | baseball position | PLATE, |
| barrel section | STAVE | | BASE, OUTFIELD, |
| barrel stopper | BUNG | | INFIELD, SECOND |
| barren | ARID, FRUITLESS, | | BASE, SHORTSTOP |
| | CHILDLESS, DEVOID | baseball stick | BAT, FUNGO |
| barrier | BAR, BLOCKADE | baseball stopover point | BASE |
| barrier around a yard | FENCE | baseball team number | NINE |
| barrister's concern | TRIAL, | based on | |
| | BRIEF, CASE | experience | EMPIRICAL |
| barroom | TAP | base in Greenland | ETAH |
| barter | SWAP, TRADE | baseman | INFIELDER |
| bartizan | TURRET | basement | CELLAR |
| Bartlett | PEAR | base of leaf | AXIL |
| Bartok | BELA | bashful | COY, SHY, TIMID, |
| base | FOUNDATION, FOUND | | MODEST |
| baseball | NATIONAL PASTIME | basic | FUNDAMENTAL |
| baseball catcher | BACKSTOP | basic food | BREAD, RICE, |
| baseball club | BAT, TEAM, | | GRAIN, WHEAT |
| | NINE | basin | TANK, SINK, VESSEL |
| baseball coup | NO-HITTER, | basis | GROUNDWORK, ROOT, |
| | SHUTOUT, HOME RUN, | | FOUNDATION |
| | TRIPLE PLAY, HOMER | basis of argument | PREMISE |
| baseballer Aaron | HANK | bask | LUXURIATE |
| baseballer Agee | TOMMY | basketball group (abbr.) | N.B.A. |
| baseballer Berra | YOGI | basketball misplay | FOUL |
| baseballer DiMaggio | JOE, DOM | basketball team | FIVE |
| baseballer Gehrig | LOU | basket twig | WATTLE |

| | | | |
|---|---|---|---|
| basket willow | OSIER | bear (Lat.) | URSUS, URSA |
| Basque game | PELOTA | bear cat | PANDA |
| Basque headwear | BERET | beard of grain | AWN |
| basslike marine fish | SNAPPER | bearded titmouse | REEDLING |
| basswood tree | LINDEN | bearing | MIEN, PRESENCE |
| bast | FIBER | bearlike | URSINE |
| baste | HEM, SEW, MOISTEN | bearlike animal | PANDA |
| bat | HIT, CLUB | bear's home | DEN |
| bastion | EPAULE | bear up under | TOLERATE |
| bath | SAUNA, TUB | bear witness to | ATTEST |
| bathe | LAVE, WASH | beast | ANIMAL, BRUTE |
| bath house | CABANA | beastly | BRUTAL, CRUEL |
| bathing place | TUB | beast of burden | ASS, CAMEL, |
| bathrobe fabric | TERRY | | HORSE, OX, MULE, |
| bathroom fixture | SHOWER, | | BURRO. LLAMA, |
| | TUB, SINK | | ELEPHANT |
| Batman or | | beast's stomach | MAW |
| Robin | CRIMEFIGHTER | beat | POUND, TEMPO, |
| baton | STICK | | RHYTHM, WHIP, THROB, |
| batter | RAM, HITTER | | PULSE, PULSATE |
| battery plate | GRID | beat back | REPULSE |
| battle | DUEL, WAR, FRAY, | beaten way | PATH |
| | FIGHT, MELEE | beatitude | JOY, HAPPINESS |
| Battle-Born State | NEVADA | Beatles' drummer | RINGO |
| battle memento | SCAR | Beatles' movie | HELP, HARD |
| battle with lances | JOUST | | DAY'S NIGHT, YELLOW |
| bauble | PLAYTHING | | SUBMARINE, LET IT BE |
| bauxite | ORE, ALUMINUM | beatnik's abode | PAD |
| bay | COVE, INLET, TREE | beau | ESCORT, LOVER, |
| bay bird | SNIPE, PLOVER | | ADMIRER |
| bayou | CREEK, ESTUARY | beautiful | FAIR, LOVELY, |
| Bay State | MASSACHUSETTS | | PRETTY |
| bay tree | LAUREL | beautify | ADORN |
| bay window | ORIEL | beauty | GRACE |
| bazaar | FAIR | beauty aid | CURLER, WIG, |
| bazaar stall | BOOTH | | COSMETIC |
| be | EXIST | beauty of movement | GRACE |
| beach | SHORE, STRAND, | beauty preparation | COSMETIC |
| | SEASIDE, PLAYA | beauty shop | SALON, PARLOR |
| beach feature | DUNE, SAND | beauty spot | MOLE |
| beacon | LIGHT | beaver skin | PELT, PLEW |
| be adjacent to | ABUT | Beaver State | OREGON |
| beadle | USHER | be beholden to | OWE |
| be afraid | FEAR | be careful of | BEWARE |
| be agitated | SEETHE | because | FOR, SINCE, AS |
| be agreeable to | PLEASE | be chief feature of | DOMINATE, |
| beak | NIB, BILL | | STAR |
| beaker | CUP | beck | BIDDING |
| beam | EMIT, GIRDER | beckon | MOTION, WAVE |
| be a match for | COPE | be clothed in | WEAR |
| be ambitious | ASPIRE | becloud | DARKEN, CONFUSE |
| be a member | BELONG | become a Benedict | WED |
| beam of light | RAY | become accustomed | INURE, |
| bean | LIMA, SOY | | ENURE |
| bear | CARRY, GRIZZLY, | become adept in | MASTER |
| | SUPPORT, KOALA, POLAR | become a nun | TAKE THE VEIL |
| | TOLERATE, STAND, | become apparent | EMERGE |
| | SUFFER, ABIDE, YIELD | become a tenant | RENT |

| | | | |
|---|---|---|---|
| become aware of | SENSE | be correct size | FIT |
| become bankrupt | FAIL | bed | COT, FOUR POSTER, |
| become better | IMPROVE | | COUCH, BUNK, |
| become buoyant | FLOAT, | | BERTH, CHAISE |
| | LEVITATE | bed and board | HOME |
| become covered with | | bedaub | SMEAR, SOIL |
| fungus | MILDEW | bedaze | STUN |
| become crooked | BEND | bed board | SLAT |
| become curved | BEND | bed cover | BLANKET, |
| become depressed | DESPOND | SPREAD, QUILT, COMFORTER, | |
| become different | ALTER | | SHEET, COVERLET |
| become dirty | SOIL | bedding | LINEN |
| become drowsy | NOD | bedeck | ADORN |
| become entangled | MAT | be deeply affected | |
| become faded | PALE | by | TAKE TO HEART |
| become firm | GEL, SET | be defeated | LOSE |
| become fond of | TAKE TO | be deficient | FALL SHORT, LACK |
| become formed | TAKE SHAPE | bedevil | HARASS, CONFUSE |
| become frayed | WEAR | bedim | CLOUD |
| become furious | RAGE | bedlam | MADHOUSE |
| become ill | AIL | Bedlington | TERRIER |
| become indistinct | BLUR | bed of flowers | GARDEN |
| become insipid | PALL | bed of straw | PALLET |
| become | | Bedouin | ARAB |
| insufficient | RUN SHORT | bedroom | CHAMBER |
| become less | ABATE | bedroom furniture | DRESSER, |
| become less stern | RELENT | | VANITY, BUREAU, |
| become lively | PERK | | NIGHTSTAND |
| become manifest | EMERGE | bedroom shoe | SLIPPER, MULE |
| become mature | RIPEN, AGE | bedside light | LAMP |
| become mellow | AGE, RIPEN | bedspread material | CHENILLE |
| become more genial | THAW | be dull | BORE |
| become more profound | DEEPEN | bee | APIS |
| become morose | SOUR | beech | TREE |
| become old | AGE | beef | MEAT |
| become one | MERGE | beef animal | STEER |
| become overcast | DIM | beef cattle | LONGHORN |
| become oxidized | RUST | beef fat | SUET |
| become reconciled | MAKE UP | Beehive State | UTAH |
| become ripe | MATURE | beekeeper | APIARIST |
| become smaller | DWINDLE | beelzebub | DEVIL, SATAN |
| become sound | HEAL | beep | HONK |
| become sour | TART | bee product | HONEY |
| become stale | STAGNATE | be enough | DO, SUFFICE |
| become submerged | SINK | be equal | TIE |
| become thin with use | WEAR | beer | LAGER, PILSNER, |
| become twisted | GNARL | | BREW, SUDS |
| become unwoven | RAVEL | beer barrel | CASK, KEG |
| become very cold | FREEZE | beer cask | BUTT |
| become visible | APPEAR | beer glass | STEIN, MUG |
| become void | LAPSE | beer ingredient | HOPS, MALT, |
| become weary | TIRE | | YEAST |
| become worn | FRAY | beerlike drink | ALE, STOUT, |
| become zealous | ENTHUSE | | PORTER |
| becoming | FIT, PROPER | beer maker | BREWER |
| be compelled | MUST | beer mug | STEIN |
| be concerned | CARE | bee's home | HIVE |
| be contiguous | ABUT | beet | CHARD, SUGAR |

beet genus **BETA**
beetle **DOR**
beetleheaded **STUPID**
beetlenut palm **ARECA**
befall **BETIDE, HAPPEN**
be festive **REVEL**
be finical **FUSS**
before (Lat.) **ANTE**
before (poet.) **ERE**
before (prefix) **PRE**
before all others **FIRST**
before birth **PRENATAL**
before deductions **NET**
beforehand **IN ADVANCE, AHEAD**
before long **ANON, SOON**
before noon (abbr.) **AM**
before this **ERE, SINCE**
beforetime **FORMERLY**
befoul **SOIL**
befriend **ASSIST, ABET**
befuddle **CONFUSE**
befuddled **ASEA, IN A FOG, AT SEA, CONFUSED, MUDDLED**
beg **PLEAD, ENTREAT, IMPLORE, CADGE, SPONGE, MOOCH, BESEECH**
beget **PRODUCE, PROCREATE**
begetter **PARENT**
beggar **MENDICANT, BUM, PANHANDLER, PAUPER**
beggarly **MEAN, INDIGENT**
begin **OPEN, START, SET OUT, FALL TO**
begin a battle **ATTACK**
begin a day **RISE, AWAKEN**
begin again **RENEW, REOPEN**
begin an ocean voyage **SAIL, EMBARK**
begin eating **DIG IN**
beginner **STARTER, TIRO, TYRO, NOVICE, GREENHORN, TENDERFOOT, NEOPHYTE, FRESHMAN**
beginning **ONSET, NASCENT, EMERGING, ROOT, START**
beginning of day **DAWN, SUNRISE**
beginning of flight **TAKEOFF**
beginning of marriage **HONEYMOON**
beginning of social career **DEBUT**
beginning socialite **DEB**

beginning worker **APPRENTICE, TRAINEE**
begin to develop **BUD**
begin war **ATTACK**
begird **SURROUND**
begone **SHOO, SCAT, GO, LEAVE, BEAT IT, VAMOOSE**
begonia **FLOWER**
begrime **SOIL**
begrudge **ENVY**
beguile **DECEIVE, CHEAT, DELUDE**
beguiled **AMUSED**
beguine **DANCE**
behalf **PART, SUPPORT**
behalf of **FOR**
behave **ACT**
behave badly **MISBEHAVE**
behave childishly **CRY**
behave foolishly **CARRY ON**
behave menacingly **THREATEN, FRIGHTEN**
behave theatrically **EMOTE**
behave with dignity **ACT ONE'S AGE**
behavior **COMPORTMENT, DEPORTMENT, MANNER**
behest **COMMAND**
behind **AFTER, LATE, SLOW**
behind a ship **ASTERN**
behind in payments **IN ARREARS**
behind the curtain **BACKSTAGE**
behold **LO**
behold (Lat.) **ECCE**
beige **TAN, ECRU**
be ill **AIL**
be imminent **IMPEND**
be in a fury **RAGE**
be in command **LEAD**
be in contact **TOUCH**
be in debt **OWE**
be indignant **RESENT**
being **ESSENCE, EXISTENCE**
being (Fr.) **ETRE**
being (Lat.) **ESSE**
being broadcast **ON THE AIR**
being in a fairy tale **OGRE**
being from Aladdin's lamp **GENIE**
be in harmony **AGREE**
be in store for **AWAIT**
be interested **CARE**
be irritated **FRET**
be kept waiting **COOL ONE'S HEELS**
belabor **ASSAIL**
beldam **HAG**

belfry **TOWER**
Belgian capital **BRUSSELS**
Belgian port **OSTEND, ANTWERP**
belie **DENY**
belief **CREDO, CREDENCE, CREED, RELIGION, FAITH**
believe **OPINE, THINK, JUDGE**
believer (suffix) **IST**
believer in facts **REALIST**
believer in God **THEIST**
belittle **DISPARAGE**
bell **CHIME, GONG**
bellicose **WARLIKE**
belligerent **HOSTILE**
bellow **ROAR**
bell-shaped flower **TULIP**
bell-shaped hat **CLOCHE**
bell sound **BONG, TINKLE, DING, GONG, PEAL, TOLL, CHIME**
bell tower **BELFRY, CAMPANILE**
be lofty **TOWER**
belonging to him **HIS**
belonging to me **MINE**
belonging to the thing **ITS**
belonging to us **OUR, OURS**
belongings **PROPERTY**
beloved **DEAR**
beloved Disciple **JOHN**
below **BENEATH, UNDER, UNDERNEATH**
below key **FLAT**
belt **STRAP, BAND**
belt fastener **BUCKLE**
belt of calm **DOLDRUMS**
beluga **CAVIAR**
be made up of **CONSIST**
be master of **POSSESS**
be merciful **SPARE**
be mistaken **ERR**
bemoan **LAMENT**
be moodily silent **SULK**
bemuse **DAZE**
Ben Cartwright's boy **HOSS, JOE**
bench **SEAT, PEW, CHAIR**
bend **CURVE**
bend down **STOOP**
bend downward **SAG**
bender **SPREE**
bend low **CROUCH**
bend over **STOOP**
bend the head **BOW**
be near **STAND BY**
beneath **BELOW, UNDER, UNDERNEATH**

beneath the earth **UNDERGROUND**
benediction **BLESSING, PRAYER**
benefactor **HELPER, PATRON**
beneficial **USEFUL**
beneficiary of a will **HEIR**
benefit **STEAD**
benevolence **KINDNESS**
Bengal capitol **CALCUTTA**
Bengal cat **TIGER**
bent pipe **SIPHON**
bent to one side **WRY**
be obedient **BEHAVE**
be of consequence **MATTER**
be of importance **MATTER**
be of one mind **AGREE**
be of the opinion **BELIEVE**
be of use **AVAIL**
be on fire **BURN**
be on one's feet **STAND**
be overly fond **DOTE**
be present **ATTEND**
be quiet **SH**
berate **NAG, SCOLD**
Berber **ARAB**
be ready for **AWAIT**
be reluctant **BALK**
beret **CAP**
be revived **COME TO**
Berliner **GERMAN**
Berlin's divider **WALL**
Bernstein, for short **LEN**
berry **CURRANT**
beseech **BEG, ENTREAT, PLEAD, IMPLORE**
be sensitive to **FEEL**
beset **ATTACK, BESIEGE**
be sick **AIL**
beside (prefix) **PARA, PAR**
besides **ALSO, ELSE, TO BOOT, TOO**
besiege **BESET, ATTACK**
be situated **LIE, SIT, SETTLED**
besmear **SOIL**
besom **BROOM**
be sorry for **PITY**
be sparing **STINT**
bespatter **DAUB, SPLASH**
best **OUTSTRIP, BEAT, OUT-DO, GREATEST, LARGEST**
bestial **BRUTAL, CRUEL**
bestow **GRANT, AWARD, GIVE**
be successful **GO FAR**
be sufficient **AMPLE, DO**
be suitable **FIT**
bet **WAGER**

| | |
|---|---|
| betel palm | ARECA |
| betray | SELL |
| betrayal | TREASON |
| be sparing | STINT |
| be undecided | WAVER |
| be unsuccessful | FAIL |
| be victorious | WIN |
| be without | LACK |
| be worthy of | DESERVE |
| be wrong | ERR |
| beach | SHORE, STRAND, SEASIDE, PLAYA |
| beach feature | DUNE, SAND |
| betrothed | ENGAGED |
| better balanced | SANER |
| betting factor | ODDS |
| betting method | PARLAY |
| betting odds | PRICE |
| between (Fr.) | ENTRE |
| between (prefix) | INTER |
| bevel | SLANT |
| bevel corners | SPLAY |
| beverage | TEA, ALE, BEER, COFFEE, MILK, SODA, WINE |
| beverage container | TEAPOT, GLASS, TUMBLER, BOTTLE, CARTON, CAN, FLASK, PITCHER, CUP |
| beverage glasses | STEMWARE, TUMBLERS |
| bevy | FLOCK |
| bewail | LAMENT, MOAN |
| bewildered | AT SEA, ASEA, BEFUDDLED, LOST, CONFUSED |
| bewitch | CHARM |
| beyond | YONDER, ABOVE |
| beyond control | OUT OF HAND |
| beyond the limit | OUT |
| bias | SLANT, PREJUDICE |
| bias binding | TAPE |
| bib | TUCKER |
| Biblical angel | RAPHAEL, GABRIEL, MICHAEL |
| Biblical boat | ARK |
| Biblical brother | ABEL, CAIN, JOSEPH, ESAU, JACOB, REUBEN, SIMEON, BENJAMIN, JUDAH |
| Biblical character | LOT, ARA, IRA, ABEL, JOAB, JOB, AMOS, MICAH, MOSES, AARON, ZADOK, ELI, BOAZ |
| Biblical dancer | SALOME |
| Biblical garden | EDEN, GETHSEMANE |
| Biblical hero | NOAH |

| | |
|---|---|
| Biblical king | ASA, HEROD, HIRAM, DAVID, SOLOMON, SAUL, JOSIAH, AHAB, OMRI, HEZEKIAH, JEHORAM, AHAZ, ELAH |
| Biblical land | OPHIR, ELAM, MOAB, CANAAN, EGYPT |
| Biblical liar | ANANIAS |
| Biblical measure | OMER |
| Biblical mountain | ARARAT, SINAI, CARMEL, JARMAK, EBAL, THABOR, NEBO, GARIZIM, LEBANON |
| Biblical name of Syria | ARAM |
| Biblical passage | TEXT |
| Biblical Patriarch | MOSES, NOAH |
| Biblical preposition | UNTO |
| Biblical pronoun | THY, THOU, THINE |
| Biblical plotter | HAMAN |
| Biblical priest | AARON, LEVI, SADOC |
| Biblical prophet | HOSEA, AMOS, MICAH, ISAIA, DANIEL, OSEE, JOEL, ABDIA, JONAH, NAHUM, HABACUC, ELIA |
| Biblical story | PARABLE |
| Biblical strong man | SAMSON |
| Biblical tower | BABEL |
| Biblical town | CANA, LOD, HEBRON |
| Biblical tribe | ANAK, LEVI, DAN |
| Biblical vessel | ARK |
| Biblical weed | TARE |
| Biblical witch's home | ENDOR |
| Biblical word | SELAH |
| bicker | ARGUE |
| bicuspid | TOOTH |
| bicycle for two | TANDEM |
| bicycle part | PEDAL |
| bid | OFFER, COMMAND |
| biddy | HEN |
| bide | TARRY, WAIT |
| big | LARGE, HUGE, IMMENSE, VAST, MAMMOTH, GIANT, GIGANTIC, COLOSSAL |
| big and strong | BURLY |
| Big Bend State | TENNESSEE |
| big book | TOME |
| big boy | MAN |
| big bundle | BALE |
| big coffee pot | URN |
| big deer | ELK |
| bigeye | FISH |
| big girl | WOMAN |
| big house | PRISON, PEN |
| big leaguer | PRO |

big man **TITAN, GIANT**
big monkey **APE, GORILLA, ORANGUTAN**
big name in golf **PALMER, SNEAD, HOGAN, CASPER, BEARD, NICKLAUS, WOOD**
bigoted **NARROW**
bigotry **PREJUDICE**
big top **TENT**
bijou **JEWEL, GEM**
bile **CHOLER, ANGER**
bilk **CHEAT, SWINDLE**
bill **NIB, BEAK, INVOICE, TARIFF, CHECK, NEB**
billabong **LAGOON**
billboard **SIGN, POSTER**
billiard shot **CAROM, MASSE, BANK, BREAK, DRAW, KISS**
billiard stick **CUE**
billiards **POOL**
bill of fare **MENU**
bill of lading (abbr.) **BL**
billow **SURGE, WAVE**
billowy expanse **OCEAN, SEA**
billy **CLUB**
billy or nanny **GOAT**
bin **CRIB, BOX**
binary **DOUBLE, DUAL, TWOFOLD**
bind **TIE, LASH, BANDAGE**
bind closely **ALLY, TIE**
binding custom **LAW**
bind up **GIRD, TRUSS**
binge **SPREE, TOOT**
bingo **GAME**
biographer Ludwig **EMIL**
biography **LIFE**
biological classification **GENUS**
biological determinant **GENE**
birchbark boat **CANOE**
bird **AUK, FINCH, ORIOLE, SERIN, TERN, CANARY, OWL, SPARROW, SWALLOW, SWAN, RAVEN, PARROT, PARAKEET, WREN, HAWK, CROW, EAGLE, DOVE, CHICKADEE, BLUEJAY, CARDINAL, GROSBEAK, REDPOL, BUZZARD, OSPREY, VULTURE, ERNE, ALBATROSS, PIGEON, LOON, QUAIL, GROUSE, PENGUIN, PETREL, BOOBIE, FALCON, STORK, SWIFT, GULL, DODO, THRUSH**
bird (Lat.) **AVIS**
bird (prefix) **AVI**

bird call **NOTE, TWEET, SONG, TRILL, CHIRP, TWEE**
bird clapper **SCARECROW**
bird class **AVES**
bird claw **TALON**
bird enclosure **CAGE**
bird feed **SUET, SEED**
bird home **NEST, AVIARY**
bird keeper **AVIARIST**
bird of Jove **EAGLE**
bird of peace **DOVE**
bird of prey **EAGLE, HAWK, KITE, OWL, FALCON, BUZZARD, VULTURE**
bird's arm **WING**
bird's beak **BILL, NEB**
bird's crop **CRAW**
bird's flapper **WING**
bird's food **SEED**
bird's home **NEST, AERIE**
bird's perch **ROOST**
bireme **GALLEY, SHIP**
birth **ORIGIN**
birthday figure **AGE**
birthmark **NEVUS, MOLE**
birthright **HERITAGE**
birthstone for April **DIAMOND**
birthstone for August **PERIDOT**
birthstone for December **TURQUOISE**
birthstone for February **AMETHYST**
birthstone for January **GARNET**
birthstone for July **RUBY**
birthstone for June **PEARL**
birthstone for March **AQUAMARINE**
birthstone for May **EMERALD**
birthstone for November **TOPAZ**
birthstone for October **OPAL**
birthstone for September **SAPPHIRE**
bis **TWICE**
biscuit **BUN**
bisect **HALVE**
bishop **PRELATE**
bishopric **SEE**
bishop's hat **MITRE**
bishop's throne **SEE**
bison **BUFFALO**
bisque **SOUP**
bistro **BAR**
bit **MORSEL, SCRAP**
bite **MOUTHFUL, NIBBLE, GNAW, NIP, SNAP, STING, TANG, CHEW**
bite impatiently **CHAMP**
bite off **GHAW**
biting **ACRID, CAUSTIC**

| | |
|---|---|
| bit of floating dust | MOTE |
| bit of news | ITEM |
| bits of fluff | LINT |
| bitter | ACRID |
| bitter nut | KOLA |
| bitter vetch | ERS |
| bivalve | CLAM, MUSSEL |
| bivouac | CAMP, ENCAMP |
| bizarre | OUTRE, ODD |
| Bizet opera | CARMEN |
| blab | TELL, TATTLE |
| black | EBON, EBONY |
| black and blue | LIVID |
| black art | MAGIC |
| black-backed gull | COB(B) |
| Black Beauty | HORSE |
| black bird | ANI, CROW, DAW, RAVEN, GRACKLE, MERLE |
| blackboard | SLATE |
| black bread | RYE |
| black buck | SASIN |
| black dairy cow | KERRY |
| black death | PLAGUE |
| black diamond | COAL |
| blacken | CHAR |
| black eye | SHINER |
| black face | MINSTREL |
| blackface music show | MINSTREL |
| blackfin | FISH, SNAPPER |
| black flag | JOLLY ROGER |
| black fuel | COAL |
| black gold | OIL |
| blackguard | SCOUNDREL |
| black hole | CELL, BRIG |
| black lacquer | JAPAN |
| black leg (Brit.) | SCAB |
| black magic | WITCHCRAFT |
| blackmail | EXTORT |
| black mark | DEMERIT |
| Blackmore heroine | LORNA |
| blacksmith shop | FORGE |
| black snake | RACER |
| black tea | BOHEA |
| blackthorn fruit | SLOE |
| black-tongued dog | CHOW |
| blacktop | PAVE |
| black widow | SPIDER |
| black wood | EBONY |
| blade | SWORD, KNIFE, DIRK |
| blade bone | SCAPULA |
| blame | ACCUSE, CENSURE |
| blameless | INNOCENT |
| blanch | ETIOLATE, WHITEN |
| blanched | PALE, WHITE |
| blank | VOID, EMPTY |
| blank book | TABLET |
| blase | BORED, JADED |

| | |
|---|---|
| blast | EXPLOSION |
| blast of wind | GUST |
| blaze | FLAME, FLARE, FIRE, CUT, FLASH |
| blaze brightly | FLARE |
| blazing | AFIRE |
| bleak | DESOLATE |
| bleat | BAA, MAA |
| blemish | SCAR, SPOT, FLAW, DEFECT |
| blend | MERGE, MIX |
| bless | HALLOW |
| blessed | BLEST, HALLOWED, SAINT |
| blessing | BOON, GRACE, BENEDICTION |
| blessing (arch.) | BENISON |
| blimp | BALLOON, DIRIGIBLE |
| blind fear | PANIC |
| blink | WINK |
| blithe | MERRY, GAY |
| blockade | SIEGE |
| blockhead | ASS, DOLT, DOPE, OAF, FOOL, DUNCE |
| bloke | CHAP |
| blond | GOLDEN, FAIR, FLAXEN |
| blood-building meat | LIVER |
| blood deficiency | ANEMIA |
| blood fluid | PLASMA |
| blood giver | DONER |
| blood (prefix) | HEMO, HEMA, HEM |
| blooper | ERROR, BLUNDER |
| blossom | BLOOM, FLOWER |
| blot | SPOT, STAIN |
| blot out | ERASE |
| blouse | WAIST |
| blouse ruffle | JABOT |
| blow | HIT, STROKE |
| blow a horn | TOOT, HONK |
| blow hard | BRAGGART |
| blue | AZURE, INDIGO, SAD, MOPEY |
| blue dye | ANIL |
| blue fin | TUNA |
| blue flag | IRIS |
| Bluegrass State | KENTUCKY |
| blue jeans material | DENIM |
| Blue Law State | CONNECTICUT |
| blue or white bird | GREAT HERON |
| blue-pencil | EDIT |
| blue pigment | BICE, SMALT |
| Blue Point | OYSTER |
| blue pottery | DELFT |
| blueprint | PLAN |
| blue-white star in Lyra | VEGA |

| | | | |
|---|---|---|---|
| bluff | GRUFF, RUDE, HOODWINK | boil | STEW, SIMMER, SEETHE |
| bluish gray | SLATE | boil down | CONDENSE, REDUCE |
| bluish-white metal | ZINC | bold | PERT, DARING, SASSY, NERVY, CHEEKY, BRAVE, VENTURESOME |
| blunder | ERR, MISTAKE, ERROR, SNAFU | boldness | COURAGE, DARING |
| blunt | DULL | bolero | DANCE, JACKET |
| blur | DIM, OBSCURE | Bolivian mountains | ANDES |
| blurt out | BLAT, BLAB | Bolshevik | LENIN, TROTSKY |
| blush | REDDEN | bolster | PILLOW |
| blushing | ROSY | bombastic speech | HARANGUE |
| boa | SERPENT, SNAKE, PYTHON, SCARF | bond | TIE, BAIL |
| | | bondage | SLAVERY |
| boar | PIG | bondsman | SLAVE |
| board | PLANK | bone | OS |
| boarder | ROOMER | boneblack | CHARCOAL |
| boardinghouse fare | HASH | bone-dry | ARID |
| boarhound | GREAT DANE | boner | BLUNDER |
| boast | BLOW, BRAG | bone structure | SKELETON |
| boat | CANOE, SHIP, VESSEL | bongo | DRUM |
| boat basin | MARINA | bonito | ALBACORE |
| boat paddle | OAR | bonnet | HAT, TOQUE |
| boat ride | SAIL | boo | HISS |
| boat rope | HAWSER, LINE | boob | SAP, DOPE, FOOL, DOLT |
| boat's company | CREW | book | FOLIO, TOME |
| boat side | GUNWALE | bookbinding leather | ROAN |
| boat's radio | SHIP-TO-SHORE | book cover | BINDING |
| boat's power source | OUTBOARD MOTOR | bookish | STODGY |
| | | bookkeeper's entry | DEBIT, CREDIT |
| boat trip | SAIL, CRUISE | bookkeeping term | ENTRY, POST |
| bobble | ERR, BUNGLE, MISS, FUMBLE | | |
| bobwhite | QUAIL | book (Lat.) | LIBER |
| bodice | WAIST | book leaf | PAGE |
| body | TORSO, TRUNK | book of a poem | CANTO |
| body builders | LIFTS, WEIGHTS | book of fiction | NOVEL |
| body height | STATURE | book of maps | ATLAS |
| body injuries | LESIONS | book of Norse myths | EDDA |
| body limb | LEG, ARM | book of photographs | ALBUM |
| body of advisers | CABINET, BOARD | book page | FOLIO, LEAF |
| | | book part | PAGE, CHAPTER, LEAF, SPINE |
| body of police | POSSE | | |
| body of ship | HULL | boom | SPAR |
| body of soldiers | REGIMENT | boon | BLESSING, FAVOR |
| body of students | CLASS | Boone | DANIEL, DANL |
| body of water | BAY, LAKE, SEA, OCEAN, POND, RIVER, STREAM, CREEK | boorish | RUDE |
| | | boost | LIFT |
| | | booster | FAN |
| Boer | AFRIKANER | boot | KICK |
| boff | JOKE | bootblack's specialty | SHINE |
| bog | MORASS, FEN, MARSH, SWAMP, MIRE | booth | LOGE, SEAT, ETALL |
| | | booty | LOOT, SPOILS |
| bog down | MIRE, SLOW, IMPEDE, HINDER | bop | HIT, PUNCH |
| | | Bordeaux wine | CLARET, MEDOC, GRAVES, SAUTERNE |
| bogus | SHAM, ERSATZ | | |
| Bohemian | ARTY | | |
| Bohemian city | PRAGUE | border | EDGE, RIM, HEM, MARGIN, SELVAGE |
| Bohemian reformer | HUSS | | |

| | | | |
|---|---|---|---|
| bordering tool | EDGER | bourbon | WHISKEY, |
| border on | ABUT | | CORN MASH |
| border saloon | CANTINA | bout | PRIZEFIGHT, MATCH, |
| bore | DRILL, TIRE, EAGRE | | SPELL |
| bore into | TAP | boutonniere | FLOWER, |
| bore witness | ATTESTED | | CARNATION |
| boreal | NORTHERN | boutonniere location | LAPEL |
| boredom | ENNUI, TEDIUM | boutique | SHOP |
| boring | TEDIOUS | bouzouki | MANDOLIN |
| boring tool | BRACE AND BIT, | bovine animal | STEER, OX, |
| | AUGER, DRILL | | COW, BULL |
| born | NEE | bovine sound | LOW, MOO |
| Borneo ape | ORANG | bow | KNOT, CURTSY, STOOP |
| borough | BURG | bowed | BENT |
| borrow dishonestly | CADGE, | bower | ARBOR |
| | PLAGERIZE | bowfin | AMIA |
| borrow money on | PAWN | bowie | KNIFE |
| Bosc | PEAR | bowl | BASIN |
| bosom | BREAST | bowler | HAT, DERBY |
| bossy | COW | bowlike curved line | ARC |
| botch | BUNGLE, MESS | bowline | KNOT |
| both | TWO | bowling alley | LANE, GREEN |
| bother | AIL, ANNOY, PESTER | bowling norm | AVERAGE |
| bottle | FLASK | bowling piece | PIN |
| bottle cap | LID | bowling place | ALLEY, GREEN |
| bottle cap remover | OPENER | bowling term | SPARE, STRIKE |
| bottle dweller | GENIE | bowling target | PIN, TENPIN |
| bottle part | NECK | bowman | ARCHER |
| bottle sealer | CAP, CORK | bow of a ship | PROW |
| bottle-shaped container | FLASK | bowsprit | BOOM, SPAR |
| bottle stopper | CORK | box | CASE, CRATE, CARTON, |
| bottle top | CAP | | FIGHT, SPAR, LOGE |
| bottom | BASE | boxberry | WINTERGREEN |
| bottomless | DEEP, ENDLESS | boxcars | TWELVE |
| bottomless pit | HELL | box cautiously | SPAR |
| bottom out | LEVEL | boxer Baer | MAX |
| bottom surface | BED, FLOOR | boxer Clay | CASSIUS |
| bottom support of a | | boxer Palooka | JOE |
| column | PEDESTAL | boxer Patterson | FLOYD |
| bough | BRANCH | boxer's nickname | CHAMP |
| boulevard | STREET, AVENUE, | box for alms | ARCA |
| | ROAD | box for coal | BIN |
| bouillon | BROTH, STOCK | boxing blow | JAB, HOOK, KO, |
| boulder | ROCK | | KNOCKOUT, KAYO, |
| bounce | DAP, REBOUND | | CROSS |
| bound | TIED, DESTINED | boxing contest | BOUT |
| boundary | LIMIT, LINE, | boxing coup | KO, KAYO, |
| | BORDER | | KNOCKOUT |
| boundary line | FENCE | boxing ring | ARENA |
| bounder | CAD, ROUE, LOUT | boxing strategy | ONE-TWO |
| boundless | ENDLESS, | box-of-evils | |
| | LIMITLESS | op'ener | PANDORA |
| bounteous | AMPLE, PLENTIFUL | box supper | SOCIAL |
| bountiful | PLENTIFUL, | box top | LID |
| | ABUNDANT | box up | CONFINE |
| bounty | REWARD | boy | LAD, SON, MALE, TAD |
| bouquet | AROMA, CORSAGE, | boycott | BLOCK |
| | ODOR, POSY, NOSEGAY | boyfriend | BEAU |

boyhood **YOUTH**
boys and girls **CHILDREN**
boy's book author **ALGER**
Boy Scout **CUB, EAGLE**
Boy Scout activity **HIKE**
Boy Scout group **TROOP**
boy's plaything **TOY SOLDIER, CAP GUN, FOOTBALL, BASEBALL**
bozo **GUY, FELLOW**
BPOE member **ELK**
brace **PAIR, TWOSOME, SUPPORT, COUPLE**
bracer **TONIC**
bracing **CRISP**
bracket candlestick **SCONCE**
brackish **SALTY, BRINY**
brad **NAIL**
brag **BOAST**
Brahman **PUNDIT, AYA**
braid **PLAIT**
brain **MIND**
brainless **STUPID**
brainstorm **IDEA**
brainwash **CONDITION, CONVINCE**
brainy **SMART**
braise **COOK**
brake **STOP**
bran **CEREAL**
branch **ARM, BOUGH**
branch (biol.) **RAMUS**
branches of learning **ARTS**
branch of the armed forces **MARINES, NAVY, ARMY, AIR FORCE, COAST GUARD, NATIONAL GUARD**
branch off **FORK**
brand **MARK, TRADEMARK**
brandish **SHAKE, WAVE**
brass hat **GENERAL**
brass instrument **BUGLE, CORNET, TUBA, TRUMPET, TROMBONE**
brassy **BOLD**
brave **DARING, COURAGEOUS, INDIAN**
brave man **HERO**
bravery **COURAGE**
brawl **FIGHT, MELEE**
Brazilian dance **SAMBA**
Brazilian export **RUBBER**
Brazilian parrot **ARA**
Brazilian port **BELEM, RIO, NATAL, CEARA**
Brazilian river **AMAZON**
Brazilian rubber tree **SERINGA**
breach **CHASM, GAP**

breadbasket **STOMACH**
bread cakes **ROLLS, MUFFINS**
bread crust **RIND**
bread made of corn meal **PONE**
breadmaking ingredient **YEAST**
bread spread **OLEO, BUTTER, MARGARINE, JELLY, JAM, CURD, MUSTARD, MAYONNAISE**
breadwinner **DAD, PAPA, FATHER, POP**
breadwinning ability **EARNING POWER**
break **SMASH, SPLIT, SHATTER**
breakable **FRAGILE**
break asunder **DISRUPT**
breakdown in law and order **ANARCHY**
breakers **SURF, WAVES**
breakfast **MEAL**
breakfast bread **ROLLS, BUN, SCONE, COFFEE CAKE**
breakfast food **CEREAL, BACON, EGGS, PANCAKE, HOTCAKE, WAFFLE, HAM, OMELET, GRITS, OATMEAL**
breakfast fruit juice **ORANGE, GRAPEFRUIT**
breakfast sweet (2 wds.) **COFFEE CAKE**
break in two **SNAP**
break into many pieces **SHATTER**
break of day **DAWN, SUNRISE**
break out **ERUPT**
break ranks **DISBAND**
break rules **DISOBEY**
break short **SNAP**
break suddenly **BURST, SNAP**
break the seal **OPEN**
break up **SEPARATE, DISPERSE**
breakwater **PIER, JETTY**
breast **BOSOM**
breastbone **STERNUM**
breathe **RESPIRE, INHALE**
breathe hard **PANT, GASP, WHEEZE**
breathe one's last **DIE, EXPIRE**
breathe spasmodically **SIGH**
breathing **ALIVE**
breathing organ **LUNG**
bred **ENGENDERED, RAISED, REARED**
breeches **TROUSERS**
breed **CLASS**
breed of cat **SIAMESE, PERSIAN**

breed of dog **SETTER, POODLE, SPANIEL, PUG, SCHNAUZER, TERRIER, SCOTTIE, WHIPPET, CHOW, SAMOYED, COLLIE, SHEPHERD**

breed of horse **ARAB, BARB, THOROUGHBRED, CLYDESDALE, MORGAN, SHIRE**

breeze **WIND, ZEPHYR**
breezy **AIRY**
breezy farewell **TATA**
Breton **CELT**
brew **STEEP**
brick carrier **HOD**
bricklayer **MASON**
brick red **SARAVAN**
bridal
attendant **MAID OF HONOR**
bridegroom's attendant **BEST MAN, USHER**
bride's mate **GROOM**
bride's portion **DOWERY**
bridge **SPAN**
bridge (Fr.) **PONT**
bridge expert **GOREN**
bridge play **SLAM**
bridge score **GAME**
bridge strategy **FINESSE**
bridge structure **ARCH**
bridle **HALTER, HARNESS**
bridle part **BIT, REIN, HEADSTALL**
brief **SHORT**
brief and compact **CONCISE**
brief excerpt **SCRAP**
brief in speech **CURT, TERSE**
brief look **GLIMPSE, GLANCE**
briefly brilliant star **NOVA**
brief news statement **BULLETIN**
brief outline **SKETCH**
brief preface **PROEM**
brief swim **DIP**
brier **THORN**
brig **BOAT**
brigand **PIRATE, THIEF**
bright **SHINY, BRILLIANT**
bright but cheap **TINNY**
bright color **RED, CRIMSON, SCARLET, YELLOW, GOLD, CORAL**
brighten **CLEAR UP, LIGHT UP**
brightly colored bird **ORIOLE, PEACOCK**
bright person **BRAIN, GENIUS**
bright planet **EVENING STAR, VENUS**

brilliance **ELAN, LUSTER, SHINE, GLOW**
brilliance of success **ECLAT**
brilliant **BRIGHT, VIVID**
brilliant Asian
pheasant **TRAGOPAN**
brilliant fish **OPAH**
brilliant planet **VENUS**
brim **EDGE, RIM**
brimless hat **CAP**
bring **CARRY, FETCH**
bring about **CAUSE**
bring back **RESTORE, RETURN**
bring forth **EDUCE**
bring into existence **CREATE, GENERATE, CONCEIVE**
bring into line **ALINE, ALIGN**
bring into play **USE**
bring legal action **SUE**
bring out **ELICIT, EDUCE, EVOKE**
bring out into the open **AIR, REVEAL**
bring to a finish **GO THROUGH WITH, END, CLOSE, FINALIZE, CONCLUDE**
bring to an end **CLOSE**
bring to bay **TREE, CORNER, TRAP**
bring to earth **LAND**
bring to life **RENEW**
bring to light **DETECT, PUBLICIZE**
bring to completion **FINISH, END**
bring together **UNITE**
bring to memory **REMIND**
bring to mind **RECALL**
bring to ruin **UNDO**
bring to the attention **REMIND, PUBLICIZE**
bring up **REAR, RAISE**
bring upon oneself **INCUR**
brink **EDGE, RIM, VERGE**
briny **SALINE, SALTY**
briny expanse **SEA, OCEAN**
brioche **ROLL**
brisk **LIVELY**
bristle **AWN, SETA**
bristle (prefix) **SETI**
British airplane **SPITFIRE**
British beverage **TEA**
British car **ROLLS ROYCE**
British carbine **STEN**
British cavalryman **DRAGOON**
British coin **SHILLING, PENNY**
British colony **BAHAMA, BERMUDA, GIBRALTAR, HONG KONG**

| | |
|---|---|
| British county | **SHIRE** |
| British daisy | **GOWAN** |
| British essayist | **STEELE, ADDISON, CHESTERTON** |
| British flag | **UNION JACK** |
| British flyers (abbr.) | **R.A.F.** |
| British foreign minister | **EDEN** |
| British gun | **STEN** |
| British imperial color | **RED** |
| British island | **MALTA** |
| British isle | **MAN, WIGHT** |
| British king | **GEORGE, HENRY, EDWARD, RICHARD, CHARLES** |
| British man-of-war | **GALATEA** |
| British manufacturing city | **LEEDS** |
| British meal | **TEA** |
| British nobleman | **EARL, LORD, BARON, BARONET, PEER, DUKE** |
| British peeress | **DAME, LADY, DUCHESS, BARONESS** |
| British pennies | **PENCE** |
| British prep school | **ETON, HARROW** |
| British prime minister | **CHURCHILL, WILSON** |
| British princess | **ANNE, MARGARET, ALEXANDRA** |
| British school | **ETON, HARROW, OXFORD, CAMBRIDGE** |
| British sea hero | **NELSON** |
| British streetcar | **TRAM** |
| British taproom | **PUB** |
| British weight | **STONE** |
| Briton | **CELT** |
| brittle | **CRISP** |
| broad | **WIDE, VAST** |
| broadcast | **AIR** |
| broaden | **WIDEN** |
| broad flat bottle | **FLASK** |
| broad humor | **FARCE** |
| broad minded | **LIBERAL** |
| broad necktie | **ASCOT** |
| broad scarf | **SHAWL** |
| broad smile | **GRIN** |
| broad street | **BOULEVARD, AVENUE** |
| broadtail | **KARAKUL** |
| broad thin piece | **SHEET** |
| Broadway backer | **ANGEL** |
| Broadway light | **NEON** |
| Broadway musical | **HAIR, CAMELOT, HELLO DOLLY, MAME, COMPANY, APPLAUSE, FANNY, FUNNY GIRL, TENDERLOIN, FIORELLO, ZORBA** |
| Broadway offering | **DRAMA, COMEDY, MUSICAL, REVUE, PLAY** |
| Broadway patron | **GOER** |
| brochette | **SKEWER** |
| brochure | **PAMPHLET** |
| brogan | **SHOE** |
| broil | **GRILL** |
| broiler | **CHICKEN** |
| broil in covered kettle | **BRAIZE** |
| broiling meat | **STEAK** |
| broil on gridiron | **GRILL** |
| broke | **PENNILESS** |
| broke bread | **ATE** |
| broken open | **SPRUNG** |
| broken pottery | **SHARD** |
| broker | **AGENT, REPRESENTATIVE** |
| broker's advice | **SELL, BUY** |
| bromide | **CLICHE** |
| bronze | **TAN** |
| brooch | **PIN** |
| brood | **COVEY, HATCH** |
| brook | **RILL, STREAM, RIVULET** |
| broom | **BESOM** |
| brose | **OATMEAL** |
| broth | **SOUP, BOUILLON** |
| brother | **FRA** |
| brother (abbr.) | **BR., BRO.** |
| brother (Fr.) | **FRERE** |
| brotherly | **LOYAL** |
| brother of Abel | **CAIN** |
| brother of Cain | **ABLE** |
| brother of Esau | **JACOB** |
| brother of Moses | **AARON** |
| brother's daughter | **NIECE** |
| brother's son | **NEPHEW** |
| brought about | **DID** |
| brought into life | **BORN** |
| brought up | **BRED, REARED** |
| brow | **FOREHEAD** |
| brown | **TAN, COCOA, BEIGE, CHOCOLATE, SEPIA** |
| brown bread | **GRAHAM, WHOLE WHEAT** |
| browned | **RISSOLE** |
| brown ermine | **STOAT** |
| brownie | **CAKE, ELF** |
| brownish | **RUSSET, UMBER** |
| brownish purple | **PUCE** |
| brownish yellow | **AMBER** |
| brown kiwi | **MOA** |
| brown pigment | **UMBER** |
| browse for bargains | **SHOP** |
| bruin | **BEAR** |
| bruise | **BUMP, WELT** |
| brusque | **CURT, TERSE, BLUNT** |

brute **ANIMAL, BEAST**
brutish **COARSE, RUDE**
bryophyte **MOSS, LIVERWORT**
bubble **GLOBULE**
bubble up **BOIL**
bubbling **BOILING**
buccaneers **PIRATES, PRIVATEER, SEA ROVER**
buckboard **WAGON**
bucket **PAIL, TUB**
bucket handle **BAIL**
Buckeye State **OHIO**
bucolic **PASTORAL, RUSTIC**
Buddha's mother **MAYA**
Buddhist monk **LAMA**
Buddhist shrine **TOPE, STUPA**
buddy **PAL, CHUM, PARTNER, MATE, FRIEND**
budge **STIR, MOVE**
budget **SCHEDULE**
buff **POLISH, TAN**
buffalo **BISON**
buffalo of India **ARNA**
buffet **CUPBOARD, MEAL**
buffet about **TOSS**
buffoon **MERRY ANDREW, JESTER, CLOWN**
bug **INSECT**
bugaboo **GOBLIN, SPECTER**
bugbear **GHOST, BOGIE, HOBGOBLIN**
buggy **CARRIAGE, PRAM**
bugle **HORN**
bugle call **TAPS, REVEILLE, RETREAT**
bugle note **MOT**
build **CONSTRUCT, ERECT, MAKE, ESTABLISH**
build castles in the air **DREAM**
building **HOUSE, SKYSCRAPER, OFFICE, CHURCH, FACTORY, SETBACK, HI RISE**
building addition **ELL, WING, ANNEX**
building beam **GIRDER**
building block **STONE**
building diagram **PLAN**
building entrance **DOOR**
building front **FACADE**
building ground **LOT, PLOT, SITE**
building location **SITE**
building material **LUMBER, STEEL, STONE, WOOD, BRICK, CONCRETE**
buildings along the Rhine **CASTLES**
building support **ANTA**

building wing **ELL, ANNEX, EXTENSION**
bulb **ROOT, GLOBE**
bulbous vegetable **ONION**
Bulgarian city **SOFIA**
Bulgarian river **DANUBE**
bulge **SWELL**
bulkhead **WALL, FIREWALL**
bulky **MASSIVE, HEAVY**
bull (Sp.) **TORO**
bulldozer **GRADER**
bullet **PELLET, SLUG**
bullet diameter **CALIBER**
bullfight cheer **OLE**
bullfighter **TORERO, MATADOR, PICADOR**
bully **MENACE, TOUGH, HOODLUM**
bulwark **RAMPART**
bum **HOBO, TRAMP, BEGGAR, PANHANDLER**
bumpkin **YOKEL, RUBE, HICK, HILLBILLY**
bun **ROLL, BREAD, CHIGNON**
bunch **CLUSTER**
bunch of grass **TUFT**
bundle **BALE, PACK, WRAP, PACKAGE**
bundle maker **BALER**
bundle of cotton **BALE**
bundle of grain **SHEAF**
bundle of sticks **FAGOT**
bungle **BOTCH**
bungling **CLUMSY**
bunk **BED**
bunny **RABBIT**
bunting **ETAMINE**
buoy **FLOAT**
burden **LOAD, ONUS**
burdened **LADEN**
burdensome **HEAVY**
bureau **CHEST, DRESSER, DESK, OFFICE, BUSINESS, DEPARTMENT**
burglar **THIEF**
burglarize **ROB**
burglary **LARCENY, THEFT**
burgle **ROB**
burgundy **WINE**
burial place **CEMETERY**
burlap fiber **JUTE**
burlesque **PARODY**
burly **BULKY, STOUT**
Burmese **LAI**
Burmese capital **RANGOON**
Burmese tribe **TAI**
burn **CHAR, SINGE, SEAR, SCALD**

| | | | |
|---|---|---|---|
| burning | AFIRE, AFLAME, FLAMING, TORRID, HOT, PASSIONATE | butter portion | PAT |
| | | butter substitute | OLEO, MARGARINE |
| Burning Bush | WAHOO | butterfly | IO, SATYR, MONARCH |
| burning glass | LENS | butterfly snare | NET |
| burning mountain | VOLCANO | butting animal | GOAT |
| burning oil | KEROSENE | buttock | RUMP |
| burn in hot water | SCALD | butt of joke | IT |
| burnish | GLAZE | button | STUD |
| burro | ASS | button-down | COLLAR |
| burrowing animal | MOLE, VOLE, GROUNDHOG | button fastener | LOOP, HOOK |
| | | buttress | PILE |
| burry | PRICKLY | buy | PURCHASE |
| bursa | CAVITY | buyer | SHOPPER |
| bursar | TREASURER | buy off | BRIBE |
| bursary | TREASURY | buzz | HUM, DRONE |
| burst | ERUPT, EXPLODE | buzzing insect | DOR, BEE, WASP, HORNET, FLY |
| burst of activity | SPASM | | |
| burst of thunder | CLAP | by | AT, NEAR |
| burst open | POP, EXPLODE, ERUPT | by and by | ANON, SOON, PRESENTLY |
| bury | INTER | by and large | MAINLY |
| bus | TRANSPORT | by birth | NEE |
| busby | HAT | bygone days | PAST, AGO |
| bush | SHRUB | by itself | ALONE, SOLO, SOLITARY, LONELY, LONE |
| bushy clump (Brit.) | TOD | | |
| business | TRADE, WORK | Byelorussian town | PINSK, MINSK |
| business agreement | DEAL | | |
| business deal | SALE | by means of | PER, THROUGH |
| business deficit | LOSS | by mouth | ORAL |
| business house | FIRM | by-pass | DETOUR |
| business man | TYCOON | by reason | RATIONAL |
| business note | MEMO, MEMORANDUM | by slow stages | GRADUAL |
| | | bystander | ONLOOKER, WITNESS |
| business program | AGENDA | | |
| business organization | CARTEL, COMPANY, CORPORATION, CONGLOMERATE | by the side of | BESIDE |
| | | byway | PATH, LANE |
| businessman | MERCHANT, WHOLESALER | by way of | VIA |
| | | byword | PROVERB |
| bus station | DEPOT, TERMINAL | by word of mouth | PAROL |
| bustle | TO-DO, HUBBUB, ADO | | |
| bus token | FARE | | |
| busybody | MEDDLER | | |
| busy insect | ANT, BEE | **C** | |
| busy place | HIVE | | |
| but | SAVE, EXCEPT | | |
| but (Gr.) | ABER | | |
| but (Lat.) | SED | ca | CALCIUM, CIRCA |
| butcher | SLAY, SLAUGHTER | cab | TAXI |
| butcher's tool | SLICER, KNIFE, CLEAVER, BLOCK, SCALE | cabal | INTRIGUE, PLOT, SCHEME |
| butch's pal | SPIKE | cabalistic | OCCULT |
| butler | SERVANT | caballero | SENOR, CAVALIER |
| butlery | PANTRY | cabana | BEACHHOUSE, LANAI |
| butt | RAM, TARGET | cabbage broth | KALE |
| butte | MESA | cabbage dish | SLAW, SAUERKRAUT |
| butter maker | CHURN | | |

cabin **STATEROOM, SHED**
cabin bed **BERTH**
cabinet **CASE, CUPBOARD**
cable **WIRE, ROPE**
cad **BOUNDER, ROUE, LOUT**
cadence **LILT, BEAT, MEASURE**
Caesar's enemy **SULLA,**
**POMPEY, CASSIUS**
Caesar's language **LATIN**
cafe employee **WAITER,**
**WAITRESS, COOK,**
**DISHWASHER, HOST,**
**HOSTESS, CASHIER**
cafe patron **EATER, DINER**
**DRINKER**
cage for poultry **COOP**
cage of an elevator **CAR, CAB**
Cain's brother **ABEL**
Cairo's river **NILE**
caisson **WAGON**
cajole **COAX, WHEEDLE**
cake **PASTRY, HARDEN**
cake mix **BATTER**
cake of soap **BAR**
cake topping **ICING, FROSTING,**
**SAUCE, FRUIT, WHIPPED**
**CREAM, ICE CREAM**
calabash **GOURD**
calaboose **JAIL, PRISON**
calamity **DISASTER**
calculate **COMPUTE**
calculate
approximately **ESTIMATE**
calculation
instrument **ABACUS,**
**ADDING MACHINE, COMPUTER**
Calcutta hemp **JUTE**
caldron **VAT, KETTLE, POT**
Caledonian **SCOT**
calendar **ALMANAC**
calf meat **VEAL**
caliber **BORE**
California city **NAPA, SALINAS,**
**SAN FRANCISCO, LOS**
**ANGELES, FRESNO,**
**SACRAMENTO**
California fruit **KUMQUAT**
California mountain **SHASTA**
California rockfish **RENA**
California tree **REDWOOD**
California wine district **NAPA**
Caliph's name **ALI**
call **SHOUT, TELL, PAGE,**
**PHONE, TELEPHONE,**
**SUMMON, VISIT, RING UP,**
**YELL, SHRIEK, HOLLER,**
**SCREAM**
call for quiet **SH, HUSH**

call forth **EVOKE, SUMMON**
calling **TRADE, VOCATION**
call it quits **STOP, CEASE**
callous **UNFEELING**
callow **GREEN**
call the roll **MUSTER**
call to the phone **PAGE**
calm **SERENITY, TRANQUILITY,**
**LULL, QUIET, PEACE,**
**PEACEFUL**
calmative **SEDATIVE**
calm endurance **PATIENCE**
calumet **PIPE, PEACE PIPE**
calumny **SLANDER, LIBEL**
calyx leaf **SEPAL**
camel-like mammal **LLAMA**
camelopard **GIRAFFE**
Camelot's king **ARTHUR**
Camelot's magician **MERLIN**
camera adjustment **FOCUS**
camera glass **LENS**
Cameroon tribe **IBO, BETI,**
**BULU**
camp bed **COT**
camp shelter **TENT**
campus building **DORM, QUAD,**
**HALL, LIBRARY, CHAPEL**
can **TIN**
Canadian capital **OTTAWA,**
**VICTORIA, EDMONTON,**
**REGINA, WINNIPEG,**
**QUEBEC, ST. JOHNS,**
**HALIFAX, FREDERICTON**
Canadian mountain **LOGAN**
Canadian peninsula **GASPE**
Canadian province **ONTARIO,**
**QUEBEC, NEW BRUNSWICK,**
**NOVA SCOTIA, BRITISH**
**COLUMBIA,**
**NEWFOUNDLAND,**
**MANITOBA,**
**SASKATCHEWAN,**
**ALBERTA**
canal **WATERWAY**
canal near Egypt **SUEZ**
canal system in northern
Michigan **SOO**
Canal Zone lake **GATUN**
canape **APPETIZER**
canard **RUMOR**
canary **BIRD, WARBLER**
canary's home **CAGE**
cancel **ANNUL, VOID**
Cancer **CRAB**
candid **HONEST, FRANK, OPEN,**
**ABOVEBOARD**
candidate **NOMINEE**
candied fruit **SWEETMEAT**

candle **TAPER**
candle drippings **WAX**
candle holder **SCONCE**
candy flavor **LEMON, ORANGE, CHERRY, PEPPERMINT, CARAMEL, CHOCOLATE, MINT, LICORICE, RUM**
cane **WHIP, BEAT, THRASH, STICK, PADDLE, STEM**
cane-cutting knife **BOLO**
cane sugar **SUCROSE**
canine **TOOTH, DOG, FOX, WOLF, EYETOOTH**
canine cry **YELP, YAP, YIP, BARK, WOOF, ARF, BOWWOW, GROWL, GRR, ROWF**
canine home **KENNEL**
canine pet **DOG**
canine tooth **FANG, EYETOOTH**
canine with rabies
(2 wds.) **MAD DOG**
canker **ULCER, SORE**
can metal **TIN**
cannon **GUN**
cannon fire **BARRAGE, BATTERY**
cannon handle **ANSE**
cannon shot **GRAPE**
canoe **BOAT, BIRCHBARK, PROA**
canoe of Malaysia **PROA**
canon **LAW, CODE, RULE, CRITERION**
canonized man **SAINT, ST.**
canonized woman (Fr.) **SAINTE, STE.**
canonized woman (It.) **SANTA**
canopy **ROOF**
cant **ARGOT, JARGON, SLANG, SLANT, INCLINE, TOP**
cantabile **FLOWING**
cantaloupe **MELON, MUSKMELON**
cantata **MOTET**
canteen **FLASK**
canter **GAIT, LOPE**
canticle **ODE, SONG, CHANT**
cantina **SALOON, BAR**
cantle **NOOK, SLICE**
canto **SONG, VERSE**
cantor **SOLOIST, PRECENTOR**
canvas **DUCK**
canvas bed **COT**
canvas frame **EASEL**
canvas home **TENT**
canvass **POLL**
canyon **GORGE, CHASM**

caoutchouc **RUBBER**
cap **BERET, HAT**
capa **CLOAK**
capability **CAPACITY**
capable **ABLE, COMPETENT**
capable of (2 wds.) **UP TO**
capable of cultivation **ARABLE**
capable of flying **VOLANT**
capable of learning **TEACHABLE**
capacious **LARGE, ROOMY**
capacity **VOLUME**
cape **CLOAK, HEADLAND, NESS, PROMONTORY**
Cape Kennedy launching
(comp. wd.) **LIFT-OFF, BLAST-OFF**
Cape Kennedy
platform **GANTRY**
Cape Kennedy rocket **AGENA, APOLLO, MERCURY, GEMINI**
Cape Kennedy
routine **COUNTDOWN**
caper **ANTIC, TRICK, FROLIC**
caper about **CAVORT**
capillus **HAIR**
Capistrano resident **SWALLOW**
capital **MAIN, MAJOR**
capital of
Alabama **MONTGOMERY**
capital of Alaska **JUNEAU**
capital of Albania **TIRANA**
capital of Arizona **PHOENIX**
capital of Arkansas **LITTLE ROCK**
capital of Austria **VIENNA**
capital of Bolivia
(2 wds.) **LA PAZ**
capital of
California **SACRAMENTO**
capital of Canada **OTTAWA**
capital of Colorado **DENVER**
capital of
Connecticut **HARTFORD**
capital of Cuba **HAVANA**
capital of Delaware **DOVER**
capital of Egypt **CAIRO**
capital of Florida **TALLAHASSEE**
capital of France **PARIS**
capital of Georgia **ATLANTA**
capital of Germany **BERLIN, BONN**
capital of Greece **ATHENS**
capital of Guam **AGANA**
capital of Haiti **PORT-AU-PRINCE**
capital of Hawaii **HONOLULU**
capital of Hungary **BUDAPEST**

capital of Idaho **BOISE**
capital of Illinois **SPRINGFIELD**
capital of
Indiana **INDIANAPOLIS**
capital of Indonesia **DJAKARTA**
capital of Iowa **DES MOINES**
capital of Iraq **BAGHDAD**
capital of Italia **ROMA**
capital of Italy **ROME**
capital of Kansas **TOPEKA**
capital of Kentucky **FRANKFORT**
capital of
Louisiana **BATON ROUGE**
capital of Lydian
Empire **SARDIS**
capital of Maine **AUGUSTA**
capital of Maryland **ANNAPOLIS**
capital of
Massachusetts **BOSTON**
capital of Michigan **LANSING**
capital of Minnesota **ST. PAUL**
capital of Mississippi **JACKSON**
capital of Missouri **JEFFERSON
CITY**
capital of Montana **HELENA**
capital of Morocco **RABAT**
capital of Nebraska **LINCOLN**
capital of Nevada **CARSON CITY**
capital of New
Hampshire **CONCORD**
capital of New Jersey **TRENTON**
capital of New Mexico
**SANTA FE**
capital of New York **ALBANY**
capital of Nicaragua **MANAGUA**
capital of Nigeria **LAGOS**
capital of North
Carolina **RALEIGH**
capital of North
Dakota **BISMARCK**
capital of North Vietnam **HANOI**
capital of Norway **OSLO**
capital of Ohio **COLUMBUS**
capital of Oklahoma
**OKLAHOMA CITY**
capital of Oregon **SALEM**
capital of Paraguay **ASUNCION**
capital of
Pennsylvania **HARRISBURG**
capital of Peru **LIMA**
capital of Philippines
**QUEZON CITY**
capital of Phoenicia **TYRE**
capital of Poland **WARSAW**
capital of Rhode
Island **PROVIDENCE**

capital of Senegal **DAKAR**
capital of South
Carolina **COLUMBIA**
capital of South Dakota **PIERRE**
capital of Soviet
Union **MOSCOW**
capital of Spain **MADRID**
capital of Tennessee **NASHVILLE**
capital of Texas **AUSTIN**
capital of Tibet **LHASA**
capital of Utah **SALT LAKE CITY**
capital of Venezuela **CARACAS**
capital of
Vermont **MONTPELIER**
capital of Virginia **RICHMOND**
capital of Washington **OLYMPIA**
capital of West Germany **BONN**
capital of West
Pakistan **LAHORE**
capital of West
Virginia **CHARLESTON**
capital of Western Samoa **APIA**
capital of Wisconsin **MADISON**
capital of Wyoming **CHEYENNE**
capital of Yemen **SANA(A)**
capital of Yugoslavia **BELGRADE**
capsule **PILL, PELLET,
TABLET**
Captain Kidd **PIRATE,
BUCCANEER**
captain of a ship **SKIPPER**
captivate **ENTRANCE**
captor **TAKER**
capture **NAB, SEIZE, CATCH,
GRAB, TAKE**
capture again **RETAKE, REGAIN**
capuchin monkey **SAI**
car **AUTO, AUTOMOBILE**
carabao **BUFFALO**
carafe **BOTTLE, DECANTER**
caramel **CANDY, FLAVOR**
carat **GEM WEIGHT**
caravansary **INN**
caravan station **SERAI**
caraway **SEED**
carbohydrate **STARCH**
carbon **COPY, SOOT**
carbonated beverage **POP,
SODA**
carcass **BODY, CORPSE**
card **ACE, DEUCE, TREY**
card (Fr.) **CARTE**
cardboard box **CARTON**
card combination **TENACE,
FLUSH, PAIR**

card game **CANASTA, GIN,
LOON, PINOCHLE, POKER,
HEARTS, RUMMY, BEZIQUE,
CRIBBAGE, CASINO, CANFIELD,
KLONDIKE, RUSSIAN BANK,
MONTE CARLO, BRIDGE,
WHIST**
cardigan **SWEATER, JACKET**
cardinal **BIRD**
cardinal point **NORTH, SOUTH,
EAST, WEST**
cardinal's office **HAT**
cardinal's symbol (2 wds.)
**RED HAT**
card of admission **PASS**
cards and letters **MAIL**
card suit **SPADES, HEARTS,
DIAMONDS, CLUBS**
card wool **COMB**
care **ANXIETY, MIND, WORRY,
TROUBLE, HEEDFUL,
CAUTION, WISH**
careen **LURCH**
career **PROFESSION, VOCATION**
career beginning **DEBUT**
carefree **HAPPY, GAY**
careful **CAUTIOUS**
careful management
**PRUDENCE**
careless **LAX, LAZY**
car entrance **DRIVEWAY**
caress **FONDLE, PET, PAT,
STROKE**
caretaker **CUSTODIAN**
car fuel **GAS, PETROL,
GASOLINE**
car gear **REVERSE, LOW,
DRIVE, PASSING**
cargo **LOAD**
cargo compartment **HOLD**
cargo ship **TRAMP, TANKER,
FREIGHTER**
cargo stower **STEVEDORE**
Caribbean island **NEVIS,
GRENADA, PUERTO RICO,
ANTIGUA, CUBA, JAMAICA,
HAITI, BARBADOS, DOMINICA,
MARTINIQUE, MONSERRAT**
caribou **MOOSE, DEER**
caricature **PARODY,
BURLESQUE**
car ignition device **STARTER**
carillon **CHIME**
Carl Sandburg creation **POEM**
carmine **SCARLET**
car model **SEDAN, COUPE,
CONVERTIBLE, HARDTOP**
carnal **EARTHY**

carnation **PINK**
carnival **FESTIVAL**
carnival attraction
(2 wds.) **SIDE SHOW**
carousel (comp. wd.)
**MERRY-GO-ROUND**
carp **CAVIL**
car part (2 wds.) **TIE ROD**
carpentry tool **AWL, HAMMER,
SAW, AUGER, RASP, MITER
BOX, LEVEL, PLUMB LINE,
PLANE**
carpet **RUG, MAT**
carpet nap **PILE**
carport **GARAGE**
carp's home **POND**
carriage **STATURE**
carriage dog **DALMATIAN**
carried away **RAPT**
carried on the back **TOTE**
carrier **PORTER**
carrion **ROTTEN, VILE**
carry **BEAR, TOTE, LUG**
carry across water **FERRY**
carry away **REMOVE**
carrying guns **ARMED**
carry into effect **EXECUTE**
carry on **WAGE, CONTINUE,
ENSUE**
carry out **PERFORM, EXECUTE**
carry tales **TATTLE**
carry the day **WIN**
cart **WAGON**
cartel **POOL, TRUST**
carter **TEAMSTER**
Carthaginian **PUNIC**
Carthaginian queen **DIDO**
cartilage **GRISTLE**
cartridge **SHELL**
carve **CUT, SLICE**
carved gem **CAMEO**
carve letters upon **ENGRAVE**
Casals' instrument **CELLO**
cascade **WATERFALL**
case **ETUI, BOX, CRATE,
CARTON**
case for small articles **ETUI**
cash **MONEY**
cash drawer **TILL**
cashew **NUT**
cashmere **WOOL**
cask **BARREL, TUN**
casket **BOX, COFFIN**
cask part **STAVE**
cask's circular strip **HOOP**
cask stave **LAG**
Caspian **SEA**
cassava starch food **TAPIOCA**

cassowary **EMU**
cast **PLAYERS, THROW, PITCH, TOSS**
cast a ballot **VOTE**
cast aside **DISCARD, REJECT**
caste **CLASS**
castle **PALACE**
castle ditch **MOAT**
castles in the air **DREAMS**
cast off **SHED, SLOUGH**
Castor or Pollux **STAR**
Castro's country **CUBA**
casual utterance **REMARK**
casualty **ACCIDENT**
cat **FELINE, TABBY, PUSSY**
cataclysm **DISASTER**
catalogue **LIST**
catamaran **FLOAT, RAFT**
catastrophe **CALAMITY, DISASTER**
catch **NAB, GRAB, SEIZE, SNATCH, TAKE**
catch on to **GLOM**
catch sight of **ESPY**
catch up with **OVERTAKE**
catching implement **HOOK**
catchword **SLOGAN**
cat command **SCAT, SHOO**
category **BRACKET, CLASS**
cater **SERVE**
catharsis **PURGE**
Catholic cleric's cap **BIRETTA**
Catholic prayer (Lat., 2 wds.) **AVE MARIA, PATER NOSTER**
Catholic service **MASS**
catkin **AMENT**
cats and dogs **PETS**
cat's foot **PAW**
cat sound **PURR, MEOW, MIAOW, MEW, MIAOU**
cat's prey **MOUSE, CANARY**
cattle (arch.) **KINE**
cattle bedding **STRAW**
cattle enclosure **CORRAL**
cattle genus **BOS**
cattleman **DROVER**
cattle thief **RUSTLER**
Caucasian **ARYAN**
Caucasian goat **TUR**
caudal appendage **TAIL**
caught in a net **ENMESHED**
cauldron **POT**
cause **GIVE RISE TO, REASON**
cause dough to rise **LEAVEN**
cause of Cleopatra's death **ASP**
cause of tension **STRESS**
cause to jump the track **DERAIL**

cause to remember **REMIND, RECALL**
cause to slant **TILT**
cause to stand out **EMBOSS**
cause to stick **MIRE**
cause to take root **RADICATE**
causeway **DIKE**
causing amusement **FUNNY**
causing feeling **EMOTIVE**
caustic **ACRID, BITTER**
caustic substance **ACID, LYE**
caustic wit **IRONIC, CUTTING, SARCASTIC**
cauterize **SEAR**
caution **WARN**
cautious **WARY**
cautiously **CAREFULLY, GINGERLY**
cavalcade **MARCH, PARADE**
Cavalier State **VIRGINIA**
cavalry **TROOP**
cavalry horse **LANCER, MOUNT**
cavalry man **TROOPER, DRAGOON**
cavalry soldiers **LANCERS**
cavalry sword **SABER, SABRE**
cavalry unit **TROOP**
cave **CAVERN**
caveat **WARNING**
cave in **COLLAPSE**
cavern **CAVE**
cavernous **DEEP, HOLLOW**
caviar **ROE**
cavil **CARP**
caviler **CRITIC**
cavity **HOLE**
cavort **PRANCE**
cay **INLET**
cayenne **PEPPER**
cease **STOP, DESIST, HALT**
cease-fire **TRUCE, ARMISTICE**
cease friendship with (2 wds.) **PART COMPANY**
ceaseless **CONTINUAL**
cebine monkey **SAI**
Cebu hemp **MANILA**
cedar **TREE, SAVINE**
cede **YIELD**
Celebes ox **ANOA**
celebrate **OBSERVE, REVEL**
celebrated **FAMOUS**
celebration **RITE, FETE, FESTIVAL**
celebrity **LION, STAR**
celerity **SPEED**
celery portion **STALK**
celestial **HEAVENLY**
celestial being **ANGEL**

celestial body **COMET, SUN, STAR, MOON, PLANET, ASTEROID**
celestial instrument **HARP**
celestial visitor **COMET**
celibate **SINGLE**
cell **ROOM**
cellar **BASEMENT, PANTRY**
Celt **GAUL, BRITON**
Celtic language **ERSE, GAELIC, MANX, WELSH, BRETON**
Celtic peasant **KERN**
Celtic priest **DRUID**
Celtic sea deity **LER**
cement **PUTTY**
cemetery **GRAVEYARD**
censurable quality **DEMERIT**
censure **BLAME, CONDEMN**
cent **PENNY**
Centennial State **COLORADO**
center **CORE, MID, MIDDLE, NUCLEUS, HUB**
center of activity **FOCUS**
center of interest **FOCUS**
center of sail **BUNT**
center of target **EYE**
Central American country **NICARAGUA, HONDURAS, GUATEMALA, EL SALVADOR, COSTA RICA, PANAMA**
Central American Indian **CARIB, MAYA**
Central American oil tree **EBOE**
Central American rodent **PACA**
central point **PIVOT**
century plant **AGAVE, MAGUEY, ALOE**
ceramic earth **CLAY**
ceramic piece **VASE, PITCHER, POT, PLATE**
ceramic square **TILE**
ceramics **POTTERY**
ceramics maker **POTTER**
cerated **WAXED**
cere **ANOINT, WAX**
cereal **GRAIN, BRAN**
cereal dish **BOWL**
cereal grain **OAT, RICE, RYE, BARLEY, WHEAT, CORN**
cereal grass **OAT, RICE, RYE, WHEAT, BARLEY**
cereal spike **EAR**
ceremonial **FORMAL, RITUAL**
ceremonial post **TOTEM**
ceremony **RITE**
cerise **RED**
certain **SURE**
certainly **OF COURSE, YES**
certainly not **NO**

certainty **FACT**
certificate **DOCUMENT**
certify **ATTEST, VERIFY**
certitude **SURENESS**
cerulean **BLUE**
cessation **LULL**
cessation of war agreement (2 wds.) **PEACE TREATY**
cetacea **WHALES**
Ceylonese canoe **BALSA**
Ceylon moss **AGAR**
chagrin **SHAME**
chain **CATENA, BIND, FETTER, SHACKLE**
chain cable **BOOM**
chain of mountains **RANGE, RIDGE**
chain of rocks **REEF**
chain part **LINK**
chain reaction **SEQUENCE**
chain sound **CLANK, CLINK**
chair **SEAT**
chair covers **TIDIES**
chair of state **THRONE**
chair part **LEG, SPLAT, SEAT, BACK, ARM**
chaise **CHAIR, CARRIAGE**
chalcedony **AGATE, SARD**
Chaldean city **UR**
chalet **CABIN, HUT**
chalice **GOBLET, CUP**
chalice cover **PALL**
chalk **CRAYON**
chalk remover **ERASER**
chalk up **SCORE**
chalky **PALE, WHITE**
challenge **DARE, DEFY**
chalumeau **CLARINET, REED**
chamber **ROOM**
chamber beneath the Vatican **CATACOMB**
chamberlain **ATTENDANT, STEWARD**
chameleon **LIZARD**
chamfer **BEVEL**
champ **BITE**
champagne **WINE**
champagne bucket **ICER, COOLER**
champion **DEFENDER, WINNER**
chance **FATE, LUCK**
chancel seats **SEDILIA**
chancel table **ALTAR**
change **ALTER, AMEND, VARY**
changeable **ERRATIC, FICKLE**
change a constitution **AMEND**
change a manuscript **REVISE**
change an alarm **RESET**
change color **DYE, FADE**

change course **VEER, TACK**
change direction **TURN, VEER**
changed state **MUTATION**
change for the better **REFORM**
change from evil **REPENT**
change into bone **OSSIFY**
changeling (arch.) **IDIOT**
change off **TAKE TURNS**
change one's address **MOVE**
change order of **TRANSPOSE**
change position **TURN OVER, MOVE, SHIFT, REVERSE**
change the decor **REDO**
change the mind **RECONSIDER**
channel **VEIN, RIVER, STRAIT**
Channel Island **JERSEY, SARK, GUERNSEY, ALDERNEY**
channel marker **BUOY**
chant **INTONE, SINGSONG**
Chantilly product **LACE**
chaos **MESS**
chap **FELLOW**
chaparral **THICKET**
chaparral cock **ROAD RUNNER**
chapeau **HAT**
chapel **SANCTUARY**
chaperon **DUENNA**
chaplain **MINISTER, PADRE, PRIEST**
chaplet **ANADEM, BEADS, WREATH**
chapter of Koran **SURA**
char **BURN, SEAR, SCORCH, TASK**
character **PERSONALITY, NATURE**
characteristic **TRAIT, EARMARK**
characterization **ROLE**
characterize **REPRESENT**
characterized by (suffix) **MORPH**
character of a people **ETHOS**
character part **ROLE**
characters in a play **CAST**
charcoal **FUEL**
charcoal grill **BRAZIER**
charge **FEE, RATE**
charged atom **ION**
charge for use of road **TOLL**
charge with crime **ACCUSE**
charge with gas **AERATE**
chariot **CART**
charisma **GRACE, CHARM**
charitable **GENEROUS**
charity **ALMS, GIVING**
charity gift **DOLE, ALMS, DONATION**
charlatan **QUACK, FRAUD**
Charles Goren's domain
(2 wds.) **CONTRACT BRIDGE**

Charles Lamb **ELIA**
charley horse **CRAMP**
Charlotte Corday's victim **MARAT**
charm **ENAMOR, ENTHRALL, FASCINATE, TALISMAN, TOKEN**
charming **WINSOME**
chart **GRAPH, MAP**
charter **HIRE, GRANT**
chary **FRUGAL, WARY, SHY**
chase **PURSUE**
chase away **ROUT**
chaste **PURE, VESTAL**
chasten **DISCIPLINE, PUNISH**
chastise **BERATE, CHASTEN, SCOLD**
chastity **PURITY, VIRTUE**
chat **GAB, CHATTER, PRATE, CHIN, CHEW THE RAG, CHEW THE FAT, GABBLE**
chatter **PRATE, PRATTLE**
cheap **INEXPENSIVE, TINNY**
cheap metal **TIN**
cheat **SWINDLE, DUPE**
check **REIN, TAB, BILL, STOP, ARREST**
check by danger **DAUNT**
checkers **DRAFTS, DRAUGHTS**
cheer **RAH, BRAVO, BRAVA, OLE, HURRAH, HURRAY, LIVEN, ELATE, GLADDEN**
cheerful **ROSY, PLEASANT**
cheerful expression **SMILE, GRIN**
cheerless **BLEAK, DRAB, DULL, DEPRESSING**
cheese dish **RAREBIT, FONDUE**
cheese variety **EDAM, GOUDA, BRIE, GRUYERE**
chef **COOK**
chef's garment **APRON**
chef's specialty **SALAD**
chelonian **TURTLE, TORTOISE**
chemical analysis **ASSAY**
chemical compound **ESTER**
chemical element **ANTIMONY, BARIUM**
chemical particle **ION**
chemical product of the body **HORMONE**
chemical salts **SALS**
chemical suffix **ANE, ASE, IDE, ITE, INE**
chemist's burner **BUNSEN, ETNA**
chemist's shop **PHARMACY**
chemist's workplace **LAB**

cherish **LOVE, TREASURE, HOLD DEAR**
cherished **DEAR**
cherished animal **PET**
cherry **OXHEART, MORELLO, BING**
cherry-colored **CERISE**
cherry orange **KUMQUAT**
cherry seed **PIT**
chess move **GAMBIT**
chess piece **MAN, PAWN, KING, QUEEN, KNIGHT, BISHOP, CASTLE, ROOK**
chess victory **CHECKMATE, MATE**
chest **BOX, CASE, STRONGBOX**
chest bone **RIB**
chestnut horse **ROAN**
chest of drawers **DRESSER, BUREAU, COMMODE**
chest sound **RALE**
chew **MASTICATE, GNAW, MUNCH, BITE**
chewing gum **CHICLE**
chewing gum flavor **SPEARMINT**
chew the cud **RUMINATE**
chewy candy **CARAMEL, TAFFY, TOFFEE, NOUGAT**
chic **MODISH, STYLISH**
chick's mother **HEN**
chicken **HEN, CAPON, FOWL, FRYER**
chicken feed **MASH**
chicken pen **COOP**
chicory **HERB, ENDIVE**
chide **SCOLD, BERATE**
chief **MAIN, HEAD**
chief character **HERO**
chief executive **PRESIDENT**
chief of fairies **PUCK**
chief ore of lead **GALENA**
chief part **MAIN**
chief ruler **GOVERNOR**
chiffonier **CABINET**
chignon **BUN, KNOT**
child **KID, TOT, YOUNGSTER, TODDLER**
childish **PUERILE, INFANTILE**
child of necessity **INVENTION**
child's cry **SNIVEL**
child's game **JACKS, TAG, MARBLES, KICK THE CAN, RED ROVER, HIDE AND SEEK, JUMP ROPE, HOPSCOTCH**
child's hat **BONNET, TAM, BERET, CAP**
child's marble **AGATE, TAW**

child's play **EASY, SIMPLE**
child's salary **ALLOWANCE**
child's sock **ANKLET**
child's stroller (comp. wd.) **GO-CART**
child's toy **YOYO**
child's vehicle **SCOOTER, BIKE, WAGON, CARRIAGE**
Chilean coin **CONDOR**
Chilean export **NITER, NITRATES**
Chilean Indian **ONA**
Chilean mountains **ANDES**
chill **FREEZE, ICE, COOL**
chilling tale (2 wds.) **GHOST STORY**
chilly attitude **STANDOFF**
chime **PEAL, RING**
chimney dirt **SOOT**
chimney passage **FLUE**
chimpanzee **APE**
chinaware **DISHES**
Chinese **SINIC**
Chinese drink **TEA**
Chinese dynasty **MING, CHING, SUNG, TANG, WEI**
Chinese fish sauce **SOY, SOYA**
Chinese fruit **LITCHI, LICHEE**
Chinese idol **JOSS, GHOS**
Chinese island **AMOY, FORMOSA**
Chinese laborer **COOLIE**
Chinese measure **LI, TU**
Chinese nurse **AMAH**
Chinese pagoda **TAA**
Chinese philosophy **TAO**
Chinese poet (2 wds.) **LI PO**
Chinese porcelain **MING**
Chinese port **AMOY**
Chinese ship **JUNK**
Chinese society **TONG**
Chinese staple grain **RICE**
Chinese temple **TAA**
Chinook State **WASHINGTON**
chip of stone **SPALL**
chirp **PEEP, PIP, TWEET, TWEE, CHEEP, CHIRRUP**
chisel **CUT, GOUGE, SHAPE**
chiseler **MOOCHER, SPONGER**
chitchat (2 wds.) **SMALL TALK**
chivalrous **VALIANT, GALLANT**
chocolate tree **CACAO**
choice **OPTION, SELECTION**
choice cut of beef **SIRLOIN**
choice morsel **TIDBIT**
choice part **ELITE**
choice seashore location **OCEANFRONT**
choir leader **CANTOR**

choir voice **ALTO, SOPRANO,**
**BASS, BARITONE, TENOR**
choke **OBSTRUCT, STRANGLE**
choke back **REPRESS, STIFLE**
choke coil **REACTOR**
choke up **CLOG, SPEECHLESS**
choler **IRE, SPLEEN**
choleric **ANGRY**
Chomolungma's other
name **EVEREST**
choose **ELECT, SELECT, OPT,**
**PICK**
choose over **PREFER**
choosy **PARTICULAR, FINICKY**
chop **HEW, CUT, DICE, MINCE**
chop-chop **QUICKLY, HURRY**
chop finely **DICE, MINCE**
chop off **LOP**
chopped cabbage dish **SLAW**
chopped meat dish **HASH,**
**MINCE, HAMBURGER**
chopping tool **AX, AXE,**
**HATCHET, KNIFE**
choppy **ROUGH, JERKY**
chord **HARMONY**
chord composition **CANTATA**
chore **ERRAND, TASK**
chortle **CHUCKLE**
chorus **REFRAIN**
Chosen **KOREA**
chosen few **ELITE**
chosen field **CAREER**
chosen people **ISRAELITES,**
**HEBREWS**
christen **DUB, NAME**
Christian **GENTILE**
Christian era (abbr.) **A.D.**
Christiania **OSLO**
Christmas **HOLIDAY, NOEL,**
**YULE, YULETIDE**
Christmas carol **NOEL**
Christmas Carol character **TIM,**
**SCROOGE**
Christmas decoration **HOLLY,**
**IVY, TREE**
Christmas plant **HOLLY,**
**MISTLETOE**
Christmas song **CAROL, NOEL**
Christmas trimming **TINSEL**
chromosome **GENE**
chronic **CONSTANT**
chronicle **ACCOUNT, HISTORY**
chubby **PLUMP**
chum **FRIEND, PAL, BUDDY,**
**PARTNER**
chunk **SLAB**
chunky **LUMPY, PLUMP**
church **BASILICA, CATHEDRAL**

church bench **KNEELER, PEW**
church body **CANON, SYNOD,**
**CONGREGATION**
church calendar **ORDO**
church canticle **VENITE**
church council **SYNOD**
church court **ROTA**
church dignitary **PRELATE**
church district **PARISH**
church fast **LENT**
church gallery **LOFT**
church hymn **ANTHEM**
church law **CANON**
church minister **PASTOR,**
**PRIEST**
church morning service **MATINS**
Church of Latter-day
Saints **MORMON**
church officer **SEXTON,**
**WARDEN**
church official **ELDER, DEACON,**
**CARDINAL**
Church of Rome **LATERAN,**
**CATHOLIC**
church part **ALTAR, APSE,**
**NAVE, CHANCEL, CHOIR**
**LOFT, VESTRY, BAPTISTRY**
church pulpit **AMBO**
church seat **PEW**
church service **MASS**
church singing group **CHOIR**
church tower **STEEPLE, SPIRE**
church vault **CRYPT**
church vestry room **SACRISTY**
churl **BOOR**
churlish **SURLY**
chute **FLUME, SLIDE**
chutney **RELISH**
CIA employee **SPY, AGENT**
cicada **LOCUST**
cicatrix **SCAR**
cider source **APPLE**
cigar **STOGIE, PANATELA,**
**PANATELLA**
cigar residue **ASH**
cigarette **FAG, CIG, BUTT**
cigarette end **STUB, BUTT**
cilium **EYELASH**
cinch **GIRTH, SNAP**
cinchona **QUININE**
Cincinnati ball club **REDS**
cincture **BELT**
cinder **ASH**
cinema house **THEATER,**
**THEATRE, MOVIE**
cinnabar **ORE**
cinnamon **CASSIA**
cipher **CODE, ZERO**

| | |
|---|---|
| circle | **SET, CLIQUE** |
| circle a planet | **ORBIT** |
| circle of light | **HALO** |
| circle of persons | **CORDON** |
| circle part | **ARC** |
| circlet | **HOOP, RING** |
| circlet of light | **AUREOLE(A)** |
| circuit | **CYCLE, LOOP** |
| circuit-breaker | **FUSE** |
| circuit rider | **ITINERANT,** |
| | **MINISTER** |
| circuitous | **ROUNDABOUT** |
| circular | **OVAL, ROUND** |
| circular cloak | **CAPE** |
| circular figure | **LOOP** |
| circulate | **DIFFUSE, MIX** |
| circumference | **PERIMETER** |
| circumscribe | **ENCLOSE, LIMIT** |
| circumspect | **DISCREET** |
| circumstance | **EVENT** |
| circumvent | **EVADE, AVOID** |
| circus | **ARENA** |
| circus (2 wds.) | **BIG TOP** |
| circus animal | **LION, TIGER,** |
| | **ELEPHANT, APE, HORSE,** |
| | **CHIMPANZEE, GORILLA,** |
| | **SEAL** |
| circus attraction | **SIDE SHOW,** |
| | **FREAK, CLOWN** |
| circus caller | **BARKER** |
| circus ring | **ARENA** |
| circus shelter | **TENT** |
| circus tent (2 wds.) | **BIG TOP** |
| Cisalpine land | **ITALY, GAUL** |
| Cistercian monk | **TRAPPIST** |
| cistern | **TANK** |
| citadel | **FORT, REFUGE** |
| citadel in Texas | **ALAMO** |
| citation | **SUMMONS** |
| cite | **QUOTE** |
| cite as proof | **ADDUCE** |
| citizen | **SUBJECT, NATIVE** |
| citrus drink | **ADE** |
| citrus fruit | **LEMON, LIME,** |
| | **ORANGE, GRAPEFRUIT** |
| city | **TOWN, METROPOLIS** |
| city dirt | **SOOT** |
| city district | **WARD** |
| city division | **DISTRICT,** |
| | **PRECINCT** |
| city executive | **MAYOR** |
| city in Alabama | **MOBILE,** |
| | **SELMA, MONTGOMERY,** |
| | **BIRMINGHAM** |
| city in Alaska | **JUNEAU,** |
| | **FAIRBANKS** |
| city in Arizona | **TUCSON,** |
| | **PHOENIX** |
| city in Brazil | **RIO** |

| | |
|---|---|
| city in Brittany | **NANTES** |
| city in California | **SAN MATEO,** |
| | **SANTA BARBARA, LOS** |
| | **ANGELES, FRESNO, SAN** |
| | **FRANCISCO, PALO ALTO,** |
| | **SACRAMENTO, SAN DIEGO** |
| city in Delaware | **WILMINGTON** |
| city in England | **OLDHAM,** |
| | **LONDON, LIVERPOOL,** |
| | **BIRMINGHAM, MANCHESTER** |
| city in Florida | **OCALA, TAMPA,** |
| | **MIAMI, MIAMI BEACH,** |
| | **TALLAHASSEE, ORLANDO** |
| city in Georgia | **ATLANTA** |
| city in Germany | **EMDEN, ESSEN,** |
| | **ULM, BERLIN, BONN** |
| city in Hawaii | **HONOLULU, HILO** |
| city in Illinois | **PEKIN, CHICAGO,** |
| | **SPRINGFIELD, PEORIA** |
| city in India | **AGRA, NEW DELHI,** |
| | **VARANASI, MADRAS,** |
| | **CALCUTTA, KAPUR** |
| city in Indiana | **SOUTH BEND,** |
| | **GARY, INDIANAPOLIS,** |
| | **TERRE HAUTE, HAMMOND** |
| city in Iowa | **AMES** |
| city in Italia | **ROMA, MILANO,** |
| | **FIRENZE, PISA, NAPOLI, SIENA** |
| city in Italy | **ASTI, MILAN, ROME,** |
| | **NAPLES, GENOA, FLORENCE,** |
| | **PARMA, VENICE** |
| city in Kansas | **HUTCHINSON,** |
| | **TOPEKA, WICHITA** |
| city in Kentucky | **LOUISVILLE** |
| city in Kwangtung | |
| province | **MACAO, CANTON** |
| city in Louisiana | **NEW ORLEANS** |
| city in Michigan | **NILES,** |
| | **LANSING, DETROIT, SAGINAW,** |
| | **ANN ARBOR** |
| city in Minnesota | **ROCHESTER,** |
| | **MINNEAPOLIS** |
| city in Mississippi | **NATCHEZ,** |
| | **JACKSON, BILOXI,** |
| | **GULFPORT, VICKSBURG,** |
| | **GREENVILLE** |
| city in Montana | **BUTTE** |
| city in Nebraska | **OMAHA,** |
| | **LINCOLN** |
| city in Nevada | **ELKO, RENO** |
| city in New Hampshire | **KEENE** |
| city in New Jersey | **ORANGE,** |
| | **NEWARK, PATERSON,** |
| | **TRENTON** |
| city in New | |
| Mexico | **ALBUQUERQUE** |
| city in New York | **OLEAN,** |
| | **SYRACUSE, UTICA, TROY,** |
| | **SCHENECTADY, WHITE PLAINS** |

| | | | |
|---|---|---|---|
| city in Nicaragua | **LEON** | city on the Mississippi gulf | |
| city in Normandy | **CAEN** | coast | **BILOXI, GULFPORT,** |
| city in North Carolina | **RALEIGH,** | | **PASCAGOULA** |
| | **DURHAM** | city on the Mohawk | **UTICA** |
| city in North Dakota | **MINOT** | city on the Nile | **CAIRO** |
| city in northern France | **LILLE** | city on the Oka | **OREL** |
| city in North Vietnam | **HANOI** | city on the Po | **TURIN** |
| city in Norway | **OSLO, HAMMAR,** | city on the Rhone | **ARLES** |
| | **BERGEN** | city on the Seine | **PARIS** |
| city in Ohio | **DAYTON, TOLEDO** | city on the Thames | **LONDON** |
| city in Oklahoma | **ADA, TULSA,** | city on the Truckee | **RENO** |
| | **ENID** | city on the Vltava | **PRAGUE** |
| city in Oregon | **SALEM, EUGENE,** | city problem | **SMOG, CRIME,** |
| | **PORTLAND** | | **HOUSING, SANITATION,** |
| city in Pakistan | **LAHORE** | | **TRAFFIC** |
| city in Pennsylvania | **ALTOONA,** | city prosecutor (abbr.) | **D.A.** |
| **YORKTOWN, SCRANTON,** | | city slicker | **DUDE,** |
| **PHILADELPHIA, PITTSBURGH,** | | | **SOPHISTICATE** |
| | **ERIE** | city square | **BLOCK, PLACE** |
| city in Peru | **LIMA** | city thoroughfare | **STREET,** |
| city in Poland | **LODZ, POSEN** | **AVENUE, BOULEVARD, ROAD** | |
| city in Quebec | **MONTREAL** | city train | **EL, SUBWAY** |
| city in Russia | **OREL, MOSCOW,** | civet | **CAT** |
| **LENINGRAD, MINSK, PINSK** | | civic | **URBAN** |
| city in Sicily | **ENNA** | civic corruption | **GRAFT** |
| city in Spain | **JAEN, AVILA,** | civil | **POLITE** |
| **CADIZ, MADRID, TOLEDO,** | | civil defense item | |
| | **BARCELONA** | (2 wds.) | **GAS MASK** |
| city in Tennessee | **MEMPHIS,** | civil disorder | **RIOT** |
| **NASHVILLE, KNOXVILLE,** | | civilian clothes | **MUFTI** |
| | **JACKSON** | civilian, to gobs | **LANDLUBBER** |
| city in Texas | **DALLAS, WACO,** | civilities | **AMENITIES** |
| **EL PASO, HOUSTON, LUBBOCK** | | civilized | **REFINED** |
| city in The Netherlands | | Civil War general | **LEE, GRANT,** |
| **ROTTERDAM, AMSTERDAM,** | | | **MEADE, SHERMAN** |
| | **THE HAGUE** | civil wrong | **TORT** |
| city in Turkey | **ISTANBUL** | clad | **ATTIRED** |
| city in Utah | **OGDEN** | claim | **ASSERT, AVER** |
| city in Washington | **TACOMA,** | claimant | **PRETENDER** |
| | **SEATTLE** | claim as due | **DEMAND** |
| city in Wyoming | **LARAMIE** | clairvoyant | **SEER** |
| city man | **DUDE, SLICKER** | clam dish | **CHOWDER** |
| city manager | **MAYOR** | clam genus | **MYA, VENUS** |
| city official | **ALDERMAN,** | clammy | **DAMP, DANK** |
| | **MAYOR** | clamor | **NOISE** |
| City of Light | **PARIS** | clamor of pursuit | |
| city of Manasseh | **ANER** | (3 wds.) | **HUE AND CRY** |
| city of Paris | **TROY** | clamorous | **LOUD** |
| city of Pied Piper | | clamp | **VISE** |
| legend | **HAMELIN** | clan | **TRIBE, FAMILY** |
| City of Rams | **CANTON** | clandestine | **SECRET** |
| City of Saints | **MONTREAL** | clan quarrel | **FEUD** |
| City of Wheels | **DETROIT** | clap | **APPLAUD** |
| city on Lake Ontario | **OSWEGO** | claret | **WINE** |
| city on the Allegheny | **OLEAN** | clash | **CONFLICT** |
| city on the Arno | **PISA** | clasp | **EMBRACE, HUG, FASTEN** |
| city on the Danube | **ULM** | class | **SORT, KIND, RANK,** |
| city on the Loire | **NANTES** | | **GENRE, TYPE, VARIETY** |

classical Chinese poet
(2 wds.)     **LI PO**
classification of plants     **GENUS**
classified item     **AD**
classify     **SORT, RATE, ASSORT**
classroom favorite
(2 wds.)     **TEACHER'S PET**
classroom period     **HOUR**
classroom talk     **LECTURE**
clatter     **RATTLE, DIN**
clause     **ARTICLE, STIPULATION**
claw     **TALON**
clay and sand mixture     **LOAM**
clay building block     **BRICK**
clayey earth     **MARL**
clay worker     **POTTER**
clean     **WASH**
clean a floor     **SCRUB, MOP,**
**SWEEP, SWAB**
clean and neat (comp.
wd.)     **WELL-GROOMED**
clean a painting     **RESTORE**
cleaning implement     **DUSTER,**
**MOP, DUSTPAN, VACUUM,**
**CLOTH**
cleanse     **PURIFY**
cleanse of impurities     **PURGE**
cleanse of soap     **RINSE**
cleanse the feathers     **PREEN**
cleansing agent     **SOAP,**
**DETERGENT, WATER**
clean up     **POLICE**
clear     **BRIGHT, LUCID**
clear a space
(2 wds.)     **MAKE ROOM**
clear-cut     **DECIDED**
clear of accusations     **ABSOLVE,**
**ACQUIT**
clear profit     **NET**
clear up     **SOLVE**
cleave     **REND, RIVE, SEVER,**
**SPLIT, CUT**
clef     **BASS, TREBLE**
cleft     **RIFT, CRACK, SPLIT**
clemency     **LENIENCY, MERCY**
clement     **MILD**
clench     **CLUTCH, GRASP**
clenched hand     **FIST**
Cleopatra's handmaiden     **IRAS,**
**CHARMIAN**
Cleopatra's river     **NILE**
Cleopatra's snake     **ASP**
clergyman     **CLERIC, PRIEST,**
**VICAR, MINISTER, PASTOR,**
**RECTOR, PARSON, RABBI,**
**MONK**
clergyman's residence     **MANSE,**
**RECTORY**

clergyman's speech     **SERMON**
clergyman's title     **REVEREND**
cleric     **CLERGYMAN**
clerical collar     **RABAT**
clerical mantle     **COPE**
clerical vestment     **ALB**
cleric of early Irish
Church     **ERENACH**
Cleveland's first name     **GROVER**
Cleveland's waterfront     **ERIE**
clever     **CUTE, WITTY**
cleverness     **WIT**
clever phrase     **MOT**
cliche     **PLATITUDE, BROMIDE**
click     **SNAP**
cliff     **BLUFF**
climate (poet.)     **CLIME**
climax     **PEAK, APEX**
climax of a joke
(2 wds.)     **PUNCH LINE**
climb     **ASCEND, SCALE**
climb down     **DESCEND**
climbing device     **LADDER**
climbing plant     **IVY, LIANA,**
**VINE**
climb on all fours     **CLAMBER**
climb on top of     **MOUNT**
clime     **CLIMATE**
clinch     **SEAL, SECURE**
cling     **ADHERE, STICK**
clinging crustacean     **BARNACLE**
clinic     **INFIRMARY, HOSPITAL**
clinical     **IMPERSONAL**
Clio     **MUSE**
clip     **SNIP, TRIM, SHEAR**
clipped     **SHORN**
clipper     **LINER, SHIP**
clique     **CLAN, SET, GROUP**
cloak     **MANTLE, ROBE**
clock     **TIMEPIECE**
clock dial     **FACE**
clock face     **DIAL**
clock sound     **TICKTOCK, TICK,**
**TOCK**
clod     **LUMP**
clodhopper     **LOUT, DOLT**
clog     **BLOCK, JAM**
cloister     **ABBEY, CONVENT**
cloistered     **SECLUDED**
cloistered woman     **NUN**
close     **NEAR, SHUT, END,**
**COVER**
close acquaintance     **FRIEND**
close at hand     **NEARBY**
close by     **AT, HANDY, NEAR**
closed car     **SEDAN**
close falcon eyes     **SEEL**
close firmly     **BAR, SEAL**

closefisted **STINGY, MISERLY**
close friend **CHUM, PAL, BUDDY**
closemouthed **TACITURN**
closeness **INTIMACY**
close noisily **SLAM**
close relative **NIECE, NEPHEW, AUNT, UNCLE, BROTHER, SISTER, MOTHER, FATHER, SON, DAUGHTER, PARENT, SIBLING**
close securely **SEAL**
close tightly **CLENCH, SEAL**
close to **AT, BESIDE, NEAR**
close to tears **SAD**
closet **WARDROBE, LOCKER**
clot **MASS, THICKEN**
cloth **FABRIC**
cloth belt **SASH**
cloth dealer **DRAPER**
clothe **DRESS, GARB**
clothe with authority **VEST**
clothes **APPAREL**
clothes (colloq.) **TOGS**
cloth gaiters **SPATS**
clothing **GARB, ATTIRE, TOGS, DRESS**
clothing fabric **HOPSACKING, TRICOT, COTTON, SERGE, WORSTED, TWEED, WOOL, CORDUROY, DENIM, LINEN, VELVET, FUR, VELOUR, PONGEE, CHIFFON, SATIN, NYLON, ACETATE, SUEDE, LEATHER, SILK, RAYON**
cloth made of flax **LINEN**
cloth measurements **YARD**
cloth of gold **LAME**
cloth piece **BOLT**
cloth ridge **WALE**
cloth scrap **RAG, REMNANT**
cloth used as wall hanging **TAPESTRY**
cloth worn over the head **SCARF, KERCHIEF, MANTILLA, VEIL**
clothes moth **TINEA**
clothespress **WARDROBE**
clothes tinter **DYER**
clothes tree **COATRACK**
cloud **CUMULUS, NIMBUS, CIRRUS, STRATUS**
clouded **OBSCURE, OVERCAST**
cloud of smoke **FUME**
cloud region **SKY**
cloudy **DIM, GLOOMY**
clout **SWAT**

clown **BUFFOON, COMEDIAN, COMIC**
clownish **AWKWARD**
cloy **GLUT, SATE**
club **BAT, CUDGEL**
club fees **DUES**
clublike weapon **MACE**
clue **HINT, INKLING**
clump **WAD**
clumsy **ALL THUMBS, AWKWARD**
clumsy boat **ARK, TUB**
clumsy fellow **LOUT, OAF**
cluster **TUFT**
cluster of flowers **BUNCH**
cluster of shrubs **BUSH**
clutch **GRASP, BUNCH, NUMBER, CLUSTER**
clutch at wildly **CLAW, GRIP**
coach **CAR, STAGE**
coach and four **TALLY-HO**
coach dog **DALMATIAN**
coagulate **CLOT, GEL, SET**
coagulum **CLOT, CURD**
coal **ANTHRACITE, FUEL**
coal bed **SEAM**
coal digger **MINER**
coalesce **MERGE, UNITE**
coal excavation **MINE**
coal fuel product **COKE**
coal hod **SCUTTLE**
coalition **ALLIANCE**
coal mine **PIT, COLLIERY**
coal oil **KEROSENE**
coal pit **MINE, STRIP-MINE**
coal product **TAR, COKE**
coal scuttle **HOD**
coal tar **EOSIN**
coal tunnel entrance **ADIT**
coal unit **TON**
coarse **ROUGH, CRUDE**
coarse and sticky **TACKY**
coarse cord **TWINE, ROPE**
coarse corn meal **SAMP**
coarse file **RASP**
coarse grain **MEAL**
coarse grass **REED**
coarse hair **SETA**
coarse hairnet **SNOOD**
coarse hominy **GRITS, SAMP**
coarse part **DREGS**
coarse tobacco **SHAG**
coarse wool cloth **TWEED**
coast **SEASHORE, SHORE**
coastal projection **CAPE, NESS**
coaster **SLED, DISK**
Coast Guard lady **SPAR**
coast of India **MALABAR**

| | | | |
|---|---|---|---|
| coat | COVER | coin of the realm | SPECIE |
| coat arm | SLEEVE | coin opening | SLOT |
| coat collar | LAPEL | coin's date space | EXERGUE |
| coat lapel | FLAP | cola purchase | SIXPACK |
| coat of arms | CREST | colander | SIEVE |
| coat of mail | ARMOR | colate | FINISH, STRAIN |
| coat sleeve | ARM | cold | ALGID, FRIGID, CHILLY, |
| coat with color | PAINT | | COOL |
| coat with gold | GILD | cold Adriatic wind | BORA |
| coat with icing | GLAZE | cold and bleak | RAW |
| coat with metal | PLATE | cold and damp | RAW |
| coating on grain | BRAN | cold cubes | ICE |
| coating on iron | RUST | cold dish | SALAD, ASPIC, ICE |
| coating on teeth | ENAMEL | | CREAM, SHERBET |
| coax URGE, WHEEDLE, CAJOLE | | cold feet | COWARDICE |
| cob vegetable | CORN | cold season | WINTER |
| cobbler's form | LAST | cold storage | DEEP FREEZE, |
| cobbler's tool | AWL | | FREEZER |
| cock | ROOSTER | cold wind (Fr.) | BISE |
| cocktail seafood | SHRIMP, | coliseum | STADIUM |
| OYSTER, CLAM, HERRING | | collaborate | AID |
| cocktail snack | CANAPE | collapse | DEFLATE |
| coconut tree | PALM | collarbone | CLAVICLE |
| codfish dish | SCROD | collar fastener STUD, BUTTON | |
| coelenterate HYDRA, POLYP, | | collar of a coat | LAPEL |
| | CORAL | collar shape | VEE |
| coerce | FORCE | collate COMPARE, ASSEMBLE | |
| coercion | DURESS | collect ASSEMBLE, AMASS, | |
| coffee (sl.) | JAVA | | GATHER |
| coffee bean | NIB | collect gradually | GLEAN |
| coffee container | CUP, MUG | collection set | GROUP |
| coffee dispenser | URN, POT, | collection of animals | ZOO, |
| PERCOLATOR, CARAFE | | | MENAGERIE |
| coffee grinder | MILL | collection of facts | ANA, DATA |
| coffee house | CAFE | collection of papers | DOSSIER |
| cogent | POTENT, STRONG | collection of sayings | ANA |
| cogitate | THINK | collection of tents | CAMP |
| cognizant AWARE, CONSCIOUS | | collection of type | FONT |
| cognomen | NAME | collective | CO-OP |
| cogwheel | GEAR | collectivism | SOCIALISM |
| coil | WIND, SPRING | colleen | LASS |
| coin MONEY, DIME, NICKEL, | | college | SCHOOL |
| QUARTER, MINT | | college administrator | DEAN |
| coincide | AGREE | college building, for short | |
| coincide in part | OVERLAP | | DORM |
| coin factory | MINT | college campus | QUAD |
| coin manufacture | MINTAGE | college cheer | RAH |
| coin of ancient Greece | OBOL, | college course SEMINAR, LOGIC | |
| | DRACHMA | college court | QUAD |
| coin of Bulgaria | LEV | college dance | HOP, PROM |
| coin of France | ECU, SOU, | college degree (abbr.) BA, BS, | |
| CENTIME, FRANC | | MA, MS, PHD, AB, BFA, | |
| coin of India | RUPEE | LLD, MD, DDS | |
| coin of Iran | RIAL | college discussion | |
| coin of Italy | LIRA | group | SEMINAR |
| coin of Japan | SEN, YEN | college examination | ORAL |
| coin of Mexico | PESO | college girl | COED |
| coin of the Bible | TALENT | college graduate | ALUMNUS |

college group **DEBATING TEAM, FOOTBALL TEAM, FRATERNITY, FRAT, SORORITY**
college half-year **SEMESTER**
college head **DEAN**
college official **DEAN**
college president (sl.) **PREXY**
college song **GLEE**
college student **JUNIOR, SENIOR**
college subject **ECONOMICS, ANATOMY, BIOLOGY, CHEMISTRY, TRIGONOMETRY, CALCULUS, LITERATURE**
college term **SEMESTER, TRIMESTER**
collegian's jacket **BLAZER**
collide **CLASH**
collie (2 wds.) **SHEEP DOG**
colliery **MINE**
collision **CRASH**
colloidal substance **GAL**
colloquy **DISCOURSE, SPEECH**
Cologne (Ger.) **KOLN**
Colombia city **BOGOTA**
colonist **SETTLER**
colonize **PLANT, SETTLE**
colonnade **STOA**
colony **SETTLEMENT**
color **DYE, HUE, TINT, PAINT, SHADE, BLUSH, REDDEN, RED, YELLOW, BLUE, CERISE, SCARLET, BEIGE, BROWN, TAN, ECRU, CORAL, OLIVE, GREEN, PURPLE, VIOLET, PINK, AZURE**
color (suffix) **CHROME**
Colorado city **ASPEN, DENVER**
Colorado Indian **UTE**
Colorado mountain (2 wds.) **PIKES PEAK**
Colorado park **ESTES**
Colorado ski resort **ASPEN**
Colorado tributary **GILA**
color a picture **TINT**
color-changing lizard **AGAMA**
color graduation **SHADE, TONE, TINE, HUE**
color of moleskin **TAUPE**
color slightly **TINGE, TINT**
colorful **PICTURESQUE, VIVID**
colorful bird **BLUE JAY, BALTIMORE ORIOLE, PEACOCK**
colorful fabric **CHINTZ PRINT**
colorful lizard **AGAMA**
colorful parrot **MACAW**

colorful warm-water denizen (2 wds.) **PARROT FISH**
colorless **ASHEN, DRAB, PALE, PALLID, TRANSPARENT**
colorless alcohol **NEROLI**
colorless crystalline compound **TAURINE**
colossal **HUGE, IMMENSE**
colt **YEARLING**
coltish **FRISKY**
colt's father **SIRE**
colt's mother **DAM, MARE**
Columbus' birthplace **GENOA**
Columbus' departure port **PALOS**
Columbus' ship **NINA, PINTA, SANTA MARIA**
Columbus' sponsor **ISABELLA, SPAIN**
column **PILLAR**
column shaft **SCAPE**
columnist's entry **ITEM**
columnist Wilson **EARL**
comatose **TORPID**
comb rat **GUNDI**
combat **FIGHT, BATTLE, WAR, DUEL**
combatant **FIGHTER**
combat vehicle **TANK**
combination **UNION, MERGER**
combine **MERGE, UNITE, WED, MARRY, MELD, MIX**
combustion **FIRE, BURNING**
combustion remnant **ASH**
come **APPROACH, ARRIVE, NEAR**
come across **FIND**
come back **RETURN**
come between **MEDDLE**
come by **GET, GAIN**
come close to **NEAR, APPROACH**
comedian Abbott **BUD**
comedian Benny **JACK**
comedian Caesar **SID**
comedian Carney **ART**
comedian Conway **TIM**
comedian DeLuise **DOM**
comedian Durante **JIMMY**
comedian Hill **NORMAN**
comedian Hope **BOB**
comedian Kamen **MILT**
comedian Kaye **DANNY**
comedian King **ALAN**
comedian Knotts **DON**
comedian Lahr **BERT**
comedian Mostel **ZERO**

comedian Shriner **HERB**
comedian Skelton **RED**
comedian Sparks **NED**
comedienne Arden **EVE**
comedienne Ball **LUCILLE**
comedienne Prentiss **PAULA**
come forth **EMERGE, EMANATE**
come in **ENTER**
come in first **WIN**
come in second **LOSE**
come into port **LAND**
come into sight **APPEAR**
come into view **LOOM**
comely **PRETTY**
come-on **TEASER**
come out **EMERGE**
come to **REACH**
come to an end **HALT, STOP, CEASE, TERMINATE**
come to earth **ALIGHT, LIGHT, LAND**
come to nothing **FIZZLE**
come to rest **STOP**
come to terms **AGREE**
come together **MEET, MERGE, UNITE, AGREE**
comet's train **TAIL**
comet tail **STREAMER**
come up **ARISE, VISIT**
come upon **FIND**
come upon (2 wds.) **MEET WITH**
come upon unawares
(3 wds.) **TAKE BY SURPRISE**
comfort **EASE, SOLACE, SOOTHE**
comfortable **PLEASANT**
comfortable chair **RECLINER**
comforter **QUILT, BLANKET**
comic **FUNNY, DROLL**
comical **AMUSING**
comic section **FUNNIES**
comic strip
detective **DICK TRACY**
comic strip sailor **POPEYE**
coming into being **GENESIS**
coming-out party **DEBUT**
comma **CAESURA, PAUSE**
command **ORDER, BID, EDICT**
commander **LEADER**
commander-in-chief **PRESIDENT**
commandment **LAW, PRECEPT**
command to a horse **GEE, WHOA, HAW, GIDDYAP**
commemorate **CELEBRATE**
commemoration **MEMORY**
commemorative pillar **STELE**
commence **BEGIN, INITIATE**

commend **PRAISE, APPROVE**
comment **REMARK**
commentator Sevareid **ERIC**
comment on **NOTE**
commerce **TRADE**
commercial building **MART**
commercial flight
(2 wds.) **AIR TRAVEL**
commercial ship **STEAMER**
commercial spiel
(2 wds.) **SALES PITCH**
commiserate **CONDOLE**
commission **PERCENTAGE**
commit a faux pas **ERR**
commit theft **ROB**
commode **CHEST**
commodious **SUITABLE, COMFORTABLE**
common **ORDINARY**
common (prefix) **CENO**
common adder **ASP**
common ailment **COLD, FLU**
common ancestor **ADAM, EVE**
common ant **PISMIRE**
common conjunction **AND**
common level **PAR**
common metal **IRON, TIN, NICKEL, STEEL, COPPER, BRASS**
common newt **EFT**
common people **DEMOS**
commonplace **TRITE, BANAL, HACKNEYED**
commonplace
remark **PLATITUDE**
common practice **USAGE**
common sailor
(2 wds.) **DECK HAND**
common tree **ELM, OAK, MAPLE, PINE**
common verb **ARE, IS, BE**
common viper **ADDER**
commonwealth **STATE**
commotion **ADO, TO-DO, NOISE, STIR, RACKET, DISTURBANCE**
communalism **SOCIALISM**
commune in Belgium **NIEL**
communicant **MEMBER**
communicate **CONVEY**
communicating instrument **TV, PHONE, TELEGRAPH, SATELLITE, TELSTAR**
communication **MESSAGE, LETTER, WIRE, CALL**
communion **FELLOWSHIP, SHARE**
communion cloth **CORPORAL**

communion plate **PATEN**
communion table **ALTAR**
communion vessel **PYX**
communique **MESSAGE**
communist **RED**
commute **EXCHANGE, SUBSTITUTE**
compact **DENSE, SOLID, SNUG, SERRIED**
compact body of troops **PHALANX**
companion **MATE, PAL, BUDDY, FRIEND, SPOUSE, ASSOCIATE, PARTNER**
companionable **SOCIAL**
companion for ham **EGGS**
companion of odds **ENDS**
company **GUESTS**
company (Fr. abbr.) **CIE**
company of people **CREW, GANG**
company of troupers **CAST**
comparable to (3 wds.) **AS GOOD AS**
comparative **RELATIVE**
comparative conjunction **THAN**
compare **CONTRAST, LIKEN**
compare critically **EXAMINE**
comparison **SIMILE**
compartment aboard a ship **CABIN, GALLEY, STATEROOM, BERTH**
compass point **ENE, NNE, SSE, SSW, ESE, WSW, WNW, NNW, NE, NW, SE, SW, NORTH, SOUTH, EAST, WEST**
compassion **TENDERNESS, PITY**
compassionate **TENDER**
compatible **AGREEABLE**
compatriot **COLLEAGUE**
compel **FORCE**
compendium **SUMMARY**
compensate **PAY**
compensate for **RECOUP**
compensation **PAY, REWARD**
compete **VIE**
compete in a race **RUN**
competence **ABILITY**
competent **ABLE, CAPABLE**
competition **CONTEST, RACE**
competition between retailers (2 wds.) **PRICE WAR**
competitive game **SPORT, TENNIS, BASEBALL, HOCKEY**
competitor **RIVAL**
compilation **REPORT, DIGEST**
compile **AMASS, EDIT**

compiler of game rules **HOYLE**
complacent **SMUG**
complacently self-satisfied **SMUG**
complain **MOAN, GRIPE, BEEF**
complainant **PLAINTIFF**
complaining **QUERULOUS**
complain loudly (3 wds.) **RAISE THE ROOF**
complaint **ILLNESS, AILMENT**
complaisance **COURTESY, AMENITY**
complaisant **CIVIL**
complement **ADJUNCT**
complete **ENTIRE, WHOLE, TOTAL, UTTER, FINISH, ACCOMPLISH**
complete agreement **UNISON**
complete collection **SET**
completed **DONE**
complete failure **WASHOUT**
completely mistaken (2 wds.) **OFF BASE**
completely waterless (comp. wd.) **BONE-DRY**
complex **INTRICATE, CONFUSED**
compliment **FLATTER**
complimentary ticket **PASS**
comply **SUBMIT, OBEY**
comply with **OBSERVE**
comply with commands **OBEY**
component **UNIT, PART**
component of atom **PROTON, ION**
comport **BEHAVE**
comportment **BEHAVIOR**
compose **WRITE**
composed **CALM**
composer **AUTHOR**
composer Bernstein **LEONARD**
composer Dvorak **ANTON(IN)**
composer Stravinsky **IGOR**
composite picture **MONTAGE**
composition **ESSAY**
composition for two **DUET**
composure **POISE, SERENITY**
compound **COMBINE, ESTER**
compound tincture **ELIXIR**
comprehend **UNDERSTAND, GRASP**
comprehensive **EXTENSIVE, WIDE**
comprise **INCLUDE**
compulsion **DURESS**
compunction **REMORSE, REGRET**
compute **CALCULATE, COUNT**

computerized production **AUTOMATION**
comrade **MATE, COMPANION, FRIEND, PAL, CHUM, COLLEAGUE**
conceal **COVER, HIDE, MASK**
conceal by false appearance **DISGUISE**
concealed **HID, HIDDEN, COVERT**
concede **ADMIT**
conceit **EGO, VANITY**
conceited **VAIN**
conceited person **EGOTIST**
conceive **IMAGINE, SUPPOSE**
concentrate **FOCUS**
concentration **ATTENTION**
concept **IDEA**
conception **NOTION, DESIGN**
concern **CARE, INTEREST**
concerned **ANXIOUS**
concerning **AS TO, IN RE, ANENT, ABOUT, RE**
concerning a title **TITULAR**
concerning origin **GENETIC**
concerning the ear **OTIC**
concernment **WORRY, ANXIETY**
concert by single performer **RECITAL**
concert grand **PIANO**
concert halls **ODEA, ODEONS**
concert instrument **OBOE, PIANO, VIOLIN, HARP, CELLO, FLUTE, TUBA**
concession **FAVOR**
conch **SHELL**
concierge **CUSTODIAN, SUPER**
conciliate **PACIFY, MOLLIFY**
conciliatory bribe **SOP**
concise **LACONIC, TERSE, BRIEF**
concise summary **PRECIS**
conclave **MEETING**
conclude **CLOSE, END, FINISH**
concluding passage **CODA**
conclusion **END, FINALE, FINIS, CLIMAX**
conclusive **DECISIVE, FINAL**
concoct **BREW**
concoction **INVENTION**
concord **AGREEMENT, UNISON**
concordat **COVENANT**
concrete **SOLID, FIRM**
concrete surface **PAVEMENT**
concretion **PEARL**
concur **AGREE**
condemn **CONVICT, DOOM**
condensation **DEW**

condense **ABRIDGE**
condensed representation **EPITOME**
condign **DESERVED, SUITABLE**
condiment **RELISH, SEASONING**
condition **CIRCUMSTANCE, STATE**
conditional release from prison **PAROLE**
conditional stipulation **PROVISO**
condition made **PREMISE**
conditions **TERMS**
condone **FORGIVE, PARDON**
conducive to peace **IRENIC**
conduct **BEHAVIOR, LEAD**
conduct oneself **BEHAVE**
conductor **DIRECTOR, LEADER**
conductor's stick **BATON**
conduit **CHANNEL, TUBE**
cone-bearing tree **FIR, PINE**
cone-shaped cap **FEZ**
confederate **ALLY**
Confederate soldier **REB**
Confederate States Army (abbr.) **CSA**
confederation **UNION, LEAGUE**
confer **BESTOW**
conference site, 1945 **YALTA**
confess (3 wds.) **OWN UP TO**
confession of faith **CREDO, CREED**
confide **TRUST, RELY**
confidence **TRUST**
confident **CERTAIN, SURE**
confine **COOP UP, PEN**
confine by bars **JAIL, CAGE**
confined to a locality **ENDEMIC**
confinement **DETENTION**
confirm **RATIFY**
confiscate **SEIZE**
conflagration **FIRE, BLAZE**
conflict **STRIFE CLASH, WAR. BATTLE, FIGHT**
conform **ADAPT**
conform to shape **FIT**
confound **AMAZE, ASTONISH**
confront **FACE, MEET**
confuse **ADDLE, MIX UP**
confused **ASEA, AT SEA**
confused fight **MELEE, FREE-FOR-ALL**
confused mess **MISHMASH**
confused state **MESS**
confusion **DISORDER, CHAOS**
confute **DENY**
congeal **FREEZE, ICE**
congenial **FRIENDLY**

conger **EEL**
congressional office **SPEAKER, SENATORSHIP, WHIP**
congressman (abbr.) **REP**
congressman's trip **JUNKET**
coniferous tree **FIR, PINE, LARCH**
conjecture **GUESS**
conjugal **BRIDAL, MARITAL**
conjunction **AND, OR, BUT, NOR**
conjunction (Fr.) **ET**
conjunction (Ger.) **UND**
conjunction (Lat.) **ET**
conjunction (Sp.) **Y**
conjure **INVOKE**
conjuror's handiwork **SPELL**
connect **JOIN, WED, MARRY, WELD**
connected group **NEXUS**
Connecticut university **YALE**
connection **LINKAGE, RELATION**
connective **AND**
conquer **BEST, BEAT, WIN**
conscious **AWARE, AWAKE**
consecrate **BLESS**
consecrated **HOLY, BLESSED, BLEST**
consent **AGREE, ASSENT**
consequence **RESULT**
conservationist **FORESTER, ECOLOGIST**
conservative group
(2 wds.) **OLD GUARD**
consider **PONDER**
considerable **NOTABLE**
considerable amount **WAD**
considerate **KIND**
consideration **ESTEEM, ATTENTION**
considering **SINCE**
consign **SEND, DELIVER**
consistent **REGULAR**
consolation **COMFORT**
console **SOLACE, COMFORT, SOOTHE**
consolidate **UNITE, COMBINE**
consomme **SOUP**
consort **SPOUSE, PARTNER**
consort of Amon-Ra **MUT**
conspicuous **NOTICEABLE, SALIENT**
conspiracy **CABAL, INTRIGUE**
constant **TRUE, STEADY, REGULAR**
constantly **AT EVERY TURN, ALWAYS**

constellation **ARA, ORION, LEO, CENTAURUS, LYRA, BOOTES, VIRGO, AQUILA, GEMINI, SCORPIUS, CYGNUS, CRUX, CETUS, COMA, ARIES, GRUS, PAVO, VELA, DORADO CARINA, AURIGA, TAURUS, LYNX**
consternation **DISMAY, ALARM**
constituent **COMPONENT, FACTOR**
constituent part **ELEMENT**
Constitution
State **CONNECTICUT**
constrain **CHECK, CURB**
constraint **DURESS**
constrict **CONTRACT**
construct **MAKE, ERECT, BUILD**
construct anew **REMAKE**
construction beam
(2 wds.) **I BAR, T BAR**
constructive **CREATIVE**
constructor **BUILDER**
construe **INTERPRET**
consul of old Rome **CATO**
consult **CONFER**
consultation **CONFERENCE, DISCUSSION**
consume **EAT, USE**
consummate **COMPLETE, IDEAL**
consumption **TUBERCULOSIS**
contact **TOUCH**
contact by phone **CALL**
contagious **INFECTIOUS**
contain **HOLD**
container **CAN, TIN, VAT, CRATE, CARTON**
container for face
powder **COMPACT**
container for oranges **CRATE**
containing air **PNEUMATIC**
containing fine soil **SILTY**
containing fire **IGNEOUS**
containing gold **AURIC**
containing iron **FERRIC**
containing orifices **POROUS**
contaminate **TAINT**
contemn **SCORN, RIDICULE**
contemplate **CONSIDER**
contemplative **THOUGHTFUL, SEDATE**
contemporary **MODERN**

contemporary painter **DALI, WYETH, WARHOL, TAMAYO, PICASSO, RAY O'KEEFFE, RIVERS, MIRO, MOTHERWELL, OLDENBURG, GUSTON, INDIANA, POLLOCK, KUPKA, LEVINE, DINE, EVERGOOD, CHIRICO, CHAGALL, ALBERS, ARP, BACON, BENTON, BRAQUE, DIX**

contempt **DISDAIN, SCORN**
contemptible **MEAN**
contemptibly cheap
person **PIKER**
contend **COPE, VIE**
content **HAPPY, PLEASED**
contention **STRIFE**
contentment **PLEASURE**
contest **COMPETITION, RACE, GAME**
contestant **ENTRANT**
contestant for
office **CANDIDATE**
contest at law **LITIGATE**
contest necessity **BOX TOP**
contiguous **TOUCHING**
continent **AFRICA, ASIA, NORTH AMERICA, EUROPE, AUSTRALIA, SOUTH AMERICA**
contingent **CAUSAL**
continual **CONSTANT**
continue **ENDURE, PERSIST**
continue a journey
(2 wds.) **PUSH ON**
continuing story **SERIAL**
contract **CHARTER**
contraction **SPASM**
contract of ownership **DEED**
contradict **DENY, REBUT**
contradiction **PARADOX, DENIAL, REBUTTAL**
contrary **UNLIKE, OPPOSITE**
contrary current **EDDY**
contrast **COMPARE**
contribute **SHELL OUT, DONATE, GIVE**
contribution **DONATION, GIFT, BEQUEST**
contrivance **DEVICE, TRICK**
contrive **CONCOCT**
control **CHECK, DIAL, MASTERY, REGULATE, MANAGE**
control of emotions **RESTRAINT**
controversial **POLEMIC**

controversy **DEBATE, DISPUTE**
conundrum **RIDDLE**
convene **MEET, SIT, CALL**
convenient **HANDY**
convent **CLOISTER**
convent inmate **NUN**
convent room **CELL**
convention **MEETING**
conventional **ACCEPTED, CORRECT**
convention
representative **DELEGATE**
conventions **MORES**
converge **FOCUS**
conversant **FAMILIAR, SKILLED**
conversation **CHAT, TALK**
conversational pause **ER, UH, AHEM**
converse **TALK, CHAT, GAB**
convert **CHANGE**
convert into money **CASH**
convert into ordinary
language **DECODE**
convertible **CAR, COUCH, SOFA**
convex molding **OVOLO**
convey **BRING**
conviction **FAITH, BELIEF**
convince **ASSURE**
convivial **FESTIVE, GAY**
convoke **SUMMON**
cook **CHEF**
cook bacon **FRY**
cook by simmering **STEW**
cooked fruit dish **COMPOTE, APPLESAUCE**
cooked sufficiently **DONE**
cooker **STOVE, RANGE, POT**
cookery **CUISINE**
cookie **SNAP**
cook in an oven **BAKE, ROAST**
cook in fat **FRY, SAUTE**
cooking device **GRIDDLE, STOVE**
cooking fat **LARD, OIL, GREASE, BUTTER, SUET**
cooking mixture **BATTER**
cooking pot **OLLA**
cooking vessel **PAN, POT, SAUCEPAN, SKILLET**
cook in water **BOIL**
cook lightly in liquid **POACH**
cookout **BARBECUE**
cook over live coals **BROIL, GRILL**
cook quickly **FRY, SEAR**
cook's formula **RECIPE**
cook's measure **TABLESPOON, TEASPOON, CUP, PINCH, DASH**

cook slowly STEW
cookstove RANGE
cook up CONCOCT, DEVISE
cook with dry heat BAKE,
ROAST
cool CHILLY, FROSTY
cool and reserved ALOOF
cooled ICED
cooled lava AA
cooler JAIL, ICER
coolheaded CALM
coolie LABORER
cooling beverage ADE
cooling device FAN
cool off CHILL
cool season FALL
cool to low point FREEZE
coonskin CAP
coop CAGE, PEN
cooperate ASSIST, CONSPIRE
cooperate secretly CONNIVE
cootie LOUSE, BUG
cope CONTEND
copious PLENTIFUL
copper and tin alloy BRONZE,
PEWTER
copper coin CENT, PENNY
Copperfield's wife DORA,
AGNES
copter GIRO
copy APE, MIMIC, CARBON,
XEROX
copycat APER
coral island ATOLL
coral reef KEY
coral ridge REEF
corbel BRACKET
Corcyra CORFU
cord STRING, TWINE
cord-and-stone weapon BOLA
corded fabric REP(P)
cordial GENIAL
cordon CIRCLE
cord on an Arab
headdress AGAL
cord ornament TASSEL
cordwood measure STERE
core HEART, CENTER
cornbread PONE
corncob PIPE
corner NOOK, TREE
cornered ANGULAR, CAUGHT
cornet TRUMPET, HORN
cornfield weed DARNEL
corn-heating utensil POPPER
Cornhusker State NEBRASKA
cornice EAVE
corn porridge SAMP, MUSH

corn spike EAR, COB
corny TRITE, BANAL
corny actor HAM
coronet TIARA, CROWN
corporal BODILY
corporation BODY
corpse BODY, CADAVER
corpulence FAT, OBESITY
corpulent FAT, OBESE
corral PEN, RING
correct AMEND, EMEND,
TRUE, REVISE, EDIT,
RIGHT
correct a manuscript EDIT
corrida cheer OLE
corridor HALL
corrode RUST, EAT
corrupt LOW, BASE
corruption VICE
corsage BOUQUET
corset string LACE
cortege PARADE, RETINUE,
PROCESSION
cortex BARK, RIND
cos LETTUCE
cosmetic ROUGE, CREAM,
LIPSTICK, SHADOW,
MASCARA, LINER, BASE,
POWDER
cost PRICE, RATE
costly DEAR, EXPENSIVE
costly fur SABLE, MINK,
ERMINE
cost of membership DUES
cost of passage FARE
costume ATTIRE, CLOTHING
cot BED
cote COOP
coterie CLIQUE, SET
cote sound COO
cottage cheese lumps CURDS
cotton bundle BALE
cotton fabric LISLE, PIMA,
MUSLIN, PERCALE, VOILE,
FLANNEL
cotton pod BOLL
cottontail HARE, RABBIT,
PETER
cottonwood TREE
couch SOFA, SETTEE, DIVAN,
DAVENPORT
cougar PUMA, CAT
counsel ADVICE
count NUMBER
count calories DIET, REDUCE
countenance FACE, VISAGE
counter OPPOSE, BAR

counterfeit **BOGUS, FAKE, PHONY, SHAM, IMITATION, ERSATZ**
counterfeit coin **SLUG**
countermand **ABOLISH, CANCEL**
counterpane **COVER**
counterpart **DUPLICATE, TWIN**
countersign **PASSWORD**
counter tenor **ALTO**
counting of votes cast **POLL**
countless **INFINITE**
Count of music **BASIE**
country **STATE, LAND, NATION, WOODS**
country bumpkin (sl.) **RUBE, HICK**
country by-way **LANE**
country estate **VILLA**
country festival **FAIR**
country hotel **INN**
country place **VILLA, CABIN, FARM**
country road **LANE**
countrywide **NATIONAL**
county **PARISH**
county in England **SHIRE**
coup **BLOW, UPSET**
coupe **AUTO, CAR**
couple **PAIR, TWO, TWOSOME, DUO, LINK**
couple together **BRACKET**
courage **HEART, METTLE, BRAVERY, NERVE**
courageous **BRAVE**
courageous man **HERO**
courant **GAZETTE**
courier **MESSENGER**
course **PATH, WAY, ROUTE, PATHWAY**
course of instruction **CLASS**
court **WOO**
court case **TRIAL, SUIT**
court cry **OYES, OYEZ, HEAR YE**
courteous **CIVIL, POLITE**
court game **TENNIS, SQUASH**
court hearing **OYER**
court order **FIAT, WRIT**
court proceedings **TRIAL**
court reporter's machine **STENOTYPE**
courtroom panel **JURY**
courtroom procedure **TRIAL, SUIT**
court session **ASSIZE**
courtyard **PATIO**
cousin of Absalom **AMASA**

couth **REFINED, POLISHED**
couturiere **MODISTE**
cove **BAY, INLET**
covenant **BOND, CONTRACT**
cover **CONCEAL, LID, TOP**
cover a package **WRAP**
covered avenue **ARCADE**
covered porch **VERANDA**
covered with frost **HOARY**
covered with moisture **DEWY**
covered with velvety growth **MOSSY**
cover girl **MODEL**
covering of trees **BARK**
coverlet **BEDSPREAD**
covert **HIDDEN, PRIVATE**
cover the face **MASK**
cover the inside **LINE**
cover up **CONCEAL**
cover with a sheath **GLOVE**
cover with asphalt **PAVE**
cover with cloth **DRAPE**
cover with concrete **PAVE**
cover with gold paint **GILD**
cover with turf **SOD**
covet **DESIRE**
covey **BEVY, FLOCK**
cow **DAUNT, TERRIFY**
coward **CRAVEN**
cowardice **FEAR**
cowbell **CAMPION**
cowboy **RIDER, ROPER**
cowboy country **WEST**
cowboy event **RODEO**
cowboy gear **STIRRUP, SADDLE, RIATA, LASSO LARIAT, CHAPS**
cowboy movie **WESTERN, OATER**
cowboy Rogers **ROY**
cowboy's breeches **CHAPS**
cowboy's concern **HERD**
cowboy's nickname **TEX**
cowboy's rope **LARIAT, RIATA, LASSO**
cowboy's shoes **BOOTS**
cower **CRINGE**
cowfish **GRAMPUS**
cow genus **BOS**
cowgirl Evans **DALE**
cowl **HOOD**
cows **CATTLE, KINE**
cow's chewed food **RUMEN, CUD**
cow's home **BARN**
cow's low **MOO**
cow's offspring **CALF**
cowskin **HIDE**

| | | | |
|---|---|---|---|
| cow sound | **MOO** | creep furtively | **SNEAK** |
| coy | **DEMUR, SHY** | creeping creature | **WORM,** |
| Coyote State | **SOUTH DAKOTA** | | **SNAKE, REPTILE** |
| cozen | **CHEAT** | Creole State | **LOUISIANA** |
| cozy | **SNUG** | crescent point | **CUSP** |
| cozy home | **NEST** | crestfallen | **ASHAMED** |
| cozy room | **DEN** | crest of hair | **TOPKNOT** |
| cozy talk | **CHAT** | crew | **TEAM, GANG** |
| crab | **CANCER** | crew member | **MAN** |
| crab's pincer | **CLAW** | cricket team | **ELEVEN** |
| crack | **BREAK, SPLIT** | crime | **SIN, OFFENSE** |
| Cracker State | **GEORGIA** | criminal | **FELON, CROOK,** |
| crackle | **SNAP, CRUNCH, POP** | | **HOODLUM, MISCREANT** |
| crackpot | **NUT, LUNATIC** | crimson | **RED** |
| crack through which water | | cringe | **COWER** |
| escapes | **LEAK** | crinkled fabric | **CRAPE, CREPE** |
| cradle | **BASSINET, CRIB** | crinoline | **PETTICOAT, SLIP** |
| cradle song | **LULLABY** | cripple | **DISABLE, MAIM** |
| craft | **BOAT, ART, SKILL** | crippled | **LAME** |
| craft of the far north | **KAYAK,** | crisis | **EMERGENCY** |
| | **ICEBREAKER** | crisp and fragile | **BRITTLE** |
| crafty | **SLY, WILY, CLEVER** | crisp cookie | **SNAP** |
| crag | **TOR, PRECIPICE** | criterion | **RULE, TEST, BASIS** |
| cram | **STUFF, RAM, STUDY** | critical | **ACUTE** |
| cramp | **SPASM, ACHE** | criticize | **CARP, CAVIL** |
| crane | **DERRICK** | criticize severely (colloq.) | **PAN** |
| crane arm | **GIB** | critic's account | **REVIEW** |
| cranium | **SKULL** | critic's place | |
| crank | **GROUCH, HANDLE** | (2 wds.) | **AISLE SEAT** |
| cranky | **TESTY, CROSS** | croak | **CAW** |
| crash against | **RAM** | Croatian | **SERBIAN** |
| crate | **CASE, CARTON** | crochet | **HOOK, KNIT** |
| cravat | **TIE** | crockery | **CHINA** |
| crave | **DESIRE** | crocodile | **ALLIGATOR** |
| craven | **AFRAID, COWARDLY** | crone | **HAG** |
| craving | **LUST, HUNGER,** | crony | **CHUM, PAL** |
| | **DESIRE** | crook | **BEND, THIEF, ROBBER** |
| crawl | **CREEP** | crooked | **ASKEW, AWRY** |
| crawling animal | **REPTILE** | croon | **SING** |
| crayon drawing | **PASTEL** | crooner Crosby | **BING** |
| craze | **FAD, MANIA** | crooner Vallee | **RUDY** |
| crazy | **DAFT, NUTS, NUTTY,** | crop | **HARVEST** |
| | **CRACKED, MAD** | cross | **TRAVERSE** |
| cream | **ELITE** | cross a river | **FORD** |
| crease | **FOLD** | crossbar | **AXLE** |
| create | **ORIGINATE, MAKE,** | crossbeam | **TRAVE** |
| | **BUILD** | crossed wood | |
| create pictures | **PAINT, DRAW** | framework | **LATTICE** |
| creative person | **ARTIST** | cross in a church | **ROOD** |
| creator of Fantasyland | **DISNEY** | cross out | **DELE** |
| creator of the | | crouch | **BEND, STOOP** |
| Thesaurus | **ROGET** | crouch in fear | **COWER** |
| creature | **ANIMAL, BEING** | crow | **ROOK** |
| credence | **TRUST** | crowbar | **LEVER** |
| credential | **VOUCHER, PASS** | crowd | **HORDE, PACK, MOB** |
| creed | **RELIGION, BELIEF** | crowded | **DENSE** |
| creek | **INLET, STREAM, BAYOU** | crown | **DIADEM, TIARA,** |
| creep | **CRAWL** | | **CORONET** |

| | |
|---|---|
| crow's call | CAW |
| crucible | POT |
| crucifix | CROSS |
| crude | RAW |
| crude metal | ORE |
| crude rubber | PARA |
| crude watercraft | RAFT |
| cruel | MEAN, BRUTAL, SADISTIC |
| cruel joke | HOAX |
| cruel person | BRUTE, MEANIE, SADIST BULLY |
| cruet | VIAL |
| cruise | SAIL |
| crumb | BIT, PIECE |
| crumble | MOLDER |
| Crusader's enemy | SARACEN |
| crush | MASH |
| crustacean | CRAB, SHRIMP |
| cry | SOB, WEEP, BAWL |
| cry of a lamb | BLEAT, BAA, MAA, BLAT |
| cry of an owl | HOOT |
| cry of despair | ALAS |
| cry of pain | OUCH, YIPE, OW |
| cry of sorrow | ALAS |
| cry of surprise | OH, HO, OHO, AHA |
| cry of triumph | AHA, EUREKA |
| cry out | SCREAM, SHOUT |
| crypt | VAULT |
| cryptic | SECRET, OCCULT |
| crystal | GLASS |
| crystalline gem | IOLITE |
| Cuban capital | HAVANA |
| Cuban dance | CONGA |
| cubicle | CELL |
| cubic meter | STERE |
| cuboid | BONE |
| cub's home | DEN |
| cuckoo | ANI |
| cuckoopoint | ARUM |
| cucumber | PICKLE |
| cud | RUMEN |
| cud chewer | COW |
| cuddle | NESTLE, SNUGGLE |
| cuddy | CABIN, GALLEY |
| cudgel | CLUB, STAVE |
| cue | HINT, SIGNAL |
| cuff | SLAP, STRIKE |
| cuff ornament | STUD, LINK, BUTTON |
| culinary expert | CHEF |
| cull | CHOOSE, SORT |
| culmination | CLIMAX, ACME |
| culpability | GUILT |
| cult | SECT |

| | |
|---|---|
| cultivate | FARM, PLOW, GROW, RAISE, REFINE |
| cultivate the soil | TILL, FARM |
| cultivator | HOER |
| culture | ART, POLISH |
| culture medium | AGAR |
| culvert | CONDUIT, UNDERPASS |
| cummerbund | SASH, BELT |
| cunning | SLY, CLEVER, ART, SLYNESS |
| cup | MUG |
| cupbearer of gods | HEBE |
| cupboard | CABINET, CLOSET, PANTRY |
| Cupid | AMOR. EROS |
| Cupid's mother | VENUS |
| Cupid's title | DAN |
| cupidity | AVARICE, GREED |
| cupola | DOME |
| cup rim | LIP |
| cuprum | COPPER |
| cup-shaped flower | TULIP |
| cur | MONGREL, MUTT |
| curate | PRIEST |
| curative | REMEDY |
| curb | ARREST, CHECK |
| cure | HEAL, REMEDY |
| curious | ODD |
| curl | TRESS, RINGLET |
| curl the lip | SNEER |
| curly cabbage | KALE, ENDIVE |
| curly-haired dog | POODLE |
| curly letter | ESS |
| curmudgeon | MISER |
| currant | BERRY |
| currency | MONEY |
| currency exchange premium | AGIO |
| current | TIDE, PRESENT |
| current events | NEWS |
| current fad | CRAZE |
| current fashion | MODE |
| current of air | DRAFT, BREEZE |
| current style | FAD, TREND |
| curry a horse | GROOM |
| curse | SWEAR, HEX, OATH |
| cursory | HASTY, CARELESS |
| curt | ABRUPT |
| curtail | SHORTEN |
| curtain | DRAPE |
| curtain fabric | NINON, SCRIM |
| curtain pole | ROD |
| curtsy | BOW |
| curve | ARC, BEND, HOOK, TWIST, BOW |
| curved bone | RIB |
| curved doorway | ARCH |
| curved garland | FESTOON |

curved glass **LENS**
curved inward **ADUNCOUS, CONCAVE**
curved molding **OGEE**
curved roof **DOME**
curvy letter **ESS**
cushion **PAD, MAT, PILLOW, SOFTEN**
Cush's father **HAM**
Cush's son **NIMROD, SEBA**
cushy **EASY**
custard **FLAN**
custodian **CARETAKER, JANITOR**
custody **CHARGE, TRUST**
custom **HABIT, USAGE, MODE**
customary **USUAL**
customary method **HABIT**
customer **BUYER, CLIENT, USER, PATRON**
customs **MORES**
cut **HEW, SEVER, SAW, SLICE**
cut across **TRANSECT**
cut apart **SEVER**
cut at random **SLASH**
cut back **PINCH, REDUCE, DECREASE**
cut dead **SNUB**
cut down **HEW**
cut down a tree **FELL**
cut down wood on land **CLEAR**
cut fine **DICE, MINCE**
cut for insertion in mortise **TENON**
cut grass **MOW**
cut hair **CLIP, BOB, STYLE, TRIM**
cut in **INTERRUPT**
cut in small pieces **HASH**
cut in squares **DICE, CUBE**
cut into cubes **DICE, MINCE**
cut into pieces **CHOP**
cut into slices **CARVE**
cut in two **HALVE, SEVER, SPLIT, BISECT**
cut it out **STOP**
cut jaggedly **SNAG**
cut lengthwise **SLIT**
cut lumber **SAW**
cut of beef **EYE ROAST, FLANK, SIRLOIN, RUMP ROAST, T-BONE, STEAK, RIB ROAST, CHUCK**
cut off **LOP, SNIP**
cut off the beard **SHAVE**
cut off tops **CROP**
cut of lamb **LEG, SHOULDER, CHOP, ROAST, CROWN**

cut of meat **CHOP, STEAK, LOIN**
cut one's teeth **TEETHE**
cut on slant **BEVEL**
cut out **OMIT, ELIMINATE**
cut out for **FIT, SUITED**
cut-price deal **SALE, BARGAIN**
cut short **CROP, LOP**
cut timber **LUMBER**
cut to deep slope **SCARP**
cut up **KIBITZ, CARVE**
cut with scissors **SNIP**
cute **ADORABLE, LOVABLE, DARLING**
cuticle **PELLICLE, SKIN**
cutter **SLOOP**
cutting **SHARP**
cutting diamond **BORT**
cutting edge **BLADE**
cutting implement **KNIFE, SHEARS, SCISSORS, SAW, BLADE, RAZOR, AX, AXE**
cuttlefish ink **SEPIA**
Cyclades island **DELOS**
cylindrical **TERETE**
cymbal **TAL**
Cymric **WELSH, BRETON, CORNISH**
cyprinoid fish **IDE**
Cyprus city **NICOSIA**
cyst **POUCH, SAC**
czar **PETER, IVAN**
czardas **DANCE**

**D**

dabber **PAD**
dad **FATHER, PAPA, DADDY, SIRE**
daffy **WACKY, BATTY, NUTS**
dagger **DIRK**
dagger thrust **STAB**
daily record **DIARY, JOURNAL**
dainty **CHIC, CUTE, FASTIDIOUS**
dairy animal **COW**
dairy product **CHEESE, MILK, CREAM, BUTTER, EGG**
dais **STAND, PLATFORM**
daisy phrase (3 wds.) **HE LOVES ME**
Dakota **SIOUX**
dale **VALLEY, VALE, DELL**
dally **LINGER**
Dalmatian (2 wds.) **COACH DOG**
dam **BLOCK, RESTRAIN**

| | | | |
|---|---|---|---|
| damage | HARM, SPOIL, MAR, RUIN | dark-haired girl | BRUNETTE |
| | | dark mood | ANGER |
| damask | LINEN, PINK | darkness (prefix) | SCOTO |
| dame | WOMAN, GIRL | dark-skinned | DUSKY, SWARTHY |
| damp | HUMID, MOIST, WET | darling | MINION, PET |
| damp and cold | DANK | darn | MEND |
| damsel | MAID | dart | ARROW, FLIT |
| damson | PLUM, BULLACE | dash | SHATTER, TEAR, RACE |
| dance | WALTZ, POLKA, | data | INFORMATION, FACTS, |
| | SAMBA, RHUMBA, CONGA, | | STATISTICS |
| | BALL, PROM, HOP, JIG, | date | APPOINTMENT |
| | TANGO, FRUG, TWIST, | date book | CALENDAR |
| | BALLET, TAP | dated | PASSE |
| dance orchestra | BAND, | date tree | PALM |
| | COMBO, GROUP | datum | FACT |
| dancer | HOOFER, TAPPER, | daub | SMEAR |
| | BALLERINA | daughter of Cadmus | INO |
| dancer Astaire | FRED | daughter of Eioneus | DIA |
| dancer Bolger | RAY | daunt | SCARE, COW |
| dancer Charisse | CYD | davenport | SOFA, COUCH, |
| dancer Chase | BARRIE | | DIVAN, SETTEE |
| dancer for Herod | SALOME | David Copperfield's first | |
| dancer Kelly | GENE | wife | DORA |
| dance routine | | David Copperfield villain | HEEP |
| (2 wds.) | TIME STEP | David's daughter | TAMAR, |
| dancer Rogers | GINGER | | THAMAR |
| dancer Tallchief | MARIA | David's father | JESSE |
| dancer Verdon | GWEN | David's son | AMNON, SOLOMON, |
| dance step | CHASSE, PAS, | | ABSALOM |
| | GLISSADE | David's wife | MICHAL, ABITAL, |
| dancing mate | PARTNER | | ABIGAIL, BATHSHEBA |
| dancing shoe | PUMP, SLIPPER | dawdle | MOPE, LINGER |
| dandelion | WEED | dawn | SUNUP, DAYBREAK, |
| dandy | FOP | | SUNRISE |
| danger | PERIL | dawn (Sp.) | ALBA |
| dangerous | RISKY | dawn moisture | DEW |
| dangerous fish | SHARK | day (Fr.) | JOUR |
| dangerous woman | SIREN | day (Heb.) | YOM |
| danger signal | ALARM, ALERT, | day before a feast | EVE |
| | SIREN | daybreak | DAWN, SUNUP, |
| dangle | HANG | | SUNRISE |
| Danish coin | KRONE | daydream | CHIMERA |
| dank | DAMP, SOGGY | day of rest | SABBATH |
| danseuse | BALLERINA | days long gone (2 wds.) | OLDEN |
| Danube tributary | ENNS, ISAR | | TIMES, ANCIENT HISTORY |
| dapper | NATTY | daytime performance | MATINEE |
| dapple | FLECK | day work | LABOR |
| dappled | PIED | daze | STUN |
| dare | CHALLENGE, VENTURE | dazzle | BLIND |
| daring | BOLD, HEROIC, NERVE | dazzling | BRILLIANT |
| daring deed | FEAT | dead city (2 wds.) | GHOST TOWN |
| dark | DIM, DUSKY, INKY, | deaden the sound of | MUFFLE |
| | BLACK, UNLIGHTED | deadfall | SNARE, TRAP |
| dark blue | NAVY | dead heat | TIE |
| dark brown fur | SABLE, MINK, | dead language | LATIN |
| | BEAVER | deadly | FATAL, LETHAL |
| darken | DIM, SHADOW | deadly snake | ASP, VIPER |
| dark gray | TAUPE | deadlock | STALEMATE |

| | |
|---|---|
| Dead Sea city | **SODOM** |
| dead tired | **WEARY** |
| deal | **PACT** |
| dealer | **DISTRIBUTOR,** |
| | **SALESMAN, RETAILER** |
| dealer in salvaged | |
| trash | **JUNKMAN** |
| deal sparingly | **DOLE** |
| deal with | |
| beforehand | **ANTICIPATE** |
| dear | **BELOVED** |
| dear one (Fr.) | **CHERI** |
| death | **DECEASE, DEMISE** |
| deathly pale | **ASHEN, ASHY** |
| debar | **EXCLUDE** |
| debase | **DEGRADE** |
| debatable | **MOOT, ARGUABLE** |
| debate | **ARGUE, DISCUSS** |
| debilitated | **FEEBLE, INFIRM** |
| debit | **CHARGE** |
| debonair | **URBANE, SUAVE** |
| debonair fellow | |
| (2 wds.) | **CITY SLICKER** |
| debris | **RUBBLE** |
| debt | **OBLIGATION** |
| debtor's note | **IOU** |
| Debussy opus (2 wds.) | **LA MER** |
| decade | **TEN** |
| decadence | **DECAY** |
| decamp | **FLEE** |
| decant | **POUR** |
| decanter | **BOTTLE** |
| decay | **ROT, SPOIL** |
| decay of timber | |
| (2 wds.) | **WET ROT** |
| deceit | **GUILE, CHICANERY** |
| deceitful | **TRICKY, FALSE** |
| deceive | **FOOL, TRICK,** |
| | **BEGUILE, DELUDE, DUPE,** |
| | **MISLEAD** |
| deceived easily | **GULLIBLE** |
| December song | **CAROL, NOEL** |
| December 24th | |
| (2 wds.) | **CHRISTMAS EVE** |
| December visitor | **SANTA** |
| decent | **PROPER** |
| deception | **FRAUD** |
| deceptive | **ILLUSORY** |
| decide | **SETTLE** |
| decimal unit | **TEN** |
| decimeter | **LITER** |
| decipher | **READ, DECODE** |
| decision | **RESOLUTION** |
| decisive | **CONCLUSIVE** |
| deck hand | **TAR, SALT, GOB,** |
| | **SAILOR** |
| deck out | **ARRAY** |
| declaim | **ORATE** |

| | |
|---|---|
| declaim violently | **RANT** |
| declamation | **ORATORY** |
| declaration | **AVOWAL,** |
| | **STATEMENT** |
| declaration of allegiance | **OATH,** |
| | **PLEDGE** |
| declare | **AVER, AVOW, ASSERT,** |
| | **ALLEGE, SAY, STATE** |
| declare invalid | **ANNUL** |
| declare untrue | **DENY** |
| declination | **REFUSAL** |
| decline | **DESCENT, EBB,** |
| | **REFUSE** |
| declining | **DECADENT** |
| declivity | **SCARP** |
| decode | **TRANSLATE** |
| decompose | **ROT, DECAY** |
| decompression sickness | **BENDS** |
| decorate | **ADORN, TRIM,** |
| | **PAINT, GILD, BEDECK, DECK,** |
| | **ORNAMENT** |
| decorated | **ORNATE** |
| decorate with | |
| woodworking | **PANEL, INLAY** |
| decorating metal | **NIELLO** |
| decoration | **DECOR, MEDAL,** |
| | **BADGE, ORNAMENT** |
| decorative | **ORNAMENTAL** |
| decorative fold | **PLEAT** |
| decorative hanging | **FESTOON** |
| decorative pellet | **BEAD** |
| decorative stamp | **SEAL** |
| decorous | **STAID** |
| decorum | **DIGNITY, PROPRIETY** |
| decoy | **LURE** |
| decrease | **ABATE, WANE, EBB** |
| decree | **EDICT, BULL** |
| decree beforehand | **DESTINE** |
| decreed | **FATED** |
| decrement | **LOSS, WASTE** |
| decrepit | **INFIRM, SENILE** |
| decry | **BELITTLE, BOO** |
| decrypt | **DECODE** |
| dedicate | **DEVOTE** |
| deduce | **DERIVE, INFER** |
| deduct | **SUBTRACT** |
| deduct from bill | **REBATE** |
| deduction | **REBATE** |
| deed | **ACT, ACTION, FEAT,** |
| | **CONTRACT, BOND** |
| deem | **JUDGE** |
| deep | **PROFOUND** |
| deep affection | **LOVE** |
| deep apprehension | **FEAR,** |
| | **FOREBODING** |
| deep blue pigment | **SMALT** |
| deep blue stone | |
| (2 wds.) | **LAPIS LAZULI** |

| | | | |
|---|---|---|---|
| deep bow | SALAAM | deform | MAIM |
| deep canyon | CHASM | defraud | CHEAT, MULCT |
| deep crimson | CARMINE | defray | MEET, SETTLE, PAY |
| deep dish | BOWL | deft | ADEPT |
| deep ditch | TRENCH | defy | OPPOSE |
| deepen a channel | DREDGE | degenerate | DECAY, DEPRAVE |
| deep gorge | RAVINE | degradation | DISHONOR, |
| deep hole | PIT | | DISGRACE |
| deep in tone | LOW | degrade | ABASE, DEBASE, |
| deeply engrossed | RAPT | | DEMEAN |
| deeply tinge | IMBUE | degree | STEP, STAGE |
| deep mud | MIRE | degree of a slope | GRADE |
| deep sleep | TRANCE | deign | CONDESCEND |
| deep space | OUTER SPACE | deity | GOD |
| deep valley | RAVINE | deity (name of) | See under |
| deer | HIND, DOE, STAG, ROE, | Greek deity. Norse deity, etc | |
| | HART | dejected | SAD, MOROSE, GLUM |
| deer meat | VENISON | Delaware Indian | LENAPE |
| deer pathway | RUN | Delaware town | CHESTER |
| deer's horn | ANTLER | delay | RETARD, DETAIN, HOLD |
| deface | MAR | | UP, PUT OFF |
| defamation | SLANDER, LIBEL | dele | ERASE |
| defamatory statement | LIBEL | delete's opposite | STET |
| defame | SMEAR, LIBEL | delegate (abbr.) | REP |
| default | FAILURE, NEGLECT | delete | ERASE, REMOVE |
| defeat | BEAT, THWART, ROUT, | deliberate | CAREFUL, CAUTIOUS |
| | SUBDUE | delicacy | TACT |
| defeat at bridge | SET | delicate | FRAIL, FRAGILE, |
| defeated one | LOSER | | TENDER |
| defeat soundly | ROUT | delicate plant | MOSS |
| defect | FLAW, IMPERFECTION | delicate skill | FINESSE |
| defection | DESERTION | delicious | TASTEFUL, TASTY |
| defective | BAD, POOR | delicious beverage | NECTAR |
| defective bomb | DUD | delight | JOY, PLEASE |
| defective vision | ANOPIA, | delightful | NICE |
| | MYOPIA | delightful abode | EDEN |
| defend | PROTECT, SHIELD | delight in | LOVE, SAVOR |
| defendant's answer | PLEA | delineate | DRAW |
| defense | BULWARK, | delirious | RAVING |
| | PROTECTION | deliver | BRING, RENDER |
| defenseless | NAKED | deliver an address | SPEAK |
| defense missile | NIKE, ICBM | deliver formally | PRESENT |
| defense organization | | dell | VALLEY, VALE, DALE |
| (abbr.) | NATO | delude | DUPE, FOOL |
| defensible | TENABLE | deluge | FLOOD, SWAMP |
| defensive slope | GLACIS | demand obedience | |
| defensive wall | PARAPET | (3 wds.) | SNAP THE WHIP |
| defensive work | FORT, | demand payment | DUN |
| | RAMPART | demean | DEBASE, ABASE, |
| defer | DELAY, RETARD | | DEGRADE |
| defer temporarily | TABLE | demeanor | MANNER |
| deficient | DEFECTIVE, SCARCE | demented | INSANE |
| defile | CORRUPT, SOIL | Democrat's symbol | DONKEY |
| define | DESCRIBE | demolish | DESTROY |
| definite | FIXED, EXACT | demon | DEVIL, FIEND |
| definite article | THE | demon of Arabian lore | JINN(I), |
| definition | MEANING | | DJINN, GENIE |
| deflect | DIVERT | demonstrate | PROVE, SHOW |

demonstrative pronoun **THAT**
demoralize **DISCOURAGE**
demos **POPULACE, PEOPLE**
demur **OBJECT, BALK, HESITATE**
demure **SHY, COY**
den **LAIR**
denomination **SECT, CULT, CLASSIFICATION**
denote **SIGNIFY, MEAN**
denounce **ACCUSE, BLAME**
dense **COMPACT**
dense growth of trees **FOREST**
dense row of shrubs **HEDGE**
dent **BATTER**
dental filling **INLAY**
dentine **IVORY**
dentist's degree (abbr.) **DDS**
denude **BARE, STRIP, EXPOSE**
deny **REPUDIATE, WITHHOLD**
depart **GO, LEAVE**
departed **GONE, LEFT, WENT, DECEASED**
department **FIELD, SECTION**
department of France **EURE**
depart secretly **ABSCOND**
depart suddenly **BOLT**
depart this life **DIE**
departure **EXIT**
departure port of
Columbus **PALOS**
depend **RELY**
dependable **RELIABLE**
dependent **SUBJECT**
depend upon **HINGE**
depict **PORTRAY**
deplete **DRAIN, EXHAUST**
deplorable **WRETCHED**
deplore **BEMOAN**
deploy **SPREAD, SCATTER**
deport **BANISH, EXILE**
deportment **AIR, BEHAVIOR**
deposit **LAY, PUT, PLACE**
deposit, as a ballot **CAST**
deposit of resources **FUND**
depositor's concern **INTEREST**
depot **WAREHOUSE, STATION, TERMINAL**
depraved **EVIL, BAD**
depravity **CORRUPTION, EVIL**
deprecate **DECRY, BELITTLE**
depress **SADDEN**
depressed **LOW, BLUE**
depression **GLOOM**
depression initials **NRA**
depress with fear **COW**
deprivation **LOSS**
deprive **DEBAR, DISPOSSESS**

deprived of (Fr.) **SANS**
deprived of social
rights **UNDERPRIVILEGED**
deprive of sensation **NUMB**
deprived of strength
**ENERVATED, DEBILITATED**
deputy **AGENT, REP, ASSISTANT**
deranged **INSANE, DEMENTED**
derby **HAT, BOWLER**
deride **RIDICULE**
derision **SCORN, CONTEMPT**
derivation **ORIGIN, CAUSE**
derive **DEDUCE, INFER, ORIGINATE**
derogatory **SNIDE**
descend (2 wds.) **GO DOWN**
descendant **SCION, HEIR**
descent **FALL**
describe grammatically **PARSE**
descriptive name **TITLE**
desert **ABANDON, STRAND, LEAVE, WASTELAND**
desert animal **CAMEL**
desert dweller **ARAB, BEDOUIN**
deserted in love **LORN, FORLORN, BEREFT**
deserter **RAT**
Desert Fox **ROMMEL**
desert green spot **OASIS**
desert hallucination **MIRAGE**
desert illusion **MIRAGE**
desert in Asia **GOBI**
desertlike **ARID**
desert nomad **ARAB**
desert plant **AGAVE, CACTUS, YUCCA**
desert region of Africa **SUDAN**
desert region of shifting
sand **ERG**
desert ship **CAMEL**
desert shrub **TETEM**
desert train **CARAVAN**
desert wind **SIROCCO, SIMOON, SAMIEL**
deserve **EARN, MERIT**
deserving of
reproach **BLAMABLE**
desiccated **DRY, ARID**
design **PATTERN, PLAN**
designate **NAME, APPOINT**
design of initials **MONOGRAM**
design on fabric **BATIK**
desirable **VALUABLE**
desire **COVET, WANT, ASPIRE, WISH, HOPE, YEN, YEARN**
desire a lofty object **ASPIRE**
desist **CEASE, STOP**

| | | | |
|---|---|---|---|
| desk | ESCRITOIRE, SECRETARY, BUREAU | detraction | DEROGATION |
| desolate | BLEAK, FORSAKEN, STARK | detriment | HARM, LOSS |
| | | Detroit baseball team | TIGERS |
| desolation | RUIN | deuce | CARD, TWO |
| despair | HOPELESSNESS | DeValera's land | ERIN, EIRE |
| desperate | FRANTIC | devastate | RAVAGE |
| despise | HATE, LOATHE, SCORN | devastation | HAVOC |
| | | develop | UNFOLD |
| | | develop into | BECOME |
| despondent | FORLORN | deviate | DEFLECT |
| despot | TSAR, TYRANT, DICTATOR | device | MACHINE, GADGET |
| | | device for runners | |
| dessert pastry | PIE, CAKE, ECLAIR, TART | (2 wds.) | STARTING BLOCK |
| | | devil | DEMON, SATAN, FIEND |
| destination | GOAL | devilfish | MANTA, RAY |
| destine | DOOM | devise | INVENT, CONTRIVE |
| destined | FATED, IN THE CARDS | devise unfairly | |
| destiny | FATE, LOT | (2 wds.) | TRUMP UP |
| destitute | DEVOID, NEEDY, POOR | devoid | LACKING |
| | | devoid of light | DARK |
| destitute of light | DARK | devotion of nine days | NOVENA |
| destitution | POVERTY, WANT | devour | EAT, CONSUME |
| destroy | RUIN | devout | HOLY, PIOUS |
| destroyed | KAPUT | dew | MOISTURE |
| destroyed by fire | BURNT | dexterity | AGILITY |
| destroyer | SHIP | dexterous | ADROIT, DEFT |
| destroy most of | DECIMATE | diabetic's need | INSULIN |
| destroy power of | ANNUL | diabolical | FIENDISH |
| destruction | ERADICATION, LOSS, RUIN | diacritical mark | TILDE |
| | | diagonal | CATERCORNER, SLANT |
| destructive | HARMFUL | | |
| destructive insect | PEST | diagram | GRAPH, MAP |
| destructive prowler | VANDAL | dialect | IDIOM, LINGO, SLANG, ARGOT |
| destructive rodent | RAT | | |
| destructive storm | TORNADO, HURRICANE, GALE, SQUALL, BLIZZARD | dial pointer | HAND |
| | | diamond | GEM, JEWEL, STONE |
| | | diamond call (2 wds.) | BATTER UP, PLAY BALL |
| desultory | CURSORY, RAMBLING | diamond man | PITCHER, CATCHER, BATTER |
| detach | SEPARATE, SEVER | | |
| detached | UNCONCERNED | diamond ring | SOLITAIRE |
| detail | ITEM | diamonds (sl.) | ICE, ROCKS |
| detain | HOLD, KEEP | Diamond State | DELAWARE |
| detect | DISCOVER | diamond surface | FACET |
| detecting device | RADAR, SONAR | diaphanous | SHEER |
| | | diary | JOURNAL, LOG |
| detective Queen | ELLERY | dictate | COMMAND, DIRECT |
| detective's case (sl.) | CAPER | diction | STYLE |
| detective Spade | SAM | dictionary | LEXICON, GLOSSARY |
| detention | DELAY | | |
| deter | WARN, DISSUADE | dido | ANTIC, TRICK, CAPER |
| detergent | SOAP | die | EXPIRE, DECEASE |
| deteriorate | DEGRADE, DEBASE | diesel engine | MOTOR |
| deterioration | DECAY, DECLINE | diet | REGIMEN |
| determination | GRIT, RESOLVE | dieter's concern | FLAB, FAT, POUNDS, CALORIES, BULGE, PAUNCH |
| determine | WILL | | |
| determined | FIRM, RESOLUTE | | |
| detest | ABHOR, LOATHE. HATE | diet fruit | GRAPEFRUIT |

differ **VARY**
different **ELSE, OTHER**
differentiate **CONTRAST, DISTINGUISH**
differently **OTHERWISE**
difficult **HARD**
difficult journey **TREK**
difficult problem **POSER**
difficult sailing
  (3 wds.) **AGAINST THE WIND**
difficult
  situation **PREDICAMENT**
difficulty **SNAG**
diffident **TIMID, SHY**
diffuse **SPREAD, EXPAND**
diffused with color **IRIDESCENT**
dig **EXCAVATE**
dig cherrystones **CLAM**
digging implement **SPADE, SHOVEL**
digit **FINGER, TOE, NUMBER, NUMERAL**
dignified **SEDATE**
dignify **ENNOBLE**
dignity **DECORUM, MAJESTY**
dig ore **MINE**
digress **DEVIATE**
dig up **UNEARTH**
dike **LEVEE**
dilate **EXPAND, WIDEN**
dilemma **PLIGHT, PROBLEM**
dilettante **AMATEUR, DABBLER**
diligence **CARE, INDUSTRY**
dill **ANET, SPICE**
dim **PALE**
dimension **LENGTH, HEIGHT, WIDTH**
diminish **ABATE, LESSEN, PETER OUT, TAPER**
diminish gradually **TAPER**
diminutive **SMALL, PETITE**
diminutive being **GNOME, ELF, DWARF, BROWNIE, GREMLIN**
diminutive suffix **ETTE, ULE**
dimwit **DUNCE, FOOL, DOLT**
din **CLATTER, NOISE, UPROAR, RACKET**
dine **EAT, SUP**
dine at home (2 wds.) **EAT IN**
diner **EATERY, EATER**
ding **RING**
dinghy **ROWBOAT**
dingy **DUSKY, DRAB, WORN, SHABBY**
dining room furniture **TABLE, CHAIR, SERVER, CART, BUFFET**

dinner **MEAL, BANQUET**
dinner bell **GONG**
dinner course **DESSERT, ENTREE, SALAD, FISH, MEAT, SOUP, APPETIZER**
dinner jacket **TUXEDO**
dinosaur **LIZARD**
Dinsmore **ELSIE**
dint **FORCE**
diocese **SEE, BISHOPRIC**
dip **IMMERSE, DUNK, SOP**
dip Easter eggs **TINT, DYE**
dip into liquid **RINSE**
diploma **CERTIFICATE, DEGREE**
diplomacy **TACT**
diplomat **CONSUL**
diplomatic **TACTFUL**
diplomat's aide **ATTACHE**
dip out **BAIL**
dipper **LADLE**
dire **DISASTROUS, DREADFUL, FATAL, CRITICAL**
direct **LEAD, MANAGE, AIM**
direct attention **REFER**
direction **GUIDANCE, EAST, NORTH, SOUTH, WEST, EASTWARD, WESTWARD, NORTHWARD, SOUTHWARD, RIGHT, LEFT**
direction mark **ARROW**
directive **ORDER**
director **LEADER, MANAGER**
director Kazan **ELIA**
director Penn **ARTHUR**
director Preminger **OTTO**
dirge **LAMENT**
dirigible **BLIMP**
dirk **DAGGER, SNEE**
dirndl **SKIRT**
dirt **FILTH, GRIME, SOIL, SOOT**
dirty **IMPURE, SOOTY, FILTHY, GRIMY, SOILED**
disability **WEAKNESS**
disable **CRIPPLE**
disadvantage **HANDICAP**
disagree **DIFFER, ARGUE**
disagreeable **NASTY, UNPLEASANT**
disagreeable child **BRAT**
disagreeable person **CRAB, GROUCH**
disagreeable sight **EYESORE**
disagreeable woman **SHREW**
disagreement **CLASH, DISPUTE**
disappear **VANISH**
disappoint **FAIL**

disapproval **CENSURE**
disarray **CONFUSION, DISORDER**
disassemble (2 wds.) **TAKE APART**
disaster **CALAMITY, CATASTROPHE**
disastrous **DIRE, TRAGIC**
disavow **RETRACT**
disburse **SPEND**
disc **RECORD**
discard **SET ASIDE, THROW AWAY, TOSS OUT, SCRAP**
discern **DETECT, PERCEIVE**
discharge **DISMISS, UNLOAD, EMIT, FIRE**
discharge a debt **PAY, PAY UP**
discharge a gun **SHOOT, FIRE**
disciple **STUDENT, FOLLOWER**
discipline **CHASTEN**
disclaim **DISAVOW**
disclaimer **DENIAL**
disclaim formally **ABJURE**
disclose **BARE, REVEAL**
discomfit **THWART, FOIL, ROUT**
discompose **UNSETTLE**
disconcert **ABASH**
disconnect **SEPARATE**
disconsolate **SAD**
discontent **RESTLESS**
discontinue **STOP, HALT**
discord **CONTENTION, STRIFE**
Discordia **ERIS**
discount **REBATE, KICKBACK**
discourage **DAUNT**
discourage through fear **DETER**
discourse **LECTURE, DEBATE**
discourteous **RUDE, IMPOLITE**
discover **ESPY, FIND, DETECT**
discover by chance
 (2 wds.) **RUN ACROSS**
discoverer of
 America **COLUMBUS**
discover suddenly
 (2 wds.) **HIT ON**
discovery-minded
 traveler **EXPLORER**
discreet **CAUTIOUS, PRUDENT**
discrepancy **VARIANCE**
discretion **TACT**
discrimination **PRUDENCE**
discuss **DEBATE**
discussion basis **TOPIC**
disdain **SCORN**
disease **AILMENT, MALADY**
disembark **LAND**
disencumber **RID, RELIEVE**
disfigure **DEFACE, MAR, SCAR**

disgrace **SHAME**
disguise **MASK, CAMOUFLAGE**
disgust **DISTASTE, DISLIKE**
disgusting **NASTY**
dish **PLATE, BOWL, SAUCER, CUP**
dishes **CHINA**
dish of appetizers
 (2 wds.) **RELISH TRAY**
dish of cabbage **SLAW**
dish of greens **SALAD**
dish of stewed fruit **COMPOTE**
dishonest **FALSE, UNTRUE**
disinclined **AVERSE**
disinclined to work **LAZY**
dislike **HATE, LOATHE, DESPISE**
disloyal **FALSE, UNTRUE**
dismal **GLOOMY, DREARY**
dismal failure **FLOP**
dismantle **STRIP**
dismantled ship **HULK**
dismay **APPALL, COW, DAUNT**
dismiss **DISCHARGE, DROP**
dismissal (Fr.) **CONGE**
dismiss forcibly **EXILE**
dismiss from office **AMOVE, REMOVE, IMPEACH**
dismount **ALIGHT, UNSEAT**
disobedient **NAUGHTY**
disobey **DEFY, REBEL**
disorder **MESS**
disorderly **UNRULY**
disorderly crowd **MOB**
disorderly flight **ROUT**
disorganize **CONFUSE**
disown **RENOUNCE**
disparage **BELITTLE**
disparaging remark **SLUR**
disparity **ODDS, INCONGRUITY**
dispatch **SEND**
dispatch boat **AVISO**
dispel **DISPERSE, BANISH**
disperse **SCATTER**
disperse in defeat **ROUT**
display **SHOW, FLAUNT**
display cards for a score **MELD, DECLARE**
display stand **RACK**
displease **ANNOY, VEX**
displeased **OUT OF HUMOR, CROSS**
dispose **ARRANGE**
disposed **PRONE**
dispossess **DIVEST**
dispute **HAGGLE, WRANGLE, QUARREL, CONTEST, FIGHT, DEBATE**

disregard **PASS OVER, IGNORE, NEGLECT**
disreputable **LOW, BASE**
disrespectful **RUDE**
disrupt **REND, TEAR**
dissent **DISAGREE, DIFFER**
dissenting vote **NAY**
dissertation **TRACT, THESIS, TREATISE**
dissipate **DIFFUSE**
dissolve **MELT, THAW**
dissuade **DETER**
distance measure **MILE, FOOT, ROD, YARD, INCH**
distant **FAR, AFAR**
distant (prefix) **TELE**
distaste **AVERSION, DISGUST**
distasteful **BITTER**
distemper **AILMENT, VIRUS**
distend **DILATE, SWELL**
distinct **CLEAR, PLAIN**
distinct (comp. wd.) **CLEAR-CUT**
distinct part **UNIT**
distinction **HONOR, RENOWN, DIFFERENCE**
distinctive **PECULIAR**
distinctive air **AURA**
distinctive character **CACHET**
distinctive manner of writing **STYLE**
distinctive mark **STAMP**
distinctive quality **TALENT**
distinctive taste **SAVOR**
distinguish **DISCERN**
distinguished **EMINENT**
distinguishing feature **TRAIT**
distort **WARP**
distorted **AWRY**
distract **DIVERT**
distress **TROUBLE, ANGUISH**
distress call **SOS, HELP**
distribute **ALLOT, DOLE, APPORTION**
distribute cards **DEAL**
district **AREA, REGION, TERRITORY**
district attorney (abbr.) **DA**
district in Saudi Arabia **ASIR**
distrust **DOUBT**
disturb **TROUBLE, WORRY**
disturbance **UPROAR**
disturb suddenly **STARTLE, ALARM**
disturb the peace **RIOT**
disunite **SEVER, DIVORCE**
disuse **DISCARD**
ditch **TRENCH, RHINE, RINE**

ditch around a castle **MOAT**
ditty **SONG, AIR**
divan **SOFA, COUCH, SETTEE**
diva's forte **ARIA**
dive **PLUNGE, RUSH**
divers **SUNDRY**
diver's disease **BENDS**
diversion **GAME, SPORT, AMUSEMENT**
divest **DEPRIVE**
divest of office **DEPOSE**
divide **CLEFT, PART, SPLIT, SEPARATE, SUNDER**
divided into two lobes **BIFID**
divide into regular steps **GRADUATE**
divide into strata **LAYER**
divide in two parts **BISECT**
dividing wall **SEPTUM, PARTITION**
divine **HOLY, SACRED**
divine being **DEITY, GOD**
divine gift **BLESSING**
diving bird **AUK, LOON, GREBE**
diving duck **SMEE, SCOTER**
divinity **FUDGE**
division **SEGMENT, SECTION, RIFT, PART, PORTION**
division of ancient Greece **ELIS**
division of a poem **PASSUS, CANTO, VERSE, COUPLET**
division of Great Britain **WALES, SCOTLAND, ENGLAND, IRELAND**
division of the year **SEASON, MONTH**
division preposition **INTO**
divorce **SEPARATE, DISUNITE**
divorce capital **RENO**
divorced person **EX**
divot **CLOD, TURF**
divulge **TELL, INFORM**
Dixie **SOUTH**
Dixieland **JAZZ**
dizziness **VERTIGO**
dizzy **GIDDY**
do **PERFORM, ACT**
do a jackknife **DIVE**
do a risky deed (3 wds.) **BELL THE CAT**
do away with **ABOLISH**
dobbin **HORSE**
docile **GENTLE, TAME**
dock **PIER, WHARF**
docket **TICKET**
doctor **PHYSICIAN**
doctor's assistant **NURSE**

doctors' group **AMA**
doctor's helper (abbr.) **RN**
doctrine **ISM, TENET, CREDO**
doctrine adherent (suffix) **IST**
doctrine of
   inevitable **FATALISM**
doctrine of selfishness **EGOISM**
doc's penmanship **SCRAWL**
document **PAPER**
document addition **RIDER**
document file **DOSSIER**
documentary **FILM**
dodder **TREMBLE, TOTTER**
dodderer **CODGER**
doddering old age **SENILITY**
do detective work
   (2 wds.) **TRACK DOWN**
dodge **DUCK, ELUDE**
dodge an issue **SIDESTEP**
dodo **FOGY**
doe **HIND, DEER**
doer **ACTOR**
doer of odd jobs
   (2 wds.) **HANDY MAN**
do farm work **HOE, SOW, MILK,**
   **REAP, PLOW, HARVEST**
doff **REMOVE**
dog **PET, CANINE**
dog doctor, for short **VET**
dog-drawn vehicle **SLED**
dogged **STUBBORN**
doggerel **NONSENSE VERSE**
doggie-in-window locale
   (2 wds.) **PET SHOP**
dog house **KENNEL**
dogie **CALF**
doglike animal **WOLF. FOX**
dogma **TENET, BELIEF,**
   **TEACHING**
dogmatic sayings **DICTA**
dog salmon **KETA**
dog-tired (2 wds.) **ALL IN**
dog's delight **BONE**
dog's foot **PAW**
dog's growl **GNAR, ROWF,**
   **GRRR**
dog's lead **LEASH**
dog's name **FIDO, ROVER,**
   **KING, REX, LADY, LASSIE**
dog's tail movement **WAG**
dog's tooth **FANG**
dog's treats **BONES**
dog's wagger **TAIL**
dogwood **TREE**
do housework **CLEAN, DUST,**
   **SWEEP, POLISH, WAX,**
   **WASH, MOP**

doily **MAT**
do in **KILL**
do intensive research **DELVE**
do laundry **WASH**
dolce **SWEET, SMOOTH**
doldrums **CALM**
dole **ALLOTMENT, ALLOCATE,**
   **DISTRIBUTE, ALLOT,**
   **APPORTION, METE, PORTION**
doleful **SAD**
doll **TOY, PUPPET**
dollar bill **ONE, SINGLE**
dollop **LUMP, HELPING**
dolman **SLEEVE**
dolor **GRIEF, SORROW**
dolphin **PORPOISE**
dolt **BLOCKHEAD**
domain **FIELD, REALM**
dome **CUPOLA**
domestic **TAME, NATIVE**
domestic animal **CAT, DOG,**
   **PET, CANARY, PARAKEET,**
   **COW, SHEEP, HORSE, HEN,**
   **ROOSTER. DUCK, BULL,**
   **STEER, RAM. EWE, GOAT**
domestic animals **CATTLE**
domesticate **TAME**
domestic employee **SERVANT,**
   **MAID, HOUSEBOY, BUTLER,**
   **COOK**
domestic
   establishment **MENAGE**
domicile **ABODE, RESIDENCE**
dominant **CHIEF, SUPREME**
dominate **REIGN, RULE**
dominating **BOSSY**
domination **RULE**
domineer **BULLY, TYRANNIZE**
domineering **OVERBEARING**
Dominican friar **JACOBIN**
dominion **TERRITORY**
domino **MASK, TILE, ROBE**
don **TUTOR**
Don Adams program
   (2 wds.) **GET SMART**
donate **GIVE. CONTRIBUTE**
donating **GIVING**
donation **GRANT, GIFT**
done **FINISHED, OVER**
done for **DEAD**
done in **TIRED**
donjon **KEEP. TOWER**
Don Juan's mother **INEZ**
do newspaper work **EDIT,**
   **REPORT. REWRITE**
donkey **ASS, BURRO**
donkey's cry **BRAY**
donna **LADY, MADAM**

donor **GIVER**
Don Quixote's steed **ROSINANTE**
doodad **TRINKET, BAUBLE**
doodle **SCRIBBLE**
doom **FATE**
door **PORTAL**
door (Ital.) **PORTA**
doorbell **CHIME**
door clasp **HASP, KNOB**
door column **ANTA**
door fastening **LATCH**
door frame **JAMB**
door joint **HINGE**
door molding **ASTRAGAL**
door-to-door
  salesman **PEDDLER**
doorway sign **EXIT**
doorway structure **ARCH**
dope **NARCOTIC, OPIUM**
dor **BEETLE**
dormant **LATENT**
dormer window **LUCARNE**
do sums **ADD**
dot **PERIOD, SPOT, SPECK**
dote on **ADORE**
do the crawl **SWIM**
doting **FOND**
double **TWIN, TWOFOLD**
double chair
  (2 wds.) **LOVE SEAT**
double curve **ESS**
doubt **DEMUR, DISTRUST**
dough **PASTE, MONEY, BREAD**
doughnut-shaped roll **BAGEL**
do up **PREPARE**
dour **GLOOMY**
dove **PIGEON**
doves' home **COTE**
dove sound **COO**
dowdy **SHABBY**
dowdy woman **FRUMP**
down **FUZZ**
down (arch.) **ADOWN**
down (prefix) **DE**
downcast **BLUE, SAD**
downpour **RAIN, TORRENT**
downright **CANDID**
downtown Chicago **LOOP**
downwind **LEEWARD**
down with (Fr., 2 wds.) **A BAS**
downy **SOFT**
downy duck **EIDER**
downy surface **NAP**
do wrong **ERR**
doxology **HYMN, FORMULA**
doze **DROWSE, NAP, SLEEP**
drab **COLORLESS, DULL**
draft **DOSE, PORTION**

draft animals **OXEN**
draftsman **DRAWER**
draftsman's need
  (2 wds.) **GRAPH PAPER**
drag **HAUL, TOW, PULL**
drag loosely **TRAIL**
drama **THEATER, PLAY**
drama division **ACT, SCENE**
dramatic part **ROLE**
dramatis personae **CAST**
draped garment **TOGA**
drastic social change **REFORM**
draught **DOSE, PORTION**
draw **PULL, SKETCH,
  DELINEATE**
draw a mark below **UNDERLINE**
draw back **RECEDE**
draw close **NEAR**
drawer knob **PULL**
drawforth **EDUCE, EVOKE**
draw game **STALEMATE**
drawing **SKETCH**
drawing room **SALON, PARLOR**
draw letters **PRINT**
draw off **SIPHON**
draw out **ELICIT**
draw through thin paper **TRACE**
draw tight **CINCH**
dread **FEAR**
dreadful **DIRE**
dream **FANTASY, REVERIE**
dreamer **VISIONARY**
dreamland **SLEEP**
dreary **BLEAK**
dreary (poet.) **DREAR**
dredge **SCOOP**
dregs **LEES, SEDIMENT**
drench **SOAK, SOP, SOUSE**
Dresden **PORCELAIN, CHINA,
  MEISSENWARE**
dress **CLOTHE, FROCK,
  GOWN, CLOTHING, GARB,
  APPAREL, ATTIRE**
dressage **HORSEMANSHIP**
dress border **HEM**
dress carefully **PREEN, PRIMP**
dress down **SCOLD**
dressed **CLAD**
dressed pelt **FUR**
dresser **BUREAU, VALET**
dress feathers **PREEN**
dress flax **TED**
dressing **TOPPING, STUFFING,
  SAUCE**
dressing gown **NEGLIGEE,
  ROBE, WRAPPER**
dressmaker **MODISTE**

| | |
|---|---|
| dress material | SILK, CREPE, COTTON, SATIN, RAYON, NYLON, ARNEL |
| dress style | EMPIRE, SACK, A-LINE, MOD |
| dress the hair | COMB |
| dress trimming | RUCHE, RUFFLE |
| dress up | PRIMP |
| dress warmly (2 wds.) | BUNDLE UP |
| dressy | STYLISH, ELEGANT |
| dribble | TRICKLE |
| dried cut grass | HAY |
| dried plum | PRUNE |
| dried up | SERE |
| drift | TENDENCY, TREND, FLOAT, PILE |
| drill | BORE |
| drill into again | RETAP |
| drink | IMBIBE, QUAFF |
| drink heavily | TOPE |
| drinking cup | MUG, TOBY |
| drinking salutation | PROSIT |
| drinking tube | STRAW |
| drinking vessel | CUP, MUG, GLASS, STEIN |
| drink like a dog | LAP |
| drink slowly | SIP |
| drink to excess | TIPPLE |
| drink to health of | TOAST |
| drip | TRICKLE |
| drip-dry | NO IRON |
| dripping wet | SODDEN |
| drive | IMPEL, PROPEL |
| drive a golf ball (2 wds.) | TEE OFF |
| drive at | AIM |
| drive away | SHOO |
| drive back | REPULSE, REPEL |
| drive backward | REVERSE |
| drive forward | IMPEL, PROPEL |
| drive frantic | BEDEVIL |
| drive-in | RESTAURANT, MOVIE |
| drive insane | MADDEN |
| drive obliquely | SLICE |
| drive out | EXPEL |
| driver | CHAUFFEUR |
| driver's compartment | CAB |
| driveway covering | GRAVEL |
| drizzle | RAIN |
| droll | FUNNY |
| dromedary | CAMEL |
| drone | HUM, BUZZ, BEE |
| drool | SLAVER |
| droop | SAG, WILT |
| drooping on one side | ALOP |
| drooping tree | WILLOW |
| droopy | TIRED |
| drop | FALL, GLOBULE |
| drop down suddenly | DIP, PLUNGE |
| drop from sight | VANISH |
| drop heavily | PLOP |
| drop in | VISIT, CALL |
| droplet | BEAD |
| drop off | DECLINE, DECREASE |
| drop slowly | SINK |
| dropsy | EDEMA |
| dross | WASTE |
| dross of metal | SLAG |
| drove | FLOCK |
| drown | INUNDATE, SUBMERGE |
| drowse | DOZE, NOD |
| drowsy | SLEEPY |
| drudge | SLAVE |
| drudgery | LABOR, GRIND |
| drug | MEDICINE, OPIATE, DOPE |
| drug container | CAPSULE |
| druggist | APOTHECARY, PHARMACIST |
| drug plant | ALOE, POPPY |
| drugstore | PHARMACY |
| drug-yielding crocus | SAFFRON |
| drum | TAMBOR, KETTLE |
| drunkard | SOT, SOUSE, TIPPLER |
| dry | ARID, SEAR, SERE |
| dryad | NYMPH |
| dry, as wine | SEC |
| dry dishes | WIPE |
| dryer | BLOWER |
| dry goods dealer (Brit.) | DRAPER |
| drying cloth | TOWEL |
| drying kiln | OAST |
| dry outer part | HUSK |
| dry river bed | WADI |
| dry rot | FUNGUS |
| dry run | REHEARSAL |
| duad | PAIR, COUPLE |
| dual | TWOFOLD |
| dub | TAP, NAME |
| dubious | DOUBTFUL |
| duck | MALLARD, TEAL, SMEE, PINTAIL |
| ducklike bird | COOT |
| duck's call | QUACK |
| duct | CANAL, TUBE |
| ductile | DOCILE, FACILE |
| dud | FLOP, FIZZLE |
| dude | TENDERFOOT |
| due | OWING |
| duel | CONTEST |

duelist's aide **SECOND**
duet **TWO, TWOSOME, DUO**
due to motion **KINETIC**
duffer's bugaboo **TRAP**
duke (Fr.) **DUC**
duke's wife **DUCHESS**
dukedom **DUCHY**
dull **DREARY, BLUNT,
BORING, TEDIOUS, DRAB**
dull blow **THUD**
dull color **GRAY, GREY**
dull fellow **CLOD**
dull pain **ACHE**
dull routine **RUT**
dull thump **THUD**
duly **PROPERLY**
Dumas character **ARAMIS**
dumb **MUTE**
dumbbell **DUNCE**
dumb girl **DORA**
dump dweller **RAT**
dun **TAN**
dunce **FOOL**
dunderhead **ASS**
duo **PAIR, TWOSOME, DUET,
TWO**
dupe **TRICK, FOOL**
duplicate **REPLICA, COPY,
CARBON**
duplicate part **SPARE**
duplication **COPY, REPLICA**
durable **LASTING, CONSTANT**
duramen **HEARTWOOD**
duration **TERM, TIME, SPAN,
TENURE**
duress **IMPRISONMENT,
FORCE**
during the time that **WHILE**
dusk **GLOAM, TWILIGHT**
dusky **DARK**
dust cloth **RAG**
dust matter **LINT**
dust speck **MOTE**
dustbowl victim **OKIE**
Dutch cheese **EDAM, GOUDA**
Dutch coin **STIVER, GUILDER**
Dutch commune **EDE**
Dutch embankment **DIKE**
Dutch flower **TULIP**
Dutch Guiana **SURINAM**
Dutch landholder **PATROON**
Dutch measure **AHM, AUM**
Dutch pottery **DELFT**
Dutch South African **BOER**
Dutch uncle **EME**
duty **TASK, TARIFF**
dwarf **ELF, RUNT**
dwell **ABIDE, RESIDE, LIVE**

dweller **TENANT**
dwelling place **ABODE, HOME,
DOMICILE, RESIDENCE,
HOUSE, APARTMENT, VILLA,
FARM, RANCH, ESTATE,
DUPLEX, PENTHOUSE, COOP**
dwell on unduly **HARP**
dwindle **TAPER, WANE**
dyad **PAIR, COUPLE**
dybbuk **SPIRIT**
dye **COLOR, STAIN, TINT,
ANIL, TINGE**
dye compound **ANILINE,
EOSIN**
dye for butter **ACHIOTE,
ANNATTO, ARNATO**
dyed rabbit fur **LAPIN**
dyeing tub **TANK, VAT**
dyer **STAINER**
dynamic **POTENT**
dynamite explosion **BLAST**
dynamo **GENERATOR**
dyspeptic **GLOOMY,
GROUCHY, MOROSE**

## E

each **APIECE, EVERY,
EVERYONE, ALL**
each and every **ALL**
eager **AGOG, ANXIOUS,
ARDENT, AVID,
ENTHUSIASTIC, KEEN,
IMPATIENT**
eagerness **ALACRITY, FERVOR**
eagerness for action **ELAN**
eagle **ERN, ERNE**
eagle's claw **TALON**
eagle's nest **AERIE, EYRIE,
EYRY, AERY**
ear **AURICLE**
ear (prefix) **OT, OTO**
earache **OTALGIA**
eared seal **OTARY**
earlier **PRIOR**
earliest **FIRST, SOONEST**
earliest born **ELDEST, FIRST**
early **PREMATURE**
early Briton **PICT, CELT,
ANGLE, JUTE**
early dwelling place **CAVE**
early mattress
stuffing **STRAW**
early part of day **MORN,
MORNING**
early part of night **EVENING**

| | |
|---|---|
| early stringed instrument | **LUTE, LYRE** |
| early violin | **REBEC** |
| earn | **MERIT, DESERVE** |
| earnest | **SINCERE, ZEALOUS** |
| earnest effort | **UTMOST, BEST** |
| earnings | **SALARY, WAGES, PROFIT** |
| ear of corn | **SPIKE** |
| ear ornament | **EARRING** |
| ear part | **LOBE** |
| ear shell | **ABALONE** |
| earshot | **HEARING** |
| earsplitting | **LOUD** |
| earth | **WORLD, LAND, SOIL, PLANET** |
| earth deity | **TARI, GEB, KEB** |
| earth deposit | **SILT** |
| earthenware | **CROCKERY** |
| earthenware jar | **OLLA** |
| earthenware vessel | **JAR, OLLA** |
| earthly | **MUNDANE, PROFANE** |
| earth mover | **BULLDOZER** |
| earthnut | **TRUFFLE** |
| earthquake | **TREMOR, SEISM** |
| earth's axis end | **POLE** |
| earth's satellite | **MOON** |
| earth's sister planet | **VENUS** |
| earth's star | **SUN, SOL** |
| earthworm | **ANNELID** |
| earthy | **SENSUAL** |
| earthy deposit | **MARL** |
| earwax | **CERUMEN** |
| ease | **ALLEVIATE, RELIEVE, LUXURY, SOOTHE** |
| easel | **STAND** |
| ease off | **ABATE** |
| ease up | **RELENT** |
| easily broken | **FRAGILE** |
| easily cut, as a steak | **TENDER** |
| easily deceived | **GULLIBLE** |
| easily fooled person | **DUPE** |
| easily frightened | **SKITTISH** |
| easily hurt | **SENSITIVE** |
| easily managed | **DOCILE** |
| east | **ORIENT** |
| Easter flower | **LILY** |
| eastern | **ORIENTAL** |
| eastern caravansary | **SERAI** |
| eastern Catholic | **UNIATET** |
| eastern potentate | **RAJAH** |
| eastern priest | **ABBA** |
| eastern title | **AGA** |
| Easter preparatory season | **LENT** |
| East Indian bird | **SHAMA** |
| East Indian cedar | **DEODAR** |
| East Indian cereal grass | **RAGI** |

| | |
|---|---|
| East Indian island | **BALI** |
| East Indian pepper plant | **BETEL** |
| East Indian sailor | **LASCAR** |
| East Indian timber tree | **TEAK** |
| East Indian tree | **POON** |
| East Indian weight | **BAHAR, SER** |
| East Indian wood | **ENG, ALOES** |
| east wind god | **EURUS** |
| easy | **FACILE** |
| easy does it | **CAREFUL** |
| easy gait | **LOPE** |
| easy gallop | **CANTER** |
| easy-going horse | **PADNAG** |
| easy-going walker | **AMBLER** |
| easy job | **SINECURE** |
| easy mark (2 wds.) | **SOFT TOUCH** |
| easy task | **CINCH, SNAP** |
| easy winner (comp. wd.) | **SHOO-IN** |
| eat | **CONSUME, DEVOUR, DINE, SUP, ERODE** |
| eat at eight | **DINE** |
| eat away | **ERODE** |
| eat by regimen | **DIET** |
| eatery | **DINER** |
| eat grass | **GRAZE** |
| eat greedily | **GOBBLE** |
| eating alcove | **DINETTE** |
| eating utensil | **FORK, SPOON, KNIFE** |
| eat noisily | **SLURP** |
| eat peanuts | **MUNCH** |
| eat sparingly | **DIET** |
| eau de vie | **BRANDY** |
| eavesdrop | **LISTEN** |
| ebb | **ABATE, RECEDE, SUBSIDE** |
| ebb and flow | **TIDE** |
| ebony | **BLACK** |
| ebullient | **BUBBLING** |
| eccentric | **ODD, QUEER** |
| eccentric piece | **CAM** |
| ecclesiastic | **PRIEST** |
| echinoderm | **STARFISH** |
| echo | **REVERBERATE, RESOUND, REPEAT, APE, MIMIC** |
| eclat | **ACCLAIM** |
| eclipse | **DARKEN** |
| economical | **FRUGAL, THRIFTY** |
| economize | **SAVE, SCRIMP** |
| ecstasy | **RAPTURE** |
| ectoskeleton | **SHELL** |
| Ecuador capital | **QUITO** |
| Ecuador islands | **GALAPAGOS** |

ecumenical **UNIVERSAL, GENERAL, WORLDWIDE, ALL**
eddy **SWIRL, WHIRLPOOL**
Eden **PARADISE**
edge **ADVANTAGE, BRINK, VERGE, BORDER, BRIM, RIM, MARGIN, LIP**
edge of a molding **ARRIS**
edge of a street **CURB, KERB**
edge of woven fabric **SELVAGE**
edging **HEM**
edgy **NERVOUS, TENSE**
edible bean **LENTIL**
edible bivalve **MUSSEL, CLAM, OYSTER**
edible bulb **ONION**
edible crustacean **LOBSTER, CRAB**
edible fish **CARP, TUNA**
edible fruit **PLUM, PEAR, APPLE, ORANGE**
edible fungus **MUSHROOM**
edible green pod **OKRA**
edible Japanese shoot **UDO**
edible marine fish **GRUNT**
edible nut **ALMOND, CASHEW, FILBERT, PECAN, WALNUT, PEANUT, HAZELNUT**
edible part of fruit **PULP**
edible root **CARROT, RADISH, APET, OPET, ISIS, AMON, POTATO, BEET, PARSNIP, TURNIP, TARO**
edibles **FOODS**
edible seaweed **DULSE**
edible seed **BEAN, PEA**
edible tuber **POTATO, OCA, YAM**
edict **DECREE**
edification **INSTRUCTION**
edifice **BUILDING**
edify **INSTRUCT, ENLIGHTEN**
edit **REVISE**
Ed Sullivan, e.g. **EMCEE**
educate **TEACH, TRAIN, SCHOOL**
education **TRAINING**
educe **ELICIT, EVOKE**
eel **LAMPREY, CONGER**
eerie **SPOOKY, WEIRD**
efface **ERASE, EXPUNGE**
effect **FINISH, FULFILL, RESULT**
effective **USEFUL, EFFICIENT**
effeminate **WOMANLY**
effervescent **VOLATILE**
efficiency **ABILITY, EFFICACY**
efficient **ABLE, CAPABLE, COMPETENT, VALID**

eft **NEWT**
egg **GOAD, INCITE**
egg (prefix) **OVI**
egg cell **OVUM**
egg center **YOLK, NUCLEUS**
egg covering **SHELL**
egg dish **OMELET, SOUFFLE**
egg drink **NOG**
egg layer **HEN**
egg on **URGE**
egg part **YOLK, WHITE**
egg-shaped **OVAL, OVATE, OVOID**
egg white **ALBUMEN**
egis **AUSPICES, PATRONAGE**
ego **SELF, CONCEIT**
egotism **CONCEIT, VANITY**
egotistic **VAIN**
egress **EXIT**
egret **HERON**
Egyptian **COPTIC, COPT**
Egyptian astral body **KA**
Egyptian beetle **SCARAB**
Egyptian boat **BARIS**
Egyptian dam site **ASWAN**
Egyptian dancing girl **ALME**
Egyptian deity **SEB, SET(H), APET, OPET, ISIS, AMON, ANUBIS, OSIRIS, BUBASTIS, MA, THOTH, RA, BES, AANI, HAPI, PTAH, SATI, HORUS, ATON, HERSHEF**
Egyptian governor **PASHA**
Egyptian king **PTOLEMY, FAROUK**
Egyptian king's crown **ATEF**
Egyptian lily **LOTUS, CALLA**
Egyptian measure **ABDAT, CUBUT**
Egyptian paper **PAPYRUS**
Egyptian peninsula **SINAI**
Egyptian queen of gods **SATI**
Egyptian reed **PAPYRUS**
Egyptian river **NILE**
Egyptian sacred bull **APIS**
Egyptian seaport **SUEZ**
Egyptian stone **ROSETTA**
Egyptian sun disk **ATEN**
Egyptian sun god **RA**
Egyptian symbol **SCARAB**
Egyptian tomb **PYRAMID**
eider **DOWN, DUCK**
eight (comb. form) **OCTO**
Eire **IRELAND. ERIN**
Eisenhower memorial museum site **ABILENE**

Eisenhower's nickname **IKE**
either **OR**
ejaculate **EXCLAIM**
eject **OUST**
eke **SUPPLEMENT**
elaborate **FANCY**
elaborate meal **FEAST**
elan **ARDOR, ENTHUSIASM, VERVE, DASH**
elapse **EXPIRE, PASS**
elastic **PLIABLE**
elate **GLADDEN**
elation **GLADNESS, JOY, HAPPINESS**
elder **OLDER, SENIOR**
elderly **AGED, OLD, ANCIENT**
elderly person
(2 wds.) **SENIOR CITIZEN**
elder statesman of Japan **GENRO**
eldest of the Pleiades **MAIA**
elect **CHOOSE, SELECT**
elector **VOTER**
electrical device **RESISTOR**
electrical engineer (abbr.) **EE**
electrically charged particle **ION, PROTON**
electrical unit **AMP, FARAD, OHM, VOLT, WATT, MHO**
electric current (abbr.) **AC, DC**
electric current path **CIRCUIT**
electrician **WIRER**
electrified particle **ION**
electromotive unit **VOLT**
electronic beam **LASER**
electronic speed-check **RADAR**
elegance **GRACE, POLISH**
elegance of manners **REFINEMENT**
elegant **REFINED, POLISHED**
elegant appetizer **CAVIAR, PÂTÉ**
elegant attire **ARRAY**
element **INGREDIENT, FACTOR**
elementary **PRIMARY**
elementary schoolbook **PRIMER**
elephant call **TRUMPET**
elephant cry **BARR**
elephant dentin **IVORY**
elephant driver **MAHOUT**
elephant saddle **HOWDAH**
elephant's ear **TARO**
elephant's tooth **TUSK**
elephant's tusk **IVORY**
elevate **EXALT, RAISE, UPLIFT, REAR**
elevated railroad **EL**
elevation **HILL**

elevator **LIFT**
elevator direction **UP, DOWN**
elf **SPRITE, PIXIE, GNOME, BROWNIE**
elicit **EVOKE, EDUCE**
elide **OMIT, SLUR**
eligible **FIT, WORTHY**
eliminate (2 wds.) **RULE OUT**
elite **CREAM**
elk **MOOSE**
elk's horn **ANTLER**
elliptical **OVAL, OVATE**
elm **TREE**
Elmo Roper item (2 wds.) **STRAW VOTE**
elongate **LENGTHEN, STRETCH**
elope **ABSCOND**
eloquence **RHETORIC, ORATORY**
eloquent **EXPRESSIVE**
else **OTHERWISE**
elucidate **EXPLAIN, ILLUSTRATE**
elude **EVADE, AVOID**
emaciated **LEAN, SKINNY**
emanate **ISSUE, FLOW**
emanation **AURA**
emancipate **LIBERATE, FREE**
embankment **LEVEE**
embark **SAIL**
embarrass **ABASH**
embarrassment **SHAME**
embellish **ADORN, DECORATE**
ember **COAL**
embezzle **STEAL**
emblem **BADGE, TOKEN**
emblem of grief **RUE**
emblem of United States **EAGLE**
embody **EMBRACE, COMPRISE**
embolden **STIMULATE**
embrace **CLASP, HUG**
embroidery **NEEDLEWORK**
embroidery silk **FLOSS**
embroil **PERPLEX, TROUBLE**
emcee Linkletter **ART**
emcee Mack **TED**
emcee Sullivan **ED**
emend **CORRECT**
Emerald Isle **EIRE, ERIN, IRELAND**
emerge from an egg **HATCH**
emergency **CRISIS, NECESSITY**
emergency sum (2 wds.) **MAD MONEY**
emery **CORUNDUM**
emigrant **SETTLER**
emigrate **MIGRATE, MOVE**

Emily Post behavior (2 wds.)
**GOOD MANNERS**
eminent **ILLUSTRIOUS, PROMINENT**
emissary **AGENT**
emit **DISCHARGE, VENT**
emit rays of light **RADIATE**
emit vapor **REEK, STEAM**
emmet **ANT**
emote **OVERACT, ACT, HAM**
emotion **SENTIMENT, FEELING**
emotionally detached **CLINICAL**
emotional shock **TRAUMA**
empathy **COMPASSION**
emperor **RULER**
emphasis **STRESS, ACCENT**
emphasize **ACCENT, STRESS, UNDERSCORE, PLAY UP**
emphatic **STRONG, FORCEFUL**
emphatic request **DEMAND**
Empire State (2 wds.) **NEW YORK**
Empire State city **OLEAN, YONKERS, UTICA, ALBANY, TROY**
Empire State of the south **GEORGIA**
employ **HIRE, TAKE ON, USE, UTILIZE**
employee **HAND, HELP**
employee's hourly record **TIME CARD**
employer **BOSS**
employment **WORK**
emporium **STORE, MART**
empower **ENABLE, ENTITLE**
empty **BARE, VOID, BLANK, INANE, UNOCCUPIED**
empty bullet **SHELL**
empty place **SPACE, BLANK, SHELL, VACANT, VOID**
emulate **IMITATE**
emulation **RIVALRY, IMITATION**
emulsion **PAP**
enable **EMPOWER, PERMIT**
enact **DECREE**
enamel **GLAZE, PAINT**
enamor **CHARM**
enchant **CHARM, BEWITCH**
enchantment **SPELL**
enchantress **SIREN**
encina **OAK**
encircle **ENCLOSE, RING**
encircled **GIRT**
encircling strap **BELT, CINCTURE**
enclose **ENVELOP, FENCE**
enclosed automobile **SEDAN**

enclosed in this **HEREWITH**
enclose in paper **WRAP**
enclosure **CAGE, PEN**
enclosure for horses **CORRAL**
encomiast **EULOGIST**
encomium **PRAISE**
encompass **INCLUDE**
encore **AGAIN, BIS**
encounter **MEET, MEET WITH**
encourage **ABET, PROD, EGG ON**
encroach **TRESPASS**
encroach on **INVADE**
encrust **CAKE**
encumber **HINDER**
encumbrance **BURDEN**
encyclopedic **COMPREHENSIVE**
end **CONCLUDE, CONCLUSION, FINISH, TERMINATE, TERMINUS, OUTCOME, RESULT, AIM, GOAL, OMEGA, PURPOSE**
end (Lat.) **FINIS**
endanger **IMPERIL**
endearment **CARESS**
endeavor **ATTEMPT, STRIVE**
endemic **NATIVE**
endless **ETERNAL**
endocrine **GLAND, GLANDULAR**
end of a pencil **STUB, ERASER**
end of a spar **YARDARM**
endowment **GIFT, BEQUEST**
endurable **BEARABLE**
endurance **PATIENCE, TOLERANCE**
endure **LAST, BEAR, TOLERATE**
enemy **FOE**
energetic **VIGOROUS**
energize **ACTIVATE**
energy **VIM, VIGOR, PEP**
energy unit **ERG**
enervate **WEAKEN, SAP**
enfeeble **WEAKEN**
enfold **WRAP, ENVELOP**
enforce **EXECUTE**
enfranchise **FREE**
engage **HIRE, WIN**
engage, as gears **MESH**
engage in a contest **COMPETE**
engage in reverie **DREAM**
engage in small talk **CHAT, GAB, JAW**
engage in sport **PLAY**
engage in winter sport **SKI, SKATE**
engagement **TROTH, DATE, BETROTHAL**

| | | | |
|---|---|---|---|
| engagement ring | **SPARKLER** | engrave | **ETCH** |
| engender | **BREED** | engraver's tool | **BURIN** |
| engine | **MOTOR** | engross | **ABSORB** |
| engineer | **DESIGNER** | engrossed | **ENRAPT, RAPT** |
| engineer's helper | **OILER** | engulf | **DROWN, SWAMP** |
| English actor | **TREE, MILLS,** | enigma | **RIDDLE** |
| | **REDGRAVE** | enjoin | **ORDER, DIRECT** |
| English admiral | **NELSON** | enjoy | **LIKE** |
| English air force | **R.A.F.** | enjoy a book | **READ** |
| English architect | **WREN** | enjoy a cigar | **SMOKE** |
| English architecture | **TUDOR** | enjoy a meal | **DINE, EAT, SUP** |
| English bard | **SCOP** | enjoyment | **FUN, AMUSEMENT** |
| English cathedral city | **ELY,** | enlarge | **WIDEN, PROJECT** |
| **COVENTRY, ST. ALBANS** | | enlarge a hole | **REAM** |
| English city | **BRISTOL,** | enlighten | **INFORM, TEACH** |
| | **LIVERPOOL** | enlist | **ENROLL** |
| English coin | **SHILLING, PENNY** | enlisted man | **GI** |
| English coins | **PENCE** | enliven | **ANIMATE** |
| English college | **OXFORD, ETON** | enmity | **MALICE** |
| English composer | **ARNOLD,** | ennui | **TEDIUM, BOREDOM** |
| **BLIS, BRITTEN, ELGAR,** | | enormity | **VASTNESS** |
| **PURCELL** | | enormous | **HUGE, VAST,** |
| English conservative | **TORY** | | **LARGE, BIG** |
| English count | **EARL** | enough | **ADEQUATE, PLENTY** |
| English county | **SHIRE** | enrage | **ANGER, MADDEN** |
| English derby town | **EPSOM** | enrapture | **ENCHANT, CHARM** |
| English dynasty | **TUDOR,** | enroll | **ENTER. REGISTER** |
| | **STUART** | en route (3 wds.) | **ON THE WAY** |
| English game | **CRICKET** | ensconce | **CONCEAL, HIDE** |
| English heather | **LING** | ensign (abbr.) | **ENS.** |
| English island | **WIGHT** | ensnare | **ENTRAP, NET** |
| English manufacturing city | | ensue | **FOLLOW** |
| **LEEDS, LIVERPOOL** | | entangle | **SNARL** |
| English nursemaid | **NANNY** | enter | **BEGIN** |
| English poet | **MILTON, BYRON,** | enter in writing | **SET DOWN** |
| **SHELLEY, KEATS** | | enterprise | **VENTURE** |
| English policeman | **BOBBY** | entertain | **AMUSE, TREAT,** |
| English porcelain | **SPODE** | | **REGALE** |
| English potter | **SPODE** | entertain at one's | |
| English prep school | **ETON,** | own expense | **TREAT** |
| | **HARROW** | entertainer | **ACTOR, STAR** |
| English princess | **ANNE,** | entertaining | **AMUSING** |
| | **MARGARET** | entertain lavishly | **FETE,** |
| English professor | **DON** | | **REGALE** |
| English pudding | **PUD** | entertainment | **FUN, PLEASURE** |
| English racetrack | **ASCOT** | | **SHOW** |
| English region (2 wds.) | | entertainment group (abbr.) | |
| **LAKE DISTRICT,** | | | **USO** |
| **HOME COUNTIES** | | enthrall | **FASCINATE** |
| English resort | **BATH,** | enthralled | **RAPT** |
| | **BRIGHTON** | enthusiasm | **ELAN** |
| English river | **AVON, DEE,** | enthusiast | **FAN** |
| **HUMBER, THAMES** | | enthusiastic | **AVID, EAGER** |
| English rowboat | **PUNT** | enthusiastic applause | **OVATION** |
| English school | **ETON, HARROW** | enthusiastic review | **RAVE** |
| English statesman | **PITT** | entice | **ALLURE, LURE, TEMPT** |
| English streetcar | **TRAM** | enticement | **TEMPTATION** |
| English tavern | **PUB, TAPROOM** | enticing woman | **SIREN** |

| | | | |
|---|---|---|---|
| entire | **ALL, TOTAL, WHOLE** | equalize (2 wds.) | **LEVEL OFF** |
| entirety (2 wds., sl.) | | equanimity | **POISE** |
| | **WHOLE HOG** | equation | **FORMULA** |
| entire range | **GAMUT** | equidistant lines | **PARALLEL** |
| entirely | **ALL** | equilibrium | **BALANCE** |
| entity | **BEING, UNITY** | equine | **HORSE, ZEBRA, ASS** |
| entourage | **TRAIN** | equine father | **SIRE** |
| entrance | **DOOR, ACCESS** | equine gait | **CANTER, TROT,** |
| entrance fee | **ADMISSION** | | **GALLOP, LOPE** |
| entrance hall | **FOYER** | equine mother | **DAM** |
| entrance to a garden | **GATE** | equine sound | **SNORT, WHINNY,** |
| entrance way | **ENTRY** | | **NEIGH** |
| entrancing | **RAVISHING** | equine trappings | **CAPARISON** |
| entrant | **CONTESTANT,** | equinox | **VERNAL, AUTUMNAL** |
| | **PARTICIPANT** | equip | **RIG, FIT OUT, OUTFIT** |
| entrap | **CATCH, ENSNARE** | equipage (arch.) | **CREW,** |
| entreat | **BEG, BESEECH, PRAY,** | | **RETINUE** |
| | **PLEAD** | equipment | **GEAR** |
| entreaty | **PLEA** | equitable | **FAIR, IMPARTIAL** |
| entrechat | **LEAP** | equitably | **FAIRLY** |
| entry | **ENTRANCE, ACCESS** | equitation | **DRESSAGE** |
| entwine | **ENLACE, LACE, TWIST** | equity | **FAIRNESS** |
| enumerate | **COUNT, LIST** | equivalent to | **TANTAMOUNT** |
| enunciate | **UTTER,** | equivocal | **UNCERTAIN** |
| | **ARTICULATE** | equivocate | **LIE** |
| enure | **HARDEN** | equivocation | **EVASION** |
| envelop | **ENCLOSE** | equivoque | **PUN** |
| envelop in paper | **WRAP** | era | **AGE, EPOCH, EON** |
| envious | **JEALOUS, COVETOUS** | eradicate (2 wds.) | **ROOT OUT** |
| environment | **LOCALE,** | erase | **DELE, EXPUNGE,** |
| | **SURROUNDINGS** | | **RUB OUT** |
| envision | **SEE** | Erato | **MUSE** |
| envoy | **MESSENGER** | ere | **BEFORE, RATHER** |
| envy | **JEALOUSY** | erect | **BUILD, UPRIGHT** |
| enzyme (suffix) | **ASE** | ere long | **ANON, SOON** |
| eoan | **AURORAL** | eremite | **HERMIT, RECLUSE** |
| eon | **ETERNITY, ERA, AGE** | eremite's hut | **CELL** |
| ephemeral | **TRANSIENT,** | erenow | **HERETOFORE** |
| | **FLEETING** | ergo | **THUS, HENCE** |
| epi | **FINIAL** | ergot | **FUNGUS** |
| epic | **HEROIC** | Erin | **IRELAND, EIRE** |
| epic poem | **EPOS, EPODE,** | Erinyes | **FURIES** |
| | **EPOPEE** | Erle Stanley Gardner stories | |
| epic story | **SAGA** | | **MYSTERIES,** |
| epicurean | **SENSUAL** | ermine | **STOAT** |
| epidemic | **PLAGUE** | ern | **OSPREY** |
| episode | **SCENE** | Ernest Borgnine role | **MARTY** |
| epistle | **LETTER, MISSIVE** | erode | **EAT, WEAR** |
| epithet | **NAME, APPELATION** | Eros | **AMOR, CUPID** |
| epitome | **SYNOPSIS, PRECIS** | erose | **WORN, JAGGED** |
| epoch | **ERA, AGE** | erotic | **SENSUAL** |
| epoxy | **ENAMEL, RESIN** | err | **MISDO, SIN** |
| equable | **EVEN, STEADY** | errand | **SHORE, MISSION, TASK** |
| equal | **EVEN, PEER** | errand boy | **PAGE, MESSENGER** |
| equal (Fr.) | **EGAL** | errant | **ITINERANT** |
| equality | **PAR** | errantry | **CHIVALRY** |
| equality (Fr.) | **EGALITE** | erratic | **ECCENTRIC** |
| Equality State | **WYOMING** | erroneous | **MISTAKEN** |

| | |
|---|---|
| error | BLUNDER, LAPSE, MISTAKE, SLIP, FALLACY |
| ersatz | SYNTHETIC, ARTIFICIAL, BUTTER, OLEO |
| Erse | GAELIC |
| erst | ONCE, FORMERLY |
| erudite | LEARNED, WISE |
| erupt | BURST, EJECT |
| Esau's brother | JACOB |
| Esau's country | EDOM |
| Esau's wife | ADA, JUDITH, BASEMATH, MAHELETH |
| escape | ELUDE, EVADE, FLEE, LAM |
| escargot | SNAIL |
| eschew | AVOID, SHUN |
| escort | CHAPERONE, USHER |
| eskers | OSAR |
| Eskimo | AMERIND, ALEUT |
| Eskimo boat | UMIAK, KAYAK, OOMIAK |
| Eskimo house | IGLOO, IGLU |
| Eskimo knife | ULU |
| Eskimo vehicle | SLED |
| espouse | EMBRACE, ADOPT |
| esprit de corps | MORALE, SPIRIT, UNITY |
| espy | SEE |
| essay | TRY, ATTEMPT, THEME |
| essay | THEME, TOPIC |
| essence | PERFUME |
| essential | IMPERATIVE, NECESSARY |
| essential part | PITH, CORE, CRUX, GIST |
| establishment | SHOP |
| establish the truth | PROVE |
| estate | MANOR, PROPERTY |
| estate employee | GARDENER, GATEMAN |
| esteem | RESPECT, REVERE |
| esthetic judgment (2 wds.) | GOOD TASTE |
| estimable | WORTHY |
| estimate | ASSESS, GUESS, RATE |
| estimated worth | VALUE |
| estimation | ESTEEM, REGARD |
| estop | BAR, PROHIBIT |
| estrange | ALIENATE |
| estuary | BAY, FIRTH |
| etape | STOREHOUSE |
| etch | ENGRAVE |
| etching fluid | ACID |
| eternal | AGELESS, ENDLESS, PERPETUAL |
| Eternal City native | ROMAN |

| | |
|---|---|
| eternally | ALWAYS, EVER, E'ER, FOREVER |
| eternity | EON |
| ethanol | ALCOHOL |
| ether | ANAESTHETIC |
| ether compound | ESTER |
| ethereal | AIRY |
| ethereal being | SYLPH |
| ethereal salt | ESTER |
| ethical | MORAL |
| ethics | MORALS |
| Ethopian lake | TANA |
| Ethiopian native | GALLA |
| Ethiopia's neighbor | ERITREA |
| Etruscan deity | LAR, LARES (PL.) |
| Eucharistic plate | PATEN |
| eulogize | LAUD, GLORIFY |
| eulogy | ELOGE |
| Euphrates tributary | TIGRIS |
| European apple | SORB |
| European beetle | DOR |
| European blackbird | MERL |
| European capital | BERN, BONN, OSLO, PARIS, ROME, MADRID |
| European dormouse | LEROT |
| European farmer | PEASANT |
| European flatfish | TURBOT |
| European gull | MEW |
| European mountain district | TYROL |
| European mountains | ALPS |
| European river | ELBE, RUHR |
| European sandpiper | TEREK |
| European shad | ALOSE |
| European shark | TOPE |
| evade | CIRCUMVENT, ELUDE, AVOID, ESCAPE |
| evade, as a question | PARRY |
| evade, as duty | SHIRK |
| evaluate | RATE |
| evanesce | DISAPPEAR, VANISH |
| evanescent | FLEETING |
| evangelical | GOSPEL |
| Evangeline's home | ACADIA |
| evaporate (2 wds.) | DRY UP |
| even | LEVEL, FLAT |
| even (Lat.) | ENIM |
| even (poet.) | E'EN |
| even a little bit (2 wds.) | AT ALL |
| evening | TWILIGHT, DUSK |
| evening (Ger.) | ABEND |
| evening (poet.) | EVE |
| evening cloak | WRAP |
| evening dress | GOWN |
| evening in Italy | SERA |
| evening party | SOIREE |

| | |
|---|---|
| evening song | SERENADE, VESPER |
| evening star | VENUS, VESPER |
| even one | ANY |
| even score | TIE |
| event | OCCURRENCE |
| eventual | ULTIMATE, FINAL |
| ever | ALWAYS |
| ever (poet.) | E'ER |
| Everglade | SWAMP |
| evergreen shrub | JUNIPER, MYRTLE |
| Evergreen State | WASHINGTON |
| evergreen tree | CEDAR, FIR, SPRUCE, YEW, PINE |
| everlasting | ETERNAL |
| evermore | FOREVER, ALWAYS |
| every | ALL, ANY, EACH |
| everyday | COMMON, ORDINARY |
| everything | ALL |
| everything counted (2 wds.) | ALL TOLD |
| every 24 hours | DAILY |
| Eve's mate | ADAM |
| Eve's origin | RIB |
| evict | EJECT, OUST |
| evidence | PROOF |
| evident | OBVIOUS |
| evil | BAD, BADNESS, SIN, MALEVOLENT, WICKED |
| evil deed | SIN |
| evil giant | OGRE |
| evil grin | LEER, SNEER |
| evil omen | KNELL |
| evil one | DEVIL, SATAN |
| evil spirit | DEMON |
| evince | SHOW, MANIFEST |
| evocation | INDUCTION |
| evoke | SUMMON |
| evolution | DEVELOPMENT |
| evolutionary | GENETIC |
| ewer | PITCHER |
| ewe's mate | RAM |
| exacerbate | IRRITATE |
| exact | PRECISE |
| exacting | STRENUOUS |
| exactitude | PRECISION, ACCURACY |
| exact likeness | COPY |
| exactly (3 wds.) | TO A T, TO A TEE |
| exactness | PRECISION |
| exact opposite | ANTIPODE |
| exact satisfaction | AVENGE |
| exaggerate | OVERDO, OVERSTATE |
| exalt | ELATE, ELEVATE, HONOR |
| exaltation of spirit | ELATION |

| | |
|---|---|
| examination | TEST, FINAL, MIDTERM |
| examine | TEST |
| examine eggs under a light | CANDLE |
| examine judicially | TRY |
| examine minutely | SIFT |
| example | MODEL, SAMPLE |
| exanimate | DEAD, INERT |
| exasperate | RILE |
| exasperation | ANNOYANCE |
| exclamation of pity | ALAS |
| excavate | DIG |
| excavation | PIT, HOLE, CAVITY |
| excavator | SHOVEL |
| exceed | OUTDO, EXCEL |
| exceedingly | VERY |
| excel | EXCEED OUTDO |
| excellence | VIRTUE |
| excellent | FINE, SPLENDID |
| excelling others | BEST |
| except | SAVE, BUT |
| except for | SAVE |
| except that | ONLY |
| exception | DISSENT |
| exceptional | UNCOMMON, RARE |
| excerpt | EXTRACT |
| excess | OVERAGE |
| excessive | EXORBITANT, UNDUE |
| excessive interest | USURY |
| excessively | UNDULY, TOO |
| exchange | SWAP, TRADE, BARTER |
| exchange discount | AGIO |
| exchange for money | SELL |
| exchange letters | CORRESPOND |
| exchange place | FAIR, MARKET, MART |
| exchange premium | AGIO |
| exchequer | TREASURY |
| excise | TAX, DUTY |
| excite | PROVOKE, WORK UP, ENTHUSE |
| excite the attention of | INTEREST |
| excite to action | ROUSE |
| excited | AGOG |
| excitement | ADO, STIR |
| exciting | HECTIC |
| exclaim | CRY OUT |
| exclamation | AHA, OHO |
| exclamation of annoyance | DRAT |
| exclamation of approval | BRAVO |
| exclamation of disappointment | AW |
| exclamation of disbelief | BAH |

| | |
|---|---|
| exclamation of disgust | UGH, POOH |
| exclamation of doubt | HUMPH |
| exclamation of horror (2 wds.) | OH NO |
| exclamation of pity | ALAS |
| exclamation of sorrow | ALAS |
| exclamation of surprise | WOW, OH, HO |
| exclamation of triumph | AHA, AH |
| exclude | BAR, RULE OUT, DEBAR |
| exclusive | SELECT |
| exclusive news story | SCOOP |
| exclusive right | PATENT |
| excoriate | CHAFE, IRRITATE |
| excruciate | TORTURE |
| excruciating | PAINFUL |
| exculpate | ACQUIT |
| excursion | JUNKET, TRIP, TREK, TOUR |
| excuse | ALIBI, PLEA |
| execrate | ABHOR, CURSE, CONDEMN |
| execute | EFFECT, PERFORM |
| executive ability | LEADERSHIP |
| executive's bag | BRIEFCASE |
| executor's responsibility | ESTATE |
| exemplar | MODEL |
| exemplify | ILLUSTRATE |
| exempt | FREE, CLEAR |
| exercise | ACTIVITY |
| exercising device (2 wds.) | LONG HORSE |
| exertion | DINT |
| exhale | RESPIRE, EMIT |
| exhaust | DEPLETE, FAG, SPEND, BUSH, WEAR OUT |
| exhausted | TIRED, SPENT |
| exhaustion | FATIGUE |
| exhibit | DISPLAY |
| exhibition at its best | SHOWCASE |
| exhilarate | ELATE |
| exhort | URGE |
| exhortation | PLEA, SERMON |
| exhume | DISCLOSE, REVEAL |
| exigency | EMERGENCY, NEED |
| exigent | URGENT |
| exile | DEPORT |
| exist | AM, ARE, IS, BE, LIVE |
| existed | BEEN, WAS, WERE |
| existence | BEING, LIFE |
| existence (Lat.) | ESSE |
| existent | ALIVE |
| exit | EGRESS |

| | |
|---|---|
| exodus | HEGIRA |
| exonerate | CLEAR |
| exorbitant | EXCESSIVE |
| exorbitant interest rate | USURY |
| exotic | ALIEN, STRANGE |
| expand | DEVELOP, DILATE, ENLARGE |
| expanse | REACH, SPREAD |
| expansion | INCREASE, GROWTH |
| expansive | BROAD, WIDE |
| expatriate | EXILE, BANISH |
| expect | AWAIT |
| expectation | HOPE |
| expedient | POLITIC, WISE |
| expedite | HASTEN |
| expedition | EXCURSION, JOURNEY |
| expel | OUST, EVICT, EJECT |
| expend | DISBURSE, CONSUME |
| expenditure | OUTLAY |
| expense | COST |
| expensive | DEAR, COSTLY |
| expensive fur | MINK, SABLE, ERMINE |
| experience anew | REENACT |
| experiment | TEST |
| expert | PRO, ADEPT, SKILLED, ACE |
| expert bridge player | MASTER |
| expert flyer | ACE |
| expert golfer | ACE, PRO |
| expertise | SKILL |
| expiate | ATONE |
| expire | DIE, RUN OUT, LAPSE |
| explain | INTERPRET, DEFINE |
| explain a word | DEFINE |
| explanation | DESCRIPTION |
| expletive | GOSH, GEE |
| explicit | CLEAR |
| explode | BURST, POP, DETONATE, ERUPT |
| explode in muffler | BACKFIRE |
| exploit | FEAT, USE, DEED |
| explore | EXAMINE, SEARCH |
| explorer | PIONEER |
| explosion | BLAST |
| explosive | TNT, NITRO |
| explosive device | BOMB, GRENADE, MINE |
| explosive noise | POP |
| expose | BARE |
| exposed | BARED, BARE, OPEN, FRANK |
| expose to view | OPEN |
| expound | ORATE |
| express | DECLARE, TELL |
| express a choice for | PREFER |

| | |
|---|---|
| express an idea | **OPINE** |
| express disapproval | **ADMONISH** |
| express discontent | **COMPLAIN** |
| express disdain | **SNIFF** |
| express gratitude | **THANK** |
| express impatience | **TUT** |
| expressing love | **ROMANTIC** |
| express in words | **PHRASE, SAY, STATE** |
| expression of contempt | **BOO** |
| expression of good will | **VIVA** |
| express merriment | **LAUGH** |
| express road | **FREEWAY** |
| express scorn | **SNEER** |
| express sorrow | **LAMENT** |
| express sympathy | **CONDOLE, CONSOLE** |
| expunge | **ERASE, DELE, DELETE** |
| exquisite | **PERFECT** |
| extant | **BEING, EXISTENT** |
| extemporaneous | **IMPROMPTU** |
| extempore (comp. wd.) | **AD-LIB** |
| extend | **OFFER, REACH** |
| extend across | **SPAN** |
| extend a loan | **LEND** |
| extend a subscription | **RENEW** |
| extend over | **COVER** |
| extend to | **REACH** |
| extend upward | **RISE** |
| extensive | **LONG, VAST** |
| extensive plain | **PRAIRIE** |
| extent | **RANGE, SCOPE, LENGTH** |
| extent of influence | **SCOPE** |
| exterior | **OUTER** |
| exterminate | **ANNIHILATE, DESTROY** |
| external | **OUTER** |
| extinct | **DEAD** |
| extinct bird | **DODO, MOA** |
| extinct wild ox | **URUS, AUROCHS** |
| extinguish | **DOUSE, QUELL** |
| extol | **PRAISE** |
| extract | **EDUCE** |
| extraction | **ORIGIN, STOCK** |
| extraneous | **EXTERNAL, FOREIGN** |
| extraordinary | **RARE, SINGULAR** |
| extra pay | **BONUS** |
| extrasensory perception (abbr.) | **ESP** |
| extra small pup | **RUNT** |
| extra supplies | **RESERVES** |
| extra tire | **SPARE** |
| extravagance | **WASTE** |
| extravagant | **FANCY** |
| extreme | **DIRE, RADICAL, DRASTIC** |
| extreme alarm | **PANIC** |

| | |
|---|---|
| extreme anger | **RAGE** |
| extreme conservative | **DIEHARD** |
| extreme fear | **HORROR, TERROR, PANIC** |
| extreme fondness | **LOVE** |
| extremely | **AWFULLY, VERY** |
| extremely poor | **DESTITUTE** |
| extremely violent argument (comp. wd.) | **KNOCK-DOWN-AND-DRAG-OUT** |
| extremist | **RADICAL** |
| extremity | **END, TOE, FINGER** |
| extricate | **DISENTANGLE** |
| exuberant | **PROLIFIC** |
| exudation | **SECRETION** |
| exude | **EMIT, SPEW, SEEP, OOZE** |
| exult | **ELATE** |
| exultant | **JUBILANT** |
| exultation | **GLEE, JOY** |
| exult maliciously | **GLOAT** |
| exuviate | **MOLT** |
| eye | **ESPY, OBSERVE, SCRUTINIZE, WATCH** |
| eye amorously | **OGLE, LEER** |
| eye boldly | **STARE** |
| eye disease | **GLAUCOMA, TRACHOMA** |
| eye drop | **TEAR** |
| eyeglass | **LENS, MONOCLE** |
| eyelashes | **CILIA** |
| eye make-up | **MASCARA** |
| eye membrane | **RETINA** |
| eyes (slang) | **GLIMS** |
| eyesight | **VISION** |
| eyetooth | **CANINE** |
| eyre | **COURT, TOUR, CIRCUIT** |

**F**

| | |
|---|---|
| fable | **PARABLE, MYTH** |
| fabled bird | **ROC** |
| fabled marine creature | **MERMAID** |
| fabled one-horned animal | **UNICORN** |
| fabliau | **TALE, STORY** |
| fabric | **TEXTILE, MATERIAL, CLOTH** |
| fabricate | **MAKE** |
| fabrication | **LIE, FIB** |
| fabric glaze | **CIRE** |
| fabric junction | **SEAM** |
| fabric woven from flax | **LINEN** |
| fabulist | **AESOP** |
| fabulous | **WONDERFUL** |
| fabulous beast | **DRAGON** |

| | |
|---|---|
| fabulous bird | ROC |
| fabulous one-horned animal | UNICORN |
| facade | FACE, FRONT |
| face | VISAGE |
| face covering | VEIL, MASK |
| face part | CHIN, NOSE, LIP, MOUTH, CHEEK, EYE |
| face with stone | REVET |
| facet | SIDE, ASPECT, PHASE |
| facetious | SARCASTIC, WITTY |
| facile | EASY |
| facilitate | AID, ASSIST |
| facility | EASE, FLUENCY |
| facing | TOWARD |
| facsimile | LIKENESS |
| fact | DATUM |
| faction | SIDE |
| factitious | ARTIFICIAL, SHAM |
| factor | AGENT, ELEMENT |
| factory | MILL, PLANT |
| factory fuel | COAL |
| factory superintendent | FOREMAN |
| factotum | HANDYMAN |
| facts and figures | DATA |
| factual | TRUE |
| faculty | ABILITY |
| fad | RAGE, CRAZE, MANIA |
| fade | PALE, DIM |
| fade away | EVANESCE |
| faded star (comp. wd.) | HAS-BEEN |
| Faerie Queene | UNA |
| fail | MISS, FLUNK |
| fail in duty | LAPSE |
| failing | FAULT |
| fail to follow suit | RENEGE |
| fail to hit | MISS |
| fail to mention | OMIT |
| fail to win | LOSE |
| failure | FLOP, DUD |
| failure at Cape Kennedy (2 wds.) | NO GO |
| faint | FEEBLE |
| fair | JUST |
| fair grade | CEE |
| fairly | SOMEWHAT |
| fair to middling | PASSABLE |
| fairy | ELF, SPRITE |
| fairy stick | WAND |
| fairy tale creature | ELF, GNOME, OGRE, TROLL |
| faith | CONVICTION, TRUST |
| faithful | TRUE, LOYAL |
| faithful counselor | MENTOR |
| faith healer Roberts | ORAL |
| faithless | FALSE |

| | |
|---|---|
| fake | COUNTERFEIT, PHONY, FRAUD, SHAM, PRETEND, ERSATZ, FORGERY |
| fake coin | SLUG |
| fake jewelry | PASTE |
| fakir | YOGI, DERVISH |
| Falasha | HAMITE |
| falchion | SWORD |
| falcon | KESTREL |
| falderal | NONSENSE |
| fall | AUTUMN |
| fallacious | CRAFTY, DECEITFUL |
| fallacy | ERROR |
| fall back | RECEDE, RETREAT |
| fall back into former state | RELAPSE |
| fall back on | RELY, DEPEND |
| fall behind | LAG |
| fall flower | ASTER, MUM |
| fall guy | PATSY, CHUMP, MARK |
| fallible | HUMAN |
| fall in | MEET, COLLAPSE |
| fall in drops | DRIP |
| fall in flakes | SNOW |
| falling sickness | EPILEPSY |
| fall month | SEPTEMBER, OCTOBER |
| fall noisily | CRASH |
| fall off | DECLINE |
| fall of rain | SHOWER |
| fall out | DISAGREE, QUARREL |
| fall over | TOPPLE |
| fallow | IDLE, INACTIVE |
| fall short | FAIL |
| fall suddenly | DROP, SLUMP, COLLAPSE |
| fall to | BEGIN, START |
| fall upon | ASSAIL, ATTACK |
| false | RECREANT, UNFAITHFUL, UNTRUE |
| false appearance | GUISE |
| false belief | DELUSION |
| false claim | PRETENSE |
| false coin | SLUG |
| false face | MASK |
| false front | POSE |
| false god | IDOL |
| false hairpiece | WIG, PERUKE, FALL, TOUPEE |
| falsehood | LIE, FIB |
| false jewelry | PASTE |
| false name | ALIAS |
| false report | CANARD, RUMOR |
| false show | TINSEL |
| false signature | FORGERY |
| false step | SLIP |
| false teeth | DENTURE |
| falsify | FORGE, LIE |

falter **HESITATE, STUMBLE**
faltering speech **STUTTER**
fame **HONOR, RENOWN, NAME, REPUTE**
familiar **INTIMATE**
familiar emblem **EAGLE**
familiarity **FRIENDSHIP**
familiar with **CONVERSANT**
family **HOUSE, CLAN**
family car **AUTO, SEDAN, COUPE, STATION WAGON**
family group **CLAN**
family imp **BRAT**
family man **FATHER**
family member **MAMA, PAPA, MOM, DAD, SISTER, BROTHER, JUNIOR, SIS**
family name **SURNAME**
family of kings **DYNASTY**
family of medieval Ferrara **ESTE**
famine **HUNGER, SHORTAGE**
famish **STARVE**
famous **EMINENT, KNOWN**
famous uncle **SAM**
fan **ENTHUSIAST, SUPPORTER**
fanatic **CRANK, ZEALOT**
fanatical **RABID**
fanatic devotion **CULT**
fanciful **WHIMSICAL**
fanciful reverie **DAYDREAM**
fancy **ELABORATE**
fancy dive **GAINER**
fancy fabric **LACE**
fancy trappings **REGALIA, FINERY**
fancy vase **URN**
fane **BANNER, PENNANT**
Fanny Farmer specialty **RECIPE**
fantastic **BIZARRE**
fantastic trick **ANTIC**
fantasy **DREAM**
far **DISTANT, REMOTE**
far (prefix) **TEL(E)**
farce **COMEDY**
farcical **ABSURD**
far down **DEEP**
fare **DIET, PASSAGE, GO**
Far East **ORIENT**
farer **TRAVELER**
farewell **ADIEU**
farewell (Sp.) **ADIOS**
farewell party (comp. wd.) **SEND-OFF**
farewell to the Islands **ALOHA**

farm animal **CALF. SOW, COW, BULL, STEER, HORSE, SHEEP, MARE, EWE, RAM, GOAT**
farm animals **LIVESTOCK, CATTLE**
farm building **BARN, SILO**
farm implement **REAPER, GIN, TRACTOR, PLOW**
farming **AGRICULTURE**
farm laborer **HAND**
farm measure **ACRE**
farm out **HIRE, LET**
farm product **CROP**
farm tenant **COTTER, COTTIER**
farmyard sound **MOO, BAA, BLEAT, OINK, CLUCK, WHINNY**
far-off **DISTANT**
far-reaching **VAST**
farrow **PIG**
far-sighted **SHREWD**
fascinate **CHARM**
fashion **CRAZE, FAD, MODE, STYLE, MODEL, FORM, MANNER, ASPECT, SORT, VOGUE**
fashionable **CHIC**
fashionable resort **SPA**
fashionable section of Boston **BACK BAY**
fashionably elegant **SWANK**
fashion name **DIOR, CHANEL, PARNIS, BROOKS, CARDIN, PUCCI, VALENTINO, GRES**
fast **FLEET, RAPID, QUICK, SPEEDY**
fast car **RACER**
fast driver (2 wds.) **SPEED DEMON**
fasten **GLUE, NAIL, RIVET, TIE, LACE, CLASP, CLIP, PIN, SNAP, LATCH**
fastener **CLASP, PIN**
fasten firmly **ANCHOR, BIND, NAIL**
fastens **CLASPS**
fasten shut **BAR**
fasten with stitches **SEW**
fasten with string **TIE**
fastidious **NEAT, DAINTY**
fastidious man **DUDE, FOP**
fasting period **LENT**
fast plane **JET**
fat **CORPULENT, OBESE, PLUMP, LARD, GREASE, STOUT, ROTUND, CHUBBY**

fatal **LETHAL**
fatality **DEATH**
fata morgana **MIRAGE**
fate **DESTINY, DOOM, KARMA, KISMET**
fateful time for Caesar **IDES**
Fates **PARCAE, ATROPOS, CLOTHO, LACHESIS**
father **DAD, SIRE, POP, DADDY, POPPA, PAPA, PA, PAW**
father (Fr.) **PERE**
father (Lat.) **PATER**
father (poetic) **SIRE**
father (Sp.) **PADRE**
fatherhood **PATERNITY**
father of Enos **SETH**
father of Horus **OSIRIS**
father of Zeus **KRONOS, CRONUS, CRONOS**
father or mother **PARENT**
father's wife **MOTHER**
fathom **DELVE**
fatigue **TIRE, WEARY, WEARINESS**
Fatima's husband **ALI, BLUEBEARD**
fat lot **LITTLE, NOTHING**
fat of swine **LARD**
fat of the land **LUXURY**
fattened, as cattle (comp. wd.) **CORN-FED**
fatty **ADIPOSE**
fatuity **STUPIDITY**
fatuous **FOOLISH**
faubourg **SUBURB, QUARTER, SECTION**
faucet **SPIGOT, TAP**
fault **FLAW, FAILING**
faultfinder **CARPER**
faultfinding **CENSORIAL**
faultless **PERFECT, PURE**
faulty **AMISS**
faun **SATYR**
faux pas **ERROR**
favor **RESPECT, INDULGENCE, PARTIALITY**
favorable **HELPFUL**
favorable to progress **LIBERAL**
favoring **FOR, PRO**
favoring neither **NEUTRAL**
favorite **PET**
favoritism **BIAS, PREJUDICE**
fawn **DEER**
fawning **SERVILE, OBSEQUIOUS**
fay **FAIRY**
faze **DISTURB, DISCONCERT**
feal **LOYAL, FAITHFUL**
fealty **LOYALTY, HOMAGE**

fear **DREAD, TERROR, FRIGHT, ALARM**
fearful **ANXIOUS, AWFUL, DREADFUL**
fearless **BOLD, BRAVE**
fearsome **AWFUL, AWESOME, TIMID**
feasible **POSSIBLE**
Feast of Booths **SUCCOTH, SUKKOTH**
Feast of Lights **CHANUKAH**
Feast of Lots **PURIM**
Feast of Nativity **CHRISTMAS**
Feast of Weeks **SHAVUOT, SHABUOTH**
feat **ACHIEVEMENT, DEED**
feather **PLUME**
feather barb **PINNULA**
feathered friend **BIRD**
feathers **PLUMAGE, DOWN**
feather scarf **BOA**
feature **QUALITY, MOTIF**
febrile **FEVERISH**
fecund **FERTILE**
federal **NATIONAL**
federate **UNITE**
federation **ALLIANCE**
fedora **HAT**
fee **CHARGE**
feeble **WEAK, PUNY**
feeble-minded person **MORON, DOLT, IDIOT, IMBECILE**
feed **NOURISH**
feed the kitty **ANTE**
feed to fill **SATE**
feel **TOUCH, SENSE**
feel affection for **LIKE**
feel contrite **REPENT**
feeler **TENTACLE, ANTENNA, BARBEL**
feel indignation **RESENT**
feel indisposed **AIL, SICK**
feeling **SENSATION, EMOTION**
feeling deeply **INTENSE**
feeling of resentment **PEEVE**
feeling of weariness **ENNUI**
feel in the dark **GROPE**
feel intuitively **SENSE**
feel melancholy **GRIEVE**
feel one's way **GROPE**
feel regret **REPENT, RUE**
feel sorrow **MOURN**
feign **SHAM, PRETEND, PUT ON, ACT**
feign illness **MALINGER**
feint **SHAM**
feisty **AGGRESSIVE**

| | |
|---|---|
| felicitate | CONGRATULATE, GREET |
| felicity | BLISS, RAPTURE |
| feline | CAT |
| feline sound | MEW, MIAO, MEOW |
| feline treat | CATNIP |
| fell | CUT, BEAT |
| fellow | CHAP |
| fellowship | COMPANY, BROTHERHOOD |
| felon | CRIMINAL |
| felonious | MALICIOUS |
| felony | CRIME |
| female | WOMAN, GIRL |
| female antelope | DOE |
| female bird | HEN |
| female child | GIRL |
| female colt | FILLY |
| female deer | DOE |
| female deity | GODDESS |
| female domestic | MAID |
| female elephant | COW |
| female goat | NANNY |
| female hog | SOW |
| female horse | MARE |
| female host | HOSTESS |
| female knight | DAME |
| female monster | GORGON, MEDUSA, STHENO, EURYALE |
| female ovine | EWE |
| female parent | MOTHER |
| female pig | SOW |
| female relative | AUNT, MOTHER, DAUGHTER, SISTER, GRANDMA |
| female religious (abbr.) | SR. |
| female ruff | REEVE, REE |
| female sailor | WAVE |
| female saint (abbr.) | STE. |
| female sandpiper | REEVE, REE |
| female servant | MAID |
| female sheep | EWE |
| female sibling | SISTER |
| female's mate | MALE, HUSBAND |
| female soldier | WAC |
| female sovereign | PRINCESS, QUEEN |
| female spirit | BANSHEE, BANSHIE |
| female student | COED |
| female swimmer | MERMAID |
| female voice | ALTO, SOPRANO |
| female warrior | AMAZON |
| feminine | FEMALE, WOMANLY |
| feminine (suffix) | ETTE |
| feminine garment | SKIP, SKIRT, DRESS, BRA |
| feminine title | MADAM, MISS, MAM |
| femininity | WOMEN |
| femme fatale | SIREN |
| femur | THIGH |
| fen | MARSH, SWAMP, BOG |
| fence | WALL, HEDGE, RAIL |
| fence opening | GATE, TURNSTILE |
| fence post | STAKE |
| fencer | DUELIST |
| fence stake | POST |
| fence step | STILE |
| fence straddler's domain (4 wds.) | MIDDLE OF THE ROAD |
| fence timber | RAIL |
| fencing hit | PUNTO, TOUCHE |
| fencing position | CARTE |
| fencing sword | EPEE, FOIL, SABER |
| fend | PARRY, RESIST |
| fender | BUMPER |
| fender mishap | DENT |
| fennel genus | NIGELLA |
| fenstra | OPENING |
| fen water | MIRE |
| feral | WILD, SAVAGE |
| fermented drink | ALE, CIDER, WINE, BEER |
| fermenting vat | GYLE |
| fern genus | ANEMIA |
| fern leaf | FROND |
| ferocious | FIERCE, VIOLENT |
| ferret | WEASEL |
| ferrous metal | IRON |
| ferry | CARRY. TRANSPORT |
| fertile | FRUITFUL, FECUND |
| fertile spot in a desert | OASIS |
| fertilizer | MARL |
| fervent | ARDENT |
| fervent appeal | PLEA |
| fervor | ARDOR, ZEAL |
| festival | FETE, GALA, FAIR, FIESTA |
| festival of Passover | SEDER |
| festive | GALA |
| festivity | MIRTH, REVEL |
| feta | CHEESE |
| fetch | BRING |
| fete | GALA |
| fetid | RANK |
| fetish | TOTEM, IDOL |
| fetter | MANACLE, CHAIN |
| fettel | CONDITION |
| feud | DISPUTE, VENDETTA |
| feudal castle | MANOR |

| | |
|---|---|
| feudal chief | **LORD, OVERLORD, BARON** |
| feudal estate | **FIEF** |
| feudal slave | **SERF, ESNE** |
| feudal tenant | **VASSAL** |
| fever | **HEAT, FIRE** |
| feverish | **FEBRILE, EXCITED** |
| fewer | **LESS** |
| fewest | **LEAST** |
| fey | **ODD** |
| fez ornament | **TASSEL** |
| fiance | **BETROTHED, INTENDED** |
| fiasco | **FAILURE** |
| fiat | **DECREE, EDICT** |
| fib | **LIE** |
| fiber | **STAPLE, SISAL, KAPOK** |
| fiber cluster | **NEP** |
| fiber plant | **FLAX, HEMP, SISAL** |
| fibril | **HAIR** |
| fibula | **BUCKLE, CLASP** |
| fickle | **UNSTABLE, FAITHLESS** |
| fiction | **NOVEL** |
| fictional story | **TALE, YARN, NOVEL, FABLE, ROMANCE** |
| fictitious | **FALSE** |
| fictitious name | **ALIAS** |
| fiddling emperor | **NERO** |
| fidelity | **DEVOTION, LOYALTY** |
| Fidel's capital | **HAVANA** |
| fidget | **FUSS, FRET** |
| fidgety | **NERVOUS, RESTIVE** |
| Fido | **DOG** |
| Fido's offspring | **PUPPY, PUP** |
| Fido's treasure | **BONE** |
| fiduciary | **TRUSTEE** |
| fief | **FEE** |
| field | **LOT, CLEARING, AREA** |
| field edge | **RAND** |
| field flower | **DAISY** |
| field mouse | **VOLE** |
| field of action | **ARENA** |
| field of granular snow | **NEVE, FIRN** |
| fiend | **DEMON, DEVIL** |
| fiendish | **MALICIOUS** |
| fierce | **VIOLENT, FIERY** |
| fiery | **ARDENT, FIERCE, HOT** |
| fiery jewel | **OPAL** |
| fiesta | **FESTIVAL, HOLIDAY** |
| fifteenth century royal family | **PLANTAGENET, YORK, TUDOR, LANCASTER** |
| fifth tire | **SPARE** |
| fifth zodiac sign | **LEO** |
| fiftieth state | **HAWAII** |
| fifty percent | **HALF** |

| | |
|---|---|
| fight | **STRUGGLE, BATTLE, WAR, QUARREL** |
| fight against | **RESIST** |
| fighter pilot | **ACE** |
| fighter's exercise | **LEG WORK** |
| fighting equipment | **ARMS** |
| figure | **NUMBER, SHAPE** |
| figure applied to fabric | **APPLIQUE** |
| figure in a Millet painting | **GLEANER** |
| figure on a card | **SPADE, HEART, CLUB, DIAMOND** |
| filament | **THREAD** |
| filament for cloth | **FIBER** |
| filch | **PILFER, STEAL** |
| file | **RASP** |
| fill | **GLUT, SATE** |
| fill again | **REPLENISH** |
| fill a gun | **LOAD** |
| fill a suitcase | **PACK** |
| filled with interstices | **AREOLAR** |
| fill with ambition | **INSPIRE** |
| fill with determination | **STEEL** |
| fill with ennui | **BORE** |
| fill with joy | **ELATE** |
| fill with love | **ENAMOR** |
| fill with pride | **ELATE** |
| filly | **MARE** |
| film | **MOVIE, CINEMA** |
| film spool | **REEL** |
| filmy | **SHEER** |
| filter | **STRAIN** |
| filth | **DIRT** |
| filthy | **CRUDDY, DIRTY, SOILED** |
| filthy hut | **STY** |
| finagle | **SCHEME, CONTRIVE** |
| final | **LAST, ULTIMATE** |
| finale | **FINISH, CODA** |
| finalize | **COMPLETE** |
| finally (2 wds.) | **AT LAST** |
| finally and decisively (4 wds.) | **ONCE AND FOR ALL** |
| final opportunity (2 wds.) | **LAST CHANCE** |
| final performer (2 wds.) | **ANCHOR MAN** |
| financial | **FISCAL, PECUNIARY** |
| financial center in N.Y. (2 wds.) | **WALL STREET** |
| financially solvent (3 wds.) | **IN THE BLACK** |
| financial sponsor | **PATRON** |
| find | **DISCOVER, LOCATE** |
| find a sum | **ADD** |
| find direction | **ORIENT** |
| find fault | **NAG, CARP, CAVIL** |

| | |
|---|---|
| find guilty | **CONVICT** |
| finding | **CONCLUSION, SOLUTION** |
| find of treasure | **TROVE** |
| find out | **DISCOVER, DETECT** |
| find position of | **LOCATE** |
| find the answer | **SOLVE** |
| fine | **EXCELLENT, PENALTY, TARIFF** |
| fine bits of thread | **LINT** |
| fine cord | **THREAD** |
| fine cotton fabric | **BATISTE** |
| fine English china | **SPODE** |
| fine jet of water | **SPRAY** |
| fine line, in printing | **SERIF** |
| fine linen | **CAMBRIC** |
| finely | **NICELY** |
| fine porcelain | **SPODE, LIMOGES** |
| fine rock debris | **SAND** |
| finery | **GAUD, LUXURY** |
| fine sensitiveness | **DELICACY** |
| fine soil | **SILT** |
| finesse | **CUNNING, SUBTLETY** |
| finest | **BEST** |
| fine suiting | **TWEED, SERGE** |
| fine whetstone | **HONE** |
| finger | **DIGIT** |
| finger jewelry | **RING** |
| fingernail moon | **LUNULE** |
| fingerprint mark | **LOOP, WHORL** |
| finial | **EPI** |
| finis | **END** |
| finish | **END, CONCLUDE, TERMINATE, COMPLETE** |
| finished | **OVER, DONE** |
| finished garment edge | **HEM** |
| finish line | **TAPE** |
| finite | **LIMITED** |
| Finland | **SUOMI** |
| Finnish city | **HELSINKI, ABO** |
| Finnish lake | **ENARE** |
| Finnish steam bath | **SAUNA** |
| fiord | **INLET** |
| fire | **FLAME, BLAZE** |
| fire a gun | **SHOOT** |
| firearm | **GUN, RIFLE** |
| firebug's crime | **ARSON** |
| firecracker | **PETARD** |
| firedog | **ANDIRON** |
| fire god | **VULCAN, YAMA** |
| fireman | **STOKER** |
| fire opal | **GIRASOL** |
| fireplace | **GRATE, HEARTH** |
| fireplace facing | **MANTEL** |
| fireplace fuel | **LOGS, COAL, PEAT** |
| fireplace shelf | **HOB, MANTLE** |
| fireplug | **HYDRANT** |

| | |
|---|---|
| fire residue | **ASH, ASHES** |
| fire-stirring rod | **POKER** |
| firewater | **WHISKEY, LIQUOR** |
| fire whistle | **SIREN** |
| firewood | **FUEL** |
| fireworks | **ROCKETS, SPARKLERS** |
| firm | **HARD, SOLID, STRICT, STERN** |
| firmament | **SKY, HEAVEN** |
| firm grasp | **GRIP** |
| firmly established | **DEEP-SET** |
| firn | **NEVE** |
| first | **PRIMAL, LEADING** |
| first appearance | **DEBUT** |
| first beginning | **ORIGIN** |
| first class | **PRIME** |
| first day | **SUNDAY** |
| first drawing | **DRAFT** |
| first garden | **EDEN** |
| first Hebrew letter | **ALEPH, ALEF** |
| first king of Israel | **SAUL** |
| first king of Rome | **ROMULUS** |
| first man | **ADAM** |
| first performance | **DEBUT, PREMIERE** |
| first person | **I, ME** |
| first principle | **ELEMENT** |
| first-rate | **SUPER, A ONE, TOP NOTCH** |
| first reader | **PRIMER** |
| first-row position (2 wds.) | **IN FRONT, UP FRONT** |
| first state | **DELAWARE** |
| first water | **BEST, PUREST** |
| first woman | **EVE** |
| first word of Caesar's boast | **VENI** |
| first word on the wall | **MENE** |
| first zodiac sign | **ARIES** |
| firth | **ESTUARY** |
| fisc | **TREASURY, EXCHEQUER** |
| fiscal | **FINANCIAL** |
| fiscal department | **TREASURY** |
| fiscal officer | **TREASURER, CONTROLLER** |
| fish | **ANGLE, DACE, IDE, TUNA, GAR, CARP, SHAD, SOLE, PIKE, PORGY, RAY, SHARK, SKATE** |
| fish appendage | **FIN** |
| fish bait | **WORM** |
| fish basket | **CREEL** |
| fish bowl | **AQUARIUM** |
| fish-catching fence | **WEIR** |
| fish-eating diving bird | **LOON** |

| | | | |
|---|---|---|---|
| fish-eating mammal | OTTER, WHALE, DOLPHIN, SEAL, PORPOISE | fix | REPAIR |
| | | fix definitely | SETTLE |
| | | fixed | SET |
| fish eggs | ROE | fixed charge | FEE, RATE |
| fisherman's boot | WADER | fixed in position | STABILE |
| fisherman's snare | NET | fixed pay | STIPEND, SALARY |
| fish fin (Sp.) | ALETA | fixed period of time | TERM |
| fish from moving boat | TROLL | fixed prices | RATES |
| fish gig | SPEAR | fixed residence | HOME |
| fish hawk | OSPREY | fixed routine | ROTE |
| fishhook leader | SNELL | fixed star | VEGA |
| fishhook part | BARB | fixed time period | TERM |
| fishing appurtenance | CORK, FLOAT | fix up | MEND |
| | | fizz | HISS, BUBBLE |
| fishing cork | FLOAT | flabby | WEAK, LIMP |
| fishing duck | MERGANSER, SHELDRAKE | flaccid | LIMP |
| | | flag | BANNER, IRIS, CATTAIL |
| fishing eagle | OSPREY | flag flower | IRIS |
| fishing float | BOBBER | flagon | FLASK, BOTTLE |
| fishing fly | LURE | flagrant | GLARING |
| fishing gear | TACKLE | flagstone | SLAB |
| fishing lure | BAIT | flail | BEAT, FLOG |
| fishing net | SEINE, TRAWL | flair | KNACK, TALENT |
| fishing pole | ROD | flair for gardening (2 wds.) | GREEN THUMB |
| fishing rod | POLE | | |
| fishing snare | NET | flaky storm | SNOW |
| fishing vessel | SMACK, BOAT, TRAWLER | flam | CHEAT, TRICK |
| | | flamboyant | ORNATE, GARISH |
| fish limb | FIN | flame | BLAZE, FIRE |
| fish lung | GILL | flaming | ARDENT |
| fish lure | BAIT | flaming light | TORCH |
| fish nostril | GILL | flame-loving insect | MOTH |
| fish of the carp family | DACE | Flanders treaty city | GHENT |
| fishpound | WEIR | flank | SIDE |
| fish roe | CAVIAR, EGGS | flare | FLAME, FLICKER |
| fish sauce | ALEC | flash | FLARE, BLAZE |
| fish spear | GIG | flash lamp | STROBE |
| fish through ice | CHUG | flashlight (Brit.) | TORCH |
| fish trap | EELPOT, WEIR | flash of lightning | BOLT |
| fish with a moving line | TROLL | flash out | GLINT |
| fishy | SUSPECT | flashy | GAUDY, GARISH |
| fissile rock | SHALE | flask | AMPULE, CANTEEN |
| fission | DIVISION | flat | LEVEL, EVEN, SMOOTH, TENEMENT, APARTMENT |
| fissure | CLEFT | | |
| fisticuffs | BOXING | flat and even | LEVEL |
| fistula | CAVITY | flatbed | TRUCK |
| fit | SUITABLE, PROPER | flat-bottomed boat | BARGE, DORY, PUNT, SCOW |
| fit for farming | ARABLE | | |
| fitful | RESTLESS | flat cap | BERET |
| fitness | DECORUM | flat circular plate | DISK |
| fit of anger | HUFF, RAGE | flat disc-like sea urchin (2 wds.) | SAND DOLLAR |
| fit of petulance | RAGE, TANTRUM | flatfish | SOLE |
| | | flat fold in cloth | PLEAT |
| fit of resentment | PIQUE | flatfoot | COP, DETECTIVE |
| fit of temper | TANTRUM | flat hat | CAP |
| fit out | EQUIP | flatland form | MESA |
| fit together closely | DOVETAIL | flat shallow container | TRAY |
| fit to one's use | ADAPT | | |

| | |
|---|---|
| flat surface | **PLANE** |
| flat tableland | **MESA** |
| flatten | **DEPRESS, EVEN** |
| flatter | **COMPLIMENT, PRAISE** |
| flattery (2 wds.) | **SWEET TALK** |
| flaunt | **BRANDISH** |
| flavor | **SAPOR, TASTE, SEASON** |
| flavoring plant | **ANISE** |
| flavorsome | **TASTY** |
| flaw | **DEFECT** |
| flawless | **PERFECT** |
| flaxen | **WHITE, TOW** |
| flax fabric | **LINEN** |
| flaxseed | **LINSEED** |
| flay | **REPROVE** |
| fled | **RAN** |
| flee | **LAM, RUN, SPLIT, ESCAPE** |
| fleecy white clouds | **CIRRI** |
| flee in panic, as cattle | |
| | **STAMPEDE** |
| fleet | **FAST** |
| fleet of ships | **NAVY, ARMADA** |
| Flemish | **DUTCH** |
| flesh | **MEAT** |
| flesh and blood | **MORTAL** |
| fleshy | **BEEFY, PLUMP** |
| fleshy berry | **PEPO** |
| fleshy fruit | **PEAR, APPLE,** |
| | **PEACH** |
| fleur de lis | **LILY, IRIS** |
| flex | **BEND, CONTRACT** |
| flexible | **LIMP, PLIABLE** |
| flexible tube | **HOSE** |
| flexor | **MUSCLE** |
| flick | **MOVIE** |
| flicker | **WAVER** |
| Flickertail State | |
| | **NORTH DAKOTA** |
| flier | **AVIATOR, PILOT** |
| flight | **FLYING, HOP** |
| flightless bird | **EMU, MOA,** |
| | **RATITE** |
| flight of steps | **STAIRS** |
| flighty person | **RATTLEBRAIN** |
| flimflam | **NONSENSE, SWINDLE** |
| flimsy | **THIN, TRANSPARENT** |
| flinch | **WINCE** |
| fling | **TOSS, CAST, THROW** |
| flint | **FIRESTONE, CHERT** |
| flip | **TOSS** |
| flippant | **GLIB** |
| flipper | **FIN** |
| flippered animal | **SEAL** |
| flirt | **OGLE** |
| flit | **DART** |
| float | **RAFT, WAFT** |
| floating home | **HOUSEBOAT** |

| | |
|---|---|
| floating ice mass | **BERG, FLOE,** |
| | **ICEBERG** |
| float in the air | **SOAR, LEVITATE** |
| float of logs | **RAFT** |
| float on water | **BOB** |
| float upward | **RISE, SURFACE** |
| flock | **BEVY, HERD** |
| flock member | **EWE, RAM, LAMB** |
| flock of herons | **SEDGE** |
| flock tender | **SHEPHERD** |
| floe | **BERG** |
| flog | **LASH** |
| flood | **DELUGE** |
| flooded stream | **FRESHET** |
| flood gate | **SLUICE** |
| floor | **STORY** |
| floor covering | **CARPET, RUG,** |
| | **MAT, TILE, LINEOLEUM,** |
| | **SKIN** |
| flooring square | **TILE** |
| flora | **PLANTS** |
| flora and fauna | **BIOTA** |
| floral emblem of Wales | **LEEK** |
| floral ornament | **ROSETTE** |
| Florentine family | **MEDICI** |
| Florentine iris | **ORRIS** |
| florid | **ORNATE** |
| Florida city | **MIAMI, TAMPA,** |
| | **SARASOTA, OCALA** |
| Florida county | **DADE** |
| Florida food fish | **POMPANO** |
| Florida game fish | **SNAPPER** |
| Florida Indian | **SEMINOLE** |
| Florida islets | **KEYS** |
| Florida key | **LARGO, WEST** |
| Florida race track | **HIALEAH** |
| Florida region | **EVERGLADES** |
| flotilla | **NAVY, FLEET** |
| flounder | **FISH** |
| flourish | **GROW, PROSPER** |
| flour manufacturer | **MILLER** |
| flout | **JEER, SCORN, SPURN** |
| flow | **RUN** |
| flow back | **EBB, RECEDE** |
| flower | **ASTER, CANNA, LILY,** |
| | **DANDELION, ROSE, DAHLIA,** |
| | **ZINNIA, PEONY, TULIP, MUM,** |
| | **DAISY, POSY, PRIMROSE,** |
| | **LILAC, ARUM, PANSY,** |
| | **GERANIUM, VIOLET, PHLOX,** |
| | **PETUNIA, BEGONIA, PINK,** |
| | **CARNATION, STOCK, SEDUM,** |
| | **MARIGOLD, ANEMONE,** |
| | **POPPY, CLOVER, IRIS,** |
| | **FOXGLOVE, GEUM, CROCUS** |
| flower band | **WREATH** |
| flower circle | **WREATH** |
| flower holder | **VASE, URN** |

| | |
|---|---|
| flowering climbing plant | **SMILAX** |
| flower leaf | **PETAL, SEPAL** |
| flowerless plant | **MOSS, VINE, FERN, IVY** |
| flower of Holland | **TULIP** |
| flower part | **PETAL, SEPAL, STEM, STALK** |
| flower plot | **BED** |
| flower stalk | **STEM** |
| flower-to-be | **BUD** |
| flowing | **FLUENT, COPIOUS** |
| flowing forth | **EMANATE** |
| flowing garment | **ROBE, CAPE** |
| flowing oil well | **GUSHER** |
| flub | **BLUNDER** |
| fluctuate | **WAVER** |
| flue | **CHIMNEY** |
| fluent | **LIQUID, SMOOTH** |
| fluent in speech | **GLIB** |
| fluff | **DOWN, FLOSS** |
| fluff from cloth | **LINT** |
| fluffy | **SOFT** |
| fluid | **LIQUID, WATER** |
| fluid measure | **DRAM, PINT, QUART, CUP** |
| fluid rock | **LAVA** |
| flunk | **FAIL** |
| flurry | **ADO, BUSTLE** |
| flush | **BLUSH, REDDEN** |
| flush with success | **ELATE** |
| flute | **WOODWIND** |
| flutelike instrument | **OBOE** |
| flutter | **FLAP, WAVE, WAVER** |
| flutter over | **HOVER** |
| fly | **SOAR, WING, AVIATE** |
| fly before the wind | **SCUD** |
| flyer | **PILOT, ACE** |
| fly high | **SOAR** |
| flying (3 wds.) | **ON THE WING** |
| flying boat | **SEAPLANE** |
| flying body | **METEOR** |
| flying creature | **BIRD** |
| flying equipment | **WING** |
| flying fish | **SAURY** |
| flying honker | **GOOSE** |
| flying machine | **PLANE** |
| flying mammal | **BAT** |
| flying saucer (abbr.) | **UFO** |
| flying toy | **KITE** |
| fly quickly | **FLIT** |
| fly's enemy | **SPIDER** |
| flyspeck | **ERROR, FLAW, SPOT** |
| foal | **HORSE, COLT** |
| foam | **SPUME, FROTH, LATHER** |
| foaming | **SPUMOUS, SUDSY** |
| fob | **POCKET, CHAIN** |
| focus | **CENTER, CONVERGE** |
| fodder | **FEED, SILAGE** |

| | |
|---|---|
| fodder storage structure | **SILO** |
| fodder tower | **SILO** |
| foe | **ADVERSARY, ENEMY** |
| fog | **MIST, HAZE** |
| fog and smoke | **SMOG** |
| foggy | **CLOUDY, DIM** |
| foghorn | **SIREN** |
| foible | **WEAKNESS** |
| foil | **FRUSTRATE, SWORD** |
| fold | **NAP, CREASE** |
| folder | **LEAFLET** |
| folding bed | **COT** |
| folding money | **DOLLAR** |
| fold of cloth | **PLEAT** |
| fold of skin | **DEWLAP** |
| fold over | **LAP** |
| foliage | **LEAVES** |
| folio | **BOOK** |
| folk | **PEOPLE** |
| folk knowledge | **LORE** |
| folklore | **LEGENDS** |
| folklore creatures | **GNOME, TROLL, ELF, SPRITE** |
| folklore genie | **SANDMAN** |
| folksinger Ives | **BURL** |
| folksinger Guthrie | **WOODY, ARLO** |
| folksinger Seeger | **PETE** |
| folk song | **BLUES** |
| folkways | **MORES** |
| follow | **ENSUE, TAIL, CHASE** |
| follower | **ITE, ADHERENT** |
| follow exactly | **TRACE** |
| following | **AFTER** |
| following story | **SEQUEL** |
| follow orders | **OBEY** |
| follow secretly | **SHADOW** |
| follow the chase | **HUNT** |
| folly | **MADNESS** |
| fond | **LOVING** |
| fondle | **CARESS, PET** |
| fondly | **TENDERLY** |
| fondness | **AFFECTION, LOVE** |
| font | **POOL, POND, BASIN** |
| food | **CHOW, EATS, VICTUALS, GRUB, EATABLES, EDIBLES, NOURISHMENT** |
| food constituent | **VITAMIN** |
| food container | **CAN, TIN, JAR, BOX** |
| food counter | **BAR** |
| food dressing | **SAUCE** |
| food fish | **COD, BASS, SOLE, SHAD, TROUT, EEL, HALIBUT, TUNA, SALMON** |
| food for animals | **FORAGE** |
| food for cattle | **FODDER** |
| food for infants | **PAP** |

| | | | |
|---|---|---|---|
| food from heaven | **MANNA** | footrest | **OTTOMAN, HASSOCK** |
| food of the gods | **AMBROSIA** | foot trail | **PATH** |
| food quickly prepared (2 wds.) | | footwear | **SHOES** |
| | **SHORT ORDER** | foozle | **BUNGLE** |
| food regimen | **DIET** | fop | **DANDY** |
| food sauce | **CONDIMENT** | for | **PRO** |
| food scrap | **ORT** | for (Sp.) | **POR** |
| food served | **MENU** | forage | **BROWSE** |
| food shortage | **FAMINE** | forage acre | **PASTURE** |
| foodstuff | **CEREAL** | forage grass | **REDTOP** |
| food topping | **SAUCE, GARNISH** | forage plant | **CLOVER** |
| fool | **ASS, IDIOT** | foray | **RAID** |
| fool away | **FRITTER** | forbear | **ABSTAIN** |
| foolhardy | **BRASH, RASH** | forbearance | **MERCY** |
| fool hen | **GROUSE** | forbid | **BAN** |
| foolish | **INANE, SILLY** | forbidden | **TABOO** |
| foolish act | **FOLLY, BONER** | Forbidden City | **LHASA, LASA** |
| foolishness | **NONSENSE** | forbidding | **GRIM** |
| foolish person | **GOOSE, DOLT** | force | **COMPEL, OBLIGE, DINT,** |
| foolish show | **FARCE** | | **POWER, STRENGTH** |
| foolproof | **SIMPLE** | force (Lat.) | **VIS** |
| foolscap | **PAPER** | forced | **COMPELLED,** |
| fool's gold | **PYRITE** | | **COMPULSORY** |
| fool's paradise | **LIMBO** | forced laborer | **SLAVE** |
| foot | **PES, HOOF** | forceful blow | **BASH** |
| foot affliction | **CORN** | force into less space | **COMPRESS** |
| footage | **LENGTH** | force onward | **URGE** |
| football cheer | **RAH** | force to go | **DRIVE OUT** |
| football in England | **RUGBY** | force unit | **DYNE** |
| football kick | **PUNT** | for credit | **ON THE CUFF** |
| football pass | **LATERAL** | ford a stream | **WADE** |
| football play | **DROP KICK,** | for each | **PER** |
| | **TOUCHDOWN, PUNT, RUN,** | for each person | **APIECE** |
| | **PASS** | forearm bone | **ULNA** |
| football player | **BACK, END,** | forebear | **ANCESTOR** |
| | **CENTER, TACKLE,** | forebode | **AUGUR** |
| | **FULLBACK, HALFBACK** | foreboding | **OMEN,** |
| football score | **TOUCHDOWN** | | **PREMONITION** |
| football team | **ELEVEN** | forebrain | **PROSENCEPHALON** |
| foot bone | **TARSUS** | forecast | **PRESAGE** |
| footboy | **PAGE** | forecaster | **SEER** |
| foot covering | **SHOE, BOOT,** | foreclose | **DEBAR, PREVENT** |
| | **SOCK** | forefather | **ANCESTOR** |
| foot digit | **TOE** | forefinger | **INDEX** |
| footed vase | **URN** | forego | **PRECEDE** |
| footing | **POSITION** | foregoing | **FORMER** |
| foot it | **SCUD** | forehead | **BROW** |
| footless | **APOD** | foreign | **STRANGE, ALIEN** |
| foot lever | **PEDAL** | foreign agent | **SPY** |
| footlike part | **PES** | foreigner | **ALIEN** |
| footlocker | **TRUNK** | foreign service residence | |
| footloose | **FREE** | | **CONSULATE** |
| footnote | **ADDITION, P.S.** | foreknow | **PRECONCEIVE** |
| foot part | **TOE, HEEL, INSTEP,** | foreknowledge | **PRESCIENCE** |
| | **ARCH, SOLE, BALL** | forlock | **BANGS** |
| footpath | **TRAIL** | foreman | **BOSS, MANAGER** |
| footprint | **STEP, TRACK** | foremost | **LEADING, FIRST** |
| footrace | **DASH** | | |

| | |
|---|---|
| forenoon (abbr.) | A.M. |
| forensic | RHETORICAL |
| foreordain | DESTINE |
| forepiece of a cap | VISOR |
| forest | WOODS |
| forestall | AVERT |
| forest animal | DEER, BEAR |
| forest clearing | GLADE |
| forest god | PAN |
| forest home | CABIN |
| forest open space | GLADE |
| forest ox | ANOA |
| forest warden | RANGER |
| foretell | BODE |
| foretoken | OMEN |
| forever | ALWAYS, AYE |
| foreword | PREFACE |
| for example (abbr.) | E.G. |
| for fear that | LEST |
| forfeit | LOSE, PENALTY |
| forge | SMITHY |
| forget | OMIT |
| forgive | CONDONE, PARDON |
| forgo | QUIT, WAIVE |
| for instance | AS |
| fork over | PAY |
| fork prong | TINE |
| forlorn | FORSAKEN, DESOLATE |
| form | MOLD, SHAPE |
| form a jelly | GEL |
| formal | STIFF |
| formal argument | DEBATE |
| formal attitude | POSE |
| formal dance | BALL |
| formal dress | GOWN |
| formal letter | EPISTLE |
| formalities | ETIQUETTE |
| formality | CEREMONY |
| formal meeting | CONFERENCE |
| formal objection | PROTEST |
| formal procession | PARADE |
| formal speech | ORATION, ADDRESS |
| formal structure | FORMATION |
| form a spider web | SPIN |
| format | PLAN |
| formed at the base of mountains | PIEDMONT |
| formed by the sea | MARINE |
| formed like a needle | ACERATE |
| formed like lips | LABIAL |
| for men only | STAG |
| former | ONE TIME, ONCE |
| former boy | MAN |
| former candidate Stevenson | ADLAI |
| former college man | ALUMNUS |

| | |
|---|---|
| former European coin | DUCAT |
| former French premier | DE GAULLE |
| former German coin | TALER, KRONA |
| former Japanese statesman | ITO |
| former labor group (abbr.) | IWW |
| formerly | ERST, ONCE |
| formerly Persia | IRAN |
| former Moslem edict | IRADE |
| former New York governor | DEWEY |
| former Russian ruler | TZAR, CZAR |
| former screen star (2 wds.) | GRETA GARBO, PEARL WHITE, THEDA BARA |
| former Soviet leader | LENIN, STALIN, KHRUSHCHEV |
| former state in Germany | PRUSSIA |
| former time | PAST |
| former Turkish president | INONU |
| former President's nickname | IKE |
| formicary | ANTHILL |
| formidable | ALARMING, APPALLING |
| forming container | MOLD |
| form of architecture | DORIC, IONIC |
| form of hoisting crane | DAVIT |
| form of polite address | MADAM |
| Formosa | TAIWAN |
| Formosa city | TAIPEI |
| formula | RECIPE |
| for nothing | GRATIS |
| forsake | LEAVE, DEPART, GO, DESERT, ABANDON, STRAND |
| forsaken | DESOLATE |
| forswear | REJECT, RENOUNCE |
| fort | STRONGHOLD |
| forth | FORWARD |
| forthcoming | DUE |
| for the most part | IN GENERAL, MAINLY |
| forthwith | AT ONCE |
| fortification | REDAN |
| fortify | ARM |
| fortitude | STRENGTH |
| fortress | TOWER |
| fortuitous | ACCIDENTAL |
| fortuity | CHANCE |
| fortunate | LUCKY |
| fortune | LOT, LUCK, FATE |

| | |
|---|---|
| forty winks | **NAP** |
| forward | **ON** |
| forward part | **FRONT** |
| forward part of a ship | **PROW,** |
| | **BOW** |
| for what reason | **WHY** |
| foss | **DITCH, MOAT** |
| fossil | **BONE** |
| foster | **PROMOTE** |
| foul | **FILTHY, NASTY** |
| foulard | **SCARF, TIE** |
| found | **BASE, ESTABLISH** |
| foundation | **BASE, BASIS** |
| founded on experience | **EMPIRICAL** |
| founder | **STUMBLE, FAIL** |
| founder of Carthage | **DIDO** |
| foundling | **WAIF, ORPHAN** |
| fountain | **WELLHEAD** |
| fountain drink | **COLA, SODA,** |
| **SHAKE, MALTED, FLOAT,** | |
| | **COOLER** |
| fountain man (2 wds.) | **SODA JERK** |
| fountain nymph | **NAIAD** |
| four | **TETRAD** |
| four (Ger.) | **VIER** |
| four (prefix) | **TETRA, TETR** |
| four-door car | **SEDAN** |
| four-flush | **BLUFF** |
| four-in-hand | **TIE, CRAVAT** |
| fourpenny | **NAIL** |
| four-poster | **BED** |
| fourth estate | **PRESS** |
| fourth month | **APRIL** |
| fowl | **BIRD** |
| fowl product | **EGG** |
| fox's foot | **PAD** |
| foxy | **SLY, CRAFTY** |
| foyer | **LOBBY** |
| fracas | **SET-TO** |
| fraction | **PART, DIVISION** |
| fractious | **CROSS, FRETFUL** |
| fracture | **BREAK** |
| fragile | **DELICATE,** |
| **BREAKABLE, FRAIL** | |
| fragment | **CHIP, PIECE, SCRAP,** |
| **SHRED, WISP, SHARD** | |
| fragment left at meal | **ORT** |
| fragment of earthern vessel | **SHARD** |
| fragrance | **AROMA, ODOR,** |
| **SCENT, BOUQUET,** | |
| | **PERFUME** |
| fragrant | **OLENT, REDOLENT** |
| fragrant ointment | **BALM, NARD** |
| fragrant plant | **MINT** |
| fragrant root in perfume | **ORRIS** |
| fragrant wood | **CEDAR** |
| frail | **WEAK, DELICATE,** |
| | **FRAGILE** |
| frailty | **WEAKNESS** |
| frambesia | **YAWS** |
| frame | **FORM, CONSTRUCT,** |
| | **OUTLINE** |
| frame for stretching | **TENTER** |
| frame of mind | **MOOD** |
| framework | **LATTICE** |
| France | **GAUL** |
| franchise | **RIGHT, LICENSE** |
| franchised | **PATENTED** |
| Franciscan | **FRIAR, MONK** |
| Franco's land | **SPAIN** |
| frangible | **FRAGILE** |
| frank | **OPEN, CANDID** |
| Frankish | **GALIC** |
| Franklin | **BEN** |
| frankness | **CANDOR** |
| frantic | **FRENZIED** |
| frantic cry | **HELP** |
| frappe | **ICED** |
| fraternal | **BROTHERLY** |
| fraternal member | **ELK** |
| fraternize | **ASSOCIATE** |
| fraud | **FAKER, FAKERY, PHONY** |
| fraud (2 wds.) | **MARE'S NEST** |
| fraudulent | **FAKE, CUNNING** |
| fraught | **LADEN** |
| fray | **RAVEL, BATTLE** |
| frazzle | **WEAR, FRAY** |
| freak | **MONSTER, QUIRK** |
| freakish | **ODD, QUEER** |
| freckle | **SPOT** |
| Fred Astaire's sister | **ADELE** |
| free | **LOOSE, UNFETTERED,** |
| **RELEASE, RID, LIBERATE,** | |
| | **GRATIS** |
| free access (2 wds.) | **OPEN DOOR** |
| free and easy | **INFORMAL** |
| free commercial | **PLUG** |
| freedom | **LIBERTY, LICENSE** |
| freedom from activity | **REST,** |
| | **RESPITE** |
| freedom from narrow restrictions | **LATITUDE** |
| freedom from strife | **PEACE** |
| freedom from worry (3 wds.) | **PEACE OF MIND** |
| freedom of access | **ENTREE** |
| freedom of action | **LEEWAY** |
| free entertainment | **TREAT** |
| free food or money | **HANDOUT** |
| free-for-all | **FRACAS** |

| | | | |
|---|---|---|---|
| free from bacteria | ASEPTIC | French river | ISERE, LOIRE, OISE, SEINE |
| free from coarseness | REFINED | | |
| free from danger | RESCUE, SAFE, SECURE | French school | ECOLE, LYCEE |
| | | French sculptor | RODIN |
| free from guilt (3 wds.) | IN THE CLEAR | French service cap | KEPI |
| | | French shooting contest | TIR |
| free from liability | EXEMPT | French short story | CONTE |
| free from suspicion | ABSOLVE, CLEAR | French singer | CHANTEUSE |
| | | French stock exchange | BOURSE |
| freely | WILLINGLY | French street | RUE |
| free ticket | PASS | French subway | METRO |
| free time | LEISURE | frenzied | FRANTIC, MAD |
| freeway | PIKE | frenzy | FUROR, RAGE |
| freeze | CHILL, ICE | frequent | FAMILIAR, USUAL |
| freezing rain | SLEET | frequent a place | HAUNT |
| freight | CARGO | frequently | OFTEN |
| freighted | LADEN | frequently (poet.) | OFT |
| freighter | SHIP | fresh | NEW, STRONG |
| French annual income | RENTE | freshen | PERK |
| French article | LE, LA, LES, UN, UNE | freshet | STREAM |
| | | freshwater duck | TEAL |
| French author | DUMAS, HUGO | freshwater fish | CARP, IDE, DACE, PIKE |
| French capital | PARIS | freshwater porpoise | INIA |
| French cheese | BRIE | fret | WORRY, STEW |
| French chemist | PASTEUR | fretful | CROSS |
| French city | BREST, PARIS, NICE, NIMES, METZ, LILLE | friar | MONK |
| | | friar's title | FRA |
| | | friend | CHUM, PAL, BUDDY, MATE |
| French cleric | ABBE, PERE | | |
| French coin | SOU, ECU, FRANC | friend (Fr.) | AMI |
| French composer | BIZET, RAVEL | friend (Sp.) | AMIGO |
| | | friendly correspondent (2 wds.) | PEN PAL |
| French conjunction | ET | Friendly Islands | TONGA |
| French dance | CANCAN | friendly talk | CHAT |
| French dog | POODLE | friend of Peter Pan | WENDY |
| French dramatist | RACINE, ANOUILH | friendship | AMITY |
| | | frieze | BORDER |
| French duke | DUC | frigate | SHIP |
| French edict | ARRET | fright | PANIC, FEAR |
| French father | PERE | frighten | SCARE, TERRIFY |
| French friend | AMI | frighten away | SHOO |
| French impressionist | MANET, MONET | frightful | AWFUL, HORRIBLE |
| | | frigid | COLD, ICY, FROZEN |
| French island | ILE | frill | RUCHE, LACE |
| French cream | CREME | frilly trimming | LACE, RUFFLE |
| Frenchman | GAUL | fringe | EDGE |
| French negative | NON | fringed ornament | TASSEL |
| French noble | DUC | frisk | FROLIC, CAVORT |
| French painter | DEGAS, MANET, MONET, RENOIR, DAVID | frisky | PLAYFUL |
| | | frisson | CHILL, SHIVER |
| French pirate in America | LAFITTE | frivolous | PETTY, TRIVIAL |
| | | frock | DRESS |
| French police | SURETE | froglike amphibian | TOAD |
| French resort | NICE, NIMES, CANNES | frog's sound | CROAK |
| | | frolic | CAPER, REVEL, ROMP, SPREE |
| French revolutionary leader | MARAT | | |

| | | | |
|---|---|---|---|
| from | **OF** | fruit seed | **PIP, PIT** |
| from a distance | **AFAR** | fruit skin | **PEEL, RIND** |
| from head to foot | | fruit spread | **JELLY, JAM,** |
| (comp. wd.) | **CAP-A-PIE** | | **PRESERVE, MARMALADE** |
| from now on | **HENCEFORTH** | fruit stone | **PIT** |
| from one side to the other | | fruit sugar | **FRUCTOSE** |
| | **ACROSS** | frump | **DOWDY** |
| from the heart | **SINCERE** | frustrate | **FOIL** |
| from the time of | **SINCE** | frustrator of plan | **MARPLOT** |
| from this place | **NATIVE** | fry | **YOUNG, BROOD** |
| frond | **LEAF** | fryer | **CHICKEN** |
| front | **FORE, VAN** | frying pan | **SPIDER, GRIDDLE,** |
| frontage | **FACADE, EXPOSURE** | | **SKILLET** |
| frontier merchant | **TRADER** | fry quickly | **SAUTE** |
| frontiersman | **BOONE,** | fuchsia | **PURPLE** |
| | **CROCKETT** | fucus | **PAINT, DYE** |
| frontier transportation | **STAGE** | fudge | **CANDY** |
| front lawn | **YARD** | fuel | **COAL, WOOD, GAS, PEAT,** |
| front part of a coat | **LAPEL** | | **OIL** |
| frontrunner | **LEADER** | fuel-carrying ship | **COALER,** |
| frost a cake | **ICE** | | **OILER, TANKER** |
| frosting | **ICE, ICING** | fuel-conveying tube. | |
| frosty | **ICY, HAUGHTY** | (2 wds.) | **GAS PIPE** |
| frothy | **FOAMY, SPUMOUS** | fugitive | **REFUGEE, RUNAWAY** |
| frothy brew | **ALE** | Fujiyama, e.g. | **VOLCANO** |
| frothy dessert | **MOUSSE** | fulcrum | **SUPPORT, PROP** |
| froufrou | **SWISH, RUSTLE** | fulfill | **FINISH, COMPLETE** |
| frown | **SCOWL** | fulfill a command | **OBEY** |
| frowsy | **UNKEMPT, MESSY** | fulfill the demands of | **SATISFY** |
| frozen dessert | **FRAPPE, ICE,** | full | **REPLETE, SATED** |
| | **ICE CREAM, GLACE** | full-length | **UNABRIDGED,** |
| frozen pendant | **ICICLE** | | **UNCUT** |
| frozen rain | **SLEET, HAIL** | fullness | **PLENUM** |
| frozen water | **ICE** | full of (suffix) | **OSE** |
| fructuous | **FRUITFUL** | full of ecstatic joy | **RAPTUROUS** |
| frugal | **SAVING, THRIFTY** | full of happenings | **EVENTFUL** |
| frugality | **ECONOMY** | full of holes, as a roof | **LEAKY** |
| fruit | **LEMON, LIME, ORANGE,** | full of life | **ANIMATE** |
| | **APPLE, PEAR, MELON,** | full of meaning | **PITHY** |
| | **PEACH** | full of ringlets | **CURLY** |
| fruit center | **CORE** | full of small openings | **POROUS** |
| fruit covering | **PERICARP** | full of vigor | **PEPPY** |
| fruit decay | **BLET** | full of zest | **RACY** |
| fruit drink | **ADE, CIDER,** | fully | **WHOLLY, UTTERLY** |
| | **NECTAR, JUICE** | fully grown | **ADULT, MATURE** |
| fruitful | **FERTILE** | fully sufficient | **ADEQUATE** |
| fruit in bunches | **BANANA,** | fulsome | **INSINCERE** |
| | **GRAPE** | Fulton's folly | **CLERMONT** |
| fruition | **FULFILLMENT** | fume | **REEK, SMOKE** |
| fruit jar rubber ring | **LUTE** | fun | **AMUSEMENT, SPORT** |
| fruitless | **VAIN, IDLE** | function | **ROLE** |
| fruit of a palm | **DATE, FIG** | fund | **STOCK, STORE** |
| fruit of Jove | **PERSIMMON** | fundamental | **BASAL, BASIC** |
| fruit of paradise | **POMELO** | funeral bell | **TOLL, KNELL** |
| fruit of pine | **CONE** | funeral hymn | **DIRGE** |
| fruit or vegetable dish | **SALAD** | fungus | **MILDEW, MOLD** |
| fruit pastry | **PIE, TART** | funny | **COMIC, AMUSING** |
| fruit preserve | **COMPOTE** | | |

| | |
|---|---|
| fur-bearing animal | **MARTEN, OTTER, SEAL, MINK, RABBIT, SABLE** |
| fur-cloak | **PELISSE** |
| furious | **IRATE, MAD, ANGRY** |
| furlough | **LEAVE** |
| furnace | **OVEN, OAST, KILN** |
| furnish | **PROVIDE, DECORATE** |
| furnished with shoes | **SHOD** |
| furnish food | **CATER** |
| furnish with weapons | **ARM** |
| furnishings | **FURNITURE** |
| furniture item | **BED, COUCH, CHAIR, TABLE, SOFA, DAVENPORT** |
| furniture polish | **WAX** |
| furniture set | **DINETTE, SUITE** |
| furniture wheel | **CASTER** |
| furor | **HOOPLA** |
| furrow | **SEAM** |
| furs | **PELTRY** |
| further | **ADVANCE** |
| further direction | **REFERRAL** |
| furthermore | **MOREOVER** |
| furtive | **SNEAKY, STEALTHY** |
| furtive glimpse | **PEEP, PEEK** |
| fur wrap | **STOLE** |
| fury | **RAGE** |
| furze genus | **ULEX** |
| fuse | **CIRCUIT** |
| fused by heat | **MOLTEN** |
| fuse together | **WELD** |
| fuss | **ADO, TO-DO, POTHER, BOTHER, STIR, STEW** |
| fusty | **MUSTY, MOLDY** |
| futile | **USELESS, VAIN** |
| fuzz | **LINT, FLUFF** |
| fylfot | **SWASTIKA** |

**G**

| | |
|---|---|
| gab | **CHAT, CHATTER, GABBLE** |
| gabble | **BABBLE, CHATTER, JABBER** |
| gaberdine | **COAT** |
| Gabriel, for one | **ANGEL** |
| gad | **ROVE, ROAM** |
| Gaelic | **ERSE** |
| gag | **JOKE** |
| gage | **SECURITY** |
| gaiety | **MIRTH** |
| gain | **ACQUIRE, PROFIT** |
| gain a victory | **WIN, TRIUMPH** |
| gain as clear profit | **NET** |
| gain by labor | **EARN** |
| gain command of | **MASTER** |
| gain control (2 wds.) | **SEW UP** |

| | |
|---|---|
| gain courage (2 wds.) | **TAKE HEART** |
| gainer | **DIVE** |
| gainful | **PROFITABLE** |
| gain knowledge | **LEARN** |
| gain on | **NEAR** |
| gain over expense | **NET, PROFIT** |
| gainsay | **DENY** |
| gain victory | **OVERCOME, WIN, TRIUMPH** |
| gait | **CANTER, PACE, TROT** |
| gaited horse | **PACER** |
| gaiters | **SPATS** |
| gala | **FESTIVAL, FETE, BALL, FESTIVE, FIESTA** |
| Galatea's lover | **ACIS** |
| gale | **STORM** |
| gall | **NERVE** |
| gallant | **NOBLE, HEROIC** |
| gallery hanging | **OIL** |
| galley sweep | **OAR** |
| Gallic affirmative | **OUI** |
| gallop | **GAIT** |
| gamble | **BET, WAGER** |
| gambler | **BETTOR** |
| gambler's capital | **STAKE** |
| gambling cubes | **DICE** |
| gambling game | **FARO, POKER, BLACKJACK** |
| gambol | **CAPER, FRISK** |
| gambrel | **ROOF** |
| game | **SPORT** |
| game animal | **DEER, ELK, MOOSE** |
| game at cards | **FARO, LOO** |
| game at marbles | **TAW, MIB** |
| gamecock spur | **GAFF** |
| game collection | **BAG** |
| game fish | **BASS, CERO, TARPON, TROUT, PIKE** |
| game like bowling | **TENPINS** |
| game of checkers | **DRAUGHTS** |
| game of strategy | **CHESS, GO** |
| game played on horseback | **POLO** |
| game played with clubs | **GOLF** |
| game result | **SCORE** |
| game stealer | **POACHER** |
| gamester | **GAMBLER** |
| gamin | **URCHIN, WAIF** |
| gaming cubes | **DICE** |
| gammon | **BACON** |
| gamut | **RANGE, SCOPE** |
| gamy | **SPOILED** |
| gander | **GOOSE** |
| gang | **CREW** |
| gangling | **LANKY** |
| gangster | **HOODLUM, THUG** |

gangster Capone **AL**
gangster's girl friend **MOLL**
gang up on **ATTACK, OPPOSE**
gaol **PRISON**
gap **OPENING, HOLE, LACUNA, HIATUS**
gape **YAWN, STARE**
gar **NEEDLEFISH**
garb **ATTIRE, CLOTHE, CLOTHING**
garbage **TRASH**
garbage barge **SCOW**
garbanzo **BEAN, CHICKPEA**
garble **DISTORT**
garcon **WAITER**
garden amphibian **TOAD, FROG**
garden flower **PETUNIA, ROSE, PEONY, ASTER, ZINNIA, DAHLIA, PANSY,**
garden for animals **ZOO**
garden implement **HOE, RAKE, TROWEL**
garden moisture **DEW**
garden party **FETE**
garden pest **APHID, WEED, BEETLE**
garden plant **RADISH, TOMATO, BEAN, CARROT, POTATO, ASPARAGUS, BEET, TURNIP, PEA**
garden plot **BED**
garden portulaca (2 wds.) **ROSE MOSS**
Garden State **NEW JERSEY**
garden tool **HOE, RAKE, TROWEL**
garden walk **PATH**
gargantuan **HUGE, GIGANTIC**
gargle **RINSE**
gargling liquid **MOUTHWASH**
gargoyle **SPOUT**
garish **GAUDY, LOUD**
garland **WREATH, LEI, ANADEM**
garlic-like herb **SHALLOT**
garlic part **CLOVE**
garment **WRAP**
garment edge **HEM**
garment maker **TAILOR**
garment of old Rome **TOGA**
garment piece **SLEEVE, YOKE, COLLAR, LAPEL**
garment protector **APRON, BIB, SMOCK**
garner **GATHER, COLLECT**
garnish **ADORN, EMBELLISH**
garret **ATTIC**
garrison **POST, FORT**

garrote **STRANGLE**
garrulous **TALKY, TALKATIVE**
garter **SUPPORT**
gas **FUEL, PETROL, VAPOR, FUME**
gas burner **JET**
gaseous compound **ETHANE**
gaseous element **ARGON, NEON**
gaseous hydrocarbon **ETHANE**
gash **CUT, SLASH**
gasoline container **TANK**
gasoline in Britain **PETROL**
gasoline rating **OCTANE**
gasp **PANT**
gastronome **EPICURE, GOURMET**
gastropod **ABALONE, SNAIL**
gastropod genus **OLIVA**
gat **CHANNEL**
gate **DOOR, PORTAL**
gatefold **FOLD-OUT, INSERT**
gatekeeper **WARDEN**
gateway **ENTRY, PORTICO**
gather **AMASS, ASSEMBLE, REAP, ACCUMULATE, COLLECT, GLEAN**
gathering of people **MEETING, ASSEMBLY**
gather in sails **FURL**
gather into folds **PLEAT, SHIRR**
gauche **AWKWARD, CLUMSY**
gaucho **COWBOY**
gaucho's weapon **BOLA(S)**
gaudy **GARISH, LOUD**
gaudy trifle **GEWGAW**
gauge **METER, MEASURE**
Gaul **FRENCHMAN**
gaunt **BONY, SKINNY**
gauntlet **GLOVE**
gay **CHEERY, JOYOUS, MERRY**
gay city **PAREE, PARIS**
gay time **LARK, SPREE**
gaze **PEER, STARE**
gazelle **ARIEL, GOA**
gaze with greed **GLOAT**
gear **EQUIPMENT**
gear tooth **COG**
gee **GOLLY**
gekko **LIZARD**
gelatinous substance **AGAR, AGAR-AGAR**
gem **JEWEL, STONE**
gem carved in relief **CAMEO**
gem face **FACET**
gem of the mountains **IDAHO**
Gem State **IDAHO**
gem surface **FACET**
gem weight **CARAT**

| | |
|---|---|
| gender | SEX |
| Gene Tierney role | LAURA |
| genealogical record | TREE |
| genealogy | LINEAGE, PEDIGREE |
| general | COMMON, UNIVERSAL |
| general course | TREND |
| general Eisenhower | IKE |
| generally | USUALLY |
| general's aides | STAFF |
| general's assistant | |
| | AIDE-DE-CAMP, AIDE |
| generate | PRODUCE |
| generation | AGE, ERA |
| generic | TYPICAL |
| generous | OPEN-HANDED, |
| | CHARITABLE |
| genesis | BIRTH, ORIGIN |
| genial | CORDIAL, WARM |
| genius | TALENT |
| genteel | POLITE, POLISHED |
| gentle | MILD, TAME, KIND, |
| | SOFT |
| gentle blow | TAP |
| gentle creature | LAMB |
| gentlefolk | NOBILITY |
| gentleman | SIR |
| gentleman (Sp.) | SENOR |
| gentleman's gentleman | VALET |
| gentlemen's agreement | |
| | HANDSHAKE |
| gentle reproof | ADMONITION |
| gentle tap | PAT |
| genuflect | KNEEL |
| genuine | REAL, BONA FIDE, |
| | PURE, TRUE |
| genus | CLASS |
| genus of African tree | COLA |
| genus of ants | ECITON |
| genus of apes | SIMIA |
| genus of apple trees | MALUS |
| genus of bees | APIS |
| genus of beetles | SITOPHILUS |
| genus of cattle | BOS |
| genus of chickpeas | CICER |
| genus of currants | RIBES |
| genus of frogs | RANA |
| genus of maples | ACER |
| genus of olive trees | OLEA |
| genus of palms | ARECA |
| genus of rodents | MUS |
| genus of sheep | OVIS |
| genus of snakes | OPHIDIA |
| geographical dictionary | |
| | GAZETTEER |
| geographical division | ZONE |
| geological period | ERA |

| | |
|---|---|
| geometrical figure | CONE, |
| | CUBE, POLYGON, |
| | SQUARE, OCTAGON |
| geometrical line | RADIUS, |
| | DIAMETER |
| George Gershwin's brother | IRA |
| George Sand classic | LELIA |
| Georgia city | AUGUSTA, |
| | MACON, ATLANTA |
| germ | SEED |
| German | TEUTON |
| German article | DAS, DER, DIE |
| German city | BADEN, ESSEN, |
| | EMDEN, BONN, BERLIN, |
| | FRANKFURT, HAMBURG |
| German coin | TALER |
| German composer | LEHAR, |
| | STRAUS, BRAHMS, WAGNER |
| German dive bomber | STUKA |
| German fascist | NAZI |
| German folk dance | ALLEMANDE |
| German goblin | KOBOLD |
| German-made pistol | LUGER |
| German measles | RUBELLA |
| German negative | NEIN |
| German philosopher | KANT, |
| | HEGEL |
| German river | ELBE, ISAR, |
| | ODER, RHINE |
| German submarine | |
| (comp. wd.) | U-BOAT |
| German title | HERR, FRAU |
| germ culture | AGAR |
| gesture | ACT, MOTION |
| get | RECEIVE, OBTAIN, |
| | PROCURE, GAIN |
| get along | MANAGE |
| get a scolding | |
| (2 wds., colloq.) | CATCH IT |
| get as deserved | EARN, MERIT |
| get away | ESCAPE, FLEE |
| get back | REDEEM |
| get better of | BEST |
| get bigger | GROW, INCREASE |
| get by force | EXTORT, PRY |
| get by reasoning | DERIVE |
| get lost | STRAY |
| get on | BOARD |
| get on a horse | MOUNT |
| get out (sl.) | SCRAM |
| get ready | PREPARE |
| get rid of (2 wds.) | CLEAR OFF |
| get the advantage of | BEST |
| get the best of | MASTER |
| get the point | UNDERSTAND, |
| | SEE |
| get up | ARISE, STAND |
| get-up | OUTFIT |

get well **RECOVER, HEAL, MEND**
gewgaw **TRINKET**
Ghandi's country **INDIA**
ghastly **HIDEOUS**
ghat **PASS, STAIRS**
gherkin **CUCUMBER, PICKLE**
ghost **SPIRIT, SPOOK, SHADE**
ghostly **EERIE, EERY**
giant **TITAN**
giant beggar of Ithaca **IRUS**
giant of fairy tales **OGRE**
gibberish **CHATTER, JARGON**
gibbon **APE**
gift **PRESENT**
gibe **SNEER, SCOFF**
giddy **DIZZY**
gift bearer **GREEK, DONOR**
gift recipient **DONEE**
gifted speaker **ORATOR**
gift to the needy **ALMS**
gigantic **HUGE, IMMENSE**
giggle **LAUGH, TITTER, SNICKER**
giggling sound **TEHEE**
gilding **GILT**
gill **SMALL LIQUID MEASURE**
gimcrack **GEWGAW, TRINKET**
gimpy **LAME**
gin-and-tonic garnish **LIME**
ginger **PEP**
ginger cookie **SNAP**
gingerly **CAREFULLY**
gingili **SESAME**
gin mixer **TONIC**
giraffe-like animal **OKAPI**
gird **BIND, BELT**
girl **GAL, LASS, MAID, MAIDEN**
girl of song **MARIE, LOLA, DAISY, MARY, JEANNIE, LAURA, MARTA, WENDY**
girl of the Twenties **FLAPPER**
girl servant **MAID**
girth **HOOP, BAND**
GI's ID (2 wds., colloq.) **DOG TAG**
gist **POINT, MEAT**
give **DONATE**
give an account of **RELATE, REPORT, TELL**
give and take **BANDY**
give a new title to **RENAME**
give another title to **RENAME**
give assent **AGREE**
give away **BESTOW, GRANT**
give back **REPAY, RETURN, RESTORE**
give claim to **ENTITLE**

give consent **ACCEDE**
give due credit **PRAISE**
give ear **HEED, LISTEN**
give evidence **TESTIFY**
give forth **EMIT**
give in **RELENT**
give information **REPORT**
give legal force to **VALIDATE**
give light **SHINE, GLOW**
give meaning to **DEFINE**
give name to **DUB, TITLE**
give notice **WARN**
given to loose chatter **GOSSIPY**
give off fumes **REEK**
give one's word **PROMISE**
give outlet to **VENT**
give out sparingly **DOLE, METE**
give silent assent **NOD**
give temporarily **LEND**
give the alarm **WARN, ALERT**
give the meaning of **DEFINE**
give up **CEDE, YIELD**
giving **GENEROUS**
glacial epoch (2 wds.) **ICE AGE**
glacial ice **SERAC**
glacial ridge **ESKER**
glacial sand **NEVE**
glacial term **STOSS**
glad **HAPPY, JOYFUL**
gladden **ELATE**
glade **VALE**
glamour **CHARM, ALLURE**
glance **LOOK, PEEK**
glare **SHINE, GLEAM**
glaring **OBVIOUS**
Glasgow resident **SCOT**
glass bottle **CARAFE**
glass container **JAR, BOTTLE**
glass-enclosed room **SOLARIUM, SUNROOM**
glasses part **LENS, FRAME**
glass to reflect image **MIRROR**
glassy **SMOOTH**
gleam **GLINT, SHINE**
glee **EXULTATION, JOY, BLISS, ELATION**
glib **FLIP, SMOOTH**
glide aloft **SOAR**
glide on snow **SKI**
glide over ice **SKATE**
glider **SWING**
glimpse **ESPY, NOTICE**
glisten **GLITTER, SHINE**
glisten brightly **SPARKLE**
glitter **GLARE, SHINE**
globe **SPHERE, ORB, WORLD, PLANET, BULB**
globule **DROP**

| | |
|---|---|
| gloom | DARKNESS |
| gloomy | GLUM, BLUE, SAD |
| glorify | PRAISE |
| glorious | SPLENDID, NOBLE |
| glory | GRANDEUR, HONOR |
| gloss | LUSTER, POLISH, SHEEN, SHINE |
| glossa | TONGUE |
| glossy | SHINY |
| glossy black bird | RAVEN |
| glossy fabric | SATEEN, SATIN |
| glossy paint | ENAMEL |
| glossy shoe material (2 wds.) | PATENT LEATHER |
| glove | GAUNTLET, MITTEN |
| glove leather | CALF, KID |
| glow | SHINE |
| glowing coal | EMBER |
| glucose | SUGAR |
| glue | PASTE |
| glue shut | SEAL |
| glum | SULLEN, SAD |
| glut | SATE, SATIATE |
| glutton (colloq.) | HOG, PIG |
| gluttony | GREED |
| glyph | CARVING |
| gnarl | KNOT, SNARL |
| gnash | GRIND |
| gnat | MIDGE |
| gnaw | CHEW |
| gnome | ELF, GREMLIN, TROLL, BROWNIE |
| gnu | WILDEBEEST |
| go | DEPART, LEAVE |
| go (poet.) | WEND |
| go aboard, at depot | ENTRAIN |
| goad | INCITE, PROD, SPUR, URGE, EGG ON |
| go ahead | CONTINUE, PROCEED |
| goal | AIM, OBJECTIVE, END, TARGET |
| go along with | AGREE |
| go around | DETOUR |
| go astray | ERR, SIN |
| goat | KID |
| go at | ATTACK |
| goatee | BEARD |
| go away | SCRAM, SHOO, DEPART, LEAVE, SCAT |
| gob | TAR, SAILOR |
| go back | RETURN |
| go back on a promise | RENEGE |
| go back to | REVERT, RETURN |
| go bad | SPOIL, ROT |
| gobble | EAT |
| gobbler | TURKEY |
| go before the wind | SCUD |
| go-between | AGENT |

| | |
|---|---|
| go beyond | OVERREACH |
| goblet | GLASS |
| goblet part | STEM |
| goblin | SPRITE, GHOST, HAUNT |
| go by | ELAPSE, PASS |
| go by car | RIDE |
| go by ship | SAIL |
| god | IDOL, DIETY |
| god-fearing | DEVOUT, PIOUS |
| godforsaken | DESOLATE, FORLORN |
| god, goddess (name of)—(See under Greek deity, Norse deity, etc.) | |
| godliness | PIETY |
| godly | DIVINE |
| god of the east | ALLAH |
| go easily | AMBLE |
| go forward | ADVANCE, PROGRESS |
| go from store to store | SHOP |
| go furtively | SNEAK, STEAL |
| goggle | STARE, GAPE |
| goggles | GLASSES |
| go in | ENTER, PENETRATE |
| gold | WEALTH, MONEY |
| gold (Sp.) | ORO |
| gold cloth | LAME |
| Gold Coast | GHANA |
| gold coin | EAGLE |
| gold color | YELLOW |
| gold in heraldry | OR |
| gold in mass | BULLION |
| gold leaf | GILT |
| gold plated statuette | OSCAR |
| golden | GILT |
| golden bird | ORIOLE |
| golden bronze | ORMOLU |
| golden calf | IDOL |
| golden fish | CARP |
| golden fleece seeker | JASON |
| golden horde | MONGOLS |
| Golden State | CALIFORNIA |
| golf club | WOOD, PUTTER, IRON, DRIVER |
| golf club face | LOFT |
| golf course | LINKS |
| golf course item | HOLE |
| golfer Hogan | BEN |
| golfer Lema | TONY |
| golfer Palmer | ARNOLD |
| golfer Sarazen | GENE |
| golfer Snead | SAM |
| golf expert | PRO |
| golf gadget | TEE |
| golf hazard | BUNKER, TRAP |
| golf hole | CUP, BYE |
| golf mound | TEE |

| | |
|---|---|
| golf norm | **PAR** |
| golf score | **BIRDIE, PAR,** |
| | **EAGLE, BOGEY** |
| golf shout | **FORE** |
| golf term | **BIRDIE, FORE** |
| Golgotha | **CALVARY** |
| goliard | **MINSTREL, JESTER** |
| Goliath | **GIANT** |
| Goliath's slayer | **DAVID** |
| golly | **GEE, GOSH** |
| gondola | **BOAT** |
| gone | **LEFT, AGO** |
| gone by | **PAST, AGO** |
| gone from home | **AWAY, OUT** |
| goober | **PEANUT** |
| good | **HONEST** |
| good (Fr.) | **BON** |
| good (Scot.) | **GUDE** |
| good-by | **FAREWELL, TA-TA** |
| good-by, in Madrid | **ADIOS** |
| good-by, in Tokyo | **SAYONARA** |
| good-for-nothing | **IDLER** |
| good fortune on first venture | |
| | **BEGINNER'S LUCK** |
| good judgment | **PRUDENCE** |
| good luck symbol | **MASCOT,** |
| | **TALISMAN** |
| good name | **CREDIT, HONOR** |
| goodness | **VIRTUE** |
| good news | **EVANGEL** |
| goods | **MATERIAL, WARES** |
| goods for sale | **WARES** |
| good turn | **FAVOR** |
| gooey | **STICKY** |
| gooey mud | **SLIME** |
| goof | **BLUNDER** |
| go off | **EXPLODE** |
| go on | **CONTINUE** |
| go on a cruise (2 wds.) | **SET SAIL** |
| go one better | **OUT DO** |
| go on foot | **WALK, MARCH** |
| goose egg | **O, ZERO** |
| goose genus | **ANSER** |
| go over | **EXAMINE** |
| go over a bridge | **CROSS** |
| go over and change | **REVISE** |
| gore | **PIERCE** |
| gorge | **CANYON** |
| gorgeous | **MAGNIFICENT,** |
| | **SPLENDID** |
| gorgon | **MEDUSA** |
| gorilla | **APE** |
| gorse | **FURZE** |
| gosh | **GEE, GOLLY** |
| go softly | **TIPTOE** |
| gospel | **TRUTH** |
| gossamer | **FILMY, THIN** |
| gossip | **TALK, TATTLER, DIRT** |

| | |
|---|---|
| go swiftly | **FLIT, RACE, RUN,** |
| | **HIE, HASTEN, SCUD** |
| go swimming | **BATHE** |
| Gothic arch | **OGIVE** |
| Gothic window | **ORIEL** |
| go through | **EXPERIENCE** |
| go through with | **COMPLETE** |
| go to bed | **RETIRE, TURN IN** |
| go together | **MATCH** |
| go too far | **OVERSTEP** |
| go to the bottom | **SINK** |
| goulash | **STEW** |
| go under | **FAIL** |
| Gounod's opera | **FAUST** |
| go up | **RISE, ASCEND, CLIMB** |
| gourd | **PEPO, MELON** |
| gourmand | **EPICURE, GOURMET** |
| govern | **RULE** |
| governess | **NANNY** |
| governing board member | |
| | **REGENT** |
| government agent | |
| (comp. wd.) | **T-MAN, G-MAN** |
| government assistance | |
| (2 wds.) | **FEDERAL AID** |
| government by a few | **OLIGARCHY** |
| government levy | **TAX** |
| governor | **REGENT** |
| Gower Champion's wife | **MARGE** |
| gown | **DRESS** |
| go wrong | **ERR, SIN** |
| grace | **CHARM** |
| graceful | **ELEGANT** |
| graceful animal | **DEER** |
| graceful bird | **SWAN** |
| graceful horse | **ARAB** |
| graceful loser (2 wds.) | **GOOD** |
| | **SPORT** |
| gracious | **BENIGN, KIND** |
| gradation | **STEP** |
| grade | **RANK** |
| gradual | **SLOW** |
| graduate | **ALUMNUS** |
| graduate of Annapolis (abbr.) | |
| | **ENS** |
| graduate's memento | |
| (2 wds.) | **CLASS RING** |
| grafted (Her.) | **ENTE** |
| grafting twig | **SCION, CION** |
| grain | **OAT, RICE, WHEAT,** |
| | **BARLEY, SEED** |
| grain for beer | **BARLEY** |
| grain for bread | **WHEAT** |
| grain for grinding | **GRIST** |
| grain for weddings | **RICE** |
| grain for whiskey | **RYE** |
| grain grinding place | **MILL** |

| | |
|---|---|
| grain mildew | **RUST** |
| grain of corn | **KERNEL** |
| grain warehouse | **ELEVATOR** |
| grainy | **GRANULAR** |
| grammarian's concern | **SYNTAX** |
| grammatical mark | **TILDE** |
| grampus | **ORC** |
| grand | **GREAT, EPIC** |
| Grand Canyon State | **ARIZONA** |
| grandee | **NOBLEMAN** |
| grandeur | **MAJESTY** |
| grange | **FARM** |
| Granite State | **NEW HAMPSHIRE** |
| grant | **CEDE** |
| granting that | **IF** |
| grant temporarily | **LEND** |
| granular | **GRAINY** |
| granular snow | **NEVE** |
| grape plant | **VINE** |
| graph | **CHART** |
| graphic | **VIVID, LUCID, CLEAR** |
| graphic layout | **MAP** |
| grapple | **WRESTLE** |
| grasp | **CLUTCH, HOLD, TAKE** |
| grasp firmly | **CLENCH** |
| grasp grimly | **GRIP** |
| grasping | **AVID, GREEDY** |
| grasping device | **TONGS** |
| grasp roughly | **GRAB** |
| grass | **LAWN, CEREAL** |
| grass cloth | **JUTE, HEMP** |
| grass cutter | **MOWER** |
| grass dried for fodder | **HAY** |
| grassland | **LEA, PASTURE** |
| grass leaf | **BLADE** |
| grasshopper's cousin | **CICADA, LOCUST, MANTIS** |
| grass roots | **BASICS** |
| grassy area | **LAWN, PASTURE, LEA, SAVANNA** |
| grassy field (poet.) | **MEAD** |
| grate | **RASP, SCRAPE** |
| grateful | **APPRECIATIVE, GLAD** |
| gratify | **PLEASE** |
| gratify one's vanity | **FLATTER** |
| grating | **GRID** |
| gratis | **FREE** |
| gratitude | **THANKS** |
| gratuitous | **BASELESS** |
| gratuity | **TIP** |
| grave | **SERIOUS, SOBER** |
| grave robber | **GHOUL** |
| gravy | **SAUCE** |
| gravy server | **BOAT** |
| gray | **DISMAL, NEUTRAL** |
| grayish blue | **SLATE** |
| grayish red (2 wds.) | **ASH ROSE** |
| gray with age | **HOARY** |

| | |
|---|---|
| grazing land | **PASTURE, LEA** |
| grease | **OIL, FAT, LARD** |
| great | **LARGE, VAST, BIG, HUGE** |
| Great Britain principality | **WALES, SCOTLAND** |
| greater in number | **MORE** |
| greatest | **EXTREME, UTMOST** |
| great folly | **MADNESS** |
| great-hearted | **BRAVE, GENEROUS** |
| great in size | **VAST, GIGANTIC** |
| great knowledge | **LORE** |
| Great Lake | **ERIE, HURON, MICHIGAN, ONTARIO, SUPERIOR** |
| great lie (colloq ) | **WHOPPER** |
| greatly | **MUCH** |
| greatly excited | **ENTHUSED, AGOG** |
| greatly happy | **BLISSFUL, JOYFUL, ELATED** |
| great misfortune | **DISASTER** |
| great Mogul emperor | **AKBAR** |
| great number | **MULTITUDE** |
| great operatic tenor | **CARUSO** |
| great part | **BULK** |
| great personage | **MOGUL** |
| great pleasure | **DELIGHT** |
| great plenty | **ABUNDANCE** |
| great realm | **EMPIRE** |
| great respect | **AWE** |
| great success | **HIT** |
| Great White Way | **BROADWAY** |
| great world | **SOCIETY** |
| greedy | **AVID** |
| greedy person | **MISER** |
| Greek assembly | **AGORA** |
| Greek biographer | **PLUTARCH** |
| Greek capital | **ATHENS** |
| Greek city | **SPARTA** |
| Greek coin | **OBOL** |
| Greek colonnade | **STOA** |
| Greek colony | **IONIA** |
| Greek column | **CARYATID** |
| Greek commune | **DEME** |
| Greek cupid | **EROS** |
| Greek cynic | **TIMON** |
| Greek dialect | **DORIC, AEOLIC, EOLIC** |
| Greek deity | **AMPHITRITE, APHRODITE, APOLLO, ARES, POSEIDON, ZEUS, HERMES, HERA, ERIS, ATHENA, EROS, EOS, DEMETER, DIONYSUS, NIKE, PAN, PLUTO, TRITON, MOIRA, CYBELE, NEMESIS, BACCHUS** |

| | |
|---|---|
| Greek district | **DEME** |
| Greek dog | **GREYHOUND** |
| Greek epic poem | **ILIAD, ODYSSEY** |
| Greek epic poet | **HOMER** |
| Greek games city | **NEMEA** |
| Greek god—(See Greek deity) | |
| Greek goddess of agriculture | **DEMETER** |
| Greek goddess of discord | **ERIS** |
| Greek goddess of peace | **IRENE** |
| Greek goddess of the dawn | **EOS** |
| Greek goddess of the moon | **ARTEMIS** |
| Greek goddess of victory | **NIKE** |
| Greek goddess of youth | **HEBE** |
| Greek god of love | **EROS** |
| Greek goddess—(See Greek deity) | |
| Greek hero | **THESEUS, AJAX** |
| Greek island | **CRETE, SAMOS, CORFU** |
| Greek Juno | **HERA** |
| Greek lawgiver | **SOLON** |
| Greek letter | **BETA, ALPHA, THETA, KAPPA, PI, PSI, RHO, OMEGA, CHI, ETA, DELTA, PHI, TAU, MU, EPSILON, GAMMA, ZETA, ETA, IOTA, LAMBDA, NU, XI, OMICRON, SIGMA, UPSILON** |
| Greek malignant spirit | **KER** |
| Greek marker | **STELE** |
| Greek mathematician and inventor | **ARCHIMEDES** |
| Greek measure | **DAKTYLOS, BEMA** |
| Greek money | **DRACHMA** |
| Greek monster | **GORGON** |
| Greek mountain | **OSSA, PELION** |
| Greek muse | **ERATO, CLIO, CALLIOPE, EUTERPE, MELPOMENE, POLYMNIA, TERPSICHORE, THALIA, URANIA** |
| Greek mythological youth | **ADONIS** |
| Greek nymph | **OREAD** |
| Greek paradise | **ELYSIUM** |
| Greek people | **DEMOS** |
| Greek philosophers | **PLATO, SOCRATES** |
| Greek philosophy school | **STOIC** |
| Greek physician | **GALEN** |
| Greek platform | **BEMA** |
| Greek poet | **HOMER, ARION** |
| Greek poetess | **SAPPHO** |
| Greek port | **CORFU, PIRAEUS** |

| | |
|---|---|
| Greek portico | **STOA** |
| Greek ruler | **EPARCH** |
| Greek sea | **AEGEAN, IONIAN** |
| Greek slave | **HELOT** |
| Greek sorceress | **MEDEA** |
| Greek sun god | **APOLLO** |
| Greek sylvan deity | **SATYR** |
| Greek temple | **NAOS** |
| Greek theater | **ODEUM, ODEA** |
| green | **UNRIPE, ENVIOUS** |
| greenback | **DOLLAR, BILL** |
| Green Bay football team | **PACKERS** |
| green citrus fruit | **LIME** |
| green-eyed | **JEALOUS** |
| green (Fr.) | **VERT** |
| green gem | **JADE, EMERALD** |
| green herbage | **GRASS** |
| Greenland's colonizer | **ERIC** |
| Greenland settlement | **ETAH** |
| green light | **GO-AHEAD, GO** |
| Green Mountain State | **VERMONT** |
| green onion | **SCALLION** |
| green plum | **GAGE** |
| green quartz | **PRASE** |
| green rock-growth | **MOSS** |
| green rust | **PATINA** |
| green spot | **OASIS** |
| green stone | **EMERALD, JADE** |
| greensward | **LAWN, SOD** |
| greet | **ACCOST, HAIL, SALUTE** |
| greeting | **HULLO, HELLO, HI** |
| greeting message | **CARD** |
| gregarious | **SOCIAL** |
| gremlin | **GNOME, BROWNIE, ELF, SPRITE** |
| Gretna Green figure | **ELOPER** |
| grief | **SORROW** |
| grieve | **LAMENT** |
| grieve bitterly (4 wds.) | **EAT ONE'S HEART OUT** |
| grievous | **LAMENTABLE** |
| grill | **BROIL** |
| grim | **AUSTERE** |
| grimace | **MOUE, SNEER** |
| grime | **DIRT, SOOT, DUST** |
| grin | **SMILE** |
| grind | **CRUSH** |
| grinding machine | **MILL** |
| grinding stone | **EMERY** |
| grinding tooth | **MOLAR** |
| grind with the teeth | **CHEW, MASH, GNASH** |
| grip | **GRASP, VALISE** |
| grisly | **GHASTLY, GRIM** |
| gristle | **CARTILAGE** |
| grit | **SAND** |

| | | | |
|---|---|---|---|
| grizzly | **BEAR** | grow drowsy | **NOD** |
| groan | **MOAN** | growing in pairs | **BINATE** |
| grooming aid | **COMB, BRUSH,** | grow in length | **ELONGATE** |
| | **TALC, TONIC, RAZOR** | growl | **SNARL** |
| groom's attendant | | grow molars | **TEETHE** |
| (2 wds.) | **BEST MAN** | grow more intense | **DEEPEN** |
| groove | **RUT** | grown boy | **MAN** |
| grotesque | **BIZARRE** | grown up ugly duckling | **SWAN** |
| grotto | **CAVE, CAVERN** | grow old | **AGE** |
| grotto (poet.) | **GROT** | grow out of | **DEVELOP** |
| grouchy person | **CRAB, CRANK** | grow quickly | **SPROUT** |
| ground | **LAND, SOIL** | growth | **RISE, INCREASE** |
| ground-breaking tool | **SPADE** | grow thin | **EMACIATE** |
| ground grain | **MEAL** | grow tiresome | **BORE** |
| groundless | **UNFOUNDED** | grow weary | **TIRE** |
| ground plot | **LOT** | grow worse | **DETERIORATE** |
| grounds | **BASIS** | grub | **FOOD, VICTUALS** |
| ground squirrel | **GOPHER** | grubby | **MESSY, UNTIDY** |
| group | **LOT** | grudge | **SPITE, ENVY** |
| grouper | **MERO** | gruesome | **LURID, MACABRE** |
| group of actors | **CAST, TROUPE** | gruff | **ABRUPT, BRUSQUE** |
| group of animals | **HERD** | grumble | **COMPLAIN** |
| group of criminals | **GANG** | Guam capital | **AGANA** |
| group of customers | **CLIENTELE** | Guam seaport | **APRA** |
| group of eight | **OCTET** | guanaco | **LLAMA** |
| group of facts | **DATA** | guarantee | **ASSURE** |
| group of families | **TRIBE, CLAN** | guaranty | **PLEDGE, WARRANTY** |
| group of five | **QUINTET, PENTAD** | guard | **SENTINEL** |
| group of Indians | **TRIBE** | guardhouse | **BRIG** |
| group of lions | **PRIDE** | guardian | **PATRON,** |
| group of musicians | **BAND,** | | **CUSTODIAN** |
| | **ORCHESTRA, COMBO,** | guard spirit of old Rome | **LAR** |
| | **DANCE BAND** | Guatemalan | **MAYAN** |
| group of nine | **ENNEAD** | Gudrun's husband | **ATLI** |
| group of persons | **TEAM, CROWD** | guess | **SUPPOSE, ESTIMATE** |
| group of pictures | **SET** | guessing game | **CHARADE** |
| group of points | **LOCI** | guest | **LODGER, VISITOR** |
| group of related species | **GENUS** | guide | **LEAD** |
| group of rooms | **SUITE** | guide a car | **STEER,** |
| group of seamen | **CREW** | | **DRIVE** |
| group of seven | **HEPTAD** | guide a plane | **PILOT** |
| group of ships | **FLEET, ARMADA** | guide to solution of | |
| group of singers | **CHOIR** | a mystery | **CLUE** |
| group of six | **SEXTET** | guidon | **PENNANT, BANNER** |
| group of states | **EMPIRE** | Guido's high note | **ELA** |
| group of students | **CLASS** | guile | **CRAFT, CUNNING** |
| group of ten | **DECADE, DECAD** | guileless | **NAIVE** |
| group of three | **TRIAD, TRIO** | guillotine | **BEHEAD** |
| group of two | **DYAD, DUET, DUO,** | guilty | **CULPABLE,** |
| | **PAIR, BRACE** | | **BLAMABLE** |
| group of Western allies | **NATO** | guilty person | **CULPRIT** |
| group spirit | **MORALE** | guilty regret | **REMORSE** |
| group transportation | | guinea pig | **CAVY** |
| (2 wds.) | **CHARTERED BUS** | guise | **ASPECT, SEMBLANCE** |
| grove of trees | **COPSE, FOREST** | gulch | **RAVINE** |
| grovel | **FAWN, CRINGE** | gulf | **ABYSS** |
| grow | **EXPAND, RAISE** | gulf between Africa | |
| grow dim | **FADE, WANE** | and Arabia | **ADEN** |

| | |
|---|---|
| gulf of Australia | **CARPENTARIA** |
| gullet | **MAW, THROAT** |
| gullible fellow | **DUPE** |
| gull-like bird | **TERN** |
| gully | **GUTTER** |
| gum | **RESIN** |
| gumbo | **OKRA, SOUP** |
| gumption | **NERVE** |
| gums | **ULA** |
| gum tree | **SAPODILLA** |
| gun | **FIREARM, MUSKET, RIFLE, PISTOL** |
| gun an engine | **REV** |
| gun barrel cleaner | **RAMROD** |
| gun cavity | **BORE** |
| gun dog | **SETTER** |
| gunny bag | **SACK** |
| gunpowder ingredient | **NITRE** |
| gun tube | **BARREL** |
| guru | **TEACHER** |
| gush | **POUR, SPURT** |
| gush forth | **SPEW** |
| gusto | **ZEST, ELAN** |
| guy | **CHAP, FELLOW** |
| gymnasium pad | **MAT** |
| gyp | **CHEAT, SWINDLE** |
| gypsy man | **ROM** |
| gyrate | **WHIRL, ROTATE** |

## H

| | |
|---|---|
| habiliment | **CLOTHING, DRESS, ATTIRE** |
| habit | **CUSTOM, WONT, OUTFIT, ATTIRE** |
| habitat | **LOCALITY** |
| habitation | **ABODE** |
| habitual | **USUAL, CUSTOMARY** |
| habitual drunkard | **SOT** |
| habituate | **INURE** |
| hack | **TAXI** |
| hackamore | **HALTER, BRIDLE** |
| hackle | **BRISTLE** |
| hackneyed | **BANAL, TRITE, STALE** |
| hack up | **CHOP** |
| hades | **HELL, INFERNO** |
| hag | **CRONE** |
| haggard | **GAUNT, WEARY** |
| Haggard novel | **SHE** |
| haggle | **BARGAIN, DICKER** |
| hail | **AVE, GREET, SLEET** |
| hair | **TRESSES, MANE** |
| hair curler | **ROLLER** |
| hair-do | **AFRO, SET, STYLE** |
| hair-do holder | **NET** |
| hair dye | **HENNA** |

| | |
|---|---|
| hair grooming aid | **COMB, BRUSH** |
| hairless | **BALD** |
| hair ointment | **POMADE** |
| hair on horse's foot | **FETLOCK** |
| hair on lion's neck | **MANE** |
| hair pad | **RAT** |
| hair piece | **SWITCH, FALL, WIG, TOUPEE** |
| hair ribbon | **SNOOD** |
| hair ringlet | **TRESS, CURL** |
| hair roll | **CHIGNON** |
| hair style | **UPDO, SHINGLE** |
| hair tint | **RINSE** |
| hairy man | **ESAU** |
| Haitian city | **PORT-AU-PRINCE** |
| Haitian magic | **OBEAH, OBI** |
| halcyon | **TRANQUIL, CALM** |
| hale | **HEALTHY, ROBUST** |
| half | **PART, PARTIAL** |
| half (prefix) | **SEMI, DEMI, HEMI** |
| half a quart | **PINT** |
| half a score | **TEN** |
| half-diameter | **RADIUS** |
| half gainer | **DIVE** |
| half hitch | **KNOT** |
| half man and half bull | **CENTAUR** |
| half mask | **DOMINO** |
| half moon | **CRESCENT** |
| half-suppressed laugh | **SNICKER** |
| halfway | **MID** |
| halfwit | **FOOL, DOLT** |
| hall | **PASSAGE, CORRIDOR** |
| Halley's constellation | **APUS** |
| hallow | **DEDICATE, BLESS** |
| hallowed place | **SHRINE** |
| Halloween alternative | **TRICK, TREAT** |
| Halloween beverage | **CIDER** |
| hall rug | **RUNNER** |
| hallucination | **DELUSION** |
| hallux | **BIG TOE** |
| halo | **AURA, NIMBUS** |
| halt | **CEASE, STOP, DESIST, ESTOP** |
| halter | **LEAD** |
| halve | **BISECT** |
| hambletonian | **TROTTER, RACE** |
| hamburger garnish | **ONION, PICKLE, MUSTARD, CATSUP, RELISH** |
| hame | **HARNESS** |
| Hamilton bill | **TEN** |
| Hamite | **SOMALI** |
| hamlet | **TOWN, VILLAGE, DORP** |
| Hamlet's home | **ELSINORE, DENMARK** |

| | |
|---|---|
| Hamlet's sweetheart | **OPHELIA** |
| hammer | **SLEDGE** |
| hammer part | **PEEN, CLAW,** |
| | **HEAD** |
| hammerhead | **SHARK** |
| hammerlike tool | **MALLET** |
| hammock cord (comp. wd.) | |
| | **TIE-TIE** |
| hamper | **BASKET, IMPEDE** |
| Ham's son | **CUSH** |
| hamstring | **DISABLE** |
| hand | **WORKER** |
| handbag | **PURSE** |
| handball point | **ACE** |
| hand blow | **SLAP** |
| handcuff | **MANACLE** |
| Handel masterwork | **MESSIAH** |
| hand down | **BEQUEATH** |
| handicap | **BURDEN, PENALTY** |
| hand implement | **SHOVEL,** |
| | **PICK, HOE** |
| handkerchief | **BANDANA,** |
| | **HANKY** |
| handle | **LEVER, TREAT** |
| handle of a knife | **HAFT** |
| handle of a sword | **HILT** |
| handle of a whip | **CROP** |
| handle roughly | **MAUL** |
| handle rudely | **PAW** |
| handle well | **COPE** |
| handling | **TREATMENT,** |
| | **CONTROL** |
| handsome man | **ADONIS** |
| hand-to-hand fight | **MELEE** |
| handy carryall (2 wds.) | |
| | **SHOPPING BAG** |
| hang | **PEND, SUSPEND** |
| hang above | **HOVER** |
| hang around | **LOITER** |
| hanger on | **PARASITE** |
| hang in folds | **DRAPE** |
| hanging tuft of threads | **TASSEL** |
| hang loosely | **LOLL, SAG, DROOP** |
| hangman's knot | **NOOSE** |
| hang on | **PERSEVERE** |
| hang on to | **HOLD, KEEP,** |
| | **RETAIN** |
| hang overhead | **HOVER** |
| hank | **SKEIN** |
| hanker | **ITCH, YEN, DESIRE** |
| hank of twine | **RAN** |
| haphazard (3 wds.) | **HIT OR MISS** |
| haphazardly (2 wds.) | |
| | **AT RANDOM** |
| happen | **BETIDE, OCCUR,** |
| | **TAKE PLACE** |
| happen again | **RECUR** |
| hapless | **UNLUCKY** |

| | |
|---|---|
| happening | **EVENT** |
| happen to | **BEFALL** |
| happily | **LUCKILY** |
| happiness | **GLADNESS, JOY,** |
| | **ELATION, BLISS** |
| happy | **GLAD, JOYFUL,** |
| | **BLISSFUL** |
| happy bird | **LARK** |
| happy cat sound | **PURR** |
| happy expressions | **SMILE, GRIN** |
| harangue | **ORATE** |
| harass | **ANNOY, PLAGUE** |
| harbinger | **HERALD** |
| harbor | **HAVEN, PORT** |
| harbor boat | **TUG** |
| harbor city | **PORT** |
| harbor craft | **FERRYBOAT,** |
| | **TUGBOAT** |
| harbor guide | **PILOT** |
| harbor sight | **SHIP** |
| hard | **DIFFICULT, SOLID** |
| hard and fast | **STRICT** |
| hard ball | **BASEBALL** |
| hard-bitten | **STUBBORN, TOUGH** |
| hard-boiled | **TOUGH, CALLOUS** |
| hard candy | **LEMON DROP** |
| hard cash | **MONEY** |
| hard coal | **ANTHRACITE** |
| hard core | **ABSOLUTE** |
| hard cover | **BOUND** |
| hard drawn | **TENSE** |
| hard drinker | **TOPER, SOT,** |
| | **SOUSE** |
| harden | **SET, STEEL, GEL, INURE** |
| hardened | **CALLOUS, FROZEN** |
| hard finish | **ENAMEL** |
| hard-fisted | **STINGY, MISERLY** |
| hard handed defense | **KARATE** |
| hard hearted | **CRUEL, MEAN** |
| hard lump of earth | **CLOD** |
| hardly | **BARELY** |
| hardly ever | **RARELY** |
| hard metal | **IRON, STEEL** |
| hardness | **RIGOR** |
| hard-nosed | **SHREWD** |
| hard of hearing | **DEAF** |
| hard question | **POSER** |
| hard resin | **COPAL** |
| hard rock | **SLATE** |
| hard-shelled fruit | **NUT** |
| hardship | **PRIVATION, RIGOR** |
| hard to describe | **NONDESCRIPT** |
| hard up | **NEEDY, LACKING** |
| hardware | **TOOLS** |
| hardwood | **TEAK** |
| hardwood tree | **MAPLE, OAK** |
| hard work | **LABOR, TOIL** |
| hard worker | **DEMON** |

hardy **BOLD, DARING**
hardy cabbage **KALE**
hardy person **SPARTAN**
Hardy's heroine **TESS**
harebrained **RECKLESS, RASH**
harem apartment **ODA**
hark **LISTEN**
harm **DAMAGE, MAR, HURT**
harmless **GENTLE, DOCILE**
harmonious **AGREEABLE**
harmonize **AGREE, BLEND**
harmony **UNISON, ACCORD**
harmony in pitch **TUNE**
harness attachment **REIN**
harry **HARASS, ANNOY**
harsh **SEVERE**
harshest **SEVEREST**
harsh speech **TIRADE**
hart **DEER, STAG**
Harvard's rival **YALE**
harvest **CROP, REAP**
harvest fly **CICADA**
hash **MINCE**
hash over **DISCUSS**
hassle **CONTENTION**
hassock **FOOTSTOOL**
haste **SPEED, SWIFTNESS**
hasten **HIE, RUN, SPEED**
hasty **HURRIED, FLEET**
hasty meal **SNACK**
hat **BONNET, CAP, BERET,
CHAPEAU**
hat accessory **VEIL, RIBBON**
hatch **PLOT, PLAN**
hatchet **AX, AXE**
hat crown **POLL**
hate **ABHOR, DETEST, LOATHE**
hateful **ODIOUS**
hat material **FELT, STRAW**
hatred **ODIUM, DISLIKE**
haughtiness **ARROGANCE,
PRIDE**
haughty **PROUD, ALOOF**
haughty one **SNOB**
haul **DRAG, TOW, TUG**
haul down flag **STRIKE**
hauling charge **CARTAGE**
hauling wagon **DRAY**
haulm **STRAW**
haul up **REST, STOP**
haunch **HIP**
haunt **DEN, HABIT**
hausen **BELUGA**
hautboy **OBOE**
have **OWN, POSSESS, HOLD**
have affection for **LIKE, LOVE**
have ambitions **ASPIRE**
have a meal **EAT, DINE, SUP**

have another opinion **DIFFER**
have a quarrel (2 wds.) **FALL OUT**
have at **ATTACK, STRIKE**
have being **ARE**
have benefit **ENJOY**
have courage (2 wds.) **BEAR UP**
have debts **OWE**
have done **FINISH**
have effect **ENURE, INURE**
have faith **TRUST**
have high regard for **ADMIRE**
have interest in **CARE**
have life **LIVE, EXIST**
have need of **LACK**
have reference to **PERTAIN**
have the ability **CAN**
have the courage **DARE TO**
have to **MUST**
have to do with **DEAL**
haven **HARBOR, PORT,
ASYLUM**
having a backbone **VERTEBRATE**
having a beak **ROSTRATE**
having a good memory
**RETENTIVE**
having antlers **HORNED**
having a tail **CAUDATE**
having auricles **EARED**
having boots **SHOD**
having equality of measure
**ISOMETRICAL**
having feet **PEDATE**
having fine scenery **SCENIC**
having knowledge **AWARE**
having leaves **FOLIAR**
having left a will **TESTATE**
having less hair **BALDER**
having liberty **FREE**
having limits **FINITE**
having little warmth **COLD**
having made a will **TESTATE**
having offensive odor **OLID**
having one foot **UNIPED**
having onionlike forms **BULBED**
having pile **NAPPY**
having ringlets **CURLY**
having wealth position, etc.
**SUCCESSFUL**
having wings **ALAR, ALATE**
Hawaiian city **HILO, HONOLULU**
Hawaiian Dance **HULA**
Hawaiian export **COPRA,
PINEAPPLE**
Hawaiian food fish **LANIA, ULUA**
Hawaiian food staple **TARO**
Hawaiian garland **LEI**
Hawaiian goddess **PELE**
Hawaiian greeting **ALOHA**

| | |
|---|---|
| Hawaiian guitar | UKULELE, UKE |
| Hawaiian hawk | IO |
| Hawaiian island | OAHU |
| Hawaiian lava | AA |
| Hawaiian mahogany | KOA |
| Hawaiian pepper | AVA |
| Hawaiian porch | LANAI |
| Hawaiian root | TARO |
| Hawaiian salutation | ALOHA |
| Hawaiian town | HILO |
| hawker | PEDDLER |
| Hawkeye State | IOWA |
| hawk-like bird | KITE |
| hawk's claws | TALON |
| hawkshaw's | SLEUTH |
| hawk's victims | PREY |
| Hawthorne heroine | HESTER |
| hay fever | POLLEN |
| hay field | MEADOW |
| hayseed | RUBE, HICK |
| haystack | STADDLE |
| haywire | CRAZY, WACKY |
| hazard | RISK |
| hazardous | UNSAFE, RISKY |
| haze | MIST, FOG |
| hazelnut | FILBERT |
| hazy | CLOUDY, MURKY |
| he (Fr.) | IL |
| head | PATE, CHIEF, NOODLE, NOGGIN, BEAN |
| headache | MIGRAINE |
| headache remedy | ASPIRIN |
| headcloth | SCARF |
| head cook | CHEF |
| head covering | CAP, HAT, HOOD, SCARF, BERET, VEIL |
| headdress | FEATHER |
| headed pin | RIVET |
| heading | TITLE, BEARING, DIRECTION |
| headland | CAPE, NESS, RAS |
| headless (Fr.) | ETETE |
| headline | CAPTION |
| headliner | STAR |
| headlong | RECKLESS, HASTY |
| headman | CHIEF |
| head money | BOUNTY |
| head of a monastery | ABBOT |
| head of a nunnery | ABBESS |
| head skin | SCALP |
| headstrong | RASH |
| heal | CURE, MEND |
| heal, as bone | KNIT |
| healer | BALM |
| healing | CURATIVE |
| healing profession | MEDICINE |
| health resort | SPA |
| healthy | HALE, ROBUST |

| | |
|---|---|
| healthy (Lat.) | SANA |
| heap | MOUND, PILE, STACK |
| heap of stone | CAIRN |
| hear | HEED, LISTEN |
| hear about | LEARN |
| hearing organ | EAR |
| hearken | HEED, LISTEN |
| hearsay | RUMOR, GOSSIP |
| heart | CORE |
| heartbeat | PULSE |
| heartbreak | GRIEF, SORROW |
| hear tell | LEARN |
| hearten | CHEER |
| hearth | FIRESIDE |
| heartless | COLD, HARD, CRUEL |
| heart of the matter | GIST |
| hearty | WARM |
| hearty enjoyment | ZEST |
| hearty laugh (comp. wd.) | HA-HA |
| hearty meat dish | STEW |
| hearty relish | GUSTO |
| heat | WARMTH, PRESSURE |
| heat content | ENTHALPY |
| heater | STOVE, OVEN |
| heath (Brit.) | MOOR |
| heathen (arch.) | PAYNIM |
| heathen deity | IDOL |
| heather | LING, ERICA |
| heath plant | ERICA |
| heath tree | BRIER, BRIAR |
| heating apparatus | ETNA, OVEN, OAST, KILN, BOILER, BRAZIER, STOVE |
| heating chambers | OVEN, OAST, KILN |
| heating material | FUEL, OIL, GAS, WOOD |
| heave | HOIST, LIFT |
| heave to | STOP |
| heaven | PARADISE |
| heavenly | DIVINE, SUBLIME, CELESTIAL |
| heavenly altar | ARA |
| heavenly being | ANGEL |
| heavenly body | COMET, STAR, PLANET, SUN, MOON, METEOR |
| heavenly city | ZION, VALHALLA |
| heavenly instrument | HARP |
| heavens | SKY |
| heavenward | UP |
| heavily built | STOCKY |
| heavily loaded | LADEN |
| heavy | WEIGHTY, LEADEN |
| heavy affliction | WOE |
| heavy board | PLANK |
| heavy blow | CLOUT |

| | | | |
|---|---|---|---|
| heavy book | **TOME** | height | **STATURE** |
| heavy burden | **LOAD** | heighten | **ENHANCE** |
| heavy cord | **ROPE** | heinous | **HIDEOUS,** |
| heavy curtain | **DRAPE** | | **OUTRAGEOUS** |
| heavy element | **LEAD** | heir | **SON, SCION** |
| heavy-footed | **SLOW, DULL** | held in readiness (2 wds.) | **ON ICE** |
| heavy grouping of reeds | **CLUMP** | hell | **HADES, INFERNO** |
| heavy-handed | **CLUMSY, HARSH** | hello | **HI, GREETING** |
| heavy-hearted | **SAD** | helmsman | **PILOT** |
| heavy hydrogen | **DEUTERIUM** | help | **ABET, AID, ASSIST** |
| heavy impact | **SLAM** | helper | **ALLY, AIDE, ASSISTANT** |
| heavy metal | **LEAD** | helpful | **USEFUL** |
| heavy nail | **SPIKE** | help in crime | **ABET** |
| heavy rainfall | **STORM** | helping | **PORTION** |
| heavy-set | **STOUT, STOCKY** | help in solving a mystery | **CLUE** |
| heavy shoe | **BOOT, BROGAN,** | helpless | **POWERLESS** |
| | **CLOG** | helpmate | **WIFE** |
| heavy sleepers | **SNORERS,** | Helsinki native | **FINLANDER** |
| | **BUNTING** | helter-skelter | **RUSHED,** |
| heavy spar | **BARITE** | | **DISORDERLY** |
| heavy string | **CORD, TWINE,** | hem | **BORDER, EDGE** |
| | **ROPE** | hemi | **HALF** |
| heavy twilled cotton | **DENIM** | hem in | **ENCLOSE** |
| heavy volume | **TOME** | hemorrhage | **BLEEDING** |
| heavy weight | **TON** | hemp | **FENNEL, SISAL** |
| heavy with moisture | **SODDEN** | hemp cord | **ROPE** |
| Hebrew | **SEMITE, SEMITIC** | hen | **CHICKEN, PULLET** |
| Hebrew abode of dead | **SHEOL** | henchman | **MINION** |
| Hebrew ascetic | **ESSENE** | hen fruit | **EGG** |
| Hebrew lawgiver | **MOSES** | hens | **POULTRY** |
| Hebrew letter | **ALEF, BETH,** | herald | **MESSENGER** |
| **GIMEL, DALETH, MEM,** | | heraldic bearing | **ORLE** |
| **TETH, PE, YOD, HE,** | | heraldic cross | **PETTEE,** |
| **VAU, ZAYIN, CHETH,** | | | **POMMEE, MOLINE, TAU,** |
| **VODH, CAPH, LAMEDH,** | | | **MALTESE, FOURCHEE,** |
| **NUN, SAMEKH, AYIN,** | | | **BOTONEE, CROSSLET** |
| **SADHE, KOPH, RESH,** | | Hera's husband | **ZEUS** |
| **SIN, SHIN, TAV** | | Hera's son | **ARES, HEPHAETOS** |
| Hebrew lyre | **ASTOR** | herb | **SAGE, ANISE, BASIL** |
| Hebrew marriage custom | | herb of the teasel family | |
| | **LEVIRATE** | | **SCABIOSA** |
| Hebrew measure | **OMER** | Hercules' captive | **IOLE** |
| Hebrew month | **TISHRI, ADAR,** | herd | **DROVE, FLOCK** |
| **ELUL, AB, KISLEV** | | here (Fr.) | **ICI** |
| Hebrew patriarch | **ABRAHAM,** | hereditary | **INHERENT, INNATE** |
| **ISAAC, JACOB** | | hereditary factor | **GENE** |
| Hebrew prophet | **MOSES,** | heretic | **DISSENTER, TRAITOR** |
| **DANIEL, AMOS,** | | heritage | **LEGACY, BIRTHRIGHT** |
| **HOSEA, MICAH** | | hermit | **EREMITE, RECLUSE** |
| Hebrew prophetess | **DEBORAH** | hermit's hut | **CELL** |
| Hebrew Sabbath | **SATURDAY,** | hernia support | **TRUSS** |
| | **SHABBAT** | hero of comics | **SUPERMAN,** |
| Hebrew school | **CHEDER** | | **BATMAN, DICK TRACY** |
| Hebrew teacher | **RABBI** | heroic | **EPIC** |
| heckle | **BADGER, PESTER** | heroic tale | **SAGA** |
| hectic | **FEVERISH** | heroine of A Doll's House | **NORA** |
| hedge shrub | **PRIVET** | heroine of The Rose Tattoo | |
| heed | **HEAR** | | **ROSA** |

| | | | |
|---|---|---|---|
| heroism | VALOR, BRAVERY | high intensity light beam | LASER |
| heron | EGRET | high in value | DEAR |
| hero's award | MEDAL | high keyed | TENSE |
| herring | CISCO, SPRAT | highlander | SCOT |
| herring alec | PICKLE | highlander's cap | TAM |
| herring family fish | ALEWIFE | highly | EXTREMELY |
| he-she dispute (2 wds.) | | highly seasoned dish | OLLA, |
| | LOVERS' QUARREL | | PODRIDA |
| hesitate | DEMUR, FALTER, | highly sensible | PRUDENT |
| PAUSE, STUMBLE, WAVER | | high male singing voice | TENOR |
| hesitation of speech | STUTTER | high-minded | NOBLE |
| heterogeneous | VARIANT, MIXED, | high mountain | ALP |
| | DISSIMILAR | high note | ELA, ALT |
| hew | CUT, CHOP | high-pitched | SHRILL |
| hew out | CARVE | high plateau | MESA |
| hex | JINX | high pointed hill | TOR |
| Heyerdahl's raft (2 wds.) | | high priced | COSTLY |
| | KON TIKI | high priest of Israel | ELI |
| Hialeah event (2 wds.) | | high rank | EMINENCE |
| | HORSE RACE | high regard | ESTEEM, RESPECT, |
| hiatus | GAP, PAUSE | | HONOR |
| Hiawatha's nurse | NOKOMIS | high rubber boot | WADER |
| Hibernian | ERSE | high school dance | HOP, PROM |
| hickory nut | PECAN | high school student | |
| hidden | INNER, LATENT, | (comp. wd.) | TEENAGER |
| | COVERT | high sea | MAIN |
| hidden obstacle | SNAG | high shoe | BOOT |
| hidden supply | CACHE | high spirits | ELATION, GLEE |
| hide | CONCEAL, COVER, | high structure | TOWER |
| MASK, PELT, SKIN | | high strung | TENSE, NERVOUS |
| hideous | GHASTLY, HORRIBLE | high temperature | HEAT |
| hideous giant | OGRE | high time | SPREE |
| hiding place | CACHE, LAIR | high up | ALOFT |
| hie | HASTEN, HURRY, | highway | ROAD, ROUTE, PIKE |
| | SPEED, RUN | highway charge | TOLL |
| hiemal | WINTRY | highway curve | ESS |
| hieratic | SACERDOTAL | highway division | LANE |
| hieroglyphic | SYMBOL | highway exit | RAMP |
| hierology | LORE, FABLE | highway inn | MOTEL |
| hi-fi | STEREO | highwayman (2 wds.) | |
| high | TALL, LOFTY | | ROAD AGENT |
| highbinder | SWINDLER | highway sight | BILLBOARD |
| highborn | NOBLE | highway to the far north | ALCAN |
| highboy | BUREAU, CHEST | high winds | GALE, SQUALL, |
| highbrow | INTELLECTUAL | | STORM, HURRICANE, |
| high card | ACE | | TORNADO, CYCLONE |
| high-class | SUPERIOR | high wire | TIGHTROPE |
| high craggy hill | TOR | hijack | STEAL, CAPTURE |
| high day | FESTIVAL, HOLIDAY | hike | MARCH, TRAMP |
| higher than | ABOVE | hilarious | FUNNY, MERRY |
| highest note | ELA | hilarious comedy | FARCE |
| highest point | ACME, APEX, | hilarity | GLEE, MIRTH |
| | SUMMIT | hill | HEAP, MOUND |
| high-flying bird | LARK, EAGLE | hill (Sp.) | MORRO |
| high-hatter | SNOB | hill dweller | ANT |
| high honkers (2 wds.) | | hillock | KNOLL |
| | WILD GEESE | hill of beans | TRIFLE |
| high in pitch | ALT | hillside (Scot.) | BRAE |

hilly **RUGGED, STEEP**
Hilo garland **LEIS**
hilt **HANDLE**
Himalayan animal **PANDA**
Himalayan monkshood **ATIS**
Himalayan mountain **EVEREST**
Himalayan ox **YAK**
hind **DOE, DEER**
hinder **DETER, STOP, SET BACK**
hinder (law) **ESTOP, ESTOPPEL**
Hindi dialect **URDU**
hindrance **OBSTACLE, BURDEN, IMPEDIMENT**
Hindu ascetic **SADHU, SADDHU, YOGI**
Hindu ascetic practice **YOGA**
Hindu chief **SIRDAR**
Hindu coin **ANAA**
Hindu cymbals **TAL**
Hindu deity **DEVI, VAC, UMA, KALI, MATRIS, AGNI, SIVA, DEVA, KAMA, RAMA, YAMA, VISHNU, KRISHNA, INDRA, USAS, SURYA, VARUNA, SHAKTI, GANESA**
Hindu doctrine **KARMA**
Hindu garment **SARI**
Hindu guitar **SITAR**
Hindu incarnation **AVATAR**
Hindu king **RAJAH**
Hindu literature **VEDA**
Hindu noble **RAJAH**
Hindu queen **RANEE, RANI**
Hindu religious teacher **SWAMI**
Hindu sacred city **BENARES, BANARAS**
Hindu social class **CASTE**
hinged tabletop folding to wall **DROP TABLE**
hint **CLUE, CUE, SUGGESTION**
hint (Brit.) **CLEW**
hinterland **BACKWOODS**
hip (sl.) **AWARE, COOL**
hipbone **ILIUM, ILIA (pl.)**
hippie's home **PAD**
hippocampus (2 wds.) **SEA HORSE**
Hippocrates **PHYSICIAN**
hippodrome **ARENA**
hippopotamus (2 wds.) **RIVER HORSE**
hire **EMPLOY, ENGAGE, RENT, LEASE, LET, CHARTER**
hired help **HAND**
hireling **SERF, MERCENARY**
hirsute **HAIRY**
hirundine **SWALLOW**

hiss **SIBILANCE**
hissing sound **SISS**
historian **CHRONICLER**
historical records **ANNALS**
historic island of the Philippines **LEYTE**
historic period **ERA, EPOCH**
history **ACCOUNT, RECORD**
histrionics **THEATRICS**
hit **STRIKE, BAT**
hitch **CATCH, TWIST**
hitchhike **THUMB**
hit hard **SWAT, SMOTE, SMITE, SLAP**
hither **HERE**
hithermost **NEAREST**
Hitler follower **NAZI**
hit lightly **TAP**
hit or miss **CARELESS**
hit out at **ATTACK, CRITICIZE**
hit-show sign (abbr.) **S.R.O.**
hit the road **SCRAM**
hit with the open hand **SLAP**
hive dweller **BEE, WASP, HORNET**
hive product **HONEY**
hoard **SAVE**
hoarder **MISER**
hoarfrost **RIME**
hoarse **HARSH, GRATING**
hoax **FOOLER**
hobble along **LIMP**
hobbling **LAME**
hobby **AVOCATION, PURSUIT**
hobgoblin **IMP, SPRITE**
hobo **BUM, TRAMP, VAGRANT**
hock **PAWN**
hockey game **BANDY**
hockey player **SKATER**
hodgepodge **MESS, MIXTURE, HOTCHPOTCH**
hoe **WEED, DIG**
hog **PIG, SWINE**
hog food **SLOP**
hog meat **HAM, PORK, BACON**
hogshead **CASK**
hoi polloi **RABBLE**
hoist **HEAVE, LIFT**
hoisting device **CRANE**
hold **GRASP, KEEP, CLASP**
hold an opinion **DEEM**
hold back **DELAY, DETAIN, PREVENT, RESTRAIN, RETARD**
hold dear **CHERISH**
hold fast **CLING, ADHERE**
hold firmly **CLASP, GRASP, GRIP**

| | |
|---|---|
| hold in check | **CURB, REIN** |
| holding device | **CLAMP, VISE** |
| holding of property | **TENURE** |
| hold in greater favor | **PREFER** |
| hold out | **ENDURE, LAST** |
| hold session | **SIT, MEET** |
| hold spellbound | **ENTHRALL,** |
| | **MESMERIZE, HYPNOTIZE** |
| hold sway | **RULE** |
| hold up | **ROB, ROBBERY** |
| hold up well | **WEAR** |
| hold within fixed | |
| limits | **CONTAIN** |
| hole | **CAVITY, PIT,** |
| | **EXCAVATION, CAVE, CAVERN** |
| hole enlarger | **REAMER** |
| hole in a mold | **SPRUE** |
| hole in a pan | **LEAK** |
| hole-in-one | **ACE** |
| hole-making tool | **AWL** |
| holey cheese | **SWISS** |
| holiday | **FESTIVAL** |
| holiness | **SANCTITY, PIETY** |
| holler | **ROAR, YELL** |
| hollow | **EMPTY** |
| hollow grass | **REED, BAMBOO** |
| holly tree | **ILEX** |
| Hollywood event | **ACADEMY** |
| | **AWARDS, PREMIERE,** |
| | **SCREENING, SHOWING** |
| Hollywood hopeful | **STARLET** |
| Hollywood luminary | **STAR** |
| Hollywood's elephant boy | **SABU** |
| holm | **AIT** |
| holm oak | **ILEX** |
| holocaust | **DESTRUCTION** |
| holy (Fr.) | **SACRE** |
| holy city of Islam | **MECCA** |
| holy image | **ICON** |
| Holy Land | **PALESTINE** |
| holy person | **SAINT** |
| Holy Roman Empire (abbr.) | |
| | **H.R.E.** |
| holy souvenir | **RELIC** |
| holy water receptacle | **FONT** |
| homage | **HONOR** |
| homard | **LOBSTER** |
| homburg | **HAT** |
| home | **ABODE, DWELLING,** |
| | **HOUSE, APARTMENT,** |
| | **FIRESIDE, HEARTH,** |
| | **RESIDENCE** |
| home base | **PLATE** |
| home-grown | **DOMESTIC** |
| home in Madrid | **CASA** |
| homeless child | **WAIF** |
| homelike | **HOMEY** |
| homely | **UGLY, PLAIN** |

| | |
|---|---|
| homemade | **DOMESTIC** |
| home of Abraham | **UR** |
| home of Adam and Eve | **EDEN** |
| home of Irish kings | **TARA** |
| home of Scarlett O'Hara | **TARA** |
| home party (2 wds.) | **OPEN** |
| | **HOUSE** |
| Homeric epic | **ILIAD, ODYSSEY** |
| Homeric poem | **EPIC, ILIAD,** |
| | **ODYSSEY** |
| Homeric wise man | **NESTOR** |
| homesickness | **NOSTALGIA** |
| homesite | **LOT** |
| homesteader | **SETTLER** |
| homicide | **MURDER** |
| homily | **ADAGE, SERMON** |
| hominy | **SAMP, GRITS** |
| homogeneous | **UNIFORM, ALIKE** |
| homo sapiens | **MAN** |
| Honduras Indian | **LENCA** |
| hone | **SHARPEN, WHET** |
| honest | **TRUTHFUL, JUST,** |
| | **FRANK, OPEN, CANDID, FAIR** |
| honesty | **SINCERITY,** |
| | **FRANKNESS, CANDOR** |
| honey (pharm.) | **MEL** |
| honey badger | **RATEL** |
| honey bee genus | **APIS** |
| honeycomb cell | **ALVEOLUS** |
| honeycomb product | **BEESWAX** |
| honey maker | **BEE** |
| honk | **TOOT, BEEP** |
| honor | **EXALT** |
| honorable | **HONEST, EXALTED,** |
| | **ESTEEMED** |
| honorary disc | **MEDAL** |
| honorary title for | |
| retired VIP's | **EMERITUS** |
| Honshu bay | **ISE** |
| hood | **COWL** |
| hooded cape | **AMICE, DOMINO** |
| hooded vestment | **COPE** |
| hoodwink | **DUPE** |
| hoofbeat sound | **CLOP, CLIP** |
| hoofer | **DANCER** |
| hook | **GAFF** |
| Hoosier State | **INDIANA** |
| hoot | **JEER, HISS** |
| hop | **LEAP, JUMP** |
| hope | **ASPIRATION, WISH** |
| hopeful time | **TOMORROW** |
| hopeless | **DESPERATE** |
| hop kiln | **OAST** |
| hopping insect | **FLEA** |
| hop stem | **BINE** |
| horde | **CROWD, MULTITUDE,** |
| | **HOST, MOB** |
| horizon | **SKYLINE** |

horizontal **PLANE, LEVEL**
horn **CORNET, BUGLE, ANTLER, CORNUCOPIA**
horn blare **FANFARE, TANTARA**
horned animal **STAG, ELK, MOOSE**
horned cud-chewer **GOAT, COW**
horned viper **ASP**
horn of plenty **CORNUCOPIA**
horns **BRASS**
horn sound **TOOT, HONK**
horrible **HATEFUL, REPULSIVE**
horror **DISGUST, AVERSION**
hors d'oeuvre mixture **DIP**
horse **FOAL, ROAN, MARE, NAG, PLUG STALLION, STEED,**
horse and buggy **RIG**
horseback game **POLO**
horse bet **PARLAY, WAGER**
horse color **ROAN**
horse command **GEE, HAW, WHOA**
horsedoctor, for short **VET**
horsefeathers **NONSENSE, BUNK**
horse food **HAY, OATS, FODDER**
horsehair **CRINOLINE**
horselaugh **GUFFAW**
horselike mammal **MULE, DONKEY, BURRO, ZEBRA**
horseman **EQUESTRIAN, RIDER, JOCKEY**
horseman's goad **SPUR**
horse measure **HAND**
horse opera **WESTERN**
horse race **DERBY**
horse racing (4 wds.) **THE SPORT OF KINGS**
horse rope **HALTER, HACKAMORE**
horse's ankle **HOCK**
horse's foot **HOOF**
horse's gait **LOPE, TROT, CANTER, GALLOP**
horse's gear **HARNESS, REIN, SADDLE, BRIDLE, BLINDER**
horse's long neck-hair **MANE**
horse soldiers **CAVALRY**
horse's shoe spur **CALK**
horse-training rope **LONGE**
horticulturist **FLORIST, GARDENER**
hose **STOCKINGS**
hospitable **FRIENDLY, CORDIAL**
hospital **INFIRMARY, CLINIC**
hospital assistant (2 wds.) **NURSE'S AIDE**

hospital doctor **INTERN, RESIDENT**
hospitalization **INSURANCE**
hospital section **WARD**
host **ARMY, MULTITUDE**
hostelry **INN, TAVERN, HOTEL, MOTEL**
hostile **CONTRARY, OPPOSED**
hostile criticism **CENSURE**
hostile feeling **ANGER**
hostile force **ENEMY, FOE**
hostile incursion **RAID**
hostility **WAR, BATTLE, FIGHT**
hostler **GROOM**
hot **TORRID**
hot and humid **STICKY, TROPIC, TORRID**
hot chocolate **COCOA**
hotel **INN, HOSTEL**
hotel guest **PATRON**
hotheaded **RASH, HASTY**
hothouse **GREENHOUSE**
hot Mexican specialty **TAMALE**
hot spring **GEYSER, SPA**
hot vapor **STEAM**
hot water tank **BOILER**
hound **DOG**
hound's quarry **HARE, FOX**
hour and minute **TIME**
hourglass **TIMER**
hourglass contents **SAND**
hourly **HORAL, HORARY**
house **RESIDENCE, DWELLING**
house (Sp.) **CASA**
house addition **ELL, WING**
house and grounds **PREMISES**
House and Senate **CONGRESS**
houseboat **BARGE**
house-breaker **BURGLAR**
housebroken **TRAINED**
house broker **REALTOR**
housecoat **ROBE**
house fuel **GAS, OIL, COAL, WOOD**
household **MENAGE**
household animal **PET, DOG, CAT**
household appliance **WASHER, DRIER, STOVE, IRON, TOASTER, BLENDER, MIXER, REFRIGERATOR**
household gods **LARES, PENATES, LARS**
household linen **NAPERY**
housekeeper **MATRON**
house member **LEGISLATOR, REP**
housemother **CHAPERONE**

house of healing **HOSPITAL**
house of logs **CABIN**
house pet **DOG, CAT, FISH, CANARY, PARAKEET**
house plant **FERN, IVY**
house projection **DORMER**
housetop **ROOF**
housetop feature **GABLE, EAVE**
housewifely **DOMESTIC**
housewife's title (abbr.) **MRS.**
house wing **ELL, ADDITION**
housing **LODGING, SHELTER**
Houston ballplayer **ASTRO**
hovel **HUT**
hover **LINGER, SUSPEND**
however **YET**
howl **BAY, WAIL**
hoyden **TOMBOY**
hub **CENTER**
hubbub **ADO, TO-DO, STIR**
hub of a wheel **NAVE**
Huckleberry Finn character **JIM**
Huckleberry Finn's craft **RAFT**
huckster **HAWKER, PEDDLER**
huddle **CONFER**
hue **COLOR, TINT, SHADE**
huffy **TESTY, TOUCHY**
hug **CLASP, CARESS, FONDLE, HOLD**
huge **BIG, ENORMOUS, LARGE, VAST**
huge animal **ELEPHANT, HIPPO, RHINO**
huge continent **ASIA**
huge stone **BOULDER**
Huguenot **PROTESTANT**
huitre **OYSTER**
hulky **HEAVY**
hull **HUSK**
hullabaloo **HUBBUB**
hulled corn **SAMP**
hum **DRONE, BUZZ**
human being **ADAMITE, MAN, MORTAL, PERSON, WOMAN**
human bondage **SLAVERY**
humane **KIND, MERCIFUL**
humanity **MANKIND**
human trunk **TORSO**
humble **ABASE, MEEK, MODEST**
humbug **ROT, BAH**
humdrum **MONOTONOUS, TRITE, BANAL**
humid **DANK, MOIST, DAMP**
humiliate **SHAME, DISGRACE**
humility **MODESTY**
hummock **KNOLL**
humor **WIT**

humorist **COMIC, WIT, WAG, COMEDIAN, SATIRIST**
humorous **COMIC, FUNNY**
humorous play **FARCE, COMEDY**
humor to excess **PAMPER**
hump **BULGE, LUMP**
hump-backed animal **CAMEL, DROMEDARY**
Hun **VANDAL**
hunch **INTUITION**
hunchback **QUASIMODO**
hundredth anniversary **CENTENNIAL**
Hungarian **MAGYAR**
Hungarian wine **TOKAY**
hunger pain **PANG**
hungery **STARVING, UNFED**
hungry rodent **SHREW**
Hung Wu dynasty **MING**
hunt **CHASE, SEARCH, SEEK**
hunt for bargains **SHOP**
hunter **NIMROD, CHASER, SEEKER**
hunter's shelter **LODGE, CAMP, TENT**
hunter's shoe **BOOT**
hunting dog **BASSET, SETTER, POINTER, BEAGLE, HOUND**
hunting expedition **SAFARI**
hurdle **JUMP, BARRIER**
hurl **THROW, FLING, SLING, TOSS**
hurly-burly **TUMULT**
hurrah, for short **RAH**
hurricane **GALE, TEMPEST, STORM**
hurricane center **EYE**
hurry **RACE, DASH, HASTEN, SPEED, RUN, HIE, SHAKE A LEG, GET A MOVE ON**
hurt **ACHE, PAIN, WOUND**
husband **MAN, SPOUSE**
husbandman **FARMER**
husband of Bathsheba **URIAH**
husband of Isis **OSIRIS**
husband of Minnehaha **HIAWATHA**
husbandry **FARMING**
hush **QUIET, CALM**
hush-hush business process (2 wds.) **TRADE SECRET**
husk **HULL**
husk of wheat grain **BRAN**
hustle **RUSH, DRIVE**
hustler **PROMOTER**
hut **HOVEL, SHANTY**

| | |
|---|---|
| hutch | **CHEST** |
| hygiene | **SANITATION** |
| hymn of joy | **PEAN, PAEAN** |
| hymn of thanksgiving | **TE DEUM** |
| hymn's finale | **AMEN** |
| hypersensitivity | **ALLERGY** |
| hyphen | **DASH** |
| hypnotic spell | **TRANCE** |
| hypocrisy | **SHAM** |
| hypocrite | **DECEIVER** |
| hypocritical | **FALSE, INSINCERE** |
| hypocritical sorrow (2 wds.) | |
| | **CROCODILE TEARS** |
| hypothesis | **THEORY** |
| hyssop | **MINT, FIGWORT** |
| | |
| I (Ger.) | **ICH** |
| Iago's wife | **EMILIA** |
| iatric | **MEDICAL** |
| Iberian lady | **DONA** |
| ibex | **GOAT** |
| Ibsen character | **ASE, NORA,** |
| **PEER GYNT, HEDDA GABLER,** | |
| **LONA, HELMER** | |
| ice | **COOL, FROST, CHILL** |
| ice carrier | **TONGS** |
| ice cream drink | **SODA, SHAKE,** |
| **MALTED, FROSTED, FLOAT** | |
| ice cream holder | **CONE** |
| iced | **GLACE** |
| ice fishing gear | **GIG** |
| Icelandic epic | **EDDA** |
| Icelandic giant | **ATLI** |
| Icelandic legend | **SAGA** |
| Icelandic literary work | **EDDA** |
| ice mass | **BERG, FLOE** |
| ice runner | **SKATE** |
| ice tower | **SERAC** |
| ichneumon | **MONGOOSE** |
| icicle | **STALACTITE** |
| icing | **GLAZE** |
| icon | **IMAGE** |
| icy | **FRIGID, FROSTY, COLD** |
| icy precipitation | **SLEET, HAIL** |
| Idaho city | **BOISE** |
| ide | **FISH** |
| idea | **BRAINSTORM, THOUGHT,** |
| **CONCEPTION, INSPIRATION,** | |
| **OPINION, CONCEPT, NOTION** | |
| idea (prefix) | **IDEO** |
| ideal | **PERFECT** |
| identical | **TWIN, SAME, ALIKE,** |
| | **SIMILAR** |
| identical sibling | **TWIN** |
| identify | **RECOGNIZE, NAME** |

| | |
|---|---|
| idiocy | **FOLLY** |
| idiom | **PHRASE** |
| idiomatic | **COLLOQUIAL** |
| idiot | **FOOL, IMBECILE** |
| idiotic | **INANE, FOOLISH** |
| idle | **INACTIVE, LAZY** |
| | **LOITER** |
| idle away time | **LOAF** |
| idle rumor | **GOSSIP** |
| idle talk | **PATTER, PRATE** |
| idler | **LOAFER** |
| idol | **HERO, GOD, IMAGE,** |
| | **DEITY, WORSHIP** |
| idolize | **ADORE, DEIFY,** |
| | **WORSHIP** |
| idyll | **POEM** |
| if | **PROVIDED, PROVISO** |
| if not | **ELSE** |
| igloo builder | **ESKIMO, ALEUT** |
| igneous rock | **BASALT** |
| ignite | **LIGHT, FIRE** |
| ignoble | **MEAN, BASE** |
| ignominious | **VILE** |
| ignominy | **SHAME, INFAMY** |
| ignorant | **UNTAUGHT, DENSE** |
| ignore | **ELIDE, NEGLECT** |
| I have found it | **EUREKA** |
| ilk | **KIND, TYPE** |
| ill | **SICK, AILING, TROUBLE,** |
| | **WOE, BAD** |
| ill-boding | **DIRE** |
| ill-bred person | **CAD** |
| illegal business | **RACKET** |
| illegal eavesdropping device | |
| | **WIRETAP** |
| Illinois city | **PEORIA, CHICAGO** |
| illiterate signature | **EX** |
| ill-tempered person | **CRAB** |
| ill-tempered woman | **SHREW** |
| illusion | **CHIMERA** |
| illustration | **EXAMPLE, DRAWING** |
| illustration placed within | |
| another | **INSET** |
| illustrator | **ARTIST** |
| illustrious | **EMINENT, GRAND** |
| ill will | **RANCOR** |
| illuminate | **LIGHT** |
| I love (Lat.) | **AMO** |
| image | **ICON, IDOL, LIKENESS,** |
| | **PICTURE** |
| imaginary | **FANCIFUL,** |
| | **ILLUSORY** |
| imaginary marine creature | |
| | **MERMAID** |
| imagination | **FANCY** |
| imagine | **DREAM, CONCEIVE** |
| imbecile | **DOLT, MORON** |
| imbed firmly (2 wds.) | **SET IN** |

| | |
|---|---|
| imbibe | **DRINK** |
| imbue | **COLOR, SUFFUSE** |
| imbue thoroughly | **STEEP,** |
| | **SATURATE** |
| imitate | **MIMIC, APE, COPY** |
| imitate Sam Spade | **TAIL** |
| imitation | **COPY, ERSATZ,** |
| | **MIMICRY** |
| immaculate | **PURE** |
| immature | **INFANTILE, YOUNG** |
| immediately | **ANON, SOON,** |
| | **AT ONCE** |
| immediately following | **NEXT** |
| immense | **VAST, HUGE, LARGE,** |
| | **ENORMOUS** |
| immerse | **DIP, DUNK** |
| imminent | **IMPENDING,** |
| | **THREATENING** |
| immoral | **CORRUPT, EVIL** |
| immortal | **ETERNAL** |
| immortal spirit | **ANGEL** |
| immunity | **EXEMPTION** |
| imp | **PIXIE** |
| impair | **MAR, WEAR, INJURE** |
| impalpable | **VAGUE, INTANGIBLE** |
| impart | **CONVEY, BESTOW** |
| impartial | **FAIR, EQUITABLE** |
| impart knowledge to | **EDUCATE,** |
| | **TEACH** |
| impassive | **STOICAL, STOLID,** |
| | **APATHETIC** |
| impatient | **EAGER** |
| impeach | **CENSURE, DENOUNCE** |
| impeccable | **SPOTLESS,** |
| | **PERFECT** |
| impede | **HINDER** |
| impediment | **OBSTACLE, SNAG** |
| impel | **URGE, PROD, EGG ON,** |
| | **SPUR, PROPEL** |
| impend | **LOOM** |
| impersonate | **MAKE LIKE, MIMIC** |
| impervious to rain | **LEAKPROOF** |
| impetuous | **RASH, BRASH,** |
| | **HASTY** |
| impetuous person | **HOTHEAD** |
| implement | **TOOL** |
| implement of warfare | **WEAPON** |
| impolite | **RUDE** |
| importance | **MOMENT, VALUE** |
| important | **VITAL** |
| important bridge card | **TRUMP** |
| important occurrence | **EVENT** |
| important part | **PITH, LEAD** |
| importune | **URGE, COAX, BEG,** |
| | **PLEAD** |
| impose a tax | **ASSESS, LEVY** |
| impose restrictions (2 wds.) | |
| | **CLAMP DOWN** |
| imposing | **IMPRESSIVE,** |
| | **STRIKING** |
| imposing series | **ARRAY** |
| imposture | **RUSE, PRETENSE** |
| impotent | **BARREN, STERILE** |
| impoverished | **NEEDY, POOR** |
| impregnable | **INVINCIBLE,** |
| | **SECURE** |
| impression | **DENT, IDEA,** |
| | **STAMP** |
| impressive | **AWESOME** |
| imprison | **IMMURE** |
| imprisonment | **DURESS** |
| impromptu (2 wds.) | **AD LIB** |
| improve | **BETTER** |
| improvident | **PRODIGAL** |
| improvise (2 wds.) | **AD LIB** |
| imprudent | **RASH, HASTY** |
| impudence | **BRASS, SASS** |
| impudent | **BRASSY, FRESH,** |
| | **SASSY, PERT** |
| impugn | **ATTACK, CHALLENGE,** |
| | **REFUTE** |
| impulse | **URGE, WHIM** |
| impulsive | **RASH, HASTY** |
| impure | **UNCLEAN, CORRUPT** |
| impute | **ASCRIBE, ATTRIBUTE** |
| inability | **IMPOTENCE** |
| in abundance | **GALORE** |
| inaccuracy | **ERROR, MISTAKE** |
| inaccurate | **FAULTY** |
| inactive | **IDLE, INERT** |
| inactivity | **INERTIA** |
| in addition | **ALSO, TOO, AND,** |
| | **YET** |
| inadequate | **WANTING** |
| in a difficult position | **TREED** |
| in a direct line (4 wds.) | |
| | **AS THE CROW FLIES** |
| in agreement (2 wds., Fr.) | |
| | **EN RAPPORT** |
| in a line | **ALONG, AROW** |
| in all places | **EVERYWHERE** |
| in ancient times | **EARLY** |
| inane | **POINTLESS, TRITE,** |
| | **FOOLISH** |
| inanimate | **INERT, LIFELESS** |
| in another direction | **AWAY** |
| in another place | **ELSEWHERE** |
| in any case | **ANYWAY** |
| in any manner | **SOMEWAY** |
| in any way (2 wds.) | **AT ALL** |
| in a pile | **AHEAP** |
| inappropriate | **INEPT, UNFIT** |
| in a row | **ALINED, AROW** |
| in a sheltered place | **ALEE** |
| in a short time | **SOON, ANON** |
| inaugurate | **START** |

| | |
|---|---|
| in bad temper | CROSS |
| in behalf of | FOR |
| in between | MID |
| inborn | INNATE, NATURAL |
| inbred | INNATE |
| Inca country | PERU |
| incandescence | GLOW |
| incapable of being obliterated | INDELIBLE |
| incapacity of | QUA |
| incarnate | EMBODIED, PERSONIFIED |
| incarnation of Vishnu | RAMA |
| in case that | IF, LEST |
| incense | ENRAGE, INFURIATE |
| incense burner | CENSER, THURIBLE |
| incentive | MOTIVE |
| inception | START, INITIATION |
| incessant | UNENDING |
| inch along | EDGE, CREEP |
| incident | EVENT |
| incidental information | SIDELIGHT, TRIVIA |
| incite | GOAD, SPUR, URGE |
| incivility | DISRESPECT |
| inclement | SEVERE, STORMY |
| inclination | SLOPE, TREND, TENDENCY |
| incline | SLANT, SLOPE, TILT |
| inclined walkway | RAMP |
| incline the head | BOW, NOD |
| include | CONTAIN, INVOLVE |
| incoherent | GARBLED |
| income | REVENUE, SALARY, WAGES |
| income from housing | RENTAL |
| in common | ALIKE |
| in company of | WITH |
| incomparable | UNRIVALED, PEERLESS, SUPREME |
| incompatible | CONTRARY |
| incompetence | INABILITY |
| incompetent | INEPT |
| incomplete | UNFINISHED |
| in conflict (2 wds.) | AT WAR |
| incongruous expression (2 wds.) | IRISH BULL |
| inconsistent | VARYING |
| inconstant | CHANGING, UNSTABLE |
| in controversy (2 wds.) | AT ISSUE |
| incorrect (prefix) | MIS- |
| increase | INCREMENT, GROWTH |
| increased by | PLUS |
| increase in size | GROW, SWELL |
| increase in wages (2 wds.) | PAY RAISE |
| increment | INCREASE |
| incrustation | SCAB |
| inculcate | INSTILL, IMBUE |
| incumbent | BINDING, REQUIRED |
| in current style | MODISH |
| incursion | RAID, INROAD |
| incus | ANVIL |
| in debt | OWING |
| indeed | AYE, YES, REALLY, OF COURSE |
| indefatigable | TIRELESS, UNTIRING |
| indefinite | UNCERTAIN, VAGUE |
| indefinite amount | SOME, ANY |
| indefinite article | AN, A |
| indefinite number | MANY, SEVERAL, SOME, ANY |
| indelible | FIXED |
| indemnify | GUARANTEE |
| independent | FREE, UNENCUMBERED, AUTONOMOUS |
| independent thing | ENTITY |
| index | FILE, LIST |
| India, class of | CASTE |
| India rubber | CAOUT CHOUC |
| Indian | CREE, ERIE, OSAGE, PAWNEE, UTE, SIOUX, APACHE, PIMA, NAVAHO |
| Indiana city | GARY, SOUTH BEND, TERRE HAUTE, FORT WAYNE, INDIANAPOLIS |
| Indianapolis competitor | RACER, DRIVER |
| Indianapolis 500 | RACE |
| Indian boat | CANOE |
| Indian buffalo | ARNA, ARNEE |
| Indian coin | ANNA |
| Indian drum | TOMTOM |
| Indian garment | SARI |
| Indian group | TRIBE |
| Indian maize | CORN |
| Indian mercenary | SEPOY |
| Indian of Peru | INCA |
| Indian of Yucatan | MAYA |
| Indian pony | CAYUSE |
| Indian rainy season | MONSOON |
| Indian ruler | RAJAH |
| Indian state | NEPAL |
| Indian tent | TEPEE, WIGWAM, TIPEE, TIPI |
| Indian territory | OKLAHOMA |
| Indian tribe | ERIE, SIOUX |
| Indian trophy | SCALP, COUP |
| Indian unit of weight | SER |
| Indian warrior | BRAVE |
| Indian woman | SQUAW |

indicate assent **NOD**
indicate beforehand **PORTEND, PRESAGE**
indication **CLUE, SIGN, HINT**
indifference **APATHY**
indifferent **ALOOF, BLASE, DISINTERESTED, SO-SO**
indigence **WANT, POVERTY, NEED**
indigenous **NATIVE, INNATE**
indignation **ANGER, IRE**
indignity **INSULT, AFFRONT**
indigo dye **ANIL**
indirect **DEVIOUS**
indirect allusion **HINT, CLUE**
indiscreet **RASH**
in disorder **ASKEW, MESSY, UNTIDY**
indispensable **ESSENTIAL, NECESSARY**
indistinct **DIM, VAGUE, FAINT**
individual **ONE, PERSON, UNIT**
Indo-European **ARYAN**
indolent **OTIOSE, LAZY**
Indonesian capital **DJAKARTA**
Indonesian island **BALI, JAVA, SUMATRA**
indorse **RATIFY, CONFIRM**
induce **EVOKE, LEAD**
indulge **PAMPER, FAVOR**
indulger in fantasy **DREAMER**
industrial fuel **COKE**
industrious **BUSY, DILIGENT**
industrious creature **ANT, BEE**
industry **ACTIVITY**
inebriated **DRUNK**
in effect **OPERATIVE**
ineffective **USELESS**
inept serviceman (2 wds.) **SAD SACK**
in equal degree **AS**
in error **WRONG, MISTAKEN**
inert **IDLE, INACTIVE, PASSIVE**
inert gas **ARGON, NEON**
inevitable outcome **DOOM, FATE, DESTINY**
in excess **OVER, TOO**
in existence **ALIVE**
inexpensive **CHEAP**
inexpensive cigar **STOGIE**
inexperienced **RAW, YOUNG, GREEN, NEOPHYTE, NOVICE, TYRO**
infallible **UNERRING**
infamous **CONTEMPTIBLE, BASE**
infamous Roman emperor **NERO**
infamy **DISHONOR, DISGRACE**

infant **BABY**
infant cupid **AMOR**
infant enclosure **CRIB, PLAYPEN**
infant food **PAP, PABLUM, FORMULA, MILK**
infant garment **DIAPER, SACQUE, BUNTING**
infant's bed **CRIB, CRADLE, BASSINET**
in favor of **PRO, FOR**
infect **POISON, POLLUTE**
infer **DEDUCE**
inference **CONCLUSION**
inferior **BENEATH, POOR**
inferior in size **PUNY, RUNTY**
inferior race horse **PLATER**
inferior ship accommodations **STEERAGE**
infernal **SATANIC, DEMONIC, HELLISH, DAMNABLE**
infielder **BASEMAN**
infiltrate **PENETRATE**
infinite **UNLIMITED, BOUNDLESS**
infinity of time **EON**
infirm **WEAK, FEEBLE**
inflame **IRRITATE, CHAFE**
inflame with love **ENAMOR**
inflate **EXPAND**
inflexible **STIFF, FIRM**
inflict **IMPOSE**
in flight (3 wds.) **ON THE WING**
influence **IMPRESS, PRESTIGE**
influence with flattery **WHEEDLE, PANDER**
infold **WRAP**
informal chat at meal (2 wds.) **TABLE TALK**
informal letter **NOTE**
informal talk **CHAT, GAB**
information **DATA, DOPE, INFO, FACTS**
informed **AWARE, HEP, HIP**
infrequent **RARE**
infrequently **SELDOM, RARELY**
infringe **TRESPASS, VIOLATE**
in front **AHEAD**
infuriate **ENRAGE**
infuse **INSTILL, IMBUE**
in general favor **POPULAR**
ingenious **CLEVER**
ingenuous **NAIVE**
in good condition **SOUND, FIT, HEALTHY**
in good order **NEAT**
ingratiate **CHARM, FLATTER**
ingredient **ELEMENT**
inhabitant **DENIZEN, RESIDENT**
inhabitant of (suffix) **ITE**

inhabited by a ghost **HAUNTED**
inherent character **NATURE**
inheritor **HEIR**
in high spirits **MERRY**
iniquity **EVIL**
initiate **START, BEGIN**
in itself (2 wds.) **PER SE**
injure **DAMAGE, HARM,**
**WOUND, MAR, HURT**
injure seriously **MAIM, CRIPPLE**
injure with a knife **STAB**
injure with horns **GORE**
injurious **DELETERIOUS**
injury **WOUND, HURT, DAMAGE**
injury mark **CICATRIX, SCAR,**
**SCAB**
injustice **WRONG, INEQUITY**
ink **DRAW, WRITE**
inkling **CLUE, HINT, IDEA**
ink stain **BLOT**
ink writing instrument **PEN,**
**QUILL, PRESS**
inky **BLACK**
inland sea **LAKE**
inlay **FILLING**
inlay work **MOSAIC**
inlet **BAY, RIA**
in line **AROW**
in lower position **DOWN, BELOW**
in manner of (Fr.) **A LA**
in motion **ASTIR**
inn **HOTEL, TAVERN, MOTEL,**
**HOSTEL**
innate **INHERENT**
innate skill **TALENT, ABILITY,**
**FLAIR**
in neat layers **STACKED**
inner **INSIDE, INTERIOR**
Inner Hebrides island **IONA**
inner self **EGO**
inner surface of the hand **PALM**
innocent **NAIVE, PURE**
innocuous **HARMLESS**
in no manner **NOT**
in no way **NOWISE**
inordinate **EXCESSIVE, UNDUE**
inordinate self-esteem **EGO,**
**CONCEIT**
inorganic substance **METAL,**
**PLASTIC**
in other words (4 wds.)
**THAT IS TO SAY**
in place of **INSTEAD**
in present conditions (2 wds.)
**AS IS**
in progress **AFOOT**
in proper manner **DULY**
in pursuit of **AFTER**
inquire **ASK, REQUEST**

inquire curiously **PRY**
inquiry **QUESTION, RESEARCH**
inquiry for lost goods **TRACER**
inquisition **PURGE, INQUEST**
inquisitive **PRYING, CURIOUS**
inquisitive (sl.) **NOSY**
in rags **TATTERED**
in recent times **LATELY**
in regard to (Scot.) **ANENT**
inroad **RAID, INCURSION**
insane **CRAZY, MAD**
insane person **LUNATIC,**
**MADMAN**
insanity **MANIA, LUNACY**
insatiable **GREEDY**
inscribe **ENGRAVE, WRITE**
inscribed tablet **STELE**
inscription **EPIGRAPH, LEGEND**
inscrutable **MYSTERIOUS**
insect **ANT, BEE, BEETLE,**
**ROACH, BUG, KATYDID,**
**MANTIS, APHID, LOCUST,**
**FLY, WASP, TICK, FLEA,**
**MOTH, TERMITE**
insect antenna **FEELER**
insect at a picnic **ANT**
insect bite **STING**
insect egg **NIT**
insect feeler **PALP**
insect pupa **CHRYSALIS**
insect stage **PUPA, LARVA,**
**EGG, ADULT**
insect trap **WEB**
insecticide **PARIS GREEN, DDT**
insidious **DECEITFUL**
insight **INTUITION**
insignificant **PETTY, SLIGHT**
insignificant matter **TRIVIALITY**
insinuate **INTIMATE, HINT**
insipid **TASTELESS, WATERY**
in so far as (Lat.) **QUA**
insolence (2 wds.) **BACK TALK**
insolent **OFFENSIVE, RUDE**
insolvent **BANKRUPT**
in some other place **ELSEWHERE**
in sour spirits **CROSS**
inspiration **IDEA**
inspire **AWE**
in spite of **DESPITE**
instant **MOMENT, SECOND,**
**WINK, MINUTE, TRICE**
instead **LIEU**
instigate (2 wds.) **STIR UP,**
**SPUR ON, ROUSE UP,**
**URGE ON**
instruct **EDUCATE, TEACH,**
**COACH, TUTOR**
instructor, for short **PROF**
instrument board **PANEL**

insubordination **DEFIANCE, REVOLT**
in such a manner **SO, THIS**
insult **AFFRONT, INDIGNITY**
in support of **FOR, BEHIND**
insurance payment **PREMIUM**
insurgent **REBEL**
intact **WHOLE, COMPLETE**
integer **NUMERAL, UNIT, ENTITY**
integrity **HONESTY**
intellect **MIND**
intellectual **EGGHEAD**
intelligence **SENSE, WIT**
intelligent **SMART, BRAINY, BRIGHT**
intelligible **CLEAR, LUCID**
intemperance **EXCESS**
intend **AIM, MEAN, PLAN**
intensify **ENHANCE**
intensity **ENERGY, FORCE**
intent **RAPT**
intent look **STARE**
intention **AIM, GOAL, END**
intentional **DELIBERATE**
intentionally (2 wds.) **ON PURPOSE**
inter **BURY**
interdict **CUT, DEBAR, BAN**
interdiction **BAN**
interest **PROFIT, CONCERN**
interest-bearing certificate **BOND**
interfere **MEDDLE, INTRUDE, TAMPER**
interfering **MEDDLESOME**
interim **MEANTIME**
interim ruler **REGENT**
interior **INNER, INSIDE**
interjection **ALAS, OH**
interlace **ENTWINE, WEAVE**
interlaced design **FRET, LACE**
interlock **KNIT, UNITE**
interloper **INTRUDER**
intermediate (law) **MESNE**
intermediate (prefix) **MES**
interminable **ENDLESS, INFINITE**
intermittent **BROKEN, PERIODIC**
intermittently (3 wds.) **OFF AND ON**
internal **INNER**
internal revenue supporter **TAXPAYER**
international monopoly **CARTEL**
international tennis cup **DAVIS**
international treaty **PACT**

international understanding **ENTENTE**
interpose **INTERCEDE**
interpret **EXPLAIN, TRANSLATE**
interpretation **EXPLANATION**
interrupt (2 wds.) **CUT IN, BUTT IN**
intersect **CROSS, CUT**
intersection of lines **ANGLE**
intersection sign **STOP, YIELD**
interstice **PORE, CHINK, CREVICE, INTERVAL**
intertwine **LACE**
interurban railroad **EL**
interval of relief **RESPITE**
intervene (2 wds.) **STEP IN, MEDDLE IN**
intervening (law) **MESNE**
interweave **MAT**
in that case **THEN**
in that place **THERE**
in the center **AMID**
in the direction of **TOWARD, TO**
in the future **LATER**
in the interim **MEANWHILE**
in the know **AWARE, HEP, HIP**
in the last month **ULTIMO**
in the middle of **AMID**
in the offing **NEAR, SOON**
in the past **AGO**
in the place **AT**
in the same place (abbr.) **IBID.**
in the time of **DURING**
in this manner **SO, THUS**
in this place **HERE**
intimate **CLOSE, FAMILIAR**
intimation **HINT, CLUE**
intimidate **DAUNT, DISMAY**
intolerable **UNBEARABLE**
intone **CHANT**
intoxicating liquor **SPIRITS**
intrepid **BRAVE, BOLD**
intricate **COMPLEX**
intrigue **CABAL, PLOT**
intrinsic **GENUINE**
introduction **PREFACE, PRELUDE**
introductory discourse **PROEM, PREFACE**
introductory performance **PRELUDE, OVERTURE**
in truth **INDEED, VERILY**
intuitive feeling **HUNCH**
inundation **FLOOD**
invading throng **HORDE, MOB**
invent **DEVISE, CREATE**
invention protection **PATENT**
inventor Whitney **ELI**

| | | | |
|---|---|---|---|
| invigorating medicine | **TONIC** | irrational | **FOOLISH, ABSURD** |
| invisible | **UNSEEN** | irregularly notched | **EROSE** |
| invisible emanation | **AURA** | irrelevant | **EXTRANEOUS** |
| invitation | **BID** | irreligious | **IMPIOUS** |
| invite | **ASK, ATTRACT, LURE** | irresolute | **UNDECIDED** |
| invocation | **PRAYER, SERMON** | irresponsible | **UNRELIABLE** |
| invoice | **BILL** | irrigate | **WATER** |
| invoke | **ELICIT** | irrigation dike | **LEVEE** |
| involve | **ENTAIL, INCLUDE** | irritable | **FRETFUL, TESTY** |
| inward | **INNER, INTERN** | irritate | **IRK, RILE, NETTLE,** |
| in what place | **WHERE** | | **TEASE** |
| in what way | **HOW** | irritated | **SORE** |
| in what way (Lat.) | **QUO MODO** | irritation | **PIQUE** |
| iota | **JOT** | is | **EXISTS** |
| IOU endorser | **OWER** | is (Sp.) | **ES, ESTA** |
| Iowa college town | **AMES** | Isaac's mother | **SARAH** |
| Iran | **PERSIA** | Isaac's son | **DSAU, JACOB** |
| Iran's neighbor | **IRAQ, IRAK** | is able to | **CAN** |
| Irani ruler | **SHAH** | is angered at | **RESENTS** |
| irate | **ANGRY, MAD, WRATHFUL,** | is appropriate | **SUITS** |
| | **FURIOUS** | is aware of | **KNOWS** |
| ire | **ANGER, CHOLER** | is compelled | **MUST** |
| Ireland | **ERIN, EIRE,** | is concerned | **CARES** |
| | **EMERALD ISLE** | is curious | **WONDERS** |
| irenic | **SERENE, PEACEFUL** | is disposed kindly toward | |
| iridescent | **OPALINE** | (2 wds.) | **TAKES TO** |
| iridescent gem | **OPAL** | is excessively fond of | **DOTES** |
| iris | **IXIA, FLAG, RAINBOW** | Ishmael's mother | **HAGAR** |
| iris with fragrant roots | **ORRIS** | is human | **ERRS** |
| Irish | **CELTIC, ERSE** | is inclined | **LEANS** |
| Irish cattle | **KERRY** | is indebted to | **OWES** |
| Irish chemist | **BOYLE** | isinglass | **MICA** |
| Irish city | **BELFAST, CORK** | is in store for | **AWAITS** |
| Irish clan | **SEPT** | Isis' husband | **OSIRIS** |
| Irish county | **MAYO, CORK** | Islamic holy city | **MECCA,** |
| Irish dagger | **SKEAN** | | **MEDINA** |
| Irish dance | **REEL** | Islamic name | **ALI** |
| Irish dish | **STEW** | island (Fr.) | **ILE** |
| Irish emblem | **SHAMROCK** | island (Ital.) | **ISOLA** |
| Irish expletive | **ARRAH, GO-ON** | island in the Mediterranean | |
| Irish fairy | **BANSHEE** | | **ELBA, MALTA, CYPRUS,** |
| Irish Free State | **EIRE** | | **CORSICA, SICILY** |
| Irish fuel | **PEAT** | island in the West Indies | **CUBA,** |
| Irish-Gaelic | **ERSE** | | **JAMAICA** |
| Irish island group | **ARAN** | island nation | **HAITI, IRELAND,** |
| Irish king's home | **TARA** | | **JAPAN, FORMOSA** |
| Irish lass | **COLLEEN** | island near Athens | **SALAMIS** |
| Irish moss | **CARRAGEEN** | island near Corsica | **ELBA,** |
| Irish poet | **WILDE, YEATS** | | **SARDINIA** |
| Irish republic | **EIRE** | island near Greece | **CRETE** |
| Irish sea god | **LER** | island near Italy | **MALTA** |
| Irish seaport | **COBH** | island of exile | **ELBA,** |
| irk | **ANNOY** | | **ST. HELENA** |
| iron bar | **ROD** | island off China | **NATSU HAINAN** |
| iron clothes | **PRESS** | island off Mozambique | **IBO** |
| iron coating | **RUST** | island off Scotland | **IONA** |
| iron compound | **FERRITE, STEEL** | island of saints | **ERIN** |
| iron rod | **BAR** | | |

island of the Aegean **LEROS, IOS, DELOS, MELOS, NAXOS**
island of the Bahamas **BIMINI**
island of the Cyclades **DELOS, ANDROS, TENOS, NAXOS, MELOS**
island of the Philippines **SAMAR**
island republic **EIRE, IRELAND, PHILIPPINES**
islands between North and South America (2 wds.) **WEST INDIES**
islands near Florida **BAHAMAS, KEYS**
island south of Australia **TASMANIA**
island south of Sicily **MALTA**
isle in a river **AIT**
isle in the Bay of Naples **CAPRI**
isle off coast of Ireland **ARAN**
islet **AIT**
ism **DOCTRINE**
is no more **GONE**
is not (arch.) **NIS**
is not well **AILS**
is obliged to **MUST**
isolate **SEPARATE, SECLUDE**
isolation **SOLITUDE**
isometrics **EXERCISES**
is on fire **BURNS**
is overfond **DOTES, SPOILS**
is possible **MAY**
is present at **ATTENDS**
Israel, formerly **PALESTINE**
Israeli coins **MILS**
Israeli folk dance **HORA**
Israeli port **HAIFA, ELATH**
Israeli round dance **HORA**
is situated **LIES**
is successful **WINS, TRIUMPHS**
issue **EMIT, FLOW**
issue forth **EMANATE**
is suitable to **BECOMES**
isthmus **NECK**
is unable to (contr.) **CAN'T**
is unsuccessful **FAILS**
is worthy of **DESERVES**
Italian actress **LOREN, MAGNANI**
Italian affirmative **SI**
Italian art center **SIENA, ROME, VENICE, FLORENCE**
Italian capital **ROME**
Italian city **GENOA, TURIN**
Italian coin **LIRA**
Italian commune **ASOLA**

Italian delicacy **RAVIOLI, SPAGHETTI, PASTA, ANTIPASTO**
Italian epic poet **TASSO**
Italian family **ESTE, BORGIA**
Italian family of violin makers **AMATI**
Italian house **CASA, VILLA**
Italian housewife's title **SIGNORA**
Italian innkeeper **PADRONE**
Italian island **LIDO, SICILY**
Italian lady **DONNA**
Italian lake **ALBANO, COMO**
Italian monetary unit **LIRA**
Italian monk **FRA**
Italian poet **DANTE**
Italian port **GENOA, NAPLES, BARI**
Italian resort **LIDO, CAPRI**
Italian river **ARNO, PO, TIBER**
Itch **HANKER, URGE**
item **DETAIL, PARAGRAPH**
itemize **DETAIL**
item of clothing **TOG**
item of gossip **RUMOR**
item often tossed **SALAD, COIN, BALL**
item of value **ASSET**
itinerant **ARRANT, ERRANT, NOMAD**
itinerary **ROUTE**
it is (contr.) **'TIS, IT'S**
itty-bitty **TINY**
Ivan the Terrible **TSAR**
ivory **DENTINE**
ivy **VINE**
Ivy League member **YALE, HARVARD, PRINCETON, DARTMOUTH, COLUMBIA**
ixia **IRIS**


**J**

jab **POKE, THRUST, BLOW, PUNCH**
jabber **CHATTER, PRATE, PRATTLE**
jabberwocky **NONSENSE, GIBBERISH**
jabot material **LACE**
jack at cards **KNAVE**
jacket **COAT**
jack-in-the-pulpit **ARUM**
jackrabbit **HARE**
jacks or better **OPENERS**

| | |
|---|---|
| Jack Sprat's meat | LEAN |
| Jack Tar's drink | GROG |
| Jacob's brother | ESAU |
| Jacob's father | ISAAC |
| Jacob's father-in-law | LABAN |
| Jacob's first wife | LEAH, LEI |
| Jacob's son | JOSEPH, LEVI, DAN, |
| RUBEN, AS(H)ER, BENJAMIN, | |
| SIMEON, JUDA, ISSACHAR, | |
| ZABULON, GAD, NEPHTHALI | |
| Jacob's wife | LEAH, RACHEL |
| jacquard | LOOM |
| jade | TIRE |
| jagged | ROUGH |
| jai alai | PELOTA |
| jail (Brit.) | GAOL |
| jail breaker | ESCAPEE |
| jail room | CELL |
| jalousie | BLIND, SHUTTER |
| Jamaican witchcraft | OBEAH |
| Jane Austen title | EMMA |
| Jane Eyre author | BRONTE |
| Japan | NIPPON |
| Japanese aborigine | AINO, AINU |
| Japanese-American | NISEI, |
| SANSEI, ISSEI, KIBEI | |
| Japanese beverage | SAKE, TEA |
| Japanese coin | SEN, YEN |
| Japanese drama | NO, NOH |
| Japanese metropolis | KYOTO, |
| | TOKYO |
| Japanese musical instrument | |
| | KOTO |
| Japanese outlaw | RONIN |
| Japanese pagoda | TAA |
| Japanese plant | UDO |
| Japanese port | KOBE, OSAKA |
| Japanese robe | KIMONO |
| Japanese sash | OBI |
| Japanese statesman | ITO |
| Japanese zither | KOTO |
| jar | JOLT, SHAKE |
| jar cover | LID, TOP |
| jardiniere | URN, VASE, POT |
| jargon | CANT, ARGOT |
| Jason's ship | ARGO |
| jaunt | TRIP |
| jaunty | PERKY |
| java | COFFEE |
| Javanese tree | UPAS |
| Jayhawk State | KANSAS |
| jazz music | BEBOP |
| jealous | ENVIOUS |
| jealousy | ENVY |
| jeer | MOCK, JIBE |
| jeer at | TAUNT |
| jelly | ASPIC, GELATIN |
| jerk (colloq.) | YANK |
| jerky | CHOPPY, MEAT |
| jest | JOKE, JAPE, QUIP |
| jesting talk | JAPERY |
| jet | FLY, BLACK, PLANE |
| jet black | RAVEN |
| jet pilot | FLYER |
| jetty | WHARF, PIER |
| Jew | SEMITE, HEBREW |
| jewel | GEM |
| jeweled coronet | TIARA |
| jeweler's weight | CARAT |
| Jewish ascetic | ESSENE |
| Jewish bible | TORAH |
| Jewish Day of Atonement | |
| | YOM KIPPUR |
| Jewish feast | PASSOVER, SEDER, |
| | PESACH |
| Jewish leader | RABBI |
| Jewish month | HESHVAN, |
| KISLEV, TEBET, SHEBAT, | |
| ADAR, VEADAR, NISAN, | |
| IYAR, SILVAN, TAMMUZ, | |
| TISHRI, AB, ELUL | |
| Jewish nation | ISRAEL |
| Jewish prayer book | SIDDUR |
| Jewish quarter | GHETTO |
| Jewish school | (C)HEDER |
| Jewish scripture | TORAH |
| Jewish spiritual leader | RABBI |
| Jewish teacher | RABBI |
| jib | BOOM, CRANE |
| jibe | TAUNT |
| jiffy | INSTANT |
| jiggle | VIBRATE |
| jingle | TINKLE, VERSE |
| jinx | HEX |
| job | CHORE, TASK |
| job for Perry Mason | CASE |
| Job's home | UZ |
| jocose | JOKING, PLAYFUL |
| jocular | COMICAL |
| jocund | CHEERFUL |
| jog | TROT |
| joggle | DOWEL |
| johnnycake | PONE |
| Johnson's vice president | |
| | HUMPHREY |
| join | ADD, CONNECT, UNITE, |
| WED, MARRY, TIE, WELD, | |
| MELD, SOLDER, YOKE | |
| join forces | UNITE |
| join securely | TENON |
| join strands | SPLICE |
| joint | ELBOW, KNEE, ANKLE |
| join the army | ENLIST |
| join the colors | ENLIST |
| join the race | RUN |

joint on which a door swings **HINGE**
joke **GAG, JEST**
joke anthology **ANA**
jokester **WAG, WIT**
jollity **MIRTH**
jolly **JOCULAR, MERRY**
jolly boat **SKIFF, YAWL**
jolt **JAR**
Jonah **JINX**
josh **TEASE**
Joshua's partner to Canaan **CALEB**
Joshua tree **YUCCA**
jostle **SHOVE, PUSH**
jot **IOTA**
jounce **JOLT, BOUNCE**
journal **NEWSPAPER, PAPER, DIARY, RECORD, LOG**
journalist **REPORTER**
journalist Sevareid **ERIC**
journey **TOUR, TRAVEL, TRIP, TREK**
journey for another **ERRAND**
journey's interruption **STOPOVER**
joust **TILT**
jovial **JOLLY**
jowl **CHOP, JAWBONE**
joy **GLEE, ELATION, HAPPINESS, BLISS**
Joyce Kilmer poem **TREES**
joyful **ELATED, GLAD, GAY MIRTHFUL, JUBILANT**
joyous **HAPPY, GLAD**
Jubal **MUSICIAN**
jubilant **ELATED, JOYFUL**
jubilation **REJOICING**
Judas tree **CERCIS, REDBUD**
Judean king **ASA, HEROD**
judge **DEEM, OPINE**
judge in a dispute **ARBITER**
judge's aide (2 wds.) **COURT CLERK**
judge's bench **BANC**
judge's chambers **CAMERAS**
judge's command (4 wds.) **ORDER IN THE COURT**
judge's concern **CASE**
judge's gown **TOGA, ROBE**
judge's hammer **GAVEL**
judgeship **CHAIR**
judgment **DECISION**
judicial order **WRIT**
judiciary **BENCH**
judicious **WISE, PRUDENT**

Judy Garland movie **WIZARD OF OZ, A STAR IS BORN, THE PIRATE, EASTER PARADE**
jug **EWER, PITCHER**
juice drink **ADE**
juicer **REAMER**
juicy **SUCCULENT**
juicy fruit **ORANGE, LEMON, GRAPEFRUIT, PEAR, PLUM, PEACH, LIME**
Juliet's lover **ROMEO**
Julliard specialty **MUSIC**
jumbled medley **OLIO**
jumbled type **PI**
jump **LEAP, HOP**
jumping insect **FLEA**
jumping stick **POGO**
jump on **SCOLD**
jump suit **OVERALLS**
junction **MEETING, UNION**
juncture **SEAM, JOINT**
june bug **DOR**
jungle cat **TIGER, PANTHER, LION**
jungle drum **TOM-TOM**
jungle snake **BOA**
junior **NAMESAKE**
Junior League event (2 wds.) **DEBUTANTE BALL**
junior or senior (2 wds.) **COLLEGE STUDENT**
junior's father **SENIOR**
juniper bush **SAVIN**
juniper tree **CEDAR**
junket **TOUR, TRIP**
jupe **SKIRT**
Jupiter **JOVE**
jurisdiction **AUTHORITY**
jury **PANEL**
just **ONLY, FAIR**
just gone by **PAST**
justice **FAIRNESS**
justify **WARRANT**
just perfect **IDEAL**
just right (3 wds., sl.) **ON THE BEAM**
Jute leader **HORSA, HENGIST**
Jutland native **DANE**
juvenile **YOUNG, YOUTHFUL, CHILDISH, CHILD**

**K**

Kaddish **PRAYER**

karate blow **CHOP**
karma **FATE**
kasha **MUSH, GROATS**
katydid **INSECT, GRASSHOPPER**
kayak **CANOE**
keen **SHARP**
keen enjoyment **ZEST**
keen insight **ACUMEN**
keen intuitive power (2 wds.) **SIXTH SENSE**
keenly desirous **EAGER, AVID**
keenly eager **AVID**
keenly honed **SHARP**
keenness **ACUMEN**
keen relish **GUSTO**
keep **RETAIN, HOLD, RESERVE, MAINTAIN**
keep afloat **BUOY**
keep clear of **EVADE, SHUN**
keeper **GUARD, WARDEN**
keeper of an elephant **MAHOUT**
keep going **SUSTAIN**
keep in check **RESTRAIN**
keeping **CUSTODY, CHARGE**
keepsake **TOKEN, MOMENTO**
keepsake box **CHEST**
keep within one's means (4 wds.) **MAKE BOTH ENDS MEET**
keg **BARREL, CASK**
kelp **ALGA**
ken **UNDERSTANDING**
kennel dwellers **CANINE, DOG**
kennel sound **YAP, YELP, YIP, WOOF, BOWWOW, ROWF, GRRR**
Kentucky blue grass **POA**
Kentucky college **BEREA**
Kentucky Derby entry **HORSE**
kernel **CORN, SEED, GERM**
kerosene **OIL**
kerosene lantern **LAMP**
ketch **SAIC**
ketone **ACETONE**
kettle **POT**
kettle drum **TYMPANUM**
key **OPENER, SOLUTION**
keyboard instrument **ORGAN, PIANO, SPINET**
keyhole **SLOT**
Keystone State **PENNSYLVANIA**
kick **BOOT**
kick a football **PUNT**
kid **CHILD, GOAT**
kill **SLAY, MURDER**
kill a fly **SWAT**
killed **SLEW, SLAIN**

killer whale **ORC**
killick **ANCHOR**
Kilmer poem **TREES**
kiln **OAST, OVEN**
kiloliter **STERE**
kilt **PLEAT, SKIRT**
kimono **ROBE**
kimono sash **OBI**
kin **FAMILY, RELATIVES**
kind **ILK, SORT, TYPE, CLASS, GENTLE, NICE, GENRE**
kindle **LIGHT, FIRE**
kindly **NICE**
kindness **COMPASSION**
kind of **SOMEWHAT, RATHER**
kind of art **POP, OP, MODERN**
kind of automobile **STATION WAGON, SEDAN, COUPE, ROADSTER, HOT ROD**
kind of bark **CANELLA**
kind of beaver **EAGER**
kind of beer **LAGER, BITTER, PILSNER**
kind of bread **RYE, WHITE, WHEAT, CORN**
kind of cheese **EDAM, BRIE, GOUDA, SWISS, CHEDDAR, STILTON**
kind of clock **ALARM**
kind of cloth **COTTON, SILK, SATIN, RAYON, NYLON, LINEN**
kind of corn bread **PONE**
kind of couch **DIVAN, SETTEE, LOVE SEAT**
kind of dog **PUG, POM, PEKE, MUTT, CUR, SPANIEL, HOUND**
kind of fabric **CORD, SCRIM**
kind of feed **BRAN**
kind of firecracker **DEVIL**
kind of fuel **GAS, OIL, PEAT, COAL, WOOD**
kind of grain **WHEAT, OATS**
kind of hammer **PEEN, GAVEL**
kind of income **RENT**
kind of lettuce **COS, BIB, BOSTON, ICEBERG, ROMAINE**
kind of marble **AGATE, TAW**
kind of meat **PORK, HAM, BEEF, VEAL, STEAK, LAMB**
kind of moth **LUNA, MILLER**
kind of music **OPERA, POP, ROCK, BLUES, COUNTRY, JAZZ**
kind of nut **PECAN, ALMOND, WALNUT**
kind of onion **LEEK**
kind of overshoe **GAITER**

| | | | |
|---|---|---|---|
| kind of paper | RICE | king's chair | THRONE |
| kind of pastry | PIE, CAKE, | king's hat | CROWN |
| | TART, COOKIE | king's representative | VICEROY |
| kind of pie | MINCE, APPLE, | king (Sp.) | REY |
| | PUMPKIN | king's son | PRINCE |
| kind of power | ATOMIC, | king's yellow | ORPIMENT |
| | ELECTRIC | kinship | AFFINITY |
| kind of race | RELAY | kinsman | RELATIVE |
| kind of rocket | RETRO | Kirghiz mountain range | ALAI |
| kind of salesmen (comp. wd.) | | kiss | SMOOCH, BUSS |
| | DOOR-TO-DOOR, | kit | OUTFIT, GEAR |
| | HOUSE-TO-HOUSE, | kitchen appliance | TOASTER, |
| | TRAVELING | | OPENER, STOVE, |
| kind of sea food | SHRIMP, CLAM, | | REFRIGERATOR, GRILL |
| | CRAB, LOBSTER | kitchen gadget | CORER, DICER, |
| kind of signal | DANGER, ALARM, | | RICER, PRESS, CUTTER, HILL |
| | STOP, GO | kitchen garment | APRON |
| kind of singing club | GLEE | kitchen implement | SPATULA, |
| kind of slipper | MULE | | KNIFE, SPOON, SCRAPER, |
| kind of soil | LOAM | | SIEVE |
| kind of stew | POTTAGE | kitchen rug | MAT |
| kind of test | ORAL | kitchen stove | RANGE |
| kind of trowel | PLANE | kitchen vessel | KETTLE, POT, |
| kind of velvet | PANNE | | PAN, SAUCEPAN |
| kind of violin (sl.) | STRAD | kite | ELANET |
| kind of weapon | BAZOOKA, | kite part | TAIL |
| | GUN, RIFLE, | kith | FRIENDS |
| | ARROW, CANNON | kitsch | SHALLOW, POP |
| kind or class | SORT | kitten's cry | MEW, MEOW |
| king | RULER, MONARCH | Kiwanis member | MAN |
| king (Fr.) | ROI | kiwi | BIRD |
| king (Lat.) | REX | klatch (klatsch) | GATHERING, |
| King Arthur's capital | CAMELOT | | HEN PARTY, BREAK |
| King David's grandfather | OBED | knack | ART, TALENT, FLAIR |
| kingdom | REALM | knapsack | BAG |
| kingfish | OPAH | knave | RASCAL, JACK |
| King James' translation | BIBLE | knead | MASSAGE |
| kingly | REGAL, ROYAL | knee | PATELLA, JOINT |
| King Minos' daughter | ARIADNE | kneehole and rolltop | DESKS |
| King Mongkut's land | SIAM | knickknack | NOTION, WHATNOT |
| King Mongkut's tutor | ANNA | knife edge | BLADE |
| king of beasts | LION | knife for dissecting | SCALPEL |
| king of birds | EAGLE | knife maker | CUTLER |
| king of fairies | OBERON | knife swinger | SLASHER |
| king of gods | JUPITER | knight | CAVALIER, SIR |
| king of Israel | AHAB, DAVID, | knight errant | PALADIN |
| | SAUL | knightly champion | PALADIN |
| king of Judah | ASA | knightly quest | GRAIL |
| king of Judea | HEROD | knight's assistant | PAGE |
| king of Norway | OLAF | knight's clothing | ARMOR |
| king of Persia | DARIUS | knight's lance banner | |
| king of the golden touch | MIDAS | | GONFALON |
| king of the Huns | ATLI, ATTILA | knight's title | SIR |
| king of the Lapithae | IXION | knit | WEAVE |
| king of the Visigoths | ALARIC | knitting stitch | LOOP, PURL, |
| king of Troy | PRIAM | | CABLE, KNIT |
| king's baton | SCEPTER | knitting wool | YARN |
| king's blue | COBALT | knives | CUTLERY |

knob **NODE**
knock **RAP, TAP**
knock about **WANDER**
knock against **BUMP**
knock down **FLOOR, KO, KAYO**
knock it off **STOP**
knock off **QUIT, KILL**
knockout **KO, KAYO**
knoll **HILL**
knot **NODE, BOW, NOOSE**
knot in cotton fiber **NEPS**
knot in wood **GNARL, KNAR**
knot in wool **NOIL**
knot of hair **BUN**
knotty **INTRICATE**
knout **FLOG**
know **WIST, REALIZE**
knowhow **SKILL**
knowing **ALERT, SCIENT, AWARE**
knowledge **KEN, LORE**
knuckle under **YIELD**
knurl **NODULE, KNOT**
kobold **GNOME, GOBLIN**
kohlrabi **CABBAGE**
Konrad Adenauer's nickname **DER ALTE**
kooky **SILLY, CRAZY**
Korea **CHOSEN**
Korean Border river **YALU**
Korean city **SEOUL**
Korean seaport **PUSAN**
kosher **CLEAN, RIGHT, PROPER**
Krupp works site **ESSEN**

**L**

laager **CAMP**
Laban's daughter **RACHEL, LEAH**
lab burner **ETNA, BUNSEN**
lab substance **AGAR**
label **STICKER, TAB, TAG, TRADEMARK**
labial **LIP**
labor **TOIL, WORK**
laboratory tube **PIPETTE**
laborer **COOLIE, TOILER, WORKER, HAND**
labor group **UNION, ILO, CIO, AFL, GUILD**
laborious **ARDUOUS, DIFFICULT**
labor stoppage **STRIKE**
Labrador dog **RETRIEVER, NEWFOUNDLAND**

labyrinth **MAZE**
lac **RESIN**
lace **DASH, FRILL, SHOESTRING**
lace collar **RUFF**
lacelike fabric **NET**
lacerate **RIP, TEAR, SCRATCH, CUT**
lachrymal drop **TEAR**
lack **ABSENCE, NEED, WANT**
lackadaisical **LISTLESS**
lackey **TOADY, FOOTMAN**
lacking **SHY, SHORT**
lacking boldness **TIMID**
lacking good taste **INDECOROUS, UNSEEMLY**
lacking hair **BALD**
lacking heat **COLD**
lacking money **POOR, NEEDY, INDIGENT**
lacking strength **WEAK**
lackluster **DULL**
lack of energy **ATONY**
lack of interest **APATHY**
laconic **TERSE, CONCISE**
lacquer **ENAMEL**
lacquered metalware **TOLE**
lacuna **GAP, HIATUS**
lacy **DELICATE, FILMY**
lacy frill **RUCHE, ROUCHE**
lacy plant **FERN**
lad **BOY, STRIPLING**
ladder round **RUNG, STEP, RUNDLE**
lade **LOAD**
laden **FREIGHTED**
ladies' man **ROMEO, CASANOVA, DON JUAN**
lading **CARGO, LOAD**
ladle **DIPPER, SCOOP**
ladrone **BANDIT, THIEF**
lady **DAME, WOMAN, MADAM, DONNA**
lady (Sp.) **SENORA**
ladylike **FEMININE**
lady's gown **DRESS, FROCK**
lag **DELAY, LINGER**
lag behind **LOITER, TARRY**
lager **BEER**
laggard **SLUGGISH, STRAGGLER**
lagniappe **GRATUITY**
lagoon **POND**
laic **SECULAR, LAITY**
lair **DEN**
laity **LAYMEN**
lake **POOL**
lam **FLEE, ESCAPE**
Lama land **TIBET**

lambaste **THRASH, SCOLD**
lambent **GLOWING, LUMINOUS**
lamblike **GENTLE, MEEK**
lamb's father **RAM**
lamb's mother **EWE**
Lamb's pen name **ELIA**
lambskin leather **SUEDE**
lame **CRIPPLED, GIMPY**
lamebrain **NUMBSKULL**
lament **BEMOAN, MOAN, RUE, SIGH, WAIL**
lamentation **GRIEF**
lamia **VAMPIRE**
lamp **LIGHT, TORCH**
lampblack **SOOT**
lampoon **SATIRE**
lamprey **EEL**
lampshade **GLOBE**
lanai **VERANDA**
lanate **WOOLLY**
lance **SPEAR**
lance contest **JOUST**
lancer **SOLDIER**
land **DISEMBARK, ALIGHT, SOIL, TERRAIN, COUNTRY, CARRIAGE, WAGON**
land broker **REALTOR**
land contract **DEED**
land drawing **MAP**
land measure **ACRE, AREA, PLOT, LOT**
land parcel **LOT**
land title **DEED**
landed property **ESTATE, REAL ESTATE**
landing boat **LST**
landing pier **WHARF**
landing place **AIRPORT, RUNWAY, AIRSTRIP, STOLPORT**
Land of Alley Oop **MOO**
Land of Enchantment **NEW MEXICO**
Land of Opportunity **ARKANSAS**
Land of Rising Sun **JAPAN**
Land of Ten Thousand Lakes **MINNESOTA**
Land of the Midnight Sun **ALASKA**
Land of the Sheiks **ARABIA**
land on **CRITICIZE, SCOLD**
landscape **SCENERY, VIEW**
landscape feature **SCENERY**
landslide **AVALANCHE**
lane **ALLEY**
language **TONGUE**

language of ancient Rome **LATIN**
language of North Africa **ARABIC**
language peculiarity **IDIOM**
language spoken in Brazil **PORTUGUESE**
languid **WEAK, SLOW**
languish **AIL, PINE, YEARN, ACHE**
languor **ENNUI**
lanky **GAUNT, THIN**
lap **FOLD, LIP**
Lapp **SCANDINAVIAN**
lap robe **BLANKET, RUG**
lapse **ERROR, MISTAKE**
larceny **THEFT, ROBBERY**
lard **FAT, SHORTENING, GREASE**
larder **PANTRY**
large **BIG, HUGE, VAST, ENORMOUS**
large amount **SCADS**
large antelope **GNU, ELAND**
large ape **GORILLA, ORANGUTAN**
large armadillo **PELUDO**
large artery **AORTA**
large Australian shark **MAKO**
large bag **SACK**
large barb of a feather **HERL, HARL**
large basin **TANK**
large bell **GONG**
large bird **EMU, MOA, OSTRICH, STORK**
large board **PLANK, SLAT**
large book **TOME**
large bundle **BALE**
large burrowing mammal **AARDVARK**
large candlestick **FLAMBEAU**
large canine **MASTIFF**
large canoe **BUNGO**
large cask **TUN**
large cat **LION, TIGER, PANTHER**
large Central American snake **BUSHMASTER**
large Central American tree **SAPODILLA**
large chest **TRUNK**
large cistern **TANK**
large conduit **MAIN**
large container **VAT, TUN**
large continent **ASIA**
large country house **CHATEAU, ESTATE, MANOR**

large crude boat **ARK**
large cup **MUG**
large cupola **DOME**
large cut **SLAB**
large deer **ELK**
large dog (2 wds.) **SAINT BERNARD**
large drinking vessel **FLAGON**
large East Indian tree **NEEM**
large fish **OPAH, TUNA**
large fruit **MELON**
large gateway **PYLON**
large gray wolf **LOBO**
large heavy hammer **SLEDGE**
large in scope **GENERAL**
large kettle **CALDRON**
large knife **SNEE, BOLO**
large ladle **SCOOP**
large-leaved beet **CHARD**
large lizard **ALLIGATOR, CROCODILE**
large mass of people **HORDE, MOB, CROWD, HOST, MULTITUDE**
large mouthed pot **OLLA**
large number **MYRIAD**
large of body **BURLY**
large parrot **MACAW**
large porch **VERANDA**
large pulpit **AMBO**
large quantity **MUCH, RAFT**
large rock **BOULDER**
large rodent **PACA, RAT**
larger than life **HEROIC**
large scissors **SHEARS**
large sea duck **EIDER**
large seagoing vessel **LINER**
large seal (2 wds.) **SEA LION**
large snake **BOA**
large sofa **DIVAN**
large South African antelope **SASSABY**
large spoon **LADLE**
largess **BOUNTY, GENEROSITY**
largest amount **MOST**
largest continent **ASIA**
large stewpot **OLLA**
largest ocean **PACIFIC**
largest of the Kuriles **ETOROFU**
large stout cord **ROPE**
largest planet **JUPITER**
large stream **RIVER**
large tooth **TUSK**
large town **CITY**
large truck **VAN**
large tub **VAT**
large vase **URN**
large volume **TOME**

large wading bird **CRANE, IBIS**
large warship (2 wds.) **AIRCRAFT CARRIER**
large wasp **HORNET**
large web-footed bird **PELICAN**
large white bear **POLAR**
large wicker basket **HAMPER**
large wooden cask **BARREL**
largo **SLOW**
lariat **LASSO, REATA, RIATA, ROPE**
laridae **GULLS**
lark **FROLIC, SPREE**
larkspur **DELPHINIUM**
larrigan **MOCCASIN**
larva **GRUB**
larval stage **PUPA**
lascivious **LEWD**
laser **BEAM**
lash **WHIP, FLOG**
lash out **STRIKE**
lass **GIRL, MAID, MAIDEN**
lassitude **TORPOR, LANGUOR**
lasso **LARIAT, REATA, RIATA, ROPE, NOOSE**
lasso expert **ROPER, COWBOY**
last **ENDURE, FINAL, PERSIST, OMEGA**
last dinner course **DESSERT**
last frontier **ALASKA**
last Greek letter **OMEGA**
lasting **PERMANENT**
lasting a brief time **EPHEMERAL**
last inning **NINTH**
last in the race **LOSER**
last letter **ZED, ZEE, OMEGA**
lastly **FINALLY**
last named **LATTER**
last offer **ULTIMATUM**
last part **END**
last queen of Spain **ENA**
last-resort device (2 wds.) **PANIC BUTTON**
last word **AUTHORITY**
latch **LEVER, LOCK**
late **OVERDUE, TARDY, RECENT**
lateen **SAIL**
lately **RECENTLY**
latent **HIDDEN, COVERT, POTENTIAL, DORMANT**
later **AFTERWARD**
lateral **SIDE, SIDEWARD**
lateral part **SIDE**
latest **NEWEST**
latest happenings **NEWS**
latex **RUBBER**
lath **SLAT**

| | |
|---|---|
| lathe operator | **TURNER** |
| lather | **FOAM, SUDS** |
| Latin | **ROMAN** |
| Latin conjunction | **ET** |
| Latin god | **DEUS** |
| Latin poet | **OVID, VIRGIL** |
| Latvia's capital | **RIGA** |
| laud | **PRAISE** |
| laudable | **WORTHY** |
| laudanum | **OPIATE** |
| laugh | **GIGGLE** |
| laughable | **COMIC, FUNNY** |
| laugh boisterously | **ROAR, SNORT** |
| laugh brokenly | **CACKLE** |
| laugh contemptuously | **SNORT** |
| laughing | **RIANT** |
| laughing bird | **LOON** |
| laughingstock | **BUTT** |
| laugh loudly | **ROAR** |
| laugh raucously | **CACKLE** |
| laugh syllable/ | **HA, HO, TEE, HEE** |
| laughter | **MIRTH** |
| laugh to scorn | **DERIDE** |
| launch | **DISCHARGE, START** |
| launching site | **PAD** |
| launder | **WASH, LAVE** |
| launderable | **TUB-FAST, WASHABLE, COLORFAST** |
| laundering finale | **RINSE** |
| laundry appliance | **WRINGER, DRYER, WASHER** |
| laureate | **DISTINGUISHED, HONORED** |
| laurel | **BAY** |
| lava | **LATITE, SCORIA** |
| lavaliere | **PENDANT** |
| lavatory | **BASIN** |
| lave | **WASH** |
| lavender | **PURPLE** |
| lavish | **PROFUSE** |
| lavish party | **FETE** |
| law | **ACT, RULE, STATUTE, CANON, DECREE, EDICT, ORDINANCE** |
| law (Lat.) | **LEX, LEGES (PL.)** |
| law charges | **COSTS** |
| law degree (abbr.) | **LLB** |
| lawful | **LEGAL, LICIT** |
| lawless | **ILLEGAL, UNRULY** |
| lawless crowd | **MOB, GANG** |
| lawmaker | **SENATOR, LEGISLATOR** |
| lawman | **SHERIFF, MARSHAL** |
| lawn | **GREENSWARD** |
| lawn covering | **GRASS, TURF** |
| lawn mower's path | **SWATH** |

| | |
|---|---|
| lawn party | **FETÉ, BARBECUE** |
| lawn wrecker | **MOLE** |
| law of Moses | **TORAH** |
| law officers | **POLICE** |
| law precedent (2 wds.) | **RES JUDICATA** |
| lawsuit | **CASE** |
| lawyer | **ATTORNEY, BARRISTER, COUNSELOR, COUNSEL, SOLICITOR, ADVOCATE** |
| lawyer's charge | **FEE, RETAINER** |
| lawyer's customer | **CLIENT** |
| lawyer's fee | **RETAINER** |
| lawyer's patron saint | **IVES** |
| lax | **NEGLIGENT** |
| laxative | **PURGATIVE, CATHARTIC** |
| laxity | **LOOSENESS** |
| lay | **PUT, PLACE, DEPOSIT** |
| lay in plaits | **FOLD** |
| layer | **PLY, TIER, STRATUM** |
| layer of cloth | **PLY** |
| layer of floors | **TILER, CARPENTER** |
| layer of eye | **UVEA** |
| layer of paint | **COAT** |
| layer of skin | **DERMA** |
| lay out | **EXPEND, SPEND, STOP** |
| layover | **DISABLE** |
| lay up | **DISABLE** |
| lay waste | **RAVAGE** |
| laze | **LOAF** |
| laziness | **LETHARGY** |
| lazy | **INDOLENT, IDLE** |
| lazy animal | **SLOTH** |
| lazybones | **SHIRKER, IDLER** |
| lazy way to fish | **TROTLINE, SETLINE, TRAWL** |
| LBJ's state | **TEXAS** |
| lea | **MEADOW** |
| leachy | **POROUS** |
| lead | **DIRECT, GUIDE** |
| leaden | **HEAVY** |
| leader | **CHIEF, HEAD** |
| lead-in | **INTRODUCTION** |
| leading | **AHEAD** |
| leading actor | **STAR** |
| leading man | **HERO, STAR** |
| lead into error | **DELUDE** |
| lead on | **LURE** |
| leaf | **PAGE, SEPAL** |
| leaf cutter | **ANT** |
| leaf fat | **LARD** |
| leafless plant | **FERN** |
| leaflet | **PAMPHLET** |
| leaf of a book | **PAGE** |
| leaf of a calyx | **SEPAL** |

leafstalk **PETIOLE**
leafstalk used for sauce **RHUBARB**
leafy-headed vegetable **CABBAGE, LETTUCE**
league **CLUB**
League of Nations city **GENEVA**
Leah's sister **RACHEL**
leak **ESCAPE, FLAW, CRACK, DRIP**
leak out **SEEP, OOZE**
lean **RARE, SPARE, THIN, LANK, GAUNT, TILT**
lean, as a ship **CAREEN, HEEL**
leaned over **CANTED**
leaning **ALOP, TREND, TENDENCY**
lean-to **SHED**
leap **JUMP, SKIP, HOP, SPRING**
leaping creature **TOAD, FROG**
leaping insect **CRICKET, FLEA**
leaps and bounds **RAPIDLY**
learn **ASCERTAIN, MASTER**
learned **VERSED**
learned man in India **PANDIT**
learned person **SCHOLAR**
learning **LORE, KNOWLEDGE**
lease **LET, RENT**
lease payment **RENT**
leash **CURB, RESTRAIN**
least **MEREST**
least appropriate (3 wds.) **OF ALL THINGS**
least bit **IOTA**
leather **HIDE**
leatherback **TURTLE**
leather belt **STRAP**
leather bottle **MATARA**
leather fastener **STRAP, THONG**
leather gaiter **PUTTEE, SPAT**
leatherneck **MARINE**
leather punch **AWL**
leather ribbon **STRAP**
leather source **STEERHIDE**
leather splitting tool **SKIVER**
leather strap **THONG, BELT**
leather strip **STRAP**
leather whip **KNOUT**
leathery **TOUGH**
leave **DEPART, GO**
leave empty **VACATE**
leave isolated **MAROON, STRAND, ABANDON, DESERT**
leavening agent **YEAST**
leave of absence **FURLOUGH, SABBATICAL**
leave off **CEASE**

leave out **OMIT, SKIP, REMOVE, CUT, DELETE**
leave port **SAIL, EMBARK**
leaves **FOLIAGE**
leave suddenly (2 wds.) **MAKE OFF**
leaving **RESIDUE**
leaving a will **TESTATE**
lectern **DESK, STAND**
lecture **DISCOURSE, SERMON**
lecture platform **DAIS**
ledge **SHELF**
ledger entry **CREDIT, DEBIT**
lee **SHELTER**
leech **PARASITE**
leek **ONION**
leer **OGLE**
leery **WARY**
leeward **DOWNWIND**
leeway **ROOM, PLAY**
left **GONE, LIBERAL**
Left Bank location **PARIS**
leftist **RADICAL, RED**
leftover **SCRAP**
leg **CALF, GAM**
legacy **BEQUEST**
legal **LAWFUL, LICIT**
legal claim **LIEN**
legal conveyance **DEED**
legal critic **CENSOR**
legal decree **EDICT**
legal defense **ALIBI**
legal document **DEED, WRIT**
legal holiday **LABOR DAY, MEMORIAL DAY, LINCOLN'S BIRTHDAY, WASHINGTON'S BIRTHDAY, COLUMBUS DAY, ARMISTICE DAY**
legally authorized **LICENSED**
legal matter **RES**
legal order **WRIT**
legal paper **WRIT**
legal plea **ALIBI**
legal profession **BAR**
legal warning **CAVEAT**
legal writ to insure payment **ELEGIT**
leg armor **GREAVE**
legate **ENVOY**
legatee **HEIR**
legation **MISSION**
leg bone **SHIN, TIBIA**
legend **MYTH, SAGA**
legendary **MYTHICAL**
legendary bird **ROC**
legendary British king **LUD, ARTHUR**

legendary enchantress **CIRCE**
legendary hero **PALADIN**
legendary magician **MERLIN**
legendary sea creature **MERMAID**
legerdemain **MAGIC, TRICKERY**
leghorn **CHICKEN**
legible **READABLE**
legion **ARMY, MULTITUDE**
legislate **ENACT**
legislative body **SENATE, CONGRESS, HOUSE, PARLIAMENT**
legislative enactment **LAW**
legislator **SENATOR, CONGRESSMAN, REPRESENTATIVE, MP, ASSEMBLYMAN**
legislature **ASSEMBLY, CONGRESS**
legitimate **LAWFUL, LICIT**
leg joint **HIP, KNEE**
legume **PEA, BEAN, VEGETABLE**
lei **GARLAND, WREATH**
leisure **REST, EASE**
leisure activity **HOBBY**
leisure time **EASE**
leitmotif **THEME**
lemming **RODENT**
lemon **DEFECTIVE, CITRUS**
lemon drink **ADE**
lemonlike fruit **CITRON, LIME**
lemur **TARSIER**
lemur of Java **LORIS**
Lenape **DELAWARE**
lend **LOAN**
lend a hand **AID, HELP, ASSIST**
lend dignity to **ENNOBLE**
lene **NONASPIRATE**
length **EXTENT**
lengthen **EXTEND**
length of office **TERM**
length of railroad **TRACK**
length of service status **SENIORITY**
length of 3/4 of an inch **DIGIT**
length unit **ROD, YARD, FOOT, INCH, MILE**
lengthwise **ALONG**
lengthy **LONG**
leniency **MERCY**
lenient **TOLERANT**
Lenin's country **RUSSIA**
Lenten observers goal (comp. wd.) **SELF-DENIAL**

lentigo **FRECKLE**
lento **SLOW**
leonine hair **MANE**
leonine sound **ROAR**
leopard **PANTHER, CHEETAH**
leotard **TIGHTS**
Leo's home **LAIR**
Leo's son **LIONET**
lepidopteran **BUTTERFLY**
leporid **HARE**
leprechauns (2 wds.) **LITTLE PEOPLE**
lesion **INJURY, WOUND**
Leslie Caron role **LILI**
less **FEWER**
less adulterated **PURER**
less bad **BETTER**
less common **RARER**
less difficult **EASIER**
lessee **RENTER, TENANT**
lessen **ABATE, WANE, EASE**
lessen the strength of **ENERVATE, DEBILITATE**
lessen the tension of **RELAX**
lesser **MINOR, INFERIOR**
less expensive **CHEAPER**
less fancy **BARER**
less good **WORSE**
lesson **EXERCISE, UNIT**
lessor **LANDLORD**
less refined **COARSER**
less risky **SAFER**
less stale **FRESHER**
less than **UNDER**
less than 100 shares stock (2 wds.) **ODD LOT**
less wild **TAMER**
let **ALLOW, HIRE, RENT, PERMIT**
let down **LOWER, DISAPPOINT**
let fall **DROP**
let go **RELEASE, RELAX**
lethal **FATAL, DEADLY**
lethargic **SLEEPY, DULL**
lethargy **STUPOR, LANGUOR, TORPOR**
let in **ADMIT**
let it stand **STET**
let off **EXCUSE**
let run out **SPILL**
letter **NOTE, PRINT, MISSIVE, EPISTLE, CHARACTER**
letter carrier **POSTMAN, MAILMAN**
letter cutter **OPENER**
lettered **LITERATE**
letterhead **STATIONERY**

letter of agreement **CARTEL**
lettuce **ICEBERG, BOSTON, ROMAINE, BIBB, HEAD, COS**
lettuce dish **SALAD**
let up **RESPITE**
Levant **EAST, ORIENT**
Levantine ketch **SAIC**
levee **DIKE, PIER**
level **EVEN, FLAT, RAZE, RASE**
leveler **PLANE**
levelheaded **SENSIBLE**
level of command **ECHELON**
level of equality **PAR**
lever **PRY, CROWBAR**
leveret **HARE**
leviathan **MONSTER**
levis **JEANS**
levitate **RISE, FLOAT**
levity **GAIETY, FRIVOLITY**
levy a fine **AMERCE**
lewd **OBSCENE**
Lewis Carroll character **ALICE**
lexicon **DICTIONARY**
liability **DEBT**
liable **APT, PRONE, LIKELY, SUBJECT**
liaison **INTIMACY**
liana **VINE**
liar **PERJURER, PREVARICATOR, FIBBER**
lias **LIMESTONE**
libation **DRINK, POTION**
Liberace's instrument **PIANO**
liberal **FREE**
liberate **FREE, RELEASE**
Liberian natives **VAI, VEI**
liberty **FREEDOM, PRIVILEGE**
libidinous **LEWD, WANTON**
library (2 wds.) **READING ROOM**
library piece **BOOKCASE**
library's study enclosure **CARREL(L)**
library treasure **BOOK**
Libyan city **TRIPOLI, BENGASI**
license **PERMIT, SANCTION**
license plate **TAG**
license tag **PLATE**
licentious **WANTON, LIBERTINE**
lichen **MOSS**
lichen dye **LITMUS**
lick an envelope **SEAL**
lick up **LAP**
licorice herb **ANISE**

lid **COVER**
lid clasp **HASP**
Lido **RESORT, BEACH**
lid remover **OPENER**
lie **EQUIVOCATE, FIB, FALSEHOOD, STORY, RECLINE, FABRICATE**
lie in ambush **LURK**
lie in warmth **BASK**
Liebfraumilch **WINE**
Liederkranz **CHEESE**
lief **WILLINGLY, GLADLY**
lieu **STEAD, PLACE**
lieutenant **SHAVETAIL, OFFICER**
life **BIOGRAPHY, EXISTENCE**
life and death **DIRE**
lifeboat **RAFT**
life jacket **MAE WEST**
lifeless **INERT, DEAD**
lifetime **AGE**
lift **RAISE, BOOST, ELEVATOR**
lifting device **LEVER, CRANE**
lifting machine **CRANE**
lift the hat **DOFF**
lift up **BOOST, ELEVATE, RAISE**
lift with effort **HEAVE, STRAIN**
light **IGNITE, LAMP, CANDLE, BLITHE, TRIVIAL, AIRY, FAIR, ASPECT**
light anchor **KEDGE**
light and airy **ETHEREAL**
light anew **REKINDLE**
light beam **RAY**
light beer **LAGER**
light boat **CANOE, SUNFISH, SAILFISH, SKIFF**
light breeze **AIR, ZEPHYR**
light brown **ECRU, TAN, BEIGE**
light coating **FILM**
light crimson **PINK**
lighted **LIT, ILLUMINATED**
lighten **EASE**
light-footed **NIMBLE**
light four-wheeled carriage **PHAETON**
light globe **BULB**
light-headed **GIDDY, DIZZY**
lighthouse **BEACON, PHAROS**
lighting device **LAMP, TORCH, CANDLE, BEACON**
light meal **LUNCHEON, SNACK, TEA**
lightning bug **FIREFLY**
light open wagon **CART**

light portable sunshade **PARASOL**
light red **PINK**
light refractor **PRISM**
light sarcasm **IRONY**
light shoe **SLIPPER, SANDAL**
light soup **BROTH**
lights out **TAPS**
light tan **ECRU, BEIGE, KHAKI**
light touch **DAB**
light up **ILLUMINE, BRIGHTEN**
light weight **DRAM**
light wood **BALSA**
lignite **COAL**
likable **NICE, PLEASING, ATTRACTIVE**
like **SIMILAR, ENJOY**
like a leopard **SPOTTED**
like a modern refrigerator (comp. wd.) **SELF-DEFROSTING**
like an old maid **SPINSTERISH, FINICKY, FUSSY**
like a routine police case (3 wds.) **OPEN AND SHUT**
like a warm spring day **BALMY**
like a wing **ALAR**
like better **PREFER**
like expensive beef (comp. wd.) **TOP-GRADE**
like metal **STEELY**
likely **APT, LIABLE, PRONE**
likely to turn out well **PROMISING**
liken **COMPARE**
likeness **IMAGE**
like peanut brittle **CRUNCHY**
like seawater **SALTY**
like some diets (comp. wd.) **SALT-FREE**
like sweater weather **COOL**
like unfilleted fish **BONY**
likewise **ALSO, DITTO, TOO**
liking **TASTE**
lilac color **MAUVE**
lilliputian **TINY**
lilt **CADENCE, AIR, TUNE, MELODY**
lily **ALOE, CALLA**
Lily Maid **ELAINE**
lily of the sea **CRINOID**
lily palm **TI**
lily plant **ALOE**
Lily Pons, for one **DIVA**
lily-white **PURE, BLAMELESS**
lima **BEAN**

limb **BRANCH, RAMAGE, LEG, ARM**
limber **AGILE, SPRY, NIMBLE**
limbo **HELL**
limbless reptile **SNAKE**
Limburger **CHEESE**
lime **CITRUS, CEMENT**
limestone pit **QUARRY**
lime twig **SNARE**
limit **END, BOUNDARY, EXTENT, RESTRICT, CONFINE, BOUND**
limited **FINITE, NARROW**
limiting **RESTRICTIVE**
limitless **VAST, INFINITE**
limp **FLACCID, FLABBY**
limpid **BRIGHT, LUCID**
Lincoln Center offering **OPERA, CONCERT, PLAY, BALLET**
Lindbergh book **WE**
line **ROPE, ROW, QUEUE, BOUNDARY**
lineage **PEDIGREE**
line delivered to the audience **ASIDE**
linen **NAPERY**
line of cliffs **PALISADES**
line of guards **CORDON**
line of travel **ROUTE**
line ornamenting type **SERIF**
liner **STEAMSHIP, PLANE**
liner's roster (2 wds.) **PASSENGER LIST**
lineup **ROSTER**
line with panels **WAINSCOT**
ling **HAKE, BURBOT**
linger **TARRY, WAIT**
linger close by **HOVER**
linger idly **LOITER**
linger over a triumph **GLOAT**
lingo **LANGUAGE, JARGON, CANT**
linguine **PASTA**
linguist **POLYGLOT**
link **CONNECTION**
linn **POOL, RAVINE, WATERFALL**
linoleum **FLOORING**
lint **FLUFF**
lion **CAT**
lioness in *Born Free* **ELSA**
lion's cry **ROAR**
lion's den **LAIR**
lion's lair **DEN**
lion's neck hair **MANE**
lion's share **ALL**
lip **LABIUM, RIM**

liquefy THAW, MELT, DEFROST, CONDENSE
liqueur CORDIAL
liqueur flavoring ANISE, MINT, COFFEE, ORANGE, CHERRY
liquid FLUID, WATER
liquidate SETTLE
liquid dressing SAUCE
liquid food SOUP, BROTH
liquid measure LITRE, PINT, CUP, QUART, GALLON
liquor SPIRITS, WHISKEY
liquor vessel DECANTER
lisle CLOTH, THREAD
lissome AGILE, SUPPLE
list CATALOGUE, REGISTER
listel FILLET, MOLDING
listen HARK, HEED, HEAR
listen furtively EAVESDROP
listening ATTENTIVE
list individually ITEMIZE
listless BORED
list of candidates SLATE
list of foods MENU
list of investments PORTFOLIO
list of names ROLL
list of performers CAST
list of persons ROTA
litany PRAYER, RECITAL
literal TRUE, EXACT
literalism REALISM
literally REALLY, ACTUALLY
literary appendix ADDENDUM
literary composition ESSAY
literary drudge HACK
literary irony SATIRE
literary man AUTHOR, WRITER
literary miscellany ANA
literary parody TRAVESTY
literature LORE, WRITINGS
lithe LIMBER, SUPPLE
litigant SUITOR
litigate CONTEST
little SMALL, TINY, WEE
little (mus.) POCO
little arrow DART
little bone OSSICLE
little branch TWIG
little brook RILL
little by little GRADUALLY
little child TOT, TAD
Little Corporal NAPOLEON
little devil IMP
little fellow SHAVER
little piece MORSEL
Little Rhody RHODE ISLAND
little whirlpool EDDY
liturgy RITE, RITUAL

live EXIST, RESIDE, DWELL
live coal EMBER
liveliness ANIMATION
lively NIMBLE, AGILE, PEPPY, ACTIVE, PERT, SPRY
lively celebration GALA
lively dance GALOP, JIG, POLKA, REEL, FANDANGO
lively frolic SPREE, CAPER
lively song LILT
liver fluid BILE
liverwort HEPATICA
livestock CATTLE
livid PALE, ASHEN
living ALIVE, VITAL
living being ANIMAL, CREATURE
living room PARLOR
living room piece DIVAN, SOFA, COUCH, END TABLE, COFFEE TABLE, LAMP, RUG
living thing CREATURE, ANIMAL
lizard ANOLE
lizardlike amphibian SALAMANDER
llama ALPACA
llano PLAIN
lo BEHOLD
load BURDEN, LADE, CARGO, PACK
loaf about LOITER, LOLL, IDLE
loafer SHOE, MOCASSIN
loam SOIL
loam deposit LOESS, SILT
loan LEND
loan shark USURER
loath UNWILLING, RELUCTANT
loathe DESPISE, HATE, DETEST, ABHOR
loathing AVERSION
loathsome DETESTABLE
lobby FOYER, HALL
lobe EARLAP
lobo TIMBERWOLF
lobster claw CHELA, PINCER
local REGIONAL, AREAL
local businessman (2 wds.) RETAIL MERCHANT
local citizen (2 wds.) NATIVE SON
local dialect IDIOM
locale AREA, SITE, ENVIRONMENT
local geography TERRAIN
localism CUSTOM
locality PLACE, SPOT, SITE
locate FIND, SITUATE

location **PLACE, SITE, SPOT**
loch in Scotland **NESS, LEVEN, TAY, KATRINE**
lock **GATE, BOLT**
lock away **STORE, SAVE**
lockjaw **TETANUS**
lock of hair **TRESS**
lock opener **KEY**
locomotive **ENGINE**
locomotive and cars **TRAIN**
locomotive cowcatcher **PILOT**
locomotive track **RAIL**
locule **CAVITY**
locus **PLACE, SITE**
locust **CICADA**
locust tree **ACACIA, CAROB**
lode **VEIN**
lodestone **MAGNET**
lodge **CABIN**
lodge member **ELK**
lodger **ROOMER**
lodging **ROOM, QUARTERS**
lodging house **HOTEL, INN, HOSTEL**
loess **LOAM, SILT**
loft **ATTIC**
lofty **HIGH, TALL, ALPINE, GRAND, NOBLE**
lofty goal **IDEAL**
lofty mountain **EVEREST**
lofty place **PEAK, PINNACLE**
log **DIARY, RECORD**
log dwelling **CABIN**
loge **BOX, MEZZANINE**
log float **RAFT**
logger's boot **PAC**
loggia **GALLERY**
logical **SOUND, VALID**
logrolling **BIRLING**
logrolling contest **ROLEO**
logy **DULL, SLUGGISH**
Lohengrin's bride **ELSA**
loiter **DALLY, LAG, LINGER, TARRY, IDLE, LOLL**
loll **LOUNGE, LAZE, LINGER**
London district **CHELSEA, SOHO, MAYFAIR**
Londoner **COCKNEY**
London literature **ADELPHIAN**
London's cafe district **SOHO**
London trolley **TRAM**
lone **SOLE, SOLITARY**
loneliness **ISOLATION, SOLITUDE**
lonely **LONESOME, SOLITARY**
lone performance **SOLO**
loner **SINGLETON**
Lone Star State **TEXAS**

long **EXTENSIVE, LENGTHY, YEARN, PINE**
long ago **YORE**
long and slender **REEDY, LANK**
long and tiresome **TEDIOUS, BORING**
long cape **CLOAK**
long creeping reptile **SNAKE**
long curl of hair **RINGLET, TRESS**
long discourse **TIRADE**
long distance (2 wds.) **COUNTRY MILE**
long distance runner **MILER**
long dry period **DROUGHT**
longe **ROPE, RING**
long essay **TREATISE**
Longfellow hero **ALDEN**
long fish **EEL, GAR**
long for **COVET, PINE, YEARN, CRAVE**
long green **MONEY**
longhair **INTELLECTUAL**
longhand **WRITTEN**
long-handled brush **BROOM**
long heroic poem **EPOS**
longing **ACHE, YEN, DESIRE**
longing for friends **LONELY, HOMESICK**
long inlet **RIA**
long journey **ODYSSEY, TREK**
long-legged bird **STORK, STILT**
long life **LONGEVITY**
long live (Fr.) **VIVE**
long narrative **SAGA**
long narrow pennant **STREAMER**
long narrow piece **STRIP**
long-necked bird **SWAN, GOOSE**
long nose **SNOUT**
long-nosed fish **GAR**
long period of time **EON, AGE, CENTURY**
long piece of timber **BEAM**
long piece of wood **POLE**
long poem's division **CANTO**
long rolling wave **SWELL**
long seat **BENCH**
longshoreman **STEVEDORE**
long spear **LANCE**
long staff **POLE**
long step **STRIDE**
long-suffering **PATIENT**
long tale **SAGA**
long time **EON, AGE**
long tooth **TUSK, FANG**
long tube **PIPE**
long vocal solo **ARIA**

| | | | |
|---|---|---|---|
| long weapon | SWORD | lorgnette | EYEGLASSES |
| look | SEE, VIEW | loris | LEMUR |
| look after | TEND, MIND | lorry | TRUCK |
| look-alike | TWIN, DOUBLE | lory | PARROT |
| look askance | LEER, OGLE | Los Angeles area | WATTS |
| look at | ESPY, EYE, SEE, | Los Angeles ball club | ANGELS, |
| | WATCH, REGARD | | DODGERS |
| look at flirtatiously | OGLE, LEER | Los Angeles quarterback | RAM |
| look back | RECALL | Los Angeles specialty | SMOG |
| look closely | PEER, PRY, | Los Angeles suburb (2 wds.) | |
| | EXAMINE | | SANTA MONICA |
| look for | SEEK, HUNT, SEARCH | lose | MISLAY, MISPLACE |
| look for game | HUNT | lose balance | TRIP |
| look for ore | PROSPECT | lose by neglect | FORFEIT |
| look forward to | ANTICIPATE | lose color | FADE, PALE |
| looking for trouble (4 wds.) | | lose courage | DESPAIR |
| | UP TO NO GOOD | lose feathers | MOLT |
| looking glass | MIRROR | lose force | WANE |
| look in on | VISIT, CHECK | lose freshness | FADE |
| look on | OBSERVE, REGARD | lose hair | SHED |
| lookout | SENTRY | lose luster | DIM, FADE |
| look over | SCAN, PORE | lose out | FAIL |
| look slyly | PEEP, PEEK | lose patience | TIRE |
| look steadily | GAZE, STARE | lose weight | REDUCE |
| look sullen | POUT | loser's alibi (2 wds.) | |
| look to | RELY | | SOUR GRAPES |
| look to be | SEEM | loss | DEPRIVATION |
| look up to | RESPECT | loss of memory | AMNESIA |
| loom | IMPEND, SHAFT | loss of reason | AMENTIA |
| loom bar | EASER | loss of speech | APHASIA |
| loom frame | LATHE | lost | GONE, MISSING |
| loom harness | LEAF | lot | GROUP, PLOT, FATE, LUCK |
| loon | DIVER | Lothario | RAKE |
| loop | CURL | lottery | RAFFLE |
| loop for lifting | TAB | loud | NOISY |
| loop in a rope | NOOSE | loud clamor | RACKET, DIN |
| loop on lace | PICOT | loud guffaw | ROAR |
| loose | BAGGY, SLACK | loud noise | BANG, DIN |
| loose garment | ROBE, SIMAR, | loud rushing noise | WHOOSH |
| | CAPE, CLOAK | loud-voiced person | STENTOR |
| loose-jointed | LIMBER | Louisiana bird | PELICAN |
| loosen | UNPIN, UNTIE, UNDO | Louisiana county | PARISH |
| loosen up | RELAX | Louisiana patois | CREOLE |
| looseness | SLACK | lounge | LOLL, LOAF, LAZE |
| loose rock particles | SAND | lout | OAF, BOOR, CAD |
| loose soil | DIRT | lovable | AMIABLE, ENDEARING |
| loot | BOOTY, PLUNDER | love | FONDNESS |
| lop | CUT | love affair | AMOUR |
| lop off | BOB | love apple | TOMATO |
| lope | STRIDE | love deity | CUPID |
| lopsided | ALIST, ATILT, AWRY | love in Rome | AMORE |
| loquacious | TALKATIVE | loveliness | PULCHRITUDE |
| lord | NOBLEMAN | lovelock | TRESS |
| lordly beast | LION | lovely | BEAUTIFUL, HANDSOME, |
| Lord's Day | SUNDAY | | COMELY |
| lord's wife | LADY | love of travel | WANDERLUST |
| lore | KNOWLEDGE | lover | ROMEO, SWEETHEART, |
| Lorelei | SIREN | | PARAMOUR |

| | |
|---|---|
| lover of Heloise | **ABELARD** |
| lover's heartbeat (comp. wd.) | |
| | **PIT-A-PAT** |
| lovers' meeting place | **TRYST** |
| lovers' quarrel | **SPAT** |
| lover's song | **SERENADE** |
| love seat | **DIVAN** |
| love story | **ROMANCE** |
| love to excess | **ADORE, DOTE** |
| love token | **AMORET** |
| loving | **FOND** |
| loving cup | **TROPHY** |
| low | **BASE, DEEP** |
| lowbred | **VULGAR, COARSE** |
| low chirping note | **TWEET** |
| low-cost dwelling | **TENEMENT** |
| lower | **ABASE** |
| lower limb | **LEG** |
| lower world | **HADES, ORCUS** |
| lowest | **LEAST** |
| lowest class of animal | **AMOEBA** |
| lowest deck | **ORLOP** |
| lowest form of wit | **PUN** |
| lowest point | **NADIR** |
| lowest singing voice | **BASS** |
| low female voice | **ALTO** |
| low green shrub | **ERICA** |
| lowland | **BOTTOM** |
| low male voice | **BASS** |
| low spirits | **BLUES** |
| low step-in shoe | **LOAFER** |
| low tide | **NEAP, EBB** |
| low tufted plant | **MOSS** |
| low waters (2 wds.) | **EBB TIDE** |
| loyal | **TRUE, CONSTANT,** |
| | **FAITHFUL** |
| loyalist | **PATRIOT, TORY** |
| loyal supporter | **FAN** |
| loyalty | **DEVOTION, FEALTY** |
| Loyolite | **JESUIT** |
| lozenge | **PASTILLE** |
| luau food | **POI** |
| lubricant, for short | **LUBE** |
| lubricate | **OIL, GREASE** |
| lucid | **BRIGHT, CLEAR** |
| Lucifer | **FALLEN ANGEL,** |
| | **SATAN, DEVIL** |
| Lucifer's state | **PERDITION** |
| luck | **CHANCE** |
| lucky | **FORTUNATE** |
| lucky event | **HIT** |
| lucky number | **SEVEN** |
| lucky token | **AMULET** |
| lucrative | **GAINFUL** |
| ludicrous | **COMICAL** |
| luggage item | **TRUNK,** |
| | **SUITCASE, BAG,** |
| | **GRIP, ETUI, VALISE** |

| | |
|---|---|
| lukewarm | **TEPID** |
| lull | **HUSH, CALM** |
| lumber | **WOOD, TIMBER** |
| lumberman's boot | **PAC** |
| lumberman's tool | **AXE, AX, SAW** |
| luminary | **SUN, STAR** |
| luminous | **RADIANT, SHINY** |
| luminous heavenly | |
| body | **COMET, STAR,** |
| | **MOON, PLANET** |
| lump | **BLOB, MASS** |
| lump of butter | **PAT** |
| lump of cottage cheese | **CURD** |
| lump of earth | **CLOD** |
| lump of earth on the | |
| fairway | **DIVOT** |
| lump of tobacco | **WAD** |
| lunar flight control | |
| center | **HOUSTON** |
| lunacy | **MADNESS, INSANITY** |
| lunatic | **MANIAC** |
| lunchroom | **TEA SHOP, SNACK** |
| | **BAR, COFFEE SHOP, CAFE,** |
| | **CAFETERIA, RESTAURANT** |
| lunchtime | **NOON** |
| lune | **MOON, CRESCENT** |
| lunge | **LEAP, SPRING** |
| lurch | **CAREEN** |
| lure | **BAIT, ENTICE, TEMPT** |
| lure by artifice | **DECOY** |
| lurid | **SENSATIONAL** |
| lurk | **SKULK, SNEAK** |
| lurk about | **SNEAK** |
| luscious | **TASTY, SWEET** |
| lush | **JUICY, PROFUSE** |
| lust | **PASSION** |
| luster | **GLOSS, POLISH, SHEEN,** |
| | **SHINE** |
| lusterless | **DEAD, MAT** |
| lustrous cloth | **PANNE** |
| lustrous resin | **COPAL** |
| luxuriate | **BASK** |
| luxurious | **SYBARITIC** |
| luxurious fabric | **SILK, SATIN,** |
| | **VELVET** |
| luxurious fur | **SABLE, MINK,** |
| | **ERMINE** |
| luxury | **EASE** |
| Luzon headhunter | **IGOROT** |
| lying | **DISHONEST, PRONE** |
| lying across | **TRANSVERSE** |
| lying flat | **PRONE** |
| lying on the back | **SUPINE** |
| lynx | **CAT, WILDCAT** |
| lyric | **POETIC** |
| lyricist Gershwin | **IRA** |
| lyric poem | **ODE, EPODE** |
| lysergic acid diethylamide | **LSD** |

# M

macabre **WEIRD, EERIE, EERY, GRIM, GHASTLY, GRUESOME**
macaco **LEMUR, MONKEY**
macadamia **NUT**
Macao coin **AVO**
macaroni **PASTA**
macaw **ARA, PARROT**
Macbeth's title **THANE**
maccaboy **SNUFF**
mace **SPICE**
macedoine **MEDLEY**
macerate **SOFTEN, TORMENT**
machination **SCHEME, PLOT**
machine **ENGINE, MOTOR, GADGET**
machine part **CAM, GEAR, TAPPET, PAWL**
machine tool **BAND-SAW, FILE, LATHE**
machismo **VIRILITY**
mackerel's relative **BONITO, CERO**
mackinaw **BLANKET, COAT**
mackintosh **RAINCOAT**
mackle **BLUR**
macrocosm **UNIVERSE**
macroscopic **VISIBLE**
macruran **LOBSTER, SHRIMP**
maculate **DEFILE**
mad **ANGRY, INSANE, RABID**
Madagascar mammal **LEMUR**
mad, as a dog **RABID**
madcap **RECKLESS**
madden **ENRAGE, CRAZE**
madder **DYE, CRIMSON**
made of (suffix) **INE**
made of a hard wood **OAKEN**
made of cereal **OATEN**
made of fired clay **EARTHEN, CERAMIC**
made of flax **LINEN**
made of grain **CEREAL**
made of iron **METALLIC**
made of silver **ARGENT**
made on a loom **WOVEN**
madhouse **BEDLAM**
Madison Avenue technique (2 wds.) **HARD SELL, SOFT SELL**
madman **LUNATIC, MANIAC**
madness **LUNACY, INSANITY**
Madras hemp **SUNN**
Madrid boulevard **PRADO**
madrigal **LYRIC, POEM**

maelstrom **WHIRLPOOL**
Mae West role **LOU, LIL**
magazine official **EDITOR**
magic **LEGERDEMAIN, SORCERY, VOODOO, ALCHEMY, NECROMANCY**
magic charm **AMULET**
magician's rod **WAND**
magic lamp owner **ALADDIN**
magic stick **WAND**
magistrate **JUDGE**
magistrate's staff **MACE**
magnanimous **GENEROUS**
magnetic metal **IRON**
magnetic recording strip **TAPE**
magnificent **GRAND**
magnify **ENLARGE**
magnitude **SIZE**
magnolia **TREE**
Magnolia State **MISSISSIPPI**
mahatma (2 wds.) **HOLY MAN**
mah-jongg piece **TILE**
maid **GIRL, LASS, SERVANT**
mail **POST, SEND**
mail container **SACK**
mail room employee (2 wds.) **OFFICE BOY**
mailbag **POUCH**
maim **CRIPPLE, DISFIGURE**
main **CHIEF, PRIME**
main artery **AORTA, BOULEVARD**
main course **ENTREE**
Maine capital **AUGUSTA**
Maine city **BANGOR**
Maine lake **SEBAGO**
main idea **GIST**
main impact **BRUNT**
mainland **CONTINENT**
main meal **DINNER**
main movie **FEATURE**
main part **BULK**
maintain **KEEP**
maintain one's dignity (2 wds.) **SAVE FACE**
maize **CORN**
majestic **REGAL, ROYAL, STATELY, GRAND**
major appliance **RANGE, STOVE, REFRIGERATOR, WASHER, DRYER, OVEN**
majority **PLURALITY**
make **CONSTRUCT, CREATE, ERECT, MANUFACTURE**
make a beginning **START, BEGIN, COMMENCE**
make a brief visit **CALL**
make a cake **BAKE**

| | | | |
|---|---|---|---|
| make a choice | **OPT, ELECT, SELECT** | make gay | **LIVEN, ELATE** |
| | | make gentle | **TAME** |
| make a contented sound | **PURR** | make happen | **CAUSE** |
| make active | **ENERGIZE** | make happy | **ELATE** |
| make a decision | **DECIDE** | make hard | **FREEZE, STEEL** |
| make a difference | **MATTER** | make headway | **ADVANCE, PROGRESS** |
| make a garment | **SEW** | | |
| make airtight | **SEAL** | make holy | **HALLOW, SANCTIFY, BLESS, CANONIZE** |
| make allusion to | **MENTION** | | |
| make a loan | **LEND** | make impossible | **PRECLUDE** |
| make amends | **REDRESS, ATONE** | make improvements | **REVISE** |
| | | make inquiry | **ASK** |
| make a mess of | **PI(E)** | make into coin | **MINT** |
| make a mistake | **ERR** | make into law | **ENACT, LEGISLATE** |
| make an address | **SPEAK, ORATE** | | |
| | | make into leather | **TAN** |
| make an edging | **TAT, BIND** | make keen, as the appetite | **WHET** |
| make angry | **RILE, MADDEN, IRE** | | |
| make an offer | **BID** | make known | **DISCLOSE, AIR, PUBLISH, ADVERTISE, REVEAL** |
| make a picture | **DRAW, PAINT, ILLUSTRATE, SKETCH** | | |
| | | make lace | **TAT** |
| make a promise | **PLEDGE, VOW** | make less dense | **RAREFY** |
| make a proposal | **OFFER** | make level | **TRUE** |
| make a rasping sound | **GRATE** | make lively | **ANIMATE** |
| make a recording | **TAPE** | make love | **WOO** |
| make a speech | **ORATE** | make lusterless | **FLATTEN** |
| make a vow | **SWEAR** | make merry | **REVEL** |
| make bare | **DENUDE** | make money | **EARN, COIN, MINT** |
| make beer | **BREW** | make muddy | **ROIL** |
| make believe | **PRETEND** | make multiform | **DIVERSIFY** |
| make beloved | **ENDEAR** | make neat | **GROOM, TIDY** |
| make better | **AMEND, REFORM, RENOVATE, REPAIR, RENEW, RESTORE, REHABILITATE** | make objection | **DEMUR, REMONSTRATE, PROTEST** |
| | | make out clearly | **DISCERN** |
| make bigger | **ENLARGE, MAGNIFY** | make over | **REDO** |
| | | make pale | **CHALK** |
| make brief note | **JOT** | make payment | **PAY, REMIT** |
| make broader | **WIDEN** | make perplexed | **BAFFLE** |
| make brown | **TAN** | make possible | **ENABLE** |
| make butter | **CHURN** | make precious | **ENDEAR** |
| make calm | **ALLAY, COMPOSE** | make preparations (2 wds.) | |
| make certain | **ENSURE** | | **GET READY** |
| make cheerful | **ENLIVEN** | make progress | **ADVANCE, GAIN** |
| make choice | **OPT, SELECT** | make proud | **ELATE** |
| make cloth | **WEAVE** | make purchases | **SHOP, BUY** |
| make cloudy | **BLUR** | make quiet | **HUSH, SILENCE** |
| make content | **SATISFY** | maker | **CREATOR, MANUFACTURER** |
| make corrections | **AMEND** | | |
| make designs on metal | **ETCH** | make ready | **PREPARE** |
| make different | **CHANGE** | make report | **TELL** |
| make even | **LEVEL** | maker of earthenware | **POTTER, CERAMIST** |
| make eyes at | **OGLE** | | |
| make float in air | **LEVITATE, FLY** | maker of laws | **LEGISLATOR** |
| | | maker of pottery | **CERAMIST** |
| make free | **RID, LIBERATE** | make slow | **RETARD** |
| make fresh again | **RENEW** | make smaller | **DECREASE, SHRINK** |
| make full | **FILL** | | |
| make fun of | **RIDICULE** | | |

| | |
|---|---|
| make small talk | CHAT |
| make soundproof | DEAFEN, |
| | INSULATE |
| make sport of | DERIDE |
| make tardy | DELAY, RETARD |
| make thread | SPIN |
| make unfriendly | ALIENATE |
| make untidy | MUSS, MESS-UP |
| makeup | COSMETICS |
| make up for | ATONE |
| make use of | AVAIL, EMPLOY |
| make void | ANNUL |
| make watertight | SEAL, CALK |
| make weary | BORE, TIRE |
| make well | CURE |
| make white | BLANCH |
| make wine | VINTAGE |
| make worse | AGGRAVATE, |
| | IRRITATE |
| making a profit (3 wds.) | |
| | IN THE BLACK |
| maladroit | INEPT |
| malady | ILLNESS, AILMENT |
| malagma | POULTICE |
| Malamud novel (2 wds.) | |
| | THE FIXER |
| malarial fever | AGUE |
| Malay ape | LAR |
| Malay archipelago garment | |
| | SARONG |
| Malay buffalo | CARIBOU |
| Malay island | JAVA |
| Malaysian state | PERAK |
| male | MASCULINE |
| male adult | MAN |
| male ancestor | SIRE |
| male bee | DRONE |
| male bird | ROOSTER |
| male bovine | BULL, STEER, OX |
| male cat | TOM |
| male chicken | ROOSTER |
| male child | SON, BOY |
| male deer | HART, STAG |
| male deity | GOD |
| male descendant | SON |
| malediction | CURSE |
| male elephant | BULL |
| malefactor | VILLAIN |
| male falcon | TERCEL, TIERCEL |
| male garment | SHIRT, TIE, |
| | TRUNKS, ASCOT, TUXEDO, |
| | OVERCOAT, JACKET |
| male horse | STALLION, STUD |
| Malemute | HUSKY |
| male or female | SEX |
| male parent | DAD, SIRE, |
| | FATHER, POP, DADDY, |
| | POPPA, PAPA, PA, PAW |

| | |
|---|---|
| male pig | BOAR |
| male sheep | RAM |
| male sibling | BROTHER |
| male singer | TENOR, BASS, |
| | BARITONE, CROONER |
| male swan | COB |
| male swine | BOAR |
| male title | MR., SIR |
| male turkey | TOM |
| male witch | WARLOCK, WIZARD |
| malevolent | EVIL |
| malice | SPITE |
| malicious | SPITEFUL |
| malicious burning | ARSON |
| malicious look | LEER |
| malign | SLANDER, DEFAME |
| malignant | POISONOUS |
| mall | PROMENADE |
| mallard | DUCK |
| mallet | GAVEL, HAMMER, |
| | SLEDGE |
| malodorous | RANK, FOUL |
| malt beverage | ALE, BEER |
| malt froth | BARM |
| malt infusion | WORT |
| malt liquor | BREW |
| maltreat | INJURE, ABUSE |
| maltworm | TOPER |
| mama | MOTHER, MOM, |
| | MOMMY, MA |
| mama hog | SOW |
| mama's husband | PAPA |
| mamba | COBRA, SNAKE |
| Mamie's man | IKE |
| mammoth | COLOSSAL, |
| | IMMENSE |
| man | MALE, MASCULINE |
| man about town | SOPHISTICATE |
| manacle | HANDCUFF |
| manage | RUN, ADMINISTER, |
| | DIRECT, OPERATE |
| manageable | DOCILE |
| management | DIRECTION, |
| | CONTROL |
| manage well (2 wds.) | GET ALONG |
| manager | BOSS, LEADER |
| manatee (2 wds.) | SEA COW |
| man child | BOY, SON |
| Manchurian border river | AMUR |
| Mandan | SIOUAN, SIOUX |
| mandrill | BABOON |
| mane | HAIR |
| man-eater | CANNIBAL, SHARK |
| maneuver | TACTIC |
| man from Amsterdam | |
| | NETHERLANDER, DUTCHMAN |
| man from Bangkok | THAI |
| man from Edinburgh | SCOT |

man from Glasgow **SCOT**
man from Stockholm **SWEDE**
man from Tel Aviv **ISRAELI**
mangle **IRON**
mangy **SORDID, SQUALID,**
**SHABBY, SEEDY**
maniac **LUNATIC, MADMAN**
manicuring tool **SCISSORS,**
**BRUSH, CLIPPER,**
**FILE, BUFFER**
manifest **CLEAR, REVEAL**
manifold **DIVERSE, SUNDRY**
manioc **CASSAVA**
man in charge **BOSS, FOREMAN**
man in the street **PEDESTRIAN**
manipulate **JUGGLE, WIELD,**
**RIG, HANDLE**
manlike device **ROBOT**
manlike robot **ANDROID**
manly **BOLD, BRAVE,**
**MASCULINE**
man-made **SYNTHETIC,**
**ARTIFICIAL**
manner **AIR, MIEN**
manner of walking **GAIT**
man next door **NEIGHBOR**
man of action **DOER**
man of God **SAINT, PRIEST,**
**RABBI, MINISTER**
man of great valor **HERO**
man of great wealth **MIDAS**
man of influence **VIP**
man of law **ATTORNEY**
man of learning **SCHOLAR**
man of letters **AUTHOR**
Man of Sorrows **MESSIAH,**
**CHRIST**
man of the hour **HERO**
man-of-war **FRIGATE, WARSHIP,**
**JELLYFISH**
man on the bench **JUDGE**
manor house **MANSION**
Mansard's extension **EAVES**
man's best friend **DOG**
manservant **VALET, BUTLER,**
**CHAUFFEUR, HOUSEBOY,**
**GARDENER, CHEF**
man's garment **SUIT,**
**SHIRT, PANTS, POLO SHIRT,**
**SPORTS JACKET, TUXEDO,**
**OVERCOAT, TIE**
man's mate **WOMAN**
man's opera headgear **TOP HAT**
man's purchase (2 wds.) **RAZOR**
**BLADE, SHAVE CREAM**
man's title **SIR, MR.**
manta **DEVILFISH, RAY**

mantle **CLOAK, CAPE,**
**CONCEAL**
manual **HANDBOOK**
manual art **CRAFT**
manual digit **THUMB**
manufacture **MAKE, PRODUCE**
manufactured products **WARE**
manuscript (abbr.) **MS,**
**MSS (pl.)**
manuscript part **PAGE, FOLIO**
many **NUMEROUS**
many times **OFTEN,**
**FREQUENTLY**
Maori tribe **ATI**
map **PLAN, CHART, ARRANGE**
map abbreviation **ALT, LAT,**
**LONG**
map book **ATLAS**
maple **TREE**
maple genus **ACER**
map within a map **INSET**
maquillage **MAKEUP,**
**COSMETICS**
mar **DAMAGE, IMPAIR, INJURE,**
**SPOIL**
marabou **STORK**
marauder **BRIGAND**
marble **AGATE, TAW, MIB**
Marc Antony's wife **OCTAVIA**
Marcel Marceau's
routine **MIME,**
**PANTOMIME**
march **DRILL, HIKE, WALK,**
**PARADE**
marching order (2 wds.) **ABOUT**
**FACE, RIGHT FACE,**
**LEFT FACE, DOUBLE TIME**
march into **ENTER**
March King **SOUSA**
Margaret Mitchell hero
(2 wds.) **RHETT BUTLER**
Margaret Mitchell heroine
(2 wds.) **SCARLETT O'HARA**
margarine **OLEO**
margin **EDGE, BORDER, RIM**
marijuana (sl.) **POT, REEFER,**
**MARY JANE, JOINT,**
**GRASS, TEA**
marina **BASIN, DOCK**
marina sight **YACHT, BOAT,**
**SAILS**
marine **NAVAL**
marine crustacean **CRAB,**
**CRAYFISH, CRAWDAD**
marine fish **HAKE, OPAH, BLUE,**
**TUNA**
marine growth **SEAWEED**
mariner **SAILOR, SEAMAN**

marionette **DOLL, PUPPET**
marital **CONJUGAL**
maritime **NAVAL, NAUTICAL**
mark **TRAIT, SCAR, STAIN**
markdown **DISCOUNT, SALE**
marked aversion **DISGUST**
marked by denial **NEGATIVE**
market **MART, STORE, SHOP, SELL, VEND**
market again **RESELL**
market place **AGORA**
mark of a wound **SCAR**
mark of disgrace **STIGMA**
mark of omission **CARET**
mark of respect **HONOR**
mark with spots **MOTTLE**
marksman **SHOT**
marksman's goal **TARGET**
marl **FERTILIZER**
marmalade **JELLY**
maroon **STRAND, ABANDON, DESERT**
marriage **WEDDING, WEDLOCK**
marriage announcement **BANNS**
marriage ceremony **WEDDING, NUPTIALS**
marriage notice **BANNS**
marriage termination **DIVORCE**
marriage vow (2 wds.) **I DO**
married **WED, WEDDED**
married woman **WIFE**
married woman's title (Fr.) **MADAME**
marron **CHESTNUT**
marrow **MEDULLA, PITH**
marrowbone **KNEE**
marry **WED**
marry again **REWED**
marry a woman **WIVE**
marry in haste **ELOPE**
Mars (2 wds.) **RED PLANET**
marsh **BOG, FEN, SWAMP, MIRE, MORASS**
marshal's badge **STAR**
Marshal Dillon's nickname **MATT**
marsh bird **RAIL, SNIPE, STILT**
marsh crocodile **GOA**
marsh elder **IVA**
marsh gas **METHANE**
marshy **BOGGY, WET**
marshy hollow part **SWALE**
marsupial **KOALA, KANGAROO**
mart **MARKET, EMPORIUM**
marten **WEASEL**
martenlike mammal **SABLE**
martial **MILITARY**

martini garnish **OLIVE, TWIST**
martini ingredient **OLIVE, GIN, VERMOUTH, TWIST, ICE, VODKA**
Martinique volcano **PELEE**
marvel **MIRACLE, WONDER**
marvelous **WONDERFUL**
mascara wearer **EYELASH**
masculine **MALE**
mash **PULVERIZE, CRUSH**
masher **WOLF**
mask **HIDE, CONCEAL, SCREEN, DOMINO**
masked animal, for short **COON**
ma's mate **PA**
masonry fence **WALL**
mass **BULK, WAD**
Massachusetts cape **ANN, COD**
Massachusetts city **SALEM, BOSTON, CAMBRIDGE**
Massachusetts island **NANTUCKET**
massacre **SLAUGHTER**
massage **RUB**
massive **HUGE, HEAVY**
mass of bread **LOAF**
mass of trees **FOREST**
mass vestment **AMICE**
mast **POLE, SPAR**
master **CHIEF, LORD**
master in India **SAHIB**
master in music **MAESTRO**
master of ceremonies **EMCEE**
master plan **STRATEGY**
Master Sawyer **TOM**
master stroke **COUP**
mastery (2 wds.) **UPPER HAND**
masticate **CHEW**
mat **RUG**
matador's opponent **TORO, BULL**
match **MATE**
matched group **SET**
matched group of china (2 wds.) **TEA SET**
matched pair **MATES**
matchless **PEERLESS**
mate **COMRADE, SPOUSE, HUSBAND, WIFE, COMPANION**
material for making molds (3 wds.) **PLASTER OF PARIS**
maternity bird **STORK**
mate's kin **IN-LAW**
mathematics **ARITHMETIC**
math exercise **PROBLEM**
math term **SINE, COSINE**

| | |
|---|---|
| matriculate | **ENROLL** |
| matrimonial | **CONJUGAL, MARITAL** |
| matter | **SUBSTANCE** |
| mature | **AGE, RIPE, RIPEN** |
| mature person | **ADULT** |
| maturing agent | **AGER** |
| maudlin | **EMOTIONAL, MUSHY** |
| mausoleum | **TOMB, CRYPT** |
| mauve | **LILAC, PURPLE** |
| maw | **CRAW, CROP** |
| maw's husband | **PAW** |
| maxilla and mandible | **JAWS** |
| maxim | **ADAGE, MOTTO, SAYING, SAW** |
| maximum | **MOST, LIMIT** |
| maybe | **PERHAPS, POSSIBLY, PERCHANCE** |
| Mayday signal | **SOS** |
| mayhem | **DESTRUCTION, VIOLENCE** |
| May 30th | **MEMORIAL DAY,** |
| (2 wds.) | **DECORATION DAY** |
| maze | **TANGLE, CONFUSION** |
| maze of the Minotaur | **LABYRINTH** |
| mazzard | **CHERRY** |
| McGuffey opus | **READER** |
| McIntosh | **APPLE** |
| McLuhan's field | **TV, MEDIA** |
| McNally's partner | **RAND** |
| m.c. Mack | **TED** |
| m.c. Sullivan | **ED** |
| mead | **DRINK, BREW** |
| meadow | **LEA** |
| meadow mouse | **VOLE** |
| meadow saffron | **COLCHIUM** |
| meager | **POOR, SCANT, SCANTY** |
| meal | **DINNER, LUNCH, SNACK, SUPPER, TEA, REPAST, BREAKFAST** |
| meal fragment | **ORT** |
| mealtime prayer | **GRACE** |
| mealy | **FRIABLE** |
| mean | **INTEND, CRUEL, NASTY, AVERAGE** |
| meander | **ROAM, WANDER** |
| mean dog | **BITER** |
| meaning | **IMPORT, SENSE, INTENT** |
| meaningful | **SIGNIFICANT** |
| meaningless | **EMPTY** |
| meaningless ritual (2 wds.) | **MUMBO JUMBO** |
| meanness | **SPITE** |
| mean proportion | **AVERAGE** |
| means | **RESOURCE, WEALTH** |

| | |
|---|---|
| means of entry | **ACCESS, DOOR, GATE, ENTRY** |
| means of escape | **LOOPHOLE** |
| meantime | **INTERIM** |
| measles | **RUBELLA** |
| measly | **SKIMPY** |
| measure | **METE** |
| measured | **UNIFORM** |
| measured duration | **TIME** |
| measure of distance | **MILE** |
| measure of heat | **CALORIE, THERM** |
| measure of land | **ACRE, ARE, LOT, PLOT** |
| measure of length | **FOOT, ROD, METER, YARD, INCH, MILE** |
| measure of paper | **REAM** |
| measure of time | **HOUR, MINUTE, SECOND, DAY, WEEK, MONTH, YEAR** |
| measure of type | **EN, EM, POINT** |
| measure of weight | **POUND, OUNCE** |
| measure of wood | **CORD** |
| measure out | **ALLOT** |
| measure swords | **DUEL** |
| measurer | **RULER, GAUGE, SURVEYOR** |
| measuring strip | **TAPE** |
| meat | **FLESH, PORK, BEEF, HAM, LAMB** |
| meat cut | **RASHER, LOIN** |
| meat dish | **HASH, STEW** |
| meat jelly | **ASPIC** |
| meat pastry | **RISSOLE** |
| meat sauce | **GRAVY** |
| meaty | **SUBSTANTIAL** |
| mechanical | **AUTOMATIC, REFLEX** |
| mechanical man | **ROBOT** |
| mechanics of motion | **DYNAMICS** |
| mechanism | **APPARATUS, TOOL** |
| medal | **BADGE, PLAQUE** |
| meddler | **BUSYBODY** |
| meddle (with) | **TAMPER** |
| Mede | **ARYAN** |
| mediate | **INTERCEDE** |
| medical fluid | **SERUM** |
| medical patient | **CASE** |
| medical picture | **X RAY** |
| medical suffix | **IATRIC, OMA** |
| medicated lozenge | **PASTILLE** |
| medicinal plant | **ALOE, HERB, SENNA** |
| medicinal remedy | **ANTIDOTE** |
| medicinal root | **IPECAC** |

| | |
|---|---|
| medicinal unit | **DOSE** |
| medicine | **DRUG** |
| medicine bottle | **VIAL** |
| medicine man | **SHAMAN** |
| medicine pellet | **PILL** |
| medicine portion | **DOSE** |
| medico | **PHYSICIAN, SURGEON** |
| medieval dance refrain | **RONDO** |
| medieval instrument | **LUTE** |
| medieval Jewish automaton | **GOLEM** |
| medieval poem | **LAI, LAY,** |
| | **BALLAD, ROMANCE** |
| medieval slave | **SERF, ESNE** |
| medieval story | **SAGA, ROMANCE** |
| medieval viol | **REBEC** |
| mediocre | **SO-SO** |
| meditate | **PONDER, BROOD,** |
| | **THINK** |
| Mediterranean | **SEA** |
| Mediterranean area | **RIVIERA** |
| Mediterranean island | **CRETE,** |
| | **CYPRUS, MALTA** |
| Mediterranean sailing vessel | |
| | **SETTEE** |
| Mediterranean tree | **CAROB** |
| Mediterranean wind | **SOLANO,** |
| | **MISTRAL** |
| medium | **MIDDLE, HALF** |
| medium (pl.) | **MEDIA** |
| medium of exchange | |
| | **CURRENCY** |
| medley | **OLIO** |
| medulla | **MARROW** |
| meek | **HUMBLE** |
| meerschaum | **PIPE** |
| meet | **ENCOUNTER, SIT,** |
| | **CONVENE, ASSEMBLE,** |
| | **CONFRONT** |
| meet by chance (2 wds.) | **COME** |
| | **ACROSS, RUN INTO** |
| meeting | **SESSION** |
| meeting program | **AGENDA** |
| mel | **HONEY** |
| melancholy | **LOW, SAD, BLUE,** |
| | **SOMBER** |
| Melanesian native | **FIJI** |
| melange | **MEDLEY, MIXTURE** |
| melee | **RIOT** |
| mellow | **RIPE, AGE, RIPEN** |
| melodic | **ARIOSE** |
| melodic sounds | **MUSIC,** |
| | **HARMONY** |
| melodious | **MUSICAL,** |
| | **AGREEABLE** |
| melodist | **COMPOSER** |
| melody | **ARIA, SONG, TUNE,** |
| | **AIR, REFRAIN** |

| | |
|---|---|
| meloid | **BEETLE** |
| melon | **CANTALOUPE, PEPO,** |
| | **HONEYDEW** |
| melon-like fruit | **GOURD** |
| melon pear | **PEPINO** |
| melt | **DISSOLVE, THAW,** |
| | **DEFROST** |
| melt away | **DWINDLE** |
| melt down, as lard | **RENDER** |
| melted rock | **LAVA** |
| melting pot | **CRUCIBLE** |
| melt ore | **SMELT** |
| melt together | **FUSE** |
| member | **LIMB, ELEMENT** |
| member of an Indian sect | |
| | **PARSI, PARSEE** |
| member of boys' group | **SCOUT** |
| member of crew | **HAND** |
| member of Parliament | |
| | **LORD, MP** |
| member of state | **CITIZEN** |
| member of the clergy | **CLERIC,** |
| | **MINISTER, PRIEST, RABBI** |
| member of the firm | **PARTNER** |
| member of a work crew | **MAN** |
| members of the fourth | |
| estate | **PRESS, REPORTER** |
| membership charge | **DUES** |
| membrane | **TELA** |
| membranous pouch | **CYST** |
| memento | **RELIC, REMINDER,** |
| | **SOUVENIR** |
| memento case | **LOCKET,** |
| | **RELIQUARY** |
| memo | **NOTE** |
| memoir | **RECORD, REPORT** |
| memorable | **NOTABLE** |
| memorial mound | **CAIRN** |
| memory | **RECOLLECTION** |
| memory aid | **MNEMONIC** |
| menace | **THREATEN** |
| menage | **HOUSEHOLD** |
| menagerie | **ZOO** |
| mend | **REPAIR, DARN, FIX,** |
| | **KNIT, HEAL** |
| mendacity | **LYING, DECEIT** |
| mender of pots | **TINKER** |
| mendicant | **BEGGAR** |
| menial | **SERVILE** |
| men in blue | **POLICE** |
| Mennonite sect | **AMISH** |
| men's party | **STAG, SMOKER** |
| mental | **RATIONAL** |
| mental acumen | **WIT** |
| mental anguish | **DOLOR** |
| mental disposition | **TEMPER,** |
| | **MOOD** |
| mentality | **ACUMEN** |

| | |
|---|---|
| mentally sound | **SANE** |
| mental position (3 wds.) | |
| | **POINT OF VIEW** |
| mental slip | **LAPSE** |
| mental strain | **TENSION** |
| mention | **CITE, NAME** |
| mentor | **TEACHER** |
| menu (3 wds.) | **BILL OF FARE** |
| menu item | **PRIME RIBS,** |
| **STEAK, CHOPS, SALAD,** | |
| **VEGETABLE, DESSERT,** | |
| **ROAST BEEF, ENTREE** | |
| Mephistopheles | **SATAN, DEVIL** |
| mephitic | **POISONOUS, FOUL** |
| mercantile | **COMMERCIAL** |
| mercenary | **HIRELING** |
| merchandise | **GOODS, WARES** |
| merchant | **DEALER, TRADER,** |
| | **SELLER, VENDOR** |
| merciful | **CLEMENT** |
| merciless | **STONY** |
| Mercury's winged cap | **PETASOS** |
| mercy | **LENIENCY, PITY** |
| mere | **ONLY, SIMPLE** |
| mere handful | **WISP** |
| merely | **JUST, ONLY** |
| merest bit | **IOTA** |
| mere taste | **SIP, BIT** |
| meretricious | **VULGAR, GAUDY,** |
| | **TAWDRY** |
| merganser | **SMEW, SHELDRAKE** |
| merge | **BLEND, MELD,** |
| | **COALESCE, COMBINE** |
| meridian | **MIDDAY, NOON** |
| merino | **SHEEP, WOOL** |
| merit | **DESERVE, EARN, WORTH,** |
| | **VALUE** |
| meritorious | **WORTHY** |
| mermaid | **SIREN** |
| mero | **GROUPER, GUASA** |
| merriment | **GAIETY, GLEE** |
| merry | **GAY, HILARIOUS** |
| merry adventure | **LARK, SPREE** |
| merry andrew | **CLOWN, ZANY,** |
| | **BUFFOON** |
| merry-go-round | **CAROUSEL** |
| merrymaking | **REVEL** |
| merry prank | **CAPER** |
| merry tune | **LILT** |
| mesa | **TABLELAND, PLATEAU** |
| mescal cactus of Mexico | |
| | **PEYOTE** |
| mesh | **NET, NETWORK** |
| mess | **HODGEPODGE** |
| message | **COMMUNICATION,** |
| | **TELEGRAM, NOTE** |
| message boy | **PAGE** |
| messenger | **ENVOY, HERALD** |

| | |
|---|---|
| messenger of the gods | **HERMES** |
| messiah | **SAVIOR** |
| messy | **UNTIDY** |
| Met solo | **ARIA** |
| metal | **LEAD, TIN, ZINC, STEEL,** |
| | **IRON** |
| metal bar | **INGOT** |
| metal-bearing lode | **VEIN** |
| metal bolt | **RIVET** |
| metal cement | **SOLDER** |
| metal container | **CAN, TIN** |
| metal cord | **WIRE** |
| metal deposit | **LODE** |
| metal disc | **PATEN, MEDAL** |
| metal dross | **SLAG** |
| metal fastener | **NAIL, PIN,** |
| | **RIVET, SNAP, BOLT, SCREW** |
| metal globe | **POME** |
| metallic paper | **FOIL** |
| metallic fabric | **LAME** |
| metallic sound | **CLING, CLANK,** |
| | **PING, BANG** |
| metallic vein | **LODE** |
| metal tag on shoelace | **AGLET** |
| metal thread | **WIRE** |
| metal tube | **PIPE** |
| metal worker | **TINNER, TINKER** |
| metal workshop | **SMITHY,** |
| | **FORGE** |
| metamorphosis | **CHANGE** |
| metaphor | **TROPE** |
| metaphysical entity | **ENTIUM,** |
| | **(pl.) ENTIA** |
| metatarsus | **FOOT** |
| mete | **ALLOT, APPORTION,** |
| | **DOLE, DISTRIBUTE** |
| meteorological device | **SONDE** |
| meter | **RHYTHM** |
| methane hydrocarbon | |
| | **PARAFFIN** |
| method | **MODE, SYSTEM, WAY** |
| method of payment (2 wds.) | |
| | **INSTALLMENT PLAN** |
| methyl alcohol (2 wds.) | |
| | **WOOD SPIRIT** |
| meticulous | **FASTIDIOUS,** |
| | **PRECISE** |
| metier | **LINE, JOB** |
| metrical | **RHYTHMIC** |
| metrical stress | **ICTUS** |
| metric foot | **IAMB** |
| metric land measure | **ARE** |
| metric measure | **STERE** |
| metric quart | **LITER** |
| metric unit | **GRAM, STERE,** |
| | **LITER, DECARE, KILO,** |
| | **METER, ARE** |
| metric weight | **KILO, GRAM** |

| | | | |
|---|---|---|---|
| mettle | SPIRIT, STAMINA | mild | GENTLE, TAME, TENDER, |
| Mexican blanket | SERAPE | | KIND, PLEASANT, NICE, |
| Mexican coin | PESO | | FAIR, CLÉMENT |
| Mexican corn cake | TORTILLA | mild cheese | GOUDA, BRIE |
| Mexican cottonwood | ALAMO | mildew | MOLD |
| Mexican dance | HAT | mild expletive | DANG, DRAT, |
| Mexican dish | TAMALE | | HECK, GAD, EGAD, |
| Mexican dollar | PESO | | PFUI, DARN, |
| Mexican garment | SERAPE, | mild oath | EGAD |
| | PONCHO | mild oath in Britain | GOR, GAD |
| Mexican gentleman | SENOR | mild pinch | TWEAK |
| Mexican Indian | AZTEC, YAQUI | militant | HOSTILE |
| Mexican laborer | PEON | military | MARTIAL |
| Mexican lake | CHAPALA | military acronym | AWOL |
| Mexican peninsula | YUCATAN | military aircraft | CHOPPER, |
| Mexican rubber tree | ULE | | PURSUIT PLANE, BOMBER, |
| Mexican sandwich | TACO | | FIGHTER PLANE |
| Mexican's hat | SOMBRERO | military assistant | AIDE |
| Mexican shrub | CHIA | military automobile | JEEP |
| Michaelmas daisy | ASTER | military award | MEDAL |
| Michelangelo masterpiece | | military base | FORT, POST, |
| | PIETA, | | CAMP |
| | DAVID, MOSES | military cap | KEPI |
| Michigan metropolis | DETROIT, | military depot | BASE |
| | LANSING, ANN ARBOR | military device | SONAR, RADAR |
| Mickey Mouse inventor | DISNEY | military ditch | TRENCH |
| microcosm | UNIVERSE | military division | PLATOON, |
| microorganism | BACTERIUM, | | SQUAD |
| | GERM, VIRUS | military dress hat | SHAKO |
| microscopic | MINUTE, TINY | military exercise | DRILL, |
| microscopic organism | AMOEBA | | PARADE, BIVOUAC |
| microwave amplifier | MASER | military expedition to Holy | |
| mid | CENTRAL | Land | CRUSADE |
| midday | NOON | military force | LEGION, TROOP |
| midday nap | SIESTA | military fugitive | AWOL |
| midday refreshment | LUNCH | military greeting | SALUTE |
| middle | CENTER, MID | military guard | SENTRY |
| Middle Eastern nation | ISRAEL, | military horsemen | CAVALRY |
| | SYRIA, JORDAN, | military inspection | REVIEW, |
| | EGYPT, LEBANON | | PARADE |
| middle (law) | MESNE | military instrument | BUGLE |
| Midianite king | REBA | military offense | DESERTION |
| midshipman | CADET | military officer | CAPTAIN, |
| midst | AMONG | | COLONEL, SERGEANT, |
| midway attraction | RIDE, SHOW, | | CORPORAL, LIEUTENANT, |
| | SIDESHOW | | MAJOR, GENERAL |
| midwestern college | ANTIOCH, | military operation | SIEGE, RAID |
| | OBERLIN, KENT, WAYNE, | military orchestra | BAND |
| | NOTRE DAME | military review | PARADE |
| mien | BEARING | military salute | SALVO |
| miff | OFFEND | military storehouse | ETAPE |
| might | POWER, MAY | military student | CADET |
| mighty | POTENT, STRONG | military supplies and | |
| mighty cataract | NIAGARA | weapons | ORDNANCE |
| mighty mite | ATOM | military truck | CAMION |
| mignon | DELICATE | military unit | REGIMENT, TROOP |
| migraine | HEADACHE | milk | DRAIN |
| migration | TREK | milk and egg dish | CUSTARD |

| | |
|---|---|
| milk cattle farm | **DAIRY** |
| milk giver | **COW** |
| milk glass | **OPALINE** |
| milkman's daily course | **ROUTE** |
| milky gem | **OPAL** |
| milquetoast | **SISSY, CASPER** |
| Milwaukee brew | **BEER** |
| mime | **CLOWN, COPY, APE** |
| mimeo master | **STENCIL** |
| mimic | **APE, COPY, IMITATE** |
| minaret | **TOWER** |
| mince | **CHOP, DICE** |
| minced dish | **HASH** |
| minced oath | **EGAD** |
| mincing | **DAINTY** |
| mind | **CARE, TEND, INTELLECT,** |
| | **OBEY, BRAIN** |
| mindful | **AWARE** |
| mind's eye | **IMAGINATION** |
| mine | **PIT, DIG** |
| mine car | **TRAM** |
| mined fuel | **COKE** |
| mine entrance | **ADIT** |
| mine explosion hole | **CRATER** |
| mine level | **STOPE** |
| mine passage | **DRIFT, ADIT,** |
| | **SHAFT** |
| mine product | **ORE, COAL,** |
| | **STONES, MINERAL** |
| mineral | **ORE** |
| mineral deposit | **LODE** |
| mineral jelly | **PETROLATUM** |
| mineral pitch | **ASPHALT** |
| mineral spring | **SPA** |
| mineral tar | **MALTHA** |
| mine shaft | **ADIT, INCLINE,** |
| | **TUNNEL** |
| mingle | **MIX** |
| miniature | **TINY** |
| minim | **SMALLEST** |
| minimal | **LEAST** |
| minimize | **BELITTLE** |
| minimum | **LEAST** |
| minister | **HELP, ATTEND** |
| minister's assistant | **DEACON** |
| minister's home | **MANSE,** |
| | **RECTORY, PARSONAGE** |
| minister's speech | **SERMON,** |
| | **HOMILY** |
| ministration | **SERVICE** |
| ministry | **CLERGY** |
| minium | **VERMILION** |
| mink | **FUR** |
| minklike animal | **WEASEL,** |
| | **STOAT** |
| minor | **LESSER, INFERIOR** |
| minority | **FACTION** |
| minor river | **BAYOU** |

| | |
|---|---|
| Minotaur's owner | **MINOS** |
| minstrel | **BARD** |
| minstrel's instrument | **LUTE** |
| minstrel's song | **LAY, LAMENT** |
| mint | **COIN, CANDY, PLANT,** |
| | **HERB, GARNISH** |
| mint camphor | **MENTHOL** |
| minuet | **DANCE** |
| minus | **LESS** |
| minuscule | **PETTY, TINY** |
| minute | **SMALL, TINY** |
| minute difference | **SHADE** |
| minute groove | **STRIA** |
| minute insect | **GNAT** |
| minute opening | **PORE** |
| minute particle | **ATOM, IOTA** |
| minutes | **RECORD, PROCEEDING** |
| minutes of court | **REGISTER,** |
| | **RECORD, ACTA** |
| minutia | **DETAIL** |
| minyan | **QUORUM, TEN** |
| miracle | **MARVEL, WONDER** |
| mirage | **CHIMERA** |
| mire | **MUD** |
| mirror | **GLASS, REFLECT** |
| mirth | **GAIETY, GLEE** |
| mirthful | **MERRY** |
| misanthrope | **CYNIC** |
| misbehave (2 wds.) | **ACT UP,** |
| | **CUT UP** |
| misbehaving (3 wds.) | |
| | **OUT OF LINE** |
| miscalculate | **ERR** |
| miscellaneous | **VARIOUS** |
| miscellaneous items | **SUNDRIES** |
| miscellany | **OLLA, MIXTURE,** |
| | **OLIO** |
| mischievous | **NAUGHTY** |
| mischievous child | **IMP** |
| mischievous person | **RASCAL** |
| mischievous sprite | **ELF** |
| miscreant | **VILLAIN, WRETCH** |
| misdeed | **CRIME** |
| misdemeanor | **CRIME** |
| misdo | **ERR, BLUNDER** |
| miser | **SCROOGE** |
| miserable | **UNHAPPY** |
| miserly | **STINGY** |
| misery | **SORROW** |
| misfortune | **ILL, EVIL, WOE** |
| mishandle | **ABUSE** |
| mishap | **ACCIDENT** |
| misinterpret | **MISREAD** |
| mislay | **LOSE, MISPLACE** |
| mislead | **DECEIVE, DELUDE** |
| misplace | **LOSE, MISLAY** |
| misrepresent | **DISTORT, BELIE** |

| | |
|---|---|
| miss | GIRL, LASS, MAID, MAIDEN |
| misshapen | DEFORMED |
| missile | DART, ARROW, ICBM, NIKE |
| missing | LOST |
| missing link | APEMAN, PITHECANTHROPUS, JAVA-MAN |
| mission | ERRAND, DELEGATION, CHURCH |
| Mississippi resort | BILOXI |
| Mississippi River sight | LEVEE |
| missive | LETTER, EPISTLE |
| Miss Kett of the comics | ETTA |
| Miss O'Hara | SCARLETT |
| Miss Oyl | OLIVE |
| misstep | ERROR, TRIP |
| mist | FOG, HAZE |
| mistake | ERR, ERROR, BLUNDER, BONER, GOOF |
| mistaken | WRONG |
| mistake in printing | ERRATUM |
| mister (Sp.) | SENOR |
| mistreat | ABUSE |
| mistress | DAME |
| mistrust | DOUBT |
| misty | FOGGY, DIM |
| misuse | ABUSE |
| Mitch Miller's instrument | OBOE |
| Mitchell novel (4 wds.) | GONE WITH THE WIND |
| mite | TICK |
| mitigate | LESSEN |
| mix | BLEND, STIR, MINGLE |
| mixed breed | MONGREL |
| mixed greens | SALAD |
| mixed type | PI |
| mixed with | AMONG |
| mix playing cards | SHUFFLE |
| mixture | MEDLEY, OLIO, HODGEPODGE, POTPOURRI, BLEND |
| mixture of snow and rain | SLEET |
| mizzen | MAST |
| moa | BIRD, OSTRICH |
| moa genus | APTERYX |
| moan | GROAN |
| moat | TRENCH, DITCH |
| mob | CROWD, RABBLE, HORDE, GANG |
| mobile | MOVABLE |
| mobile home | TRAILER, CAMPER |
| mocassin | PAC, SHOE |
| mock | DERIDE, RIDICULE, APE, MIMIC |
| mocker nut | HICKORY |
| mockery | FARCE |

| | |
|---|---|
| mock sun | PARHELION |
| mock-up | MODEL, LAYOUT |
| mode | CUSTOM, MANNER, FASHION, STYLE |
| model | PATTERN, SAMPLE, EXAMPLE |
| model of perfection | PARAGON |
| model of solar system | ORRERY |
| mode of speech | PARLANCE |
| mode of standing | POSTURE |
| moderate | LIMITED, FAIR |
| moderately cold | COOL |
| moderation | RESTRAINT |
| moderator | ARBITER |
| modern | NEW |
| modern appliance | WASHER, DRYER |
| modern epiclike narrative | SAGA |
| modern fabric | NYLON, RAYON, ARNEL, ORLON, DACRON |
| modernize | RENOVATE |
| modern painter | DALI, STELLA, WARHOL, PICASSO, MIRO |
| modern philosophy | EXISTENTIALISM |
| modern phonograph | STEREO |
| modest | SHY |
| modesty | HUMILITY |
| mod fashion | MINISKIRT, MIDISKIRT, MAXICOAT |
| modify | AMEND, ALTER, CHANGE, DEFINE |
| modish | CHIC, STYLISH |
| modiste | DRESSMAKER, COUTURIERE |
| mod paintings (2 wds.) | POP ART |
| modulation | TONE |
| Mohammedan prince | AMIR, EMIR, AMEER |
| Mohammedan religion | ISLAM |
| Mohammed's birthplace | MECCA |
| Mohammed's daughter | FATIMA |
| Mohammed's flight | HEGIRA |
| Mohammed's son | ALI |
| moist | DAMP, WET |
| molar | TOOTH |
| molasses | SIRUP, SYRUP |
| molasses (Brit.) | TREACLE |
| mold | FORM, SHAPE |
| moldy | MUSTY |
| moleskin color | TAUPE |
| molest | INJURE, DISTURB |
| mollify | ASSUAGE |
| mollusk | CLAM, OYSTER |
| molt | SHED |
| molten rock | LAVA |

| | |
|---|---|
| moment | **IMPORT, MINUTE, TRICE, SECOND** |
| mom or dad | **PARENT** |
| mom's mate | **DAD** |
| monastery | **PRIORY, CONVENT, ABBEY** |
| monastery head | **ABBOT** |
| monastery occupant | **MONK, FRA** |
| monastery room | **CELL** |
| monastic | **ASCETIC** |
| monastic officer | **PRIOR, ABBOT** |
| monastic title | **DOM** |
| monetary | **FINANCIAL** |
| monetary penalty | **FINE** |
| monetary unit | **DOLLAR** |
| monetary unit of Japan | **YEN, SEN** |
| money | **CURRENCY** |
| money factory | **MINT** |
| money handler | **CASHIER** |
| money holder | **WALLET, BANK, PURSE** |
| money in India | **RUPEE** |
| money in Rome | **LIRA** |
| money on hand | **CASH** |
| money opening | **SLOT** |
| money saving campaign (2 wds.) | **ECONOMY DRIVE** |
| money (sl.) | **GREEN, MOOLAH, GELT, BREAD** |
| money vault | **SAFE** |
| Mongol conqueror | **TAMERLANE** |
| Mongolian monk | **LAMA** |
| mongrel dog | **CUR, MUTT** |
| monk | **FRIAR** |
| monkey | **APE** |
| monkey's treat | **BANANA** |
| monk's hood | **ATIS, COWL** |
| monk's title | **FRA** |
| monocle | **EYEGLASS, LENS** |
| monogram | **INITIAL, CIPHER** |
| monolith | **MENHIR, PILLAR** |
| monomania | **LUNACY, DELIRIUM** |
| monopoly | **GAME** |
| monotonous | **HUMDRUM, TEDIOUS** |
| monotonous song | **CHANT** |
| monotony | **TEDIUM** |
| monster | **GIANT, OGRE, TROLL** |
| monstrous | **ATROCIOUS, VAST** |
| Montana city | **BUTTE, MISSOULA** |
| Montana river | **TETON** |
| month | **JANUARY, FEBRUARY, MARCH, APRIL, MAY, JUNE, JULY, AUGUST, SEPTEMBER, OCTOBER, NOVEMBER, DECEMBER** |
| month (Fr.) | **JANVIER, FEVRIER, MARS, AVRIL, MAI, JUIN, JUILLET, AOUT, SEPTEMBRE, OCTOBRE, NOVEMBRE, DECEMBRE** |
| month (Sp.) | **ENERO, FEBRERO, MARZO, ABRIL, MAYO, JUNIO, JULIO, AGOSTO, SEPTIEMBRE, OCTUBRE, NOVIEMBRE, DICIEMBRE** |
| monument | **TOMBSTONE** |
| moo | **LOW** |
| mood | **TEMPER** |
| moody | **CAPRICIOUS** |
| moody person | **MOPER** |
| moon goddess | **LUNA, DIANA, ARTEMIS** |
| moor | **ANCHOR, HEATH** |
| mooring post | **BITT** |
| mop | **SWAB** |
| mope | **SULK, BROOD** |
| moppet | **BABY, DOLL** |
| moral | **ETHICAL** |
| morale | **SPIRIT** |
| morale-raising speech (2 wds.) | **PEP TALK** |
| moralist | **PRIG** |
| morals | **ETHICS** |
| moral transgression | **SIN** |
| morass | **SWAMP, BOG, FEN, MIRE** |
| moray | **EEL** |
| morbid | **UNHEALTHY** |
| morbid sound | **RALE** |
| mordant | **CAUSTIC** |
| more | **ADDITIONAL, GREATER** |
| more agreeable | **NICER** |
| more ancient | **OLDER** |
| more arid | **DRIER** |
| more austere | **STERNER** |
| more banal | **TRITER** |
| more cautious | **WARIER** |
| more cerulean | **BLUER** |
| more clever | **SMARTER** |
| more competent | **ABLER** |
| more crafty | **FOXIER, SLYER** |
| more cunning | **SLYER** |
| more delicate | **FINER** |
| more difficult | **HARDER** |
| more disabled | **LAMER** |
| more distant | **FARTHER, REMOTER** |
| more distended | **FULLER** |
| more docile | **TAMER** |
| more domesticated | **TAMER** |
| more elegant | **FINER, SMARTER** |
| more expensive | **DEARER** |
| more famous | **GREATER** |

| more fastidious | NEATER, TIDIER, DAINTIER, NICER, |
| more foxy | SLYER, SLIER |
| more frigid | ICIER, COOLER, COLDER |
| more gentle | TAMER |
| more inclement | RAWER, ROUGHER |
| more infrequent | RARER |
| more insolent | BRASHER, SASSIER |
| more intelligent | SMARTER, BRIGHTER |
| more learned | WISER |
| more likely | APTER |
| morello | CHERRY |
| more mature | OLDER, RIPER |
| more meager | SCANTIER |
| more mellow | RIPER |
| more miserly | MEANER |
| more modern | NEWER |
| more optimistic | ROSIER, BRIGHTER |
| more or less | SOME |
| more orderly | NEATER, TIDIER |
| moreover | AND, BESIDES |
| more painful | SORER |
| more pallid | PALER |
| more precious | DEARER |
| more precipitous | STEEPER |
| more profound | DEEPER |
| more rapid | FASTER |
| more rational | SANER |
| more recent | LATTER |
| more refined | NICER |
| mores | CUSTOMS |
| more sagacious | WISER |
| more scarce | RARER |
| more secure | SAFER |
| more seedy | SHABBIER |
| more severe | STERNER |
| more slippery | ICIER, SLICKER |
| more so | YEA |
| more sour | TARTER |
| more spacious | ROOMIER, LARGER |
| more strange | ODDER |
| more suitable | BETTER |
| more tardy | LATER |
| more tender | SORER |
| more than | ABOVE, OVER |
| more than enough | AMPLE |
| more than one | MANY, PLURAL |
| more tidy | NEATER |
| more uncanny | EERIER |
| more uncivil | RUDER |
| more uncommon | RARER |

| more up-to-date | NEWER |
| more wary | CAGIER |
| more willingly | RATHER |
| moribund | DYING |
| morion | HELMET |
| Mormon of secret sect | DANITE |
| Mormon State | UTAH |
| morning | DAWN |
| morning (poetic) | MORN |
| morning after | HANGOVER |
| morning coat | CUTAWAY |
| morning glory genus | IPOMOEA |
| morning moisture | DEW |
| morning performance | MATINEE |
| morning prayer | MATINS |
| morning reception | LEVEE |
| morning's light | DAWN |
| morning song | ALBA |
| morning star | MARS, VENUS |
| Moroccan capital | RABAT |
| Moroccan native | BERBER |
| Moroccan ruler | SULTAN |
| Moroccan soldier | ASKAR |
| moro chief | DATO |
| moron | IMBECILE |
| morose | GLUM |
| morphine derivative | HEROIN |
| morro | HILL |
| morsel | BIT, BITE, ORT |
| morsel left at meal | ORT |
| mortal | HUMAN, PERSON, FATAL |
| mortar | BOWL, PUTTY |
| mortar mixer | RAB |
| mortar tray | HOD |
| mortgage | LIEN, LOAN |
| mortification | CHAGRIN |
| mosaic piece | INSET, TILE |
| moselle (2 wds.) | WHITE WINE |
| Moses' brother | AARON |
| Moslem bible | KORAN |
| Moslem commander | AGA |
| Moslem countries | ISLAM |
| Moslem deity | ALLAH |
| Moslem headgear | FEZ, TURBAN |
| Moslem judge | CADI |
| Moslem lawyer | MUFTI |
| Moslem nymph | HOURI |
| Moslem officer | AGA |
| Moslem priest | IMAM |
| Moslem prince | AMIR, EMIR, AMEER |
| Moslem title | AGA |
| mosquito-eating bird | MARTIN |
| mosquito genus | AEDES |
| mosquito larva | WIGGLER |
| most attractive | PRETTIEST, CUTEST |

| | |
|---|---|
| most beloved | **DEAREST** |
| most brazen (sl.) | **NERVIEST** |
| most courageous | **GAMEST,** |
| | **BRAVEST** |
| most desirable | **BEST** |
| most difficult | **HARDEST** |
| most distant planet | **PLUTO** |
| most distant point in | |
| an orbit. | **APOGEE** |
| most excellent | **BEST** |
| most ill-boding | **DIREST** |
| most independent | **FREEST** |
| most intelligent | **SMARTEST** |
| mostly | **CHIEFLY, USUALLY** |
| most modern | **NEWEST** |
| most outstanding | **BEST** |
| most pallid | **PALEST** |
| most peculiar | **ODDEST** |
| most pleasant | **NICEST** |
| most precious | **DEAREST** |
| most precipitous | **STEEPEST** |
| most profound | **DEEPEST** |
| most rapid | **FASTEST** |
| most recent | **LATEST** |
| most ridiculous | **SILLIEST** |
| most sagacious | **WISEST** |
| most savory | **TASTIEST** |
| most sensible | **SANEST** |
| most sensitive | **SOREST** |
| most spirited | **LIVELIEST** |
| most tardy | **LATEST** |
| most terrible | **DIREST** |
| most unique | **ODDEST** |
| most untouched | **PUREST** |
| most unusual | **ODDEST, RAREST** |
| most wonderful | **BEST** |
| mot | **RETORT, SAYING** |
| mote | **PARTICLE** |
| motel feature | **POOL** |
| motet | **ANTHEM** |
| moth-eaten | **OLD, WORN** |
| mother | **MA, MOM, MAW, MAMA,** |
| | **MOMMY, MOMMA, DAM,** |
| | **MADONNA** |
| mother (Lat.) | **MATER** |
| mother (Sp.) | **MADRE** |
| mother and father | **PARENTS** |
| Mother Carey's chicken | **PETREL** |
| Mother Carey's goose | **FULMAR** |
| Mother Goose author | **PERRAULT** |
| Mother Hubbard | **GOWN** |
| mother of Castor and Pollux | |
| | **LEDA** |
| mother of Hiawatha | **NOKOMIS** |
| mother of mankind | **EVE** |
| mother-of-pearl | **NACRE** |
| mother of Peer Gynt | **ASE** |
| mother of Perseus | **DANAE** |

| | |
|---|---|
| mother of Romulus | |
| and Remus | **ILIA** |
| mother or father | **PARENT** |
| mother sheep | **EWE** |
| mother's sister | **AUNT** |
| mother turned to stone | **NIOBE** |
| motherly | **MATERNAL** |
| moth larva | **CATERPILLAR** |
| motif | **THEME** |
| motion | **GESTURE** |
| motionless | **INERT, STILL** |
| motion picture | **FILM** |
| motion picture light | **KLIEG** |
| motion picture machine | |
| | **PROJECTOR** |
| motivate | **INSPIRE** |
| motive | **REASON** |
| motive force | **POWER** |
| motley | **DIVERSE, MIXED** |
| motor | **ENGINE, TURBINE** |
| motorcar | **AUTOMOBILE** |
| motor coach | **BUS** |
| motor control | **STARTER** |
| motor court | **MOTEL** |
| motorist | **DRIVER** |
| motorist's nightmare (2 wds.) | |
| | **TRAFFIC JAM** |
| motorist's problem (2 wds.) | |
| | **PARKING SPACE** |
| motorist's tool | **JACK, WRENCH** |
| motorless airplane | **GLIDER** |
| motorman | **CONDUCTOR** |
| mottled horse | **PINTO** |
| mottled marking | **DAPPLE** |
| mottled soap | **CASTILE** |
| motto | **ADAGE, MAXIM, SAW** |
| mould | **MATRIX** |
| mound | **HEAP, TEE** |
| mount | **ASCEND, CLIMB** |
| mountain at earth's center | |
| | **MERU** |
| mountain cat | **BOBCAT,** |
| | **COUGAR, PUMA** |
| mountain crest | **ARETE, RIDGE** |
| mountain home | **CHALET** |
| mountain in Thessaly | **OSSA** |
| mountain lake | **TARN** |
| mountain lion | **PUMA** |
| mountain near ancient | |
| Troy | **IDA** |
| mountain nymph | **OREAD** |
| mountain pass | **COL, GAP** |
| mountain pass in India | **GHAT,** |
| | **GHAUT** |
| mountain peak | **TOR** |
| mountain pheasant | **GROUSE** |
| mountain pool | **TARN** |
| mountain ridge | **ARETE, CREST** |

Mountain State **WEST VIRGINIA**
mountain system in Europe **ALPS**
mountain system in South America **ANDES**
mountaintop **PEAK**
mourn **LAMENT, GRIEVE**
mournful **DOLEFUL**
mournful cry **ALAS, ALACK, WOE IS ME**
mournful poem **ELEGY, LAMENT**
mournful song **DIRGE**
mournful sound **KNELL, MOAN, KEEN**
mourning **SORROW, GRIEF**
mouse family **RODENT**
mouser **CAT**
mouth **SPEAK, SAY**
mouthful **BITE, MORSEL, SIP**
mouth organ **HARMONICA**
mouth part **LIP, PALATE, TONGUE, GUM, TOOTH**
movable **MOBILE**
movable cover **LID, AWNING**
movable door part **HINGE**
move **STIR, BUDGE**
move along **MOSEY**
move apart **SEPARATE**
move, as Fido's tail **WAG**
move aside (2 wds.) **MAKE WAY**
move aside suddenly **DODGE**
move, as the wind **BLOW**
move back **RECEDE, RETREAT**
move back and forth **SHUTTLE**
move before the wind **SCUD, SAIL**
move forward **ADVANCE**
move furtively **LURK, SLINK, SNEAK, TIPTOE, CREEP, STEAL, SIDLE**
move in water **SWIM, FLOAT**
move like a crab **SIDLE**
move lazily **LOLL**
movement **MOTION**
movement of the hands **GESTURE**
move out **VACATE**
move over water **SAIL, FLOAT**
move quickly **RUN, SCUD, HIE, SPEED, HASTEN, BUSTLE, HUSTLE, RACE**
mover's truck **VAN**
move rhythmically **DANCE**
move sideways **SIDLE**
move slightly **BUDGE, STIR**
move slowly **EDGE, INCH**
move smoothly **SLIDE, GLIDE**
move spasmodically **TWITCH**

move stealthily **SLINK**
move suddenly **DART**
move swiftly **SCUD, DART**
move with an easy gait **LOPE, AMBLE, STROLL**
move with difficulty **WADE**
movie house **THEATRE, CINEMA**
movie queen **STAR**
movie version of a novel **ADAPTATION**
movie V.I.P. **DIRECTOR, STAR, ACTOR, PRODUCER, WRITER**
moving **ASTIR, ACTIVE**
moving air **WIND**
moving force **AGENT**
moving mechanical part **ROTOR**
moving stairway **ESCALATOR**
Mr. Bumpstead **DAGWOOD**
Mr. Claus **SANTA**
Mr. Heep **URIAH**
Mr. Kettle **PA**
Mr. Spade **SAM**
Mr. Van Winkle **RIP**
Mrs. Charles Chaplin **OONA**
Mrs. Dick Tracy **TESS**
Mrs. Eddie Cantor **IDA**
Mrs. Eisenhower **MAMIE**
mrs. in Madrid **SRA.**
Mrs. Kettle **MA**
Mrs. Nixon **PAT**
Mrs. Roosevelt **ELEANOR**
Mrs. Roy Rogers (2 wds.) **DALE EVANS**
Mrs. Truman **BESS**
Mrs. Washington **MARTHA**
much **LOTS**
much larger **HUGER**
much loved **DEAR**
much the same **ALIKE**
mucilage **GLUE, ADHESIVE**
muck **MIRE, MUD**
mud **MIRE**
muddle **MESS**
muddy **MURKY, OBSCURE**
mudguard **FENDER**
mud pie **PATTY**
mud puppy **SALAMANDER**
mud volcano **SALSE**
muffin **CRUMPET, POPOVER, SCONE**
muffle **DAMPEN, MUTE, DEADEN**
muffler **SCARF**
mug **CUP**
mugger **HAM**
muggy **HUMID, DAMP**
muir **MOOR**

mukluk **BOOT**
mulberry cloth **TAPA**
mulch **SAWDUST**
mulct **FINE, AMERCE**
mule **SLIPPER**
muley **COW, HORNLESS**
mulish **STUBBORN**
mull **PONDER**
muller **PESTLE**
mullet hawk **OSPREY**
mulligan **STEW**
mulligatawny **SOUP**
multicolored **ROAN, PIED**
multifold **MANY**
multiform **DIVERSE**
multiplication word **TIMES**
multitude **HORDE, HOST, MOB**
munch, comic strip style
**CHOMP**
mundane **WORLDLY**
municipal corporation **CITY,**
**BOROUGH**
municipality **CITY**
municipal official **MAYOR**
munificent **GENEROUS**
mural painting **FRESCO**
murder **KILL, SLAY**
murder mystery character
**SUSPECT**
murky **OBSCURE, DARK**
murmur **WHISPER**
murmuring, as a brook
**BABBLING**
murmuring sound **HUM**
muscle **TENDON**
muscle cramp **CRICK**
muscular **HUSKY**
muscular tone **TONUS**
muse **MEDITATE, PONDER**
muse **CALLIOPE, CLIO, ERATO,**
**EUTERPE, MELPOMENE,**
**POLYHYMNIA, TERPSICHORE,**
**THALIA, URANIA**
musette **BAGPIPE**
museum keeper **CURATOR**
museum pieces **ART,**
**COLLECTION**
mush **ATOLE**
music **HARMONY, TUNE**
musical **TUNEFUL, MELODIC,**
**SHOW**
musical adaptation
**ARRANGEMENT**
musical author **COMPOSER**
musical bells **CHIME**
musical character **CLEF, NOTE**
musical chord **TRIAD**

musical composition **ETUDE,**
**CONCERTO, SONATA,**
**SYMPHONY, RONDO**
musical direction **PIANO,**
**LARGO**
musical disk **RECORD**
musical drama **OPERA**
musical ending **CODA**
musical exercise **ETUDE, SCALE**
musical feature **MOTIF**
musical group **OCTET, TRIO,**
**QUARTET, QUINTET, BAND,**
**ORCHESTRA, COMBO**
musical group of nine **NONET**
musical half-tone **MINIM**
musical instrument **FLUTE,**
**PIPE ORGAN, BASS DRUM,**
**FIFE, TUBA, PIANO, ORGAN,**
**DRUM, KETTLE DRUM,**
**TRIANGLE, LUTE, OBOE,**
**VIOLA, VIOLIN, WOODWIND,**
**CORNET, TRUMPET, HORN,**
**TROMBONE, HARP, LYRE,**
**PICCOLO, BASSOON, CELLO,**
**GUITAR, BANJO, CLARINET,**
**SAXOPHONE,**
**TIMPANI, BASS**
musical interval **SEMITONE,**
**REST**
musical measured beat **PULSE**
musical medley **OLIO**
musical movement **RONDO**
musical nocturne **SERENADE**
musical note **BREVE**
musical organization **BAND,**
**ORCHESTRA**
musical pair **DUO, DUET**
musical pause **REST**
musical performance **CONCERT**
musical phrase **LEITMOTIF**
musical pipe **REED**
musical pitch **TONE**
musical play **OPERA**
musical show **OPERETTA,**
**REVUE**
musical sign **REST, CLEF,**
**NOTE, STAFF, SHARP, FLAT**
musical sound **NOTE, TONE**
musical staff **BAR**
musical study **ETUDE**
musical syllable **DO, RE, MI, FA,**
**SO, SOL, LA, TI, TRA**
musical term **TACET**
musical time marker
**METRONOME**

musical tone **CHORD**
musical work **OPUS, OPERA, OPERETTA, SYMPHONY, CONCERTO, SONG**
music buff's purchase **STEREO, ALBUM, LP, HIFI, RECORD, SPEAKER**
music by two **DUET**
music hall **ODEUM**
musician **PLAYER**
music played under lady's window **SERENADE**
music syllable **DO, RE, MI, FA, SO, LA, TI**
musk cat **CIVET**
musket **GUN**
muskmelon **CASABA**
Muslim judge **CADI**
Muslim mendicant **FAKIR**
musty **MOLDY, FUSTY**
mute **SILENT, SPEECHLESS, MUFFLE, SILENCE, QUIET**
mutilate **MAIM, CRIPPLE, DISABLE**
mutineer **REBEL**
mutinous **RESTIVE, REBELLIOUS**
mutiny **REVOLT**
mutter **MUMBLE, GRUMBLE**
muttonchop **SIDEBURN, WHISKERS**
muzzle **GAG, RESTRAIN**
my (Lat.) **MEA**
myopic **NEARSIGHTED**
myself **ME**
mysterious **EERY, SECRET, STRANGE, WEIRD, PUZZLING**
mystery **SECRET, ENIGMA**
mystery tale **STORY**
mystery writers' award **EDGAR**
mystic **OBSCURE, OCCULT**
mystic art **CABALA, CABBALA, CABBALAH**
mystify **BAFFLE**
myth **FABLE, LEGEND, TALE, BELIEF**
mythical **FABULOUS, LEGENDARY**
mythical aviator **ICARUS**
mythical bird **ROC**
mythical Greek bowman **EROS**
mythical hunter **ORION**
mythical king of Pylos **NESTOR**
mythical one-horned animal **UNICORN**

## N

nab **GRAB, SEIZE, SNATCH**
nabob **VIP, CELEBRITY, BIG WHEEL, BIG SHOT**
nag **HORSE, SCOLD, FIND FAULT, CAVIL, CARP, WHINE**
nagging pain **ACHE**
nail container **KEG**
naive **UNSOPHISTICATED, ARTLESS**
naked **BARE, NUDE**
name **TITLE**
name for a cat **TABBY, PUSS, PUFF, KITTY**
name for a dog **SPOT, FIDO, ROVER, LASSIE, REX, LADY, KING**
nameless **INDEFINABLE, ANONYMOUS, OBSCURE**
namely (2 wds.) **TO WIT**
name of a thing **NOUN**
name the letters of a word **SPELL**
name to office **APPOINT**
nanny **NURSE**
nap **DOZE, SLEEP, SNOOZE, FORTY WINKS**
nape **SCRUFF**
napery **LINEN**
Naples island **CAPRI**
nappy leather **SUEDE**
narcotic **OPIATE, DRUG**
narrate **RELATE, TELL**
narration **ACCOUNT**
narrative **TALE, YARN, STORY**
narrative poem **BALLAD, EPIC**
narrator **RACONTEUR**
narrow **SLENDER, THIN**
narrow aperture **SLOT, SLIT**
narrow band **STRIPE, TAPE, RIBBON**
narrow board **SLAT, LATH**
narrow boat **CANOE**
narrow channel **STRAIT**
narrow country road **LANE**
narrow gauge **RAILROAD**
narrow inlet **RIA**
narrow-minded **BIGOTED, PREJUDICED**
narrow opening **SLIT, SLOT**
narrow path **LANE**
narrow ravine **GORGE**
narrow shelf **LEDGE**
narrow squeak (2 wds.) **CLOSE SHAVE**

| | |
|---|---|
| narrow strip of cloth | **TAPE, RIBBON** |
| narrow strip of leather | **THONG** |
| narrow strip of wood | **SLAT** |
| narrow thoroughfare | **ALLEY, LANE** |
| narrow valley (Brit.) | **COMBE** |
| narrow waterway | **STRAIT** |
| narthex | **VESTIBULE** |
| nary | **NO, NOT ANY** |
| nary a soul (2 wds.) | **NO ONE** |
| nasal intonation | **TWANG** |
| NASA's capsule booster | **ROCKET** |
| NASA's realm | **SPACE** |
| nascent | **BEGINNING** |
| nasty | **DIRTY, SOILED, UNPLEASANT** |
| natal | **NATIVE** |
| natator | **SWIMMER** |
| nation | **COUNTRY, LAND** |
| national | **COUNTRYWIDE** |
| national bird | **EAGLE** |
| national monogram | **USA** |
| native | **SON** |
| native-born | **INDIGENOUS** |
| Native Dancer | **HORSE** |
| native lump of gold | **NUGGET** |
| native metal | **ORE** |
| native name for Norway | **NORGE** |
| native of (suffix) | **ITE** |
| native of Attu | **ALEUT** |
| native of Copenhagen | **DANE** |
| native of Dundee | **SCOT** |
| native of Edinburgh | **SCOT** |
| native of Glasgow | **SCOT** |
| native of Istanbul | **TURK** |
| native of Madagascar | **HOVA** |
| native of Muscat | **OMANI** |
| native of Ontario | **CANADIAN** |
| native of Stockholm | **SWEDE** |
| native of Tel Aviv | **ISRAELI** |
| native of the United States | **AMERICAN** |
| native South African village | **STAD** |
| nativity | **CHRISTMAS, CRECHE** |
| natty | **NEAT, SPRUCE** |
| natural | **INNATE, INBORN, NATIVE** |
| natural ability | **TALENT, GIFT** |
| natural color | **ECRU, FLESH** |
| natural condition | **NORM** |
| natural incline | **SLOPE** |
| naturalism | **REALISM** |
| naturalize | **ACCUSTOM** |
| nature | **DISPOSITION, ESSENCE** |
| nature's mythical maiden | **NYMPH** |
| nature spirit | **GENIE** |
| naught | **ZERO, NOTHING** |
| naughty | **BAD** |
| naughty look | **LEER** |
| nausea | **QUALM** |
| nauseate | **SICKEN** |
| nauseous | **DISGUSTING** |
| nautical | **MARITIME** |
| nautical assent | **AYE** |
| nautical command | **AVAST, BELAY** |
| nautical cry | **AHOY, AVAST** |
| nautical line | **MARLINE, RATLINE** |
| nautical measure | **KNOT, FATHOM** |
| nautical mop | **SWAB** |
| nautical pole | **SPAR, MAST** |
| nautical rope | **TYE, LINE, SHEET** |
| nautical speed unit | **KNOT** |
| nautical term | **ALEE** |
| Nautilus | **SUBMARINE** |
| Navaho hut | **HOGAN** |
| naval | **MARINE, NAUTICAL** |
| naval commander in ancient Sparta | **LYSANDER** |
| naval force | **FLEET** |
| naval meal | **MESS** |
| naval officer | **REAR ADMIRAL, ENSIGN, CAPTAIN** |
| naval strength (2 wds.) | **SEA POWER** |
| nave | **HUB** |
| navel | **ORANGE** |
| navigate | **GUIDE, SAIL** |
| navigate in air | **AVIATE** |
| navigating instrument | **COMPASS** |
| navigation device | **LORAN, SONAR** |
| navy | **BLUE** |
| navy force | **FLEET** |
| navy line officer | **MUSTANG** |
| navy recruit (sl.) | **BOOT** |
| naysay | **DENIAL** |
| near | **APPROACH, AT, CLOSE** |
| nearest | **NEXT** |
| nearly | **ALMOST** |
| nearly all | **MOST** |
| nearly corresponding | **SIMILAR** |
| near-sighted | **MYOPIC** |
| near-sighted cartoon character | **MAGOO** |
| near the beginning | **EARLY** |
| near the horizon | **LOW** |
| neat | **TIDY, TRIM** |
| neatly smart in dress | **NATTY** |
| neb | **BILL, BEAK** |
| Nebraska city | **OMAHA** |

Nebraska county **OTOE**
Nebraska Indian **PAWNEE**
necessary **ESSENTIAL**
necessitate **COMPEL, OBLIGE**
necessity **MUST**
neck and neck **EVEN, CLOSE**
neck artery **CAROTID**
neckerchief **SCARF**
neck frill **RUFF**
neck hair **MANE**
necklace bauble **BEAD**
neck of water **STRAIT**
neckpiece **SCARF, TIE, CRAVAT, ASCOT, COLLAR**
necktie **CRAVAT, ASCOT**
nectar of the gods **AMBROSIA**
nee **BORN**
need **LACK, REQUIRE, WANT**
neediness **POVERTY**
needing support **DEPENDENT**
needle case **ETUI**
needle (comb. form) **ACU**
needlefish **GAR**
needle hole **EYE**
needle-like body **SPICULE**
needle puncture **PRICK**
needlework **SEWING, DARNING, CREWEL, EMBROIDERY**
needy **IMPOVERISHED, POOR**
nefarious **EVIL, BAD**
negate **DENY**
negation **NOT**
negative **MINUS, NO**
negative answer **NAY, NO**
negative conjunction **NOR**
negative electrode **CATHODE**
negative ion **ANION**
negative particle **NOT**
negative prefix **NON, UN**
negative sign **MINUS**
neglect **OMIT, OVERLOOK, FORGET, SLIGHT, SHIRK**
negligence **CARELESSNESS**
negligent **LAX, REMISS, CARELESS**
negligible **NOMINAL**
negotiate **TREAT**
Negrito of Philippines **ATA, ITA**
neigh **WHINNY**
neighborhood **VICINITY**
neighborhood playing area **SANDLOT, PLAYGROUND**
neighboring **ADJACENT**
neighborly **FRIENDLY, SOCIABLE**
neither masculine nor feminine **NEUTER**
nemesis **FATE**

neophyte **NOVICE, TYRO**
Nepal capital **KATMANDU**
nephew of Daedalus **TALUS**
nepotism **PATRONAGE**
Neptune's scepter **TRIDENT**
Nero's successor **GALBA**
nerve **DARING, CHEEK, COURAGE**
nerve part **AXON**
nervous **EDGY, JITTERY, TENSE**
nervous twitch **TIC**
ness **HEADLAND**
nest **AERIE, EYRIE**
nestle **CUDDLE**
nestling pigeon **SQUAB**
nest of pheasants **NIDE**
net **MESH, SEINE, SNARE, PROFIT**
nether **LOWER, UNDER**
Netherlander **DUTCH**
Netherlands city **HAGUE, UTRECHT**
Netherlands commune **EDE, TIEL**
nethermost **LOWEST**
nether world **HELL**
netlike fabric **LACE**
netlike hat **SNOOD**
nettle **IRK, IRRITATE**
network **MESH, RETE, RESEAU, WEB**
neuter pronoun **IT**
neutral **IMPARTIAL**
Nevada city **RENO, CARSON**
Nevada lake **TAHOE**
neve **FIRN, GLACIER**
never (contr.) **NE'ER**
nevertheless **ALL THE SAME, JUST THE SAME, YET, STILL**
new **MODERN, RECENT, UNUSED**
new (prefix) **NEO**
newborn infant **BABE, BABY**
newborn threesome **TRIPLETS**
newcomer **STRANGER**
New England cape **COD, ANN**
New England native **YANKEE**
New England university **YALE, DARTMOUTH, HARVARD, BOSTON**
newel **STAIRPOST**
New Guinea export **COPRA**
New Hampshire city **DOVER, KEENE**
New Hampshire resort **SUNAPEE**
New Haven tree **ELM**
New Jersey city **NEWARK, TRENTON, ORANGE**

New Jersey river **RARITAN**
New Mexico art colony **TAOS**
New Mexico river **GILA, PECOS**
newly married woman **BRIDE**
news **TIDINGS**
news article **ITEM**
news gatherer **REPORTER**
newspaper **GAZETTE, JOURNAL**
newspaper article **ITEM**
newspaper columnist (2 wds.)
**ROVING REPORTER**
newspaper edition **DAILY,
WEEKLY, ISSUE, MORNING,
FIRST, LATE**
newspaper executive (abbr.) **ED.**
newspaper files **MORGUE**
newspaper notice (abbr.) **OBIT,
AD**
newspaperman **REPORTER,
EDITOR, COLUMNIST,
JOURNALIST**
news sheet **PAPER, JOURNAL**
newsstand fiction of 1930's
(2 wds.) **DIME NOVEL**
news story beginning **DATELINE**
news story title **HEADLINE**
new star **NOVA**
new suit (2 wds.) **SUNDAY BEST**
newt **EFT**
New Testament book **ACTS,
COLOSSIANS, CORINTHIANS,
EPHESIANS, GALATIANS,
HEBREWS, JAMES, JOHN,
JUDE, LUKE, MARK,
MATTHEW, PETER, PHILEMON,
PHILIPPIANS, REVELATION,
ROMANS, THESSALONIANS,
TIMOTHY, TITUS**
newton ingredient **FIG**
New Year's, Christmas, etc.
**HOLIDAYS**
New York ball club **METS, JETS,
YANKEES, GIANTS, KNICKS**
New York City stadium **SHEA,
YANKEE**
New York ghetto **HARLEM**
New York Indian **ONEIDA,
MOHAWK**
New York lake **SARANAC**
New York newspaper **TIMES,
NEWS, POST**
New York river **HUDSON, EAST,
HARLEM**
New York State city **ELMIRA,
OLEAN, UTICA, ALBANY,
BUFFALO, ITHACA**
New Zealand aborigine **MAORI**
New Zealand bird **MOA**

New Zealand clan **ATI**
New Zealand parrot **KEA**
New Zealand tree **AKE,
MAKOMAKO**
next **NEAREST, AFTER**
nice **PLEASANT, FINE**
niche **ALCOVE, NOOK**
nick **DENT**
nickel **COIN**
nickname for a
good dancer **TWINKLETOES**
nickname for a Scot **MAC**
nicotinic acid **NIACIN**
Nigerian city **EDE, LAGOS**
Nigerian tribesman **EBOE, IBO**
niggardly **STINGY**
nigh **NEAR, CLOSE**
night before a holiday **EVE**
night bird **OWL**
night clothes **PAJAMAS**
nightclub **CAFE**
nightclub solo (2 wds.)
**TORCH SONG**
nightcrawler **WORM, BAIT**
nightfall **DARK, TWILIGHT, DUSK**
night letter **TELEGRAM**
nightmare **INCUBUS**
nightshade **MOREL**
night twinkler **STAR**
nihil **NOTHING**
nil **NOTHING**
Nile bird **IBIS**
Nile queen, for short **CLEO**
Nile River dam **ASWAN**
Nile River falls **RIPON**
nilgai **ANTELOPE**
nimble **AGILE, SPRY**
nimbus **AURA, HALO**
nine days' devotion **NOVENA**
nine-headed monster **HYDRA**
ninny **FOOL, GOOSE**
nip **BITE, PINCH**
nippy **BITING, BRISK**
niter **SALTPETER**
nitrate **ESTER, SALT**
nitric acid **AQUAFORTIS**
Nixon **REPUBLICAN,
PRESIDENT, DICK**
Nixon's V.P. **AGNEW**
no (colloq.) **NIX**
Noah's boat **ARK**
Noah's son **SHEM, HAM**
nob **HEAD**
nobility **RANK, PEERAGE**
noble **GRAND, HIGH**
nobleman **BARON, EARL, LORD,
PEER, THANE, COUNT, DUKE**

| | |
|---|---|
| noblewoman | **DAME, LADY, DUCHESS, COUNTESS** |
| nobody | **NONE, NONENTITY** |
| no charge | **GRATIS, FREE** |
| nocturnal bird | **OWL, BULLBAT, NIGHTINGALE** |
| nocturnal mammal | **LEMUR** |
| nocturne | **LULLABY, SERENADE** |
| Noel | **CHRISTMAS, YULE** |
| noise | **DIN, CLATTER, RACKET, SOUND** |
| noiseless | **SILENT, STILL** |
| noisome | **NOXIOUS, ROTTEN** |
| noisy dispute | **FRACAS, ROW, BRAWL** |
| noisy impact | **SLAM** |
| noisy swallow | **SLURP** |
| no kidding | **REALLY** |
| no longer active | **RETIRED** |
| no longer are | **WERE** |
| no longer chic | **PASSE** |
| nomad | **MIGRANT, VAGRANT** |
| no matter which | **ANY** |
| nom de plume (2 wds.) | **PEN NAME** |
| nominal | **FORMAL, MERE** |
| nominate | **NAME** |
| no more than | **MERE, ONLY** |
| no one | **NONE** |
| nonchalant | **INDIFFERENT, CASUAL** |
| non-citizen | **ALIEN** |
| nonconforming belief | **HERESY** |
| none (Scot.) | **NANE** |
| non-iron fabric (2 wds.) | **DRIP DRY, PERMANENT PRESS** |
| nonmetallic element | **BORON, IODINE** |
| nonpareil | **PEERLESS** |
| nonplus | **PERPLEX, STUMP** |
| non-productive | **STERILE** |
| non-professional | **AMATEUR, LAYMAN** |
| nonsense | **INANITY, ROT** |
| nonsense poem | **LIMERICK** |
| non-union laborer | **SCAB** |
| nonworker | **DRONE** |
| nook | **ALCOVE** |
| noon | **MIDDAY, TWELVE** |
| noonday rest | **SIESTA** |
| noon meal | **LUNCH** |
| noose | **LOOP** |
| norm | **STANDARD, PAR** |
| normal | **PAR** |
| Norse | **SCANDINAVIAN** |

| | |
|---|---|
| Norse deity | **BALDUR, ODIN, FRIGGA, LOKI, HELA, BRAGI, THOR, FREY, FREYA, FRIGG, TYR, URDUR, VERDANDI, SKULD, IDUNA, HEIMDALL, FENRIS, HERMOD** |
| Norse god | **(see Norse deity)** |
| Norse legend | **SAGA, EDDA** |
| Norse letter | **RUNE** |
| Norseman | **VIKING** |
| Norse navigator | **ERIC** |
| Norse night | **NATT, NOTT** |
| Norse patron saint | **OLAF** |
| Norse poets | **SKALDS** |
| Norse tale | **SAGA, EDDA** |
| Norse toast | **SKOAL** |
| North African capital | **TUNIS** |
| North African colony | **IFNI** |
| North African fruit | **DATE** |
| northeaster | **STORM, GALE** |
| northern Britisher | **SCOT** |
| northern constellation | **LYRA** |
| northern European | **FINN, DANE, SWEDE, LAPP** |
| northern horned mammal | **REINDEER** |
| North Pole discoverer | **PEARY** |
| North Star State | **MINNESOTA** |
| North Vietnamese capital | **HANOI** |
| Norwegian | **NORSE** |
| Norwegian dramatist | **IBSEN** |
| Norwegian sea inlet | **FJORD, FIORD** |
| nose | **PROBOSCIS, SNOUT, SNOOT** |
| nosegay | **POSY** |
| nostalgic | **WISTFUL, HOMESICK** |
| nostrils | **NARES** |
| nosy | **SNOOPY, PRYING** |
| notable | **KNOWN, FAMOUS** |
| not aboveboard | **EVASIVE** |
| not alike | **UNEQUAL, DIFFERENT** |
| not alive | **DEAD** |
| not all | **SOME** |
| notandum | **ENTRY, MEMO** |
| not any | **NO, NONE** |
| not appropriate | **INAPT** |
| notarize | **SEAL** |
| not artificial | **NATURAL** |
| not as advanced | **SLOWER** |
| not as common | **RARER** |
| not as early | **LATER** |
| not as high | **LOWER** |
| not as large | **SMALLER** |
| not asleep | **AWAKE** |
| not as much | **LESS** |
| not a soul (2 wds.) | **NO ONE** |

| | | | |
|---|---|---|---|
| not as strong | WEAKER | not general | LOCAL |
| not as taut | LOOSER | not genuine | ERSATZ, FAKE, |
| not at all | NEVER, NOHOW, | | COUNTERFEIT |
| | NOWISE | not good | BAD |
| not at home | AWAY, OUT | not hard | EASY, SOFT |
| notation | MEMO, ENTRY, | not having made a will | |
| | RECORD | | INTESTATE |
| not at leisure | BUSY, WORKING | not heavy | LIGHT |
| not a winner | LOSER | not high | LOW |
| not bad | GOOD | nothing | NIL, ZERO, NAUGHT |
| not better | WORSE | nothing but | ONLY, MERE |
| not boastful | MODEST, SHY | nothing doing | NIX |
| not brave | TIMID | nothing (Fr.) | RIEN |
| not brief | LONG | nothing less than | SAME |
| not bright | PALE, STUPID, DUMB | nothing more than | MERE |
| not busy | IDLE | not hollow | SOLID, FILLED |
| notch | NICK | notice | SEE, ESPY, OBSERVE |
| notched bar | RATCH | noticeable | SIGNIFICANT |
| not clearly defined | INDISTINCT | notify | ANNOUNCE, INFORM |
| not closed | OPEN | not illuminated | DARK |
| not C.O.D. | POSTPAID, CHARGED | not imaginary | REAL |
| not cold | HOT, WARM | not in | OUT |
| not cooked | RAW | not in motion | STABLE, FIXED |
| not covered | BARE | not interested | BORED |
| not dead | ALIVE | notion | IDEA, THOUGHT, |
| not definite | TENTATIVE | | OPINION |
| not difficult | EASY | not joking | EARNEST, SERIOUS |
| not docile | WILD | not living | DEAD |
| not down | UP | not long | SHORT |
| not dry | WET | not long ago | RECENTLY |
| note | MESSAGE, MEMO | not many | FEW |
| note contents of | LABEL | not minor | MAJOR |
| noted | FAMOUS, FAMED, | not moist | DRY |
| | RENOWNED, SEEN | not new | OLD, USED |
| note duration of | CLOCK, TIME | not now | LATER |
| not efficient | LAME | not odd | EVEN |
| not either | NEITHER | not of the clergy | LAIC, LAY |
| note (Lat.) | NOTA | not one | NONE |
| not employed | IDLE | not open | CLOSED, SHUT |
| note of Guido's scale | UT, DO, | notoriety | ECLAT, PUBLICITY |
| | RE, MI, FA, SOL, LA | notorious | INFAMOUS |
| note of the scale | DO, RE, MI, | not out | IN, HOME, AVAILABLE |
| | FA, SO, LA, TI | not plump | LEAN, SLIM, THIN |
| noteworthy | SPECIAL | not pretty | UGLY, PLAIN |
| noteworthy act | FEAT | not professional | AMATEUR, LAIC |
| not even a soul (2 wds.) | NO ONE | not qualified | UNFIT, |
| not false | TRUE | | INEXPERIENCED |
| not fast | SLOW | not quite | NEARLY |
| not fastened | LOOSE | not ready | UNPREPARED |
| not fat | LEAN, SLIM, THIN | not regular | UNSTEADY, |
| not feral | TAME | | SPORADIC |
| not figurative | LITERAL | not rich | POOR |
| not firm | LOOSE | not rigid | LIMP, SOFT |
| not flexible | RIGID | not ripe | GREEN |
| not for publication (3 wds.) | | not separable | INDIVISIBLE |
| | OFF THE RECORD | not shaky | STEADY, SOLID |
| not forward | MODEST, SHY | not sharp | DULL |
| not fresh | STALE | not short | LONG |

not shortened, as a book **UNABRIDGED**
not shut **OPEN**
not skinny **FAT, PLUMP, STOUT**
not slow **FAST**
not smooth **ROUGH**
not so, in law **SECUS**
not soft **HARD**
not so much **LESS**
not sound **LAME**
not speaking **MUTE, SILENT**
not straight **CROOKED**
not straightforward **EVASIVE**
not suitable **INAPT, UNFIT**
not sweet **SOUR**
not talking **SILENT**
not tame **WILD**
not taut **SLACK**
not these **THOSE**
not thick **THIN**
not those **THESE**
not tight **LOOSE**
not to be considered (4 wds.)
**OUT OF THE QUESTION**
not to be pacified **IMPLACABLE**
not together **APART, SPLIT**
not tough **TENDER**
not true **FALSE**
not up **ABED, DOWN, SLEEPING**
not warm **COOL, COLD**
not waterproof **POROUS,
LEAKY**
not well **BADLY, ILL**
not well planned (comp. wd.)
**HALF-BAKED**
not wide **NARROW**
not wild **TAME**
notwithstanding **DESPITE, YET,
HOWEVER**
not working **IDLE**
not yet settled **MOOT**
not young **OLD**
nougat **CANDY, TAFFY**
nought **BAD, WORTHLESS**
noun **WORD, NAME**
noun suffix **ENT, ESE, IER, IST,
ITE**
nourish **FEED**
nourishment **FOOD, NUTRIENT**
Nova Scotia **ACADIA**
Nova Scotia mountain ash
**DOGBERRY**
Nova Scotian **BLUENOSE**
Nova Scotian resort **DIGBY**
novel **STORY, BOOK,
UNUSUAL, NEW**
novelist Bagnold **ENID**
novelist Ferber **EDNA**

novelist Glasgow **ELLEN**
novelist Hunter **EVAN**
novelist Jackson **SHIRLEY**
novelist Kazan **ELIA**
novelist on the Orient (2 wds.)
**PEARL BUCK**
novelist Uris **LEON**
novelist Zola **EMILE**
novelty **NEWNESS**
November event **ELECTION**
novice **TYRO, TIRO**
novice athlete **ROOKIE**
novocain **PROCAINE**
now **PRESENT**
now and then **SOMETIMES**
noxious **HARMFUL, POISONOUS**
nozzle **SPOUT, NOSE**
nuance **SHADE**
nub **POINT**
nubble **LUMP, KNOB**
nubby fabric **TWEED**
nucleus **CORE, HEART**
nude **BARE, NAKED**
nudge **POKE, PROD, JAB**
nugget **LUMP**
nuisance **PEST, ANNOYANCE**
null **INVALID**
nullah **GULLY, RAVINE**
nullify **CANCEL, ANNUL**
numb **TORPID, FROZEN**
number **DIGIT, NUMERAL**
number again **RENUMERATE**
numbered chart **TABLE**
number one **FIRST, BEST**
number's third power **CUBE**
numeral style **ARABIC, ROMAN**
numerous **MANY**
nun **SISTER**
nuncio **DELEGATE**
nunnery **CLOISTER, CONVENT**
nun's dress **HABIT**
nun's headdress **WIMPLE**
nun's room **CELL**
nuptial **BRIDAL**
nuptials **WEDDING**
Nureyev's milieu **BALLET**
Nureyev specialty **LEAP**
nurse **TEND, FEED**
nursemaid **NANNY**
nursery bed **CRIB**
nurse's assistant **AIDE**
nurture **FEED**
nut **ACORN, PECAN, WALNUT,
HAZELNUT, FILBERT,
PEANUT, ALMOND**
nutant **NODDING, DROOPING**
nut-bearing tree **BEECH**

| | | | |
|---|---|---|---|
| nutmeg spice | MACE | objurgation | REBUKE, REPROOF |
| Nutmeg State | CONNECTICUT | obligate | BIND |
| nut of the oak | ACORN | obligation | DEBT, DUTY |
| nut pine of the | | obligatory | REQUIRED |
| Southwest | PINON | oblige | GRATIFY, PLEASE |
| nutramin | VITAMIN | obliging | AGREEABLE |
| nutriment | FOOD, ALIMENT | oblique | INDIRECT, ASKEW |
| nutritious | HEALTHY | obliterate | ERASE |
| nutty | CRAZY | oblivious | UNAWARE, |
| nuzzle | NESTLE, SNUGGLE | | FORGETFUL |
| nyala | ANTELOPE | obloquy | REPROACH, DISGRACE |
| nylon | STOCKING, FABRIC | obnoxious | HATEFUL |
| nymph | SYLPH, SIREN | oboe | HAUTBOY, REED, |
| | | | HAUTBOIS |
| | | obscene | LEWD, DIRTY |
| | | obscuration | ECLIPSE |
| **O** | | obscure | DIM, MURKY, BLUR, |
| | | | DARK, DARKEN |
| oaf | BLOCKHEAD, LOUT, CLOD | obscure corner | NOOK |
| oak | TREE | obscurity | DIMNESS |
| oak-to-be | ACORN | obsequious | SERVILE, FAWNING |
| oakum | HEMP | observance | CEREMONY, RITE |
| oar | PADDLE, ROW | observant | ATTENTIVE, |
| oar blade | PEEL | | WATCHFUL |
| oarlock | THOLE | observe | NOTE, NOTICE, SEE, |
| oarsman | ROWER | | EYE |
| oasis | WADI, REFUGE | observe Lent | FAST, ABSTAIN |
| oasis feature (2 wds.) | | observer | WITNESS, SPECTATOR |
| | WATER HOLE | obsess | PREOCCUPY |
| oast | KILN, OVEN | obsession | MANIA, PASSION |
| oat | GRAIN | obsolete | PASSE |
| oath | CURSE, VOW | obstacle | IMPEDIMENT, SNAG |
| oatmeal | PORRIDGE | obstinate | STUBBORN, MULISH |
| obdurate | STUBBORN | obstreporous | TURBULENT, |
| obeah | WITCHERY, VOODOO | | UNRULY |
| obedience | SUBMISSION | obstruct | BAR |
| obedient | DUTIFUL, LOYAL | obstruction | BARRIER, SNAG |
| obeisance | HOMAGE | obtain | GET, FIND, PROCURE |
| obelisk | NEEDLE, PILLAR, | obtain as profit | GAIN |
| | MONOLITH | obtain by reasoning | DERIVE |
| obelus | DAGGER | obtain by searching | FIND |
| obese | FAT, STOUT, PLUMP, | obtain by threat | EXTORT |
| | OVERWEIGHT | obtain information | LEARN |
| obey | HEED, MIND, LISTEN | obtest | BEG, PLEAD, ENTREAT |
| obfuscate | BEWILDER, | obtrusive | MEDDLING, PUSHY |
| | CONFUSE, DIM | obtuse | BLUNT, DULL |
| obi | SASH | obverse | FRONT |
| object | AIM, END, INTENT, | obviate | AVOID, PREVENT |
| | THING | obvious | EVIDENT, PATENT |
| objection | QUARREL, PROTEST | ocarina | FLUTE |
| objective | END, INTENTION, | occasion | TIME, EVENT |
| | AIM, GOAL | occasional | IRREGULAR, CASUAL |
| object of art | CURIO | occasionally (2 wds.) | AT TIMES |
| object of dread | BOGEY | occident | WEST |
| object of worship | IDOL, GOD | occlusion | BITE, BLOCK |
| object to | DEMUR, PROTEST | occult | SECRET, DARK |
| objurgate | ABUSE, CHIDE, | occultism | CABALA |
| | SCOLD, REBUKE | occult power | MAGIC |

| | | | |
|---|---|---|---|
| occupant | **TENANT** | of a branch | **RAMOUS** |
| occupation | **VOCATION,** | of a chamber | **CAMERAL** |
| | **CAREER, JOB** | of a few words | **TERSE** |
| occupied | **BUSY, ENGAGED** | of age (Lat., abbr.) | **AETAT, AET** |
| occupy | **FILL** | of aircraft | **AREO** |
| occupy a chair | **SIT** | of a musical | |
| occur | **HAPPEN, TAKE PLACE,** | group | **ORCHESTRAL** |
| | **COME TO PASS** | of an artery | **AORTAL** |
| occurrence | **EVENT** | of an era | **EPOCHAL** |
| occurring after death | | of an opposite color | |
| | **POSTHUMOUS** | | **CONTRASTING** |
| occurring frequently | **COMMON** | of a part of the brain | **CORTICAL** |
| occurring occasionally | | of a wife | **UXORIAL** |
| | **SPORADIC** | of basic alteration | **MUTANT** |
| occurring often | **FREQUENT** | of better quality | **FINER** |
| ocean | **SEA, ATLANTIC,** | of cities | **URBAN** |
| | **PACIFIC, INDIAN, ARCTIC,** | of course | **YES** |
| | **ANTARCTIC, MAIN** | of course not | **NO** |
| oceanic | **PELAGIC, VAST, HUGE** | of course (sl.) | **NATCH** |
| ocean liner (abbr.) | **SS** | of different kinds | **MOTLEY** |
| ocean mammal | **WHALE** | of equal score | **EVEN, PAR, TIED** |
| ocean movement | **TIDE** | off base illegally (Army sl.) | |
| ocean route | **LANE** | | **AWOL** |
| ocean ship | **LINER** | offend | **DISPLEASE** |
| ocean shore | **SEACOAST,** | offend God | **SIN, BLASPHEME** |
| | **STRAND, BEACH** | offense | **AFFRONT** |
| oceans of the world (2 wds.) | | offensive | **ABOMINABLE** |
| | **SEVEN SEAS** | offensively obtrusive | **BLATANT** |
| ocellus | **EYESPOT** | offer | **BID, TENDER** |
| ocelot | **CAT** | offering | **GIFT, SACRIFICE** |
| ocher | **PIGMENT, YELLOW** | offer marriage | **PROPOSE** |
| octave | **EIGHT** | offhand | **IMPROMPTU** |
| octopus | **POLYP** | office | **CHARGE, FUNCTION** |
| octopus arm | **TENTACLE** | office cabinet | **FILE** |
| ocular | **OPTIC** | office expense account | |
| odalisque | **SLAVE, CONCUBINE** | (2 wds.) | **PETTY CASH** |
| odd | **PECULIAR, STRANGE** | office holder | **IN** |
| odd-jobs doer (2 wds.) | | office item (2 wds.) | **RUBBER** |
| | **HANDY MAN** | | **BAND, PAPER CLIP,** |
| oddly amusing | **DROLL** | | **CARBON PAPER** |
| oddment | **SCRAP, REMNANT** | office machine | **ADDER,** |
| odds | **ADVANTAGE** | | **TYPEWRITER** |
| odds (Scot.) | **ORRA** | office record | **FILE** |
| odds and ends | **SCRAPS** | office routine (2 wds.) | |
| ode | **POEM, CANTICLE** | **DESK WORK, PAPER WORK** | |
| odeon | **GALLERY, HALL** | officer's assistant | **AIDE** |
| odious | **HATEFUL** | officer's insignia | **STRIPE** |
| odium | **HATRED** | office table | **DESK** |
| odontalgia | **TOOTHACHE** | office worker | **STENO, CLERK,** |
| odor | **AROMA, BOUQUET,** | | **TYPIST** |
| | **SCENT, FRAGRANCE,** | official | **AUTHENTIC, REAL** |
| | **SMELL, PERFUME** | official decree | **FIAT** |
| odorous | **REDOLENT** | official grade | **RANK** |
| Oedipus' father | **LAIUS** | official proclamation | **UKASE,** |
| Oedipus' mother | **JOCASTA** | | **EDICT** |
| oeillade | **GLANCE, OGLE** | official records | **ACTA,** |
| of | **FROM** | | **REGISTER** |
| of (Fr.) | **DE** | official seal | **STAMP** |

| | |
|---|---|
| officious | **OBTRUSIVE** |
| offshore coral growth | **REEF** |
| offshore radar platform (2 wds.) | **TEXAS TOWER** |
| offspring | **SON, DAUGHTER, CHILD, CHILDREN, PROGENY, DESCENDANT** |
| off the rack (comp. wd.) | **READY-TO-WEAR** |
| off the track | **ASTRAY** |
| off-white | **GRAY, GREY, ECRU, CREAM, IVORY** |
| of government | **POLITICAL** |
| of great depth | **PROFOUND, DEEP** |
| of great importance | **MOMENTOUS** |
| of great size | **HUGE** |
| of great weight | **PONDEROUS, HEAVY** |
| of healing (abbr.) | **MED** |
| of highest quality | **BEST** |
| of little importance | **TRIVIAL** |
| of low birth | **IGNOBLE, COMMON** |
| of marriage | **MARITAL, NUPTIAL** |
| of medicine | **MEDICAL** |
| of milk | **LACTIC** |
| of mothers and fathers | **PARENTAL** |
| of musical quality | **TONAL** |
| of no avail | **FUTILE** |
| of no value | **USELESS** |
| of ocean movement | **TIDAL** |
| of one's country | **NATIONAL** |
| of planet's path | **ORBITAL** |
| of punishment | **PENAL** |
| of secondary importance | **INCIDENTAL** |
| of sound | **TONAL** |
| of speech | **PHONETIC** |
| of superior quality | **BETTER** |
| often | **FREQUENTLY** |
| often-dented item | **FENDER** |
| often-pickled vegetable | **BEET, CUCUMBER, MELON, CAULIFLOWER, BEAN, ARTICHOKE, MUSHROOM** |
| often-read item | **PALM** |
| of that kind | **SUCH** |
| of the backbone | **SPINAL** |
| of the cheek | **MALAR** |
| of the city | **URBAN** |
| of the country | **RURAL** |
| of the ear | **OTIC** |
| of the hour | **HORAL, TIMELY, CURRENT** |
| of the mouth | **ORAL** |
| of the nose | **NASAL** |
| of the Orient | **EASTERN** |
| of the pope | **PAPAL** |
| of the same kind | **AKIN** |
| of the sea | **MARINE, MARITIME** |
| of the side | **LATERAL** |
| of the skull | **CRANIAL** |
| of the spring | **VERNAL** |
| of the sun | **SOLAR** |
| of the teeth | **DENTAL** |
| of the USN | **NAVAL** |
| ogee | **ARCH** |
| ogle | **EYE, LEER, FLIRT, MAKE EYES** |
| ogre | **MONSTER, GIANT** |
| Ohio city | **TOLEDO, AKRON** |
| oil | **LUBRICATE, OLEO, FAT, GREASE, LUBRICANT** |
| oil (suffix) | **OL, OLE** |
| oilbird | **GUACHARO** |
| oil of rose petals | **ATTAR** |
| oil plant | **SESAME** |
| oil source | **OLIVE, PEANUT** |
| oily | **UNCTUOUS, GREASY** |
| oily fruit | **OLIVE** |
| oily tissue | **FAT, ADIPOSE** |
| ointment | **SALVE, NARD** |
| okay | **ALL RIGHT, YES, SATISFACTORY** |
| Oklahoma city | **ADA, TULSA** |
| Oklahoma Indian | **OSAGE, PAWNEE** |
| Oklahoma mountain | **OZARK** |
| Oklahoma river | **RED** |
| old | **ANCIENT, ELDERLY, AGED** |
| old boat | **TUB** |
| old car | **CRATE, JALOPY** |
| old card game | **LOO, WHIST** |
| Old Colony State | **MASSACHUSETTS** |
| old Dominion | **VIRGINIA** |
| old English bard | **SCOP** |
| old English coin | **GROAT, RYAL, NOBLE** |
| old English pronoun | **YE** |
| older | **ELDER, SENIOR** |
| old expletive | **EGAD** |
| Old Faithful | **GEYSER** |
| old-fashioned | **DATED, PASSE, QUAINT** |
| old-fashioned heating unit (2 wds.) | **FRANKLIN STOVE** |
| old-fashioned photo | **TINTYPE** |
| Old Franklin State | **TENNESSEE** |
| old French coin | **ECU, SOU, SOL, LOUIS** |
| old French dance | **GAVOTTE** |

old frontier region of US
(2 wds.) **WILD WEST**
Old Glory **FLAG**
old Greek music hall **ODEON**
old Greek township **DEME**
old horse **NAG**
Old Line State **MARYLAND**
old maid **SPINSTER**
old movie **RERUN**
old musical instrument **LUTE**
old musical note **ELA, UT**
Old North State
**NORTH CAROLINA**
old pal **CRONY**
old picture card **TAROT**
old poet **BARD, SCOP**
old Roman official **AEDILE,
EDILE, MAGISTRATE**
old sailor **SALT**
old salt **TAR, GOB**
old saying **ADAGE, SAW**
old Scottish chief **THANE**
old slave **ESNE, SERF**
old sledge **SEVEN-UP**
old sol **SUN**
old squaw **DUCK**
old stringed instrument **LUTE,
LYRE**
Old Testament Apocrypha book
**TOBIT, JUDITH, WISDOM OF
SOLOMON, ECCLESIASTICUS,
MACCABEES**
Old Testament book **AMOS,
CHRONICLES, DANIEL,
DEUTERONOMY, ESTHER,
ECCLESIASTES, EXODUS,
EZEKIEL, EZRA, GENESIS,
HABAKKUK, HAGGAI, HOSEA,
ISAIAH, JEREMIAH, JOB, JOEL,
JONAH, JOSHUA, JUDGES,
KINGS, LAMENTATIONS,
LEVITICUS, MALACHI, MICAH,
NAHUM, NEHEMIAH,
NUMBERS, OBADIAH,
PROVERBS, PSALMS, RUTH,
SAMUEL, SONG OF SOLOMON
(SONG OF SONGS), ZECHARIAH,
ZEPHANIAH**
old time **YORE**
old violin **AMATI, STRADIVARI**
old wagon train route
**OREGON TRAIL**
old weapon **MACE, LANCE**
old witch **CRONE**
old woman **CRONE, HAG**
old-womanish **ANILE**
oleaginous **OILY, UNCTUOUS**
oleo **MARGARINE**

oleoresin **ELEMI**
olfactory organ **NOSE**
olid **FETID**
olio **HODGEPODGE, MEDLEY,
MIXTURE**
olive genus **OLEA**
oliver **HAMMER**
olla **JUG, POT**
oloroso **SHERRY**
Olympic event **SHOT-PUT,
DASH, RELAY, GAME,
MARATHON, RACE**
ombre **SHADED**
omega **END, LAST**
omen **AUGURY, FOREBODING,
FORETOKEN, PORTENT,
PRESAGE, SIGN**
ominous **FATEFUL, SINISTER**
omit **EXCLUDE, OVERLOOK**
omit a vowel in pronunciation
**ELIDE**
omit, in printing **DELE**
on **ATOP, UPON**
on (prefix) **EPI**
on a cruise **ASEA**
on a large scale **GIANT**
on all sides **AROUND, ABOUT**
on and on **TEDIOUSLY**
on behalf of **FOR**
once **FORMERLY**
once and again **TWICE**
once and future king **ARTHUR**
once around a track **LAP**
once famous person
(comp. wd.) **HAS-BEEN**
once, formerly **ERST**
once in a while **OCCASIONALLY**
once more **AGAIN, ANEW**
once upon a time **FORMERLY**
on condition that **IF**
one **AN, UNIT, UNITED,
UNITY, SINGLETON**
one (Fr.) **UN, UNE**
one (Ger.) **EINE, EIN**
one (Sp.) **UNO, UNA**
one against **ANTI**
one and all **EVERY**
one and only **SOLE**
one at a time (2 wds.) **SINGLE
FILE**
one-celled animal **AMOEBA**
one devoted to religious work
**OBLATE**
on edge **TENSE, WARY,
NERVOUS**
one having special talents
**GENIUS**

one horse carriage **CARIOLE, GIG**
one hundred cents **DOLLAR**
one hundred per cent **ALL, ENTIRETY WHOLE, ENTIRE**
one in authority **MANAGER, FOREMAN, CHAIRMAN BOSS**
one in favor of **FOR, PRO**
one in opposition **ANTI**
one issue of a newspaper **EDITION**
one kind of secretary **DESK, EXECUTIVE**
one lacking courage **COWARD**
one-man performance **SOLO**
one missing **ABSENTEE**
one of a deck **CARD**
one of an ancient race **MEDE**
one of Atilla's followers **HUN**
one of Columbus' ships **NINA, PINTA, SANTA MARIA**
one of Hamlet's alternatives **TO BE, NOT TO BE**
one of the Barrymores **ETHEL, JOHN, LIONEL**
one of the Bears **URSA**
one of the Evangelists **MARK, MATTHEW, LUKE, JOHN**
one of the Gershwins **IRA, GEORGE**
one of the Kettles **PA, MA**
one of the Muses **ERATO, CLIO, CALLIOPE, EUTERPE, MELPOMENE, POLYHYMNIA, TERPSICHORE, THALIA, URANIA**
one of the reindeer **DASHER, DANCER, PRANCER, VIXEN, COMET, CUPID, DONNER, DONDER, BLITZEN, RUDOLPH**
one of the senses **SIGHT, TOUCH, HEARING, TASTE, SMELL**
one of the Twelve **MATTHEW, JOHN, PETER, JUDAS, THOMAS, ANDREW, JAMES, PHILIP, BARTHOLOMEW, JUDE, SIMON, MATTHIAS**
one of two equal parts **HALF**
one or the other **EITHER**
one racing circuit **LAP**
onerous **HEAVY, DIFFICULT**
one seeking political asylum **REFUGEE**
one-sided **BIASED, SLANTED, PARTIAL**

one-spot **ACE**
one's self **EGO**
one's strong point **FORTE**
one time **QUONDAM**
one time only **ONCE**
one undergoing change **MUTANT**
one way up **STAIR**
one who abandons **DESERTER**
one who avoids the company of others **LONER**
one who consumes food **EATER**
one who dies for a cause **MARTYR**
one who digs for coal **MINER**
one who entertains **HOST**
one who excels **ACE**
one who fails to win **LOSER**
one who feels superior **SNOB**
one who fights for noble cause **CRUSADER**
one who forwards goods **CONSIGNOR**
one who fustrates a plan **MARPLOT**
one who goes by **PASSER**
one who governs **RULER**
one who lubricates **OILER**
one who makes forays **RAIDER**
one who roams about furtively **PROWLER**
one who stitches **SEAMSTRESS, TAILOR**
one who tells **RELATER, NARRATOR, SNITCH**
one without courage **COWARD**
on grand scale **EPIC**
on guard **ALERT**
onion **BULB**
onion genus **ALLIUM**
onion-like herb **CHIVE**
onion-like vegetable **LEEK, SCALLION**
on its way **GONE**
onlooker **WITNESS**
only **MERE, SOLE**
only fair (comp. wd.) **SO-SO**
onset **BEGINNING, START, OPENING**
onslaught **ATTACK**
Ontario capital **TORONTO**
on the affirmative side **PRO**
on the bottom **SUNK**
on the briny **ASEA, AT SEA**
on the contrary **BUT**
on the decline **DECADENT**
on the fritz **OUT OF WHACK, BROKEN**

| | | | |
|---|---|---|---|
| on the go | ACTIVE | opinion | IDEA, THOUGHT |
| on the left side | | opinionated | BIASED |
| (nautical) | APORT | opinionated faction | SECT |
| on the move | ASTIR | opinion opposed to doctrine | |
| on the ocean | ASEA | | HERESY |
| on the peak | ATOP | opinion register | POLL |
| on the roof of | ATOP | opium | DRUG, DOPE |
| on the sheltered side | ALEE | opium drug | CODEINE, |
| on the summit | ATOP | | MORPHINE |
| on this | HEREON | opponent | ENEMY, RIVAL, FOE, |
| onus | BURDEN | | COMPETITOR |
| onward | FORWARD | opportune (comp. wd.) | |
| oodles | LOTS | | HEAVEN-SENT |
| Oolong | TEA | opportunity | CHANCE, OPENING |
| oomph | ENERGY | oppose | RESIST, COMBAT |
| Oopak | TEA | opposed | ANTI |
| ooze | SEEP, EXUDE | opposite | ANTITHESIS, |
| opah | FISH | | ANTONYM |
| opal | GIRASOL | opposite side | REVERSE |
| opaque | DARK, OBSCURE | oppress | AFFLICT, PERSECUTE |
| open | AJAR, FRANK, CANDID, | oprobrious | INFAMOUS |
| | UNFOLD, UNWRAP, UNLOCK | opt | CHOOSE |
| open a package | UNDO, UNTIE | optic | EYE |
| open declaration | AVOWAL | optical glass | LENS |
| open for discussion | MOOT | optical illusion | MIRAGE |
| open-handed blow | SLAP | optical membrane | RETINA |
| opening | GAP, HOLE, MOUTH, | optical organ | EYE |
| | VENT | optimist | HOPER |
| opening for coins | SLOT | optimistic | ROSY |
| openings | ORA | option | CHOICE |
| open-mouthed | AGAPE | optional | VOLUNTARY |
| open out | SPREAD | oracular | WISE |
| open place in forest | GLADE | oral | SPOKEN, VOCAL, VERBAL |
| open shoe | SANDAL | oral cavity | MOUTH |
| open to view | OVERT | orange and black bird | ORIOLE |
| open wide, as the mouth | YAWN | orange genus | CITRUS |
| openwork fabric | LACE | orange oil | NEROLI |
| opera by Bizet | CARMEN | orange pekoe | TEA |
| opera by Massenet | MANON | orange-red | CORAL |
| opera by Verdi | AIDA | orange seed | PIP |
| opera division | ACT | orange skin | RIND, PEEL |
| opera glass | LORGNETTE | orangutan | APE |
| opera hat | TOPPER | orate | DECLAIM, HARANGUE, |
| opera highlight | ARIA | | TALK, SPEAK |
| opera prince | IGOR | oration | SPEECH |
| opera singer (2 wds.) | | orator | SPEAKER |
| | PRIMA DONNA | oratory | ELOCUTION |
| opera star | DIVA | orb | EYE |
| operate | MANAGE, RUN | orbit | CIRCUIT |
| operate a car | DRIVE | orbital point | APSIS |
| operation | WORK, PROCEDURE | orc | GRAMPUS |
| operational | READY | orchestra | BAND |
| operative | AGENT | orchestra leader | CONDUCTOR |
| ophidian | REPTILE, SERPENT | orchestra leader's stick | BATON |
| opthalmic | OCULAR | orchestra section | REEDS, |
| opthamologist | OCULIST | | BRASS, STRINGS, TYMPANY |
| opiate | NARCOTIC | orchestra's location | PIT, |
| opine | THINK | | BANDSTAND |

| | |
|---|---|
| orchestrate | **ARRANGE** |
| ordain | **ENACT** |
| ordeal | **TEST, TRIAL** |
| order | **COMMAND, DIRECT, DIRECTIVE, NEATNESS, BID** |
| order for girl Friday (3 wds.) | **TAKE A LETTER** |
| order for writ | **PRECIPE, PRAECIPE** |
| order of frogs and toads | **ANURA** |
| order of whales | **CETE** |
| orderly | **NEAT** |
| ordinal | **REGULAR** |
| ordinance | **STATUTE, LAW** |
| ordinary | **MERE, COMMON** |
| ordinary writing | **PROSE** |
| ordnance | **ARMOR, ARMS** |
| ore deposit | **MINE, LODE, VEIN** |
| ore digger | **MINER** |
| ore vein | **LODE** |
| Oregon city | **SALEM, PORTLAND** |
| Oregon mountain | **HOOD** |
| Orel's river | **OKA** |
| organ | **MEDIUM, VEHICLE** |
| organic compound | **ESTER** |
| organic substance | **RESIN** |
| organization | **SETUP, ASSOCIATION** |
| organize | **ARRANGE, FORM** |
| organized athletics | **GAMES, SPORTS** |
| organized criminal society | **MAFIA, COSA NOSTRA, SYNDICATE** |
| organized march | **PARADE** |
| organized migration | **TREK, EXODUS** |
| organ of hearing | **EAR** |
| organ of sight | **EYE** |
| organ of speech | **TONGUE, LIP** |
| organ part | **REED, STOP** |
| organ pipe | **FLUE, REED** |
| organ stop | **OBOE, ORAGE** |
| organ tube | **PIPE** |
| Orient | **ASIA, EAST** |
| Oriental caravansary | **SERAI** |
| Oriental chief | **KHAN** |
| Oriental coin | **DINAR** |
| Oriental cymbal | **TAL** |
| Oriental destiny | **KISMET** |
| Oriental flower | **LOTUS** |
| Oriental grain | **RICE** |
| Oriental guitar | **SITAR** |
| Oriental headdress | **TURBAN** |
| Oriental marketplace | **BAZAAR** |
| Oriental nation | **JAPAN, CHINA, KOREA, VIETNAM** |
| Oriental nurse | **AMAH** |
| Oriental pagoda | **TAA** |
| Oriental periodic wind | **MONSOON** |
| Oriental potentate | **AMIR, EMIR, AMEER, EMEER** |
| Oriental river boat | **SAMPAN** |
| Oriental ruler | **CALIPH, SULTAN** |
| Oriental salute | **SALAAM** |
| Oriental sash | **OBI** |
| Oriental sauke | **SOY** |
| Oriental staple grain | **RICE** |
| Oriental title | **PASHA, AGA** |
| Oriental women's quarters | **ODA, HAREM** |
| origin | **GERM, ROOT, SEED** |
| original | **FIRST, PRIMARY** |
| originate | **ARISE, CREATE, DERIVE** |
| Orion | **CONSTELLATION, HUNTER** |
| orison | **PRAYER** |
| ormer | **ABALONE** |
| ornament | **BANGLE** |
| ornamental | **DECORATIVE** |
| ornamental ball | **BEAD** |
| ornamental bottle | **DECANTER** |
| ornamental button | **STUD** |
| ornamental fabric | **LACE** |
| ornamental flower holder | **URN, JARDINIERE** |
| ornamental knob | **STUD** |
| ornamental knot | **BOW** |
| ornamental setting | **DECOR** |
| ornamental stamp | **SEAL** |
| ornamental tuft | **TASSEL** |
| ornamental vase | **URN** |
| ornate | **OPULENT, FLORID** |
| orthodontist's concern | **BITE** |
| osar | **ESKER** |
| Oscar | **AWARD** |
| oscillate | **WAVER, VACILLATE** |
| osier | **WILLOW** |
| Osiris' wife | **ISIS** |
| osprey | **ERN** |
| ostentation | **DISPLAY, BRAVADO** |
| ostentatious | **POMPOUS, PRETENTIOUS** |
| ostentatiously fashionable (sl.) | **SWANK** |
| ostiole | **APERTURE, STOMA** |
| ostracize | **BLACKBALL, OUST** |
| ostrichlike bird | **EMU** |
| Othello villain | **IAGO** |
| other | **ELSE** |
| others (Lat.) | **ALIA** |
| otherwise | **ELSE, OR** |
| otiose | **VAIN, FUTILE** |

| | | | |
|---|---|---|---|
| ottoman | SOFA, STOOL, FOOTREST | outward | EXTERNAL |
| Ottoman Empire | TURKEY | outwit | FOIL, THWART |
| Ottoman governor | PASHA | ova | EGGS |
| oubliette | DUNGEON | oval | ELLIPTICAL |
| ought to | SHOULD | oven | KILN, OAST |
| ouija | PLANCHETTE | oven device | TIMER |
| our (Fr.) | NOTRE | over | ABOVE, ATOP, ACROSS, DONE, FINISHED |
| our country (abbr.) | USA | over (Ger.) | UBER |
| our planet | EARTH | over (poetic) | O'ER |
| oust | EJECT, EVICT | over (prefix) | SUR |
| out | ABSENT, AWAY | overabundance | EXCESS, SURPLUS |
| out-and-out | ARRANT | overact | EMOTE |
| outback | BUSH | over-adorned | ORNATE |
| outbreak | RASH | over again | ANEW, ENCORE |
| outbuilding | SHED, LEAN-TO, WC | overalls material | DENIM |
| outcast | VAGRANT, CASTAWAY | over and above | TOO |
| out class | EXCEL, SURPASS | over and over | REPEATEDLY |
| outcome | END, RESULT | overbearing | ARROGANT, HAUGHTY |
| outcry | HUE | overburden | OPPRESS |
| outdo | EXCEED, BEAT | overcast | CLOUDY |
| outdoor activity | SPORT | overcome | SUBDUE, CONQUER |
| outdoor blaze | CAMPFIRE, BONFIRE | overcome with fear | DAUNT |
| outer | ECTAL | overdue | LATE |
| outer (prefix) | ECTO | overflow | SPILL |
| outer garment | COAT, JACKET | over fond of | DOTE |
| outer layer | SKIN | over-friendly politician | HANDSHAKER |
| outer skin | EPIDERMIS | overhang | JUT, PROJECT |
| outfit | KIT, RIG | overhasty | RASH |
| outgrowth | EMERGENCE | overhaul | RENOVATE |
| outing | EXCURSION, JAUNT | overhead | ABOVE |
| out in the open | OVERT | overhead railroad | EL |
| outlandish | UNUSUAL | overjoy | ELATE |
| outlaw | CRIMINAL, FUGITIVE | overlapping part | FLAP |
| outlet | VENT | overlook | CONDONE, NEGLECT, FORGET, MISS, OMIT |
| outline | DRAFT, SKETCH | overpass approach | RAMP |
| out-migrant | EMIGRE | overpower | CRUSH, MASTER |
| outmoded | PASSE, DATED | overrun | RAVAGE, BESET |
| out of | FROM | oversee | SUPERINTEND |
| out of bed | ARISEN, RISEN | overseer of morals | CENSOR |
| out of danger | SAFE | overshadow | ECLIPSE |
| out of date | PASSE, DATED, OLD-FASHIONED | oversight | OMISSION, SLIP |
| out of place | INEPT, INAPPROPRIATE | oversized | BIG |
| out of style | PASSE, DATED, OLD-FASHIONED | overt | PUBLIC |
| out of the way | ASIDE | overtake | PASS |
| out of town | AWAY | over there | YONDER |
| outrage | INSULT, FURY | overthrow | DEFEAT, ABOLISH |
| outrageous | WANTON, FLAGRANT | overture | PRELUDE |
| outside portion | RIM | overturn | UPEND, UPSET, CAPSIZE |
| outspoken | CANDID, FRANK | overweight | OBESE, FAT, PLUMP |
| outstanding | PROMINENT | | |
| outstrip | BEST | overwhelm | AWE, CRUSH |

| | |
|---|---|
| overwrought | **SPENT, DISTURBED** |
| overzealous | **FANATIC** |
| ovine creature | **EWE, RAM, LAMB, SHEEP** |
| ovine mama | **EWE** |
| ovine papa | **RAM** |
| ovolo | **ELLIPSE** |
| ovule | **EGG, SEED** |
| ovum | **EGG** |
| owed | **DUE** |
| owl-like | **STRIGINE** |
| owl parrot | **KAKAPO** |
| owl's cry | **HOOT** |
| own | **ACKNOWLEDGE, HAVE, POSSESS** |
| own (Scot.) | **AIN** |
| owner | **PROPRIETOR** |
| own up | **CONFESS, ADMIT** |
| oxalis plant | **OCA** |
| oxen harness | **YOKE** |
| oxeye | **DUNLIN** |
| oxford | **SHOE** |
| ox-headed antelope | **GNU** |
| oxidation | **RUST** |
| oxide of iron | **RUST** |
| oxygen | **ELEMENT, AIR** |
| oxygen compound | **OXIDE** |
| oyster | **BIVALVE** |
| oyster eggs | **SPAWN** |
| oyster gem | **PEARL** |
| Ozark State | **MISSOURI** |
| ozone | **GAS, AIR** |

**P**

| | |
|---|---|
| pac | **MOCCASIN** |
| paca | **RODENT** |
| pace | **STEP, WALK, STRIDE, GAIT, MEASURE** |
| pace the field | **LEAD** |
| pachyderm | **ELEPHANT, RHINO, HIPPO** |
| pacific | **CALM, SERENE** |
| Pacific island | **BALI, SAMOA, WAKE, GUAM, TAHITI** |
| Pacific shark | **MAKO** |
| pacify | **ASSUAGE, PLACATE** |
| pack | **STUFF, BIND, BUNDLE, HEAP, GROUP, SET, GANG, BAND, RIG** |
| package | **PARCEL, ENCASE, BUNDLE, WRAP** |
| package of pepper | **ROBBIN** |
| package of wool (Australian) | **FADGE** |
| pack animal | **BURRO, LLAMA** |

| | |
|---|---|
| pack animal of Tibet | **YAK** |
| pack away | **STOW** |
| pack down | **TAMP** |
| packet | **BUNDLE, PARCEL** |
| pack in | **CRAM, WEDGE** |
| packing box | **CASE, CRATE, CARTON** |
| packing plant | **CANNERY** |
| pack it in | **GIVE UP, ADJOURN, QUIT** |
| pack off | **DISCHARGE, FIRE, DISMISS** |
| pack of hounds | **KENNEL** |
| pack of playing cards | **DECK** |
| pack the jury | **RIG** |
| packthread | **TWINE** |
| pack together | **COMPRESS** |
| pact | **AGREEMENT, ENTENTE, TREATY** |
| pad | **CUSHION** |
| paddle | **OAR, ROW, SPANK, TODDLE** |
| paddock | **FIELD, ENCLOSURE** |
| pad for hair | **RAT** |
| pad for horse's saddle | **HOUSING, TRAPPINGS** |
| padre | **CHAPLAIN, PRIEST** |
| padrone | **MASTER, PROPRIETOR** |
| paean | **HYMN, PRAISE** |
| pagan | **HEATHEN** |
| pagan image | **IDOL** |
| page | **FOLIO, LEAF** |
| pageantry | **POMP, SPECTACLE** |
| pagoda | **TA, TAA** |
| pagoda finial | **TEE** |
| paid escort | **GIGOLO** |
| paid golfer | **PRO** |
| paid notice | **AD** |
| pail | **BUCKET** |
| paillette | **SPANGLE** |
| pain | **HURT, ACHE** |
| painful | **SORE, ACHING** |
| painkiller | **ANALGESIC** |
| painstaking | **DILIGENT** |
| paint | **COLOR, ENAMEL** |
| painter | **ARTIST** |
| painter's stand | **EASEL** |
| painting and sculpture | **ART** |
| painting medium | **TEMPERA, OIL, ACRYLIC, PASTEL** |
| paint layer | **COAT** |
| paint splash | **BLOB** |
| paint the town | **CAROUSE** |
| pair | **COUPLE, DUO, DUET, TWO, TWOSOME, BRACE** |
| pair-oar | **SHELL, BOAT** |
| pair of horses | **TEAM, SPAN** |
| paisley | **SHAWL, DESIGN** |

| | |
|---|---|
| pal | **BUDDY, CHUM, FRIEND, COMRADE, MATE** |
| palace | **CASTLE, RESIDENCE** |
| palace officer | **PALATINE** |
| paladin | **KNIGHT, HERO** |
| palatable | **SAPID, TASTY, SAVORY, FLAVORFUL** |
| palate | **TASTE** |
| palate part | **UVULA** |
| palatial | **ORNATE** |
| palaver | **CONFER, CHATTER** |
| pale | **ASHEN, ASHY, DIM, FADE, PALLID, WAN** |
| pale bluish-green | **BERYL** |
| pale bluish-purple | **MAUVE** |
| pale color | **PASTEL** |
| pale red | **PINK** |
| Palestine | **HOLY LAND, ISRAEL** |
| paletot | **OVERCOAT** |
| pale yellow | **FLAXEN, MAIZE** |
| paling | **FENCE** |
| palisade | **CLIFF** |
| pall | **CLOY, SICKEN** |
| pallet | **BED, QUILT** |
| palliate | **CONCEAL** |
| pallid | **PALE, WAN, ASHY, ASHEN** |
| palm | **ARECA** |
| Palmetto State | **SOUTH CAROLINA** |
| palm fiber | **TAL** |
| palm fruit | **DATE** |
| palmyra palm fiber | **TA** |
| palpable | **PLAIN, OBVIOUS** |
| palpitation | **PITAPAT** |
| paltry | **PETTY, VILE, TRASH** |
| pamper | **CODDLE, FONDLE, SPOIL** |
| pan | **SKILLET, BASIN** |
| panacea | **CURE, REMEDY** |
| Panama city | **COLON** |
| Panama passage | **CANAL** |
| pandemonium | **RIOT, RACKET, HUBBUB** |
| pander | **CATER** |
| pane (2 wds.) | **WINDOW GLASS** |
| panel | **JURY** |
| pang | **THROE, SPASM** |
| panhandler | **BEGGAR, BUM** |
| panic | **ALARM, TERROR** |
| pant | **GASP** |
| pantomime | **MIME** |
| pantry | **LARDER** |
| papa | **DADDY, FATHER, DAD** |
| Papal court | **CURIA** |
| Papal envoy | **LEGATE** |
| Papal letter | **BULL** |
| Papal ring | **FISHERMAN'S** |
| Papal scarf | **ORALE** |
| Papal seal | **BULLA** |
| Papal throne | **PETER'S** |
| papa's wife | **MAMA** |
| paper | **BOND, TISSUE, DOCUMENT, JOURNAL** |
| paper container | **POKE, BAG, SACK** |
| paper of indebtedness | **IOU** |
| paper quantity | **REAM** |
| paper size | **LEGAL, CROWN, NOTE** |
| par | **NORMAL, EQUAL** |
| parade feature | **FLOAT, BAND** |
| paradise | **HEAVEN, EDEN** |
| paradise dweller | **ADAM, EVE** |
| "Paradise Lost" author | **MILTON** |
| paradox | **ENIGMA, PUZZLE** |
| paragon | **MODEL, IDEAL** |
| paragraph | **ITEM** |
| Paraguay tea | **MATE** |
| parallel | **CONCENTRIC** |
| parallelogram | **RHOMBUS, RHOMBOID** |
| paramount | **SUPREME, EMINENT** |
| parapet | **RAMPART, WALL** |
| paraphernalia | **APPARATUS, GEAR, TRAPPINGS, EQUIPMENT** |
| parasite | **SYCOPHANT** |
| parasitic insect | **TICK, LOUSE, FLEA** |
| parcel | **PACKAGE** |
| parcel of land | **ACRE, LOT** |
| parcel out | **METE** |
| parch | **SCORCH, SEAR** |
| parched | **SERE, ARID** |
| parchment | **VELLUM, FORREL** |
| parchment roll | **SCROLL** |
| pardon | **FORGIVE** |
| pare | **PEEL** |
| parent | **MOTHER, FATHER** |
| pariah' | **OUTCAST** |
| parley | **CONFER** |
| Paris airport | **ORLY** |
| Paris art exhibition | **SALON** |
| Paris subway | **METRO** |
| park for wild animals | **ZOO** |
| park in Copenhagen | **TIVOLI** |
| parking area | **LOT, GARAGE** |
| parking payment container | **METER** |
| paroxysm | **FIT, ATTACK, OUTBURST, SPASM** |
| parrot | **LORY, MACAW** |
| parsimonious | **STINGY** |
| parsonage | **MANSE, RECTORY** |

part SEPARATE, SPLIT, PORTION, SHARE, ROLE, PIECE, DIVORCE
partake SHARE
parterre GARDEN
partial BIASED, UNFAIR
partiality FAVOR
partial refund REBATE
participant ENTRANT
participant on a discussion show PANELIST
participate SHARE
participate in an auction BID
participle ending ING
particle ATOM, IOTA
particle, as of dust MOTE
parti-colored PIEBALD, PIED
particular EXACT, DISTINCT, FASTIDIOUS
particular instance CASE
particular place SPOT
particular taste SAVOR
particularly ESPECIALLY
particularly miserable WRETCHED
partisan FOLLOWER
partition SCREEN, WALL
partly fermented grape juice STUM, MUST
partly fused FRIT
partly open AJAR
partner PARD, MATE, PAL
part of a bird's wing ALULA
part of a book LEAF, PAGE, CHAPTER
part of a bottle NECK
part of a bridle BIT
part of a chain LINK
part of a church NAVE, APSE, CHANCEL
part of a circle ARC
part of a day HOUR
part of a desk set PEN, PENCIL
part of a dogma TENET
part of a door lock BOLT
part of a dovetail TENON, MORTISE
part of a flower SEPAL, PETAL
part of a fortress REDAN
part of a goblet STEM
part of a leaf STIPEL
part of a list ITEM
part of an old auto CRANK
part of a plant SEPAL, ROOT, PETAL, LEAF, STEM, STALK
part of a poem STANZA, VERSE, CANTO

part of a printing press PLATEN
part of Arabia ASIR
part of a ship KEEL, BRIDGE, DECK
part of a ship's bottom BILGE
part of a shoe SOLE, UPPER, LACE, TONGUE, TOE, HEEL
part of a sonnet SESTET
part of a stair RISER, TREAD
part of a theater LOGE, STAGE, GALLERY, BALCONY, PARTERRE, LOBBY, MEZZANINE, BOX
part of a typewriter PLATEN, ROLLER, KEY, RIBBON
part of a yard FOOT
part of chow mein NOODLES
part of infinitive TO
part of speech NOUN, VERB, ADVERB, ADJECTIVE, CONJUNCTION, PREPOSITION, PRONOUN
part of telephone number (2 wds.) AREA CODE
part of the day MORN, NOON, MORNING, EVENING, AFTERNOON, NIGHT
part of the ear LOBE, DRUM
part of the eye IRIS, LENS, UVEA, CORNEA, RETINA
part of the hand FINGER, NAIL, KNUCKLE, PALM, THUMB
part of the leg CALF, SHIN, KNEE, THIGH, ANKLE
part of the mouth LIP, PALATE, TONGUE
part of the psyche EGO, ID, SUPEREGO
part of to be AM, IS, ARE, WAS, WERE
part of Viet Nam ANNAM
part of Yugoslavia CROATIA
part played ROLE
partridge flock COVEY
part worked with feet PEDAL, TREADLE
party COMPANY, FACTION
party for a bride SHOWER
party for men STAG
party giver HOST, HOSTESS
pascal CELERY
pa's mate MA
pass OVERTAKE
passable SOSO, NOT BAD, NOT SO BAD

| | | | |
|---|---|---|---|
| passage | **CORRIDOR** | patience | **FORTITUDE,** |
| passageway | **AISLE** | | **ENDURANCE** |
| passageway of shops | **ARCADE** | patient | **COOL, CALM,** |
| pass a law | **ENACT** | | **CONSTANT, TOLERANT** |
| pass, as time | **ELAPSE** | patio | **COURTYARD, TERRACE** |
| passe | **DATED** | patio stove | **GRILL, BARBECUE** |
| passenger | **FARE, RIDER** | Patrick Dennis creation | **MAME** |
| passenger vehicle | **BUS, CAB,** | patrimony | **HERITAGE, LEGACY** |
| | **TRAIN** | patriotic monogram | **USA** |
| passenger vessel | **LINER** | patron | **CLIENT, CUSTOMER,** |
| passing fashion | **FAD, CRAZE** | | **BENEFACTOR** |
| passion | **ARDOR, ZEAL** | patron of shepherds | **PAN** |
| passionate | **ARDENT, FERVENT** | patron saint of | |
| passive | **INERT** | England | **GEORGE** |
| pass lightly over | **SKIM, SLUR** | patron saint of sailors | **ELMO** |
| pass on | **RELAY** | patronymic | **SURNAME** |
| Passover feast | **SEDER** | pattern | **MODEL, MOLD** |
| pass over smoothly | **GLIDE** | pause | **HESITATE, RESPITE,** |
| passport | **CONGE** | | **LETUP, BREATHER, REST** |
| passport endorsement | **VISA** | pave | **BLACKTOP** |
| pass slowly | **DRAG** | paving liquid | **TAR** |
| pass through a sieve | **SIFT** | paving stone | **SETT** |
| past | **AGO** | paw | **PATTE** |
| pasta | **SPAGHETTI, MACARONI,** | pawn | **HOCK, CHESSMAN** |
| **FETTUCINE, PASTINA, PASTE** | | Pawnee | **INDIAN** |
| paste | **GLUE** | pay | **REMIT, SETTLE** |
| pastel | **CRAYON, HUE, PALE** | pay a bill | **REMIT** |
| past events | **HISTORY** | payable | **DUE** |
| pastime | **SPORT, HOBBY** | pay a call | **VISIT** |
| pastoral | **RURAL** | pay attention | **HEED, LISTEN** |
| pastoral cantata | **SERENATA** | pay court to | **WOO** |
| pastoral deity | **FAUN** | pay dirt | **ORE** |
| pastoral home | **FARM** | pay heavily | **SMART** |
| pastoral pipe | **REED** | payment back | **REBATE** |
| pastoral poem | **BUCOLIC, IDYL** | payment for recovered item | |
| pastry | **PIE, TART** | | **REWARD** |
| pastry chef | **BAKER** | payment owing | **DUE** |
| past time | **YORE** | payoff | **BRIBE** |
| pasturage | **GRASS** | payola | **GRAFT** |
| pasture grass | **GRAMA** | pay one's share | **ANTE** |
| pasture ground | **FIELD,** | pay out | **SPEND, EXPEND** |
| | **PASTURAGE** | pea | **LEGUME, VEGETABLE** |
| pasture land | **LEA** | peace | **AMITY, SERENITY,** |
| pasture sound | **MOO, MAA, BAA** | | **TRANQUILITY** |
| pat | **TAP, CARESS, PET,** | peace agreement | **TREATY** |
| | **FONDLE, STROKE** | peace disturbance | **RIOT** |
| patch | **COVER, MEND** | peaceful | **IRENIC** |
| patch of ground | **PLOT** | peace pipe | **CALUMET** |
| patchwork | **QUILT** | peace symbol | **DOVE** |
| pate | **HEAD** | peach | **FREESTONE, PEEN-TO** |
| patella | **KNEE** | peach-like fruit | **APRICOT,** |
| paten | **PLATE** | | **NECTARINE** |
| patent | **PLAIN, GRANT,** | peach seed | **PIT** |
| | **OBVIOUS** | Peach State | **GEORGIA** |
| pat gently | **DAB** | peacock genus | **PAVO** |
| path | **LANE, ROUTE, TRAIL** | peacock ore | **BORNITE** |
| pathetic | **SAD, PITIFUL** | peacock wing marking | **EYESPOT** |
| | | peage | **WAMPUM** |

| | |
|---|---|
| pea holder | **POD** |
| peak | **SUMMIT, APEX** |
| peal | **RING** |
| peal of thunder | **CLAP** |
| peanut | **GOOBER** |
| pear | **BOSC, ANJOU** |
| pearl | **GEM, ORIENT** |
| pear-like fruit | **AVOCADO** |
| peasant | **BOOR, RUSTIC, RUBE** |
| peasant's shoe | **SABOT** |
| pea's home | **POD** |
| peat | **FUEL, MOSS** |
| pebble | **STONE** |
| pecan | **NUT** |
| pecan covering | **SHELL** |
| peccadillo | **FAULT** |
| peck | **PRICK, JERK** |
| peculate | **EMBEZZLE, DEFRAUD** |
| peculiar | **ODD, STRANGE, OUTLANDISH** |
| peculiarity | **QUIRK, ODDITY** |
| pedal digit | **TOE** |
| pedant | **PRIG, TEACHER** |
| pedant's specialty | **LESSON** |
| peddle | **HAWK, SELL** |
| peddler | **VENDOR, HAWKER, MONGER** |
| pedestal part | **DADO** |
| pedestal rest | **PLINTH** |
| pedestrian | **WALKER** |
| pedicel | **STEM, STALK** |
| peel | **PARE, RIND, SKIN** |
| peen | **HAMMER** |
| peep | **PEEK, SPY** |
| peep out | **PEER** |
| peer | **GAZE, LOOK, STARE, DUKE, EARL, BARON** |
| peerage | **RANK, LINEAGE** |
| peeress' coronet | **TIARA** |
| Peer Gynt's mother | **ASE, AASE** |
| peerless | **MATCHLESS** |
| peer of the realm | **LORD** |
| peer's cognomen | **TITLE** |
| peeve | **ANNOY, PROVOKE** |
| peevish | **PETULANT** |
| peg | **STAKE, PIN** |
| peignoir | **NEGLIGEE, DRESSING GOWN** |
| pekoe | **TEA** |
| pelage | **HAIR, FUR, WOOL** |
| pelagic | **MARINE, OCEANIC** |
| pelerine | **CAPE** |
| pelf | **BOOTY, SPOIL** |
| Pelican State | **LOUISIANA** |
| pellet | **BULLET** |
| pellucid | **LIMPID, CLEAR, TRANSPARENT** |
| pelota | **JAI ALAI** |

| | |
|---|---|
| pelt | **SKIN, FUR** |
| pelvic bones | **ILIA** |
| pen | **BALLPOINT, WRITE, CONFINE, STY, PIGSTY** |
| penalize | **PUNISH, FINE** |
| penalty | **FINE, PUNISHMENT, HANDICAP** |
| penance | **CONTRITION** |
| penchant | **BENT** |
| pencil | **DRAW, SKETCH** |
| pencil point | **LEAD** |
| pencil rubber | **ERASER** |
| pend | **AWAIT** |
| pendant | **AIGLET, AGLET** |
| pending | **DUE** |
| penetrate | **ENTER** |
| penetrating | **SHARP, ACUTE** |
| penetrating ointment | **LINIMENT** |
| penetration | **ENTRANCE** |
| penetration in perception | **ACUMEN** |
| pen fluid | **INK** |
| penicillin | **MIRACLE DRUG** |
| penitence | **REMORSE, REGRET** |
| penitential period | **LENT** |
| penitentiary inmate | **PRISONER** |
| penman | **SCRIBE** |
| pen name (Fr., 3 wds.) | **NOM DE PLUME** |
| pen name of Charles Lamb | **ELIA** |
| pennant | **FLAG, BANNER** |
| penniless | **BROKE, POOR** |
| pennon | **BANNER, PENNANT, FLAG** |
| Pennsylvania city | **ALTOONA, READING** |
| Pennsylvania port | **ERIE** |
| penny | **CENT** |
| pennypincher | **MISER** |
| pen point | **NEB, NIB** |
| pension | **SUBSIDY, INN** |
| pensive | **THOUGHTFUL** |
| Pentateuch | **TORAH** |
| penury | **PRIVATION, LACK, DEARTH, DESTITUTION** |
| peon | **SLAVE** |
| people | **PERSONS, RACE** |
| people in church | **LAYMEN** |
| people in general | **FOLK** |
| people of action | **DOERS** |
| people of ancient Iran | **MEDES** |
| people of Belgrade | **SERBS** |
| people of County Cork | **IRISH** |
| people on the town (2 wds.) | **CAFE SOCIETY** |
| people waiting for relief | **BREADLINE** |

| | |
|---|---|
| pep | ENERGY, ZEST, VIM, VIGOR |
| peplum | FLOUNCE |
| pepo | FRUIT |
| pepper | SPICE |
| pepper beverage | KAVA |
| peppermint stick (2 wds.) | CANDY CANE |
| pepper pot | STEW, SOUP |
| peppery | FIERY |
| peppy | ENERGETIC |
| Pepys' signoff (4 wds.) | AND SO TO BED |
| per | THROUGH |
| perambulator | PRAM, CARRIAGE |
| perceive | SEE, NOTICE, ESPY |
| perception | SENSE |
| perch | ROOST, FISH, SIT |
| percheron | HORSE |
| percolate slowly | SEEP |
| percussion instrument | DRUM, CYMBAL |
| peremptory | ARBITRARY |
| peremptory request | DEMAND |
| perennial | PERPETUAL, CONSTANT |
| perfect | IDEAL |
| perfect model | IDEAL |
| perfecto | CIGAR |
| perfect serve in tennis | ACE |
| perfidious | DISLOYAL, FALSE |
| perfidious fellow | SNEAK |
| perfidy | TREACHERY, TREASON |
| perforate | PUNCH, BORE, PIERCE |
| perforation | BORE, HOLE |
| perform | ACT, DO |
| performance | ACT, EXPLOIT, PRESENTATION, DEED, FEAT |
| performer | ACTOR |
| perform in a play | ACT |
| perform surgery | OPERATE |
| perfume | AROMA, SCENT, ESSENCE, ATTAR |
| perfume bottle | VIAL, ATOMIZER, FLACON |
| perfume ingredient | ATTAR, AMBERGRIS |
| perfume quantity | OUNCE, DRAM |
| perfumery root | ORRIS |
| perfume with spice | INCENSE |
| perfunctory | INDIFFERENT |
| perhaps | MAYBE |
| peril | DANGER |
| perimeter | BOUNDARY |
| period | AGE, DOT, ERA, TIME |

| | |
|---|---|
| periodical | REGULAR, RECURRENT, PUBLICATION, MAGAZINE |
| period in history | ERA, EPOCH, AGE |
| period of dryness | DROUGHT |
| period of holding | TENURE |
| period of time | SPELL, YEAR, MONTH, WEEK |
| period of work | SHIFT |
| period without war | PEACE |
| periphery | PERIMETER |
| perish | DIE |
| perjurer | LIAR |
| perk up | LIVEN |
| perky | JAUNTY, LIVELY |
| permanent | LASTING |
| permanent acting group | REPERTORY |
| permeate | IMBUE, PENETRATE |
| permission | CONSENT, LICENSE |
| permission granted | LEAVE |
| permit | ALLOW, LET, LICENSE |
| perpetual | ETERNAL |
| perplex | PUZZLE, BEWILDER |
| perplexing point | PROBLEM |
| perplexity | DOUBT |
| perquisite | PRIVILEGE, RIGHT |
| persecute | HARASS, OPPRESS |
| perseverance | TENACITY |
| persevere | PLOD, CARRY ON |
| Persia | IRAN |
| Persian cat | ANGORA |
| Persian coin | RIAL, RIYAL |
| Persian fairy | PERI |
| Persian hat | FEZ, TURBAN |
| Persian king | SHAH |
| Persian lynx | CARACAL |
| Persian money | DINAR |
| Persian nymph | PERI, HOURI |
| Persian or Siamese | CAT |
| Persian poet | OMAR |
| Persian priest | MAGUS |
| Persian product | RUG |
| Persian ruler | KHAN |
| person | INDIVIDUAL, ONE |
| person against | ANTI |
| personal | PRIVATE |
| personal affair (2 wds.) | PRIVATE MATTER |
| personal belongings | EFFECTS |
| personal conviction | OPINION |
| personality | SELF, EGO |
| person held prisoner | CAPTIVE |
| person loved to excess | IDOL, HERO |
| personnel | STAFF |
| person of power | TITAN |

person of prominence **BIG SHOT** **NABOB**

person regarded as the finest (4 wds.) **SALT OF THE EARTH**

persons **PEOPLE**

person's manner **MIEN, STYLE**

persons over here **THESE**

person under age **MINOR**

person with very loud voice **STENTOR**

perspicacity **ACUMEN**

perspire **SWEAT, SWELTER**

persuade **ACTUATE, URGE, PROD, COAX**

pert **LIVELY, SASSY, SAUCY, SPRIGHTLY, PEPPY**

pertain **RELATE**

pertaining to (suffix) **AR**

pertaining to a city **URBAN**

pertaining to a kidney **RENAL**

pertaining to an age **ERAL**

pertaining to bees **APIAN, APIARIAN**

pertaining to birds **AVIAN, ORNITHIC**

pertaining to dawn **EOAN**

pertaining to dogs **CANINE**

pertaining to form **MODAL**

pertaining to Middle Ages **MEDIEVAL**

pertaining to Norway **NORSE**

pertaining to poles **POLAR**

pertaining to sheep **OVINE**

pertaining to ships **NAVAL**

pertaining to the moon **LUNAR**

pertaining to the pope **PAPAL**

pertaining to touch **TACTUAL**

pert girl **MINX**

pertinent **RELEVANT**

perturbation **WORRY**

Peru's capital **LIMA**

Peruvian beast of burden **LLAMA**

Peruvian coin **SOL**

Peruvian Indian **INCA**

Peruvian plant **OCA**

perverse **CONTRARY, STUBBORN**

pessimistic **GLOOMY, CYNICAL**

pest **NUISANCE**

pester **ANNOY, TEASE**

pet **FAVORITE, DOG, CAT, FONDLE, CARESS, STROKE**

petard **BOMB**

pet bird's home **CAGE**

petiole **STALK, STEM**

petite **SMALL, TINY, LITTLE**

petition **SUE, PLEAD**

petitioner **PLEADER**

petits fours **CAKES**

pet mammal **CAT, DOG, HORSE**

peto **WAHOO**

petrified body **FOSSIL**

petrol **GAS**

petroleum **OIL**

petroleum processor **REFINER**

petroleum product **NAPHTHA**

petroleum source (2 wds.) **OIL WELL**

petticoat **SLIP**

pettish **PEEVISH, CROSS**

petty **SMALL, TRIVIAL, SPITEFUL, MEAN**

petty malice **SPITE**

petty objection **CAVIL**

petty prince **SATRAP**

petty quarrel **SPAT, TIFF**

petulant **FRETFUL, TOUCHY**

Pfc's bed **COT**

phantom **GHOST, SHADE, SPOOK, HAUNT, JET**

Pharaoh's ancestor **RA**

pharos **BEACON, LIGHTHOUSE**

phase **ASPECT, STAGE, FACET**

pheasant duck **MERGANSER**

philatelist **COLLECTOR**

Philippine island **LEYTE, SAMAR, BOHOL**

Philippine knife **BOLO**

Philippine native **MORO**

Philippine plant **ABACA**

phlegmatic **DULL, SLUGGISH**

phone greeting **HELLO**

phonograph disc **RECORD**

phonograph machine **HI-FI, JUKE BOX, STEREO**

phonograph machine part **ARM TURNTABLE, CHANGER, SPEAKER, TUNER**

phonograph record **DISC**

phosphate **SODA**

photograph **SHOT, SNAP**

photographer's flash tube **STROBE**

photographer's request **SMILE**

photographic bath **TONER**

photographic device **CAMERA**

phrase **SLOGAN, SENTENCE**

phrase of apology (2 wds.) **PARDON ME**

phrase of dismay (2 wds.) **OH NO**

phrase of understanding (2 wds.) **I SEE**

phrase with two meanings
(2 wds.)    **DOUBLE ENTENDRE**
Phrygian god of vegetation
    **ATTIS**
Phyllis Diller's husband    **FANG**
physical    **CORPORAL,**
   **TANGIBLE, CHECK-UP**
physician    **DOCTOR**
physician's association (abbr.)
    **AMA**
physiognomy    **FACE,**
   **EXPRESSION**
physique    **BUILD**
pianist Brubeck    **DAVE**
pianist Cliburn    **VAN**
piano adjuster    **TUNER**
piano key    **IVORY**
piano piece    **SONATA, ETUDE**
piano student's exercise    **SCALE**
piazza    **SQUARE**
picayune    **PETTY, TRIVIAL**
pick    **CULL, PLUCK**
pick carefully    **CULL**
picket    **FENCE, FORTIFY,**
   **STRIKER, STAKE**
pickle    **MARINATE**
pickle bottle    **JAR**
pickled fruit    **OLIVE**
pickling spice    **DILL**
pick out    **CHOOSE, SELECT**
pick up the check    **TREAT**
picnic    **OUTING**
picnic dishes (2 wds.)
    **PAPER PLATES**
picnic pest    **ANT**
picture    **IMAGE**
picture exhibit room    **GALLERY**
picture house    **CINEMA**
picture mounting    **FRAME**
picture puzzle    **REBUS**
picturesque **SCENIC, CHARMING**
picture stand    **EASEL**
picture taker    **CAMERA,**
   **PHOTOGRAPHER**
pie    **CHAOS, JUMBLE, MESS**
piebald horse    **PINTO**
piece    **PART, PORTION**
piece of a tree trunk    **LOG**
piece of baked clay    **TILE**
piece of candy    **KISS**
piece of china **PLATE, SAUCER,**
   **CUP, BOWL, TEACUP**
piece of coal    **LUMP**
piece of corn    **EAR**
piece of cutlery    **FORK, KNIFE,**
   **SPOON**
piece of evidence    **FACT**
piece of garlic    **CLOVE**

piece of ice    **FLOE, BERG,**
   **CUBE, BLOCK**
piece of information    **DATUM**
piece of jewelry    **CLIP, RING,**
   **EARRING, HATPIN,**
   **BRACELET, NECKLACE,**
   **EARDROP, BROOCH**
piece of land    **FARM, LOT,**
   **ACRE**
piece of luggage **GRIP, TRUNK,**
   **BAG, ETUI, VALISE**
piece of lumber    **BOARD**
piece of mail    **LETTER**
piece of merchandise    **WARE**
piece of money    **COIN**
piece of open ground    **FIELD**
piece of pasteboard    **CARD**
piece of postage    **STAMP**
piece of property    **ASSET**
piece of rock    **STONE**
piece of sculpture    **BUST**
piece of stage scenery    **PROP,**
   **FLAT**
piece of sugar    **LUMP**
piece of work    **TASK, CHORE**
piece out    **EKE**
pie covering    **CRUST**
pied    **DAPPLED**
pied animal    **PINTO**
pied diver (Brit.)    **SMEW**
pie fruit    **APPLE, PEACH,**
   **LEMON, BERRY**
pieplant    **RHUBARB**
pie plate    **TIN**
pier    **WHARF**
pierce    **GORE, STAB**
piercing    **SHRILL, ACUTE**
piercing tool    **AWL, NEEDLE**
pierce with the horns    **GORE**
pier glass    **MIRROR**
pie shell    **CRUST**
piety    **DEVOTION, HOLINESS**
piffle    **NONSENSE, TWADDLE**
pig    **HOG, PORKER, SWINE**
pigeon    **DOVE**
pigeonhole    **CLASSIFY**
pigeon pea    **DAL**
pigeon shelter    **COTE**
piggery    **PEN, STY**
piggin    **PAIL, DIPPER**
piggish    **GREEDY, SELFISH**
pigheaded    **STUBBORN**
pig meat    **HAM, PORK, BACON,**
   **CHITLINS, TENDERLOIN**
pigment    **COLOR, PAINT**
pigmy    **DWARF**
pigpen    **STY, HOVEL**
pigpen sound    **GRUNT, OINK**

| | |
|---|---|
| pigskin | FOOTBALL |
| pigsty | HOVEL, PEN |
| pigtail | QUEUE |
| pike | FREEWAY, HIGHWAY, ROAD |
| piker | SHIRKER |
| pilaster | COLUMN |
| pile | HEAP |
| pile driver head | TUP |
| pile of hay | MOW, STACK |
| pile up a fortune | AMASS |
| pilfer | FILCH, STEAL, SWIPE |
| pilgrim | TRAVELER |
| pilgrimage | JOURNEY |
| Pilgrim settler | PURITAN |
| Pilgrims' ship | MAYFLOWER |
| pill | PELLET, TABLET |
| pillage | PLUNDER, SACK, LOOT, ROB, BOOTY |
| pillar | COLUMN, POST |
| pillar of air course | PYLON |
| pillar of a staircase | NEWEL |
| pillar projecting from wall | PILASTER |
| pillbox | HAT, FORT |
| pillory | STOCKS |
| pillow | CUSHION, PAD |
| pillow covering | SHAM, TICK |
| pillow material | FOAM RUBBER, HAIR, DOWN |
| pilot | AVIATOR, FLYER, AIRMAN, GUIDE, STEER |
| pilot biscuit | HARDTACK |
| pilsener | BEER |
| pima | COTTON |
| pimento | ALLSPICE |
| pin | BROOCH, PEG, FASTEN |
| pinafore | APRON |
| pince-nez | LORGNETTE |
| pincer | CLAW |
| pincers | FORCEPS, PLIERS |
| pinch | NIP, SQUEEZE |
| Pindar opus | ODE |
| pine | FIR, TREE, EVERGREEN |
| pineapple | PINA |
| pine fruit | CONE, NUT |
| pine gum | SANDARAC |
| pine leaf | NEEDLE |
| pine tar hydrocarbon | RETENE |
| pine tree | LARCH, SPRUCE |
| pine tree exudation | RESIN |
| Pine Tree State | MAINE |
| pinion | FEATHER |
| pink | CARNATION |
| pinnacle | PEAK, APEX |
| pin one's ears back | DEFEAT, SCOLD |
| pintail | SMEE |

| | |
|---|---|
| pioneer | SETTLER, EARLIEST, FIRST |
| pious | DEVOUT |
| pipe | TUBE, MEERSCHAUM, CORNCOB |
| pipe fitting | TEE |
| pipe of peace | CALUMET |
| pipette | DROPPER |
| piquant | SHARP, ZESTY, SPICY |
| pique | IRE, ANGER |
| pirate | SEA ROVER, BUCCANEER, PRIVATEER |
| pirate flag (2 wds.) | JOLLY ROGER |
| pismire | ANT |
| pistol attachment | SILENCER |
| pistol (sl.) | PIECE, ROSCOE, GAT |
| pit | HOLE, CAVITY |
| pitch | TAR, THROW, TOSS |
| pitcher | EWER |
| pitcher ear | HANDLE |
| pitcher handle | EAR |
| pitcher's motions | WINDUP |
| piteous | PATHETIC |
| pitfall | TRAP |
| pith | GIST, ESSENCE |
| pith helmet | TOPEE |
| pithy statement | APHORISM |
| pitiful | WOEFUL, SAD |
| Pius | POPE |
| pivot | SLUE, TURN, SWING |
| pivotal | FOCAL |
| pixie | ELF, IMP, SPRITE, BROWNIE, FAIRY |
| placard | POSTER |
| place | PUT, LAY, LOCATION, LOCALE, LIEU, STEAD, SET |
| place (prefix) | TOPO |
| place a bet | WAGER |
| place a phone call | DIAL |
| place at intervals | SPACE |
| place between | INSERT |
| place confidence in | RELY, TRUST |
| place end for end | REVERSE |
| place for a drama critic | AISLE |
| place for animals | ZOO, MENAGERIE |
| place for art exhibit | MUSEUM, GALLERY |
| place for coal | BIN |
| place for exercise | GYM, GYMNASIUM, HEALTH CLUB |
| place for fish | AQUARIUM |
| place for money | BANK |

place for sheets, towels, etc. (2 wds.) **LINEN CLOSET**
place for skating **RINK**
place for the press **BOX**
place for unclaimed mail (abbr.) **DLO**
place in proximity **APPOSE, NEAR**
place of business **OFFICE, STORE, SHOP, MARKET**
place of entrance **ENTRY, FOYER, LOBBY**
place of recreation **PARK, RESORT**
place of retreat **HIDEAWAY, DEN**
place of shelter **HAVEN, REFUGE**
place of worship **ALTAR, CHURCH, CHAPEL, TEMPLE**
places **LOCI**
place to live **HOUSE, FLAT, APARTMENT**
place to sit **CHAIR, BENCH, SEAT**
place to ski **SLOPE**
place to sleep **BED, COT, BEDROOM**
placid **SERENE**
plagiarize **CRIB, PURLOIN**
plague **HARASS, FEVER**
plague carrier **RAT**
plaid **TARTAN**
plain **HOMELY, EVIDENT**
Plains Indian **OTOE, SIOUX, CROW**
plain song **CHANT**
plaintiff **SUER, PETITIONER, COMPLAINANT**
plaintive **WISTFUL, PATHETIC**
plait **FOLD, BRAID**
plan **SCHEME, PLOT, BLUEPRINT, MAP**
plane **EVEN, LEVEL**
planet **MARS, PLUTO, VENUS, NEPTUNE, MERCURY, EARTH, URANUS, SATURN, SPHERE, JUPITER**
planet nearest sun **MERCURY**
planet nearest us **VENUS**
planet's orbit **ELLIPSE**
plan frustrater **MARPLOT**
plank **BOARD**
plant **SEED, SOW, FACTORY, MILL**
plantain **BANANA**

plant beginning **SEED**
plant by strewing **SOW**
plant disease **ERGOT, SMUT**
plant embryo **SEED**
plant exudation **SAP, RESIN**
plant firmly **IMBED**
plant fluid **SAP**
plant hemp **JUTE**
plant louse **APHID**
plant opening **STOMA**
plant part **ROOT, STEM, STALK, LEAF, PETAL, CORM, SEPAL**
plant protection **MULCH**
plant root **RADIX**
plants, collectively **FLORA, VEGETATION**
plant seed **SOW**
plant stalk **STEM**
plant superintendent **FOREMAN**
plant with prickly leaves **THISTLE**
plasterer **MASON**
Plaster of Paris **GESSO**
plastic **DUCTILE, PLIANT**
plate **DISH, PATEN, PLATTER, REPRODUCTION, METALWARE**
platform **STAGE, ELEVATION, POLICIES**
plating metal **TIN**
platitude **CLICHE**
platoon **UNIT**
platter **PLATE, RECORD, DISC**
plaudit **APPLAUSE, PRAISE**
plausible **LIKELY, PROBABLE**
play **DRAMA, SPORT**
play a banjo **STRUM**
play area **YARD, PARK**
play a role **ACT**
play at courtship **FLIRT**
play at tenpins **BOWL**
play boisterously **ROMP**
play busybody **NOSE, SNOOP, PRY**
play characters **CAST**
play division **ACT, SCENE**
player **ACTOR, GAMBLER**
player's morale (2 wds.) **TEAM SPIRIT**
player's part **ROLE**
play for time **STALL**
playful talk **BADINAGE, BANTER**
playful water mammal **OTTER**
playing card **ACE, DEUCE, TREY, TEN, KING, QUEEN, JACK, KNAVE**
playing field **DIAMOND, GRIDIRON, COURT**

| | | | |
|---|---|---|---|
| playing marble | **AGATE, TAW, MIB** | plot | **PLAN, SCHEME** |
| playing the wrong role | | plot of land | **LOT, PLAT** |
| | **MISCAST** | plowed land (Sp.) | **ARADA** |
| playlet | **SKIT** | pluck | **COURAGE, GRIT, PICK** |
| play on words | **PUN** | pluck a guitar | **STRUM** |
| play outline | **SCENARIO** | plug | **PEG** |
| play setting | **SCENE** | plug up | **STOP** |
| play the first card | **LEAD** | plume | **FEATHER** |
| plaything | **TOY** | plump | **FAT, OBESE, PUDGY, ROLY-POLY** |
| play unfairly | **CHEAT** | plunder | **LOOT, SACK, RANSACK, BOOTY, SPOILS** |
| play up | **PLUG, ADVERTISE** | | |
| play up to | **FLATTER** | plunge | **DIVE** |
| play without dialogue | **MIME, PANTOMIME** | plunge in boiling liquid | **POACH** |
| | | plunge in liquid | **DIP** |
| playwright | **DRAMATIST** | plunk | **STRUM, TWANG** |
| playwright Albee | **EDWARD** | plurality | **MAJORITY** |
| playwright Anouilh | **JEAN** | plus | **AND, ALSO** |
| playwright Coward | **NOEL** | plus fours | **KNICKERS** |
| playwright Jones | **LE ROI** | plush | **RICH, ELEGANT** |
| playwright Rattigan | **TERENCE** | Plutarch work | **LIVES, BIOGRAPHY** |
| plaza | **SQUARE, MALL** | | |
| plaza cheer | **OLE** | ply | **FOLD, LAYER, STRAND, WIELD, SUPPLY, SAIL, WORK, STEER** |
| plea | **APOLOGY, ENTREATY, PRAYER** | | |
| pleach | **PLAIT, PLASH** | PM beverage | **TEA** |
| plead | **BEG, ENTREAT, PRAY, PETITION** | poach | **TRESPASS** |
| | | pocketbook | **BAG, PURSE, HANDBAG, BILLFOLD** |
| pleader | **ADVOCATE, SUER** | pocosin | **SWAMP** |
| pleasant | **AGREEABLE, NICE** | pod | **COCOON, HERD** |
| pleasant expression | **SMILE** | podagra | **GOUT** |
| pleasant manners | **AMENITIES** | podium | **DAIS** |
| please | **SUIT** | pod vegetable | **PEA** |
| pleased | **GLAD, HAPPY** | poem | **ODE, VERSE, SONG, SONNET** |
| please greatly | **DELIGHT** | | |
| pleasing odor | **AROMA, PERFUME, BOUQUET, FRAGRANCE** | poem part | **REFRAIN, EPODE** |
| | | Poe's bird | **RAVEN** |
| | | poesy | **VERSE** |
| pleasure | **JOY, PREFERENCE** | poet | **BARD** |
| pleasure boat | **BARGE, YACHT** | poetess Lowell | **AMY** |
| pleasure ground | **PARK** | poetic | **LYRIC** |
| pleasure seeker | **EPICURE** | poetic contraction | **E'EN, E'ER, 'TIS** |
| pleasure ship | **YACHT** | | |
| pleasure trip | **JAUNT, JUNKET, CRUISE, VACATION** | poetic fiction | **MYTH** |
| | | poetic foot | **IAMB, IAMBUS** |
| pleat | **FOLD** | poetic possessive | **THINE, THY** |
| plebeian | **COMMON, VULGAR** | poetic preposition | **ERE** |
| plebiscite | **DECREE, VOTE** | poetic unit | **VERSE, LINE** |
| pledge | **PROMISE, OATH, TOAST** | poet Pound | **EZRA** |
| | | poetry | **POESY, VERSE** |
| pledged faith | **TROTH** | poet Sandburg | **CARL** |
| plenary | **COMPLETE, FULL** | poet-singer McKuen | **ROD** |
| plentiful | **AMPLE** | pogonip | **FOG** |
| plenty | **ENOUGH** | pogrom | **SLAUGHTER, PERSECUTION** |
| plethora | **EXCESS** | | |
| pliant | **SUPPLE** | | |
| plight | **DILEMMA** | poignant | **PIERCING, BITTER, MOVING** |
| plod | **TRUDGE** | | |

| | |
|---|---|
| point | MEANING, NUB, PROMONTORY |
| point a gun | AIM |
| point at stake | ISSUE |
| point-blank | BLUNT, DIRECT |
| pointed (Heb.) | URDE |
| pointed arch | OGIVE |
| pointed tool | AWL |
| pointed weapon | DAGGER, SPEAR, SWORD, ARROW, DART, LANCE |
| pointer | SETTER |
| pointing signal | ARROW |
| pointless | INANE, SILLY |
| point of departure | ZERO |
| point of difference | CONTRAST |
| point of land | SPIT |
| point of orbit, in astronomy | APSIS |
| point of view | ANGLE, SLANT |
| point opposite zenith | NADIR |
| point out | INDICATE |
| points in a game | SCORE |
| point the way | DIRECT |
| poise | BALANCE, CALM |
| poison | VENIN, ARSENIC, VENOM |
| poison ash | SUMAC |
| poison from a snake | VENOM |
| poisonous | NOXIOUS, TOXIC |
| poisonous shrub | SUMAC |
| poisonous snake | ASP, COBRA, VIPER, ADDER, RATTLER |
| poke | JAB, PROD, NUDGE, SACK, BAG |
| poke around | ROOT |
| poke fun at | RIDICULE, DERIDE |
| poker game | STUD, DRAW |
| poker holding | PAIR, STRAIGHT, FULL HOUSE, FLUSH |
| poker kitty | ANTE |
| poker money | CHIP |
| poker player | GAMBLER |
| poker stake | ANTE |
| Polar exploration base | ETAH |
| polar explorer | BYRD, PEARY |
| polar lights | AURORA BOREALIS |
| polar region | NORTH, ARCTIC, ANTARCTICA |
| pole | ROD, SHAFT |
| polecat | SKUNK |
| polemic | CONTROVERSIAL |
| police (colloq.) | COPS, FUZZ |
| police action | RAID |
| policeman (sl.) | FLATFOOT |
| policeman's shield | BADGE |
| policy | PRINCIPLE, PLAN |

| | |
|---|---|
| polish | BUFF, GLOSS, LUSTER, SHINE, SHEEN, RUB |
| Polish city | CRACOW, WARSAW |
| polished | ELEGANT, REFINED |
| polishing stone | EMERY |
| polite | CIVIL, REFINED |
| polite society (2 wds.) | BON TON |
| politic | PRUDENT |
| political group | BLOC, PARTY, CLUB, LOBBY |
| political meeting | RALLY |
| political party | REPUBLICAN, DEMOCRATIC, LIBERAL, COMMUNIST, CONSERVATIVE, SOCIALIST |
| politician | STATESMAN, CANDIDATE |
| pollack fish | SEY, COD |
| pollen bearer | BEE |
| polliwog | TADPOLE |
| pollute | CONTAMINATE, TAINT, DEFILE |
| polo stick | MALLET |
| Polynesian | HAWAIIAN, SAMOAN, TAHITIAN, MAORI, TONGAN |
| Polynesian dance | HULA |
| Polynesian fabric | TAPA |
| Polynesian god | ATEO, TIKI |
| Polynesian occupation (2 wds.) | PEARL DIVER |
| pompous | HAUGHTY, ARROGANT |
| pompous show | PARADE |
| poncho | SARAPE, SERAPE |
| pond | POOL, LAGOON |
| pond duck | MALLARD |
| ponder | MULL, MUSE, THINK |
| ponderous | HEAVY, INERT, DULL, MASSIVE |
| pone | CORNBREAD |
| pongee | SILK, SHANTUNG, TUSSAH |
| Pons specialty | ARIA |
| pontiff | BISHOP |
| pontoon | BOAT, BRIDGE |
| pooch | DOG |
| pool | LINN, RESERVOIR |
| poolside dressing room | CABANA |
| poop | STERN, DECK, DATA |
| poor | MEAGER, NEEDY |
| poor area | SLUM, GHETTO |
| poor person (comp. wd.) | HAVE-NOT |

pop **SODA, BURST, FATHER, DADDY**
pope's headdress **MITRE**
pope's scarf **FANON, ORALE**
pop into the oven **BAKE**
poplar **ASPEN, TREE**
popover **MUFFIN**
poppycock **NONSENSE**
pop's wife **MOM**
pop the question **PROPOSE**
populace **DEMOS**
popular **LIKED**
popular dessert **PIE, CAKE, ICE CREAM**
popular flower **ROSE, DAISY, MUM**
popular girl **BELLE**
popularly supposed **REPUTED**
popular Mother's Day gift (2 wds.) **POTTED PLANT**
popular snack **BURGER, CHIPS, WIENER, FRANK, DANISH**
popular success **HIT**
popular TV program **WESTERN, SOAP OPERA, COMEDY**
populate **PEOPLE**
population center **CITY, MEGALOPOLIS**
porcelain clay **KAOLIN**
porcelain ware **CHINA**
porch **PORTICO, VERANDA, STOA**
porch swing **GLIDER**
porcine animal **PIG, HOG**
porcine home **PIGSTY, STY, PEN**
porcine mother **SOW**
porcupine **HEDGEHOG**
porcupine quill **SPINE**
pore **STUDY, STOMA**
pork fat **LARD**
pork pie **HAT**
porpoise **DOLPHIN**
porridge **CEREAL, MEAL**
porringer **BOWL**
port **WINE, HARBOR, HAVEN**
portable **MOVABLE, MOBILE**
portable home **TRAILER**
portable light **LANTERN, FLASHLIGHT**
portable lodge **TENT, CAMPER**
portable steps **LADDER**
portable sunshade **PARASOL**
portal **GATE, DOOR**
portcullis **GATE, SHUT, BAR, GRATING**
portend **BODE, FORETOKEN**
portent **OMEN, SIGN, EVENT**

porter **ALE, DOORMAN**
portico **STOA, PORCH, COLONNADE**
portion **PART, SHARE**
portion of bacon **RASHER**
portion of land **LOT, PARCEL, ACRE**
portion of medicine **DOSE**
portion out **ALLOT, DOLE, METE**
portly **OBESE, PLUMP, FAT**
portmanteau **BAG, CASE**
port of Rome **OSTIA**
port of the South Seas **APIA**
port on the Weser River **BREMEN**
portrait **PHOTO, PICTURE**
portrait by Da Vinci (2 wds.) **MONA LISA**
portrait on fifty dollar bill **GRANT**
portrait on five dollar bill **LINCOLN**
portrait on one dollar bill **WASHINGTON**
portrait on one hundred dollar bill **FRANKLIN**
Portugal and Spain **IBERIA**
Portuguese coin **REI**
Portuguese islands **AZORES**
Portuguese lady **DONA**
Portuguese title **DOM**
pose **SIT**
posh **ELEGANT**
position **PLACE, POST, SITE, STANCE, ARRANGE, JOB**
position halfway between **MIDPOINT, CENTER**
position in education **DEAN, TEACHERAGE, CHAIR, PROFESSORSHIP, CHAIRMAN, PRESIDENT, PRINCIPAL**
positive **CERTAIN, SURE**
positive electrode **ANODE**
positive pole **ION**
positive quantity **PLUS**
possess **HAVE, OWN, HOLD**
possessed **MAD, BEWITCHED**
possession **ASSET**
possessive pronoun **HER, HERS, HIS, MY, YOUR, OUR, THEIR, MINE, THEIRS, OURS**
possible **FEASIBLE, LIKELY**
possibly **MAYBE**
post **PILLAR, COLUMN, MAIL**
postage stamp paper **PELURE**
post a letter **MAIL, SEND**

| | | | |
|---|---|---|---|
| post and wire barrier | FENCE | pour forth | GUSH, SPOUT |
| post boat | PACKET | pout | SULK, MOPE |
| postcard message (4 wds.) | | poverty | LACK, INDIGENCE |
| | WISH YOU WERE HERE | poverty-stricken | NEEDY, |
| poster | BILL, PLACARD | | POOR, DESOLATE |
| postpone | DEFER, DELAY, | powder base | TALC |
| | TABLE | powdery dirt | DUST |
| postpone indefinitely | SHELVE | power | ENERGY, STRENGTH, |
| postponement | RESPITE, RAIN | | LEVERAGE |
| | CHECK, DELAY, | powerful | HEFTY, POTENT, |
| | DEFERMENT | | STRONG |
| post service | MAIL | powerful businessman | |
| postulate | CLAIM, STIPULATE | | TYCOON, |
| posture | ATTITUDE, STANCE | | MAGNATE |
| posy | NOSEGAY, FLOWER, | powerful explosive | TNT |
| | BOUQUET | powerful light beam | LASER |
| pot | PAN, KETTLE, SAUCEPAN | powwow | CONFERENCE |
| potash | NITER, SALIN | practical | PRAGMATIC, |
| potassium carbonate | POTASH | | WORKABLE |
| potassium compound | ALUM | practical joke | HOAX, CAPER, |
| potation | DRAFT, DRINK | | TRICK |
| potato | SPUD, TUBER | practice | CUSTOM, DRILL |
| potato bud | EYE | practice a performance | |
| potato masher | RICER | | REHEARSE |
| potato squasher | MASHER | pragmatic | PRACTICAL, |
| pot cover | LID | | DOGMATIC |
| potent | POWERFUL, STRONG | prairie | PLAIN, STEPPE |
| potentate | RULER | Prairie State | ILLINOIS |
| potential | LATENT, POSSIBLE | praise | COMPLIMENT, LAUD, |
| potential prune | PLUM | | EXALT |
| potential steel | IRON | praise insincerely | FLATTER |
| potential trouble source | | prance | CAPER, CAVORT, |
| | TINDERBOX | | CURVET |
| pother | ADO, FUSS, ROW | prank | DIDO, TRICK, CAPER, |
| potiche | VASE | | ANTIC |
| potion | DRAFT, DOSE | prate | CHATTER, PRATTLE, |
| potpourri | OLIO, COMBINATION, | | TWADDLE |
| | MIXTURE | prattle | PRATE, CHATTER |
| potsy | HOPSCOTCH | prawn | SHRIMP |
| pottage | SOUP, STEW | pray | ASK, PLEAD |
| potter's clay | ARGIL | prayer | PLEA, ENTREATY, |
| pottery | CERAMICS | | AVE, THANKS |
| pottery clay | KAOLIN | prayer beads | ROSARY |
| pottery fragment | SHARD | prayer book | MISSAL |
| | SHERD | prayer ending | AMEN |
| potto | LEMUR, KINKAJOU | prayer shawl | TALLIS, TALLITH |
| pouch | BAG, SAC | praying insect | MANTIS |
| poultry | CHICKENS, HENS | praying figure | ORANT |
| poultry product | EGG, CHICKEN, | preach | ORATE, SERMONIZE |
| | DUCK | preacher | PARSON, MINISTER |
| pounce | SPRING, LEAP | pre-adult insect | PUPA |
| pound | BEAT | Preakness | RACE |
| pound (abbr.) | LB. | preamble | PREFACE |
| pound down | TAMP | precarious | INSECURE, |
| pounder | PESTLE | | DUBIOUS |
| pour | TEEM | precarious situation (3 wds.) | |
| pourboire | TIP | | TOUCH AND GO |
| pour down | RAIN | precedence | PRIORITY |

preceding **PRIOR, PREVIOUS**
precept **LAW, RULE**
precious **DEAR**
precious jewel **GEM, PEARL, DIAMOND, RUBY, EMERALD, OPAL, GARNET**
precious metal **GOLD, SILVER, PLATINUM**
precious stone **GEM, AGATE**
precipice **CRAG**
precipitate **HASTY, RASH, RUSH, HURRY**
precipitation **RAIN, SNOW, SLEET, HAIL**
precipitous **STEEP**
precis **SUMMARY, EPITOME**
precise **ACCURATE, CORRECT**
preclude **BAR, AVERT**
predatory **PREYING, DESTRUCTIVE**
predecessor of the bus **HORSECAR, TROLLEY**
predetermine **DESTINE, ORDAIN**
predicament **SCRAPE**
predicate (abbr.) **PRED**
predict **AUGUR, BODE**
prediction **PROPHECY, FORECAST**
predominant **UPPERMOST**
preen **PRIMP**
preface **FOREWORD, PROLOGUE**
prefer **FAVOR, SELECT**
preferably **RATHER**
preference **TASTE, CHOICE**
prehistoric dwelling **CAVE**
prehistoric era (2 wds.) **STONE AGE**
prehistoric man (2 wds.) **CAVE DWELLER, APE MAN**
preholiday period **EVE**
prejudice **BIAS**
preliminary draft **SKETCH, OUTLINE**
prelude **PREFACE, PROEM**
premeditated **INTENTIONAL**
premier **CHIEF, FIRST**
preoccupied **ENRAPT**
prep school in England **ETON, HARROW**
prepare **ARRANGE**
prepare a salad **TOSS**
prepare, as beer **BREW**
prepare copy **EDIT**
prepared **READY, READIED**

prepare food by canning **PRESERVE**
prepare for war **ARM**
prepare the way for **PAVE**
prepare to fire **AIM**
prepare to testify (3 wds.) **TAKE THE STAND, TAKE AN OATH**
preposition **INTO, OF, ON, IN, OFF, FROM, BY, FOR, ONTO**
preposterous **ABSURD, SILLY**
prerecord a broadcast **TAPE**
prerogative **PRIORITY, RIGHT**
presage **OMEN, PORTEND**
presbyter **MINISTER, ELDER**
prescribe **LIMIT, ORDER**
prescribed amount **DOSE**
presence **AIR, MIEN**
present **HERE, GIVE, GIFT**
present as a gift **BESTOW, DONATE**
present for acceptance **OFFER**
presentiment **PREMONITION**
presently **ANON, SOON**
present time **NOW, TODAY**
preserve **SAVE**
preserve vegetables **CAN, FREEZE, PICKLE**
president **GEORGE WASHINGTON, JOHN ADAMS, THOMAS JEFFERSON, JAMES MADISON, JAMES MONROE, JOHN QUINCY ADAMS, ANDREW JACKSON, MARTIN VAN BUREN, WILLIAM HENRY HARRISON, JOHN TYLER, JAMES KNOX POLK, ZACHARY TAYLOR, MILLARD FILLMORE, FRANKLIN PIERCE, JAMES BUCHANAN, ABRAHAM (ABE, HONEST ABE) LINCOLN, ANDREW JOHNSON, ULYSSES SIMPSON (HIRAM ULYSSES) GRANT, RUTHERFORD B. HAYES, JAMES ABRAM GARFIELD, CHESTER ALAN ARTHUR, GROVER CLEVELAND, BENJAMIN HARRISON, WILLIAM McKINLEY, THEODORE ROOSEVELT, WILLIAM HOWARD TAFT, WOODROW WILSON, WARREN G. HARDING, JOHN CALVIN (CAL, SILENT CAL) COOLIDGE, HERBERT CLARK HOOVER, FRANKLIN DELANO**

ROOSEVELT, HARRY S.
TRUMAN, DWIGHT DAVID
(IKE) EISENHOWER, JOHN
FITZGERALD KENNEDY,
LYNDON BAINES JOHNSON,
RICHARD MILHOUS NIXON

president (abbr.) **PRES.**
presidential advisers **CABINET**
president of the Confederacy
**DAVIS**
president of Yugoslavia **TITO**
president's no **VETO**
presiding officer **CHAIRMAN**
presiding officer of the House
**SPEAKER**
presiding officer's mallet
**GAVEL**
press **FORCE, URGE**
press agent's concern
**PUBLICITY**
press clothes **IRON, STEAM**
press down **RAM, TAMP**
press for payment **DUN**
pressure **STRESS**
prestidigitator **MAGICIAN,**
**CONJURER, JUGGLER**
prestige **INFLUENCE**
presume **ASSUME**
presumption **AUDACITY**
presumptuous **INSOLENT,**
**ARROGANT**
presuppose **POSIT**
pretend **SHAM, LET ON,**
**SUPPOSE, ACT, FAKE,**
**FEIGN, POSE, SEEM**
pretender **CLAIMANT**
pretense **ACT, POSE, SHAM**
pretentious **AFFECTED**
pretext **EXCUSE**
pretty **BONNY, CUTE,**
**BEAUTIFUL**
prevail **REIGN**
prevail upon **PERSUADE**
prevalent **RIFE**
prevaricate **LIE, FIB**
prevent **AVERT, DETER, WARD**
**OFF, ESTOP, BAR, DEBAR**
previous **PRIOR, FORMER**
prey **QUARRY**
prey upon **HUNT, PLUNDER**
price **RATE, COST, FARE, FEE**
price label **TAG, TAB**
price of passage **FARE**
price per unit **RATE**
prick **PIERCE**
prickle **THORN, NETTLE**
prickly fin **ACANTHA**
prickly heat **MILIARA**

prickly plant **THISTLE**
prickly seed **BUR, BURR**
prickly sensation **TINGLE**
prickly shrub **BRIAR**
prick painfully **STING**
pride **VANITY, CONCEIT**
priest **PASTOR, CLERIC,**
**FATHER, PADRE**
priest's assistant **ACOLYTE**
priest's mantle **COPE**
priest's vestment **STOLE, ALB,**
**EPHOD, AMICE**
prig **PRUDE, PEDANT**
priggish **PRIM**
prim **SEDATE, PRISSY**
prima donna **DIVA**
primary **PRINCIPAL, CHIEF**
primary color **BLUE, RED,**
**YELLOW**
primate **APE-MAN, APE,**
**HUMANOID**
prime **FIRST, ORIGINAL**
prime minister **PREMIER**
primeval **ANCIENT, PRIMITIVE**
primitive **CRUDE, SIMPLE**
primitive chisel **CELT**
primitive wind instrument
**PANPIPE**
primitive word **ETYMON**
primp **PREEN**
primrose **YELLOW**
Prince Albert **COAT**
prince in India **RAJA, RAJAH**
princely **REGAL, AUGUST**
Prince of Darkness **DEVIL,**
**SATAN**
Prince of Denmark **HAMLET**
prince of evil **DEVIL, SATAN,**
**LUCIFER, MEPHISTOPHELES**
Prince of the Church **CARDINAL**
Princeton's mascot **TIGER**
principal **MAIN, CHIEF**
principal actor **STAR**
principal commodity **STAPLE**
principle **TENET**
print **PUBLISH, LETTER**
printed defamation **LIBEL**
printed fabric **PERCALE,**
**CHINTZ**
printer's aid **DEVIL**
printer's commodity **INK, TYPE,**
**PLATE**
printer's direction **STET, DELE**
printer's mark **CARET**
printer's measure **EN, EM**
printing error **ERRATUM**
printing for the blind **BRAILLE**
printing machine **PRESS**

printing necessity **INK**
printing process **OFFSET**
prior to **ERE, BEFORE**
priority **PRECEDENCE**
priory **CLOISTER**
prison **JAIL, CAGE, GAOL, PEN**
prison dweller **INMATE**
prisoner **CAPTIVE, INMATE**
prison official **WARDEN**
prison room **CELL**
pristine **PURE, UNTOUCHED**
private **PERSONAL, SOLDIER**
private entrance **POSTERN**
privateer **RAIDER, PIRATE, BUCCANEER**
private eye **SHAMUS**
private high school (colloq.) **PREP**
private pupil **TUTEE**
private road **DRIVEWAY**
private room **DEN**
private teacher **TUTOR**
privation **NEED, WANT**
privilege **RIGHT**
prize **AWARD, TROPHY, CUP**
prize bestowed **AWARD**
prizefight **BOUT**
prize money **PURSE**
prize ring **ARENA**
pro **FOR**
proa **OUTRIGGER**
probable **LIKELY**
probe **EXAMINE, SEARCH**
problematic **UNCERTAIN, UNSETTLED**
proboscis **NOSE, SNOUT, TRUNK**
procedure **ORDER, SYSTEM**
proceed **GO, GET ON**
proceeding **ACTION, PROCESS**
proceeds **PROFIT, INCOME**
process **METHOD**
process crude oil **REFINE**
procession **PARADE**
process leather **TAN**
proclaim **DECLARE**
proclamation **EDICT**
proclivity **BENT, LEANING**
procrastinate **DELAY, PUT OFF**
proctor **AGENT**
procurator of Judea **PILATE**
procure **ACQUIRE, SECURE**
prod **GOAD, NUDGE, POKE, URGE**
prodigy **MARVEL**
produce **GENERATE, YIELD, BEAR**

produce offspring **BREED, PROCREATE**
producer-director Preminger **OTTO**
productive **FERTILE, CREATIVE**
product of milk coagulation **CURD**
product of Pittsburgh **STEEL**
product of worms **SILK**
proem **PRELUDE, PREAMBLE**
profane **IMPURE, SECULAR**
profess **AVOW, STATE, SAY**
profession **CAREER, JOB, VOCATION, DECLARATION**
professional **EXPERT, PAID**
professional charge **FEE**
professional poet **BARD**
professional tramp **HOBO**
professor **TEACHER**
proffer **TENDER, OFFER**
proficient **ABLE, CAPABLE**
profile **CONTOUR, OUTLINE**
profit **GAIN, NET**
profit by **CAPITALIZE**
profligate **CORRUPT, VICIOUS**
profound **DEEP**
profound sleep **SOPOR, COMA, STUPOR**
profuse **LAVISH, COPIOUS**
profusion **ABUNDANCE**
progenitor **SIRE, FATHER**
progeny **SONS, OFFSPRING, CHILDREN, DESCENDANTS**
prognosis **FORECAST**
program **AGENDA, SCHEDULE**
programmer's direction (2 wds.) **READ OUT**
progress **GROWTH, ADVANCE**
progressive **LIBERAL**
prohibit **BAN, TABU, TABOO, DEBAR, ESTOP, FORBID**
prohibition **DRY**
prohibition on commerce **EMBARGO**
project **JUT, PLAN, SCHEME**
projectile **MISSILE**
projecting work, in fortification **REDAN**
prolix **WORDY, VERBOSE**
prolonged and wordy **PROLIX**
prominent **IMPORTANT**
promise **PLEDGE, WORD**
promise solemnly **VOW**
promontory **CAPE, NESS, HEADLAND, POINT**
promote **ADVANCE, ADVERTISE**

| | |
|---|---|
| promulgate | **PUBLISH, DECLARE** |
| prone | **LIKELY** |
| prone to change | **MUTABLE** |
| prong | **TINE** |
| pronged instrument | **FORK** |
| pronoun | **HER, HIM, IT, ME, YOU, US, WE, HE, SHE, THEY, THEM, THIS, THOSE** |
| pronounce | **ARTICULATE** |
| pronounce indistinctly | **SLUR, GARBLE** |
| pronouncement | **DICTUM, DICTA (pl.)** |
| pronto | **QUICK** |
| proof | **EVIDENCE** |
| proof of ownership | **DEED** |
| proof of payment | **RECEIPT** |
| proofreader's mark | **CARET** |
| pro or con | **VOTE** |
| prop | **LEG, SUPPORT, BRACE** |
| propel | **DRIVE** |
| propel with oars | **ROW** |
| propensity | **INCLINATION** |
| proper | **DUE, MEET** |
| property | **ASSET, ESTATE, LAND, REAL ESTATE** |
| property manager | **TRUSTEE** |
| property right | **LIEN** |
| prophecy | **ORACLE** |
| prophesy | **AUGUR, PREDICT** |
| prophet | **SEER, AMOS, HOSEA, MICAH, ISAIAH, JOEL, OBADIAH, JONAH, NAHUM, HABAKKUK, ZEPHANIAH, HAGGAI, ZECHARIAH, MALACHI** |
| prophetic | **FATEFUL** |
| prophetic sign | **OMEN** |
| propinquity | **NEARNESS** |
| propitiate | **CONCILIATE, APPEASE** |
| propitious | **FAVORABLE** |
| proportion | **RATIO** |
| proposal | **OFFER, DESIGN** |
| propose | **OFFER, BID** |
| proprietor | **OWNER** |
| propriety | **DECORUM** |
| prosaic | **DRAB, INSIPID** |
| proscribe | **FORBID, OUTLAW** |
| prosecute | **SUE** |
| proselyte | **CONVERT** |
| prospect | **VISTA, VIEW** |
| prospector's find | **ORE** |
| prosper | **SUCCEED, THRIVE** |
| prosperity | **WEAL, WELFARE** |
| Prospero's helper | **ARIEL** |

| | |
|---|---|
| prosperous (2 wds.) | **WELL OFF** |
| prostrate | **POWERLESS, OVERCOME** |
| protagonist | **HERO** |
| protean | **VARIABLE** |
| protect | **DEFEND, PRESERVE** |
| protect an invention | **PATENT** |
| protect from the sun | **SHADE** |
| protection | **EGIS** |
| protective barrier | **SCREEN, GATE** |
| protective case for a light | **LANTERN** |
| protective covering | **ARMOR** |
| protective ditch | **MOAT** |
| protective garment | **APRON, COAT, SMOCK, OVERALLS** |
| protective layer | **COAT** |
| protective slope | **GLACIS** |
| protege | **WARD** |
| proteinase | **PEPSIN, TRYPSIN** |
| protozoan | **AMEBA** |
| protract | **EXTEND** |
| protracted | **LONG** |
| protracted speech | **TIRADE** |
| protrude | **JUT** |
| protuberance | **BULGE, NODE** |
| protuberance on a camel | **HUMP** |
| proud | **ARROGANT, VAIN** |
| prove | **VERIFY, TEST** |
| provender | **FODDER** |
| provenience | **ORIGIN, SOURCE** |
| proverb | **ADAGE, MAXIM, SAW** |
| proverbial back-breaker (2 wds.) | **LAST STRAW** |
| prove satisfactory (3 wds.) | **RING THE BELL** |
| prove to be false | **BELIE, REFUTE** |
| provide | **FURNISH** |
| provide food and service | **CATER** |
| provide free food | **TREAT** |
| provident | **FARSIGHTED, FRUGAL** |
| provide schooling for | **EDUCATE** |
| provide weapons | **ARM** |
| provide (with qualities) | **ENDUE, IMBUE** |
| province in Canada | **ONTARIO, ALBERTA, BRITISH COLUMBIA, MANITOBA, NEW BRUNSWICK, NOVA SCOTIA, QUEBEC, SASKATCHEWAN, NEWFOUNDLAND** |
| provincial | **RURAL** |

| | |
|---|---|
| provincial bishop | **PRIMATE** |
| provision | **FOOD** |
| proviso | **IF, CLAUSE** |
| provoke | **EXCITE, STIR** |
| prow | **STEM** |
| prowess | **ABILITY, VALOR** |
| prowl | **SNOOP, PRY, SNEAK** |
| proximal | **NEXT** |
| proximity | **NEARNESS** |
| proxy | **AGENT, PROCURATOR** |
| prudent | **DISCREET, WISE** |
| prudish one (colloq.) | |
| | **BLUENOSE** |
| prune | **TRIM** |
| pry | **WRENCH, LEVER, SNOOP** |
| pry bar | **LEVER** |
| prying | **CURIOUS** |
| psalm | **HYMN** |
| psalmist | **DAVID** |
| pseudonym | **ALIAS, NOM DE** |
| | **PLUME, PEN NAME** |
| psyche | **MIND** |
| psychotic | **INSANE** |
| pub | **TAVERN, BAR, SALOON** |
| pub beverage | **ALE, STOUT,** |
| | **BEER** |
| public | **OPEN, OVERT** |
| public discussion | **DEBATE** |
| public disturbance | **RIOT** |
| public garden | **PARK** |
| public house | **INN, TAVERN,** |
| | **PUB** |
| publicity | **BALLYHOO** |
| public notice | **AD** |
| public official | **NOTARY** |
| public park | **COMMONS** |
| public procession | **PARADE** |
| public road | **STREET, AVENUE,** |
| | **BOULEVARD, PIKE** |
| public service | **UTILITY** |
| public speaker | **LECTURER,** |
| | **ORATOR** |
| public storehouse | **ETAPE** |
| public vehicle | **BUS, CAB,** |
| | **TAXI, TRAIN** |
| public walk | **MALL** |
| publish | **ISSUE, PRINT** |
| puck | **SPRITE, ELF, DISC** |
| puddle | **POOL** |
| pudgy | **DUMPY** |
| Pueblo Indian | **HOPI, ZUNI** |
| puerile | **CHILDISH, JUVENILE** |
| Puerto Rican resort | **PONCE** |
| puff | **PANT, GASP** |
| Puff's friend | **SPOT** |
| pugilist | **BOXER** |
| pugnacious | **MILITANT** |

| | |
|---|---|
| puissance | **STRENGTH,** |
| | **MIGHT, FORCE,** |
| | **POWER** |
| pulchritude | **BEAUTY,** |
| | **COMELINESS** |
| pull | **HAUL, TOW, TUG, LUG,** |
| | **DRAG, YANK, DRAW** |
| pull down | **DEMOLISH** |
| pullet | **HEN** |
| pull into a fold | **TUCK** |
| pullman | **SLEEPER** |
| pull one's leg | **HOAX** |
| pull out | **EXTRACT** |
| pullover | **SWEATER** |
| pull to pieces | **TEAR, RIP, REND** |
| pulpit | **ROSTRUM** |
| pulpy substance | **POMACE** |
| pulsate | **THROB, BEAT** |
| pulse | **THROB** |
| pulverize | **GRIND, MASH** |
| pulverizing machine | |
| (2 wds.) | **ROD MILL** |
| puma | **COUGAR** |
| pummel | **BATTER, BEAT** |
| pump | **SHOE** |
| punch | **CUFF, SOCK** |
| Punch and Judy | **PUPPETS** |
| punching tool | **AWL** |
| punch server | **LADLE, BOWL** |
| punctilious | **FORMAL, PRECISE** |
| punctual | **PROMPT** |
| punctuation mark | **COLON,** |
| | **PERIOD, COMMA** |
| pungent | **ACRID, SPICY,** |
| | **TANGY, ZESTY** |
| pungent bulb | **ONION** |
| pungent flavoring | **GARLIC** |
| pungent refrigerant | **AMMONIA** |
| pungent shrub | **SAGE** |
| punish | **DISCIPLINE,** |
| | **CHASTISE, FINE** |
| punish a child | **SPANK** |
| punishing | **PENAL** |
| puny | **FEEBLE, LITTLE** |
| pupil | **STUDENT** |
| pupil (Fr.) | **ELEVE** |
| pupil's assignment | **LESSON,** |
| | **HOMEWORK** |
| pupil's record (2 wds.) | **REPORT CARD** |
| puppet | **DOLL** |
| puppeteer Lewis | **SHARI** |
| puppy sound | **YIP, YAP, YELP** |
| purchase | **BUY** |
| purchase back | **REDEEM** |
| purdah | **VEIL** |
| pure | **CHASTE,** |
| | **UNADULTERATED** |

| | | | |
|---|---|---|---|
| pure air | **OZONE** | put to proof | **TEST** |
| purified wool fat | **LANOLIN** | put to use | **APPLY** |
| purify | **REFINE** | put upon | **IMPOSE** |
| purl | **LOOP** | put up stake | **ANTE** |
| purloin | **STEAL, FILCH** | put up with | **ABIDE, TOLERATE** |
| purple | **AMETHYST, VIOLET** | puttee | **GAITER** |
| purple flower | **VIOLET, IRIS** | putty | **CEMENT, SOFT, PLIABLE** |
| purple fruit | **PLUM, GRAPE** | puzzle | **ENIGMA, POSER,** |
| purple plum | **DAMSON** | | **CROSSWORD, RIDDLE** |
| purport | **OBJECT, SENSE** | puzzler's friend | **DICTIONARY** |
| purpose | **AIM, INTENT, END,** | pyramid | **TOMB** |
| | **DESIGN, MEANING** | pyxis | **VASE, CASE** |
| purse | **BAG, HANDBAG,** | | |
| | **POCKETBOOK** | | |
| pursue | **CHASE, GO AFTER,** | **Q** | |
| | **TAIL, FOLLOW** | | |
| purvey | **CATER, PROVIDE,** | quadrille | **DANCE, SQUARE** |
| | **FURNISH** | quaff | **DRINK** |
| push | **SHOVE** | quagmire | **MARSH, BOG** |
| push aside | **SHUNT** | quahog | **CLAM** |
| pushcart | **BARROW** | quail | **COWER, QUAKE, BIRD** |
| push gently | **NUDGE** | quaint | **CURIOUS, ODD** |
| push up | **BOOST** | quake | **TREMBLE** |
| push with the head | **BUTT** | qualified | **ABLE, CAPABLE,** |
| pussy cat | **TABBY, KITTY** | | **COMPETENT** |
| put | **DEPOSIT, PLACE, SET** | quality | **ESSENCE, CHARACTER** |
| put away for later (2 wds.) | | quality of sound | **TONE** |
| | **SET ASIDE** | qualm | **TWINGE, PANG** |
| put back | **RESTORE, REPLACE** | quandary | **DILEMMA** |
| put down | **LAY** | quantity of coal | **TON** |
| put forth | **EXERT** | quantity of cookies | **BATCH** |
| put in | **INSERT** | quantity of medicine | **DOSE** |
| put in glass container | **BOTTLE** | quantity of one baking | **BATCH** |
| put in opposition | **PIT** | quantity of paper | **REAM** |
| put in order | **ARRANGE** | quantity of yarn | **HANK** |
| put in place | **SET** | quarrel | **ROW, SPAT, FEUD,** |
| put in scabbard | **SHEATHE** | | **FALL OUT, TIFF** |
| put in shape | **TRIM** | quarry | **PREY** |
| put in tins | **CAN** | quart | **FOURTH** |
| put into a secret language | | quarter-acre | **ROOD** |
| | **CODE, ENCODE** | quarterly item due I.R.S. | |
| put into cipher | **ENCODE** | (2 wds.) | **ESTIMATED TAX** |
| put into office | **ELECT** | quarter-round molding | **OVOLO** |
| put into practice | **USE** | quartet | **FOUR, FOURSOME** |
| put into words | **STATE,** | quartet member | **TENOR,** |
| | **EXPRESS, VERBALIZE** | | **BARITONE, BASS** |
| put in writing | **REDACT** | quartz | **AGATE, SILICA** |
| put it there | **SHAKE** | quaver | **TREMBLE, FALTER** |
| put off | **DELAY, POSTPONE** | quay | **LEVEE, EMBANKMENT** |
| put on | **DON** | queasy | **DELICATE** |
| put on guard | **WARN** | queenly | **REGAL** |
| put on the payroll | **HIRE,** | queen of Carthage | **DIDO** |
| | **EMPLOY** | queen of India | **RANEE, RANI** |
| put out | **ANGER, OUST** | queen of Olympian deities | |
| put out a tenant | **EVICT** | | **HERA** |
| put out money | **SPEND** | queen of the fairies | **MAB** |
| put out of sight | **HIDE, HID,** | queer | **ODD, STRANGE, EERIE,** |
| | **CONCEAL, CONCEALED** | | **EERY, WEIRD** |

| | |
|---|---|
| queer (Scot.) | **ORRA** |
| quell | **SUBDUE, ALLAY** |
| quench the thirst | **SLAKE** |
| querulous | **FRETFUL, PEEVISH** |
| query | **QUESTION, ASK** |
| quest | **SEARCH** |
| question | **INTERROGATE, QUERY** |
| questionable | **IFFY, FISHY** |
| queue | **LINE** |
| quibble | **EVADE** |
| quick | **FAST, SPEEDY, HASTY, RAPID** |
| quick look | **PEEK, GLIMPSE** |
| quick lunch place | **DINER, EATERY** |
| quick plunge | **DIP** |
| quicksilver | **MERCURY** |
| quick sound | **POP** |
| quick to learn | **APT, CLEVER, BRIGHT** |
| quidnunc | **GOSSIP** |
| quiescent | **STILL, SERENE** |
| quiet | **STILL, SILENT, PEACEFUL** |
| quill | **PEN, FEATHER** |
| quilt part | **PATCH** |
| quilting party | **BEE** |
| quintessential | **PUREST** |
| quintet | **FIVE, FIVESOME** |
| quip | **SALLY, RETORT** |
| quit | **STOP, GIVE UP, LEAVE** |
| quite a few | **MANY** |
| quiver | **SHAKE, QUAKE, TREMBLE** |
| quivering motion | **TREMOR** |
| quixotic | **IDEALISTIC** |
| quiz | **EXAM, TEST, QUESTION** |
| quondam | **FORMER** |
| Quonset | **HUT** |
| quota | **PORTION, RATION** |
| quote as an authority | **CITE** |
| quote by Poe's raven | **NEVERMORE** |
| quote from memory | **RECITE** |
| quotidian | **DAILY, COMMON** |

**R**

| | |
|---|---|
| rabbet | **GROOVE, JOINT** |
| rabbit | **BUNNY, HARE** |
| rabbit snare | **NOOSE** |
| rabbit tail | **SCUT** |
| rabble | **MOB, RIFFRAFF** |
| rabid | **MAD, FRANTIC** |
| raccoon-like animal | **PANDA, COATI** |

| | |
|---|---|
| race | **CONTEST, RUN, SPEED** |
| race between teams | **RELAY** |
| racecourse | **TRACK, OVAL** |
| racehorse | **PACER, TROTTER** |
| racetrack character | **TOUT** |
| racetrack shape | **OVAL** |
| racetrack surface | **TURF** |
| racetrack term | **ODDS** |
| Rachel's father | **LABAN** |
| Rachel's sister | **LEAH** |
| racing program | **CARD** |
| racket | **NOISE, CLATTER, DIN** |
| racket string material | **GUT, CATGUT** |
| radar screen image | **BLIP** |
| radiance | **BRILLIANCE** |
| radiate | **SHINE, GLOW** |
| radical | **EXTREME** |
| radio detecting device | **RADAR** |
| radio interference | **STATIC** |
| radio or television system | **NETWORK** |
| radio waves' medium | **ETHER** |
| radium discoverer | **CURIE** |
| radium emanation | **RADON** |
| radius | **SCOPE** |
| radix | **ROOT** |
| rag | **TATTER** |
| rage | **RAVE, STORM** |
| ragged edge | **JAG** |
| raging woman | **MENAD, MAENAD** |
| raglan | **COAT, SLEEVE** |
| ragout | **STEW** |
| rah | **CHEER** |
| raid | **FORAY** |
| raider | **PRIVATEER, PIRATE** |
| rail at | **SCOLD** |
| rail bird | **SORA** |
| railroad bridge | **TRESTLE** |
| railroad car | **COACH, DINER, SLEEPER, PULLMAN** |
| railroad car connecting rod | **DRAWBAR** |
| railroad locomotive | **ENGINE, DIESEL** |
| railroad signal | **SEMAPHORE** |
| railroad sleeper | **TIE** |
| railroad station | **DEPOT, TERMINAL** |
| railroad track layer (2 wds., sl.) | **GANDY DANCER** |
| railroad vehicle | **CAR** |
| rail-splitter | **LINCOLN** |
| railway car | **TRAM** |
| railway mail service (abbr.) | **R.M.S.** |
| raiment | **APPAREL** |

| | | | | |
|---|---|---|---|---|
| rain | DOWNPOUR, POUR, SHOWER | rapid | FAST, SWIFT, QUICK, SPEEDY | |
| rain and snow | SLEET | rapidity | HASTE | |
| rainbow | IRIS | rapidly | APACE | |
| rainbow fish | GUPPY | rapier | SWORD | |
| raincoat | SLICKER | rap on the knuckles | | |
| rain hard | POUR | | REPRIMAND | |
| rain sound | PATTER | rapport | ACCORD | |
| rain unit | INCH | rapture | BLISS | |
| rainy | WET | rapturous feeling | EXALTATION | |
| rainy season in India | | rare | INFREQUENT, SCARCE, UNCOMMON, UNUSUAL | |
| | MONSOON | | | |
| raise | ELEVATE, REAR, ERECT, GROW, LIFT, BREED, UP, HOIST, BOOST | rare art object | CURIO | |
| | | rarefy | DILUTE | |
| | | rarely | SELDOM | |
| raise crops | FARM | rare thing | ODDITY | |
| raised border | RIM | rascal | ROGUE, SCAMP | |
| raised platform | DAIS, STAGE | rash | HEEDLESS, IMPRUDENT, OUTBREAK | |
| raised stripe | RIDGE | | | |
| raise high | EXALT | rasher | SLICE | |
| raise nap | TEASE | rasp | FILE, GRATE | |
| raise to the third power | CUBE | rat | RODENT | |
| rajah's wife | RANEE, RANI | ratchet | BOBBIN, WHEEL | |
| rake | ROUE, BOUNDER | rate | APPRAISE, PRICE, RANK, CLASSIFY, CLASS | |
| rakish | DASHING, JAUNTY | | | |
| rally | SUMMON, STIR | rate of movement | PACE, SPEED | |
| ram | TUP, SHEEP | | | |
| ramadan | FAST | rather | SOMEWHAT | |
| Rama's spouse | SITA | rather than | INSTEAD | |
| ramble | ROVE, WANDER, STROLL, STRAY | rather than (poetic) | ERE | |
| | | ratification | AMEN | |
| rambunctious | UNRULY, WILD | ratify | CONFIRM | |
| ramification | OFFSHOOT, BRANCH | ration | PORTION, SHARE | |
| | | rational | SANE | |
| ram in the zodiac | ARIES | rationale | REASON | |
| ram into | CRASH | ratite | OSTRICH | |
| ramp | GRADING | rat-like rodent | VOLE | |
| rampant | VIOLENT, RIFE | ratline | RIGGING | |
| rampart | PARAPET, REDAN | rattan | CANE | |
| ram's horn | SHOFAR | rattle | AGITATE, CLATTER | |
| ram's mate | EWE | rattler's sound | HISS | |
| ranch animal | EWE, RAM, COW, SHEEP, HORSE, MARE, BULL, STEER | rattling sound | CLATTER | |
| | | raucous | HOARSE | |
| | | ravage | DESTROY, DESPOIL | |
| rancher | COWBOY | rave | RAGE, RANT | |
| rancid | FOUL, ROTTEN | ravel | FRAY | |
| rancor | SPITE, BITTERNESS | ravelings | LINT | |
| random | CASUAL, AIMLESS | raven | BLACK | |
| range | COOKSTOVE, STOVE | raven-haired girl | BRUNETTE | |
| range of sight | KEN, SCOPE | ravenous | STARVING | |
| range of stables | MEWS | ravine | ARROYO, GULCH | |
| rank | CLASS, DEGREE, GRADE, RATE | ravish | ENRAPTURE | |
| | | raw | INEXPERIENCED, UNCOOKED, GREEN | |
| rankle | FESTER | | | |
| ransack | PILLAGE, PLUNDER | rawboned | LEAN | |
| ransom | REDEEM | raw herb dish | SALAD | |
| rant | RAVE | rawhide | PELT | |
| rap | KNOCK, TAP | rawhide whip | QUIRT | |
| rapacious | GREEDY | raw metal | ORE | |

| | | | |
|---|---|---|---|
| raw steel | IRON | reata | LARIAT, LASSO |
| ray | BEAM, SKATE | rebate | DISCOUNT |
| raze | TEAR DOWN, LEVEL | rebel | RISE, REVOLT |
| razorback | HOG | rebellion | REVOLT, MUTINY |
| razor clam | SOLEN | rebellious demonstration | RIOT |
| razor sharpener | STROP | rebound | BOUNCE |
| razz | HECKLE | rebuff | REJECT, SLAP, |
| re | CONCERNING, REGARDING | | REPULSE, SNUB |
| reach | EXTEND | rebuild | RENEW |
| reach across | SPAN | rebuke | REPROACH, CHIDE |
| reach a destination | COME, | rebus | PUZZLE |
| | ARRIVE | rebut | DISPROVE |
| reach in time | CATCH | recalcitrant | STUBBORN, |
| reach maturity | RIPEN | | REBELLIOUS |
| reach out | STRETCH | recall | REMEMBER, RECOLLECT |
| react | RESPOND | recant | RETRACT |
| reaction | RESPONSE | recap | TIRE |
| reactionary | TORY | recapitulate | SUMMARIZE |
| reactivation | RENEWAL | recede | EBB |
| read | SCAN, PORE, PERUSE | receive | GET, GAIN, ACCEPT |
| readable | LEGIBLE | receive advantage | BENEFIT |
| reader | PRIMER, LECTOR | receive a scolding (2 wds.) | |
| readily | WILLINGLY | | GET IT |
| reading desk | LECTERN | receive information | HEAR |
| reading room | DEN, STUDY, | receiver of property | ALIENEE |
| | LIBRARY | receiver of stolen property | |
| reading table | DESK | | FENCE |
| read rapidly | SKIM | receiving set | RADIO |
| read up on | STUDY | recent | NEW |
| ready | PREPARED, RIPE | recently | OF LATE, LATELY |
| ready (arch.) | YARE | recently acquired | NEW |
| ready answers | REPARTEE | recent (prefix) | NEO |
| ready cash | MONEY | receptacle | CASE |
| ready for action (2 wds.) | | receptacle for carrying | |
| | IN SHAPE, ON TAP | things | TRAY |
| ready for harvest | RIPE | reception | LEVEE, TEA |
| ready money | CASH | reception room | HALL, ENTRY, |
| ready to act (3 wds.) | | | PARLOR, FOYER |
| | ON THE ALERT | recess | NOOK |
| ready to receive visitors | | recession | WITHDRAWAL |
| (2 wds.) | AT HOME | recipe | FORMULA |
| reaffirm | REASSERT | recipient of a bequest | |
| Reagan's state | CALIFORNIA | | LEGATEE |
| real | GENUINE, TRUE, ACTUAL | recipient of a gift | DONEE |
| real estate map | PLAT | recipient of a gratuity | TIPPEE |
| real event | FACT | recite | READ, RELATE |
| realistic | VIVID | recite musically | CHANT, |
| reality | FACT | | INTONE |
| realize | KNOW | reckless | HASTY, RASH, |
| realm | DOMAIN | | IMPRUDENT |
| realm of fancy (2 wds.) | | reckon | CONSIDER, SUPPOSE |
| | DREAM WORLD | reclaim | RECOVER, REDEEM |
| reamer | JUICER | recline | LIE |
| reap | HARVEST | recline indolently | LOLL |
| rear | RAISE, FOSTER | recluse | EREMITE, HERMIT |
| reason | CAUSE, MOTIVE | recognize | KNOW |
| reasonable | LOGICAL, | recoil | SHY |
| | SENSIBLE | recollect | RECALL, REMEMBER |

| | | | |
|---|---|---|---|
| recollection | MEMORY | reduce | BATE, CUT, LESSEN |
| recommence | RESUME | reduced price offers | TWOFERS |
| recompense | REWARD, WAGE, | reduce gradually | TAPER |
| | PAY | reduce in rank | DEMOTE |
| recondite | ERUDITE, LEARNED | reduce in value | LOWER |
| reconnoiter | SCOUT, SURVEY | reduce light | DIM |
| record | DISC, ENTER | reduce speed | SLOW |
| record for TV | TAPE | reduce to a lower grade | |
| record holder | FILE | | DEMOTE, DEGRADE |
| record keeper | REGISTRAR | reduce to a mean | AVERAGE |
| record of a patient | CHART, | reduce to ashes | CREMATE |
| | MEDICAL HISTORY | reduce to fine spray | ATOMIZE |
| record of events | ANNAL | reduce to powder | GRIND |
| record of the past | HISTORY | reducing program | DIET |
| record player, for short | | reduction | DISCOUNT, REBATE |
| | STEREO, PHONO | redundant | EXCESS, WORDY |
| record speed | TIME, RPM | red wine | CLARET, PORT |
| recount | REPORT | redwood | TREE |
| recover | REGAIN, MEND | ree | SANDPIPER, ARIKARA |
| recreation | SPORT | reed instrument | OBOE |
| recreation area | CAMP, PARK | reef material | CORAL |
| rectify | CORRECT, REVISE | reek | FUME |
| recurring pattern | CYCLE | reel | STAGGER |
| red | CERISE, CRIMSON, | reel's companion | ROD |
| | SCARLET, COMMUNIST | refer | ALLUDE, MENTION |
| red (prefix) | RHOD | referee | UMPIRE |
| redact | EDIT | reference book | ATLAS, |
| redan | FORTIFICATION | | DICTIONARY |
| red-breasted bird | ROBIN | reference mark | ASTERISK |
| red chalcedony | SARD | reference table | INDEX |
| redden | BLUSH | refer to (Lat. abbr.) | VID. |
| reddish | RUDDY | refinement | POLISH |
| reddish brown | RUST, | refine metal | SMELT |
| | AUBURN, MAROON | reflect | CONSIDER |
| reddish horse | ROAN | reflection | IMAGE |
| reddish liqueur (2 wds.) | | reform | IMPROVE, BETTER |
| | SLOE GIN | refrain | CHORUS, FORBEAR, |
| reddish yellow | AMBER, CORAL | | MELODY |
| redeem | SAVE, RESCUE | refrain from noticing | IGNORE |
| redeem from captivity | | refresh | REVIVE, BRACE |
| | RANSOM | refreshing beverage | ICED TEA, |
| red gem | GARNET, RUBY | | ICED COFFEE, ADE, |
| red herring | DISTRACTION | | SODA, POP |
| red-letter day | HOLIDAY | refrigerate | ICE, CHILL, COOL |
| red light | DANGER | refuge | HAVEN, OASIS, |
| red man | INDIAN | | SHELTER |
| red meat | STEAK, BEEF | refugee | EMIGRE |
| redness of skin | RUBOR, | refund money | REPAY |
| | BLUSH | refuse | DECLINE, PASS UP, |
| redolent | FRAGRANT | | BALK, DENY, |
| redolent wood | CEDAR | | DROSS, TRASH |
| red planet | MARS | refuse from mills | SLAG |
| redress | REPAIR | refuse from sugar making | |
| red root vegetable | BEET, | | BAGASSE |
| | RADISH | refuse to accept | REJECT |
| red round vegetable | TOMATO | refuse to give up | PERSIST, |
| Red Sea gulf | AQABA | | PERSEVERE |
| Red Square name | LENIN | refute | DENY, DISPROVE |

| | |
|---|---|
| regal | GRAND, KINGLY, ROYAL, STATELY |
| regal attendant | COURTIER |
| regal chair | THRONE |
| regale | TREAT, FETE |
| regal fur | ERMINE |
| regal residence | PALACE, CASTLE |
| Regan's father | LEAR |
| regard | RESPECT, ESTEEM, LOOK, WATCH |
| regard highly | ADMIRE, ADORE, ESTEEM, RESPECT |
| regarding | RE, IN RE |
| regardless | DESPITE |
| regatta | RACE |
| regent | RULER |
| regimen | DIET |
| regimental commander | COLONEL |
| regimented trip | TOUR |
| regina | QUEEN |
| region | AREA, ZONE |
| regional | LOCAL |
| region of the patella | KNEE |
| register | LIST, ENROLL |
| registering of votes | POLL |
| register opposition | PROTEST |
| regret | REPENT, RUE |
| regretful | PENITENT, SORRY, RUEFUL |
| regular | CUSTOMARY, ORDINARY |
| regular method | SYSTEM |
| regulate | ADJUST |
| regulate food intake | DIET |
| regulate pitch | KEY |
| regulation | RULE |
| rehearsal | DRILL |
| rehearse | PRACTICE, REPEAT |
| reign | RULE |
| reigning beauty | BELLE |
| reimburse | REPAY, REFUND |
| rein | CHECK, CONTROL |
| reindeer | CARIBOU |
| reinforce | BOLSTER |
| reiterate | REPEAT |
| reject | REBUFF, SPURN, TURN DOWN, VETO |
| rejoice | CELEBRATE |
| rejoice in triumph | EXULT |
| rejoinder | RETORT |
| relapse | BACKSLIDE |
| relate | PERTAIN, TELL, REPORT |
| related | AKIN, KINDRED |
| related group | CLAN |
| relating to branches | RAMAL |

| | |
|---|---|
| relating to ebb and flow | TIDAL |
| relating to grandparents | AVAL |
| relating to Hindu literature | VEDIC |
| relating to measurement | METRICAL |
| relating to Paul VI | PAPAL |
| relating to the eye | OPTIC |
| relating to the moon | LUNAR |
| relating to time | ERAL |
| relative | KIN |
| relative of bingo | KENO |
| relatives | KIN |
| relax | REST, SLACKEN |
| relaxation | EASE, REST |
| relay | RACE |
| release | FREE, UNTIE |
| release from an obligation | EXEMPT |
| release from restraint | FREE |
| release on condition | PAROLE |
| relegate | ASSIGN, REFER |
| relent | YIELD, DEFER |
| relentless | IMPLACABLE |
| relevant | PERTINENT |
| reliable | CERTAIN, SURE, DEPENDABLE |
| reliance | HOPE, DEPENDENCE |
| relic | SOUVENIR |
| relief | SUCCOR, COMFORT |
| relief-carved gem | CAMEO |
| relief organization | CARE |
| relieve | ALLAY, EASE |
| religion | BELIEF, CREED |
| religious | DEVOUT |
| religious assembly | CONGREGATION |
| religious belief | CREED |
| religious ceremony | RITE, RITUAL, MASS |
| religious denomination | SECT |
| religious discourse | SERMON |
| religious holiday | EASTER, CHRISTMAS, PASSOVER |
| religious observance | FAST |
| religious poem | PSALM |
| religious recluse | EREMITE |
| religious service | MASS, RITE, RITUAL |
| religious sister | NUN |
| relinquish | WAIVE, CEDE, YIELD |
| relinquish throne | ABDICATE |
| reliquary | SHRINE |
| relish | GUSTO, SAVOR |
| reluctant | AVERSE |
| rely | DEPEND |
| remain | STAY |

| | |
|---|---|
| remainder | **REST** |
| remaining | **LEFT, OVER** |
| remain on the feet | **STAND** |
| remains | **ASHES, CORPSE,** |
| | **STAYS** |
| remain suspended above | |
| | **HOVER** |
| remain undecided | **PEND** |
| remark | **NOTICE** |
| remarkable | **NOTEWORTHY** |
| remarkable person (sl.) | **ONER,** |
| | **CORKER, LULU** |
| remedy | **CURE, ANTIDOTE** |
| remember | **RECALL,** |
| | **RECOLLECT** |
| remembrance | **MEMENTO,** |
| | **SOUVENIR** |
| remind | **REMEMBER** |
| reminder | **MEMO** |
| remiss | **NEGLIGENT, LAX** |
| remit | **PAY** |
| remnant | **LEFTOVER** |
| remodel (2 wds.) | **MAKE OVER** |
| remonstrate | **PROTEST** |
| remorse | **COMPUNCTION,** |
| | **REGRET** |
| remorseful | **SORRY** |
| remote | **FAR, DISTANT, ALOOF** |
| remount a gem | **RESET** |
| remove | **DISPLACE, SUBTRACT** |
| remove by cleaning | **SCOUR,** |
| | **SCRUB** |
| remove by clipping | **TRIM** |
| remove cover | **UNCAP** |
| removed | **DISTANT, REMOTE** |
| remove from office | **OUST,** |
| | **DISPLACE** |
| remove from print | **DELETE,** |
| | **DELE, ERASE** |
| remove moisture | **WRING, DRY** |
| remove rind | **PARE, SKIN** |
| remove the beard | **SHAVE** |
| remove the clothes | **STRIP** |
| remunerate | **PAY** |
| Remus' brother | **ROMULUS** |
| renaissance | **REBIRTH** |
| rend | **SPLIT, TEAR, RIP,** |
| | **DELIVER** |
| render | **GIVE, DEPICT** |
| rendezvous | **TRYST** |
| rendition | **VERSION, DELIVERY** |
| renegade | **TRAITOR** |
| renege (colloq., var.) | **RENIG** |
| renege (3 wds.) | **GO BACK ON** |
| renew | **REBUILD, RESTORE,** |
| | **REACTIVATE, REDO,** |
| | **RENOVATE** |
| Reno's river | **TRUCKEE** |

| | |
|---|---|
| renounce (2 wds.) | **SWEAR OFF** |
| renovate | **REDO, RENEW,** |
| | **REMODEL** |
| renown | **ECLAT, FAME, NOTE,** |
| | **ACCLAIM** |
| rent | **HIRE, LET, LEASE** |
| rental contract | **LEASE** |
| rental sign (2 wds.) | **TO LET** |
| renter | **TENANT** |
| renunciation | **DISCLAIMER** |
| rep | **CORD, RIBBING** |
| repair | **MEND, FIX** |
| repair shoes | **SOLE** |
| reparation | **ATONEMENT** |
| repartee | **RETORT, RIPOSTE** |
| repast | **MEAL** |
| repayment | **REBATE** |
| repeal | **CANCEL, RECALL** |
| repeat | **ECHO, RECUR,** |
| | **ITERATE** |
| repeatedly (3 wds.) | |
| | **OVER AND OVER** |
| repeat from memory | **RECITE** |
| repeating from memory | **ROTE** |
| repeat mechanically | **PARROT** |
| repeat performance | **ENCORE** |
| repeat showing | **RERUN** |
| repel | **REPULSE, DISGUST** |
| repent | **RUE** |
| repentance | **REMORSE** |
| repercussion | **EFFECT** |
| repertory | **THEATER** |
| repetition | **ROTE, ECHO** |
| repetition, in psychology | |
| | **ECHOLALIA** |
| repetition of a note | **TREMOLO** |
| repetitive | **REDUNDANT** |
| repine | **COMPLAIN, FRET** |
| replace | **RESET, RESTORE** |
| replenish | **RENEW** |
| replete | **SATED, FULL** |
| replica | **COPY, DUPLICATE** |
| reply | **ANSWER, RESPOND** |
| report | **RUMOR** |
| reporter | **JOURNALIST** |
| repose | **REST, SLEEP** |
| repository | **VAULT** |
| reprehension | **GUILT, BLAME** |
| represent (2 wds.) | **STAND FOR** |
| representation | **PORTRAYAL** |
| representative | **AGENT,** |
| | **ENVOY, DELEGATE** |
| representative part | **SAMPLE** |
| reprimand | **ADMONISH,** |
| | **CENSURE** |
| reproach | **SLUR** |
| reproach insultingly | **TAUNT** |
| reprobate | **IMMORAL, SINNER** |

| | |
|---|---|
| reproduction | **REPLICA** |
| reprove | **TAKE TO TASK,** |
| | **CHASTISE, REPRIMAND** |
| reptile | **SNAKE, LIZARD** |
| reptilian | **SAURIAN** |
| Republican party, | |
| familiarly | **GOP** |
| Republican symbol | **ELEPHANT** |
| Republic of Ireland | **EIRE** |
| repudiate | **DENY** |
| repugnant | **ADVERSE, INIMICAL** |
| repulse | **REPEL** |
| repulsive | **OFFENSIVE** |
| reputation | **FAME, RENOWN** |
| repute | **CREDIT, REGARD** |
| request | **ASK, PRAYER** |
| requiem | **DIRGE** |
| require | **DEMAND, NEED** |
| requisition | **ORDER** |
| rescind | **REVOKE, CANCEL** |
| rescue | **SAVE, REDEEM** |
| research | **STUDY** |
| research room | **LAB** |
| reseau | **NETWORK** |
| resemblance | **LIKENESS,** |
| | **SIMILARITY** |
| resembling | **LIKE** |
| resembling bone | **OSSEOUS** |
| resembling man | **ANDROID** |
| resembling sheep | **OVINE** |
| resembling wool | **LANATE** |
| resentment | **ANGER, IRE** |
| reserve | **HOLD** |
| reserved | **TAKEN** |
| reserved in manner | **ALOOF** |
| reserve fund (2 wds.) | |
| | **NEST EGG** |
| reservoir | **STORE** |
| reside | **DWELL, LIVE, ABIDE** |
| residence | **ABODE, DWELLING,** |
| | **DOMICILE, HOME** |
| residency | **TENURE** |
| resident of (suffix) | **ITE** |
| resident of Ankara | **TURK** |
| resident of Avila | **SPANIARD** |
| resident of Bagdad | **IRAQI** |
| resident of Bahia | **BRAZILIAN** |
| resident of Bali | **INDONESIAN** |
| resident of Berlin | **GERMAN** |
| resident of Boise | **IDAHOAN** |
| resident of Buda | **HUNGARIAN** |
| resident of Cebu | **PHILIPPINE,** |
| | **FILIPINO** |
| resident of Copenhagen | **DANE** |
| resident of Edinburgh | **SCOT** |
| resident of Ghent | **BELGIAN** |
| resident of Glasgow | **SCOT** |
| resident of Havana | **CUBAN** |

| | |
|---|---|
| resident of Helsinki | **FINN** |
| resident of Mecca | **ARAB** |
| resident of Ocala | **FLORIDIAN** |
| resident of Perth | **AUSTRALIAN** |
| resident of Rangoon | **BURMESE** |
| resident of Rotterdam | **DUTCH** |
| resident of Selma | **ALABAMAN** |
| resident of Sitka | **ALASKAN** |
| resident of Sophia | **BULGARIAN** |
| resident of Stockholm | **SWEDE** |
| resident of Tirana | **ALBANIAN** |
| resident of Vienna | **AUSTRIAN** |
| resident of Warsaw | **POLE** |
| resident of Yuma | **ARIZONAN** |
| residue | **ASH, SIFTINGS,** |
| | **DREGS, LEES** |
| resign | **BOW OUT, QUIT,** |
| | **ABDICATE** |
| resilient | **ELASTIC, SUPPLE** |
| resin | **LAC** |
| resinous | **PINY** |
| resinous wood | **TEAK** |
| resist | **OPPOSE** |
| resist authority | **REBEL** |
| resist change (2 wds.) | |
| | **STAND PAT** |
| resister | **OPPOSER, REBEL** |
| resolute | **DETERMINED** |
| resolve | **DECIDE** |
| resonance | **SONORITY** |
| resonant | **SONOROUS,** |
| | **VIBRATING** |
| resort | **SPA** |
| resort city in Florida | **MIAMI,** |
| | **MIAMI BEACH** |
| resort hotel feature | **CABANA,** |
| | **POOL** |
| resort near Venice | **LIDO** |
| resort of New Mexico | **TAOS** |
| resound | **ECHO, PEAL,** |
| | **REVERBERATE** |
| resound vibrantly | **TRILL** |
| resource | **ASSET** |
| resourceful | **SHARP** |
| resources | **MEANS** |
| respect | **ESTEEM, HONOR,** |
| | **REGARD** |
| respectable | **DECENT** |
| respectful title | **SIR** |
| respective | **INDIVIDUAL** |
| respiratory organ | **LUNG** |
| respire | **BREATHE** |
| respite | **LETUP, REST, LULL,** |
| | **POSTPONEMENT** |
| resplendent | **RADIANT,** |
| | **SPLENDID** |
| respond | **REACT, ANSWER** |
| response | **REPLY** |

responsibility **ONUS**
responsible **RELIABLE, LIABLE**
rest **PAUSE, RELAX, REPOSE, REMAINDER**
restaurant **CAFE, DINER**
restaurant bill **CHECK, TAB**
restaurant employee **WAITER, WAITRESS, COOK, BUSBOY, HEADWAITER**
restful **SERENE, SOOTHING**
resting **ABED, DORMANT**
restitution **REPARATION**
restive **FIDGETY, UNEASY, IMPATIENT, EDGY**
restless **NERVOUS, ANXIOUS**
rest on the knees **KNEEL**
restore **RENEW, RENOVATE**
restore confidence to **REASSURE**
restore to health **HEAL, CURE**
restrain **LEASH, REIN, HOLD BACK, CHECK, REPRESS**
restraint **CONTROL**
restrained in actions **RESERVED**
restrict **LIMIT**
restyle **REDO, REMODEL**
result of rainy weather **MUD**
result of supply and demand **PRICE**
resumé **SUMMARY**
resurface **RETOP**
resurface a building **FACE**
resuscitate **REVIVE**
ret **SOAK**
retail shop **STORE, BOUTIQUE**
retain **KEEP, HOLD**
retainer **FEE**
retaining wall **REVETMENT**
retaliate **AVENGE, REVENGE, PAY BACK**
retard **SLACKEN, SLOW**
rete **NETWORK**
retention **MEMORY**
reticent **TACITURN**
retinue **ENTOURAGE**
retired **ABED**
retirement allotment **PENSION**
retiring **SHY, MODEST, TIMID**
retort **RIPOSTE, REPARTEE**
retract **RECANT, TAKE BACK**
retreaded tire **RECAP**
retreat **DEN, LAIR**
retrieve **RECOVER**
retriever **DOG**
retribution **REPRISAL, REVENGE**
return **REVERT, COME BACK**

return a loan **REPAY**
return an argument **RETORT**
return like for like **RETALIATE**
reveal **DIVULGE, DISCLOSE**
reveler **MERRYMAKER**
reveler's cry **EVOE**
revelry **RIOT**
revenant **GHOST, PHANTOM**
revenge **RETALIATE**
revengeful **VINDICTIVE**
revenue **INCOME**
revenue (Fr.) **RENTE**
reverberant **RESONANT**
reverberate **ECHO, RESOUND**
revere **VENERATE, WORSHIP**
reverence **AWE, RESPECT**
reverent fear **AWE**
reverential regard **HOMAGE**
reverie **FANTASY, DREAM**
reversal **HINDRANCE, SNAG**
reverse **CONTRARY, OPPOSITE**
revert **RETURN, REGRESS**
review **GO OVER, RECAP**
revise **EDIT, EMEND, CHANGE**
revive **WAKE, FRESHEN**
revoke a law **REPEAL**
revoke at cards **RENEGE**
revolt **ARISE, REBEL, RISE UP**
revolting **OFFENSIVE**
revolution **ROTATION, REBELLION, UPRISING**
revolutionary **RED, REBEL**
revolutions per minute (abbr.) **RPM**
revolve **ROTATE, TURN, SPIN**
revolver **PISTOL, GUN**
revolving **ROTARY**
revolving machine part **CAM**
revolving storm **TORNADO, CYCLONE**
revulsion **AVERSION**
reward **BONUS, RECOMPENSE**
rewarding **BENEFICIAL**
rhea **EMU**
Rhine nymph **LORELEI**
Rhine tributary **RUHR**
Rhine wine **MOSELLE**
Rhone tributary **YSER**
rhumba country **CUBA**
rhythm **BEAT, TEMPO, METER, CADENCE**
rhythmic **POETIC**
rhythmical beating **PULSE**
rhythmic movement **LILT**
rhythm instrument **DRUM**
ria **INLET**
Rialto **BROADWAY**
Rialto sign **S.R.O.**

| | |
|---|---|
| riata | LARIAT, LASSO |
| rib | BONE, TEASE |
| ribbed fabric | REP |
| ribbon | BOW, FILLET |
| ribbonlike flag | STREAMER |
| ricebird | BOBOLINK |
| rice field | PADDY |
| rich | WEALTHY, OPULENT |
| rich cake | TORTE |
| rich in ideas | MEATY |
| richly ornate | PLUSHY |
| rich milk | CREAM |
| rich soil | LOAM |
| rich tapestry | ARRAS |
| rickety car or truck | JALOPY, RATTLETRAP |
| ricochet | CAROM, REBOUND |
| rid | DISENCUMBER, FREE |
| riddle | ENIGMA |
| ride a bike | PEDAL |
| rider | PASSENGER, TRAVELER |
| Rider Haggard novel | SHE |
| ride shank's mare | WALK |
| ride-sharing plan (2 wds.) | CAR POOL |
| ride to hounds | HUNT |
| ridge | CREST |
| ridge of rock near water | REEF |
| ridge of sand | DUNE |
| ridicule | DERIDE, MOCK, TAUNT, TWIT |
| ridiculous | LUDICROUS, ABSURD |
| ridiculous failure | FIASCO |
| riding costume | HABIT |
| riding crop | WHIP |
| riding exhibition | RODEO |
| riding horse | STEED |
| riding shoe | BOOT |
| riding stick | CROP |
| riding whip | CROP, QUIRT |
| rife | PREVALENT |
| rifle | GUN, SHOTGUN |
| rifle noise | SHOT |
| rift | SPLIT |
| rig | OUTFIT |
| right | FAIR, JUST, CORRECT |
| righteous | VIRTUOUS, PURE |
| righteously angry | INDIGNANT |
| rightfully | DULY |
| right-hand page | RECTO |
| right of legal ownership | TITLE |
| right or left part of the body | SIDE |
| right to choose | OPTION |
| rigid | TENSE, UNYIELDING |
| rigor | HARDSHIP |
| rigorous | SEVERE, STRICT |

| | |
|---|---|
| rile | ANNOY, IRRITATE, ANGER |
| rill | STREAM, BROOK, RIVULET |
| rim | BORDER, EDGE, LIP |
| rime | HOAR, HOARFROST, ICE |
| rimose | CRACKED |
| rind | PEEL, PEELING, SKIN |
| ring | HOOP, CIRCLET, PEAL, TOLL |
| ring a bell | REMIND |
| ringed boa | ABOMA |
| ringed planet | SATURN |
| ringed worm | ANNELID |
| ringing device | BELL |
| ringing sound | PLINK, TINKLE, DING, DONG |
| ringlet | CURL, TENDRIL, TRESS |
| ring of light | HALO, NIMBUS |
| ring slowly | TOLL |
| rinky-dink | CHEAP, SHODDY |
| rinse | WASH |
| rinsing | DREGS |
| Rio's beach | COPACABANA |
| riot | MELEE, PANDEMONIUM, TUMULT |
| rip | TEAR, REND |
| ripe | MATURE, MELLOW |
| ripen | AGE, MATURE |
| riposte | REPARTEE, RETORT |
| ripped | TORE, TORN |
| ripple | WAVE |
| rise | ASCEND, CLIMB, STAND, SOAR, ELEVATE |
| rise and fall | HEAVE, TIDE |
| rise up | REBEL |
| risible | FUNNY |
| risky | CHANCY, PERILOUS |
| risque | BLUE, NAUGHTY |
| rissole | MEATBALL |
| rite | CEREMONY, RITUAL |
| ritual | RITE, LITURGY |
| ritzy | SWANK |
| rivage | BANK, SHORE |
| rival | COMPETE, COMPETITOR |
| rive | SPLIT |
| river | STREAM |
| river (Sp.) | RIO |
| river arm | ESTUARY |
| river bank | RIPA |
| river barrier | DAM |
| river bed | CHANNEL |
| river boat | BARGE, FERRY |
| river bottom | BED |
| river bottom land | HOLM |
| river crossed by Caesar | RUBICON |
| river crossing | FORD |
| river deposit | DELTA |
| river dragon | CROCODILE |

| | | | |
|---|---|---|---|
| river duck | **TEAL** | river in the Netherlands | **LEX,** |
| river embankment | **LEVEE** | | **AMSTEL** |
| river fish | **SHAD, TROUT,** | river in the Southwest | **PECOS** |
| | **SALMON** | river into the Bay of Biscay | |
| river freighter | **SCOW** | | **LOIRE** |
| river in Africa | **CONGO, NIGER,** | river in Turkey | **ARAS** |
| | **NILE, VELE** | river in Tuscany | **ARNO** |
| river in Alaska | **YUKON** | river in Wales and | |
| river in Arizona | **GILA** | England | **WYE** |
| river in Australia | **SWAN** | river in Yorkshire | **LEEDS, AIRE** |
| river in Austria | **ENNS** | river island | **AIT** |
| river in Bavaria | **ISAR, NAAB** | river mouth formation | **DELTA** |
| river in Belgium | **LYS** | river nymph | **NAIS** |
| river in Bohemia | **ELBE** | river passage | **FORD** |
| river in China | **TARIM, YALU** | river rat | **THIEF** |
| river in Egypt | **NILE** | river sediment | **SILT** |
| river in England | **AVON, TRENT,** | riverside | **BANK** |
| | **THAMES, TEES** | river siren | **LORELEI** |
| river in Ethiopia | **ABBAI** | river through Burgundy | **SAONE** |
| river in Europe | **DANUBE,** | rivet | **BOLT, PIN** |
| | **SAAR, ODER, YSER,** | riviere | **NECKLACE** |
| | **RHINE, RHONE, AAR** | rivulet | **BROOK, STREAM** |
| river in Flanders | **YSER** | road | **PIKE, ROUTE, HIGHWAY,** |
| river in France | **SEINE, ORNE,** | | **AVENUE, STREET,** |
| | **EURE, LOIRE** | | **BOULEVARD, LANE** |
| river in Germany | **ELBE, RHINE,** | road closed at one end | |
| | **RUHR, ODER, WESER** | (2 wds.) | **BLIND ALLEY,** |
| river in Greece | **ARTA** | | **DEAD END** |
| river in Hades | **STYX** | roadhouse | **TAVERN, INN** |
| river in Hungary | **RAAB** | roadrunner | **CUCKOO** |
| river in India | **INDUS, GANGES** | roadside eatery | **DINER** |
| river in Ireland | **ERNE, BANN** | roadside hotel | **MOTEL** |
| river in Italy | **ARNO, TIBER, PO** | roadster | **CAR** |
| river in Kansas | **OSAGE** | road-surfacing material | |
| river inlet | **RIA** | | **BLACKTOP** |
| river in Nebraska | **PLATTE** | roam | **ROVE, WANDER** |
| river in Nigeria | **BENIN** | roam about idly | **GAD** |
| river in Normandy | **ORNE** | roan | **HORSE** |
| river in Norway | **TANA** | roar | **BELLOW, HOLLER** |
| river in Oregon | **KLAMATH** | roast | **BAKE** |
| river in Poland | **WARTA,** | roasting chamber | **OVEN** |
| | **NAREV(W)** | roasting ear | **CORN** |
| river in Romania | **SIRET** | roasting stick | **SPIT** |
| river in Rome | **TIBER** | roast on a spit | **BARBECUE** |
| river in Russia | **URAL, OKA,** | roast over a fire | **PARCH** |
| | **NEVA** | rob | **PILLAGE, STEAL, THIEVE** |
| river in Scotland | **DEE, AYR** | robalo | **SNOOK** |
| river in South Africa | **VAAL** | robber | **STEALER, BURGLAR,** |
| river in South America | **APA,** | | **THIEF, FELON** |
| | **AMAZON, PLATA** | robe | **HOUSECOAT, DUSTER,** |
| river in South Carolina | **EDISTO,** | | **WRAPPER, TOGA** |
| | **SANTEE** | robin | **BIRD** |
| river in Spain | **EBRO** | Robin Goodfellow | **PUCK** |
| river in Sweden | **UME, LULE** | Robinson Crusoe's man | |
| river in Switzerland | **AAR** | | **FRIDAY** |
| river in Texas | **NUECES, RED,** | roble | **OAK** |
| | **PECOS** | robot | **AUTOMATON** |
| river in the Congo | **UELE** | robust | **HALE, LUSTY** |

| | |
|---|---|
| rocambole | **ONION, LEEK** |
| rock | **STONE, PEBBLE,** |
| | **BOULDER** |
| rocket fuel | **LOX** |
| rock growth | **MOSS** |
| rock hawk | **FALCON** |
| rocking bed | **CRADLE** |
| rock lobster | **CRAYFISH** |
| rock moss | **LICHEN** |
| rock salt | **HALITE** |
| rocky crag | **TOR** |
| Rocky Mountain park | **ESTES** |
| Rocky Mountain range | **TETON** |
| Rocky Mountain sheep | |
| | **BIGHORN** |
| rococo | **FLORID, ORNATE** |
| rod | **FISHING POLE, FERULE** |
| rodent | **RAT, RABBIT, MOUSE,** |
| | **VOLE** |
| rodeo | **ROUNDUP** |
| roe | **CAVIAR** |
| Roger Moore role | **SAINT** |
| rogue | **RASCAL, SCAMP** |
| roil | **ANNOY, DISTURB** |
| role | **PART, FUNCTION** |
| roll | **BUN, TURNOVER,** |
| | **LIST, ROSTER** |
| rollaway | **BED** |
| roll call answer | **HERE,** |
| | **PRESENT** |
| roller | **WAVE, CURLER** |
| rollick | **ROMP** |
| roll of butter | **PAT** |
| roll of cloth | **BOLT** |
| roll of hair | **RAT, CHIGNON** |
| roll of meat | **RISSOLE** |
| roll of parchment | **SCROLL** |
| roll of postage stamps | **COIL** |
| roll of tobacco | **CIGAR** |
| roll tightly | **FURL** |
| roll up a flag | **FURL** |
| roly-poly | **CHUBBY, PLUMP** |
| romaine | **COS** |
| Roman | **ITALIAN, LATIN** |
| Roman bishop | **POPE** |
| Roman bronze | **AES** |
| romance | **NOVEL, FICTION** |
| Roman comedy writer | |
| | **TERENCE** |
| Roman date | **IDES** |
| Roman deity | **VENUS, MARS,** |
| **DIANA, MINERVA, JOVE,** | |
| **AURORA, BACCHUS,** | |
| **CERES, CUPID, FAUN,** | |
| **APOLLO, JUNO, JUPITER,** | |
| **MERCURY, JANUS,** | |
| **NEPTUNE, VULCAN, DIS,** | |
| **LUNA, AMOR, NONA** | |

| | |
|---|---|
| Roman emperor | **NERO** |
| Roman entrance hall | **ATRIUM** |
| Roman fates | **PARCAE** |
| Roman galley | **TRIREME** |
| Roman goddess of plenty | **OPS** |
| Roman hearth goddess | **VESTA** |
| Roman highway | **ITER** |
| Roman historian | **LIVY** |
| Roman household gods | **LARES,** |
| | **PENATES** |
| Roman judge | **(A)EDILE** |
| Roman matron's wear | **STOLA** |
| Roman orator | **CICERO** |
| Roman patriot | **CATO** |
| Roman philosopher | **SENECA** |
| Roman poet | **OVID, VIRGIL** |
| Roman prelate | **POPE** |
| Roman river | **TIBER** |
| Roman road | **ITER** |
| Roman robe | **TOGA** |
| Roman shoe | **SANDAL** |
| Roman statesman | **CATO** |
| romantic exploit | **GEST** |
| romantic flower | **ROSE** |
| Roman tyrant | **NERO** |
| Roman underworld god | **PLUTO** |
| Romany | **GYPSY** |
| Romeo | **LOVER** |
| romp | **PLAY, GAMBOL, CAVORT** |
| Romulus' brother | **REMUS** |
| rood | **CROSS** |
| roof | **GABLE** |
| roof beam | **RAFTER** |
| roof edge | **EAVE** |
| roofing liquid | **TAR** |
| roofing material | **TILE, SLATE,** |
| | **SHINGLE, ASBESTOS** |
| roof of the mouth | **PALATE** |
| roof overhang | **EAVE** |
| rook | **CASTLE, CROW** |
| rookie | **TYRO, NOVICE** |
| rook's cry | **CAW** |
| room | **CHAMBER, SPACE** |
| room entrance | **DOOR** |
| roomer | **LODGER** |
| room in a tower | **BELFRY** |
| room of the Last Supper | |
| | **CENACLE** |
| room shape | **ELL** |
| room side | **WALL** |
| room to move | **LEEWAY** |
| roomy | **SPACIOUS** |
| roost | **PERCH** |
| rooster | **COCK** |
| rooster's mate | **HEN** |
| rooster's pride | **COMB** |
| root | **RADIX, TUBER** |
| rootstock | **TARO** |

root vegetable **BEET, RADISH, CARROT, POTATO, TURNIP, PARSNIP**
rope **LASSO, LINE, RIATA, REATA, CORD**
rope connection **KNOT**
rope fiber **HEMP**
rope loop **NOOSE, BIGHT**
rope of flowers **GARLAND, LEI**
rope of onions **REEVE**
rope to limit animal's range **TETHER**
Rorschach **INKBLOT**
rosary bead **AVE**
roselike flower **CAMELLIA**
rose noble **RYAL**
rose oil **ATTAR**
roster **LIST, ROTA, ROLL**
rosy **BLUSHING, RED, CRIMSON**
rot **DECAY, SPOIL**
rota **COURT, ROSTER**
rotary motor **TURBINE**
rotate **SPIN, TWIRL, REVOLVE, TURN, WHIRL**
rotating machine **DYNAMO**
rotating machine part **ROTOR**
rotating piece **CAM**
rote **REPETITION, ROUTINE**
rotisserie skewer **SPIT**
rotund **ROUND, STOUT**
roue **RAKE**
rough **UNEVEN**
rough drawing **SKETCH**
rough hair **SHAG**
rough tire surface **TREAD**
round **CIRCULAR**
roundabout course **DETOUR**
rounded lump **NODULE, NODE**
rounded roof **DOME, CUPOLA**
round of applause **HAND**
round platter **DISC**
Round Table knight **GALAHAD, LANCELOT**
roundup **RODEO**
roundworm **NEMATODE**
rouse from sleep **AWAKE, WAKE, AWAKEN, WAKEN**
rouse to action **BESTIR**
rout **SCATTER, CONQUER**
route **HIGHWAY, ROAD, WAY**
route used by planes (2 wds.) **AIR LANE**
routine **ROTE**
routine job **CHORE**
rove **ROAM, WANDER**
rover's friend **FIDO, MAN**

row **LINE, TIER, LAYER, OAR, PADDLE**
rowboat pin **THOLE**
rowdy **HOODLUM**
rowel **SPUR**
rowing blade **OAR, PADDLE**
royal **REGAL, KINGLY, PRINCELY**
royal headdress **TIARA,**
royal mace **CORONET, CROWN**
royal mace **SCEPTRE**
royal order **EDICT, DECREE**
royal purple **CRIMSON**
royal residence **PALACE, CASTLE**
Royal Scottish Academy (abbr.) **R.S.A.**
rozzer **POLICEMAN, COP**
rub **MASSAGE, STROKE, ERASER**
rubber band **ELASTIC**
ruber city **AKRON**
rubber hoop **TIRE**
rubber overshoe **ARCTIC**
rubber rug **MAT**
rubber-soled shoe **SNEAKER**
rubber tree **ULE**
rubber tubing **HOSE**
rubbish **LITTER, TRASH, GARBAGE**
rubble **DEBRIS**
rubdown artist **MASSEUR**
rube **HICK, RUSTIC**
rubella **MEASLES**
rubicund **ROSY**
rub out **ERASE**
rubric **HEADING, TITLE**
rub the wrong way **IRRITATE**
rub together **GRATE**
ruby type **AGATE**
ruche **LACE**
ruckus **TO-DO**
ruddy **RED, REDDISH**
rude **DISCOURTEOUS, IMPOLITE, CURT**
rude cabin **HOVEL, HUT, SHACK**
rude person **BOOR**
rudimental **ELEMENTARY, INITIAL**
rue **REGRET**
rueful **DISMAL, SAD**
ruffed grouse **PARTRIDGE, PHEASANT**
ruffian **THUG, RASCAL**
ruffle **FRILL**
rug **MAT, CARPET**
Rugby's river **AVON**

| | |
|---|---|
| rug fuzz | **LINT** |
| rugged | **ROBUST, ROUGH** |
| rugged guy (comp. wd.) | **HE-MAN** |
| rugged rock | **TOR** |
| rug surface | **NAP** |
| ruin | **DESTROY, SPOIL** |
| ruinous | **FATAL** |
| rule | **GOVERN, REIGN, LAW, REGULATION** |
| rule out | **EXCLUDE** |
| ruler | **SOVEREIGN, GOVERNOR, KING** |
| Rumanian city | **BUCHAREST** |
| rumble | **THUNDER** |
| rumen | **CUD** |
| ruminant mammal | **DEER, COW** |
| ruminate | **REFLECT, PONDER** |
| rumor | **REPORT** |
| rumple | **WRINKLE, CRINKLE** |
| run | **LOPE, GALLOP, TROT, FLOW, HIE, HASTEN, HURRY, SCURRY** |
| run after | **CHASE, PURSUE** |
| run aground | **FOUNDER** |
| run along | **LEAVE, DEPART** |
| run away | **FLEE, DECAMP, ESCAPE** |
| run away to marry | **ELOPE** |
| run before the wind | **SCUD** |
| run-down | **SUMMARY** |
| rune | **MYSTERY, SECRET** |
| run-in | **QUARREL, FIGHT** |
| run in haste | **SCUTTLE** |
| run into | **MEET** |
| run machinery | **OPERATE** |
| runner | **RACER** |
| runnered vehicle | **SLED** |
| runner-up | **LOSER** |
| run off the track | **DERAIL** |
| run out | **ELAPSE, EXHAUST** |
| run out on | **ABANDON, DESERT** |
| run swiftly, as water | **FLOW** |
| runt | **DWARF** |
| runway | **RAMP** |
| rupture | **BURST, BREAK** |
| rural | **PASTORAL** |
| rural backcountry (sl.) | **BOONDOCKS** |
| rural restaurant | **INN** |
| ruse | **STRATAGEM, TRICK** |
| rush | **SURGE** |
| rush hour | **PEAK** |
| rush hour at the diner | **NOON** |
| rusk of wheat grains | **BRAN** |
| russet | **APPLE** |
| Russian beer | **KVASS** |

| | |
|---|---|
| Russian beet dish | **BORSCH, BORSCHT** |
| Russian citadel | **KREMLIN** |
| Russian city | **OREL, MOSCOW** |
| Russian community | **MIR** |
| Russian co-op | **ARTEL** |
| Russian desert | **TUNDRA** |
| Russian edict | **UKASE** |
| Russian emperor | **TSAR, CZAR, TZAR** |
| Russian fighter plane | **MIG** |
| Russian hemp | **RINE** |
| Russian inland sea | **ARAL** |
| Russian lake | **ARAL, ONEGA** |
| Russian log hut | **ISBA** |
| Russian monetary unit | **RUBLE** |
| Russian monk | **RASPUTIN** |
| Russian mountains | **URALS** |
| Russian news agency | **TASS** |
| Russian novelist Turgenev | **IVAN** |
| Russian peninsula | **CRIMEA** |
| Russian plain | **STEPPES** |
| Russian river | **NEVA, URAL** |
| Russian ruler | **TSAR, TZAR, CZAR** |
| Russian satellite | **SPUTNIK** |
| Russian sea | **ARAL** |
| Russian secret police | **N.K.V.D., O.G.P.U.** |
| Russian tea urn | **SAMOVAR** |
| Russian trade union | **ARTEL** |
| Russian turnip | **RUTABAGA** |
| Russian veto word | **NIET, NYET** |
| Russian village | **MIR** |
| Russian wolfhound | **BORZOI** |
| rustable metal | **IRON** |
| rustic | **PEASANT, RURAL** |
| rustic retreat | **BOWER** |
| rustic step | **STILE** |
| rustic vehicle | **CART** |
| rustle | **SWISH** |
| rut | **FURROW, GROOVE** |
| rutabaga | **TURNIP** |
| ruthenium (chem. symbol) | **RU** |
| ruthless | **BRUTAL, CRUEL** |
| Ruth's husband | **BOAZ** |
| ruttish | **LUSTFUL** |
| rye fungus | **ERGOT** |

**S**

| | |
|---|---|
| sabbath | **SATURDAY, SUNDAY** |
| sabbatical | **REST, LEAVE** |
| saber | **SWORD** |
| sable | **FUR** |
| sabot | **SHOE** |

| | |
|---|---|
| sabotage | DESTROY |
| sabra | ISRAELI, CACTUS |
| sac | BURSA, POUCH |
| saccharine | SWEET |
| sachet | POUCH |
| sack | BAG, POKE, PILLAGE, LOOT |
| sack material | GUNNY |
| sacrament | RITE |
| sacred | HOLY, HALLOW |
| sacred bird of the Nile | IBIS |
| sacred book | BIBLE, KORAN, TALMUD, TORAH |
| sacred Egyptian beetle | SCARAB |
| sacred Egyptian bull | APIS |
| sacred flower of India | LOTUS |
| sacred fruit | LOTUS |
| sacred hymn | CHORALE |
| sacred image | ICON |
| sacred memento | RELIC |
| sacred song | MOTET, HYMN, CANTATA |
| sacrifice | OFFERING |
| sacrilegious | IMPIOUS, PROFANE |
| sacristy | VESTRY |
| sad | DOWNCAST, SORROWFUL, UNHAPPY, BLUE |
| saddleback | HILL, RIDGE |
| saddlebag | PANNIER |
| saddle for an elephant | HOWDAH |
| sad-faced hound | BASSET |
| safari | HUNT, TREK, JOURNEY |
| safe | SECURE, VAULT |
| safecracker | YEGG |
| safe from harm | SECURE |
| safe harbor | HAVEN |
| safekeeping | STORAGE |
| safety | SECURITY, REFUGE |
| saffron | YELLOW, ORANGE |
| saffron plant | CROCUS |
| sag | DROOP, WILT |
| saga | TALE, EPIC, EDDA, STORY |
| sagacious | WISE |
| sage | HERB, WISE |
| Sagebrush State | NEVADA |
| sage hen | GROUSE |
| sago | STARCH |
| saguaro | CACTUS |
| Sahara | DESERT |
| said further | ADDED |
| said positively | DECLARED |
| sail | NAVIGATE, JIB, MAIN |
| sail against the wind | TACK |
| sailcloth | CANVAS |

| | |
|---|---|
| sail fast | SCUD |
| sailing | ASEA |
| sailing vessel | BARK, BOAT, SHIP, SLOOP, SCHOONER, YACHT, YAWL |
| sailor | TAR, GOB, SEA DOG, SEAMAN, SALT |
| sailor's command | AVAST |
| sailor's holiday (2 wds.) | SHORE LEAVE |
| sailor's jacket | REEFER, PEA |
| sailor's mop | SWAB |
| sailor's patron saint | ELMO |
| sailor's song | CHANTY |
| sailplane | GLIDER |
| sail rope | SHEET |
| sails, to sailors | SHEETS |
| sail upward | SOAR |
| sainte (abbr.) | STE. |
| saint's tomb | SHRINE |
| Saint Vitus' dance | CHOREA |
| salacious | LEWD |
| salad fish | TUNA, SALMON, SHRIMP, HERRING, LOBSTER |
| salad green | CRESS, LETTUCE, ENDIVE, ESCAROLE, CHICORY WATERCRESS |
| salad ingredient | RADISH, TOMATO, LETTUCE, CUCUMBER, AVOCADO, ONION, SCALLION, WATERCRESS, CABBAGE |
| salamander | EFT, NEWT |
| salary | PAY, WAGE |
| salary increase | RAISE |
| sale | AUCTION |
| sales figure, before deductions | GROSS |
| sales representative | AGENT |
| salient | PROMINENT |
| salient point | FEATURE |
| saline | SALTY |
| saline drop | TEAR |
| saline solution | BRINE |
| sally of troops | SORTIE |
| saloon | BAR, TAVERN, PUB |
| salt | SEASONING, SAILOR |
| salt away | SAVE |
| saltine | CRACKER |
| salt lake | SALINE |
| salt marsh | SALINE |
| saltpeter | NITER |
| salt water | BRINE |
| salty | SALINE |
| salud | TOAST |
| salutary | HEALTHFUL |

| | | | |
|---|---|---|---|
| salutation | AVE, GREETING, HELLO | sardonic | DERISIVE, BITTER |
| salvage | SAVE | sash | BELT, OBI, WAISTBAND, CUMMERBUND |
| salve | ANOINT, BALM | sassy | IMPUDENT |
| salver | TRAY | Satan | DEVIL |
| salvo | BURST | satanic | EVIL, VILE |
| Samantha or Endora | WITCH | Satan's domain | HELL, INFERNO |
| same | IDENTICAL, LIKE | satchel | VALISE |
| same (Fr.) | MEME | sate | GLUT, FILL |
| same thing | ILK | satellite | MOON |
| Samoan bird | IAO | satellite of Uranus | ARIEL |
| Samoan city | APIA | satiate | CLOY, FILL, SATE |
| Samoan seaport | APIA | satire | RIDICULE, BURLESQUE |
| samovar | URN | satisfaction | CONTENTMENT |
| Samoyed | SIBERIAN, HUSKY | satisfactory | OK |
| samp | PORRIDGE, MUSH | satisfy | SATE, SATIATE, GLUT |
| samphire | GLASSWORT | Saturn | PLANET |
| sample | TASTE, TRY | Saturn's wife | OPS |
| Samuel's teacher | ELI | satyr | FAUN |
| sanctify | BLESS | sauce | ALEC, GRAVY |
| sanction | ABET, ENDORSE | saucepan | POT |
| sanctuary | HAVEN, REFUGE | saucer of a kind | COASTER |
| sanctum | RETREAT | saucer-shaped bell | GONG |
| sand | GRIT | saucer's mate | CUP |
| sandal | SHOE | saucy | PERT |
| Sandalwood island | SUMBA | saucy girl | MINX |
| sandarac tree | ARAR | sauerkraut | CABBAGE |
| sand hill | DUNE, DENE | Saul of Tarsus | PAUL |
| sand lizard | ADDA | sauna | BATH |
| sandpiper | REE, RUFF, TEREK | saunter | AMBLE |
| sand trap | HAZARD | saurian | LIZARD |
| Sandwich Islands | HAWAII | saute | FRY, BROWN |
| sandwich meat | HAM, PORK, BOLOGNA, BEEF, SPAM, SALAMI, CHICKEN | savage | FERAL |
| | | savage island | NIUE |
| sandy region | DESERT, SHORE, BEACH | savannah | PLAIN |
| | | savant | SCHOLAR |
| sane | RATIONAL, SENSIBLE, SOUND | save | RESCUE, ECONOMIZE, SALVAGE, SALT AWAY |
| sanguine | CONFIDENT | savine | JUNIPER |
| sanitary | HYGENIC | savior | REDEEMER |
| sanity | REASON | savoir-faire | TACT, POISE |
| Sanskrit dialect | PALI | savor | TASTE |
| Santa's sound | HO | savory | PIQUANT |
| sap | DRAIN, EXHAUST | savory dish | RELISH |
| sapajou | CAPUCHIN | savvy | SKILL |
| sapid | PALATABLE | saw | ADAGE, MAXIM |
| sapient | WISE | sawbones | DOCTOR, SURGEON |
| sapling | TREE | sawbuck | TEN |
| sapor | TASTE | sawfish's snout | SERRA |
| Saracen | ARAB, MOSLEM | sawing frame | HORSE |
| Sarah's original name | SARAI | saw lengthwise | RIP |
| Saratoga | SPA | saw-toothed | SERRATE |
| Sarazen | GENE | saxhorn | TUBA |
| sarcasm | IRONY | Saxon serf | ESNE |
| sarcastic | IRONIC, FACETIOUS | say | SPEAK, DECLARE |
| sarcastic grin | SNEER | say again | REPEAT, REITERATE |
| sarcastic remark | TAUNT | say casually | REMARK |

| | | | |
|---|---|---|---|
| say further | ADD | scenic | PICTURESQUE |
| saying | BYWORD, QUOTE | scenic river | RHINE |
| scab | STRIKEBREAKER | scenic view | SCAPE |
| scabbard | HOLSTER, SHEATH | scent | AROMA, ODOR, SMELL, |
| scalawag | RASCAL, SCAMP | | PERFUME, BOUQUET, |
| scale | CLIMB | | SPOOR |
| scale note | DO, RE, MI, FA, | scented bag | SACHET |
| | SO, LA, TI, SOL | scepter | STAFF, BATON |
| scallion | SHALLOT, LEEK | schedule | SCROLL, TIME, |
| scallop | BIVALVE, MOLLUSK | | LIST, AGENDA |
| scalpel | KNIFE | scheme | PLAN, PLOT |
| scaly anteater | PANGOLIN | schism | SPLIT |
| scamp | RASCAL, SCALAWAG, | schnitzel | CUTLET |
| | ROGUE, IMP | scholar | SAVANT, STUDENT |
| scampi | PRAWNS, SHRIMP | scholarly | ACADEMIC, ERUDITE |
| scan | READ, SCRUTINIZE | school | EDUCATE, TEACH, |
| scandal | DISGRACE, SLANDER | | COLLEGE |
| scandalize | SHOCK | school assignment | LESSON, |
| Scandinavian | LAPP, NORSE, | | HOMEWORK |
| | FINN, SWEDE, DANE | school book | PRIMER, READER, |
| Scandinavian capital | OSLO, | | SPELLER, TEXT |
| COPENHAGEN, HELSINKI, | | school cafeteria (2 wds.) | |
| | STOCKHOLM | | LUNCH ROOM |
| Scandinavian god | ODIN, THOR, | school composition | ESSAY, |
| WODEN, BALDER, FRIGGA, | | | THEME |
| LOKI, BRAGI, HEL, FREYA | | school (Fr.) | ECOLE, LYCEE |
| Scandinavian literature | SAGAS | school group | CLASS |
| scanty | MEAGER | school intermission | RECESS |
| scapegoat (2 wds.) | FALL GUY | school mark | GRADE |
| scar | CICATRIX | schoolmaster | DOMINIE |
| scarab | BEETLE | school of modern art | DADA |
| scarce | RARE | school of seals | POD |
| scarcely | HARDLY | school organization (abbr.) | |
| scare | FRIGHTEN, ALARM | | P.T.A. |
| scared | AFRAID, FRIGHTENED | schoolroom item | CHALK, |
| scarf | NECKERCHIEF | | ERASER, SLATE |
| scarfskin | EPIDERMIS, CUTICLE | school semester | TERM |
| scarlet | RED | school sport | TRACK, |
| scarlet songbird | TANAGER | | FOOTBALL, SWIMMING |
| Scarlett O'Hara's home | TARA | school task | LESSON |
| scarp | CLIFF | school term | SEMESTER |
| scary | EERIE | schooner | SHIP, GLASS |
| scary word | BOO | science | ART |
| scat | BEGONE, SHOO | science-fiction | |
| scathing | CAUSTIC, | creature | ROBOT, |
| | SCORCHING | | MUTANT, MONSTER, |
| scatter | STREW | | ANDROID |
| scatter hay | TED | science-fiction topic | TIME, |
| scatter seeds | SOW | | FUTURE |
| scatter trash | LITTER | science of government | |
| scatter water | SPLASH | | POLITICS |
| scaup | DUCK | science of law | |
| scene | VISTA, VIEW | | JURISPRUDENCE |
| scene of action | ARENA | science of life | BIOLOGY |
| scene of great disorder | | science of reasoning | LOGIC |
| | SHAMBLES | scientific study of | |
| scene of the crime | VENUE | lawbreaking | CRIMINOLOGY |
| scenery | VIEW | scintillate | SPARKLE |

| | | | |
|---|---|---|---|
| scion | **SON, HEIR, DESCENDANT** | scow | **BARGE** |
| | | scowl | **GLOWER** |
| scissors | **SHEARS** | scrabble piece | **TILE** |
| scoff | **SNEER, JEER, DERIDE, GIBE** | scramble | **JUMBLE, RUSH** |
| | | scrambled eggs | **OMELET** |
| scold | **JAW, NAG, CHIDE, UPBRAID, BERATE, FLAY, RANT, RAIL** | scrap | **FRAGMENT, ORT, SHRED** |
| | | scrape | **PREDICAMENT, SCRATCH** |
| scolding woman | **SHREW** | | |
| sconce | **BRACKET** | scraper | **STRIGIL** |
| scone | **CAKE** | scratch | **MAR, SCORE, SCRAPE, ABRADE** |
| scoop | **LADLE, SHOVEL** | | |
| scoop of ice cream | **DIP** | scratch out | **ERASE** |
| scoop out water | **BAIL** | scratch with nails | **CLAW** |
| scope | **RANGE** | scrawl | **SCRIBBLE** |
| scorch | **CHAR, SEAR, SINGE** | scrawny | **LANKY, SKINNY** |
| score | **TALLY, TWENTY** | scream | **SHRIEK, YELL** |
| score a victory | **WIN** | screech | **SHRIEK** |
| scoring play in football | **TOUCHDOWN** | screen | **MASK** |
| | | screen from light | **SHADE** |
| scoring point | **ACE, GOAL** | screen off | **SECLUDE** |
| scorn | **DESPISE** | scribble | **SCRAWL** |
| Scot | **GAEL** | scribble aimlessly | **DOODLE** |
| Scotch accent | **BIRR, BURR** | scribe | **PENMAN** |
| Scotch beret | **TAM** | scrimp | **ECONOMIZE, SAVE** |
| Scotch cake | **SCONE** | scrimshaw | **CARVE** |
| Scotch child | **BAIRN** | scriptural canticle | **ODE** |
| scotch cocktail (2 wds.) | **ROB ROY** | scroll | **LIST, ROLL** |
| | | Scrooge | **MISER** |
| Scotch cup | **TASS** | scrounge | **PILFER** |
| Scotch Gaelic | **ERSE** | scrub | **SCOUR** |
| Scotch hill | **BRAE** | scruff | **NAPE** |
| Scotch lake | **LOCH** | scruff hair | **MANE** |
| Scotch musical instrument | **BAGPIPE** | scrumptious | **DELICIOUS** |
| | | scruple | **QUALM** |
| Scotch plaid | **TARTAN** | scrutinize | **SCAN, EYE** |
| Scotch poet | **BURNS** | scuba man | **DIVER** |
| Scotch river | **DEE** | scud | **SKIM** |
| Scotch uncle | **EME** | scuffle | **TUSSLE, MELEE** |
| Scot's tiny | **WEE** | scull | **OAR** |
| Scottish biscuit | **SCONE** | sculpting plaster | **GESSO** |
| Scottish cap | **TAM** | sculptured piece | **BUST** |
| Scottish fabric | **TWEED** | scurry | **FLURRY, SCAMPER** |
| Scottish family | **CLAN** | sea | **OCEAN, CASPIAN, MEDITERRANEAN, RED, BLACK, DEAD** |
| Scottish Gaelic | **ERSE** | | |
| Scottish girl | **LASS** | | |
| Scottish heath | **MOOR** | sea (Fr.) | **MER** |
| Scottish highlander | **GAEL** | sea (Ger.) | **MEER** |
| Scottish hillside | **BRAE** | sea anemone | **POLYP** |
| Scottish island | **ARRAN** | sea bird | **ERN, ERNE, TERN, GULL, OSPREY** |
| Scottish landowner | **LAIRD** | | |
| Scottish skirt | **KILT** | sea biscuit | **HARDTACK** |
| scoundrel | **RASCAL, ROGUE** | sea bottom | **BED** |
| scour | **SCRUB** | sea calf | **SEAL** |
| scourge | **BANE** | seacoast | **SHORE** |
| scouring rush | **HORSETAIL** | sea cow | **DUGONG, MANATEE** |
| scout | **SPY** | sea dog | **SALT, TAR, GOB, SAILOR** |
| scouting group | **PATROL** | | |

| | | | |
|---|---|---|---|
| sea duck | **EIDER** | seaside | **SHORE, COAST** |
| sea eagle | **ERN, ERNE** | sea soldier | **MARINE** |
| sea eel | **CONGER** | season | **SALT** |
| seafaring man | **MARINER,** | seasonable | **TIMELY** |
| | **SAILOR** | seasonal song | **NOEL, CAROL** |
| sea food | **SHRIMP, LOBSTER,** | seasoned egg dish | |
| | **CLAM, CRAB, CRAYFISH,** | (2 wds.) | **SPANISH OMELET** |
| | **CRAWDAD, OYSTER** | seasoning | **CONDIMENT, SALT,** |
| sea god | **NEPTUNE** | | **PEPPER, SPICE, HERB,** |
| seagoing vessel | **LINER, SHIP** | | **MACE, SAGE, OREGANO,** |
| sea gull | **COB, MEW** | | **THYME, ROSEMARY,** |
| sea in Central Asia | **ARAL** | | **CHERVIL, TARRAGON,** |
| seal | **CLOSE, STAMP, SYMBOL** | | **MUSTARD, NUTMEG, DILL,** |
| sealant | **WAX** | | **GARLIC, CAYENNE,** |
| sea lettuce | **ALGA, ULVA** | | **PAPRIKA, CLOVE, BASIL,** |
| seal's limb | **FLIPPER** | | **BAY LEAF** |
| seam | **SUTURE, LINE** | season of fasting | **LENT** |
| sea mammal | **MANATEE,** | season of the year | **WINTER,** |
| | **WHALE, DOLPHIN, SEAL,** | | **SUMMER, SPRING,** |
| | **PORPOISE, GRAMPUS,** | | **AUTUMN, FALL** |
| | **ORC** | sea spray | **SPINDRIFT** |
| seaman | **MARINE, TAR, GOB,** | sea squirt | **ASCIDIAN** |
| | **SAILOR** | sea swallow | **TERN** |
| seaman's chapel | **BETHEL** | sea swell | **SURF** |
| sea mile | **NAUT** | seat | **BENCH, CHAIR** |
| sea monster | **SERPENT** | sea term | **AHOY, BELAY** |
| seamstress | **DRESSMAKER** | seat of justice | **BANC** |
| seamy | **SQUALID, SORDID** | sea unicorn | **NARWHAL** |
| seance sound | **RAP** | sea vessel | **STEAMER, TANKER** |
| sea nymph | **NEREID** | sea wall | **LEVEE** |
| sea onion | **SQUILL** | sea wave | **BREAKER** |
| seaport in Alaska | **NOME** | seaweed | **ALGA, ALGAE, KELP** |
| seaport in Algeria | **ORAN** | seaweed product | **IODINE** |
| seaport in Arabia | **ADEN** | seaweed substance | **AGAR** |
| seaport in Australia | **BRISBANE** | sea wolf | **PIRATE** |
| seaport in Bombay | **SURAT** | seaworthy | **STURDY** |
| seaport in Brazil | **RECIFE** | seckel | **PEAR** |
| seaport in Chile | **ARICA** | seclude | **SCREEN** |
| seaport in Italy | **GENOA,** | secluded | **ALOOF, APART** |
| | **NAPLES** | secluded valley | **GLEN, VALE,** |
| seaport in Oregon | **ASTORIA** | | **DALE** |
| seaport in Samoa | **APIA** | seclusion | **PRIVACY** |
| seaport in West Africa | **DAKAR** | second | **INSTANT, MOMENT,** |
| seaport of the Philippines | | | **MIN** |
| | **ILOILO** | secondary school | **PREP, HIGH** |
| sear | **SCORCH, SINGE, CHAR** | secondhand | **USED** |
| search | **HUNT, SEEK, PROBE** | second lieutenant (sl.) | |
| searchlight | **BEAM** | | **SHAVETAIL** |
| search out | **FERRET** | second-mentioned | **LATTER** |
| sea robber | **PIRATE,** | second of a series | **BETA** |
| | **BUCCANEER** | second of two | **OTHER** |
| sea's ebb and flow | **TIDE** | second order of angels | |
| sea shell | **CONCH** | | **CHERUB** |
| seashore | **COAST, BEACH** | second person | **YOU** |
| seashore attraction | **BEACH,** | second-placer (comp. wd.) | |
| | **SURF** | | **RUNNER-UP** |
| seashore bird | **GULL** | second selling | **RESALE** |
| seashore feature | **SAND** | secrecy | **PRIVACY** |

| | |
|---|---|
| secret | MYSTERY |
| secret agent | SPY |
| secretaire | DESK |
| secretary | AMANUENSIS, STENO |
| secretary's note | MEMO |
| secret Chinese society | TONG |
| secrete | HIDE |
| secreting organ | GLAND |
| secretive | SILENT |
| secret language | CODE |
| secret scheme | PLOT, CABAL |
| secret store | CACHE |
| sect | DENOMINATION |
| sectarian | PAROCHIAL |
| section | AREA, PART |
| sector | DISTRICT, SEGMENT |
| secular | LAIC |
| secure | SAFE |
| secure in place | ANCHOR |
| securing device | CLEVIS, VISE |
| securing pin | TOGGLE |
| security | GAGE, BOND |
| sedan | CAR, AUTO |
| sedate | DIGNIFIED, SOBER, STAID |
| sedative | SECONAL, SOOTHING |
| sedentary | FIXED, SEATED |
| seder | FEAST, ORDER |
| sediment | LEES, SILT |
| sedition | TREASON |
| seditious | INSURGENT, DISLOYAL |
| seduce | ENTICE, ABDUCT |
| seducer | SIREN |
| sedulous | BUSY |
| see | BISHOPRIC, ENVISION, OBSERVE, DISCERN, VISUALIZE, WITNESS, PERCEIVE, UNDERSTAND, ESPY |
| seecatch | SEAL |
| seed | GERM, GRAIN, OVULE, SOW |
| seed appendage | ARIL |
| seed container | POD |
| seed covering | ARIL, HULL, POD |
| seedless raisin | SULTANA |
| seedlet | SPORE |
| seedling | PLANT |
| seed of a mighty tree | ACORN |
| seed oysters | SPAT |
| seed planter | SOWER |
| seedpod | CARPEL, PISTIL |
| seed shrimp | OSTRACOD |
| seedsman | SOWER |
| seedy | SHABBY |

| | |
|---|---|
| seek | HUNT, SEARCH |
| seek ambitiously | ASPIRE |
| seeker of Moby Dick | AHAB |
| seek for by entreaty | SOLICIT |
| seel | CLOSE, BLIND |
| seem | APPEAR |
| seeming | APPARENT |
| seemingly | QUASI |
| seemly | PROPER, FAIR |
| seep | OOZE |
| seer | PROPHET |
| seeress | SIBYL |
| seesaw | TEETER |
| seethe | BOIL |
| segment | PART |
| segment of a curve | ARC |
| sego | LILY, BULB |
| segregate | ISOLATE, SEPARATE |
| seine | NET |
| seize | GRAB, NAB, GRIP, TAKE, GRASP |
| seize forcibly | USURP |
| seizure | ATTACK |
| seldom | RARELY |
| select | PICK OUT, CHOOSE, ELECT, OPT |
| select group | ELITE |
| selection | CHOICE |
| selective service | DRAFT |
| self | EGO |
| self-acting | AUTOMATIC |
| self-centered | EGOCENTRIC |
| self-confidence | POISE, APLOMB |
| self-esteem | PRIDE, EGO |
| self-evident | CLEAR |
| selfish individual | EGOIST |
| selfless | ALTRUISTIC |
| self-possession | POISE |
| self-reproach | REMORSE |
| self-righteous person | PRIG |
| selfsame | IDENTICAL |
| self-satisfied | SMUG |
| self-sufficient | INDEPENDENT |
| sell | VEND, RETAIL |
| sell direct to consumer | RETAIL |
| selling place | MARKET |
| sell out | BETRAY |
| semblance | LIKENESS |
| semester | TERM |
| semi-diameter | RADIUS |
| Seminole chief | OSCEOLA |
| semiprecious gem | OPAL, AGATE, GARNET |
| Semite | ARAB, JEW |
| Semitic deity | BAAL |
| Semitic language | ARAMAIC, HEBREW, ARABIC |

| | |
|---|---|
| semolina | **MEAL, FLOUR** |
| semper | **ALWAYS** |
| senate | **ASSEMBLY, COUNCIL** |
| senate attendant | **PAGE** |
| send | **TRANSMIT, DISPATCH, MAIL** |
| send a letter | **MAIL** |
| send away | **DISPATCH** |
| send back | **REMAND** |
| send flying | **ROUT** |
| send forth | **EMIT** |
| send into exile | **DEPORT** |
| send off | **MAIL, DISMISS** |
| send payment | **REMIT** |
| senile | **OLD, INFIRM** |
| senility | **DOTAGE** |
| senior | **ELDER, OLDER** |
| senorita's aunt | **TIA** |
| sensation | **SENSE, FEELING** |
| sensational | **LURID** |
| sense | **FEEL** |
| senseless | **INANE** |
| sense of sight | **VISION** |
| sense of taste | **PALATE** |
| sensible | **SANE** |
| sensitive | **TENDER** |
| sentence | **DECREE, JUDGMENT** |
| sententious | **CONCISE, TERSE** |
| sentimental person (colloq.) | **SOFTY** |
| sentinel | **GUARD** |
| separate | **PART, RIFT, APART, DIVIDE, DETACH** |
| separate article | **ITEM** |
| separate from | **ALOOF** |
| separate from others | **ISOLATE** |
| separate metal from ore | **SMELT** |
| sepia | **DUN, PIGMENT** |
| sept | **CLAN** |
| sequence of rulers | **DYNASTY** |
| sequestered | **SOLITARY** |
| sequoia | **TREE, REDWOOD** |
| seraglio | **HAREM** |
| Serb | **EUROPEAN, SLAV** |
| sere | **WITHERED** |
| serene | **CALM, PLACID, TRANQUIL** |
| serenity | **COMPOSURE** |
| serf | **ESNE, PEON** |
| serf of Sparta | **HELOT** |
| series | **SEQUENCE** |
| series of boat races | **REGATTA** |
| series of contests | **TOURNEY, TOURNAMENT** |
| series of happenings (3 wds.) | **CHAIN OF EVENTS** |
| series of heroic events | **EPOS** |

| | |
|---|---|
| series of names | **LIST, ROLL, ROSTER, ROTA** |
| series of propositions in logic | **SORTIES** |
| series of rooms | **SUITE** |
| series of steps | **STAIRS** |
| series of tones | **SCALE** |
| serin | **BIRD** |
| serious | **SOBER, SOLEMN** |
| seriousness | **GRAVITY** |
| sermon | **PREACH, DISCOURSE** |
| sermon giver | **PREACHER** |
| sermon topic | **TEXT** |
| serpent | **SNAKE, ASP** |
| serpentine | **SNAKY** |
| serpent's tooth | **FANG** |
| serrate | **NOTCHED** |
| serve as a lesson | **TEACH** |
| serve food | **CATER** |
| server | **TRAY** |
| serve tea | **POUR** |
| service charge | **FEE** |
| service station | **GARAGE** |
| servile | **MENIAL** |
| serving bowl | **TUREEN** |
| serving dish | **PLATTER** |
| serving spoon | **LADLE** |
| serving vessel | **TEAPOT, TRAY** |
| sesame plant | **TIL** |
| set | **CLIQUE, GEL, JELL, HARDEN, KIT** |
| seta | **BRISTLE** |
| set afloat | **LAUNCH** |
| set aside | **TABLE** |
| set at liberty | **FREE** |
| set back | **HINDER** |
| set fire to | **IGNITE, KINDLE** |
| set free | **RELEASE, BAIL OUT** |
| Seth's father | **ADAM** |
| Seth's son | **ENOS(H)** |
| set into motion | **ACTUATE** |
| set of actors | **CAST** |
| set of garments | **SUIT** |
| set of inquiries | **QUESTIONNAIRE** |
| set of matched furniture | **SUIT, SUITE** |
| set of organ pipes | **STOP** |
| set of principles | **CODE** |
| set of three | **TRIO** |
| set of tools | **KIT** |
| set of two | **DUAD, PAIR, DUO, COUPLE, DUET, BRACE** |
| set on fire | **IGNITE** |
| set out | **START** |
| setting | **LOCALE** |
| settle | **DECIDE, DETERMINE** |
| settle a bill | **PAY** |

| | | | |
|---|---|---|---|
| settle a question | DECIDE | Shakespearean king | LEAR, |
| settle by intercession | MEDIATE | | HENRY, RICHARD, JOHN |
| settled | SEDATE | Shakespearean poem | ODE, |
| settlement | COLONY | | SONNET |
| settlement in Greenland | ETAH, | Shakespearean sprite | ARIEL |
| | THULE | Shakespearean villain | IAGO |
| settler | PIONEER | Shakespeare's river | AVON |
| settlings | DREGS, SEDIMENT | Shakespeare's wife | ANNE |
| set-to | FIGHT | shake the tail | WAG |
| set up | ESTABLISH | shake up | JAR, SHOCK |
| setup | ARRANGEMENT | shaky | WOBBLY |
| set upon | ATTACK | shale | ROCK |
| seven days | WEEK | shallow | SUPERFICIAL |
| seventh day | SABBATH | shallow area | SHOAL |
| sever | CUT, SPLIT, DISUNITE | shallow dish | PLATE |
| several | VARIOUS, DIVERSE | shallow river crossing | FORD |
| severe | STERN, HARSH | shalom | GREETING, PEACE |
| severe experience | ORDEAL | sham | PRETEND, TRICK, FAKE, |
| severely | SHARPLY | | COUNTERFEIT, BOGUS |
| severe snowstorm | BLIZZARD | shamas | SEXTON |
| sew | BASTE, STITCH | shame | FIE, DISHONOR, |
| sewage | WASTE | | DISGRACE |
| sewing implement | NEEDLE, | shameless | BRAZEN |
| | DARNER | shamrock | CLOVER |
| sewing machine inventor | HOWE | Shandy's creator | STERNE |
| sew lightly | BASTE | Shangri-La | UTOPIA |
| sex | GENDER | shanty | HUT |
| sgt. | NCO | shape | FIGURE, FORM |
| shabby | SEEDY | shaped like an egg | OVATE, |
| shabby clothing | RAGS | | OVAL |
| shack | CABIN, HUT, HOVEL | shaped with an ax | HEWN |
| shackle | FETTER, CHAIN | shapeless | AMORPHIC |
| shade | COLOR, HUE, TINT, | shaping form | MOLD |
| | SHADOW, GHOST, | shard | FRAGMENT |
| | GOBLIN, SPOOK | share | PARTICIPATE, |
| shaded walk | ARBOR, MALL | | PORTION, PART |
| shade of difference | NUANCE | shark | GATA |
| shade of green | KELLY, OLIVE, | sharp | KEEN, ACUTE |
| | LEAF, PEA | sharp bark | YIP, YAP, YELP |
| shade of red | CORAL, CERISE, | sharp bite | NIP |
| | CRIMSON, SCARLET | sharp blow | SLAP |
| shade of tan | ECRU, BEIGE, | sharp disc on a plow | COLTER |
| | KHAKI | sharpen | HONE, WHET |
| shade tree | ASH, ELM, OAK, | sharp end | POINT |
| | ELDER | sharpener | EDGER, STROP |
| shadow | SHADE | sharp flavor | TANG |
| shadowbox | SPAR | sharp mountain ridge | ARETE |
| shady | DISHONEST, DEVIOUS | sharpness | EDGE |
| shaft | POLE | sharp of mind | KEEN |
| shag | NAP, PILE | sharp pain | STING |
| shaganappi | RAWHIDE | sharp pointed | ACUTE |
| shaggy | FURRY, UNKEMPT | sharp projection | BARB, JAG, |
| shah country | IRAN | | SNAG |
| shake | QUIVER, TREMBLE, | sharp rebuke | SLAP |
| | SHIVER, QUAKE | sharpshooter | MARKSMAN |
| shakedown | EXTORTION | sharp-sighted | ASTUTE |
| Shakespearean hero | ROMEO, | sharp sound | PING |
| | OTHELLO | sharp spear | LANCE |

| | | | |
|---|---|---|---|
| sharp tap | **RAP** | sheltered side | **LEE** |
| sharp taste | **TANG, NIP** | shelter for bees | **HIVE** |
| shasta | **DAISY** | shepherd | **PASTOR** |
| shatter | **DASH, SMASH** | shepherd's pipe | **REED** |
| shave | **PARE** | sherbet | **ICE** |
| shavetail | **LIEUTENANT** | sheriff's badge | **STAR** |
| shaving tool | **RAZOR** | sheriff's band | **POSSE** |
| shawl | **WRAP, STOLE, SCARF** | sherry | **WINE** |
| Shawnee Indian chief | | shield | **PROTECT, COVER** |
| | **TECUMSEH** | shield boss | **UMBO** |
| shay | **CARRIAGE** | shield from harm | **PROTECT** |
| she (Fr.) | **ELLE** | shift responsibility (3 wds.) | |
| sheaf | **BUNDLE, CLUSTER** | | **PASS THE BUCK** |
| shear | **CLIP** | shimmer | **GLEAM, GLINT** |
| sheath | **SCABBARD, GLOVE** | shin | **SHANK** |
| sheave | **PULLEY** | shinbone | **TIBIA** |
| she-bear (Lat.) | **URSA** | shine | **GLEAM, GLOW, GLOSS,** |
| shed | **HUT, LEAN-TO** | | **RADIATE, GLISTEN** |
| shed feathers | **MOLT, MOULT** | Shinto temple | **SHA** |
| shed light | **SHINE** | shiny fabric | **SATIN** |
| shed tears | **SOB, WEEP, CRY** | ship | **BOAT** |
| sheen | **LUSTER** | ship biscuit | **HARDTACK** |
| sheep | **EWE, RAM, LAMB** | ship boarding platform | |
| sheep enclosure | **FOLD** | | **GANGPLANK** |
| sheeplike | **OVINE** | ship bow | **PROW** |
| sheep's bleat | **BAA, MAA** | shipbuilding wood | **TEAK** |
| sheep's child | **LAMB** | ship canvas | **SAIL** |
| sheep's coat | **FLEECE** | ship deck | **POOP, ORLOP** |
| sheep's hair | **WOOL** | ship deserter | **RAT** |
| sheep shelter | **COTE** | shipmates | **HEARTIES** |
| sheepskin | **PELT, DIPLOMA** | ship-model housing | **BOTTLE** |
| sheepskin shoe | **PAC** | ship mop | **SWAB** |
| sheer | **STEEP** | ship of Noah | **ARK** |
| sheer curtain | **SCRIM** | ship of the Argonauts | **ARGO** |
| sheer fabric | **TOILE, TULLE,** | ship of the desert | **CAMEL** |
| | **VOILE** | ship part | **KEEL, RUDDER** |
| sheerlegs | **SHEARS** | shipping box | **CRATE** |
| sheet | **ROPE, SHROUD** | shipping unit | **TON** |
| sheeting fabric | **PERCALE,** | ship prison | **BRIG** |
| | **LINEN, MUSLIN** | ship record | **LOG** |
| sheet of glass | **PANE** | ship's backbone | **KEEL** |
| sheets and tablecloths | **LINEN** | ship's bed | **BUNK** |
| sheik's ladies | **HAREM** | ship's boat | **DINGHY** |
| sheik's land | **ARABIA** | ship's body | **HULL** |
| sheldrake | **MERGANSER** | ship's cargo space | **HOLD** |
| shelf | **LEDGE** | ship's clerk | **PURSER** |
| shell | **ECTOSKELETON** | ship's commanding officer | |
| shellac | **LAC** | | **CAPTAIN** |
| Shelley | **POET** | ship's complement | **CREW** |
| Shelley work | **ODE** | ship's contour (naut.) | **HANCE** |
| shellfish | **ABALONE, CLAM,** | ship's diary | **LOG** |
| | **CRAB, SHRIMP** | ship section | **BILGE, HOLD,** |
| shell out | **PAY** | | **GALLEY** |
| shelter | **HAVEN, LEE** | ship's floor | **DECK** |
| shelter (Fr.) | **ABRI** | ship-shaped clock | **NEF** |
| sheltered from wind | **ALEE** | ship's kitchen | **GALLEY** |
| sheltered glen | **DELL, DALE** | ship's longboat | **GIG** |
| sheltered nook | **COVE** | ship's lowest deck | **ORLOP** |

| | |
|---|---|
| ship's master | **CAPTAIN** |
| ship's officer | **MATE, PURSER** |
| ship's parking place | **MOORING,** |
| | **BERTH** |
| ship's petty officer | **BOSUN** |
| ship's pole | **MAST, SPAR** |
| ship's rope | **HALYARD,** |
| | **HAWSER** |
| ship's station | **BERTH** |
| ship's tiller | **HELM** |
| ship's track | **WAKE** |
| ships under unified control | |
| | **FLEET** |
| shirk | **EVADE** |
| shirtwaist | **BLOUSE** |
| shiver | **SHAKE, TREMBLE** |
| shoal | **BANK, REEF** |
| shoat | **PIGLET** |
| shock | **STARTLE, IMPACT** |
| shoe | **FOOTGEAR, SLIPPER,** |
| | **BROGAN, FOOTWEAR,** |
| | **OXFORD, PUMP, GILLIE,** |
| | **SANDAL, LOAFER,** |
| | **SNEAKER, SPECTATOR,** |
| | **CLOG, MULE** |
| shoe bottom | **SOLE** |
| shoe fastener | **LACING, LACES,** |
| | **BUTTONS, BUCKLES** |
| shoe form | **LAST, TREE** |
| shoe grip | **CLEAT** |
| shoemaker | **COBBLER** |
| shoe material | **LEATHER** |
| shoe part | **HEEL, TOE, SOLE,** |
| | **UPPER, TONGUE** |
| shoestring | **LACE, POTATO** |
| shoe tie | **LACING** |
| shoji | **PANEL, SCREEN** |
| shoo | **SCAT** |
| shoofly | **PIE** |
| shoot | **TWIG** |
| shoot from ambush | **SNIPE** |
| shoot game | **POT** |
| shooting capacity | **FIREPOWER** |
| shooting iron | **GUN, PISTOL** |
| shooting marble | **TAW** |
| shooting match (Fr.) | **TIR** |
| shooting star | **METEOR** |
| shoot out | **DART** |
| shop | **STORE, MART, MARKET** |
| shopper's convenience | |
| (2 wds.) | **CHARGE ACCOUNT** |
| shopping center | **MALL** |
| shopping reminder | **LIST** |
| shore | **COAST, SEASIDE,** |
| | **BEACH, STRAND** |
| shore bird | **AVOCET, HERON,** |
| | **RAIL, TERN** |
| shore recess | **COVE, INLET** |

| | |
|---|---|
| short | **BRIEF, SMALL** |
| shortage | **DEFICIT** |
| short and pointed | **TERSE** |
| short and pudgy | |
| (comp. wd.) | **ROLY-POLY** |
| short article | **ITEM** |
| short blunt end | **STUB** |
| short boot | **SHOE** |
| short business trip | **ERRAND** |
| shortcoming | **FAULT** |
| short dagger | **DIRK** |
| short dash | **HYPHEN** |
| shorten | **ABRIDGE** |
| shortening | **LARD** |
| short explosive sound | **POP** |
| short firearm | **PISTOL** |
| short for gentleman | **GENT** |
| short for hurrah | **RAH** |
| short gaiter | **SPAT** |
| short haircut | **BOB, PIXIE,** |
| | **BUTCH, CREW** |
| shorthand | **STENO** |
| short intermission | **RECESS** |
| short jacket | **ETON, BOLERO** |
| short lance | **DART, DAGGER** |
| short-legged hound | **BASSET** |
| short letter | **NOTE, MEMO** |
| short-lived style | **FAD** |
| shortly | **ANON, SOON** |
| short note | **LINE** |
| short pencil | **STUB** |
| short period of calm | **LULL** |
| short pin | **PEG** |
| short playlet | **SKIT** |
| short poem | **SONNET** |
| short race | **DASH, SPRINT** |
| shortsighted | **MYOPIC** |
| short skirt | **MINI** |
| short sleep | **NAP, SNOOZE,** |
| | **CAT NAP, FORTY WINKS,** |
| | **DOZE** |
| short sock | **ANKLET** |
| short song | **DITTY** |
| short-spoken | **LACONIC** |
| short story | **CONTE** |
| short swim | **DIP** |
| short sword | **ESTOC** |
| short-tailed rodent | **HAMSTER** |
| short telegraphic click | **DOT** |
| short-tempered | **EDGY, TESTY** |
| short thick piece | **CHUNK** |
| short tree shoot | **SPUR** |
| short visit | **CALL** |
| shortwave | **RADIO** |
| Shoshonean Indian | **UTE** |
| shotgun | **RIFLE** |
| shoulder band | **STRAP** |
| shoulder blade | **SCAPULA** |

| | |
|---|---|
| shoulder of a road | **BERM** |
| shoulder ornament | **EPAULET** |
| shoulder scarf | **SHAWL, STOLE** |
| shout | **SCREAM, YELL, HOLLER** |
| shout of applause | **CHEER,** |
| | **BRAVO** |
| shout of contempt | **HOOT** |
| shout of good will (Ital.) | **VIVA** |
| shout to | **HAIL** |
| shout with joy | **SING** |
| shove | **PUSH** |
| shovel | **SPADE** |
| show | **DEMONSTRATE, EXHIBIT** |
| show a decline | **DROP** |
| show appreciation | **APPLAUD,** |
| | **CLAP** |
| showcase | **EXHIBIT** |
| show disapproval | **HISS,** |
| | **SNEER, SNORT** |
| show displeasure | **POUT** |
| shower | **RAIN** |
| shower down | **CASCADE** |
| showery | **RAINY** |
| showery month | **APRIL** |
| show favorable reaction | |
| | **RESPOND** |
| showing courage | **SPIRITED** |
| showing good judgment | **SANE,** |
| | **SENSIBLE, LOGICAL** |
| Show-Me State | **MISSOURI** |
| show of affection | **KISS** |
| show of hands | **VOTE** |
| show ostentatiously | **FLAUNT** |
| show plainly | **EVINCE** |
| show to a seat | **USHER** |
| show up | **SURPASS** |
| showy | **SPORTY** |
| showy clothes | **FINERY** |
| showy covering | **VENEER** |
| showy feather | **PLUME** |
| showy flower | **PEONY, ROSE,** |
| | **MUM** |
| showy red flower | **POINSETTIA** |
| shred | **FRAGMENT, STRIP,** |
| | **RAG, TATTER, TEAR** |
| shrew | **VIXEN** |
| shrewd | **ASTUTE, WILY,** |
| | **CLEVER, WISE, SLY** |
| shriek | **SCREAM, SCREECH** |
| shrill | **SHARP, KEEN** |
| shrill and piping tone | **REEDY** |
| shrill cry | **SCREECH** |
| shrimp | **PRAWN** |
| shrine | **TOMB, ALTAR** |
| shriner's hat | **FEZ** |
| shrink | **SHRIVEL** |
| shrink in fear | **COWER** |
| shrivel | **PARCH, SHRINK** |

| | |
|---|---|
| shroud | **SHEET, VEIL** |
| Shrove Tuesday | **MARDI GRAS** |
| shrub | **BUSH, PLANT** |
| shrub of the southwest | |
| | **MESQUITE** |
| shrug off | **DISMISS** |
| shuck | **SHELL, HUSK** |
| shudder | **SHAKE, TREMBLE** |
| shuffle along | **MOSEY** |
| shun | **AVOID** |
| shush | **HUSH, QUIET** |
| shut | **CLOSE** |
| shutdown | **LAYOFF** |
| shut noisily | **SLAM** |
| shut out | **DEBAR** |
| shutter | **BLIND, JALOUSIE** |
| shuttlecock | **BIRD** |
| shut up | **SILENCE** |
| shy | **COY, TIMID, MODEST,** |
| | **BASHFUL** |
| shylock | **USURER** |
| Siam | **THAILAND** |
| Siamese | **TAI** |
| Siamese capital | **BANGKOK** |
| Siamese coin | **ATT** |
| Siamese language | **THAI, TAI** |
| Siamese river | **ME NAM** |
| sib | **RELATIVE** |
| Siberian city | **IRKUTSK** |
| Siberian gulf | **OB** |
| Siberian mongoloid | **TARTAR** |
| Siberian treeless tract | **STEPPE** |
| sibilant sound | **HISS** |
| sibling | **BROTHER, SISTER** |
| sibyl | **SEERESS** |
| sic | **THUS** |
| Sicilian harbor | **PALERMO** |
| Sicilian resort | **ENNA** |
| Sicilian volcano | **ETNA** |
| sick | **ILL** |
| sick bay | **INFIRMARY,** |
| | **DISPENSARY** |
| sicken | **AIL** |
| sickly | **FEEBLE, INFIRM** |
| Siddhartha | **BUDDHA** |
| side | **FLANK** |
| side bone | **RIB** |
| side by side | **TOGETHER** |
| side dish of greens | **SALAD** |
| sidekick | **COMPANION,** |
| | **PARTNER** |
| side of a room | **WALL** |
| side post of a doorway | **JAMB** |
| sidereal hour angle | |
| (abbr.) | **SHA** |
| sidestep | **AVOID, ELUDE,** |
| | **EVADE, SLIDE, GLIDE** |
| sidetrack | **DIVERT, DIGRESS** |

| | | | |
|---|---|---|---|
| sideways | **ASKANCE** | silt remover | **DREDGE** |
| sidewinder | **SNAKE, RATTLER** | silver (chem. abbr.) | **AG.** |
| sidewise | **LATERAL** | Silver State | **NEVADA** |
| sidle along | **EDGE** | silvery fish | **SMELT** |
| siesta | **NAP** | s'il vous plait | **PLEASE** |
| sieve | **SIFT, STRAINER** | simian | **APE** |
| sift | **DREDGE, SIEVE** | similar | **AKIN, ALIKE** |
| sigh | **EXHALE, SOB** | similar in kind | **SUCH, LIKE,** |
| sight | **VISION, SCENE** | | **AKIN** |
| sight for travelers | **RUINS** | similarity | **ANALOGY, LIKENESS** |
| sight organ | **EYE** | similarly defined word | |
| sight-seeing trip | **TOUR** | | **SYNONYM** |
| sigil | **SEAL, SIGNET** | similar to | **LIKE** |
| sign | **BILLBOARD, BILL, NEON** | simile | **LIKE, AS** |
| signal | **CUE** | simmer | **STEW** |
| signal fire | **FLARE** | simpatico | **CONGENIAL** |
| sign at a sellout | **S.R.O.** | simper | **SMIRK** |
| signature | **MARK** | simple | **STUPID, EASY,** |
| signet | **SEAL, STAMP** | | **MERE, PLAIN** |
| significant | **IMPORTANT** | simple song | **LAY** |
| signify | **MEAN, DENOTE,** | simple story | **PARABLE** |
| | **CONNOTE** | simple substance | **ELEMENT** |
| sign of approaching | | simple sugar | **KETOSE** |
|   cold | **SNEEZE, SNIFFLE** | simpleton | **NEDDY, OAF,** |
| sign of assent | **NOD** | | **DOLT, DUNCE** |
| sign of disapproval | **BOO** | simulate | **FAKE** |
| sign of fire | **SMOKE** | sin | **ERR, TRANSGRESSION** |
| sign of full house | **S.R.O.** | Sindbad's bird | **ROC** |
| sign of life | **PULSE** | since | **AS, BECAUSE** |
| sign of sorrow | **SOB** | sincere | **HONEST** |
| sign of the future | **OMEN** | sinew | **TENDON, THEW** |
| sign of the times | **TREND** | sinewy | **ROPY, WIRY** |
| sign of the zodiac | **ARIES, LEO,** | sinful | **EVIL, IMMORAL** |
| | **PISCES, AQUARIUS,** | sing | **CROON, VOCALIZE,** |
| | **GEMINI, CANCER,** | | **WARBLE, CHANT** |
| | **SCORPIO, TAURUS,** | | |
| | **LIBRA, VIRGO,** | singer Ames | **ED** |
| | **SAGITTARIUS,** | singer Bennett | **TONY** |
| | **CAPRICORN** | singer Boone | **PAT** |
| sign up | **ENROLL, ENLIST** | singer Collins | **JUDY** |
| silence | **HUSH, STILLNESS** | singer Como | **PERRY** |
| silent | **MUM, QUIET,** | singer Crosby | **BING** |
| | **MUTE, TACIT** | singer Fitzgerald | **ELLA** |
| silhouette | **SHADOW** | singer Garland | **JUDY** |
| silicate | **MICA** | singer Horne | **LENA** |
| silk cotton | **KAPOK** | singer Ives | **BURL** |
| silken | **SMOOTH** | singer Jolson | **AL** |
| silk fabric | **CREPE, GROS** | singer Martin | **DEAN, TONY** |
| silk net | **TULLE** | singer Peerce | **JAN** |
| silk voile | **NINON** | singer Presley | **ELVIS** |
| silkworm | **ERI, ERIA** | singer Sinatra | **FRANK** |
| sill | **LEDGE** | singer's list | **REPERTOIRE** |
| silly | **APISH, FOOLISH,** | singer Stevens | **RISE** |
| | **INANE, GOOFY** | singer Streisand | **BARBRA** |
| silly action | **FOLLY** | singer Torme | **MEL** |
| silly bird | **GOOSE** | singer Williams | **ANDY** |
| silly talk | **DRIVEL, PRATTLE** | singing bird | **LARK** |
| silt | **SEDIMENT** | singing syllable | **TRA, LA** |

| | |
|---|---|
| singing voice | ALTO, BASS, SOPRANO, TENOR, BARITONE, CONTRALTO |
| single | ONE, SOLE |
| single-handed | UNAIDED |
| single-hearted | SINCERE |
| single-masted vessel | SLOOP |
| singleness | UNITY |
| single step | STAIR |
| singlestick | FENCING |
| single thing | ONE, UNIT, ITEM |
| single time | ONCE |
| singleton | LONER, ONE |
| sing like Bing | CROON |
| singly (4 wds.) | ONE AT A TIME |
| sing Swiss style | YODEL |
| singular | UNIQUE |
| sing under the breath | HUM |
| sinister | EVIL |
| sinister look | LEER |
| sinitic | CHINESE |
| sink | BASIN, SUBMERGE |
| sink down | SAG, DROOP |
| sink plug | STOPPER |
| sinuous | SNAKY |
| sinus cavity | ANTRUM, |
| Siouan Indian | OTOE |
| Siouan language | TETON, DAKOTA |
| Sioux Indian | CROW, OTOE, TETON |
| Sioux State | NORTH DAKOTA |
| sip | TASTE |
| siphon | TUBE, SUCTION |
| sire | FATHER, PROGENITOR |
| siren | CHARMER, ALARM |
| sire's mate | DAM |
| sir (Sp.) | SENOR |
| sir, in India | SAHIB |
| sir, in Malaya | TUAN |
| sirloin | STEAK |
| sisal | HEMP |
| sismo | SEXTO |
| sisterhood | SORORITY |
| sister of Orestes | ELECTRA |
| sister's daughter | NIECE |
| sit | REST, ROOST |
| sit back | RELAX |
| sit-down | STRIKE |
| site | LOCATION |
| site of 1898 Alsakan gold rush | NOME |
| site of witch trials | SALEM |
| sit for a portrait | POSE |
| sitsang | TIBET |
| sitting room | PARLOR |
| situate | LOCATE |

| | |
|---|---|
| situation | POSITION, PREDICAMENT |
| Siva's consort | DEVI |
| six-sided figure | CUBE |
| sixth sense (abbr.) | ESP |
| sixty-five usually (2 wds.) | RETIREMENT AGE |
| sixty minutes | HOUR |
| size | DIMENSION |
| size of paper | DEMY |
| size of type | ELITE, PICA |
| sizzle | STEAM |
| skate | STINGRAY, RAY |
| skate blade | RUNNER |
| skating arena | RINK |
| skean | DAGGER, DIRK |
| skein of yarn | HANK |
| skeleton part | BONE, SKULL, RIB, AITCHBONE, TIBIA, ULNA |
| skeptic | AGNOSTIC |
| sketch | PLAN, DRAW, INK |
| sketcher of comic pictures | CARTOONIST |
| sketch through thin paper | TRACE |
| sketchy | ROUGH |
| skewer | PIN, ROD |
| skid | SLIDE |
| skiff | BOAT |
| skilful | ADEPT, ADROIT |
| skill | ART, CRAFT, TALENT |
| skilled | ABLE, ADEPT, DEFT |
| skillet | PAN, FRYPAN |
| skim | GLANCE, GLIDE |
| skimpy | SCANTY |
| skin | PELT, HIDE, RIND, PEEL, DERMIS |
| skin ailment | ACNE |
| skin decoration | TATTOO |
| skin diver's attire (2 wds.) | WET SUIT |
| skinflint | MISER |
| skink | LIZARD |
| skin layer | DERMA |
| skinned (dial.) | SKUN |
| skinny | THIN, LEAN |
| skin opening | PORE |
| skin problem | ACNE |
| skin tone | TAN |
| skip | LEAP, OMIT |
| skip on water | DAP |
| skip over | ELIDE |
| skipper | CAPTAIN |
| skipper butterfly | HESPERID |
| skipper of the Pequod | AHAB |
| ski race | SLALOM |
| skirl | PIPE |

| | | | |
|---|---|---|---|
| skirmish | MELEE | sleep | NAP, DOZE, REST, |
| skirt | MIDI, MINI, KILT, | | SLUMBER |
| | DIRNDL, BROOMSTICK, | sleeper | PULLMAN |
| | GORE | sleep image | DREAM |
| skirt edge | HEM | sleep inducer | SEDATIVE |
| skirt feature | SLIT, PLEAT, | sleeping | DORMANT |
| | WAISTBAND | sleeping place | BED, BEDROOM |
| skit | SKETCH | sleepless | ALERT, AWAKE |
| skittish | JITTERY, JUMPY | sleep lightly | DOZE |
| skittish horse | SHIER | sleep noisily | SNORE |
| skoal | TOAST | sleepwalker | SOMNAMBULIST |
| skulk | LURK | sleepwear | PAJAMAS, |
| skull | CRANIUM | | NIGHTGOWN, NIGHTIE, |
| skunk | POLECAT | | NIGHTSHIRT |
| skunk-like animal | CIVET | sleepy | DROWSY |
| sky | HEAVEN | sleeve | ARM |
| sky-blue | AZURE | sleeveless garment | CAPE, |
| skye | TERRIER | | CLOAK, VEST |
| sky twinkler | STAR | sleeve part | CUFF |
| skyward | UP, ALOFT | sleigh | SLED, PUNG |
| slack | LOOSE | sleight of hand | MAGIC, |
| slacken | ABATE, RELENT, | | HOCUS-POCUS |
| | RETARD, EASE, LET UP, | slender | SKINNY, SVELTE, |
| | LOOSEN | | LEAN, SLIM, |
| slackening bar on a loom | | | TENUOUS, THIN |
| | EASER | slender candle | TAPER |
| slacks | PANTS | slenderize | REDUCE |
| slag | DROSS, SCORIA | slender pinnacle | EPI |
| slake | ALLAY, QUENCH | slender pipe | TUBE |
| slam | BANG | sleuth | DETECTIVE |
| slander | ASPERSE, DEFAME | slice | CARVE, CUT |
| slanderous gossip | DIRT | slice a roast | CARVE |
| slang | CANT, ARGOT | slice of meat | CUTLET, STEAK, |
| slangy affirmative | YEP, YEAH, | | CHOP |
| | OKAY | slice of toasted bread | RUSK |
| slangy denial | NOPE | slick | SLIPPERY, SMOOTH |
| slant | BIAS, INCLINE, TILT, | slicker | RAINCOAT |
| | SLOPE, ATTITUDE | slide | SLIP, SKID, GLIDE, |
| slanting | SLOPING, OBLIQUE | | SLITHER |
| slap | CUFF, REBUFF, SMACK | slight | SMALL, SLIM |
| slap-happy | GIDDY | slight coloring | TINT |
| slash | CUT, LASH | slight depression | DENT |
| slate | BLACKBOARD, TILE | slightest | LEAST |
| slattern | CARELESS | slighting remark | SLUR |
| slaughter | CARNAGE, BUTCHER | slight intentionally | SNUB |
| slaughterhouse | ABATTOIR | slightly open | AJAR |
| Slav | CROAT, SERB | slightly tapering | TERETE |
| slave | SERF, ESNE, PEON, | slightly wet | DAMP, MOIST |
| | BONDSMAN, DRUDGE | slight quarrel | TIFF, SPAT |
| slave owner | MASTER | slight sound | PEEP |
| slaver | SLOBBER, DROOL | slight taste | SIP |
| slavery | BONDAGE | slim | SLENDER, THIN, |
| Slavic language | CROAT | | LEAN, SVELTE |
| slay | KILL | slime | MUD, OOZE |
| slayer of Goliath | DAVID | sling | CAST, FLING |
| sled | COASTER, TOBOGGAN | slink | LURK |
| sleek | LUSTROUS | slinky | STEALTHY, FURTIVE |
| sleek black animal | PANTHER | slip | SLIDE |

| | | | |
|---|---|---|---|
| slip backwards | RELAPSE, REGRESS | sly fellow | FOX |
| | | sly glance | LEER |
| slip by | ELAPSE | slyly spiteful | CATTY |
| slipknot | NOOSE | sly trick | WILE |
| slip-on garment | TUNIC | smack | SLAP |
| slipper | MULE, SHOE, SCUFF | small | LITTLE, PETITE, TINY, TEENY, WEE |
| slippery | EELY, ICY | | |
| slipshod | SLOVENLY | small African antelope | ORIBI |
| slip sideways | SKID | small amount | BIT, DAB, DRAM, IOTA, MITE, MORSEL |
| slipsole | INSOLE | | |
| slip the memory | FORGET | small anchor | KEDGE |
| slip-up | ERROR, MISHAP | small and trim | PETITE |
| slit | CRACK, SPLIT | small and unimportant | TRIVIAL |
| slither | SLIDE | | DINKY, |
| sliver of wood | SPLINTER | small antelope | GAZELLE |
| slivovitz | BRANDY | small anvil | TEEST |
| slobber | DROOL | small aperture | VENT |
| sloe | PLUM | small arms | PISTOLS |
| slog | PLOD, TOIL | small arrow | DART |
| slogan | CRY, CATCHWORD, MOTTO | small articles case | ETUI |
| | | small automobile | RUNABOUT |
| slop | SPLASH | small bag | SATCHEL |
| sloping roadway | RAMP | small barn | SHED |
| slop over | SPILL | small barrel | KEG |
| sloppy person | SLOB | small bay | COVE |
| slosh | SPLASH, SLUSH | small bed | COT |
| sloth | AI, UNAU | small beetle | WEEVIL |
| slothful | INDOLENT, LAZY | small bill | DOLLAR |
| slot machine success | JACKPOT | small bird | WREN, TIT |
| slouch | DROOP, SAG | small bit | NIP |
| slovenly | UNTIDY, MESSY | small bit of food | MORSEL |
| slow | SLUGGISH | small body of water | POND |
| slow but flowing (mus.) | ANDANTE | small bottle | VIAL |
| | | small boy | TAD |
| slow down (2 wds.) | LET UP | small branch | TWIG |
| slow-moving mollusk | SNAIL | small brook | RILL |
| slow (mus.) | LENTO, ADAGIO, LARGO | small brown bird | WREN |
| | | small bunch | WISP |
| slowpoke | LAGGARD, SNAIL | small cabin | HUT |
| slow train | LOCAL | small candle | TAPER |
| slow-witted | DULL, STUPID | small carrying bag | SATCHEL, GRIP, ETUI |
| sludge | MUD, MIRE | | |
| slug | SNAIL | small cask | KEG |
| slugger's special | HOMER, KAYO | small change | SILVER |
| | | small chicken | BANTAM |
| sluggish | LOGY, SLOW | small child | TAD, TOT, TODDLER |
| sluggishness | TORPOR | | |
| sluice | GATE, CHANNEL | small chunk | WAD |
| sluice gate | CLOW | small city | TOWN |
| slumber | SLEEP | small coin | CENT, PENNY, DIME, NICKEL |
| slum dwelling | TENEMENT | | |
| slumgullion | STEW, HASH | small compact heap | WAD |
| slump | DROP, FALL | small cord | STRING |
| slur | INSULT | small cube | DIE |
| slur over | ELIDE | small cuckoo bird | ANI |
| slurp | SUCK, GULP | small cushion | PAD |
| slush | MIRE | small deer | ROE |
| sly | CUNNING, WILY, FOXY | small depression | DENT |

| | | | |
|---|---|---|---|
| small distance | INCH | small measure | OUNCE |
| small dog | TERRIER, PUPPY, | small-minded | NARROW, PETTY |
| | CHIHUAHUA | small monkey | TITI |
| small donkey | BURRO | small mound | HILL |
| small drum | TABOR | small mountain lake | TARN |
| small duck | SMEW, TEAL | smallmouth | BASS |
| small engine | MOTOR | small nail | BRAD, TACK |
| smallest | LEAST | small narrow valley | RAVINE |
| smallest bit | IOTA, WHIT | small nocturnal mammal | LEMUR |
| smallest of the litter | RUNT | | |
| smallest part | WHIT, MINIM | small opening | FORAMEN, |
| small European fish | DACE | | PORE |
| small explosion | POP | small orange fruit | KUMQUAT |
| small falcon | KESTREL | small part | BIT |
| small field | CROFT | small particle | ATOM, MOTE |
| small finch | SERIN, SISKIN | small photo | SNAPSHOT |
| small fish | SARDINE, SMELT, | small piano | SPINET |
| | MINNOW, GUPPY | small pie | TART |
| small flap | TAB | small piece | BIT, FRAGMENT, |
| small fly | GNAT | | MORSEL, SNIP |
| small forest ox | ANOA | small piece of food | MORSEL |
| small fragment | CHIP, SHRED | small piece of ground | PLAT |
| small fresh-water duck | TEAL | small pigeon | DOVE |
| small fried cake | FRITTER | small pillow | PAD |
| small garden spade | TROWEL | small pincers | PLIER |
| small glass of brandy | PONY | small plateau | MESA |
| small green finch | SERIN | small pond | POOL |
| small group of secret | | small porch | STOOP |
| plotters | CABAL | small potatoes | UNIMPORTANT |
| small gull | TERN | small pouch | SAC |
| small harpsichord | SPINET | small quantity | BIT, DAB, |
| small heavenly body | | | DROP, IOTA |
| | PLANETOID, ASTEROID, | small quarrel | SPAT, TIFF |
| | SATELLITE | small restaurant | CAFE, DINER |
| small herring | SPRAT | small river | STREAM, CREEK, |
| small hooter | OWLET | | BROOK |
| small horse | PONY, COLT | small river duck | TEAL |
| small hotel | INN | small rock | PEBBLE |
| small hound | BEAGLE | small rodent | LEROT, MOUSE, |
| small house | CABIN, COTTAGE, | | VOLE |
| | HUT | small roll | BUN |
| small in amount | SLIGHT | small room | CLOSET |
| small in figure | PETITE | small rug | MAT |
| small inlet | COVE, CREEK, RIA | small sailing vessel | LUGGER |
| small insect | GNAT | small salamander | NEWT |
| small island | AIT, CAY, ISLE, | small sample of cloth | SNIP |
| | KEY, ISLET | small satellite | MOONLET |
| small jazz group | COMBO | small-scale | LIMITED |
| small job | CHORE | small seed | PIP |
| small juicy fruit | BERRY | small shelter | SHED, LEAN-TO |
| small lace mat | DOILY | small ship | BOAT, TUG |
| small lake | MERE, POND | small shoot | TWIG |
| small leafy branch | SPRIG | small shrub | ELDER |
| small liquid measure | GILL, | small sofa | LOVE SEAT, DIVAN |
| | PINT | small songbird | WREN, |
| small lizard | EFT, NEWT | | CANARY |
| small mallet | GAVEL | small souvenir | KNICKKNACK |
| small mass | WAD | small spar | SPRIT |

| | | | |
|---|---|---|---|
| small spear | DART | smoked meat | HAM |
| small spot | SPECK, DOT | smoked pork | BACON |
| small steep waterfall | CASCADE | smoke flue | STACK, CHIMNEY |
| small stone | PEBBLE | smoker | STAG |
| small store | SHOP | smoker's item | CIGARET, PIPE, |
| small stream | CREEK, RILL, | | CIGARETTE, CIGAR |
| | BROOK | smokestack | CHIMNEY |
| small sturgeon | STERLET | Smokey | BEAR |
| small Sumatra deer | NAPU | smoking tube | PIPE |
| smallsword | EPEE | smoky | HAZY |
| small table | STAND, TABORET | smoky quartz | CAIRNGORM |
| small talk | CHAT | smolder | SMOTHER, SMUDGE |
| small task | CHORE | smooch | KISS, BUSS, NECK |
| small taste | SIP, BITE | smooth | EVEN, LEVEL, FLAT, |
| small-time | MINOR, PETTY | | GLIB, EASY |
| small tower | TURRET | smoothbore | GUN |
| small-town | PROVINCIAL | smooth cotton cloth | PERCALE |
| small tree branch | TWIG | smooth-faced | SHAVEN |
| small tropical cuckoo bird | ANI | smooth feathers | PREEN |
| small twig | SPRIG | smoothing tool | FILE, PLANE |
| small typewriter type | ELITE | smoothly courteous | URBANE |
| small valley | DALE, DELL, | smooth-spoken | GLIB |
| | GLEN, VALE | smorgasbord | BUFFET |
| small vegetable | PEA, BEAN | smother | STIFLE |
| small wagon | CART | smudge | SMEAR, SPOT, |
| small weight | GRAM, OUNCE | | STAIN, BLUR, |
| small wheeled vehicle | CART | | DIRTY, SOIL |
| small whirlpool | EDDY | smug | COMPLACENT |
| small wild ox | ANOA | smuggler | RUNNER |
| smalt | GLASS, BLUE | smug person | PRIG |
| smart | INTELLIGENT,BRIGHT, | smut | SOOT, DIRT |
| | STING, BURN | Smyrna | IZMIR |
| smart in appearance | CHIC, | Smyrna figs | ELEMI |
| | NATTY | snack | BITE |
| smart-looking | TRIG | snaffle | BIT |
| smash | SHATTER, BREAK | snag | OBSTACLE |
| smashup | WRECK, COLLISION | snail | SLUG |
| smear | SMUDGE, DEFAME, | snail genus | MITRA, TRITON |
| | DAUB | snail-paced | SLOW |
| smell | ODOR, REEK, SCENT | snake | SERPENT, VIPER, |
| smelly vegetable | ONION | | ADDER, ASP |
| smelting by-product | SLAG | snake eyes | TWO, DEUCE |
| smelting chamber | OVEN | snake-killing mammal | |
| smelt ore | REFINE | | MONGOOSE |
| smew | MERGANSER | snakeless land | EIRE |
| smile | GRIN, BEAM | snakelike fish | EEL |
| smile in a silly manner | SIMPER | snakemouth | POGONIA |
| smile scornfully | SNEER | snake's sound | HISS, RATTLE |
| smiling | RIANT | snakeweed | BISTORT |
| smirch | TAINT, STAIN, SULLY | snaky | SINUOUS |
| smirk | LEER, SIMPER | snaky letter | ESS |
| smite | STRIKE | snap | CLICK |
| smithy | FORGE | snap back | RECOVER |
| smock | CHEMISE, SHIFT | snappish bark | YAP |
| smog | MIST | snappy | SPICY, LIVELY |
| smoke | REEK, FUME | snappy comeback | RETORT |
| smoke a cigarette | PUFF | snapshot | PHOTO |
| smoke and fog | SMOG | snapshot, for short | PIC |

| | | | |
|---|---|---|---|
| snare | NET, TRAP | soap | LATHER |
| snarl | TANGLE | soapbark | SAPONIN |
| snarling dog | CUR | soap flake | CHIP |
| snarly | CROSS | soap foam | SUDS |
| snatch | GRAB, NAB | soap-frame bar | SESS |
| snazzy | FLASHY | soap ingredient | LYE |
| sneak | LURK, STEAL | soap opera | SERIAL |
| sneaker | SHOE | soap plant | AMOLE |
| sneaky | STEALTHY | soapstone | TALC |
| snee | DIRK | soapweed | YUCCA |
| sneer | GIBE, SCOFF | soar | FLY, RISE |
| sneeze | ACHOO | sob | CRY, WEEP |
| snicker | TITTER | so be it | AMEN |
| snide | MEAN, LOW | sober | SERIOUS, SOLEMN |
| sniff | SMELL, NOSE | sobriquet | EPITHET, |
| sniffles | COLD | | NICKNAME |
| snifter | GOBLET | sociable | COMPANIONABLE |
| snip | CLIP | social | POLITE |
| snitch | PILFER, INFORM | social appointment | DATE |
| snivel | WHINE | social bud | DEB |
| snobbish | SNOOTY | social class | CASTE |
| snood | NET | social division | TRIBE |
| snoop | PRY | social event | PARTY, BALL, |
| Snoopy's adversary | | | RECEPTION, TEA |
| (2 wds.) | RED BARON | social gathering | BEE |
| snooty person | SNOB | social gathering for men | STAG, |
| snooze | DOZE, NAP | | SMOKER |
| snoozing | ASLEEP | social grace | POISE |
| snout | NOSE | social group | CLAN, TRIBE |
| snout beetle | WEEVIL | social insect | ANT, BEE |
| snowbell | STYRAX | social outcast | PARIAH |
| snow coaster | SLED, | social rank | CASTE, CLASS |
| | TOBOGGAN | social set | COTERIE, CLIQUE |
| snow field | NEVE | social studies | CIVICS |
| snowflake | CRYSTAL | society | UNION, PARTNERSHIP |
| snow particle | FLAKE | society bud | DEBUTANTE |
| snow removal implement | | society game | POLO, CROQUET |
| | SHOVEL, PLOW | society in Chinatown | TONG |
| snow runner | SKI | Society of Friends | QUAKERS |
| snow shoe | PAC | sock | ANKLET, PUNCH |
| snowslide | AVALANCHE | socked in | FOGGY |
| snow slider | SLED | sockeye | SALMON |
| snow vehicle | SLED, SLEIGH, | sod | GREENSWARD, TURF |
| | TOBOGGAN | soda | POP |
| snowy | WHITE | soda sipper | STRAW |
| snub | IGNORE | soda water | SELTZER |
| snuffle | SNIFF, PANT | sodden | WET |
| snug and warm | COZY | sodium chloride | SAL, SALT |
| snuggle | NESTLE | sofa | DAVENPORT, DIVAN, |
| snug retreat | NEST | | COUCH, SETTEE |
| so | THUS | sofa bed | CONVERTIBLE |
| soak | DRENCH, SATURATE, | so far | YET |
| | SOP | soft | GENTLE, PLIANT |
| soaked | WET | soft alkali metallic element | |
| soak flax | RET | | SODIUM |
| soak thoroughly | SATURATE | soft and pliable | WAXEN |
| soak through | OOZE | soft breeze | ZEPHYR |
| soak up | ABSORB | soft cap | BERET |

| | |
|---|---|
| soft chancre | CHANCROID |
| soft cheese | BRIE |
| soft coal | BITUMINOUS |
| soft drink | COLA, POP, SODA, ADE, PUNCH |
| soft-drink nut | COLA |
| soften | ALLAY, ASSUAGE |
| softening device | MUTE |
| soften in temper | RELENT |
| soft feathers | DOWN |
| soft felt hat | FEDORA |
| soft food | PAP |
| softgoods | TEXTILES |
| soft hair | FUR |
| soft hat | CAP |
| soft in texture | SUPPLE |
| soft leather | CORDOVAN, SUEDE |
| softly | LOW, PIANO |
| soft mass | PULP |
| soft metal | MERCURY, LEAD, TIN |
| soft metal alloy | SOLDER |
| soft mineral | TALC |
| soft mud | SLIME, OOZE |
| soft palate | VELUM |
| soft part of fruit | PULP |
| soft pedal | DAMPER |
| soft plug | WAD |
| soft round cap | BERET |
| soft-shell | CRAB |
| soft-shoe | TAPDANCE |
| soft-soaper | FLATTERER |
| soft-spoken | QUIET, SUAVE |
| software | PROGRAM, DATA |
| soggy | WET, MOIST, DAMP |
| soigne | NEAT, TIDY |
| soil | DIRT, EARTH |
| soil deposit | SILT |
| soil mixture | LOAM |
| soil with dirt | BEGRIME |
| soiree | PARTY |
| sojourn | ABIDE |
| sol | SUN |
| solace | CONSOLE, SOOTHE |
| solan | GANNET |
| solar disc | ATEN |
| solar system model | ORRERY |
| soldering flux | ROSIN |
| soldering piece | LUG |
| soldier | PRIVATE, GI |
| soldier on guard | SENTRY |
| soldier's address (abbr.) | APO |
| soldiers' meal | MESS |
| soldier's overcoat | CAPOTE |
| soldier's quarters | BARRACKS |
| soldier's vacation | LEAVE, FURLOUGH |

| | |
|---|---|
| soldier's water flask | CANTEEN |
| sole | LONE, ONLY, SOLITARY |
| solecism | BARBARISM |
| solemn | SOBER |
| solemnity | GRAVITY |
| solemnize | CELEBRATE |
| solemn pledge | VOW, OATH, PROMISE |
| solemn wonder | AWE |
| solenocyte | FLAGELLUM |
| solicit | ASK, REQUEST |
| solicit individually | CANVASS |
| solicitor | LAWYER |
| solicitude | CARE |
| solid | FIRM, HARD |
| solid figure | CUBE, CONE |
| solidify | SET, GEL |
| soliloquy | MONOLOGUE |
| solitaire | DIAMOND |
| solitary | ALONE, LONE, SOLE |
| solitary person | LONER |
| solitude | SECLUSION, LONELINESS |
| solo | ALONE |
| Solomon | SAGE |
| so long | TA-TA |
| solo performance (2 wds.) | ONE-MAN SHOW |
| solution | KEY, ANSWER |
| solvent | ABOVE WATER |
| soma | BODY |
| somber | MELANCHOLY |
| sombrero | HAT |
| some | ANY |
| somersault | TUMBLE, FLIP |
| something dependable (comp. wd.) | STAND-BY |
| something easy to accomplish (sl.) | PUSHOVER |
| something extra | ACCESSORY |
| something inferior | PUNK |
| something landlubbers lack (2 wds.) | SEA LEGS |
| something learned | LESSON |
| something oppressive | BURDEN |
| something remarkable | LULU, ONER |
| something similar | ANALOGUE |
| something small | ATOM, IOTA |
| something that entertains | AMUSEMENT, DIVERSION |
| something to smoke | CIGAR, CIGARET, CIGARETTE, PIPE, TOBACCO |
| something unexplained | MYSTERY |
| something unique | ONER |
| something worthless | TRIPE |

| | | | |
|---|---|---|---|
| sometime | ONCE | son of Isaac | JACOB, ESAU |
| sometime salt ingredient | | son of Jacob | LEVI, DAN, |
| | IODINE | | JOSEPH, GIDEON, |
| sometimes wild card | DEUCE | | ASHER, GAD, JUDAH |
| somewhat | TO A DEGREE, | son of Judah | ER |
| | RATHER | son of Lancelot | GALAHAD |
| somewhat alike | SIMILAR | son of Noah | SHEM, HAM |
| somewhat colorless | PALISH | son of Obed | JESSE |
| somewhat youthful | YOUNGISH | son of Odin | THOR |
| sommelier | STEWARD | son of Ruth | OBED |
| somnambulist | SLEEPWALKER | son of Saul | JONATHAN |
| somniferous | SOPORIFIC | son of Seth | ENOS |
| somniloquy | SLEEP-TALK | sonorous | RESONANT |
| somnolent | SLEEPY | soon | ANON, PRESENTLY |
| son | BOY, HEIR, SCION | Sooner State | OKALAHOMA |
| sonance | TONE | sooner than | ERE |
| song | BALLAD, LAY, TUNE, | soot | LAMPBLACK, SMUT, GRIT |
| | ARIA, MELODY | sooth | TRUTH, FACT |
| songbird | LARK, SKYLARK, | soothe | EASE, COMFORT |
| | CANARY, TANAGER, | soothing ointment | BALM, |
| | WREN | | SALVE |
| song for a diva | ARIA | soothing substance | BALSAM |
| song for a sailor | CHANTEY | soothing word | THERE |
| song for one | SOLO | soothsayer | AUGUR |
| song for two | DUET | sop | DRENCH, SOAK |
| songlike | ARIOSO, LYRIC | sophism | FALLACY |
| song of joy | PAEN | sophisticated | WORLDLY |
| songstress Adams | EDIE | | BLASE |
| songstress Bailey | PEARL | soporific | SEDATIVE, NARCOTIC |
| songstress Brewer | TERESA | soprano Lehmann | LOTTE |
| songstress Cantrell | LANA | sora | RAIL |
| songstress Della | REESE | sorcerer | WIZARD |
| songstress Diahann | CARROLL | sorceress of myth | CIRCE |
| songstress Fitzgerald | ELLA | sordid | FOUL, FILTHY |
| songstress Horne | LENA | sore | PAINFUL |
| songstress Judy | GARLAND | sorely | URGENTLY |
| songstress Lanie | KAZAN | sorghum | SYRUP |
| songstress Lee | BRENDA, | sorrel | OCA, OXALIS |
| | PEGGY | sorrow | GRIEF, WOE, DOLOR |
| songstress Logan | ELLA | sorrowful | SAD |
| songstress Martin | MARY | sorry | RUEFUL |
| songstress Minnelli | LIZA | sorry horse | NAG |
| songstress Page | PATTI | sort | TYPE, ILK, CLASS, |
| songstress Piaf | EDITH | | CLASSIFY, KIND |
| songstress Reese | DELLA | sortie | FORAY, RAID |
| songstress Shirley | BASSEY | sot | TOPER, TOSSPOT, DRUNK |
| songstress Smith | KATE | sotto voce | WHISPER |
| songstress Starr | KAY | souchong | TEA |
| songstress Stevens | CONNIE | souk | MARKET |
| songstress Streisand | BARBRA | soul | SPIRIT, PSYCHE |
| song thrush | MAVIS | soul (Fr.) | AME |
| songwriter | COMPOSER | soul seller | FAUST |
| sonnet | POEM, VERSE | sound | NOISE, TONE, VALID |
| son of Adam | SETH, ABEL, | sound a horn | TOOT |
| | CAIN | sound, as a bell | RING, PEAL, |
| son of Agamemnon | ORESTES | | TOLL |
| son of Aphrodite | EROS | sound detector | SONAR |
| son of Hagar | ISHMAEL | sound equipment of TV | AUDIO |

| | |
|---|---|
| sounder | PLUMB |
| sound from a kennel | YELP, |
| | YIP, YAP, WOOF, ROWF, |
| | BARK, BOWWOW |
| sound harshly | GRATE |
| sound in harmony | CHIME |
| sound loudly | BLARE |
| sound made by sheep | BAA, |
| | MAA |
| soundness of mind | SANITY |
| sound of a bell | DONG, DING |
| sound of a blow | WHAM |
| sound of a cat | MEW, MEOW, |
| | MIAW |
| sound of a clock | TICK, TOCK, |
| | ALARM, TICKING |
| sound of a cow | MOO |
| sound of a dove | COO |
| sound of a rifle shot | CRACK |
| sound of a snake | HISS, |
| | RATTLE |
| sound of contempt | BOO, BAH |
| sound of disapproval | BOO, |
| | HISS, CATCALL, |
| | RASPBERRY |
| sound of dismissal | SCAT, |
| | SHOO |
| sound of hesitation | ER, UM, |
| | AH, AHEM |
| sound of relief | SIGH |
| sound of rustling skirts | SWISH |
| sound of surf | ROAR |
| sound of today's music | ROCK |
| sound quality | TONE |
| sound reasoning | LOGIC |
| sounds having melody | MUSIC |
| sound system | STEREO |
| sound the alarm | ALERT |
| sound track | AUDIO |
| soup | BROTH, BISQUE, |
| | CHOWDER |
| soupcon | SUSPICION, HINT |
| soup dish | BOWL, TUREEN |
| soupfin shark | TOPE |
| soup green | OKRA |
| soup ingredient | ONION, LEEK, |
| | SPLIT PEA, CHICKEN, |
| | RICE, BARLEY, NOODLE |
| sour | ACID, TART |
| source | ORIGIN, BEGINNING, |
| | ROOT, SPRING |
| source of honor | CREDIT |
| source of income | REVENUE |
| source of iodine | KELP |
| source of light | SUN |
| source of metal | ORE |
| source of ore | MINE |
| source of poi | TARO |

| | |
|---|---|
| source of power | ATOM, STEAM |
| source of revenue | TAX |
| source of the mighty oak | |
| | ACORN |
| source of wood | TREE |
| sourdine | MUTE |
| sourdough | BREAD |
| sour fruit | LEMON |
| sour-leaved plant | SORREL |
| sour mash | WHISKEY |
| sousaphone | TUBA |
| souse | PICKLE, BRINE |
| soused | DRUNK |
| soutane | CASSOCK |
| South | DIXIE |
| south (Fr.) | SUD |
| South African | BOER |
| South African antelope | ELAND, |
| | GNU |
| South African city | DURBAN |
| South African grassland | VELDT |
| South African native | BANTU |
| South African plant | ALOE |
| South African republic | |
| | TRANSVAAL |
| South African tribe | BANTU, |
| | ZULU |
| South African village | KRAAL |
| South American aborigine | |
| | ARAWAK |
| South American animal | LLAMA, |
| | TAPIR |
| South American beast of | |
| burden | LLAMA |
| South American country | PERU, |
| | BRAZIL, CHILE, |
| | URUGUAY, PARAGUAY, |
| | ARGENTINA, VENEZUELA, |
| | COLUMBIA |
| South American drink | ASSAI |
| South American Indian | CARIB, |
| | INCA |
| South American Indian | |
| group | INCA |
| South American knife | |
| | MACHETE |
| South American liberator | |
| | BOLIVAR, MARTIN |
| South American monkey | SAI |
| South American mountains | |
| | ANDES |
| South American ostrich | RHEA |
| South American parrot | MACAW |
| South American plains | |
| | LLANOS, PAMPAS |
| South American river | PLATA, |
| | AMAZON |
| South American rodent | PACA |

South American rubber tree **PARA**
South American tree **CACAO**
South American vulture **CONDOR**
South American weapon **BOLAS**
South Dakota city **PIERRE**
southdown **SHEEP**
southeast wind **EURUS**
southern beauty **BELLE**
southern bread **PONE**
southern constellation **ARA, ARGO, LIBRA, CENTAURUS**
southern crop **COTTON, SOYBEANS, PEANUTS, TOBACCO**
southern drink **JULEP, COMFORT**
Southern France **MIDI**
southern general **LEE**
South Pacific island group **SAMOA, HAWAII, FIJI, MICRONESIA**
southpaw **LEFTY**
South Pole bird **PENGUIN**
South Pole region **ANTARCTICA**
South Seas canoe **PROA, PRAU**
South Seas paradise **TAHITI**
South Seas plant **TARO**
Southwestern river **GILA, RED**
Southwestern saloon **CANTINA**
souvenir **RELIC, MEMENTO**
sovereign **RULER**
sovereign authority **DOMINION**
sovereign of Iran **SHAH**
sovereign power **THRONE**
sovereign's domain **EMPIRE**
sovereign's residence **PALACE**
soviet **COUNCIL**
Soviet city **OREL, MOSCOW, LENINGRAD**
Soviet commune **MIR**
Soviet news agency **TASS**
Soviet plane **MIG**
Soviet police **OGPU**
Soviet refusal **NYET, NIET**
Soviet river **URAL, VOLGA, LENA**
sow **SEED, PLANT**
sowbelly **SALT PORK**
space **ROOM**
space beside one **SIDE**
space between two points **DISTANCE**
space for laying up goods **STORAGE, ETAPE**
spaceman **ASTRONAUT**

space of time **INTERVAL**
space vehicle **APOLLO**
space-vehicle booster **SATURN**
spacious **ROOMY, AMPLE**
spade **SHOVEL**
spaghetti **PASTA**
Spain and Portugal **IBERIA**
span **BRIDGE**
spangle **SPARKLE, GLITTER**
Spanish-American laborer **PEON**
Spanish-American priest **PADRE**
Spanish-American shawl **SERAPE**
Spanish article **EL, LA, UNO, LOS**
Spanish aunt **TIA**
Spanish bayonet **YUCCA**
Spanish chaperone **DUENNA**
Spanish cheer **OLE**
Spanish city **CADIZ, TOLEDO, MADRID**
Spanish conqueror **CORTEZ, PIZARRO**
Spanish dance **TANGO, FLAMENCO, BOLERO**
Spanish fleet **ARMADA**
Spanish gambling game **MONTE**
Spanish gentleman **SENOR, CABALLERO**
Spanish gold **ORO**
Spanish hero **CID, EL CID**
Spanish holiday **FIESTA**
Spanish house **CASA**
Spanish jar **OLLA**
Spanish legislature **CORTES**
Spanish mackerel **PINTADO**
Spanish matron **DONA, SENORA**
Spanish nobleman **GRANDEE**
Spanish painter **DALI, GOYA, EL GRECO**
Spanish peninsula **IBERIA**
Spanish river **EBRO, RIO**
Spanish room **SALA**
Spanish sherry **JEREZ**
Spanish title **DON, SENOR**
spanker **SAIL**
spanking **LICKING**
spar **MAST, SHADOWBOX**
spare **EXTRA**
sparing **FRUGAL, CHARY**
spark **FLASH**
sparkle **SHINE, TWINKLE, GLISTEN**
sparrowgrass **ASPARAGUS**

| | |
|---|---|
| sparse | SCANT |
| spartan | SEVERE |
| Spartan king | MENELAUS |
| Spartan slave | HELOT |
| spasm | TIC |
| spasmodic | FITFUL |
| spat | QUARREL |
| spate | FRESHET |
| spatter | SPLASH, SPRINKLE |
| spatula | SCRAPER |
| spawn | ROE |
| speak | MOUTH, SAY, TALK, UTTER |
| speak conceitedly | BOAST, BRAG |
| speak eloquently | ORATE |
| speaker | ORATOR |
| speaker's platform | ROSTRUM |
| speak from memory | RECITE |
| speak imperfectly | LISP |
| speak in undertone | MURMUR |
| speak slightingly of | DEBASE |
| speak slowly | DRAWL |
| speak tearfully | SNIVEL |
| speak wildly | RAVE |
| spear | LANCE |
| special | NOTEWORTHY |
| special ability | TALENT |
| special approach | ANGLE |
| special edition | EXTRA |
| special event | OCCASION |
| specialist | EXPERT |
| specialist in crime | SAFECRACKER, PICKPOCKET |
| species | KIND, SORT |
| species of deer | ROE |
| species of moth | EGGER |
| species of pheasant | RINGNECK |
| species of water lily | LOTUS |
| specific | EXACT, PRECISE |
| specimen | SAMPLE |
| specious | PLAUSIBLE, LIKELY |
| speck | DOT, MOTE |
| speck of dust | MOTE |
| speck of moisture from the eyes | TEARDROP |
| spectacle | PAGEANT |
| spectacles | GLASSES |
| spectator | WITNESS |
| spectator's roofed area | GRANDSTAND |
| spectre | SHADE, GHOST, HAUNT |
| spectrum | RANGE |
| speculate | WONDER |
| speech | ADDRESS, TALK |
| speech impediment | LISP |

| | |
|---|---|
| speechless | MUTE, SILENT |
| speech to the audience | ASIDE |
| speed | RUN, SWIFTNESS, HASTEN, RACE, HIE |
| speed contest | RACE |
| speedily | APACE, QUICKLY |
| speed rate | TEMPO |
| speed up | ACCELERATE |
| speed upward, like a plane | ZOOM |
| speedy | FAST, QUICK, RAPID, HASTY, SWIFT |
| speedy horse | ARAB |
| spell | CHARM |
| spellbound | RAPT |
| spelling contest | BEE |
| spell of cold weather | SNAP |
| spelt | EMMER |
| spelunker's specialty | CAVE |
| spencer | TRYSAIL |
| spend | EXHAUST, DISBURSE |
| spend foolishly | SQUANDER |
| spend money | BUY |
| spend the summer | VACATION, (A)ESTIVATE |
| spendthrift | PRODIGAL |
| spent | EXHAUSTED, PUT OUT MONEY, EXPENDED |
| sphere | ORB, GLOBE |
| sphere of action | ARENA |
| sphere of operation | THEATER |
| spherical | ROUND |
| spherical body | BALL, GLOBE |
| sphinx land | EGYPT |
| spice | SEASON, PEPPER |
| spicy | RACY |
| spicy bud | CLOVE |
| spicy perfume | INCENSE |
| spicy quality | TANG, ZEST |
| spider | ARACHNID, TARANTULA |
| spider monkey genus | ATELES |
| spider's handiwork | WEB |
| spider trap | WEB |
| spieler | BARKER |
| spigot | TAP, FAUCET |
| spike | EAR, NAIL |
| spike of corn | EAR |
| spile | TAP, SPIGOT |
| spillikin | JACKSTRAW |
| spill over | SLOP |
| spin | TWIRL, WHIRL, REEL, REVOLVE, ROTATE, TURN |
| spindle | AXLE, AXIS |
| spindrift | SPRAY |
| spine | BACKBONE, SETA |
| spine bone | SACRUM |

| | | | |
|---|---|---|---|
| spinet | **PIANO** | spoor | **TRACK** |
| spinnaker | **SAIL** | sporadic | **INFREQUENT** |
| spinner of webs | **SPIDER** | sport | **GAME, PASTIME,** |
| spinning toy | **TOP** | | **BASEBALL, FOOTBALL,** |
| spinster (2 wds.) | **OLD MAID** | | **SQUASH, HOCKEY** |
| spiny anteater | **ECHIDNA** | sporting a Van Dyke | **BEARDED** |
| spiny dogfish | **SHARK** | sportive | **PLAYFUL** |
| spiny-finned fish | **COD** | sport of kings | **RACING** |
| spire | **STEEPLE, TOWER** | sport of shooting clay | |
| spire finial | **EPI** | pigeons | **SKEET** |
| spire ornament | **FINIAL, EPI** | sports enthusiast | **FAN** |
| spirit | **ELAN, SOUL** | sports field | **ARENA** |
| sprited | **SPUNKY, BRISK** | sports group | **TEAM** |
| spirited horse | **STEED** | sports palace | **COLISEUM** |
| spirit lamp | **ETNA** | sportswear | **SLACKS, JERSEY,** |
| spiritless | **VAPID** | | **SWEATER, SHORTS** |
| spiritual being | **ANGEL** | sporty | **FLASHY** |
| spiritualist | **MEDIUM** | spot | **BLOT, STAIN,** |
| spiritus frumenti | **WHISKEY** | | **FLECK, DOT** |
| spirochete | **BACTERIA** | spot card | **PIP** |
| spit | **SKEWER, ROD** | spotless | **CLEAN** |
| spite | **MEANNESS** | spot of color | **BLOB** |
| spiteful | **VINDICTIVE, MALIGN** | spotted | **DAPPLED** |
| spiteful woman | **CAT** | spotted dog | **BRINDLE** |
| Spithead | **SOLENT** | spotted feline | **LEOPARD** |
| spittoon | **CUSPIDOR** | spotted horse | **PINTO** |
| splash | **SPLATTER, SPATTER** | spotted wildcat | **OCELOT** |
| splash through mud | **SLOSH** | spotty | **UNEVEN** |
| splendid | **SUPERB** | spouse | **MATE, WIFE,** |
| splendor | **POMP** | | **HUSBAND** |
| splicing machine | **EDITOR** | spout | **GUSH, SPURT** |
| splinter | **SLIVER** | spout for drawing sap | **SPILE** |
| split | **CUT, CLEAVE, REND,** | spray | **ATOMIZE** |
| | **RIVE, DIVIDE** | spread | **WIDEN, DISPERSE** |
| split into thin layers | **LAMINATE** | spread abroad | **STREW** |
| split second | **MOMENT, WINK** | spread between supports | **SPAN** |
| splotch | **STAIN, SPOT** | spread by rumor | **NOISE** |
| Spode | **CHINA** | spread defamation | **LIBEL** |
| spoil | **MAR, ROT** | spread for bread | **BUTTER,** |
| spoiled child | **BRAT** | | **JAM, JELLY** |
| spoiler of plans | **MARPLOT** | spread for drying | **TED** |
| spoiler on a plane | **FLAP** | spread on thick | **SLATHER** |
| spoils | **BOOTY, LOOT,** | spread out | **OPEN** |
| | **PLUNDER** | spread out battle line | **DEPLOY** |
| spoke | **RUNG, BRACE** | spread outward | **FLARE** |
| spoken | **ORAL, VERBAL** | spread over | **COVER** |
| spoken exam | **ORAL** | spree | **BINGE, BENDER, TOOT** |
| sponge | **CADGE** | sprig | **SHOOT, TWIG** |
| sponger | **MOOCHER, CADGER** | sprightly | **PERT** |
| sponsor | **BACKER** | sprightly tune | **LILT, AIR** |
| spontaneous | **IMPULSIVE** | spring | **SOURCE, FONT, LEAP,** |
| spoof | **PARODY, SATIRE** | | **HOP, JUMP, COIL** |
| spook | **GHOST, HAUNT,** | spring back | **REBOUND** |
| | **GOBLIN, SHADE** | spring bloomer | **IRIS, TULIP,** |
| spooky | **EERIE** | | **CROCUS, VIOLET, LILAC,** |
| spool | **REEL, BOBBIN** | | **HYACINTH, LILY** |
| spoon | **NECK, SMOOCH, LADLE** | spring festival | **EASTER,** |
| spoonbill | **SHOVELER** | | **PASSOVER** |

| | |
|---|---|
| spring-like | VERNAL |
| spring month | MARCH, APRIL, MAY, JUNE |
| spring on one foot | HOP |
| spring suddenly | BOUNCE |
| spring up | ARISE |
| springy | ELASTIC |
| sprinkle | SPATTER |
| sprinkle a lawn | WATER |
| sprinkle with flour | DREDGE |
| sprinkle with powder | DUST |
| sprint | RACE, RUN |
| sprite | ELF, FAIRY, GOBLIN |
| sprite in *The Tempest* | ARIEL |
| sprout | SHOOT, SPRIG |
| sprout artificially | MALT |
| spruce | NATTY, TRIM, NEAT, TIDY, NEATEN |
| spry | AGILE, NIMBLE |
| spud | POTATO |
| spun | WOVE, WOVEN |
| spur | GOAD, ROWEL, IMPEL, STIMULUS |
| spurious | FALSE |
| spurious imitation | SHAM |
| spurn | DISDAIN, SCORN |
| spy | AGENT |
| spy employed by police | NARK |
| spy group (abbr.) | CIA |
| squabble | QUARREL, BICKER |
| squalid | SORDID |
| squander | SPEND, WASTE |
| square | CORNY |
| square of butter | PAT |
| square of three | NINE |
| squaring tool | EDGER |
| squash | GOURD |
| squat | STUBBY |
| squatter | NESTER |
| squeal | TATTLE |
| squeamish | DELICATE |
| squeeze | WRING, PINCH |
| squint | PEER |
| s-shaped molding | OGEE |
| stab | PIERCE |
| stable | FIXED, STEADY |
| stable compartment | STALL |
| stack role | NESS |
| stadium cheer | RAH |
| staff | PERSONNEL, POLE |
| staff officer | AIDE |
| staff of life | BREAD |
| staff of office | MACE, SCEPTER |
| stag | DEER, HART |
| stage | PLATFORM |
| stage comedy | FARCE |
| stage direction | ENTER, EXEUNT |

| | |
|---|---|
| stage hint | CUE |
| stage in development | PHASE |
| stage of a journey | LEG, LAP |
| stage of civilization | CULTURE |
| stage of history | ERA, EPOCH |
| stage of insect growth | LARVA |
| stage of travel (obs.) | GEST |
| stage parentheses | ASIDE |
| stage presentation | REVUE, PLAY, DRAMA, REVIEW |
| stage setting | SCENE |
| stage whisper | ASIDE |
| stagger | REEL |
| stagnant | FOUL, INERT |
| stagnate | ROT |
| stag's mate | DOE |
| staid | SEDATE, SOBER |
| stain | BLOT, BLEMISH, FLAW, SPOT, DYE |
| stair | STEP |
| stair part | RISER, TREAD |
| stair post | NEWEL |
| stairwell | SHAFT |
| stake | PEG, WAGER, ANTE |
| stalactite | ICICLE |
| stale | OLD, TRITE |
| stalemate | DRAW |
| stalk | HUNT, STEM |
| stalk game | HUNT |
| stalk of grain | STRAW |
| stalk vegetable | CELERY |
| stall | BOOTH |
| stallion | STUD, HORSE |
| stalwart | STRONG, STURDY |
| stamina | ENDURANCE |
| stammer | STUTTER |
| stamp | POSTAGE, SEAL, TRAMP, STOMP |
| stampede | DEBACLE |
| stamping device | DIE |
| stamp out | CRUSH |
| stance | POSE |
| stanch | STOP, STEM |
| stand | RISE, REAR |
| stand against | RESIST |
| standard | NORM |
| standard of perfection | IDEAL |
| standard quantity | UNIT |
| stand by | AID |
| standby | ALTERNATE |
| stand for | REPRESENT |
| stand for office | RUN |
| stand in | SUBSTITUTE |
| standing | STATUS |
| stand off | EVADE |
| stand on edge | UPEND |
| stannum | TIN |
| stanza | VERSE |

stanza of eight lines **TRIOLET**
staple grain **RICE, WHEAT**
star **TWINKLER, SUN,
ASTERISK**
starch **SAGO**
starchy edible root **TARO**
star cluster **NEBULA**
stare **GAPE, OGLE, GAZE,
GAWK**
stare open-mouthed **GAPE**
stare sullenly **GLOWER**
stark **BARE**
star (prefix) **ASTRO**
star-shaped **ASTRAL,
STELLATE**
start **LEAD, BEGIN, ONSET,
BEGINNING, INITIATE**
start again **REOPEN, RESUME**
start a Model T **CRANK**
start aside **DODGE**
startle **SURPRISE**
start of college cheer **HIP**
start off **LEAD**
start of the fiscal year
(2 wds.) **JANUARY FIRST**
start of the weekend
**SATURDAY**
start on a cruise **EMBARK**
start out **EMBARK**
start up again **RENEW**
starve **FAMISH**
stash **HIDE**
state **DECLARE, AVER, SAY,
CONDITION, STATUS**
state (Fr.) **ETAT**
state as a fact **POSIT**
state further **ADD**
state in India **ASSAM, SIKKIM**
stately **REGAL, TALL**
stately residence **MANOR**
state meaning of **DEFINE**
statement **ASSERTION**
statement of belief **CREDO**
state of anxiety **SUSPENSE**
state of disorder **MESS**
state-of-emergency crime
**LOOTING**
state of extreme happiness
(2 wds.) **SEVENTH HEAVEN**
state of feeling **MOOD**
state of health **CONDITION**
state of mind **MOOD, TEMPER**
state of perfection
(comp. wd.)
**FARE-THEE-WELL**
state of unconsciousness **COMA**
state policeman **TROOPER**
state positively **ASSERT, AVER**

state's leader **GOVERNOR**
state without proof **ALLEGE**
station **TERMINAL, DEPOT**
stationary **FIXED, SET**
stationer's item **INK, PAPER**
station in life **RANK**
station wagon **CAR**
statistics **DATA**
statue **BUST**
statue base **PLINTH**
statue support **PEDESTAL**
statue trunk **TORSO**
stature **HEIGHT**
status **RANK, GRADE**
statute **LAW**
staunch **LOYAL, FAITHFUL**
stave **CUDGEL**
stay **ABIDE, REMAIN**
stay for **WAIT**
stead **LIEU**
steadfast **STAUNCH, FIRM**
steadiness **STABILITY**
steady **STABLE, SOLID**
steady pain **ACHE**
steak **MEAT**
steal **SNEAK, ROB, THIEVE**
steal cattle **RUSTLE**
steal furtively **SLINK**
stealthy **SNEAKY**
steam **VAPOR**
steam bath **SAUNA**
steamer **CLAM**
steamship **LINER**
steamship company **LINE**
steatite **TALC**
steed **HORSE, MOUNT**
steel **HARDEN, INURE**
steel beam **GIRDER**
steelhead **TROUT**
steep **PRECIPITOUS**
steeple **SPIRE**
steeplechase **RACE**
steep slope **SCARP, BLUFF,
CLIFF**
steer **GUIDE, PILOT, DRIVE**
steer clear of **AVOID**
steer enclosure **CORRAL,
KRAAL**
steering apparatus **RUDDER**
steer meat **BEEF**
steersman **PILOT, HELMSMAN**
steeve **LADE, STORE**
stein **MUG**
steinbok **ANTELOPE**
stem **STALK**
stem-like part **STIPE**
stench **ODOR, STINK**

| | |
|---|---|
| step | **PACE, STAIR, TREAD, WALK** |
| step and hop | **SKIP** |
| step of a ladder | **RUNG** |
| steppe | **PLAIN** |
| steps over a fence | **STILE** |
| stereo attachment (2 wds.) | **TAPE RECORDER, TAPE DECK** |
| stereotype | **PATTERN** |
| sterile | **BARREN** |
| stern | **GRIM, SEVERE, REAR, AFT** |
| stern-faced | **GRIM** |
| sternward | **ABAFT, AFT** |
| stevedore union (abbr.) | **ILO** |
| stew | **RAGOUT, SIMMER, OLLA** |
| stewed fruit | **COMPOTE** |
| stick | **ADHERE, CANE** |
| sticker | **LABEL** |
| stick out | **JUT** |
| stick together | **COHERE** |
| sticky stuff | **GOO, PASTE, GLUE, OOZE, SAP** |
| stiff | **TENSE, RIGID** |
| stiff-legged bird | **STORK** |
| stiff-necked | **STUBBORN** |
| stifle | **CHOKE, SMOTHER** |
| stigma | **BLOT, STAIN** |
| still | **MOTIONLESS, QUIET, YET, SILENT** |
| still picture | **SLIDE, SNAP, PHOTOGRAPH, SNAPSHOT** |
| stimulant | **TONIC** |
| stimulate | **STIR, ROUSE** |
| stimulus to creative thought | **INSPIRATION** |
| sting | **BITE, NIP** |
| stinging insect | **BEE, WASP, HORNET** |
| stinging plant | **NETTLE, SMARTWEED** |
| stingray | **SKATE, MANTA** |
| stingy | **MISERLY, MEAN** |
| stink | **STENCH, SMELL** |
| stint | **DUTY** |
| stipend | **ALLOWANCE** |
| stipulation | **PROVISO** |
| stir | **BUDGE, AROUSE, AGITATE, ROUSE, MIX, MOVE, BUSTLE** |
| stir the fire | **STOKE** |
| stitch | **SEW** |
| stitched line | **SEAM** |
| St. Louis ball club | **CARDINALS** |
| stoa | **PORTICO** |
| stoat | **ERMINE, WEASEL** |

| | |
|---|---|
| stock | **STORE** |
| stockade (Fr.) | **ETAPE** |
| stock exchange | **BOURSE** |
| stock farm | **RANCH** |
| stockholder's unit | **SHARE** |
| stocking disaster | **RUN** |
| stocking line | **SEAM** |
| stocking mishap | **SNAG** |
| stocking run (Brit.) | **LADDER** |
| stockings | **HOSE, HOSIERY, NYLONS** |
| stockings (Fr.) | **BAS** |
| stock of goods | **LINE** |
| stock of wealth | **CAPITAL** |
| stock-quoting machine | **TICKER** |
| stogie | **CIGAR** |
| stoic | **UNEMOTIONAL, STAID, STERN** |
| stoicism | **PATIENCE** |
| stoke | **FEED** |
| stoker | **FIREMAN** |
| stole | **ROBBED, SHAWL, VESTMENT, WRAP** |
| stolen property | **PELF, LOOT, BOOTY** |
| stone | **ROCK, PEBBLE, GEM, JEWEL** |
| stonecrop | **SEDUM** |
| stonecutter | **MASON** |
| stone monument | **STELA(E)** |
| stoneware (Fr.) | **GRES** |
| stone worker | **MASON** |
| stony | **HARD, ROCKY, COLD** |
| stooge | **FOOL** |
| stool | **SEAT** |
| stool pigeon | **INFORMANT** |
| stoop | **BEND, PORCH** |
| stop | **CEASE, HALT, DESIST, QUIT, PAUSE** |
| stop (naut.) | **AVAST** |
| stopgap | **RESOURCE** |
| stop gradually (2 wds.) | **TAPER OFF** |
| stopper | **CORK, PLUG** |
| stop talking (2 wds.) | **PIPE DOWN, SHUT UP** |
| stop up | **CLOG, PLUG** |
| stopwatch | **TIMER** |
| storage battery plate | **GRID** |
| storage bin | **GRANARY, MOW** |
| storage box | **BIN** |
| storage building | **SHED, ETAPE** |
| storage place | **ATTIC** |
| storage place for weapons | **ARMORY** |
| storax | **BALSAM, RESIN** |
| store | **ACCUMULATE, SHOP, MARKET, MART** |

| | |
|---|---|
| store correspondence | **FILE** |
| stored fodder | **ENSILAGE** |
| store employee | **CLERK** |
| store event | **SALE** |
| store fodder | **ENSILE** |
| store for future use | **STASH, SAVE** |
| storehouse (Fr.) | **ETAPE** |
| storekeeper | **RETAILER, MERCHANT** |
| store label (2 wds.) | **PRICE TAG** |
| store up | **AMASS** |
| storm | **GALE, RAGE, RAVE, FURY, TEMPEST, CYCLONE, TORNADO, HURRICANE** |
| storm center | **EYE** |
| stormy | **WINDY** |
| story | **TALE, YARN, FLOOR** |
| story fabricator | **LIAR** |
| storyteller | **RACONTEUR** |
| stout | **ALE, FAT, OBESE** |
| stouthearted | **BRAVE** |
| stout stick | **BAT** |
| stout string | **CORD, TWINE** |
| stove | **COOKER, RANGE, OVEN** |
| stove compartment | **OVEN** |
| stove fuel | **GAS** |
| stow | **PACK, STORE** |
| stow cargo | **STEEVE** |
| straggle | **STRAY, WANDER** |
| straight | **DIRECT, UNBENT** |
| straight course | **BEELINE** |
| straight edge | **RULER** |
| straighten | **ALINE, ALIGN** |
| straightforward | **CANDID, FRANK** |
| strain | **STRESS** |
| strained | **TENSE, TAUT** |
| strainer | **SIEVE** |
| strait | **NECK, NARROW** |
| strand | **ABANDON, MAROON, DESERT** |
| strange | **FOREIGN, ALIEN, ODD, QUEER, UNUSUAL** |
| strange (prefix) | **XENO** |
| strangle | **CHOKE, STIFLE** |
| strap | **BELT, STROP** |
| strap on a falcon's leg | **JESS** |
| strapping | **TALL, ROBUST** |
| strass | **PASTE** |
| stratagem | **RUSE, WILE** |
| Stratford's river | **AVON** |
| strath | **VALLEY** |
| stratum | **LAYER** |
| stratum of ore | **VEIN, SEAM** |
| straw | **HAY, SIPPER** |
| strawberry bass | **CRAPPIE** |

| | |
|---|---|
| strawberry-colored horse | **ROAN** |
| straw hat | **PANAMA** |
| straw man | **SCARECROW** |
| straw rug | **MAT** |
| straw vote | **POLL** |
| stray | **ROAM, ROVE, ERR, RAMBLE, WANDER** |
| stray dog | **CUR** |
| stray from course | **STRAGGLE** |
| streak | **STRIPE** |
| streak in marble | **VEIN** |
| stream | **BROOK, RILL, RIVER, RIVULET, CREEK** |
| stream along | **FLOW** |
| streamer | **RIBBON** |
| streamlet | **RILL, RUNLET** |
| streamline | **ORGANIZE** |
| street | **BOULEVARD, ROAD, AVENUE** |
| street (Fr.) | **RUE** |
| street Arab | **GAMIN, URCHIN** |
| streetcar | **TRAM** |
| street drain | **SEWER** |
| street peddler | **VENDOR** |
| street sign | **SLOW, STOP, YIELD** |
| street urchin | **GAMIN** |
| strength | **FORCE, POWER, SINEW, THEW** |
| strengthen | **BRACE, TOUGHEN** |
| strengthen a levee | **REVET** |
| strengthening medicine | **TONIC** |
| strenuous | **SEVERE, ARDUOUS** |
| stress | **EMPHASIZE, STRAIN, ACCENT** |
| stretch | **DISTEND, EXPAND** |
| stretched tight | **TAUT** |
| stretcher | **LITTER** |
| stretch injuriously | **SPRAIN** |
| stretch of land | **TRACT, FIELD** |
| stretch out | **EKE** |
| stretch the neck | **CRANE** |
| stretchy | **ELASTIC** |
| strew | **SCATTER** |
| stria | **GROOVE, CHANNEL** |
| striate | **STRIPE, FURROW** |
| strict | **STERN, SEVERE** |
| strictness | **RIGOR** |
| stricture | **CENSURE, RESISTANCE** |
| stride | **STEP** |
| strident | **SHRILL** |
| strife | **WAR, TROUBLE** |
| strigil | **SCRAPER** |
| strike | **POKE, PUNCH, HIT, SMITE, SWAT** |
| strikebreaker | **SCAB** |
| strike lightly | **PAT, TAP, RAP** |
| strike out | **DELE, DELETE** |

strike repeatedly **BEAT**
strike with the hand **SLAP, SMACK**
strike with the head **BUTT**
strike with violence **SLAM**
striking **REMARKABLE**
striking effect **ECLAT**
string **CORD, LACE**
stringed instrument **FIDDLE, HARP, VIOL, VIOLA, VIOLIN, LUTE, LYRE, UKULELE, BANJO, GUITAR, CELLO, MANDOLIN, PIANO**
stringent **RIGID, SEVERE**
stringy **ROPY**
strip **SHRED, DENUDE**
stripe **BAR, STREAK**
striped horse **ZEBRA**
strip of cloth **TAPE**
strip off skin **FLAY**
strip of leather **STRAP, THONG**
strip of wood **SLAT**
stripling **LAD**
strive **AIM, CONTEND**
strive for (2 wds.) **SHOOT AT**
strive mightily **STRAIN**
strive with **VIE**
strobe **FLASH, LIGHT**
stroke **PAT, CARESS, PET**
stroke of luck (sl.) **FLUKE**
stroll **AMBLE, SAUNTER**
strong **STURDY, POWERFUL, POTENT**
strong affection **LOVE**
strong and healthy **ROBUST**
strong and resolute **STALWART**
strong and tough **RUGGED**
strongbox **CHEST**
strong breeze **WIND**
strong cart **DRAY**
strong cloth **SCRIM**
strong cord **ROPE**
strong cotton **PIMA**
strong herb **GARLIC**
stronghold **FORT**
strong man of myth **ATLAS, HERCULES, TITAN**
strong-minded **DETERMINED**
strong point **FORTE**
strong request **DEMAND**
strong taste **TANG**
strong upward movement **SURGE**
strong wind **GALE**
strong yearning **ITCHING, ACHE**
strop **STRAP**

strop a razor **HONE, SHARPEN**
strophe **STANZA**
structure **BUILDING, FRAME**
structure on a roof **CUPOLA**
struggle **VIE, CONTEND**
strum **THRUM**
strut **SWAGGER, PRANCE**
stub **STUMP**
stubble **BEARD**
stubborn **BALKY, DOGGED**
stubborn animal **MULE, DONKEY, BURRO**
stubby **SHORT**
stuck-up person **SNOB**
stud **BUTTON, SCREW**
student **PUPIL**
student monitor **PREFECT**
student of an English school **ETONIAN**
student pilot **CADET**
student's p.m. assignment **HOMEWORK**
stud for shoe sole **HOBNAIL**
studio **ATELIER**
stud with ornaments **BESET, BEJEWEL**
study **CON, READ, PERUSE, PORE**
study closely **EXAMINE**
study course **SEMINAR**
stuff **CRAM**
stuffed shirt **PRIG**
stuffing **FILLING**
stuffy **PRIM, STODGY**
stumble **TRIP, FALL**
stumbling block **OBSTACLE**
stun **AMAZE, DAZE**
stunt **FEAT, TRICK**
stunted animal **RUNT**
stupe **COMPRESS**
stupefy **DAZE**
stupid **SIMPLE, IDIOTIC, ASININE**
stupid fellow **SIMPLETON, ASS, OAF, DUNCE**
stupidity **DULLNESS**
stupor **LETHARGY, TORPOR**
sturdy **STRONG, STOUT**
sturdy fabric **DENIM**
sturdy tree **OAK, MAPLE**
sturgeon roe **CAVIAR**
stutter **STAMMER**
sty **PEN, PIGPEN**
Stygian **INFERNAL**
style **FASHION, MODE**
style of singing (2 wds.) **BEL CANTO**

| | | | |
|---|---|---|---|
| style of type | ELITE, ROMAN, ITALIC | suburban shopping area | MALL, CENTER |
| stylet | STILETTO | subvert | SUPPRESS, DEMOLISH |
| stylish | CHIC, CLASSY | succeed | ENSUE, ARRIVE, MAKE GOOD, WIN |
| stylish Britisher | TOFF | | |
| stylus | NEEDLE | succeeding | NEXT |
| styptic | ALUM | success | PROSPERITY, HIT |
| suave | SOFT, SMOOTH | succession | SERIES |
| subcontinent of Asia | INDIA, ASIA MINOR | successful move | COUP |
| | | succinct | TERSE, CONCISE |
| subdivision | SECTION | succotash ingredient | CORN |
| subdue | TAME, CALM | succulent | TASTY |
| subject | TEXT, THEME | succulent plant | ALOE |
| subject of discussion | TOPIC | succumb | SUBMIT, YIELD |
| subject of verb | NOUN | such and no more | MERE |
| subject to argument | MOOT | suck | DRAW, INHALE |
| sublime | GRAND | sucker | DUPE, LOLLIPOP |
| submarine missile | POLARIS | suckerfish | REMORA |
| submarine sandwich | HERO | suckle | NURSE |
| submerge | SINK | suction | INTAKE |
| submissive | MEEK, TAME, DOCILE | sudden | ABRUPT |
| | | sudden attack | RAID, SORTIE, SWOOP |
| submit | DEFER, BEND | sudden blast of wind | GUST |
| submit evidence | PROVE | sudden blaze | FLARE |
| subordinate | INFERIOR | sudden bump | JOLT |
| subordinate ruler | SATRAP | sudden burst of energy | SPURT |
| subpoena | SUMMONS | sudden death | OVERTIME |
| subscription department's delight | RENEWAL | sudden decline | LAPSE, SLUMP |
| subsequently | AFTER, LATER, THEN, LATER ON | sudden downpour | |
| | | | CLOUDBURST, STORM, SHOWER |
| subside | EBB, SETTLE, ABATE | | |
| subsidiary | AUXILIARY | sudden fear | ALARM, PANIC |
| subsidy | GRANT, SUPPORT | sudden gush | SPURT |
| subsist | LIVE | sudden inspiration | |
| substance | GIST | | BRAINSTORM |
| substance for violin strings | | sudden loud noise | BANG |
| | ROSIN | suddenly, like magic | PRESTO |
| substantial | MEATY | sudden muscular contraction. | |
| substantiate | CONFIRM | | TIC, SPASM |
| substantive | NOUN, PRONOUN | sudden pain | PANG, TWINGE |
| substitute | PROXY, SURROGATE | sudden shock | JOLT |
| substitute in office | DEPUTY | sudden start | JERK |
| substitute squad (2 wds.) | SCRUB TEAM, SECOND STRING | sudden stroke | COUP |
| | | sudden thrust | STAB |
| | | suds | FROTH |
| substructure | FOUNDATION | suds maker | SOAP, DETERGENT, SHAMPOO |
| subterfuge | ARTIFICE, EXCUSE | | |
| subtle | SLY | sue | PLEAD |
| subtle air | AURA | suet | FAT |
| subtle sarcasm | IRONY | suffer | ENDURE, BEAR |
| subtract | DEDUCT | sufferer | VICTIM |
| suburban builder | DEVELOPER | suffer from heat | SWELTER |
| suburban residence | VILLA, SPLIT-LEVEL, BUNGALOW, RANCH | suffer remorse | RUE |
| | | suffering | PAIN |
| | | suffice | SERVE |
| suburban restaurant | INN | sufficient | AMPLE |

| | | | |
|---|---|---|---|
| suffocate | CHOKE, SMOTHER | summon | CALL, CITE |
| suffrage | FRANCHISE, | summon by name | PAGE |
| | VOTE | summon forth | EVOKE |
| sugar | SUCROSE, GLUCOSE | summon together | MUSTER |
| sugar ladle | SCOOP | summon up | RALLY |
| sugar portion | CUBE, | sump | PIT |
| | TEASPOON | sumptuous | LAVISH |
| Sugar State | LOUISIANA | sumptuous meal | REPAST, |
| sugar tree | MAPLE | | FEAST |
| sugary | SWEET | sun | STAR, SOL |
| suggest indirectly | HINT, | sunbeam | RAY |
| | ALLUDE | sunburn | TAN |
| suggestion | ADVICE, OPINION | sunburn preventative (2 wds.) | |
| sui generis | UNIQUE | | TANNING LOTION |
| suit | BEFIT, BECOME | sundae topping | NUTS, SYRUP, |
| suitable | APT, FIT | | CHOCOLATE, CHERRY |
| suitable for farming | ARABLE | sunday cut of meat | ROAST |
| suitable place | NICHE | sunday lecture | SERMON |
| suit at cards | SPADES, | sunday speech (abbr.) | SER |
| | DIAMONDS, | sunder | TEAR, RIP, SHRED |
| | HEARTS, CLUBS | sundial arm | GNOMON |
| suit at law | CASE | sundog | PARHELION |
| suitcase | GRIP, VALISE, | sundown | EVE, DUSK |
| | ETUI | sundry | VARIOUS, DIVERS |
| suitmaker | TAILOR | sunfish | BREAM |
| suit material | SERGE | Sunflower State | KANSAS |
| suit of mail | ARMOR | sunken fence | HAHA |
| suite of rooms | FLAT | sunless spot | SHADE |
| suitor | SWAIN, BEAU | sunny | BRIGHT, CHEERFUL |
| sulk | MOPE, POUT, BROOD | sun parlor | SOLARIUM |
| sulky | SULLEN | sun ring | CORONA |
| sullen | DOUR, GLUM, | sunrise | SUNUP, DAWN |
| | MOROSE | sunrise direction | EAST |
| sully | SMEAR, DEFILE | sun satellite | PLANET |
| sulphur | BRIMSTONE | sunshade | PARASOL |
| sultan's wives | HAREM | Sunshine State | FLORIDA, |
| sultry | HOT, TORRID | | NEW MEXICO, |
| sulu | SARONG | | SOUTH DAKOTA |
| sum | TOTAL, ADD | sunup | DAWN, SUNRISE |
| sum of money | FUND | Suomi | FINLAND |
| sum total | ENTIRETY | sup | DINE, EAT |
| sum up | TOT | super | GREATER, BETTER |
| summarize | TOT UP, | superannuate | RETIRE |
| | RECAP | superannuated | OBSOLETE |
| summary | PPECIS, BRIEF | superb | SPLENDID |
| summer (Fr.) | ETE | supercilious | SNOBBISH |
| summer drink | ICED COFFEE, | superego | CONSCIENCE |
| | ICED TEA, ADE | superficial | CURSORY, |
| summer flounder | FLUKE | | SHALLOW |
| summer hat | PANAMA, | superfluous | EXCESSIVE, |
| | BOATER | | PROFUSE |
| summer house | COTTAGE | superior | ABOVE |
| summer resort area | SHORE, | superlative | MOST |
| | BEACH, MOUNTAINS | superlative suffix | EST |
| summer skin tone | TAN | Superman's girl | LOIS |
| summer tendency | LETHARGY | supermarket | STORE |
| summit | ACME, APEX, | supernatural | MIRACULOUS |
| | CREST, PEAK, TOP | supersede | REPLACE |

| | | | |
|---|---|---|---|
| supervise | **OVERSEE** | surgical probe | **STYLET** |
| supervisor | **BOSS,** | surgical saw | **TREPAN** |
| | **OVERSEER, DIRECTOR,** | surgical stylet | **TROCAR** |
| | **CONDUCTOR** | surgical thread | **SETON** |
| supine | **INDOLENT,** | surly | **MOROSE, SULLEN** |
| | **LISTLESS** | surmise | **GUESS** |
| supper | **MEAL, DINNER** | surmount | **CONQUER,** |
| supplant | **REPLACE, UPROOT** | | **SUBDUE** |
| supple | **PLIANT, ELASTIC,** | surmounting | **ATOP** |
| | **FLEXIBLE** | surname | **COGNOMEN** |
| supplement | **EKE** | surpass | **EXCEL, OUTDO,** |
| supplementary | **ADDITIONAL** | | **BEST** |
| supplicate | **PRAY, PLEAD** | surplus | **EXCESS** |
| supplication | **PLEA** | surprise | **STARTLE** |
| supply | **PROVIDE** | surprise attack | **RAID** |
| supply food | **CATER,** | surrender | **CEDE, YIELD** |
| | **NOURISH** | surrender rights | **WAIVE** |
| supply of money | **FUNDS** | surround | **BESET** |
| supply provisions | **PURVEY** | surrounded by | **AMID** |
| supply station | **DEPOT** | surrounding (prefix) | **PERI** |
| supply with fuel | **STOKE** | surroundings | **DECOR,** |
| supply with funds | **ENDOW** | | **ENVIRONMENT** |
| supply with weapons | **ARM** | surveyor | **LINEMAN** |
| support | **BEAR, LEG, PROP,** | suspend | **HANG** |
| | **BRACE, MAINTAIN,** | suspense | **ANXIETY,** |
| | **BOOST** | | **UNCERTAINTY** |
| support a motion | **SECOND** | suspension | **DELAY** |
| support for a glass | **COASTER** | | **FAILURE** |
| suppose | **GUESS, OPINE,** | suspicion | **DISTRUST** |
| | **DEEM, THINK** | suspicious | **LEERY** |
| supposing (2 wds.) | **AS IF** | sustain | **SUPPORT, ENDURE** |
| supposition | **HYPOTHESIS,** | sustenance | **FOOD** |
| | **THEORY** | Sutherland specialty | **ARIA** |
| suppress | **ELIDE, STIFLE,** | suture | **SEAM** |
| | **SIT ON, STOP,** | swab | **MOP** |
| | **ESTOP** | swagger | **STRUT** |
| supremacy | **MASTERY** | swaggering pretense of | |
| supreme | **UTMOST** | courage | **BRAVADO** |
| Supreme Court group | **NINE** | swain | **SUITOR, ADMIRER** |
| supreme Egyptian deity | **AMON** | swallow | **BIRD, GULP** |
| surcease | **RESPITE** | swallow up | **EAT, ENGULF,** |
| sure | **IN THE BAG,** | | **DEVOUR** |
| | **CERTAIN** | swami | **PUNDIT** |
| sure-footed | **NIMBLE** | swamp | **BOG, FEN, MARSH,** |
| surf | **BREAKERS** | | **MORASS** |
| surface | **AREA, TOP** | swamp grass | **REED** |
| surface a street | **PAVE** | swampish | **MIRY** |
| surface coating | **SCUM** | swampland tract | |
| surface depression | **DENT** | | **EVERGLADES** |
| surface drain | **SEWER** | swan | **CYGNUS, COB** |
| surface of a gem | **FACET** | swanky dwelling place | |
| surfeit | **SATE, GLUT** | (2 wds.) | |
| surf roar | **ROTE** | | **DUPLEX APARTMENT** |
| surge | **TIDE** | swansdown | **FLANNEL** |
| surge of emotion | **THRILL** | swap | **BARTER, TRADE** |
| surgeon's instrument | **SCALPEL** | sward | **SOD, TURF** |
| surgical compress | **STUPE** | swarm | **TEEM, HIVE** |
| surgical knife | **SCALPEL** | swarming | **ALIVE** |

| | | | |
|---|---|---|---|
| swarthy | DARK, DUSKY | swing around | SLUE |
| swat | STRIKE, SMACK | swinging bed | HAMMOCK |
| sway | SWING | swing music | JIVE |
| sway in the breeze | WAVE | swipe | STEAL, SWEEP |
| swearword | OATH, CURSE | swirl | TWIST, EDDY |
| Swedish beer | OL | Swiss cabin | CHALET |
| Swedish canton | LAN | Swiss canton | URI, ZUG |
| Swedish city | STOCKHOLM, UPSALA | Swiss capital | BERN |
| | | Swiss city | BASEL, |
| Swedish clover | ALSIKE | | ZURICH, GENEVA |
| Swedish Nightingale | | Swiss cottage | CHALET |
| | JENNY LIND | Swiss district | CANTON |
| sweet | SUGARY | Swiss lake | ZUG |
| sweet confection | CANDY | Swiss mountain | ALP |
| sweeten | CANDY, SUGAR | Swiss mountaineer's song |
| sweetened drink | JULEP | | YODEL |
| sweetheart | DREAMBOAT, | Swiss river | AAR |
| | LOVER, PARAMOUR, | switch | CHANGE, DIVERT |
| | DARLING | sword | RAPIER, SABER |
| sweet liqueur | CREME | swordfish's snout | SERRA |
| sweetmeat | BONBON | sword handle | HILT |
| sweet potato | YAM | sycophant | PARASITE, |
| sweet roll | BUN | | TOADY |
| sweet-scented plant | JASMINE | sylvan demigod | SATYR |
| sweet-smelling | REDOLENT | symbol | EMBLEM |
| sweet song | BALLAD | symbol for tellurium | TE |
| sweet substance | HONEY, | symbol for tin | SN |
| | SUGAR, SYRUP | symbol of bondage | YOKE |
| sweet wine | PORT | symbol of peace | DOVE |
| swell | EXPAND, DISTEND | symbol of ruthenium | RU |
| swelling | EDEMA | symbol of victory | PALM, |
| swell out | BULGE | | VEE |
| swerve | SKEW, VEER, | symmetry | BALANCE, |
| | CAREEN, DIVERGE | | HARMONY |
| swift | FAST, RAPID, QUICK | sympathize | CARE, PITY |
| swiftly | APACE, FAST, | sympathy | COMPASSION |
| | QUICKLY | syncopated rhythm | RAGTIME |
| swiftness | HASTE, SPEED | synonomous | SAME, SIMILAR |
| swig | DRAFT | synthetic fabric | ORLON, |
| swill | SLOP, GARBAGE | | RAYON, NYLON, |
| swim | FLOAT, FLOOD | | ARNEL, DACRON |
| swim fin | FLIPPER | synthetic material | PLASTIC, |
| swimming | NATANT | | FIBERGLAS, FORMICA |
| swimming mammal | OTTER, | syrup tree | MAPLE |
| | SEAL, WHALE, | system | METHOD |
| | BEAVER, PORPOISE, | systematic | REGULAR, |
| | DOLPHIN, WALRUS | | PRECISE |
| swimming place | POOL | system of belief | CREED, |
| swimming pool | TANK, | | DOGMA |
| | NATATORIUM | system of moral principles |
| swindle | DUPE, GYP, | | ETHICS |
| | BILK, CON | system of signals | CODE |
| swindling scheme | BUNCO | system of weights |
| swine | HOG, PIG, BOAR | | AVOIRDUPOIS |
| swine-like | PORCINE | syzygy | PAIR |
| swing | SWAY | | |

## T

| | |
|---|---|
| taa | PAGODA |
| tab | LABEL, TAG, BILL |
| tabanid | HORSEFLY |
| tabby | CAT |
| table | BOARD |
| tableau | SCENE, SKIT |
| tablecloth linen | DAMASK |
| table dish | TUREEN |
| table extension | LEAF |
| tableland | MESA |
| table linen | DAMASK, NAPKIN |
| tablemount | GUYOT |
| table of contents | INDEX |
| table protector | TRIVET |
| table scrap | ORT |
| table support | LEG |
| tablet | PAD, SLATE |
| table tennis | PING PONG |
| tabloid | NEWSPAPER |
| taboo | FORBID, BAN |
| tacit | SILENT, UNSPOKEN |
| taciturn | SILENT |
| tack | NAIL |
| tackle | HARNESS, GEAR |
| tact | DIPLOMACY |
| tad | BOY |
| tadpole | POLLIWOG |
| tag | LABEL, TAB |
| tag of lace | AGLET |
| Tahiti capital | PAPEETE |
| tailboard | ENDGATE |
| tailed amphibians | SALAMANDER, NEWT |
| tailless amphibian | TOAD, FROG |
| tailor | SEW |
| taint | CONTAMINATE, ADULTERATE |
| Taiwan | FORMOSA |
| Taj Mahal site | AGRA |
| take | GRASP, SEIZE |
| take a bite | TASTE |
| take a break | REST |
| take a chair | SIT |
| take a chance | RISK, DARE |
| take a dip | SWIM |
| take a direction | STEER |
| take advantage of | USE |
| take advice | HEED |
| take after | FOLLOW, PURSUE |
| take along | BRING, CARRY |
| take a meal | EAT |
| take another spouse | REWED |
| take an upright position | STAND |
| take a shower | BATHE |
| take as one's own | ADOPT |
| take a stroll | WALK |
| take a trip | TRAVEL, TREK |
| take away | REMOVE |
| take away by force | WREST |
| take back | RECANT, RETRACT |
| take by surprise (2 wds.) | BOWL OVER |
| take care | BEWARE |
| take care of | TREAT, LOOK AFTER, SEE TO, TEND |
| take cognizance of | NOTICE |
| take cover | HIDE |
| take evening meal | DINE, SUP |
| take first prize | WIN |
| take five | REST, BREAK |
| take food | EAT |
| take for granted | ASSUME, PRESUME |
| take from | DEPRIVE, SUBTRACT |
| take in oxygen | BREATHE, INHALE |
| take in sail | REEF |
| take into custody | ARREST |
| take it easy | RELAX, REST |
| take long steps | STRIDE |
| take meals for pay | BOARD |
| take notice | HEED, ESPY, WATCH |
| take off | DOFF |
| take offense at | RESENT |
| take on cargo | LADE |
| take out | DELE |
| take-out order (2 wds.) | TO GO |
| take part (2 wds.) | SIT IN |
| take pleasure in | ENJOY |
| take prisoner | ARREST, CAPTURE |
| take the bus | RIDE |
| take the car | DRIVE |
| take the sun | TAN |
| take to court | SUE |
| take to jail | ARREST |
| take to the air | FLY AWAY, SOAR, FLY |
| take turns | ROTATE, ALTERNATE, SPELL |
| take umbrage at | RESENT |
| take up again | RESUME |
| take up weapons | ARM |
| take up with | BEFRIEND |
| taking everything into account | OVERALL |

| | | | |
|---|---|---|---|
| tal | CYMBALS | tank | VAT, CISTERN |
| talc | STEATITE | tankard | STEIN |
| tale bearer | TATTLER, | tank farming | HYDROPONICS |
| | GOSSIP | tanned hide | LEATHER |
| talent | SKILL, GIFT | tansy | WEED |
| tale of adventure | GEST | tantalize | TEASE |
| tale of daring | SAGA | Tantalus' daughter | NIOBE |
| talipes | CLUBFOOT | tantamount | EQUAL |
| talisman | OMEN, CHARM, | tantara | FANFARE |
| | AMULET | tantrum | TEMPER |
| talk | JAW, GAB, CHAT, | tap | FAUCET, SPIGOT |
| | SPEAK, DISCUSS, | tap down | TAMP |
| | CONVERSE, | tape | RECORD, BIND |
| | CHATTER, PRATE | taper | CANDLE |
| talkative | GARRULOUS, | tapering object | WEDGE |
| | CHATTY | tapering solid | CONE |
| talk back | SASS | tapestry | ARRAS |
| talk foolishly | PRATE | tapioca | CASSAVA |
| talk idly | GAB, PRATE | tapioca-like food | SALEP |
| talk imperfectly | LISP, | taproom | BAR, SALOON, |
| | STUTTER, STAMMER | | PUB |
| talk indistinctly | SPUTTER, | tar | PITCH, SAILOR |
| | MUMBLE | tarantula | SPIDER |
| talking bird | MINA, | tarboosh | FEZ |
| | MYNA, PARROT | tardy | LATE, SLOW |
| talk slowly | DRAWL | tare | VETCH, WEED |
| talk up | PROMOTE | target | MARK, OBJECT |
| talk wildly | RANT, RAVE | target center | EYE, |
| tall | LOFTY, HIGH | | BULLSEYE |
| tall and thin | LANKY | Tar Heel State | |
| tall grass stalk | REED | | NORTH CAROLINA |
| tallow | SUET | tariff | DUTY |
| tall spar | MAST | Tarkington hero | PENROD |
| tall structure | TOWER, | tarnish | SMUDGE, |
| | SKYSCRAPER | | DISCOLOR |
| tall tale | YARN, FIB | taro paste | POI |
| tall wading bird | CRANE | taro root | EDDO |
| tally | SCORE | tarry | BIDE, LINGER, STAY |
| Talmud commentary | GEMARA | tarsier | LEMUR |
| Talmud text | MISHNA | tarsus | ANKLE |
| talon | CLAW | tart | ACID, SOUR |
| talus | ANKLE | tartan fabric | PLAID |
| tamarisk salt tree | ATLE | tartar | CALCULUS |
| tambour | DRUM | task | CHORE, JOB, |
| tame | DOMESTICATE, | | ERRAND, DUTY |
| | GENTLE, SUBDUE, | tassel | FRINGE |
| | DOCILE, HARMLESS | taste | FLAVOR, SAVOR, |
| tame animal | PET | | SAMPLE, SIP |
| Tamil | DRAVIDIAN | taste a lollipop | LICK |
| tamp | PACK | taste center | PALATE |
| tamper | MEDDLE | tasteful luxury | ELEGANCE |
| tan | BROWN, SUNBURN, | tasteless | INSIPID, VAPID |
| | ECRU, KHAKI | taste with pleasure | SAVOR |
| tandem | TEAM, BICYCLE | tasty | SAVORY |
| tangle | KNOT, SNARL, | ta-ta | GOODBYE |
| | RAVEL, MAT | Tatar lancer | UHLAN |
| tangled mass | MOP | tatter | RAG, SHRED |
| tangy herb | MINT | tatting | LACE |

| | | | |
|---|---|---|---|
| tattle | SQUEAL, RAT ON, TELL, SNITCH | technicality | DETAIL |
| taunt | TEASE, TWIT, GIBE | technique | METHOD |
| taupe | MOLESKIN | tedious | LONG, BORING |
| taut | TENSE | tedium | ENNUI |
| tavern | PUB, BAR, INN, SALOON | tee-hee | TITTER, SNICKER |
| | | teel | SESAME |
| tavern beverage | ALE, BEER | teem | ABOUND |
| tavern employee | BARMAID, BOUNCER | teeming | FULL, REPLETE |
| | | teeny | WEE |
| taw | MARBLE | teeter-totter | SEESAW |
| tawdry | CHEAP, GAUDY | teetotum | TOP |
| tawny | TANNED, DUSKY | tegula | TILE |
| tax | TOLL, LEVY, TARIFF | Teheran native | IRANI |
| taxi | CAB, HACK | tela | TISSUE |
| taxi chauffeur | CAB DRIVER, CABBIE | telegram | WIRE, MESSAGE |
| | | telegraphy inventor | MARCONI |
| taxi rider | PASSENGER, FARE | telephone | CALL |
| | | telephone book | DIRECTORY |
| taxi ticker | METER | telephone rod | POLE |
| tax official | ASSESSOR | telephone wire | LINE |
| taxus | YEW | telescope | GLASS |
| T-bone | STEAK | television award | EMMY |
| tea | CHA, OOLONG, PEKOE | television cabinet | CONSOLE |
| | | television porpoise | FLIPPER |
| teaberry | WINTERGREEN | television sound | AUDIO |
| tea cake | SCONE | tell | NARRATE, RELATE |
| teach | EDUCATE, TRAIN, TUTOR | teller of tall stories | LIAR, FIBBER |
| | | | |
| teacher | PROFESSOR | telling | VALID |
| teacher's concern | CLASS, STUDENT, PUPIL, LESSON | tell secrets | TATTLE |
| | | tell tales | BLAB, LIE, FIB |
| | | temblor | EARTHQUAKE |
| teaching staff | FACULTY | temerity | BOLDNESS, AUDACITY |
| tea container | CANISTER | | |
| teak | WOOD | temper | DANDER, MOOD |
| teal | DUCK | tempera | PAINT |
| team race | RELAY | temperament | DISPOSITION, MOOD |
| teamster | CARTER | | |
| team's turn at bat | INNING | temperance | MODERATION |
| tear | RIP, REND, RIVE, SPLIT | temperate | MILD |
| | | temper display | RAGE, TANTRUM |
| tear down | RAZE, DEMOLISH | | |
| tearful | SAD | tempered iron | STEEL |
| tear into | ATTACK | tempest | STORM, GALE |
| tear into shreds | TATTER | tempestuous | INCLEMENT |
| tear out | UPROOT | tempo | PACE, TIME |
| tear producer | ONION | temporal | SECULAR, EARTHLY |
| tear roughly | LACERATE | | |
| tear salad greens | SHRED | temporary | TRANSIENT |
| teary | CRYING | temporary breather | LULL |
| tease | IRRITATE, TANTALIZE, TAUNT, WORRY, RAZZ, TORMENT, ANNOY, PESTER, BADGER, TUM | temporary fashion | FAD, CRAZE |
| | | | |
| | | tempt | ENTICE, LURE |
| tease wool | TUM | temptress | SIREN |
| teatime | FOUR | ten | DECAD, DECADE |
| tea urn | SAMOVAR | tenacious | PERSISTENT |

| | | | |
|---|---|---|---|
| tenant | ROOMER, LODGER, BOARDER, LESSEE, RENTER | term | PERIOD, COURSE |
| | | termagant | SHREW |
| | | terminal | STATION, DEPOT |
| ten cents | DIME | terminal pole | ANODE, ELECTRODE |
| tend | LEAN, LEAD | | |
| tendency | DRIFT, TREND | terminate | END, FINISH |
| tender | SORE | term in logic | SORITES |
| tenderfoot | DUDE | term in office | TENURE |
| tending to arouse feelings | EMOTIVE | terminology | NOMENCLATURE |
| | | termite | ANT |
| tending to be silent | UNCOMMUNICATIVE, TACITURN | term of address | SIR |
| | | term of imprisonment | SENTENCE |
| tending to check | REPRESSIVE | term of royal address | SIRE, MAJESTY, HIGHNESS |
| tending to drive away | REPELLENT | | |
| | | terms | CONDITIONS |
| tending to wear away | EROSIVE | tern genus | STERNA |
| ten dollars (sl.) | SAWBUCK | terra alba | MAGNESIA |
| tendon | MUSCLE, THEW, SINEW | terrace | PATIO, VERANDA |
| | | terra cotta | POTTERY |
| tendril | SPRIG | terra firma dweller | EARTHMAN |
| tend to | MIND, NURSE | terrain | LAND |
| tenebrous | DARK, GLOOMY | terrapin | TURTLE |
| tenement | FLAT, APARTMENT, SLUM | terrene | EARTHLY, WORLDLY |
| tenement pest | RAT, ROACH | terret | RING |
| tenet | DOGMA, DOCTRINE | terrible | AWFUL, DREADFUL |
| tennis barrier | NET | terrible tsar | IVAN |
| tennis instructor | PRO | terrier | SKYE, FOX |
| tennis point | ACE | terrific | EXCITING |
| tennis pro | ACE | terrify | ALARM, FRIGHTEN, SCARE |
| tennis score | LOVE | | |
| tennis shoe | SNEAKER | territory | AREA |
| tennis stroke | LOB | terror | PANIC |
| tennis term | LOVE, SERVE, FAULT | terse | CONCISE, PITHY |
| | | test | EXAM, EXAMINE, EXAMINATION, TRIAL, TRY |
| tennis trophy | CUP | | |
| Tennyson hero | ENOCH | | |
| tenpenny | NAIL | test for fit (2 wds.) | TRY ON |
| tenpins | BOWLING | testify | DEPONE, DEPOSE |
| tense | EDGY TAUT, TIME | testimony | ATTESTATION |
| tension | STRESS, STRAIN | testimony weighers in court (2 wds.) | PETIT JURY |
| tensor | MUSCLE | | |
| tent | TEPEE, WIGWAM | test ore | ASSAY |
| tentacle | FEELER, PALP | testy | CRANKY |
| tentative | PROVISIONAL, TEMPORARY | Teuton | GERMAN |
| | | Texas bronco | MUSTANG |
| tent city | CAMP | Texas city | WACO, EL PASO, DALLAS, HOUSTON |
| tent-dwelling nomad | ARAB | | |
| tent show | CIRCUS | Texas evergreen shrub | BARETTA |
| tenth of a decade | YEAR | | |
| tenure | TERM | | |
| tenuous | DELICATE, THIN | Texas longhorn | STEER |
| ten years | DECADE | Texas shrine | ALAMO |
| tepee | TENT, WIGWAM | textiles | MERCERY |
| tepid | LUKEWARM | text of an opera | LIBRETTO |
| teredo | SHIPWORM | text of a play | SCRIPT |
| tergal | DORSAL | texture | WALE, GRAIN |

| | |
|---|---|
| Thackeray's Miss Sharp | **BECKY** |
| Thailand | **SIAM** |
| Thailand's neighbor | **LAOS** |
| thalium (chemical symbol) | **TL** |
| thankful | **GRATEFUL** |
| thankless person | **INGRATE** |
| thanks (Fr.) | **MERCI** |
| that boy | **HE, HIM** |
| that certain air | **AURA** |
| thatch palm | **NIPA** |
| that girl | **HER, SHE** |
| that is (Lat., 2 wds.) | **ID EST** |
| that is to say | **NAMELY** |
| that place | **THERE** |
| that thing | **IT** |
| that which follows | **SEQUEL** |
| that which gives relief | **BALM** |
| that which must be done | **DUTY** |
| that which one does best | **FORTE** |
| that which unlocks | **KEY** |
| thaumaturgy | **MAGIC** |
| thaw | **MELT** |
| the (Fr.) | **LE, LA, LES** |
| the (Ger.) | **DAS, DER** |
| the (Sp.) | **LA, EL, LOS, LAS** |
| theater | **ARENA, STAGE** |
| theater attendant | **USHER** |
| theater award | **TONY** |
| theater box | **LOGE** |
| theater lobby | **FOYER** |
| theater passageway | **AISLE** |
| theater platform | **STAGE** |
| theater play | **DRAMA** |
| theater sign | **SRO, EXIT** |
| theatrical | **DRAMATIC** |
| theatrical company | **TROUPE** |
| theatrical couple | **LUNTS** |
| theatrical performer | **ACTOR** |
| theatrics | **DRAMATICS** |
| Theban prince | **OEDIPUS** |
| the best within record (comp. wd.) | **ALL-TIME** |
| the bounding main | **OCEAN** |
| the briny deep | **SEA** |
| the bull (2 wds., Span.) | **EL TORO** |
| the devil | **SATAN** |
| the e in est | **EASTERN** |
| the end | **OMEGA, FINIS** |
| the 400 | **ELITE** |
| theft | **ROBBERY, BURGLARY** |
| the good book | **BIBLE** |
| the inevitable | **DESTINY, FATE** |
| the intellect | **MIND** |
| the last | **OMEGA** |
| the last frontier | **ALASKA, SPACE** |
| theme | **ESSAY, TOPIC, SUBJECT** |
| the merchant of Venice | **ANTONIO** |
| the m in USMC | **MARINE** |
| the night club set (2 wds.) | **CAFE SOCIETY** |
| theological school | **SEMINARY** |
| the one here | **THIS** |
| the ones here | **THESE** |
| the one there | **THESE** |
| the ones there | **THOSE** |
| theorbo | **LUTE** |
| the Orient | **EAST** |
| theorize | **SPECULATE** |
| theory | **CONJECTURE, HYPOTHESIS** |
| the p in mph | **PER** |
| the planet earth | **TERRA** |
| the populace | **PEOPLE** |
| the present | **NOW** |
| the present age | **TODAY** |
| therapeutic | **CURATIVE** |
| therapeutic draught | **DOSAGE** |
| there | **YONDER** |
| therefore | **ERGO, HENCE, SO** |
| the r in HRH | **ROYAL** |
| the r in IRS | **REVENUE** |
| therm | **CALORIE** |
| Therma | **SALONIKA** |
| thermal | **WARM** |
| thermos | **BOTTLE, JUG** |
| the same (Lat.) | **IDEM** |
| thesaurus creator | **ROGET** |
| these (Fr.) | **CES, CETTES** |
| thesis | **ESSAY** |
| the smallest bit | **IOTA** |
| thespian | **ACTOR** |
| thespian's signal | **CUE** |
| Thessaly mountain | **IDA, OSSA** |
| the sun | **SOL** |
| the sun (prefix) | **HELIO** |
| "the terrible" | **IVAN** |
| the thing | **IT** |
| "The Thinker" sculptor | **RODIN** |
| the three wise men | **MAGI** |
| the tube | **TELEVISION** |
| the two of us | **WE** |
| the two together | **BOTH** |
| thew | **SINEW, MUSCLE** |
| the way out | **EXIT** |
| the whole amount | **ALL** |
| thick | **DENSE** |
| thick and short | **SQUAT** |
| thick black liquid | **TAR** |

| | |
|---|---|
| thick board | **PLANK** |
| thick cluster | **CLUMP** |
| thick cord | **ROPE** |
| thicken | **CLOT** |
| thicket | **COPSE, GROVE** |
| thicket fence | **HEDGE** |
| thick mist | **FOG** |
| thickness | **DIAMETER, PLY** |
| thick piece | **CHUNK** |
| thick porridge | **MUSH** |
| thick set | **STOCKY** |
| thick skinned | **CALLOUS** |
| thick skulled | **STUPID, OBTUSE** |
| thick slice | **SLAB** |
| thick soup | **PUREE** |
| thick string | **CORD, TWINE, ROPE** |
| thick sweet liquid | **SYRUP** |
| thick wire ropes | **CABLE** |
| thighbone | **FEMUR** |
| thimblerig | **CHEAT, SWINDLE** |
| thin | **LEAN, SLIM, SLENDER, SKINNY** |
| thin and haggard | **GAUNT** |
| thin and limp | **LANK** |
| thin and vibrant | **REEDY** |
| thin and withered | **WIZENED** |
| thin as air | **RARE** |
| thin board | **SLAT** |
| thin cookie | **WAFER** |
| thin cord | **STRING** |
| thin fog | **MIST** |
| thing | **OBJECT, ARTICLE** |
| thing (Lat.) | **RES** |
| thing abandoned by its owner | **DERELICT** |
| thingamajig | **GADGET** |
| thing done | **DEED, FEAT, FACT** |
| thing in law | **RES** |
| thing of small value | **TRIFLE** |
| thing of value | **ASSET** |
| thing owed | **DEBT** |
| things for sale | **MERCHANDISE** |
| things given | **DATA** |
| things to be done | **AGENDA** |
| think | **REASON, DEEM, OPINE, SUPPOSE** |
| think ahead | **PLAN** |
| think hard | **CONCENTRATE** |
| think logically | **REASON** |
| think over | **PONDER** |
| think the world of | **IDOLIZE** |
| think twice | **RECONSIDER** |
| thin layer | **FILM** |
| thinly metallic | **TINNY** |

| | |
|---|---|
| thinly scattered | **SPARSE** |
| thin metal disk | **PATEN** |
| thin nail | **BRAD** |
| thinner | **TURPENTINE** |
| thin out | **PETER** |
| thin pasteboard | **CARD** |
| thin plate of metal | **LEAF** |
| thin screen | **VEIL** |
| thin shelled nut | **PECAN** |
| thin silk fabric | **PONGEE** |
| thin-skinned | **SENSITIVE** |
| third in number | **TERTIARY** |
| third largest planet | **URANUS** |
| third person | **HE, SHE, THEY** |
| third power | **CUBE** |
| third-rate | **INFERIOR** |
| thirst quencher | **WATER, DRINK** |
| thirsty | **DRY** |
| thirteen (2 wds.) | **BAKER'S DOZEN** |
| thirty (Fr.) | **TRENTE** |
| this (Lat.) | **HOC** |
| this (Sp.) | **ESTA, ESTE** |
| this way | **HERE** |
| thole | **PIN, OARPIN** |
| thong | **STRAP** |
| Thonga | **BANTU** |
| thorn | **BRIAR, SPINE** |
| thorny, as a plant | **SPINY** |
| thorny shrub | **ROSE** |
| thorough | **COMPLETE** |
| thoroughfare | **AVENUE, STREET, ROAD, BOULEVARD, HIGHWAY** |
| those in office | **INS** |
| those summoned for jury duty | **TALESMEN** |
| thought | **IDEA, NOTION, COGITATION** |
| thoughtful | **PENSIVE, KIND, GENEROUS** |
| thoughtless | **CARELESS, STUPID** |
| thousandth | **MIL** |
| thrash soundly | **DRUB, TAN, BEAT** |
| thread | **FIBER, FILAMENT** |
| threaded nail | **SCREW, BOLT** |
| threaded steel pin | **BOLT** |
| thread of smoke | **WISP** |
| thread-winding machine | **REELER** |
| threaten | **MENACE** |
| threatening | **OMINOUS** |
| three (Ger.) | **DREI** |
| three (prefix) | **TRI, TRE, TER** |

| | | | |
|---|---|---|---|
| three-banded armadillo | **APAR** | thug | **HOODLUM** |
| three-base hit | **TRIPLE** | thumb | **POLLEX** |
| three-dimensional | **CUBIC** | thumbnail | **BRIEF, CONCISE** |
| three feet | **YARD** | thump | **POUND, KNOCK** |
| three-fifths of the earth's | | thunder | **RUMBLE** |
| surface | **OCEAN** | thunder peal | **CLAP** |
| threefold | **TRINE** | thurible | **CENSER** |
| three-legged stand | **TRIPOD** | thus | **SO** |
| three lines of verse | **TRIPLET** | thus (Lat.) | **SIC** |
| three-masted vessel | **SCHOONER** | thus far | **YET** |
| three musicians | **TRIO** | thwart | **FOIL, SPITE** |
| threescore | **SIXTY** | thyme | **HERB** |
| three-sided figure | **TRIANGLE** | thymus | **GLAND** |
| threesome | **TRIO** | tiara | **CORONET** |
| three-spot card | **TREY** | Tibetan capital | **LHASA** |
| three-toed sloth | **AI** | Tibetan chief | **POMBO** |
| three-wheeler | **TRICYCLE** | Tibetan gazelle | **GOA** |
| threnody | **DIRGE, ELEGY** | Tibetan grand lama | **DALAI** |
| thresh | **BEAT** | Tibetan guide | **SHERPA** |
| threshing tool | **FLAIL** | Tibetan monk | **LAMA** |
| threshold | **SILL** | Tibetan ox | **ANOA, YAK** |
| thrice (mus.) | **TER** | Tibet's neighbor | **BURMA** |
| thrift | **FRUGALITY** | tibia | **SHIN** |
| thriftless | **LAVISH** | Tibur | **TIVOLI** |
| thrifty | **ECONOMICAL** | tic | **SPASM** |
| thrill | **SHIVER** | tical | **MONEY** |
| thrill-seeking parachutist | | tick | **OPERATE, WORK** |
| (2 wds.) | **SKY DIVER** | ticker | **WATCH, HEART** |
| thrive | **PROSPER** | ticket | **CARD** |
| throat-clearing word | **AHEM** | ticket (sl.) | **DUCAT** |
| throat sound | **RALE** | ticket half | **STUB** |
| throaty | **HUSKY, HOARSE** | tickle | **TITILLATE** |
| throb | **PULSE, PULSATE,** | tidal wave | **EAGRE** |
| | **DRUM, BEAT** | tidbit | **GOODY** |
| throbbing sound | **PITAPAT** | tide | **CURRENT** |
| throes | **PANGS** | tidings | **NEWS** |
| throng | **HORDE, HOST,** | tidy | **NEAT, TRIM** |
| | **CROWD** | tie | **ASCOT, CRAVAT,** |
| throttle | **CHOKE** | | **BIND, FASTEN,** |
| through | **PER** | | **TETHER** |
| throw | **CAST, PITCH, LOB,** | tie clasp | **TACK** |
| | **HEAVE, TOSS,** | tie off | **BELAY** |
| | **SLING, HURL** | tier | **LAYER, ROW** |
| throw away | **DISCARD** | tie the knot | **WED, MARRY** |
| throw cold water on | | tie up | **BIND, TRUSS** |
| | **DISCOURAGE** | tie-up | **JAM** |
| throwing rope | **LASSO, REATA** | tiff | **SPAT** |
| throw lightly | **TOSS** | tiffin | **LUNCH** |
| throw light upon | **ILLUMINE** | tiger | **CAT** |
| throw off | **EMIT** | tiger cat | **OCELOT, MARGAY** |
| throw off the track | **DERAIL** | tight | **TENSE, TAUT** |
| throw out | **EJECT, EVICT** | tightfisted | **STINGY** |
| throw slowly | **LOB** | tight-lipped | **TACITURN** |
| thrum | **FRINGE** | tightrope | **WIRE** |
| thrush | **MAVIS, ORIOLE** | tights | **LEOTARD** |
| thrust | **PROD, STAB** | til | **SESAME** |
| thrusting weapon | **SPEAR** | tile | **SLATE** |
| thud | **BLOW** | tillable | **ARABLE** |

| | | | |
|---|---|---|---|
| tiller | HELM | tint | DYE, HUE, COLOR, |
| till the soil | FARM, | | SHADE, TINGE |
| | CULTIVATE | tiny | LILLIPUTIAN, |
| tilt | LEAN, CANT, TIP, | | SMALL, WEE |
| | INCLINE | tiny branch | SPRIG |
| tilt, as a ship | LIST | tiny distance | HAIR, NOSE |
| tilted | ALIST | tiny morsel | CRUMB |
| tilting match | JOUST | tiny parasite | MITE |
| tilting over | ALOP | tiny particle | ATOM, MOTE, |
| timber | LOG, WOOD | | IOTA |
| timber hitch | KNOT | tiny speck | DOT, MOTE |
| timber tree | ASH, OAK, ELM | tip | END, GRATUITY, |
| timber wolf | LOBO | | TILT, LEAN, ADVICE |
| timbre | TONE | tippet | SCARF |
| time | DURATION, HOUR | tipping | ATILT |
| time being | NONCE | tipple | BIB |
| time division | YEAR, DAY, | tiptoe | CREEP |
| | HOUR, MINUTE, | tirade | PHILIPPIC, |
| | MONTH, WEEK, | | HARANGUE |
| | SECOND | tire | FATIGUE, WEARY |
| time gone by | PAST | tired | WEARY, SLEEPY |
| time limit | DEADLINE | tiresome | WEARY, TEDIOUS |
| timely | OPPORTUNE | tire support | RIM |
| time of life | AGE | tissue | TELA |
| time of year | FALL, | Tisza tributary | SOMES |
| | WINTER, SPRING, | titan | GIANT |
| | SUMMER, SEASON | tithe | TENTH |
| timeout | REST | titian | AUBURN |
| timepiece | CLOCK, WATCH | titillate | TICKLE |
| timer | STOPWATCH | title | NAME, SIR, MADAM |
| timetable | SCHEDULE | title role | LEAD |
| time-tested literary work | | titter | GIGGLE, TEEHEE |
| | CLASSIC | tittle | IOTA, JOT |
| time waster | IDLER | tizzy | FRENZY |
| timeworn | TRITE | to | TOWARD |
| timid | SHY | toad | FROG |
| timid creature | MOUSE | toadstool | MUSHROOM |
| timid person | FAINTHEART | toady | PARASITE, |
| timing | PACING | | SYCOPHANT |
| timing device | METER | to a great extent | LARGELY |
| timor | DREAD, FEAR | toast | BROWN, SKOAL |
| timorous | FEARFUL | toasty | WARM |
| timothy | HAY | tobacco chew | QUID |
| timpany | DRUMS | tobacco container | HUMIDOR |
| tin | CAN, METAL | tobacco disease | WALLOON |
| tin alloy | PEWTER | tobacco kiln | OAST |
| tincal | BORAX | tobacco pipe | CORNCOB |
| tincture | MYRRH | tobacco roll | CIGAR |
| tine | PRONG | to be (Fr.) | ETRE |
| tinge | TINT, HUE | to be (Lat.) | ESSE |
| tinge deeply | IMBUE | to be of use | AVAIL |
| tingle | PRICKLE | to be sure | INDEED |
| tingling reaction | THRILL | toboggan | SLED |
| tiniest bit | IOTA | toby | JUG |
| tinkle | CLINK | tocsin | ALARM |
| tinkling sound | PLINK | today | NOW, PRESENT |
| tinsel | GLITTER | toddler | TOT |

| | | | |
|---|---|---|---|
| to-do | **COMMOTION, FUSS** | toot | **BLAST, WHISTLE** |
| toe ailment | **GOUT** | tooth | **MOLAR, CANINE, INCISOR, FANG** |
| toe hold | **FOOTING** | tooth covering | **ENAMEL** |
| toenail beauty treatment | **PEDICURE** | tooth decay | **CARIES** |
| | | tooth doctor | **DENTIST** |
| toe the line | **OBEY** | toothed wheel | **GEAR, RATCHET** |
| toff | **DANDY** | | |
| toffee | **CANDY** | tooth of a gear wheel | **DENT** |
| toga | **ROBE** | toothpaste container | **TUBE** |
| togetherness | **UNITY** | toothsome | **TASTY** |
| toggle | **PIN, BOLT** | top | **SUMMIT, APEX, ACME, PEAK** |
| togs | **CLOTHES** | | |
| toil | **LABOR, WORK** | topaz | **YELLOW** |
| toilet case | **ETUI** | top banana | **HEADLINER** |
| tokay | **WINE** | topee | **HELMET, HAT** |
| token | **SYMBOL** | toper | **SOT** |
| token move | **GESTURE** | topic | **THEME, SUBJECT** |
| token of affection | **CARESS KISS** | top military officers | **BRASS** |
| | | top-notch | **BEST** |
| token of regard | **TESTIMONIAL** | top of altar | **MENSA** |
| token of right | **TICKET** | top of an apron | **BIB** |
| token of victory | **PALM** | top of a wave | **CREST** |
| Tokyo's former name | **EDO** | top of the head | **PATE** |
| tolerant | **LENIENT, ENDURING** | topper | **HAT** |
| | | topple | **TUMBLE, COLLAPSE** |
| tolerate | **ENDURE, BEAR, STAND** | topside | **DECK** |
| | | topsy-turvy (2 wds.) | |
| toll | **RING, TAX** | | **UPSIDE DOWN** |
| tollhouse | **COOKIE** | toque | **HAT, CAP** |
| toll road | **PIKE** | Torah | **PENTATEUCH** |
| tomahawk | **HATCHET** | torch | **FLARE** |
| to make fun of | **DERIDE** | torero | **MATADOR** |
| to make love | **WOO** | torment | **PESTER, TEASE, TAUNT** |
| tomato (2 wds.) | **LOVE APPLE** | | |
| tomato relish | **CATSUP, KETCHUP** | tornado | **TWISTER, CYCLONE** |
| tomb | **CRYPT, VAULT** | torpid | **INERT, NUMB** |
| tomboy | **HOYDEN** | torpor | **APATHY, LETHARGY** |
| tomcat | **GIB** | torrent | **DOWNPOUR** |
| tome | **VOLUME** | torrid | **HOT** |
| tommyrot | **RUBBISH** | torso | **BODY** |
| tomorrow (Sp.) | **MANANA** | torte | **CAKE** |
| tom-tom | **DRUM** | torture | **PAIN, ANGUISH** |
| tone | **SOUND** | to set in type | **PRINT** |
| tone color | **TIMBRE** | to some extent (2 wds.) | **IN PART** |
| tongue | **LANGUAGE** | toss | **THROW, HEAVE, CAST, HURL, FLING** |
| tonic | **BRACER** | | |
| to no purpose (2 wds.) | **IN VAIN** | toss carelessly | **FLIP** |
| too | **ALSO, AND** | tossed greens | **SALAD** |
| tool | **AUGER, PLANE, AWL, HAMMER, SAW, IMPLEMENT** | tot | **TODDLER** |
| | | total | **ADD, ALL, SUM, ENTIRE** |
| tool for writing | **PENCIL, PEN** | totally | **QUITE** |
| too much (Fr.) | **TROP** | tote | **CARRY** |
| toon | **MAHOGANY** | to that time | **UNTIL** |
| to one side | **APART** | to the larboard | **APORT** |

| | |
|---|---|
| to the left | HAW |
| to the point | TERSE |
| to the rear | ASTERN |
| to the sheltered side | ALEE |
| to this place | HERE, HITHER |
| toucan | ARACARI |
| touch | FEEL, ABUT |
| touch down | LAND |
| touchdown | GOAL |
| touch gently | DAB, PAT |
| touching | MOVING |
| touch up | FINISH |
| touch with color | PAINT |
| touchy | TESTY |
| tough, as meat | STRINGY |
| toughen | HARDEN, TEMPER |
| toughen by exercise | INURE, ENURE |
| tough question | POSER |
| toupee | WIG |
| tourist attraction | RUINS |
| tourist lodging | MOTEL, HOTEL, RESORT |
| tournament | CONTEST |
| tournament bridge award (2 wds.) | MASTER POINT |
| tow | PULL |
| toward | TO |
| toward shelter | ALEE |
| toward the center | INTO |
| toward the front | ANTERIOR |
| toward the interior | INLAND |
| toward the left side (naut.) | APORT |
| toward the stern | AFT |
| towel | DRY, RUB |
| towel fabric | TERRY |
| towel word | HERS, HIS |
| tower | FORTRESS, SPIRE, STEEPLE, BELFRY |
| towering | TALL |
| tower of ice | SERAC |
| towhead | BLOND |
| town (colloq.) | BURG |
| town in New Guinea | LAE |
| town map | PLAT |
| townsman | CIT |
| town's position | SITE |
| town's principal street (2 wds.) | MAIN STEM |
| tow rope | HAWSER |
| toxic | POISON |
| toy | PLAYTHING |
| toy baby | DOLL |
| trace | VESTIGE |
| trace of an ancient animal | FOSSIL |

| | |
|---|---|
| trace of color | TINGE |
| tracer | INQUIRY, BULLET |
| trachea | WINDPIPE |
| tracing | COPY |
| track | TRAIL, SPOOR |
| track circuit | LAP |
| track down | TRACE |
| track event | SELLING RACE, RELAY RACE |
| track race | RELAY |
| track runner | MILER |
| tract | AREA |
| tract | DISSERTATION |
| tractable | DOCILE, PLIANT |
| tractate | TREATISE |
| traction | PULL, FRICTION |
| tract of wasteland | MOOR |
| trade | SWAP, BARTER, EXCHANGE, COMMERCE |
| trade center | MART, MARKET |
| trade combination | MERGER |
| trade for money | SELL |
| trademark | BRAND, LABEL |
| trade name | BRAND |
| trade on | EXPLOIT |
| tradesman | MERCHANT |
| trading station | POST |
| tradition | LEGEND, CUSTOM |
| traditional knowledge | LORE |
| traditional restriction | TABOO |
| traditional tale | SAGA |
| traduce | DEFAME, MALIGN |
| traffic | COMMERCE, TRADE |
| traffic light color | AMBER, RED, GREEN |
| traffic route | LANE |
| traffic violation | SPEEDING |
| traffic violation charge | FINE |
| tragedy | DISASTER, DRAMA |
| tragic | DIRE |
| trail | TRACE, TRACK, SPOOR |
| trail blazer | PIONEER |
| trailing plant | VINE |
| train | TEACH, EDUCATE |
| train (Sp.) | TREN |
| train berth (2 wds.) | BUNK BED |
| trainer of wild animals | TAMER |
| train terminal | DEPOT, STATION |
| train track | RAIL |
| train whistle | TOOT |
| traipse | TRAMP, WANDER |
| trait | MARK |
| traitor (sl.) | RAT |
| traitorous | PERFIDIOUS |

| | |
|---|---|
| tram | **TROLLEY** |
| trammel | **ENTANGLE** |
| tramp | **BUM, HOBO, VAGABOND** |
| tramp vessel | **STEAMER** |
| trample | **TREAD** |
| tranquil | **CALM, PEACEFUL, SERENE** |
| tranquility | **PEACE, SERENITY, QUIET** |
| transaction | **SALE** |
| transcend | **SURPASS** |
| transcendental | **OBSCURE** |
| transcribe | **COPY** |
| transcribe shorthand | **TYPE** |
| transect | **DIVIDE** |
| transfer | **SHIFT, MOVE** |
| transfer sticker | **DECAL** |
| transfix | **PIERCE** |
| transform | **CONVERT, CHANGE** |
| transgress | **SIN** |
| transient | **BRIEF, TEMPORARY** |
| transistor set | **RADIO** |
| transit | **PASSAGE** |
| transit coach | **BUS** |
| transition | **CHANGE, CONVERSION** |
| transitory | **TEMPORAL, FLEETING** |
| translate | **INTERPRET** |
| translation | **TROT, PONY** |
| translucent | **LIMPID, CLEAR** |
| transmit | **SEND** |
| transmit in succession | **HAND DOWN** |
| transom | **WINDOW** |
| transparent | **CLEAR, SHEER** |
| transparent liquid | **WATER** |
| transpire | **HAPPEN, OCCUR** |
| transplant | **GRAFT** |
| transport | **CARRY** |
| transportation charge | **FARE** |
| transportation to the top floor | **ELEVATOR** |
| transpose | **REVERSE** |
| transverse | **BEAM, AXIS** |
| trap | **SNARE, CAPTURE** |
| trap door | **DROP** |
| trapeze artist | **ACROBAT** |
| trappings | **GEAR** |
| trash | **WASTE, RUBBISH** |
| trauma | **SHOCK** |
| travail | **LABOR, WORK** |
| travel | **TOUR, RIDE, JOURNEY, VISIT** |
| travel across snow | **MUSH** |
| traveler | **FARER** |
| traveler's choice | **TOUR, TRAIN, BUS, PLANE, SHIP, CAR, JET** |
| traveler's concern (2 wds.) | **DEPARTURE DATE** |
| traveler's home | **HOTEL, MOTEL** |
| travel fast (2 wds.) | **MAKE TIME** |
| traveling bag | **VALISE, SUITCASE** |
| traveling salesman | **DRUMMER** |
| travel on foot | **WALK, HIKE, MARCH** |
| travel on horseback | **RIDE** |
| traverse | **CROSS** |
| travesty | **PARODY, SATIRE** |
| tray | **SALVER, SERVER** |
| treacherous | **FALSE** |
| tread | **STEP, TRAMPLE** |
| treasure box | **CHEST** |
| Treasure State | **MONTANA** |
| treat | **AMUSE, ENTERTAIN** |
| treaty | **PACT** |
| treble | **SOPRANO, TRIPLE** |
| treble clef | **GEE** |
| tree | **ASH, CEDAR, CHESTNUT, FIR, LARCH, OAK, POPLAR, SAPLING, ELM, PINE, MAPLE, LINDEN, WALNUT** |
| tree (Ger.) | **BAUM** |
| tree branch | **LIMB** |
| tree covering | **BARK** |
| tree dwelling | **NEST** |
| tree exudation | **LAC, RESIN** |
| tree fluid | **SAP** |
| tree groups | **GROVE** |
| treeless | **UNWOODED, BARE** |
| treeless Arctic plain | **TUNDRA** |
| tree-snake | **LORA** |
| tree stump | **STUB** |
| treetop chatter (2 wds.) | **BIRD TALK** |
| treetop home | **NEST** |
| tree trunk | **BOLE** |
| trek | **TRAVEL, TOUR** |
| trellis | **ARBOR, LATTICE** |
| tremble | **QUAKE, SHAKE, SHIVER, QUIVER, VIBRATE** |
| trembling tree | **ASPEN** |
| tremendous | **HUGE** |
| tremor | **VIBRATION** |

| | | | |
|---|---|---|---|
| trench | **DITCH** | Trojan king | **PRIAM** |
| trenchant | **KEEN, CUTTING** | Trojan mountain | **IDA** |
| trencherman | **EATER** | trolley | **TRAM** |
| trend | **DIRECTION, TURN** | trophy | **AWARD, PRIZE** |
| trepidation | **FEAR** | tropical | **HOT, TORRID** |
| trespass | **INTRUDE** | tropical arum plant | **TARO** |
| tresses | **HAIR, CURLS** | tropical basket fiber | **ISTLE** |
| trestle | **BRIDGE** | tropical cuckoo | **ANI** |
| triad | **THREE** | tropical fruit | **BANANA,** |
| trial | **TEST** | | **DATE, FIG, MANGO,** |
| trial package | **SAMPLE** | | **PAPAW, PINEAPPLE** |
| triangle side | **LEG** | tropical grouper | **MERO** |
| triangular piece in skirts | **GORE** | tropical lizard | **AGAMA** |
| tribal emblem | **TOTEM** | tropical nut | **KOLA** |
| tribe | **CLAN, FAMILY,** | tropical plant | **ALOE** |
| | **BAND** | tropical tree | **EBOE, PALM** |
| tribulation | **WOE** | tropical vine | **LIANA** |
| tribunal | **COURT** | tropical water lily | **LOTUS** |
| tributary | **ARM** | trot | **CANTER, JOG, LOPE** |
| tribute | **PRAISE** | troth | **LOYALTY, PROMISE** |
| trice | **INSTANT** | trottoir | **SIDEWALK** |
| trick | **RUSE, HOAX, SHAM,** | troubador | **MINSTREL** |
| | **WILE, DUPE** | trouble | **AIL, WOE, ANNOY,** |
| trickle | **SEEP** | | **ADO, ILL** |
| trifle | **FIG, JOT** | trouble (Scot.) | **FASH** |
| trifle fault | **PECCADILLO** | troublesome plant | **RAGWEED,** |
| trifling | **PETTY, TRIVIAL** | | **WEED** |
| trig | **SPRUCE, TRIM** | troublesome weed | **TARE** |
| trigonometric function | **SINE,** | trough | **CONDUIT, CHUTE** |
| | **COSINE** | trough to hold hay | **MANGER** |
| trill | **QUAVER, WARBLE** | trounce | **DEFEAT** |
| trim | **DECORATE, NEAT** | trousers | **PANTS** |
| trimming | **RUCHE, FRINGE** | trousers' fabric | **TWILL** |
| trim off branches | **LOP,** | trousers' pocket | **FOB** |
| | **PRUNE** | trove | **TREASURE** |
| trim the hair | **CLIP** | Troy | **ILIUM** |
| trim trees | **PRUNE** | truce | **ARMISTICE** |
| Trinacria | **SICILY** | trucker | **HAULER,** |
| trine | **THREEFOLD** | | **TEAMSTER** |
| trinity | **TRIAD** | truculent | **SAVAGE, FIERCE** |
| trinket | **BEAD** | trudge | **PLOD** |
| trip | **JOURNEY, STUMBLE,** | true | **LOYAL, REAL,** |
| | **TREK, FALL,** | | **GENUINE, CORRECT** |
| | **VOYAGE, TOUR** | true to fact | **LITERAL** |
| triple | **THREE** | truffle | **TUBER** |
| tripod | **EASEL, TRIVET** | truism | **AXIOM** |
| trireme | **GALLEY** | truly | **YEA, VERILY** |
| Tristan's beloved | **ISOLDE** | Truman's opponent | **DEWEY** |
| trite | **BANAL, HACKNEYED,** | trump | **RUFF** |
| | **CORNY** | trumpet | **HORN** |
| triton | **EFT, NEWT** | trumpet fanfare | **TANTARA** |
| triumph | **WIN, VICTORY** | trumpet sound | **BLARE** |
| triumphant exclamation | **AHA,** | trunk of a body | **TORSO** |
| | **EUREKA** | trust | **BELIEVE, CREDIT** |
| trivial | **PETTY** | trustworthy | **RELIANT** |
| troche | **LOZENGE** | truth | **FACT, HONESTY** |
| Trojan hero | **PARIS,** | truthful | **HONEST** |
| | **AENEAS** | | |

| | | | |
|---|---|---|---|
| try | TEST, ATTEMPT | turn on axis | ROTATE |
| trying age | TEENS | turn on pivot | SWIVEL |
| try to secure (2 wds.) | GO FOR | turn outward | EVERT |
| tub activity | BATH | turn over | OVERSET, |
| tube | CYLINDER, PIPE | | REVERSE, FLOP |
| tuberous vegetable | POTATO | turn over a new leaf | REFORM |
| tug | HAUL, DRAG | turnpike | ROAD, HIGHWAY |
| tumble | FALL | turnpike charge | TOLL |
| tumbledown dwelling | SHACK, | turnpike exit | RAMP |
| | SHANTY | turn sharply | VEER |
| tumbler | GLASS | turpentine distillate | RESIN |
| tumid | POMPOUS | turret | TOWER |
| tumult | RIOT, STIR | turtle shell | CARAPACE |
| tumultuous | TURBULENT, | tusk | FANG, TOOTH |
| | VIOLENT | tusk material | IVORY |
| tune | AIR, MELODY, SONG | tussle | STRUGGLE, WRESTLE |
| tune in secretly | WIRETAP | tuxedo (2 wds.) | DINNER COAT |
| Tunisian ruler | BEY, DEY | TV emcee Linkletter | ART |
| turbid | MUDDY | TV emcee Mack | TED |
| turbine power | STEAM | TV emcee Parks | BERT |
| turbulent | DISTURBED, | TV in England | TELLY |
| | RESTLESS | TV outlet | CHANNEL |
| turf | PEAT, SOD, SWARD | TV part | TUBE |
| turgid | SWOLLEN, BLOATED | TV program | NEWS, SERIES, |
| Turk | OTTOMAN | | SOAP OPERA, |
| turkey gobbler | TOM | | WESTERN, SPECIAL |
| Turkish caliph | ALI | TV repeat show | RERUN |
| Turkish cap | FEZ | TV sponsor's concern | RATINGS |
| Turkish capital | ANKARA | TV statuette | EMMY |
| Turkish cavalryman | SPAHI | TV's Uncle Miltie | BERLE |
| Turkish decree | IRADE | twang | NASALITY |
| Turkish governor | PASHA | tweak | PINCH |
| Turkish gulf | COS | tweedle | CAJOLE, WHINE |
| Turkish hat | FEZ | tweet | CHIRP |
| Turkish inn | IMARET | tweezers | PINCERS |
| Turkish judge | CADI | twelfth of a year | MONTH |
| Turkish money | LIRA, PARA | twelve inches | FOOT |
| Turkish mountain | ARARAT | twelvemonth | YEAR |
| Turkish name | ALI | twenty four hours | DAY |
| Turkish standard | ALEM | twice | BIS |
| Turkish title | AGA, AMIR, | twig | SHOOT, SPRIG |
| | EMIR | twilight | EVENING |
| Turkish tobacco | LATAKIA | twilled woolen fabric | SERGE |
| Turkish vessel | SAIC | twin | DOUBLE |
| turmoil | ADO, MELEE | twine | CORD |
| turn | REVOLVE, ROTATE, | twine about | ENLACE |
| | SPIN, WHIRL | twinge | PANG, QUALM |
| turn about | SLUE | twining shoot | BINE |
| turn aside | AVERT, DETER | twining stem | VINE |
| turn away | REPEL | twinkle | WINK |
| turn back | REVERSE | twirl | SPIN |
| turn down | VETO | twirlers wand | BATON |
| turn for help | RESORT | twist | WIND |
| turning part of a dynamo | | twist about | SLEW, SLUE |
| | ROTOR | twisted | WRY |
| turn in trading stamps | REDEEM | twister | TORNADO, |
| turn of duty | SPELL | | CYCLONE |

| | | | |
|---|---|---|---|
| twist out of shape | **WARP** | type of magazine | |
| twist to one side | **SLUE** | | **PERIODICAL, GLOSSY,** |
| twist together | **ENTWINE** | | **MONTHLY, WEEKLY,** |
| twit | **TEASE, TAUNT** | | **ANNUAL** |
| twitch | **JERK** | type of ode | **PINDARIC** |
| twitter | **CHATTER, GIGGLE** | type of painting | **OIL COLOR,** |
| two | **DUET, DUO, PAIR,** | | **PORTRAIT,** |
| | | | **WATER COLOR,** |
| two below par, in golf | **EAGLE** | | **LANDSCAPE, STILL LIFE** |
| two bit gambler (sl.) | **PIKER** | type of pay | **DAY RATE,** |
| two cups | **PINT** | | **PIECE WORK** |
| two door auto | **COUPE** | type of perfection | **PARAGON** |
| two family quarrel | **FEUD** | type of piano | **GRAND,** |
| twofold | **DOUBLE,** | | **UPRIGHT,** |
| | **DUAL, TWIN, TWICE** | | **BABY GRAND** |
| two-footed animal | **BIPED** | type of poem | **ODE, SONNET** |
| two-masted vessel | **YAWL,** | type of puzzle | **JIGSAW** |
| | **KETCH** | type of race | **RELAY** |
| two pints | **QUART** | type of race track | **SPEEDWAY** |
| two (poetic) | **TWAIN** | type of record player | **STEREO** |
| two (quartets) | **OCTET** | type of rock | **SANDSTONE,** |
| | | | **SHALE** |
| two singers | **DUO, DUET** | type of rubber | **LATEX** |
| twosome | **DUO, PAIR** | type of ruby | **SPINEL** |
| two spot | **DEUCE** | type of skylight | **LUNETTE** |
| two times | **TWICE, BIS,** | type of waistcoat | **JERKIN** |
| | **DOUBLE** | type of word game | **FILL-IN,** |
| two-toed sloth | **UNAU** | | **CROSSWORD, LOTTO** |
| two-wheeled vehicle | **CART,** | type of wrench | **SPANNER** |
| | **SCOOTER, BIKE** | type row | **LINE** |
| tycoon | **SHOGUN** | type size | **ELITE, PICA** |
| tyke | **SHAVER** | typewriter bar | **SPACER,** |
| type | **SORT, KIND, CLASS,** | | **PLATEN** |
| | **ILK, GENRE** | typhoon | **CYCLONE** |
| type collection | **FONT** | typical | **REGULAR, NORMAL** |
| type measure | **EM, EN** | typographer | **PRINTER** |
| type of agent | **UNDERCOVER** | tyrant | **DESPOT, DICTATOR** |
| type of beer | **LAGER,** | Tyre king | **HIRAM** |
| | **PILSNER** | Tyrian | **PURPLE** |
| type of cabbage | **KALE** | tyro | **NOVICE** |
| type of canoe | **PIROGUE,** | tzigane | **GYPSY** |
| | **PROA, DUGOUT** | | |
| type of car | **SEDAN, COUPE** | **U** | |
| type of cross | **TAU** | | |
| type of drapery | **VALANCE** | u-boat | **SUBMARINE,** |
| type of employment | | | **SUB** |
| (comp. wd.) | **PART-TIME,** | ugly | **HOMELY, HIDEOUS** |
| | **FULL-TIME** | ugly old woman | **HAG, CRONE** |
| type of fabric | **LENO** | uh-huh | **YES** |
| type of fastener | **HASP** | uh-uh | **NO** |
| type of fuel | **COAL, GAS,** | ukase | **EDICT, DECREE** |
| | **OIL, PEAT** | ulna | **BONE** |
| type of glazed paper | **GLASSINE** | ulster | **COAT** |
| type of jacket | **ETON,** | ultimate | **EVENTUAL** |
| | **EISENHOWER, IKE** | ultimate end | **GOAL** |
| type of joke | **PUN** | ultimately (2 wds.) | **IN FINE** |
| | | ultra | **EXTREME** |

| | |
|---|---|
| ululate | HOWL, WAIL |
| umber | PIGMENT |
| umbrage | HATRED, CONTEMPT, OFFENSE |
| umpire | REFEREE, ARBITER |
| unable | CANNOT |
| unabridged | COMPLETE, UNCUT |
| unaccompanied | ALONE |
| unadorned | BARE, PLAIN |
| unadulterated | PURE |
| unaffected | SINCERE |
| unanimity | ACCORD, UNITY |
| unanimously | SOLIDLY |
| unapt | DULL, SLOW |
| unaroused | ASLEEP, DORMANT |
| unaspirated | LENE |
| unassisted | ALONE |
| unassumed | NATURAL |
| unattached | SINGLE |
| unbalanced | ALIST, ALOP |
| unbelievable | INCREDIBLE |
| unbeliever | INFIDEL, HERETIC |
| unbend | RELAX |
| unbroken | INTACT |
| unburden | EASE, RELIEVE |
| unburnt and dried brick | ADOBE |
| unbusy | IDLE |
| uncanny | EERIE |
| unceremonious | ABRUPT, INFORMAL |
| uncertain | DOUBTFUL |
| unchecked | FREE, RAMPANT |
| uncivil | RUDE, IMPOLITE, CRUSTY |
| unclaimed ground (comp. wd.) | NO-MAN'S-LAND |
| uncle (Scot.) | EME |
| uncle (Sp.) | TIO |
| unclean | DIRTY |
| unclose (poetic) | OPE |
| unclosed | OPEN |
| unclothed | NUDE, NAKED, BARE |
| uncommon | ODD, RARE |
| uncomplaining | STOICAL |
| uncomplicated | EASY |
| uncompromising | RIGID |
| unconcealed | BARE, OPEN |
| unconcerned | DETACHED |
| unconcerned, ethically | AMORAL |
| unconditional | ABSOLUTE |
| unconfined | LOOSE |

| | |
|---|---|
| unconfirmed gossip | RUMOR |
| unconfused | CALM, CLEAR |
| unconventional (Fr.) | OUTRE |
| uncooked | RAW |
| uncopied | ORIGINAL |
| uncouth | CRASS, RUDE |
| uncovered | BARE, OPEN |
| unctuous | OILY, GUSHY |
| uncultivated | FALLOW, WILD |
| uncultivated plant | WEED |
| uncultured | CRUDE |
| undaunted | BOLD, BRAVE |
| undecided (4 wds.) | UP IN THE AIR |
| undecorated | BARE |
| undeniable | TRUE |
| under | BENEATH |
| under an assumed name | INCOGNITO |
| undercover | SECRET |
| undercover man | SPY, AGENT |
| underground hollow | CAVE |
| underground plant part | ROOT |
| underground worker | MINER |
| underhand | SECRETLY |
| underling | MENIAL, INFERIOR |
| underlying reason | RATIONALE |
| undermine | SAP |
| undershirt | VEST |
| undersized | TINY, SMALL, WEE |
| undersized animal | RUNT |
| understand | SEE, REALIZE, KNOW |
| understanding | KEN |
| understood | TACIT |
| understood by a select few | ESOTERIC |
| undertake | ASSUME, ENGAGE |
| undertaker | MORTICIAN |
| undertaking | TASK |
| under tension (sl.) | UPTIGHT |
| under the weather | ILL |
| undertone | ASIDE |
| underwater | AWASH |
| underworld | HADES, SHEOL |
| underworld god | DIS |
| underworld of myth | HADES |
| undetermined | VAGUE |
| undeveloped stem | BUD |
| undiluted, as liquor | NEAT |
| undisguised | NAKED |
| undistinguished multitude | RUCK |

| | |
|---|---|
| undivided | ENTIRE, ONE, UNITED |
| undo knitting | RAVEL |
| undoing | RUIN, DOWNFALL |
| undomesticated | WILD, FERAL |
| undue hurry | HASTE |
| undulate | SWAY, RIPPLE |
| unearned cash (2 wds.) | EASY MONEY |
| unearth | UNCOVER, EXHUME |
| unearthly | EERIE |
| uneasy | RESTIVE, RESTLESS |
| unemotional | STOIC |
| unemployed | OUT OF WORK, IDLE |
| unencumbered | FREE |
| unequal | UNEVEN, DIFFERENT |
| unequal things | ODDS |
| unequivocal | PLAIN, SINCERE |
| unerring | SURE, TRUE |
| unescorted male | STAG |
| uneven | ROUGH, EROSE |
| unexpected difficulty | SNAG |
| unexpected stroke of luck | WINDFALL |
| unexpected win | UPSET |
| unexplored region | FRONTIER |
| unfamiliar | STRANGE |
| unfasten | UNDO |
| unfavorable | ADVERSE, BAD |
| unfeeling | STONY, COLD |
| unfettered | LOOSE |
| unfit | INEPT, INCOMPETENT |
| unfold | OPEN |
| unfortunate | ILL |
| unfounded report | RUMOR |
| unfreeze | THAW, MELT |
| unfrequented | LONE |
| unfriendly | COOL, HOSTILE |
| unfruitful | BARREN |
| unfulfilled desire | WISH |
| unfurl | SPREAD, UNROLL |
| ungainly | CLUMSY, AWKWARD |
| ungentlemanly man | CAD, LOUT, BOOR |
| unhappy | SAD |
| unhappy expression | FROWN |
| unharmed | INTACT |
| unhealthy color | SALLOW |
| unhealthily pallid | PASTY |
| unheard of | STRANGE |
| unheeding | DEAF |
| unheralded | UNSUNG |

| | |
|---|---|
| uniform | MEASURED |
| uniform ornament | EPAULET |
| unilateral | ONE-WAY |
| unimaginative | DULL, PROSAIC |
| unimportant | ONE-HORSE, PETTY |
| uninformed | IGNORANT |
| union weapon | STRIKE |
| unique | RARE, CHOICE |
| unique person | ONER |
| unison | HARMONY, CONCORD |
| unit | ONE |
| unite | WELD, WED, JOIN, ALLY, MARRY, SPLICE, MERGE |
| united | ONE, WED |
| unit of cavalry | TROOP |
| unit of energy | ERG, DYNE |
| unit of heat | THERM, CALORY, CALORIE |
| unit of heredity | GENE |
| unit of illumination | LUX, PHOT |
| unit of length | METER, FOOT, YARD, INCH, MILE |
| unit of light | LUX, PYR |
| unit of weight (India) | SER |
| unit of work | ERG |
| unity | ONE |
| universal | GENERAL, TOTAL |
| universal language | IDO |
| universal remedy | PANACEA |
| universe | COSMOS |
| university post | PROFESSORSHIP |
| unkempt | SHAGGY, TOUSLED |
| unkind | CRUEL, MEAN |
| unkind remark | SLUR |
| unlawful | ILLEGAL |
| unlawful act | CRIME |
| unleavened corn cake | TORTILLA |
| unlighted | DARK, DIM |
| unlock | OPEN |
| unlucky | UNTOWARD |
| unmarried | SINGLE |
| unmarried woman | MAIDEN |
| unmetered writing | PROSE |
| unmixed | PURE |
| unmounted | AFOOT |
| unmoved | FIRM |
| unnamed person | SOMEONE |
| unnecessary | NEEDLESS |
| unnerve | UPSET |

| | | | |
|---|---|---|---|
| unobtrusive | MODEST, RETIRING | untidy person | SLOVEN |
| | | untidy pile | HEAP |
| unoccupied | EMPTY, IDLE | untidy woman | SLATTERN |
| unpaved road edges | | untie | LOOSEN |
| | SHOULDER, BERM | until now (2 wds.) | SO FAR |
| unpleasant | NASTY | untoward | UNLUCKY |
| unpretentious | MODEST | untrammeled | FREE |
| unreasoning fear | PANIC | untried | NEW, GREEN |
| unrefined | CRUDE | untrue | FALSE |
| unrefined metal | ORE | untutored | ILLITERATE |
| unresisting | PASSIVE | untwist | RAVEL |
| unrestrained pleasure | FLING, SPREE | unused | NEW |
| | | unusual | NOVEL, RARE, |
| unrestricted | OPEN | | UNCOMMON, ODD, |
| unrhymed poetry (2 wds.) | | | OUTLANDISH, STRANGE |
| | BLANK VERSE | unusually good | EXCELLENT |
| unripe | GREEN | unusually sensitive | ALLERGIC |
| unroll | OPEN | unusual person (sl.) | ONER |
| unruffled | CALM | unveil | REVEAL |
| unruly | RESTIVE | unverified report | RUMOR |
| unruly child | BRAT | unwanted plant | WEED |
| unruly crowd | MOB, HORDE | unwarranted | UNDUE |
| unsatisfactory, as an excuse | LAME | unwavering | RESOLUTE |
| | | unwearied | TIRELESS |
| unsavory | TASTELESS | unwelcome person | INTRUDER |
| unseal | OPEN | unwieldy | BULKY |
| unseam | RIP | unwieldy object | HULK |
| unseat a monarch | DEPOSE | unwilling | AVERSE |
| unseemly | INAPT, IMPROPER | unwooded | TREELESS |
| | | unwrap | OPEN |
| unseen | HIDDEN | unyielding | FIRM, RIGID |
| unselfish | ALTRUISTIC | up | ALOFT, ABOVE, OVER |
| unsightly | UGLY | up and around | ACTIVE |
| unskilled worker (2 wds.) | | upbraid | SCOLD |
| | DAY LABORER | upheave | LIFT, REAR |
| unskillful | INEPT | uphold | BACK, ABET |
| unsoiled | CLEAN | uplift | RAISE |
| unsophisticated | NAIVE, CORNY | uplift spirits | ELATE |
| | | upon | ATOP, ON, ONTO |
| unsound | INSECURE | upper | HIGHER, BERTH |
| unsparing | PROFUSE | upper air | ETHER |
| unspecified amount | SOME, ANY | upper Canada | ONTARIO |
| | | upper-case letter | CAPITAL |
| unspecified person | ONES | upperclassman | JUNIOR, SENIOR |
| unspecified time | WHENEVER | | |
| unspoiled | FRESH | uppercut | PUNCH, BLOW |
| unspoken | TACIT | upper end | TOP |
| unstable | ERRATIC | upper house of the legislature | SENATE |
| unsteady glaring light | FLARE | | |
| unsuitable | INEPT, UNFIT | upper limb | ARM |
| unsung | UNHERALDED | uppermost | TOP |
| unswerving in allegiance | LOYAL | upper Nile native | NILOT |
| untamed | FERAL, WILD | upper part | TOP |
| untanned hide | PELT | upper story | ATTIC |
| unthankful person | INGRATE | uppish person | SNOB |
| untidy | MESSY | uppity | SNOOTY |
| untidy heap | MESS | upright | ERECT |

| | | | |
|---|---|---|---|
| uprightly | RECTLY | use bad posture | SLOUCH |
| uprising | RIOT, REVOLT, | use boat oars | ROW |
| | MUTINY | used | SECONDHAND |
| uproar | CLAMOR, DIN, | used up (2 wds.) | PLAYED OUT |
| | HURLY-BURLY, RIOT | use dynamite | BLAST |
| uproarious | RIOTOUS | use experimentally | TRY |
| uproot | ERADICATE | useful | HELPFUL, UTILE |
| upset | OVERTURN | useful quality | ASSET |
| upshot | RESULT, OUTCOME | useless plant | WEED |
| upside down | INVERTED | use hindsight (comp. wd.) | |
| upstanding | UPRIGHT, | | SECOND-GUESS |
| | HONORABLE | use logic | REASON |
| upstart | PARVENU | use money | SPEND, BUY |
| up to | UNTIL | use needlessly | WASTE |
| up-to-date | MODERN | use oars | ROW |
| up to now (2 wds.) | SO FAR | use pressure | EXERT |
| up to the time of | UNTIL | use scissors | SNIP, CUT |
| up to this point | AS YET, | use sparingly | STINT, |
| | SO FAR | | RATION |
| urban area | CITY | use subterfuge | CHICANE |
| urbane | SUAVE, POLISHED | use the brain | THINK |
| urban eyesore | SKID ROW, | use up | CONSUME, EAT |
| | SLUM | U.S. flag | OLD GLORY, |
| urban need (2 wds.) | | | STARS AND STRIPES |
| | RAPID TRANSIT | U.S. frigate Constitution | |
| urchin | TAD, GAMIN | (2 wds.) | OLD IRONSIDES |
| urd | BEAN | usher | SEATER, ESCORT |
| urge | COAX, IMPEL, | using speech | ORAL |
| | PROD, SPUR, | U.S. president's home | |
| | EGG ON, PERSUADE | (2 wds.) | WHITE HOUSE |
| urgent | PRESSING | U.S. service branch | NAVY, |
| urgent wireless signal | SOS | | ARMY, AIR FORCE, |
| urn | VASE | | MARINES |
| ursa | BEAR | U.S. symbol | EAGLE |
| urticate | STING | usual | NORMAL, FAMILIAR |
| Uruguay river | PLATA | usually | GENERALLY |
| us | WE | usurp | SEIZE, CLAIM |
| usable | FIT | Utah's flower | SEGO |
| usage | HABIT, CUSTOM | Ute | INDIAN |
| use | EMPLOY, UTILIZE | utensil | TOOL. IMPLEMENT |
| use a broom | SWEEP | utilitarian | ECONOMIC, |
| use a chair | SIT | | PRACTICAL |
| use a crayon | DRAW | utility | USE |
| use a gun | SHOOT | utmost | SUPREME |
| use a hammer | NAIL | utopian | IDEAL |
| use a knife | SLICE, CARVE, | utopian region | EDEN |
| | STAB | utter | SAY, SPEAK, SHEER |
| use a lever | PRY | utter affectedly | MINCE |
| use a loom | WEAVE | utter a shrill cry | YELP |
| use a needle | SEW | utter brokenly | GASP |
| use an oven | BAKE, ROAST | utter confusion | CHAOS |
| use a pencil | WRITE | utter in a low tone | MUTTER |
| use a phone | CALL, DIAL | utterly | TOTALLY, FULLY |
| use a razor | SHAVE | utterly perplexed and | |
| use a shovel | DIG | confounded (4 wds.) | |
| use a sieve | SIFT | | AT ONE'S WITS' END |
| use a spade | DIG | | |

utter musical tones **SING**
uxorial **WIFELIKE**

## V

v-shaped cut **NOTCH**
vacancy **GAP, BLANK, OPENING**
vacant **EMPTY, UNRENTED**
vacate **EVACUATE, LEAVE**
vacation **HOLIDAY, RECESS**
vacation specialist (2 wds.) **TRAVEL AGENT**
vacation spot **RESORT, SPA**
vacillate **WAVER**
vagabond **TRAMP, HOBO, GYPSY**
vagrant **HOBO, TRAMP, BUM, ROVER**
vague **OBSCURE, DIM**
vain **IDLE, TRIVIAL**
vain bird's mate **PEAHEN**
valentine's day archer **CUPID**
valentine symbol **HEART**
valet **MANSERVANT**
valiant **BRAVE, DARING**
valid **COGENT, SOUND**
valise **GRIP, SUITCASE**
valley **DALE, VALE, DELL**
valley of Argolis **NEMEA**
valley on the moon **RILLE**
valor **PROWESS, COURAGE**
valorous person **HERO**
valuable **DEAR, PRECIOUS**
valuable card **TRUMP, ACE**
valuable fur **ERMINE, MINK, SABLE**
valuable moth larva **SILKWORM**
valuable possession **ASSET**
valuable violin **AMATI, STRAD**
value **WORTH**
value highly **TREASURE**
vamoose **SCRAM**
vampire **LAMIA**
van **TRUCK, FRONT**
vandal **HUN**
Van Druten character **MAMA**
vane **COCK**
Van Gogh **ARTIST**
vanish **DISAPPEAR**
vanity **CONCEIT, PRIDE**
vanity box **ETUI**
van man **MOVER**
vanquish **CONQUER**
vapid **INSIPID, BLAND**
vapor **GAS, STEAM, FUME, SMOKE**

vaporizing easily **VOLATILE**
vaquero **COWBOY**
vaquero's rope **RIATA**
vaquero's weapon **BOLA**
variable **PROTEAN**
variable star in Cetus **MIRA**
variation **DEVIATION**
variegated **PIED**
variety **DIVERSITY, MEDLEY**
variety of agate **ONYX**
variety of apple **WINESAP, DELICIOUS, McINTOSH**
variety of beet **CHARD**
variety of cabbage **CAULIFLOWER, KALE**
variety of cheese **EDAM, BRIE, GOUDA, CHEDDAR**
variety of grape **MALAGA**
variety of moth **LUNA**
variety of wheat **SPELT**
various **SEVERAL, SUNDRY, ASSORTED**
varlet **SCOUNDREL, KNAVE**
varmint **PEST**
varna **CASTE**
varnish **ELEMI, LAC, RESIN**
vary **DIFFER, ALTER**
varying weight of India **SER, SEER**
vase **JAR, URN**
vase-shaped jug **EWER**
vase with a pedestal **URN**
vassal **SLAVE**
vast **HUGE, ENORMOUS**
vast desert **SAHARA**
vast expanse **OCEAN, SEA**
vast number **MYRIAD**
vast period of time **EON, AEON**
vat **CALDRON, TUB**
vault **LEAP, SAFE**
vaulter's shaft **POLE**
vaunt **BOAST, BRAG**
veal **MEAT**
veal steak **CHOP**
veer **SWERVE**
vega **STAR**
vegetable **BEET, KALE, LEEK, PEA, BEAN, POTATO, CARROT, RADISH, CORN, LETTUCE, CABBAGE, TOMATO, OKRA, SQUASH, LEGUME**
vegetable box **BIN**

| | |
|---|---|
| vegetable ferment | **YEAST** |
| vegetable oyster | **SALSIFY** |
| vegetable punk | **AMADOU** |
| vegetable silk | **KAPOK** |
| vehemence | **FURY, RAGE** |
| vehicle | **AUTO, BUS, TRAIN, TRUCK** |
| vehicle dispatch man | **STARTER** |
| vehicle for hauling | **TRUCK** |
| vehicle on runners | |
| | **SLED, SLEIGH** |
| veil | **SCREEN, VELUM** |
| veiling material | **TULLE** |
| veil of gauze | **VOLET** |
| vein | **LODE, STREAK, VESSEL** |
| vein of a leaf | **RIB** |
| vellum | **PARCHMENT** |
| velocity | **SPEED** |
| velvet-like fabric | **PANNE, VELURE** |
| venal | **MERCENARY** |
| vend | **SELL, RETAIL** |
| vendetta | **FEUD** |
| vendue | **AUCTION** |
| veneer | **SURFACE** |
| venerable | **OLD, WISE, AUGUST** |
| venerate | **REVERE** |
| veneration | **AWE, RESPECT** |
| Venetian blind part | **SLAT** |
| Venetian boat | **GONDOLA** |
| Venetian painter | **TITIAN** |
| Venetian red | **SIENA** |
| Venetian resort | **LIDO** |
| Venetian ruler | **DOGE** |
| Venetian water taxi | **GONDOLA** |
| vengeful Greek goddess | **ERIS** |
| venom | **POISON** |
| venomous ill-will | **SPITE** |
| venomous snake | **ADDER, ASP, COBRA** |
| venomous spider | |
| | **TARANTULA** |
| vent | **OPENING, OUTLET** |
| ventilate | **AIR** |
| ventilator | **AIR SHAFT** |
| venture | **DARE, RISK** |
| venturesome | **BOLD** |
| Venus' son | **CUPID** |
| Venus' sweetheart | **ADONIS** |
| veracity | **TRUTH, REALITY** |
| veranda | **PORCH, STOOP, TERRACE, PATIO** |
| verb form | **TENSE** |
| verbatim | **WORD FOR WORD** |
| verbose | **WORDY** |

| | |
|---|---|
| verboten | **FORBIDDEN** |
| verdant | **LUSH, GREEN** |
| verdict | **FINDING, DECISION** |
| Verdi opera | **AIDA** |
| verge | **BRINK** |
| verglas | **GLAZE** |
| verify | **AVER, CONFIRM** |
| verily | **AMEN, TRULY** |
| veritable | **ACTUAL, REAL** |
| vermilion | **RED** |
| Vermont tree | **MAPLE** |
| vernacular | **NATIVE** |
| vernal | **SPRING** |
| Verne hero | **NEMO** |
| versatile | **ADAPTABLE** |
| verse | **POEM, ODE, SONNET** |
| verse maker | **POET, BARD** |
| version | **RENDITION** |
| versus | **AGAINST** |
| vertical | **ERECT** |
| vertigo | **DIZZINESS** |
| verve | **ELAN** |
| very | **EXTREMELY, EXCEEDINGLY** |
| very (Fr.) | **TRES** |
| very cold | **ICY** |
| very dry | **ARID** |
| very eager | **AVID** |
| very fat | **OBESE** |
| very good | **FINE** |
| very heavy | **LEADEN** |
| very hot | **TROPICAL** |
| very important persons (abbr.) | **VIPS** |
| very impressive | **AWESOME** |
| very large | **HUGE** |
| very large nail | **SPIKE** |
| very nervous (4 wds.) | |
| | **ON PINS AND NEEDLES** |
| very pale | **ASHY** |
| very powerful | **POTENT** |
| Very signal | **FLARE** |
| very skillful | **EXPERT** |
| very small | **TEENY, TINY, WEE** |
| very small (prefix) | **MICRO** |
| very small paintings | **MINIATURE** |
| very small quantity | **IOTA** |
| very thin | **SHEER, SKINNY, LEAN, GAUNT** |
| very unpleasant | **NASTY** |
| very warm | **HOT** |
| very wealthy person | |
| | **MILLIONAIRE** |
| very wet | **SOPPY** |
| vesicate | **BLISTER** |
| vesicle | **SAC, CAVITY** |

| | |
|---|---|
| vespers (2 wds.) | |
| | **EVENING PRAYER** |
| vespid | **WASP, HORNET** |
| vessel | **CRAFT, BOAT,** |
| | **VEIN, BOWL** |
| vessel for preserves | **JAR** |
| vessel in Genesis | **ARK** |
| vessel's bow | **PROW** |
| vessel's frame | **HULL** |
| vest | **WAISTCOAT** |
| vestal | **CHASTE, PURE** |
| vestibule | **ENTRY, HALLWAY,** |
| | **FOYER** |
| vestige | **TRACE** |
| vestment | **STOLE, ALB, COPE** |
| vestry | **SACRISTY** |
| vetch | **ERS, TARE** |
| veteran sailor | **TAR** |
| veto | **DENY, NYET,** |
| | **PROHIBIT** |
| vex | **IRK, RILE, PESTER,** |
| | **ANNOY, NETTLE** |
| vexed | **SORE, ANNOYED** |
| via | **WAY, ROUTE** |
| viable | **LIKELY, WORKABLE** |
| viaduct | **TRESTLE, BRIDGE** |
| vial | **BOTTLE, PHIAL** |
| vibrant | **ALIVE, VITAL** |
| vibrate | **SWING, QUIVER** |
| vibration | **TREMOR** |
| vicar | **PARSON** |
| vice | **CRIME, EVIL** |
| vicinity | **AREA** |
| vicious | **MEAN** |
| victim | **PREY, SLAVE** |
| victor | **WINNER** |
| victory | **WIN, TRIUMPH,** |
| | **CONQUEST** |
| victory symbol | **LAUREL, VEE** |
| victrola | **PHONOGRAPH** |
| victuals | **FOOD** |
| video's predecessor | **RADIO** |
| vie | **CONTEND** |
| view | **LOOK, VISTA, SCENE** |
| vigil | **WAKE, WATCH** |
| vigilant | **ALERT, AWAKE** |
| vignette | **PICTURE** |
| vigor | **ENERGY, PEP, VIM** |
| vigorous | **ENERGETIC, HARDY** |
| vigorous colloquial | |
| language | **SLANG** |
| vigorous scuffle | **TUSSLE** |
| viking | **NORSEMAN** |
| vile | **BASE, FOUL** |
| vilify | **ABUSE, DEFAME** |
| village | **HAMLET** |
| village in Ireland | **TARA** |

| | |
|---|---|
| village in South Africa | **STAD** |
| village square in ancient | |
| Greece | **AGORA** |
| villain in "Othello" | **IAGO** |
| villainous | **VICIOUS** |
| villain's exclamation | **AHA** |
| villain's nemesis | **HERO** |
| vim | **ENERGY** |
| vindicate | **AVENGE** |
| vindictive | **MALICIOUS,** |
| | **VENGEFUL** |
| vine | **IVY, LIANE, LIANA** |
| vine fruit | **BERRY** |
| vinegar | **ACETUM** |
| vinous | **WINY** |
| vintage | **YEAR** |
| vinyl square | **TILE** |
| viola | **ALTO** |
| violate | **DESECRATE** |
| violation of law | **CRIME** |
| violence | **FEROCITY, RAGE,** |
| | **FORCE** |
| violent | **FURIOUS, RAGING** |
| violent anger | **RAGE** |
| violent downpour | **TORRENT** |
| violent outbreak | **ERUPTION** |
| violent pain | **PANG, THROE** |
| violent storm | **TEMPEST** |
| violent wind | **SIMOON(M),** |
| | **TYPHOON, HURRICANE,** |
| | **TORNADO, TWISTER,** |
| | **CYCLONE, MONSOON** |
| violet | **MAUVE** |
| violin | **FIDDLE** |
| violin bar | **FRET** |
| violin maker | **AMATI** |
| viper | **ADDER, ASP, SNAKE** |
| Virgil's poem | **AENEID** |
| Virginia willow | **ITEA** |
| virile | **MANLY** |
| virtue | **EXCELLENCE, PURITY** |
| virtuous | **PURE, CHASTE,** |
| | **MORAL** |
| virulent | **DEADLY** |
| visage | **FACE** |
| viscid | **STICKY, WAXY** |
| viscid liquid | **TAR** |
| viscous | **THICK, VISCID** |
| visible | **SEEN** |
| visible outline | **SILHOUETTE** |
| visible vapor | **STEAM** |
| Visigoth king | **ALARIC** |
| vision | **DREAM** |
| visit | **CALL, SEE** |
| visit a pawnbroker | **HOCK** |
| visit frequently | **HAUNT** |
| visitor | **CALLER** |

| | | | |
|---|---|---|---|
| vison | MINK | vouch | ATTEST |
| vista | SCENE, VIEW | vouchsafe | GRANT, GIVE |
| visual | SEEN | vow | OATH, SWEAR, PROMISE |
| visualize | SEE | vowel combination | DIPHTHONG |
| vital | ALIVE | Vulcan's creation | TALOS |
| vital organ | HEART, LIVER, | vulgar | COMMON, RUDE |
| | KIDNEY | vulgarity | OBSCENITY |
| vitality | VIGOR | vulnerable | WEAK |
| vitamin B₁ | THIAMIN | vying | COMPETING, |
| vitamin B₂ | RIBOFLAVIN | | STRUGGLING |
| vitriolic | CAUSTIC, SCATHING | | |
| vivid | LIVELY, BRIGHT, | | |
| | INTENSE, BRILLIANT, | **W** | |
| | ACTIVE, STRONG, | | |
| | DARING, CLEAR | wad | LUMP, BALL, MASS, |
| vixen | SCOLD, SHREW | | PLUG, STUFF |
| vocal | ORAL | wading bird | CRANE, CURLEW, |
| vocalize | SING | | HERON, IBIS, RAIL, |
| vocation | PROFESSION, CAREER | | STILT, STORK |
| vociferous | BLATANT, LOUD | wafer | BISCUIT, CAKE |
| vogue | STYLE, MODE | waff | PUFF, GUST |
| voice | SPEECH | waft | BLOW, BREEZE, BECKON |
| voice box | LARYNX | wag | HUMORIST |
| voice inflection | TONE | wage | SALARY |
| voice of the people | | wager | BET |
| (Lat., 2 wds.) | VOX POPULI | wages | SALARY, PAY |
| void | EMPTY | wagon | CART |
| void court proceeding | | wagon journey | TREK |
| | MISTRIAL | wagon track | RUT |
| volatile | LIGHT, AIRY, | wagtail | LARK |
| | UNSTABLE | wahoo | PETO |
| volcanic ash | LAVA | waif | STRAY, ORPHAN |
| volcanic cavity | CRATER | wail | HOWL, BAWL |
| volcanic rock column | BASALT | wainscot | PANELING |
| volcanic scoria | SLAG | waist | BLOUSE |
| volcano in Italy | ETNA | waist band | BELT, SASH |
| volcano mouth | CRATER | waistcoat | VEST |
| volcano of Martinique | PELEE | wait | LINGER, TARRY, BIDE |
| vole | RODENT | wait close by | HOVER |
| Volga tributary | KAMA, OKA, | waiter | SERVANT, GARCON |
| | SAMARA | waiter at a drive-in | CARHOP |
| volition | WILL | waiter's item | TRAY |
| volley | BARRAGE | waiter's reward | TIP |
| voluble | GLIB, CHATTY | waiting | EXPECTANT |
| volume | TOME, BOOK | wait on tables | SERVE |
| volume of maps | ATLAS | waive | RELINQUISH |
| voluntary | INTENTIONAL | wake | ROUSE |
| volunteer | ENLIST | wale | WELT, WEAL, RIDGE |
| Volunteer State | TENNESSEE | walk | PACE, TRED, STEP, |
| voluptuous | SENSUAL | | STRIDE |
| voracious | GREEDY, HUNGRY | walk back and forth | PACE |
| voracious eel | MORAY | walk clumsily | LUMBER |
| vortex | EDDY | walk drunkenly | STAGGER |
| vote against | CON | walk fast | RUN |
| vote down | DEFEAT | walk for pleasure | HIKE, |
| vote into office | ELECT | | STROLL, AMBLE |
| voting place | POLLS | walk heavily | TRAMP, TREAD, |
| | | | LUMBER |

| | |
|---|---|
| walking shorts | **BERMUDAS** |
| walking stick | **CANE** |
| walk in water | **WADE** |
| walk lamely | **LIMP** |
| walk leisurely | **AMBLE, STROLL** |
| walk like a duck | **WADDLE** |
| walk off with | **STEAL** |
| walk on | **TREAD** |
| walkout | **STRIKE** |
| walk out on | **ABANDON** |
| walk over | **TRAMPLE** |
| walk pompously | **STRUT** |
| walk softly | **TIPTOE** |
| walk the floor | **PACE** |
| walk uncertainly | **TOTTER** |
| walk wearily | **TRUDGE** |
| walk with an easy gait | **LOPE** |
| wall | **BASTION, RAMPART** |
| wallaba tree | **APA** |
| wall border | **DADO** |
| wall bracket | **SCONCE** |
| wall covering | **PLASTER, VINYL, MURAL** |
| wall end | **GABLE** |
| wallet | **PURSE, BILLFOLD** |
| walleye | **FISH, HORSE** |
| wall hanging | **TAPESTRY** |
| wall lining | **WAINSCOT** |
| wall ornament | **PLAQUE** |
| wallow | **FLOUNDER** |
| wall painting | **MURAL** |
| wall recess | **NICHE** |
| Walt Disney elephant | **DUMBO** |
| waltz | **DANCE** |
| wampum | **BEADS** |
| wan | **PALE, ASHEN** |
| wand | **BATON, ROD** |
| wander | **ERR, ROAM, ROVE, GAD, MEANDER, STRAY** |
| wander aimlessly | **MEANDER** |
| wanderer | **NOMAD, ROVER, VAGRANT, VAGABOND** |
| wanderer from duty | **TRUANT** |
| wander from subject | **DIGRESS** |
| wandering | **ERRANT, ERRATIC** |
| wandering laborer | **MIGRANT** |
| wane | **DECREASE, DECLINE** |
| wangle | **MANIPULATE** |
| want | **DESIRE, LACK, NEED, CRAVE, WISH** |
| want and expect | **HOPE** |
| wanting | **ABSENT, LACKING** |
| wanting in color | **PALE** |
| wanton | **LOOSE, OBSCENE** |
| wanton look | **LEER** |
| wapiti | **DEER, ELK** |
| war | **BATTLE, HOSTILITY** |

| | |
|---|---|
| warble | **SING, TRILL** |
| war club | **MACE** |
| ward | **DISTRICT, DIVISION** |
| ward off | **AVERT** |
| wardrobe | **CLOSET** |
| warehouse | **DEPOT, STORAGE, ETAPE** |
| wares | **MERCHANDISE, GOODS, PRODUCTS** |
| war fleet | **ARMADA** |
| war hero | **ACE, AVIATOR** |
| war horse | **STEED** |
| warlike | **HOSTILE** |
| warlock | **SORCERER, WIZARD** |
| warm | **TEPID, HOT, HEAT** |
| war machine | **TANK** |
| warmhearted | **TENDER** |
| warm season | **SUMMER** |
| warmth | **HEAT** |
| warmth of color | **GLOW** |
| warm up a motor | **REV** |
| warm up an oven | **PREHEAT** |
| warm wind | **SOUTHERLY** |
| warn | **ALARM, ALERT** |
| warning | **CAUTION** |
| warning device | **HORN, SIREN, ALARM** |
| warning sound at sea | **FOGHORN** |
| warp | **DISTORT, PERVERT, CORRUPT** |
| warrant | **PERMIT, WRIT, GUARANTEE** |
| warrior | **SOLDIER** |
| Warsaw citizen | **POLE** |
| wary | **LEERY, CAUTIOUS** |
| wash | **LAVE, LAUNDER, CLEANSE** |
| wash away | **ERODE, RINSE** |
| wash basin | **LAVABO, SINK** |
| washbowl | **SINK, BASIN** |
| wash by draining | **LEACH** |
| washday | **MONDAY** |
| wash for gold | **PAN** |
| washing bar | **SOAP** |
| Washington ballplayer | **SENATOR** |
| Washington city | **SEATTLE** |
| Washington sound | **PUGET** |
| wash lightly | **RINSE** |
| wash the hair | **SHAMPOO** |
| wash vigorously | **SCRUB, SCOUR** |
| washy | **PALE, DILUTED** |
| wasp | **HORNET** |
| waspish | **TESTY** |
| waste | **LOSS, SQUANDER** |
| waste allowance | **TRET** |

waste away **MOLDER, DECAY, CRUMBLE**
waste cloth **RAG**
wasteful **EXTRAVAGANT**
wasteland **DESERT**
waste matter **DROSS, SLAG**
wastepaper receptacle **BASKET**
waste time **DALLY, LOAF, IDLE**
watch **OBSERVE, REGARD, VIGIL**
watch chain **FOB**
watch closely **EYE**
watch face cover **CRYSTAL**
watch for **AWAIT**
watchful **ALERT, AWAKE, VIGILANT**
watchman **GUARD**
watch over **TEND**
watch pocket **FOB**
watch secretly **SPY**
watch sound **TICK, TOCK**
watchtower **BEACON**
watchword **CRY**
water **WET, IRRIGATE, SPRINKLE**
water (Fr.) **EAU**
water after liquor (colloq.) **CHASER**
water barrier **DAM**
water bird **PELICAN, ERNE, TERN, GULL, DUCK, SWAN**
water bottle **CARAFE**
water channel **FLUME**
water cow **MANATEE**
water craft **SHIP, BOAT**
water down **WEAKEN**
water drain **SEWER, SUMP**
water eagle **OSPREY**
watered silk **MOIRE**
water enthusiast (2 wds.) **SKIN DIVER**
waterfall **CATARACT**
waterfall (Scot.) **LINN**
water flask **CANTEEN**
waterfront **HARBOR, DOCK**
water grass **REED**
water hole **WELL**
watering place **SPA**
watering tube **HOSE**
water jug **OLLA**
water lily **LOTOS, LOTUS**
waterless **ARID, BONE-DRY**
waterlogged **SOAKED**
water main **PIPE**
water moccasin **COTTONMOUTH**

water monster's home (2 wds.) **LOCH NESS**
water nymph **NAIAD**
water passage **CANAL**
water (pharm.) **AQUA**
water pipe **MAIN, SPOUT**
water pitcher **EWER**
water plant **LOTUS**
water rat **MUSKRAT**
water sound **SPLASH**
water sprite **NIX, NIXIE**
water vapor **MIST, STEAM**
waterway **CANAL**
waterway under a road **CULVERT**
water willow **OSIER**
water witch **DOWSER**
watery **AQUEOUS**
watusi or frug **DANCE**
wave **FLUTTER, FLICKER, BREAKER**
wave (Fr.) **ONDE**
waver **TEETER, VACILLATE, REEL, FALTER**
wave (Sp.) **OLA**
wave to and fro **FLAP**
wavy **CURLY**
wax **CERE**
wax (Lat.) **CERA**
waxy ointment **CERATE**
waxy substance in cork **CERIN**
way **METHOD, ROUTE, SYSTEM**
way of behaving **MANNER**
waylay **AMBUSH**
way out **EXIT**
wayside hotel **INN, TAVERN, MOTEL**
way train **LOCAL**
wayward **ERRATIC**
weak **NERVELESS, VULNERABLE**
weaken **ENERVATE, SAP**
weakness **DEBILITY**
weak point **FOIBLE**
weal **WALE, WELT**
wealth **RICHES, ABUNDANCE**
wealthy **OPULENT, RICH, AFFLUENT, ABUNDANT**
weapon **GUN, RIFLE, ARROW, DART, ARM, SWORD**
weapons **ARMS**
wear and tear **DAMAGE**
wear at edge **FRAY**
wear away **ERODE**
wear down **EXHAUST**
weariness **FATIGUE**

| | |
|---|---|
| wearing apparel | **SUITS, CLOTHES, DRESSES, ATTIRE, CLOTHING** |
| wearing boots | **SHOD** |
| wearing clothes | **CLAD** |
| wearisome | **TEDIOUS, FATIGUING** |
| wear out | **TIRE** |
| weary | **TIRED, BORED** |
| weasel | **STOAT, ERMINE** |
| weathercock | **VANE** |
| weather condition | **CLIMATE** |
| weather forecast | **FAIR, SUNNY, RAIN, CLOUDY, HOT, COLD, MILD, SLEET, SNOW, WARM, HUMID, CLEAR** |
| weave | **INTERLACE** |
| weaving device | **LOOM** |
| webbing | **MEMBRANE** |
| web-footed bird | **GOOSE, DUCK** |
| web spinner | **SPIDER** |
| wed | **MARRY** |
| wedding | **MARRIAGE, NUPTIALS, UNION** |
| wedding attendant | **USHER, BRIDESMAID** |
| wedding band | **RING** |
| wedding grain | **RICE** |
| wedding party member | **BEST MAN, BRIDESMAID, MAID OF HONOR** |
| wedding proclamation | **BANNS, BANS** |
| wedding ring | **BAND** |
| wedge in | **JAM** |
| wedlock | **MATRIMONY** |
| wed secretly | **ELOPE** |
| wee | **SMALL, TINY** |
| weed | **TARE** |
| weeding implement | **HOE** |
| wee drink | **NIP** |
| weep | **CRY** |
| weep aloud | **SOB** |
| weeping daughter of Tantalus | **NIOBE** |
| weevil | **BOLL, RICE, PEA, SEED** |
| weft | **WOOF, FILLING, WEB** |
| weigh | **SCALE** |
| weigh down | **BURDEN** |
| weighing device | **SCALE** |
| weigh in mind | **PONDER** |
| weight | **OUNCE, POUND, TON** |
| weight allowance | **TARE** |
| weight for gems | **CARAT** |
| weight of India | **SER** |
| weight system | **METRIC** |
| weighty | **MASSIVE, BULKY** |
| weir | **DAM, FENCE** |
| weird | **EERIE, EERY, MACABRE, STRANGE** |
| weird sisters | **FATES** |
| welcome | **GREET** |
| weld | **UNITE** |
| welfare | **PROSPERITY** |
| well | **HEALTHY** |
| well-being | **WELFARE, PROSPERITY** |
| well-bred | **GENTEEL** |
| well done! | **BRAVO** |
| well-heeled | **RICH** |
| well-informed | **LEARNED** |
| well-known | **FAMOUS** |
| well-liked | **POPULAR** |
| well-skilled | **ADEPT, ABLE** |
| well-to-do | **RICH** |
| well-ventilated | **AIRY** |
| well-worn course | **PATH, TRAIL** |
| Welsh dog | **CORGI** |
| welt | **SLASH, STRIP** |
| wench | **MAIDEN** |
| went back over | **RETRACED** |
| went before | **LED** |
| went beyond the mark | **OVERSHOT** |
| went by car | **RODE** |
| went by ship | **SAILED** |
| went past one's bedtime (2 wds.) | **SAT UP** |
| went quickly | **SPED** |
| went to bed (2 wds., colloq.) | **TURNED IN** |
| went to the bottom | **SANK** |
| weskit | **VEST** |
| west | **OCCIDENT** |
| western | **OMELET, MOVIE, FILM** |
| Western farm | **RANCH** |
| Western halter | **HACKAMORE** |
| Western lily | **SEGO** |
| Western marsh plant | **TULE** |
| Western mountains | **SIERRAS** |
| Western resort | **TAHOE, ASPEN** |
| Western rope | **LASSO, REATA, RIATA, LARIAT** |
| Western show | **RODEO** |
| Western shrub | **SAGE** |
| Western song (4 wds.) | **HOME ON THE RANGE** |
| Western weed | **LOCO** |
| West German capital | **BONN** |
| West Indian magic | **OBE(AH)** |
| West Indian product | **RUM** |
| West Indian volcano | **PELEE** |
| West Indies rodent | **AGOUTI** |

| | | | |
|---|---|---|---|
| West Point freshman | PLEBE | whir | BUZZ, VIBRATE |
| West Point student | CADET | whirl | ROTATE, SPIN, SWIRL, |
| wet | MOIST, DAMP, WATER | | TURN, EDDY, REEL, |
| wet behind the ears | YOUNG | | GYRATE, REVOLVE |
| wet earth | MUD | whirligig | PINWHEEL |
| wet falling sound | PLOP | whirlwind | CYCLONE, TORNADO |
| wet ground | BOG, MIRE, | whirlybird | HELICOPTER, |
| | SWAMP | | COPTER, CHOPPER |
| wet sludge | MIRE | whisk | TUFT, WISP |
| wet smack | SPLAT | whiskers | BEARD |
| wet thoroughly | DRENCH | whisper | MURMUR |
| whack | SLAP | whistle sound | TOOT |
| whale | CETE, SPERM | whit | BIT, IOTA |
| whale school | GAM, POD | white | PALE, WAN |
| whale secretion | AMBERGRIS | white admiral | BUTTERFLY |
| whale's passenger | JONAH | white and shining | PEARLY |
| whammy | JINX | white ant | TERMITE |
| wharf | DOCK, PIER | whitebait | SMELT |
| whatever the meal is | POTLUCK | white bear | POLAR |
| what for | WHY | white beet | CHARD |
| what person | WHO | whitecap | WAVE |
| wheat | GRAIN | white coal | WATER |
| wheat chaff | BRAN | whitefish | BELUGA |
| wheedle | COAX, CAJOLE | white flower | GARDENIA |
| wheel animalcule | ROTIFER | white frost | RIME, HOAR |
| wheel covering | TIRE | white jade | ALABASTER |
| wheel edge | RIM | white lie | FIB |
| wheel hoop | TIRE | white merganser | SMEW |
| wheel hub | NAVE | whiten | BLEACH, PALE |
| wheelman | HELMSMAN | white-plumed heron | EGRET |
| wheel projection | CAM | white poplar | ABELE |
| wheel rut | TRACK | white sheep | MERINO |
| wheel shaft | AXLE | white vestment | ALB |
| wheel stopper | TRIG | whitewall | TIRE |
| wheel track | RUT | white walnut | BUTTERNUT |
| wheeze | GASP | white water | RAPIDS |
| whelk | SNAIL | white whale | BELUGA |
| when | AS, UNTIL | white with age | HOARY |
| wherewithal | MEANS | whiting | CHALK |
| whet | HONE, SHARPEN | whitlow | FELON |
| which | THAT | whittle | CUT |
| which thing | WHAT | whizz | EXPERT |
| whiff | GUST, PUFF, SNIFF | whoa | STOP |
| Whig's opponent | TORY | whole | ALL, ENTIRE, TOTAL, |
| while | AS | | INTACT |
| whilom | FORMER | wholehearted | SINCERE, |
| whim | CAPRICE | | EARNEST |
| whimper | PULE, WHINE | whole number | INTEGER |
| whimsical | FANCIFUL | wholesome | HEALTHY, |
| whin | FURZE, GORSE | | VIGOROUS |
| whine | SNIVEL, WHIMPER | wholly engrossed | RAPT |
| whining complainer | | whoop | HOOT, CHEER |
| (arch.) | PULER | whoop-de-do | HOOPLA, |
| whinny | NEIGH | | BALLYHOO |
| whip | CANE, BEAT | whooping cough | PERTUSSIS |
| whip handle | CROP | whopper | LIE |
| whipping boy | SCAPEGOAT | whorl | SPIRE |

| | | | |
|---|---|---|---|
| wick | FUSE | wild iris | FLAG |
| wicked | BAD, EVIL | wild mustard | CHARLOCK |
| wickedness | EVIL | wild ox | YAK, ANOA |
| wicker basket | HAMPER, PANNIER | wild party | ORGY |
| | | wild pig | BOAR |
| wicker container | BASKET | wild plum | SLOE |
| wicker cradle | BASSINET | wild rabbit | HARE |
| wicket | WINDOW, GATE | wild rose | SWEETBRIER |
| wide | BROAD | wild sheep | ARGAL |
| wide-awake | ALERT | wild talk | RAVING |
| wide-brimmed hat | SOMBRERO | wild turnip | RUTABAGA |
| wide extent | EXPANSE | wild west show | RODEO |
| wide inlet | BAY | wile | STRATEGEM, TRICK |
| widely accepted | PREVALENT | will | VOLITION, MIND |
| widemouthed jug | EWER | willful | INTENTIONAL |
| widen | DILATE, ENLARGE, BROADEN | willing | AGREEABLE |
| | | willow | OSIER |
| wide smile | GRIN | Wilson's thrush | VEERY |
| widespread | GENERAL | wilt | DROOP, SAG |
| wide stream | RIVER | wily | ARTFUL, SHREWD, CRAFTY, SLY |
| wide street | AVENUE, BOULEVARD | | |
| | | win | TRIUMPH, PREVAIL |
| widgeon | SMEE, DUCK | wince | CRINGE, FLINCH |
| widget | GADGET | winch | HOIST, HAUL |
| width | GIRTH, DIAMETER | wind | BREEZE, AIR |
| width of a circle | DIAMETER | wind (prefix) | ANEM(O) |
| wield | BRANDISH, PLY | wind about | COIL |
| wiener | HOT DOG, FRANK | windbreaker | JACKET |
| wife | SPOUSE, MATE | windflower | ANEMONE |
| wife of Abraham | SARAH | wind gauge | VANE |
| wife of Chuchulain | EMER | windhover | KESTREL |
| wife of Hiawatha | MINNEHAHA | wind indicator | VANE |
| wife of Jason | MEDEA | winding sheet | SHROUD |
| wife of Zeus | HERA | wind instrument | BUGLE, OBOE, TUBA, FLUTE, HORN, SAX, CLARINET |
| wig | PERUKE, TOUPEE | | |
| Wight | ISLE | | |
| wigwam | TEPEE, TENT | windlass | WINCH |
| wild | FERAL, SAVAGE, UNTAMED | windmill sail | AWN |
| | | window compartment | PANE |
| wild allspice | SPICEBUSH | window covering | BLIND, SHADE, DRAPE, SHUTTER, AWNING |
| wild animal | BEAST | | |
| wild arum | CUCKOOPINT | | |
| wild banana | PAWPAW | window curtain material | SCRIM, LACE |
| wild beast's covert | LAIR, DEN | | |
| wild buffalo of India | ARNA | window part | SASH, SILL, PANE |
| wild disorder | RIOT | windpipe | TRACHEA |
| wild dog of Australia | DINGO | windshield gadget | WIPER |
| wild donkey | ONAGER | wind spirally | COIL |
| wildebeest | GNU | windstorm | GALE |
| wilderness | DESERT | windy | STORMY |
| wild fancy | VAGARY | Windy City | CHICAGO |
| wild goat | IBEX | windy month | MARCH |
| wild grape vine | LIANA | wine barrel | CASK, TUN |
| wild headlong flight | STAMPEDE | wine bottle | DECANTER |
| wild hog | BOAR | wine cask deposit | TARTAR |
| wild horse | MUSTANG | wine colored | PURPLE |
| wild indigo | BAPTISIA | wine cup | CHALICE |

winesap **APPLE**
wing **ALA**
winged **ALAR, ALATE**
winged god **EROS**
winged horse **PEGASUS**
winged insect **BEE, FLY,**
**BUTTERFLY, WASP**
winged monster **HARPY**
winglet **ALULA**
winglike **ALAR**
winglike part **ALA**
wing movement **FLUTTER**
wing-shaped **ALARY, ALATE,**
**ALAR**
wing tip **SHOE**
wink **BLINK**
winner **CHAMPION, VICTOR**
winnow **SEPARATE, SIFT**
winsome **CHARMING,**
**ATTRACTIVE**
winter apple **WINESAP**
winter bird food **SUET**
wintergreen **SHINLEAF**
winter hand warmer **MUFF,**
**MITTEN, GLOVE**
winter jacket **PARKA**
winter melon **CASABA**
winter moisture **SNOW**
winter sport **SLEDDING,**
**SKATING, SKIING**
winter vehicle **SLED, SLEIGH,**
**SNOWMOBILE, TOBOGGAN**
winter weapon **SNOWBALL**
winter white stuff **SNOW, ICE**
win the regatta **OUTSAIL**
wintry **HIEMAL**
wintry glaze **ICE**
wipe **DRY, RUB, CLEAN**
wipe out **ERASE**
wipe the dishes **DRY**
wire **CABLE, TELEGRAM**
wire fastener **NAIL**
wirehair **TERRIER**
wireless communication **RADIO**
wire measure **MIL**
wire nail **BRAD**
wire rope **CABLE**
wire-stitching machine
**STAPLER**
wiretap device **DETECTAPHONE**
wireless signal **SOS**
wiry **RANGY, SINEWY**
Wisconsin city **OSHKOSH,**
**MADISON**
wisdom **SAGACITY**
wise **SAGACIOUS, SAPIENT,**
**SENSIBLE, SHREWD**

wise bird **OWL**
wise counselor **NESTOR**
wisecrack **GIBE, RETORT**
wise king of Pylos **NESTOR**
wise lawgiver **SOLON,**
**SOLOMON**
wisely cautious **PRUDENT**
wise man **SAGE, SEER**
wisent **BISON**
wise saying **ADAGE**
wisest Greek in the
Trojan War **NESTOR**
wise to **AWARE**
wish **DESIRE, HOPE, WANT**
wish undone **RUE**
wish well **BLESS**
wishy-washy (comp. wd.)
**NAMBY-PAMBY**
wisp **STRAND**
wist **KNOW, GAME**
wistful **LONGING**
wit **CLEVERNESS, HUMOR,**
**HUMORIST**
witchcraft **SORCERY**
witch trial city **SALEM**
with (Fr.) **AVEC**
withdraw **RETRACT, RETREAT,**
**SECEDE**
withdraw a statement **RECANT**
withdraw from
association **SECEDE**
withdraw from business **RETIRE**
with force **AMAIN**
withhold **DENY**
wither **SEAR, WILT**
with ice cream, as pie
(3 wds.) **A LA MODE**
within **IN**
within the time of **DURING**
with less hair **BALDER**
with one **ALONG**
without (Fr.) **SANS**
without (Lat.) **SINE**
without charge **FREE, GRATIS**
without company **ALONE**
without emotion **DULLY**
without end **ETERNAL**
without energy **LANGUID**
without equal **PEERLESS**
without face value
(comp. wd.) **NO-PAR**
without fat **LEAN**
without knowledge **IGNORANT**
without much meat **BONY**
without purpose **AIMLESS, IDLY**
without reason **NEEDLESS**
without vigor **SPIRITLESS**

| | |
|---|---|
| without warning | **SUDDENLY** |
| without work | **IDLE** |
| withstand | **RESIST, OPPOSE, HOLD OFF** |
| with the mouth wide open | **AGAPE** |
| with unlimited power | **PLENIPOTENTIARY** |
| witless | **FOOLISH, STUPID** |
| witness | **SEE** |
| witticism | **MOT** |
| witty | **CLEVER** |
| witty answer | **REPARTEE** |
| witty person | **WAG** |
| wizard | **SORCERER, MAGICIAN** |
| wizen | **DRY UP, WITHER, SHRIVEL** |
| wobble | **SHAKE** |
| woe | **GRIEF, SORROW** |
| woeful | **SAD, WRETCHED** |
| woe is me | **ALAS** |
| wolf | **LOBO** |
| wolfhound | **BORZOI** |
| wolfish | **LUPINE** |
| wolfram | **TUNGSTEN** |
| wolfsbane | **ACONITE** |
| Wolverine State | **MICHIGAN** |
| woman | **LADY, FEMALE** |
| woman entertainer | **HOSTESS** |
| woman hater | **MYSOGYNIST** |
| woman in the U.S. Army | **WAC** |
| womanish | **FEMALE** |
| womanless party | **STAG, SMOKER** |
| womanly | **FEMININE** |
| woman of breeding | **LADY** |
| woman of rank | **DAME** |
| woman's crowning glory | **HAIR** |
| woman's dress | **GOWN** |
| woman's dressing gown | **NEGLIGEE** |
| woman's dressing jacket | **CAMISOLE** |
| woman's fur garment | **STOLE, WRAP** |
| woman's garment | **SLIP, BRA, SKIRT, BLOUSE, DRESS, COAT** |
| woman singer (Fr.) | **CHANTEUSE** |
| woman's secret | **AGE** |
| women's patriotic society (abbr.) | **D.A.R.** |
| womera (2 wds.) | **SPEAR THROWER** |
| wonder | **MARVEL** |
| wonderful | **AMAZING, MARVELOUS** |

| | |
|---|---|
| wonderful thing | **MIRACLE** |
| wonderland girl | **ALICE** |
| wondrous | **MARVELOUS** |
| wont | **HABIT, CUSTOM** |
| woo | **COURT** |
| wood | **LUMBER, OAK, TEAK, EBONY, WALNUT, CHERRY, BIRCH** |
| wood alcohol | **METHANOL** |
| wood bundle | **FAGOT** |
| wood carver | **HEWER** |
| woodchopper | **LOGGER, AXEMAN** |
| wood chopping tool | **AXE, AX** |
| wood clearing | **GLADE** |
| woodchuck | **MARMOT** |
| wood coal | **CHARCOAL, LIGNITE** |
| wood deities | **FAUNS, SATYRS** |
| wood-eating ant | **TERMITE** |
| wooded valley | **GLEN** |
| wooden box | **CRATE** |
| wooden container | **BARREL, CASE** |
| wooden joint part | **TENON** |
| wooden match | **FUSEE, FUZEE** |
| wooden nail | **PEG** |
| wooden shoe | **SABOT, CLOG** |
| wooden tub | **SOE** |
| wood knot | **GNARL, KNUR** |
| woodland | **FOREST** |
| woodland animal | **DEER** |
| woodland deity | **FAUN, SATYR** |
| wood plant | **TREE** |
| wood sorrel | **OCA** |
| wood strip | **LATH, SLAT** |
| woodwind instrument | **FLUTE, OBOE, REED, CLARINET, BASSOON** |
| woodwork | **MOLDING** |
| woodworking tool | **ADZE** |
| woody plant | **TREE** |
| wooer | **SUITOR** |
| woof | **FILLING, WEFT** |
| wool | **FLEECE** |
| wool blemish | **MOTE** |
| woolen cap | **TAM** |
| woolen dress fabric | **DELAINE** |
| wool fat | **LANOLIN** |
| wool fiber | **NEP** |
| woolly | **LANATE** |
| woozy | **DIZZY, FAINT** |
| wordbook | **DICTIONARY, LEXICON** |
| word for opening doors | **SESAME** |
| word for word | **LITERAL, VERBATIM** |

| | |
|---|---|
| word game | LOTTO, SCRABBLE |
| wordiness | VERBIAGE |
| wording | DICTION |
| word in Japanese ship names | MARU |
| word inventor | COINER |
| wordless actor | MIME |
| word of action | VERB |
| word of approval | BRAVO |
| word of assent | YES |
| word of disgust | BAH |
| word of division | INTO |
| word of farewell | ADIEU, ADIOS |
| word of gratitude | THANKS |
| word of greeting | HELLO, HI |
| word of honor | PAROLE, OATH |
| word of negation | NOT |
| word of regret | ALAS |
| word of reproof | TUT |
| word on a towel | HIS, HERS |
| word on the wall | MENE, TEKEL |
| word puzzle | REBUS, CROSSWORD, ACROSTIC |
| words of understanding (2 wds.) | I SEE |
| word to call attention | HEY |
| word with silver or glass | WARE |
| wordy | PROLIX, VERBOSE |
| work | LABOR, TOIL |
| workaday | COMMON, ORDINARY |
| work at | PLY |
| work cattle | OXEN |
| work crew | GANG |
| work diligently | DRILL, PEG |
| work dough | KNEAD |
| worker with rattan | CANER |
| worker's concern (2 wds.) | LIVING WAGE |
| worker's cooperative | ARTEL |
| worker's meal (2 wds.) | BOX LUNCH |
| work for | SERVE |
| work for a candidate | ELECTIONEER, CAMPAIGN |
| working class | PROLETARIAT |
| working space (2 wds.) | ELBOW ROOM |
| work into a mass | KNEAD |
| workman | ARTISAN, LABORER |
| work of art | ETCHING, OPUS |
| work of charity (3 wds.) | ACT OF LOVE |
| work of fiction | NOVEL |
| work of sculpture | FOUNTAIN, STATUE, BUST |
| workout | EXERCISE |
| work out | SOLVE |
| workplace for students (2 wds.) | DAY SCHOOL |
| work soil | TILL |
| work too hard | OVERDO |
| work unit | ERG |
| work with | COOPERATE |
| work with a needle | SEW, KNIT |
| work with oils | PAINT |
| world | UNIVERSE, EARTH |
| world goal | PEACE |
| worldly | MUNDANE, EARTHLY |
| world of canines | DOGDOM |
| world of illusions | DREAMLAND |
| world's highest mountain | EVEREST |
| world-wide | UNIVERSAL |
| world-wide complex of statutes | INTERNATIONAL LAW |
| worm | ERIA |
| worn and gaunt | HAGGARD |
| worn away | EROSE |
| worn out | EFFETE, TIRED, JADED |
| worn trail | PATH |
| worrisome offspring (2 wds.) | PROBLEM CHILDREN, ENFANT TERRIBLE |
| worry | FRET, FUSS, TEASE |
| worry at persistently | NAG |
| worsen | DETERIORATE |
| worship | ADORE, LOVE, REVERE, IDOLIZE, VENERATE |
| worsted suit fabric | SERGE |
| worth | MERIT |
| worthless | TRIVIAL, PALTRY |
| worthless bit | ORT |
| worthless plant | WEED |
| worthy | RELIABLE, VIRTUOUS |
| worthy of belief | CREDIBLE |
| would-be socialite (comp. wd.) | NAME-DROPPER |
| would-be-smoker's tobacco (2 wds.) | CORN SILK |
| wound | INJURY, HARM |
| wound covering | BANDAGE, SCAB |
| wound mark | SCAR, SCAB |
| woven container | BASKET |
| wrack | TORTURE, CONVULSE |
| wraith | GHOST, SPECTRE |
| wrangle | SPAR |
| wrangler | COWBOY |
| wrap | CAPE, SWADDLE, COAT |

| | |
|---|---|
| wraparound | **SKIRT** |
| wrap in bandage | **SWATHE** |
| wrapper | **ENVELOPE** |
| wrap up **FOLD, PACKAGE, END** | |
| wrath | **IRE, ANGER** |
| wreak | **INFLICT, CAUSE** |
| wreath | **GARLAND, LEI** |
| wreathe | **ENTWINE, COIL** |
| wreath of honor | **LAUREL** |
| wreck | **SMASHUP** |
| wrecker (2 wds.) | **TOW CAR** |
| wren | **BIRD** |
| wrench | **TWIST, TEAR** |
| wrest | **EXTORT** |
| wrestle | **GRAPPLE** |
| wrestling pad | **MAT** |
| wretched hut | **HOVEL** |
| wretched (sl.) | **RATTY** |
| wriggle | **SQUIRM, WRITHE** |
| wriggly fish | **EEL** |
| wrinkle | **CREASE** |
| wrist | **CARPUS** |
| wristwatch feature | |
| (2 wds.) | **RADIUM DIAL** |
| write | **INSCRIBE, PEN** |
| write by machine | **TYPE** |
| write carelessly | **SCRAWL,** |
| | **SCRIBBLE** |
| write down | **PEN** |
| write hastily | **SCRAWL, JOT,** |
| | **SCRIBBLE** |
| write music | **COMPOSE** |
| write off **CANCEL, AMORTIZE** | |
| writer of drama | **PLAYWRIGHT** |
| writer of fiction | **NOVELIST,** |
| | **AUTHOR** |
| writer of plays | **DRAMATIST** |
| writer of travesty | **PARODIST** |
| writer of verse | **POET** |
| writing | **DOCUMENT,** |
| | **MANUSCRIPT** |
| writing desk | **SECRETARY** |
| writing fluid | **INK** |
| writing implement | **PEN, NIB,** |
| | **PENCIL, BALL-POINT** |
| writing master | **STYLIST,** |
| **CALLIGRAPHER, PENMAN,** | |
| | **ENGROSSER** |
| writing material | **PAPER,** |
| | **PARCHMENT** |
| writings | **LITERATURE** |
| writing sheet | **PAPER** |
| writing table | **DESK** |
| written acknowledgment | |
| of a debt | **IOU** |
| written agreement | **CARTEL** |
| written characters | **SCRIPT** |

| | |
|---|---|
| written communication | **NOTE,** |
| **EPISTLE, LETTER, MEMO** | |
| written in verse | **POETIC** |
| wrong | **AMISS, INCORRECT** |
| wrong (prefix) | **MIS** |
| wongdoing | **EVIL** |
| wrong name | **MISNOMER** |
| wry | **TWISTED, ASKEW** |
| wurst | **SAUSAGE** |
| WW II area | **ETO** |
| Wyandotte abode | **NEST** |
| Wyoming city | **LARAMIE,** |
| | **CASPER** |
| Wyoming mountain range | |
| | **TETON** |

**X**

| | |
|---|---|
| xanthic | **YELLOWISH** |
| Xanthippe | **SHREW** |
| xebec | **BOAT** |
| xeres | **SHERRY** |
| xylograph | **WOODCUT** |
| xyloid | **WOODY** |

**Y**

| | |
|---|---|
| yabber | **TALK, JABBER** |
| yacht basin | **MARINA** |
| yachting affair | **REGATTA** |
| Yale man | **ELI** |
| yam (2 wds.) | **SWEET POTATO** |
| yank | **JERK, PULL** |
| Yannigan | **ROOKIE, RECRUIT** |
| yard (2 wds.) | **THREE FEET** |
| yard entrance | **GATE** |
| yardstick | **RULER** |
| yarn | **TALE, STORY** |
| yarn fluff | **LINT** |
| yawn | **GAPE** |
| yawning fissure | **CHASM** |
| yea | **TRULY** |
| year | **TWELVEMONTH** |
| yearbook | **ALMANAC, ANNUAL** |
| yearling | **COLT** |
| yearn | **PINE, LONG, ACHE** |
| years of life | **AGE** |
| years thirteen to nineteen | |
| | **TEENS** |
| yeast | **FERMENT, LEAVEN** |
| yell | **CRY, SHOUT, HOLLER** |
| yellow | **GOLDEN, SAFFRON** |
| yellow-belly | **COWARD** |
| yellow bugle | **IVA** |

yellow condiment **MUSTARD**
yellow fever mosquito **AEDES**
yellow gem **TOPAZ**
Yellowhammer State **ALABAMA**
yellowish-green pear **BOSC**
yellowjacket **WASP, HORNET**
yellow metal **BRASS, GOLD**
yellow of an egg **YOLK**
yellow pigment **OCHER, OCHRE**
yellow poplar **TULIPWOOD**
yellow root **CARROT**
yellow shade **AMBER**

Yellowstone attraction **GEYSER**
yelp **ULULATE, YIP**
Yemenite **ARAB**
yen **DESIRE, URGE,**
**HANKERING**
yeoman **EXON**
yes **AYE**
yes (Sp.) **SI**
yesterday (Fr.) **HIER**
yet **HOWEVER, STILL**
yield **CEDE**
yield a result (2 wds.)
**PAN OUT**
yield control (2 wds.)
**HAND OVER**
yielding **SUBMISSIVE**
yield under pressure **SAG**
yock **YAK, LAUGH**
yoke **HARNESS, BIND**
yokel **RUSTIC**
yonder **THERE**
yore **PAST**
Yorkshire river **AIRE, URE**
you and I **WE, US**
you don't say (2 wds.) **DO TELL**
young **JUVENILE, FRESH**
young animal **PUP, CUB**
yound bear **CUB**
young bird **NESTLING**
young blood **YOUTH, VIGOR**
young boy **LAD**
young chicken **FRYER**
young child **TOT, TODDLER**
young conger **ELVER**
young cow **CALF**
young deer **FAWN**
young dog **PUP, PUPPY**
young fellow **CHAP**
young flower **BUD**
young girl **LASS**
young goat **KID**
young hog **SHOAT, SHOTE**
young horse **COLT, FOAL**
young lady **GIRL, LASS,**
**DAMSEL, MAID**

young man **BOY, LAD**
young pig **SHOAT, PIGLET,**
**SHOTE**
young salmon **GRILSE, PARR,**
**SMOLT**
young seal **PUP**
young sheep **LAMB**
young socialite, for short **DEB**
youngster **CHILD, TOT**
young tough **PUNK**
young tree **SEEDLING**
young woman **GIRL, LASS,**
**MAID, MAIDEN**
yours and mine **OURS**
youth **BOY, LAD**
youthful years **TEENS**
yowl **HOWL, CRY**
Yugoslav city **BELGRADE,**
**ZAGREB**
Yugoslav commune **STIP**
Yugoslav leader **TITO**
Yugoslav money **DINAR**
Yugoslav region **BOSNIA,**
**SLAVONIA**
Yugoslav river **DANUBE, SAVA,**
**MORAVA, DRAVA**
yukata **KIMONO**
Yule **CHRISTMAS, NOEL**
yummy **TASTY, DELICIOUS**

# Z

zany **CLOWN, BUFFOON,**
**SIMPLETON, COMICAL,**
**FOOLISH, CRAZY**
zeal **ARDOR**
zealot **FANATIC**
zealous **EARNEST**
zenith **APEX**
zephyr **BREEZE**
Zeppelin **DIRIGIBLE**
zero **NAUGHT, NIL,**
**NOTHING, CIPHER**
zest **PEP**
zesty flavor **TANG**
zibeline **SABLE**
zigzag **OBLIQUE, AWRY**
zilch **NOTHING, ZERO**
zing **SPIRIT, VIM**
zip **PEP, FLY**
zodiac sign **ARIES, LEO, LIBRA,**
**PISCES, VIRGO, CANCER,**
**AQUARIUS, TAURUS,**
**SAGITTARIUS, GEMINI,**
**CAPRICORN, SCORPIO**
Zohar **CABALA**

| | | | |
|---|---|---|---|
| Zola heroine | **NANA** | zoo resident | **ANIMAL** |
| zombie | **CORPSE** | Zoroastrian | **PARSEE, PARSI** |
| zone | **REGION, SECTOR** | zounds | **EGAD** |
| zoo | **MENAGERIE** | zowie | **WOW** |
| zoo animal | **LION, TIGER, APE,** | Zsa Zsa's sister | **EVA** |
| | **PANDA, BEAR, SEAL** | zucchini | **SQUASH** |
| zoo enclosure | **CAGE** | zwieback | **RUSK, BISCUIT** |
| zoology | **FAUNA** | | |

# YOU'RE A WHOLE LOT SMARTER WITH WEBSTER'S.

## GET A HANDY BOXED SET CONTAINING 6 MAJOR REFERENCE BOOKS!

___**WEBSTER'S NEW WORLD DICTIONARY OF THE AMERICAN LANGUAGE**
David B. Guralnik,  *Single copies: (Q31-299, $3.50, U.S.A.)*
editor  *(Q31-416, $4.50, Canada)*

___**WEBSTER'S NEW WORLD THESAURUS**
by Charlton Laird  *Single copies: (Q31-418, $3.50, U.S.A.)*
*(Q31-417, $4.50, Canada)*

___**A DICTIONARY OF SYNONYMS AND ANTONYMS**
by Joseph Devlin  *Single copies: (Q31-310, $2.95, U.S.A.)*
*(Q31-419, $3.95, Canada)*

___**HOW TO BUILD A BETTER VOCABULARY**
by Maxwell Nurnberg  *Single copies: (Q31-306, $3.50, U.S.A.)*
and Morris Rosenblum  *(Q31-307, $4.50, Canada)*

___**A NEW GUIDE TO BETTER WRITING**
by Rudolph Flesch  *Single copies: (Q31-304, $3.50, U.S.A.)*
and A.H. Lass  *(Q31-305, $4.50, Canada)*

___**SPEED READING MADE EASY**
by Nila Banton Smith  *Single copies: (Q31-308, $3.50, U.S.A.)*
*(Q31-309, $4.50, Canada)*

**All six books in handy boxed set for only**
**(Q11-237, $19.90, U.S.A.)**
**(Q11-238, $24.95, Canada)**

WARNER BOOKS
P.O. Box 690
New York, N.Y. 10019

Please send me the books I have checked. I enclose a check or money order (not cash), plus 50¢ per order and 50¢ per copy to cover postage and handling.* (Allow 4 weeks for delivery.)

_____ Please send me your free mail order catalog. (If ordering only the catalog, include a large self-addressed, stamped envelope.)

Name _____

Address _____

City _____

State _____ Zip _____

*N.Y. State and California residents add applicable sales tax.      47